Teach Reading Creatively

Teach Reading Creatively

Reading and Writing as Communication

Seventh Edition

Frank B. May
Portland State University, Emeritus

With Contributions by
Louise Fulton
California State University

PEARSON

Merrill
Prentice Hall

Upper Saddle River, New Jersey
Columbus, Ohio

Library of Congress Cataloging in Publication Data

May, Frank B.
  Teach reading creatively : reading & writing as communication / Frank B. May, Louise Fulton.
      p. cm.
Includes bibliographical references and index.
Rev. ed. of: Reading as communication / Frank B. May, Louis Rizzardi. 6th ed. c2002.
ISBN 0-13-171379-5
1. Reading. 2. Literacy. I. Fulton, Louise. II. May, Frank B. Reading as
communication. III. Title.

LB10150.M358 2006
372.4—dc22

2004065613

Vice President and Executive Publisher: Jeffrey W. Johnston
Senior Editor: Linda Ashe Montgomery
Senior Editorial Assistant: Laura Weaver
Senior Development Editor: Hope Madden
Senior Production Editor: Mary M. Irvin
Design Coordinator: Diane C. Lorenzo
Production Coordination and Text Design: Carlisle Publisher Services

Cover Designer: Ali Mohrman
Cover Image: Linda Bronson
Production Manager: Pamela D. Bennett
Director of Marketing: Ann Castel Davis
Marketing Manager: Darcy Betts Prybella
Marketing Coordinator: Brian Mounts

This book was set in Garamond by Carlisle Communications, Ltd. It was printed and bound by R.R. Donnelley & Sons Company. The cover was printed by Phoenix Color Corp.

Earlier editions published under the title *Reading as Communication.*

Photo Credits: Alicia Christiansen, p. 5; Stephen Chen, p. 12; Anthony Magnacca/Merrill, p. 16; Patrick White/Merrill, pp. 35, 41, 64, 104, 107, 115, 119, 124, 147, 159, 199, 285, 306, 340; David Mager/Pearson Learning Photo Studio, pp. 37, 155; Karin Labby, pp. 56, 61, 179, 233, 288, 325, 382; Anne Vega/Merrill, pp. 83, 250; Pearson Learning Photo Studio, p. 185; Nancy Croning, p. 214; Rosalie Watters, p. 232; Ivey Burton, p. 246; Tom Watson/Merrill, p. 256; Scott Cunningham/Merrill, p. 322; Louise Fulton, pp. 370, 425; Richmond Burton, p. 376; Frank May, p. 406; Shirley Zeiberg/ PH College, p. 423.

Pearson Education Ltd.
Pearson Education Singapore Pte. Ltd.
Pearson Education Canada, Ltd.
Pearson Education—Japan

Pearson Education Australia Pty. Limited
Pearson Education North Asia Ltd.
Pearson Educación de Mexico, S.A. de C.V.
Pearson Education Malaysia Pte. Ltd.

10 9 8 7 6 5 4 3 2 1
ISBN: 0-13-171379-5

This book is dedicated to Louise Fulton
A thin long golden box floated down softly from heaven
And when opened
A brand new goddess stepped out onto Mt. Olympus

Educator Learning Center: An Invaluable Online Resource

Merrill Education and the Association for Supervision and Curriculum Development (ASCD) invite you to take advantage of a new online resource, one that provides access to the top research and proven strategies associated with ASCD and Merrill—the Educator Learning Center. At **www.educatorlearningcenter.com,** you will find resources that will enhance your students' understanding of course topics and of current educational issues, in addition to being invaluable for further research.

How the Educator Learning Center Will Help Your Students Become Better Teachers

With the combined resources of Merrill Education and ASCD, you and your students will find a wealth of tools and materials to better prepare them for the classroom.

Research
- More than 600 articles from the ASCD journal *Educational Leadership* discuss everyday issues faced by practicing teachers.
- A direct link on the site to Research Navigator™ gives students access to many of the leading education journals, as well as extensive content detailing the research process.
- Excerpts from Merrill Education texts give your students insights on important topics of instructional methods, diverse populations, assessment, classroom management, technology, and refining classroom practice.

Classroom practice
- Hundreds of lesson plans and teaching strategies are categorized by content area and age range.
- Case studies and classroom video footage provide virtual field experience for student reflection.
- Computer simulations and other electronic tools keep your students abreast of today's classrooms and current technologies.

Look into the Value of Educator Learning Center Yourself

A four-month subscription to Educator Learning Center is $25 but is FREE when packaged with any Merrill Education text. In order for your students to have access to this site, you must use this special value-pack ISBN number WHEN placing your textbook order with the bookstore: 0-13-226734-9. Your students will then recieve a copy of the text packaged with a free ASCD pincode. To preview the value of this website to you and your students, please go to **www.educatorlearningcenter.com** and click on "Demo."

Preface

Imagine the exquisite happiness I'm feeling as I say goodbye to **Reading as Communication,** Sixth Edition. Once my long-term project of winning the battle with cancer was over, I threw myself into a two-year, six days a week, total and complete revision of **Reading as Communication.** But lo and behold, halfway through, I realized that I was creating an exciting new book called **Teach Reading Creatively.**

What's New in Teach Reading Creatively?

An unusually powerful emphasis on creative thinking, teaching, and learning is infused throughout the entire book. For teachers reading TRC (**Teach Reading Creatively**), this means you can learn to teach both reading and writing with excitement and enjoyment, especially when too many rigid standard requirements seem to make life a bit too dull for comfort. My goal is to put the magic back into teaching reading!

Waiting to be introduced to creative and critical thinking teachers at the end of each chapter is a **Creativity Training Session.** And, although diversity threads its way through most of the book, there's a bold and timely chapter (13) where numerous diversity and multicultural projects are explained and applied. Teachers are taught new and old ways of meeting the dramatically changing demographics affecting their classrooms. I'm particularly pleased with this chapter because of its vital importance at this time in our society.

What Else Is New?

New to this edition is a major use of qualified studies, with more than 300 **NEW** references. I have also included more than 100 new websites and related technology activities; more than 100 application and field experiences for professors' supplementary teaching (right in the book); and as a bonus for my readers, a huge decrease of academic language. After all, do we want teachers to speak academically with their young students, most of whom, as Vygotsky and Piaget have demonstrated, are naturally allergic to abstract speech and text?

Finally, because of the current emphasis on standards, I have decided to align my text with the standards developed by the International Reading Association and the National Council of Teachers of English. Throughout the text there are examples of standards stated on the page in such a way as to honor the teachers who are reading this book.

What's New in Each Chapter: Brief Samples

Chapter One focuses on how preschool children learn to think. It begins with a new teacher successfully learning how to deal with the state standards without losing her own voice and style. The rest of the chapter shows what preschool children are like and how they correct their own mistakes. It also shows that teachers can teach the students without spoiling their chance to problem solve—the most important learning teachers can ever have.

Chapter Two demonstrates that the nature of reading and creativity are tightly connected. Reading is a thought process and so is creative thinking. Reading often requires creative thinking in order to understand the author. The author often requires creative thinking in order to produce something worth reading. This is one reason why this book is infused with demonstrations of teaching creatively.

Chapter Three concentrates on phonological awareness with a bold and noisy emphasis on how to teach phonemic awareness. The other half of phoneme awareness, of course, is grapheme awareness, discussed in this text as The Alphabetic Principle. This chapter creatively shows how to teach phonemic awareness and the Alphabetic Principle. The intense use of rhymes and rhyming games is actually the beginning of teaching phonics.

Chapter Four is about phonics and spelling via the right side of the brain. Yes, the right side, which "thinks" in terms of patterns—the crucial ingredient of phonics and the rapid learning of the 75% of words that are regular. The chapter shows several ways to actually use phonics, but emphasizes the creative method of using phonograms—rimes and also onsets and rimes. Learning phonics through onsets and rimes is a highly creative and effective method and is often much easier than the analytic and synthetic ways of approaching phonics teaching.

Chapters Five and Six are both about learning vocabulary, but there is a major difference between the two chapters. Chapter Five deals mainly with the top 100 sight words in the English language. Learning those particular words makes one essentially a moderately literate person, and that's why it's important to teach them to our students. However, it's a lot of fun for children to experience the many enjoyable ways of learning those 100 words. The vocabulary words in Chapter Six are called content-laden words, and teachers have to work harder in helping students use these words. What's taught the most in this chapter is the need to teach concepts along with the words that represent the concepts.

Chapters Seven, Eight, and Nine take reading to a higher level. In Chapter Seven, the teacher concentrates on helping students learn to use a variety of strategies that will enable them to understand what an author is saying. Without a packful of strategies, experienced and struggling students alike can lose their self-confidence. In Chapter Eight the teacher concentrates on helping students increase their fluency. Why? Because fluent reading enables you to understand what an author is saying. If you read too slowly, you'll forget what you just read, and that can lead to zero comprehension. In Chapter Nine the teacher helps students apply their knowledge and skills toward reading bushels and baskets of books and other literature of various kinds, genres, depths, pages, and shapes.

Chapters Ten and Eleven lead us, believe it or not, to the land of pencils and paper. In Chapter Ten the teacher focuses on helping students refine their creative thinking and writing abilities. Writing has been discussed throughout the book so far, but Chapter Ten treats writing as an equal partner in communication, and also presents writing as important in its own right.

In Chapter Eleven, the teacher evaluates thinking and writing abilities, using many informal and formal ways to show how each student can learn the art of self-assessment. In a sense we've gone back to Chapter One, where much younger students have corrected their own mistakes, miscues, incorrect beliefs, and sour attitudes.

Chapters Twelve and Thirteen focus on helping every child succeed through motivation and relevant teaching. In Chapter Twelve we find teachers learning how to help students become keenly motivated and, therefore, involved learners. In Chapter Thirteen we find teachers who are tying to motivate a classroom of diverse students with different levels of skills, cultural expectations, and uses of English. In this book, especially in Chapter Thirteen, you will find well-tried and new solutions to the challenge of teaching literacy in diverse classrooms. Do you realize, for example, how useful Bloom's Taxonomy can be when struggling to teach children of many ages, varieties of scholastic skills, abilities of speaking and writing English, and possibly somewhat conflicting cultures?

I'm eager to meet you inside.

Acknowledgments

Louise and I wish that you would open your mind and heart to our feelings of devotion for all of you for your vital assistance in making this book possible.

To the publishing team:

Jeff Johnston, for standing behind Louise and me whenever we waxed creatively or requested change after change; Linda Montgomery, for always standing up for us against those who are rigid, and especially for explaining the seventh edition to our hard-working reps; Hope Madden and Mary Irvin, for answering our multitude of questions, soothing our fearful minds, and cheerleading us when we need it; Mary Benis, for keeping our writing sharp and organized and helping us correct our mistakes before "we go to print"; Carol Sykes, for encouraging Frank over many editions—and in this edition, encouraging us both to keep the photographs coming in on time.

To the reviewers of the sixth edition, who spent so many hours giving Louise and me their very significant feedback. Your reviews were invaluable to us as we recreated the seventh edition. Bless you, dear friends and colleagues: Mary Ann Dzama, George Mason University; Daniel Holm, Indiana University South Bend; Grace Nunn, Eastern Illinois University; Barbara Perry-Sheldon, North Carolina Wesleyan College; Barbara Pettegrew, Otterbein College; Debra Price, Sam Houston State University; Beth A. Richmond, University of Southern Mississippi; and Michael S. Smith, Missouri Western State College.

To the contributors—those beautiful beings often called Angels: Karin Labby, an accomplished photographer and homemaker; Stephen Chen, an inventive, always-there-for-you, M.D. psychiatrist; John King, a well-known music producer; Richmond Burton, an internationally recognized artist; Mary Gaborko, a talented reading coach for other teachers; Ivey Burton, a popular clinical psychologist (and Frank's goddaughter); Rebecca Silva, the Curriculum and Staff Development Coordinator in the Riverside County Office of Education; Lee Burton, a highly successful marketing executive; Nancy Cronig, a fine actor and a disability specialist; Alicia Christiansen, a nurturing teacher of children with special needs; Rosalie Watters, a beloved principal in Pullman, Washington, who helped us learn from her teachers and students; Vicky Rank and the other teachers at Los Angeles Family School; and let us not forget the teachers and children living in Asia, Africa, Europe, South and Central America, and the United States who have taught us so much over the years.

Brief Contents

Contents

CHAPTER 2

CHAPTER 7

CHA**8**TER

CHAPTER

CHAPTER 11

CHAPTER **12**

Note: Every effort has been made to provide accurate and current Internet information in this book. However, the Internet and information posted on it are constantly changing, so it is inevitable that some of the Internet addresses in this textbook will change.

Teach Reading Creatively

Chapter One

Children Are Investigators

First Objective for your Teaching Success:

Encourage children to think of themselves as investigators.

Alicia Christiansen, a very creative teacher living in California's San Bernardino County, sat in the in-service district meeting, feeling both stunned and frustrated. The new state standards that were to be the basis for curriculum and statewide assessment were being explained by a teacher-turned-administrator who might not have experienced the creative side of life very often. He appeared to be enamored with his new position and seemed to be basking in his own power. In a rather loud voice he announced to the group of 30 elementary school teachers, "Get rid of the Butterfly Unit. We are going to teach the content standards."

Alicia felt an unpleasant twinge in her stomach and grumbled to herself, "As if the *fun* of learning doesn't matter—just as long as we teach the standards." She found the assumption behind his statement so incredibly short-sighted, she became determined to teach that very unit about the butterfly, while at the same time integrating the appropriate grade-level content standards within the unit.

Alicia vowed to help her students find the love of learning that she had treasured from early childhood. "I want to inspire them—not just prepare them for a districtwide test," she said aloud. But in her mind she worried that the standards might not be met by the butterfly unit.

Bringing Creativity to State Standards

Professional Standard: Understands central concepts

As Alicia flipped through the *Science Frameworks for California Public Schools* (2003), she came to the content standards for life sciences and smiled broadly.

There under Grade 2 Alicia found two standards that perfectly matched her objectives for the butterfly unit: (2.a) "Organisms reproduce offspring of their own kind. The offspring resemble their parents and each other" and (2.b.U) "The sequential stages of life cycles are different for different animals such as butterflies, frogs, and mice."

In the *Reading and Language Arts Frameworks for California Public Schools* (California Department of Education, 1999), she found three more perfect standards. Under Grade 2 writing she found (2.1) "Write a brief narrative based on their experiences," and under listening and speaking she found (1.2) "Ask for clarification and explanation of stories" and (2.1) "Recount experiences or stories." Voila! The butterfly unit was on!

Alicia's own objectives in doing a butterfly unit were, first of all, to study the life cycle of butterflies through direct observation. Second, she wanted her students to become familiar with the name of each stage of butterfly development. Third, she wanted them to determine how long it takes for the metamorphosis to be complete.

But where could Alicia find caterpillars? No caterpillars, no butterflies. Within an hour she had looked up *butterflies* on the Internet and had contacted a site that sold caterpillars, complete with their own environment, food, and plastic figurines of the life-cycle stages of a painted lady butterfly.

Getting the Students Engaged

Professional Standard: Understands how children learn and develop

Once the butterflies arrived, Alicia began engaging her students, a group of 8- to 10-year-old struggling readers and learners. First she asked this simple but intriguing question: "What was a butterfly before it was a butterfly?" With great certainty they said unanimously, "It was a baby butterfly!" How's that for straightforward beginners' reasoning!

Children's Literature to the Rescue

Professional Standard: Provides learning opportunities

Alicia had gotten Eric Carle's *The Very Hungry Caterpillar* from the library, and although most of the children did understand the meaning of "a very hungry caterpillar," they were still not aware of any connection between a caterpillar and a butterfly. After Alicia read the book, though, and showed them the beautiful paintings, the kids were full of questions, most of which began with "how"?

Over the next 2 weeks they watched their caterpillars grow at an astonishing rate. They read about butterflies, wrote about them, drew pictures of them, and had

more caterpillar/butterfly discussions than Alicia could recount. Most important of all, her students were *involved* in the learning process, utterly enraptured by a meaningful topic to which they personally related.

Let's let Alicia share the end of the story:

> When the day finally came for us to release our butterflies (all of whom had been given a name), it was truly a bittersweet feeling for my kids. Their excitement was overwhelming and awe inspiring. The expressions on their shining faces, as the butterflies landed on them for the last time, were eternally etched in my memory . . . and forever planted in the warmest space in my heart. I love my job and cherish each day as a new opportunity to broaden my students' educational horizons—and especially their passion for learning.

Would you say that Alicia is a creative teacher who understands children and how they learn? I would, too. Would you say that her keen ability is a waste of time? I wouldn't either.

This chapter has been developed to help you understand how children learn how language works and how creative they are as they necessarily remake the wheel. This chapter will help you communicate with your students, no matter what age they might be. In addition, the book will help you satisfy state standards while meeting your needs and your students' needs for flexible and creative thinking, planning, and learning.

Understanding How Young Children Learn

A wise teacher was once asked who are the easiest to teach. He replied, "The beginners, for they know how to teach themselves." With this advice in mind, let's begin this book with the beginners, those children from 1 month to 8 years of age who unconsciously and eagerly build their brain power through observations and experiences.

Let's carefully study how these novice learners begin to master the communication skills of reading and writing. That study will make it clear how you, personally, can effectively teach phonemic awareness, phonics, and many other language skills that children need to become good readers and writers.

We're also talking here about multi-age students who are struggling readers, who don't understand what reading is all about. Why include them? Because your teaching career may involve students at the kindergarten level of success or the third-grade level or even teen-age levels. But if you don't clearly understand how children learn from the beginning, you're not as likely to become the creative, sensitive, and effective teacher that you want to be.

Vygotsky Leads the Way

Professional Standard: Perceives reading as the process of constructing meaning

Lev Vygotsky was a famous researcher, teacher, and founder of special education departments as well as his own institute for "defectology" (the study of children with special needs) back in the 1920s and 1930s. He died of tuberculosis at the age of 38 but had already published 12 important books and 120 articles and had demonstrated in his research this previously unknown concept: The thinking abilities of children develop primarily as a result of attempting to communicate with adults.

This process can be understood by watching young children communicate with parents or caregivers. Children whose parents or caregivers spend a great deal of time with them—conversing, making decisions together about what to have for supper, sharing books, making cookies, making a shopping list together, and so on—often become what others refer to as precocious or advanced.

The children, of course, are not motivated to become precocious ("Mom, would you please teach me how to be precocious?"), nor are parents or caregivers necessarily *trying* to make the children precocious. What motivates the learning interaction seems to be a natural environment of parental love in addition to a child's sense of belonging, both of which cause children to want to communicate effectively with the people they need and love. The same motivation can come from teachers who make children feel that they belong.

Listening to Learn Language

Listening to parents or teachers or caregivers reveals how sounds are put together to make messages. "I'll be right back," the caregiver says. The listening child hears a long string of blurred-together sounds: i/el/be/rie/bak/. Successful listening often motivates the child to repeat the verbal message and see how the adult responds to it.

This kind of teaching and learning behaviour probably occurs frequently in the most successful classrooms. After all, we teachers are extremely important communication models, and kids often spend more face-to-face hours with us than with anyone else.

Communication and Problem Solving

For children, communication is a major form of problem solving—a way of making or responding to speech noises as a *secondary tool* for getting what they want. (A *primary tool* would be something like a stick to knock a cookie jar off a shelf.) Vygotsky (1986) saw that the use of language as a secondary tool gradually leads to complicated thinking. The following experiment shows what he meant.

Let's start with questions that Vygotsky's experimenters asked themselves: What would happen if you took candy from a box and fed some to a chimpanzee? Then you put the box of candy up on the higher of two shelves and handed the chimp a short stool, a taller stool, and a stick? Well, you know the answer. After a lot of frustrated experimentation, some chimpanzees would hit on the right combination and get the candy down without help.

But what would a child do, especially one who has had experience talking with adults? She would first try to get an adult to get the candy down for her. But suppose the adult politely says no, then hands her the stools and the stick, and tells her he's not allowed to talk to her. Now what does she do? In most of the experimental situations, children turned their language back on themselves (Vygotsky, 1978, p. 25), perhaps the way you and I do when we're home alone.

Let's watch as one 4-year-old stands on the short stool, feeling along the lower shelf—quietly looking, realizing she's not getting the candy, but not knowing what to do about it. She looks at the experimenter but gets no help. Suddenly she brings her secondary tool into action, her language. "That stool," she says, pointing to the higher stool. "I can get it from that stool; stand and get it." So having used language to *plan* her actions, she's ready to act.

She takes the higher stool and stands on it, but alas, she's still too short to reach the candy. She analyzes her attempt as most adults would: "No, that doesn't get it." So once more she uses her secondary tool and says, "I could use the stick" (a primary tool).

She has to test her verbal solution by climbing down from the tall stool, grabbing the stick, and climbing back up. This time she can reach the candy and jab at it. "It will move now," she tells herself. Excitedly she jabs at the candy again. "It moved!" she tells the adult (who can't help communicating with a smile). "The stick worked!" she says to him. Finally, she succeeds completely by jabbing the candy hard enough to push it down to the floor (Vygotsky, 1978, p. 25).

The Effect of Language Development on Thinking

Fortunately for you and me, we have developed the ability to reason at a high level through the use of language, thereby avoiding the need to learn only through bitter experience. Language provides us with *symbols* (i.e., words) that stand for actual experiences.

By using language instead of an ax, we learn to use the proper tool and cutting method. By using language, we can learn without accidentally chopping our fingers off.

How do writing and reading fit into all this? Writing and reading, like speech, are social acts that require thinking. Reading actually is a form of thinking, as is writing, and both are forms of communication. Writing and reading—like painting a picture or interpreting a song—are problem-solving acts. Both reading and writing allow us to make connections—with each other, with authors, with any person or place or a marvelous thing like a box of candy.

A child who solves the problem of getting the candy off the shelf is very much like the child who solves the problem of getting the meaning off the printed page. In both problem-solving situations the child must rely on past experiences that have helped her form minitheories about how life on Earth works.

In both problem-solving situations the child must use language as a secondary tool, boldly making predictions and attempting to confirm them. Reading and writing—like searching for candy, like playing cards, like finding a soul mate—are problem-solving events (Rorty, 2000).

Why Early Readers Are Early

It's now common knowledge that the vast majority of early readers have simply been born to parents who enjoy writing and reading and who love to share a good book with their children (Davis & McCaul, 1990; Durkin, 1966; Holdaway, 1979, 1986; Sulzby, 1985; Teale, 1986). Such parents have certain behaviors in common:

1. Reading to their children daily—sometimes many times per day

2. Reading to themselves, an activity their children imitate

3. Having books and magazines or other reading materials in more than one place in the house

4. Writing letters or e-mailing messages to their friends and letting their children watch (In some cases the parents watch the *children!*)

5. Listening to their children and answering their questions

6. Allowing their children to have their own books, paper, pencils and pens, computers, calculators, and so on

7. Accepting their children's funny spelling as honest attempts to communicate

8. Allowing their children to read or try to read without correcting them and also encouraging self-correction

In short, these parents or other caregivers treat the tightly connected processes of writing and reading as natural parts of the home environment, not as something their children must wait to learn in school. You should use these eight behaviors of smart parents to guide your teaching. You won't regret it.

Piaget Identified Concrete and Abstract Stages of Thinking

Professional Standard: Understands different learning styles

Jean Piaget (1955) was a cognitive psychologist who, like Lev Vygotsky, was fascinated with the learning processes of young children. Piaget discovered that children tend to stay at a relatively *concrete stage of thinking* until around age 12, when it becomes more evident to the adults around them that they are now engaging in much more abstract thinking processes. For example, Vygotsky observed that when young children are asked what a snail is, they say things like "It's little and slimy" or "It has only one foot." When asked what a grandmother is, they might say something like "A grandmother has a soft lap" (1978, p. 50). When I asked several hundred children what a daddy is, the most common response was "He fixes things for me."

Young children often define something according to their memories of encounters with it (Piaget, 1955). This is one of the meanings that Piaget attached to the concrete stage of thinking—that is, real or actual, not abstract or symbolic.

Eventually children become less concrete and more abstract in their thinking. Instead of saying that a snail is little and slimy, as a 6-year-old might put it, a 12-year-old is more likely to say that a snail is a small animal that lives in a shell—you know, one of those spiral shells. Instead of referring to memories of personal experiences with an object, 12-year-olds usually refer to descriptive categories. These language apprentices have picked up such adult categories as animals, shells, and spiral things (and for all we know, things that go bump in the night).

To encourage language apprentices, you and I need to expect and enjoy young children's concrete views of their environment. We should not rigidly expect them to perceive things according to our adult abstract and symbolic ways of seeing things. *Instead we can learn to communicate with them in concrete rather than abstract ways.*

Later we can gradually help them use adult categories or types in their thinking. But we shouldn't consider ourselves or our students to be failures when they don't spontaneously switch to abstract and symbolic ways of perceiving their environment. The goal is to communicate well with your students.

Children Need to Be Apprentices

Vygotsky's views imply that teachers should let children be apprentices to them but they should gradually turn over the responsibility of learning to the children. Barbara Rogoff, a follower of Vygotsky, has written extensively on this topic. She notes that adults can help children find connections between their existing knowledge and the knowledge they must have to solve a new problem (Rogoff, 1990). Rogoff advocates the procedure that she calls guided participation and others call scaffolding.

With *guided participation* the teacher and the child apprentice start with a problem that they wish to solve together. The teacher doesn't solve the problem for the child (Schwartz, 1997), nor does the apprentice sit passively while the teacher does all of the thinking. Instead, the child "carries out simple problem solving under the adult's guidance, while participating in the problem's solution process" (Rogoff, 1986, pp. 31–32).

This method of guided participation, or *scaffolding*, will be demonstrated for you several times as you read this book. Basically it means that you and your students are challenged to take more and more responsibility for learning success. This approach can cause anxiety for the teacher. As Margaret Meek Spencer said, "Teachers are caught between their desire to be skillful professional practitioners and the knowledge that comes from their own experience—that pupils have to be encouraged to believe that, in the end, they teach themselves" (1986, pp. 56–57).

Young Children Teach Themselves

Now comes perhaps the most important advice in this chapter, not from me but from two of the most famous child psychologists in the 20th century. Jean Piaget and Lev Vygotsky observed children in experimental settings for over 50 years combined and came to believe that teachers can be expert guides, but the real teaching is carried on by the child. Young children teach themselves, they said, one with a French accent and one with a Russian accent. This idea has profound implications for those involved in teaching reading and writing.

Young Children Learn by Correcting Their Own Mistakes

What we know about young readers and writers today is based partly on the work of Piaget and Vygotsky and partly on our recent years of studying how children self-correct their miscues as they read (M. M. Clay, 2001; Y. Clay, 2002; Schwartz, 2005; Goodman & Goodman, 1994).

> Guided by their teacher, students learn to negotiate a variety of ways to discover and self-correct reading miscues. Teachers can create many opportunities for beginning readers to practice self-monitoring strategies that eventually result in self-corrections and accurate reading (Forbes, Poparad & McBride, 2004, p. 568).

What you just read should remind you of what Vygotsky and Piaget were saying: The real teaching is carried on by the child; young children teach themselves. How? By being bold, making mistakes, and then fixing the mistakes. This sequence can occur with very young children, as you'll soon see. Much of the research related to self-correction has been done by M. M. Clay (1991, 2001), Y. Clay (2002), Y. M. Goodman (1985a, 1985b, 1990), and Y. M. Goodman and K. S. Goodman (1994) and will be a major topic in Chapter 2.

Teachers Can Teach as Mentors

So how can a teacher teach reading and writing in such a way that children of any age don't lose confidence in what they've already learned from their own experiences? How can they be helped to learn in such a way that they usually feel that they're doing most of the discovery and correction themselves? You need to understand how children first learn to write and read—on their own, without excessive intervention by adults. If you gain that understanding, you will learn how to intervene on their behalf without spoiling their chance to develop their own thinking and learning powers.

Young Children Play the Role of Reader

Professional Standard: Understands major theories of language development

Both Piaget and Vygotsky believed that children's play is their form of meaningful work. And what's their job? Learning how to be like the bigger people they admire. My own observations of children have shown me the same thing, and your observations probably have, too. The most amazing thing about this drive of children is how early it begins—even before the age of 1. Raja, a case study by Doake (1986), illustrates my point.

Vignette

 ## What Can We Learn from Raja?

Raja was read to on the day he was born and on virtually every day following. A few of the books read to him were Mercer Mayer's *Just for You*; Bill Martin's *Brown Bear, Brown Bear, What Do You See?*; and Ethel and Leonard Kessler's *Do Baby Bears Sit In Chairs?* These and other stories were easy to listen to, repetitive, rhyming, flowing, and therefore highly predictable.

For the first 2 months, Raja paid little obvious attention to the books but would simply lie passively in the reader's arms, looking around the room, at the reader's face, and occasionally at the book. At 2 months, 3 days, however, as he was lying in his rocker and beginning to cry, *Just for You* was held up in front of him and read. He stopped crying immediately, looked at the pages of the book, and never took his eyes off them until the story was finished. Two more familiar stories were then read to him, and he listened with the same continuous attending behavior. From that time on he would sit and listen and look with a high degree of attention as familiar stories were read and reread. (Doake, 1986, p. 4)

It was as if during those first 2 months Raja had gradually developed a nonverbal association between reading books and comfort. He didn't understand much of what was going on in the stories, of course, but the rhythms and soothing sounds of his parents' reading voices had become familiar, just as lullabies do (and just as a mother's heartbeats do before birth). The associations between colorful pictures and comfort added even more familiarity.

Let's look at what happens next. While Raja was still only 2 months old, he began to show signs of wanting to make a book his—to own it with hands and mouth. Not only did he become more animated when a familiar book was read to him, but he also wanted to touch the pages.

At 3 to 4 Months. By this time Raja has become restless when an unfamiliar book is read to him; he has to be introduced to new books slowly only a few more pages each time. He identifies with the sound of the language and not just the pictures. One of the stories most familiar to him acts as a pacifier, no matter how disturbed

he is. Even his piercing scream (produced by a vaccination shot) is stilled by his father reciting "Brown Bear, Brown Bear, what do you see?" With the needle still in his arm, Raja starts to laugh. Such is the power of the joyful associations he has developed with the language of his repeatedly read stories. (Doake, 1986, p. 4)

At 5 Months. Raja has an attention span of at least 40 minutes and a repertoire of 15 familiar stories.

At 6 Months. Raja responds with smiles and excited stretching to particular words—such as *meow, boom,* and *no-oooo!*—when the reader emphasizes them.

At 8 Months. He sighs contentedly or smiles when the last page has been read, points to illustrations with enjoyment, and sometimes pulls a page up to his mouth.

At 9 Months. His attention span with familiar stories is at least 75 minutes. That's right, he sits with his mother or father for 75 minutes reading books. He has a repertoire of 22 familiar stories. He turns pages by himself and flattens them down delicately (obviously something he has picked up from watching Mom and Dad).

At 10 Months. Raja turns the pages from front to back, either at his parents' request or whenever he thinks the page is finished. His attention is now inexhaustible; his parents' is not. He closes a book he doesn't like; he takes charge.

At 11 Months. He brings to a parent books that are requested by title. His parents can draw him away from almost any other activity by beginning to read one of his favorites out loud. He spends up to 45 minutes playing with his books by himself—turning pages like an adult and laughing at favorite scenes. He now has a library of 32 favorites (Doake, 1986, p. 6).

You can draw your own conclusion as to how soon a child is capable of desiring to be a reader like an adult. It's common knowledge, though, that many very young children love to "read" to even younger children—as a visit to a day care center will demonstrate. If they don't read to another child, children read to a doll or a stuffed animal or themselves: ("Now, just sit still, dear, and I'll read you a nice story. . . . Once upon a time. . . . ").

Reading and Writing Become Natural Forms of Play

What's my point? Young children do use reading as a form of play. They play house, they play school, they play going to the store, they play professional athletics, they play reading, they play writing, they play whatever they see those admired bigger people doing. This is why the parents' and grandparents' roles are so important in developing readers, as is the older sibling's role, the aunt's or uncle's role, and equally important, the admired teacher's role.

Children Play the Role of Writer, Too

Professional Standard: Understands principles of new language acquisition

Now let's get back to the beginners. Writing is often the skill that children admire and desire the most. The stages that child apprentices go through as they learn to write are quite a testimony to their desire to imitate those adults they like.

And yet, children are not mere apprentices; they are apprentices with style— more like inventive followers. As they struggle to understand their world and to imitate their heroes and heroines, they end up reinventing the wheel, over and over again. This behavior is hard for some parents and teachers to accept with grace. They are prone to step in and point out how inefficient it is to reinvent or reconstruct: "Tis better to do it my way, little one. *Would* is not spelled *w-d*; it's spelled *w-o-u-l-d*."

Let's postpone discussing the dilemma this attitude poses for children. Instead watch how effectively children play the role of writer if we just stand back and observe, rather than showing off our aged wisdom.

Writing May Be Play, but It's Also Challenging

Keep in mind that playing the role of writer is sometimes a hardball game, even when it's played with little friends of the same age. It's exciting and challenging for children, because using symbols is somewhat foreign to their concrete stage of thinking. The idea of three rocks or three mud pies is not foreign, but three written words—that's something else. How do grown-ups know how many words to use when they're writing? And what *is* a word? Is it three of those things called letters? You do have to have at least three letters, don't you?

As Margaret Meek Spencer (2003) said at the 19th World Congress on Reading, "Just how hard children work to make sense of the world is evidenced in their play and in research analyses of it . . . ." Let's watch them build their reasoning power through problem solving. For example, they might ask, "Why do we need four words to write *Mama baked three cakes*?" A 3- to 5-year-old might hear only *two* "words" (*mamabaked* and *threecakes*) or even five (*ma ma baked three cakes*). Other children decide that four words are needed because you need one for mama and three more for the three cakes (Goodman, 1990, p. v). Do you see what I mean by children's concrete stage? Their motto is I'll Believe It When I Feel It!

But why spoil their fun in solving such a delicious mystery? Are we adults so afraid to let go of our know-it-all attitude for a few days or weeks? Are we afraid of developing students who are capable of thinking for themselves? Perhaps we're afraid our children or students won't need us. Or they might surpass our abilities.

Children First Distinguish Between Writing and Drawing

When children are just beginning to play the game of writing—and it doesn't seem to matter too much which language we're talking about (Ferreiro, 1990)—they first have to figure out the difference between writing procedures and drawing procedures. For example, to a young child at the early part of the concrete stage of thinking, drawing is a mysterious way of creating rocks without actually picking them up. You may have noticed their awe in watching an adult draw something.

Writing, on the other hand, moves the mind a great deal further from reality than drawing does. From the child's standpoint the written words *three rocks* are enormously different from either a picture of three rocks or the rocks themselves. The written words *three rocks* are a very *abstract*, adult way of communicating about the rocks. A picture of three rocks is less abstract, and three actual rocks are not abstract at all.

Kids aged 2 through 5 gradually develop enough skill to draw their own three rocks, their house, their own body, their pet—although they often have to explain what they've drawn to their not-so-wise older siblings. Around the same time they might also play the role of a fantastic writer—like Mom or Dad or Aunt Bertha. They might sit on the grass with their own private drawing board, saying out loud to themselves and their nearby playmates, "See my writing?" and showing off their nice straight lines. The playmate is likely to respond, "That's drawing, not writing. If you're gonna write, you have to use crooked lines" (Ferreiro, 1990).

This new theory may work for a few minutes or hours or days. But eventually our eager learners experience bewilderment because the new theory stops working. Soon they argue their way into a different theory: "I need straight lines to draw houses, but Mom used some round ones when she wrote on my birthday card" pointing to the *O* and the *U* in "I love you."

Eventually kids realize that it's not the *kind* of marks that makes the difference between writing and drawing; both activities use straight lines, curves, and even dots. But the marks are moved around differently. Intuitively kids come to realize that when you draw, the lines follow the "object's contours" (Ferreiro, 1990, p. 15). But when you write, you use the lines and curves to create meaningless marks called letters. "The basic concept eventually learned *intuitively* is that linear strings of letters are not real objects; they're not drawn objects; they're 'substitute objects'" (Ferreiro, 1990, p. 15). Whew! That's a hard but glorious concept to learn, yet researcher Emilia Ferreiro (1990) says that these children are still working only on the first of three main developmental levels.

Kids Discover the Purpose of Letters

Before you know it, kids have used their problem-solving abilities to realize intuitively that drawings are used as pictures of actual things and letters are used for labeling those pictures. This concept can be easily discovered when parents and teachers write children's names above pictures they have drawn, especially those of themselves, or when grown-ups write a label like *three rocks* right above a picture the child has drawn of . . . (drum role please) . . . *three* . . . *beautiful* . . . *rocks.*

"Now I'm as smart as my brother," they might be feeling. But children keep right on wondering how to *produce* those things called words. In what order should they place the letters? How do adults actually make those funny squiggles they call letters? And how do we know which ones are used for which objects? Of course, early readers have already learned the answers and often take on the role of teaching their peers—and usually do a good job.

Answers to these unvoiced questions arrive *intuitively* from much observation and often through discussion with peers or siblings. Children frequently tackle the quantitative problem first: How many letters do we need to make a word? They argue about this, but most choose three letters as a minimum (Ferreiro, 1990, p. 17). As for the qualitative problem: Will any three letters do, and can they all be the same letter, like *bbb?* As you can see, at this level of writing and print awareness, preschool children and a few kindergartners are still concerned about form rather than meaning. They have not yet discovered how to represent differences in meaning.

Children Learn to Show Differences in Meaning with Words

Let's go on to Level 2, where the main challenge is how to show differences in meaning through written language. Michael wants to write, "The boys and girls are here." He already knows the conventional way of writing *the* from seeing *The End* so often, and he has decided that *and* is spelled like the name of his friend Ann. So, using part of *his own name,* he writes "the mich ann mich r_____." For the blank he draws a picture of an ear, figuring that's close enough to the word *here.* This boy is actually at an advanced stage of Level 2.

Most children at this level begin to realize that two identical strings of *letters* (like *mich* and *mich*) can't possibly say different things like *boys* and *girls.* So they may try different letters to label different things, hoping to communicate what they want to say. Instead of *mich* and *mich,* Michael decides to use *mich* for *boys* and *ael* for *girls.*

Do you begin to feel like you're on another planet? I'm not making this up. Adults and young children really do see literacy development from a very different perspective. Unfortunately, this discrepancy often leads adults to try to teach kids to read in abstract ways that don't match their concrete thinking processes. But more about that later.

Learn More About the Second Level of Writing

Professional Standard: Understands that written language is a symbolic system

Children at this stage usually notice that adults use more letters with some words than they do with others (Ferreiro, 1990, p. 18). Occasionally kids deal with this on a conscious level. "Hmmm," Bertrand theorizes out loud, "maybe I should use lottsa letters if the thing is big and only a few letters if the thing is little. I'll write *mouse* like this—*BTD*—and *elephant* like this—*BTDERABNTDBRE*." Notice how Bertrand used the letters of his own name—a great neophyte problem solver!

Patricia's theory is even more intriguing. "Maybe I should use more letters for many things and only a few letters for one thing. I'm gonna write *girl* like this—*PTC*—and my whole family like this—*PTCRATIRA*." Ingenious, right? Other kids have been known to try more letters for an older person and fewer for a young person. Here's an actual conversation that Esther Grossi (1990) overheard:

Boy 1: How many letters do I need to write *bread?*

Boy 2: It depends on the size of the bread.

Boy 1: What do you mean?

Boy 2: If you're talking about a loaf of bread, you need more letters than you do for rolls.

Did you notice the visual, concrete thinking: How big? How many? What's it like? Is it a roll or a loaf of bread?

More and more rapidly—with gentle guidance by teachers and parents, with the realization that their theories aren't quite working, and with a developing phonemic awareness and phonics awareness (coming up in Chapter 3)—young children come around to phonemic spelling, such as *fone* for *phone*, or *razinz* for *raisins*. And soon after the phonemic approach has been tried, they usually show their desire to please themselves, their parents, caregivers, and teachers by purposely searching for the "correct" way to spell, the way bigger people do.

By learning in this seminatural way, children have become accustomed to learning with and through others. They have become used to testing their own hypotheses as scientists do. And they have gained the most precious gift of all: a sense of self-confidence based on trusting their own learning and thinking powers.

I realize that the natural road can't always be followed without some deviation. The modern world is far from natural, and direct and specific adult intervention can be more helpful with some children than the preferred gentle coaching mode. Try to adhere to children's natural tendencies wherever you can, but keep in mind that for some children those tendencies may stem less from their nature than from their need for survival in a confusing school and home environment.

Children Become Creative Constructivists

In order to discuss the constructivist theory, we have to define its important terms:

1. *Implicit learning* is the process of understanding an idea without necessarily being able to express it clearly.

2. *Explicit learning* is the process of understanding an idea to the point of being able to express it clearly.

3. *Intuitive learning* is the process of understanding an idea through experience and insight rather than through verbal analysis.

Constructivists rely more on the concepts of implicit and intuitive learning than on explicit learning.

Let's examine certain principles of teaching that can help you succeed in encouraging all three of those forms of learning. Piaget (1974) is said to have put it this way: "To understand is to invent. Children need to be physically and mentally active rather than passive learners." In almost every presentation of his theory, Piaget emphasized the need to see a functional organism, active rather than passive, in the acquisition of knowledge—whether implicit, intuitive, or explicit. "By *activity* Piaget implied not only physical manipulation but also mental action that transforms into creation" (Landsman, 1990, p. 44).

Even more important is something Piaget called *mental transformation*, during which a young child reinvents the wheel. We saw this when we watched children re-create the writing system. Young Esther went so far with her transformation that she changed the spelling of her name to *ET*, which I suppose indicated Es-Ter.

Piaget and his followers considered such a constructivist stance as an actual need—not because children are ornery creatures who just have to do it their way. Actually, this is the way they naturally behave in order to understand their world, in order to master it and make it their own. All of us at any age attempt to create our own meaning from our experiences, whether those experiences are physical or mental or both.

Developing literacy is a perfect example of this type of re-creation or reconstruction. When writing, reading, speaking, or listening to someone else speak, it is unnatural for children and adults *not* to reinvent the wheel (Tovey & Kerber, 1986). There's a reason the song "I Did It My Way" continues to be popular decade after decade. To do things *your* way is the natural way to make things meaningful to you. When someone tells you a story, it is only natural for you to add and subtract and exaggerate so you can make the story a little more meaningful (or juicy) to you.

Use this understanding of your students to communicate with them, whether through listening, speaking, reading, or writing. You and I may want to be more than tolerant of a student's flexibility and creativity—it's the nature of the beast. Children's need to reinvent the system is so inborn, it's almost as though there's a constructivist gene hidden in their DNA. As Piaget implied, the child is a producer of knowledge.

Children are also the purveyors of what Sternberg, Grigorenko, and Jarvin (2001) and Sternberg, Troff, and Grigorenko (1998) refer to as the triarchic model, and what I call three avenues for developing and using our marvelous cognitive skills. The three parts correspond to analytical, creative, and practical thinking. Our students think analytically when they are allowed to judge, evaluate, compare, contrast, and critique. They think creatively when they invent, discover, imagine, and suppose. They think practically when they implement, use, apply, and put into practice what they have learned.

"This kind of teaching does not conflict with teaching for memory," Sternberg says, and I wholeheartedly agree. Memory is the glue that allows creative people to think in three different ways at the same time. Our students enjoy learning that way, and we enjoy teaching that way.

Imagination Becomes the Core of Learning

I agree with Margaret Meek Spencer (2003) that when children are learning to read and write, their imagination should not be something simply added to their learning experience like salt and pepper. We can't keep thinking and imagination apart, she says, "especially in the first-ness of children's early encounters with the world they have to learn to make sense of" (p. 106).

> Children at this stage are probably at the most creative part of their life. Teach them to communicate well but let them keep their imagination right under their hat. If we stifle their imagination just to please us teachers, we can do serious damage to our students' spirit. (Green, 2000)

We may need to keep this in mind if we wish to be successful and caring teachers. As we share other ideas together let's let our motto remain something like this: Reading Is Imagination.

Why Creative Thinking Is So Important to You and Your Students: In Praise of Paul Torrance

I consider Paul Torrance to have been the master of creative thinking (Torrance, 1995) and a person who has influenced my own thinking and writing. As he once said, "Creativity is an ability to identify or prepare original solutions to problems." *Problems* and *original solutions* are what you and I and our students must deal with every single day. Difficult problems such as reading a book that's not easy to read, working with a kid who other teachers refer to as a knothead, writing a paper or a book about a subject you really believe in—these all require original solutions, or what I call *thinking beyond the problem.*

Most of us stay with a problem, wallow in the problem, even dream about the problem. But if you want to really help yourself and your students the most, you'll train yourself and your students to think *outside* the problem. How do you do that? That's what I'm going to help you discover as you read this book.

I'd like to start by paraphrasing Davis and Rimm (1998): Creative thinking requires three components:

1. *Fluency*—the ability to produce many ideas that might lead to a solution. In other words, rather than sticking to the same weak solution, try brainstorming the situation. Make yourself write down at least 10 solutions to choose from.

2. *Flexibility*—the ability to break away from an established set or way and change your perceptions and attitudes. Try this: take a deep, deep breath and blow it out hard. Then close your eyes and visualize yourself as someone who is with it, happy-go-lucky, full of yourself because you're great. Then spend the whole day flexing, relaxing, and flexing, doing things the way you really want to do them.

3. *Originality*—turning yourself into a vigorous generator of fresh ideas and fresh perceptions, seeing what you've never seen before within yourself. Aim for originality that makes positive changes. Imagine yourself being the first person to see a great solution for a major problem in the world.

Teach your students what you learn from me about creative thinking. And please notice throughout the book that I am modeling creative thinking—for you and for you to pass on to your students. The world deserves a lot more creative thinking, don't you agree?

Focus on Students with Special Needs: Comments by Louise Fulton

The following narrative account has been written by Dr. Louise Fulton, whose reputation as a long-time leader of the special education movement has spread throughout a large portion of the world. I have asked her to share her wisdom with you by presenting a piece of advice and experience in each chapter. More about Dr. Fulton can be found at the beginning of the book. Happy reading!

Brett: A Child with a Behavior Problem

As a new student admitted to my classroom, Brett was a challenge from Day 1. Here I was, a brand new teacher eager to teach *all* of my students, and yet this new student was labeled as a "special needs student with behavior disorders." An accurate label, I might add, since he was suddenly interrupting all of my beautiful plans. And yet, Brett could be charming, he was cute as a bug, and his verbal language seemed well developed. Truthfully, I liked him right from the start.

But Brett could suddenly turn order to chaos in my classroom. How? By throwing something across the room, pestering another student, making excessive noise, or simply by refusing to do what he was supposed to do. The day he turned over his desk and hit my classroom volunteer I was more than at my wits' end. I told him to go to the office, of course, and he turned to me with a smirk and said, "All I have to do is tell them I am sorry and I'll be right back here tomorrow."

Well! What would you do? This kid had figured out the system and was feeling his power, which translated to the word *trouble*. I knew I had to get Brett under control—but how? They sure don't prepare you for these kinds of things in college courses, do they? I suddenly felt like my Band-Aid approach wouldn't work for this child. I needed an emergency room, but none of those existed.

So in desperation, I decided to take time to examine his behavior carefully rather than always reacting to it. What do I really know about Brett? Why is he doing these things? What is he getting out of it? What is Brett really trying to tell me? What is Brett really feeling?

Focusing on Brett in this way was hard, especially since he seemed intent on wrecking my classroom. But off and on for the next 3 days I stepped back and took a look at the whole picture through my imaginary spyglass and asked myself: What happens right before his disruptive behavior occurs? What seems to be triggering it? What happens afterwards? What is reinforcing it?

No luck at all—not until I contacted Brett's grandmother, who filled my ears with enough clues to satisfy the most fastidious of detectives. First of all, Brett had recently been separated from both of his parents. Second, his mother was incarcerated. Third, Brett could not read. Fourth, he was angry about moving in with his grandmother. Fifth, he had been forced to go to this strange new school.

My detective work paid off. It was easy now to see that the troublesome behaviors almost always occurred when I announced that we were going to read aloud or begin preparation for reading exercises or after I asked the students to work on something at their desks alone.

(continued)

Focus on Students with Special Needs *(cont.)*

I made my first hypothesis: Brett is having so much difficulty succeeding with reading and writing tasks, especially reading in front of his peers, that he is taking the easy way out. Second guess: He is cleverly distracting me from my plans so I will focus on his behavior and he can successfully avoid another public failure experience of reading in front of his peers. When I interviewed Brett in a friendly way, I managed to get him to open up and tell me his absolute truth: "I hate reading and I hate school!" He also revealed that he missed playing soccer in his neighborhood and he was angry about losing his collection of bugs-in-jars when he moved. I was determined to make school and learning fun for Brett and to help him develop the love for reading that I have.

That interview opened the trust-door a fairly decent crack. From that time on I vowed to build a mutually respectful relationship with Brett. Meanwhile, I began to work with his grandmother to set some consistent be-

havioral limits for both school and home. Reading was going to be a top priority. Grandmother and I quickly became a united front.

Over the next few weeks I did brief on-the-spot emergency interviews as needed and encouraged Brett to make other choices in the future. He needed to know what was expected, what the consequences were, and he needed to be empowered to make choices for himself. Because he loved different insects so much, I helped him find pictures of different insects on the Internet. His reading skills leaped forward as he searched for insects, read about them in simple books, and became curious about the name of each new one.

The day I let him sit in the teacher's chair at the reading rug and read his favorite book to the class was a thrill beyond my imagination. He had truly made it. As for me, I felt like the teacher of the year. These times are better than any award you can get!

Summary of Main Ideas

- Vygotsky taught us the importance of social interaction and problem solving in learning to think, write, and read.
- Piaget taught us the importance of allowing children to be constructivists who come to understand by inventing their own knowledge.
- Higher level thinking abilities develop through the process of learning to communicate and problem solve in social situations.
- Learning influences rather than waits for development. Thus, literacy learning requires continual, moderate adult guidance.
- Literacy apprentices basically teach themselves, but under the inspiration and guidance of caring adults.
- Children learn to read and write partly by playing the roles of reader and writer.
- There is a strong need for abundant, functional learning in the classroom.
- Creative teaching requires fluency, flexibility and originality.

Literacy Through Technology

A. With a partner visit one of these Web sites, which encourage using arts and creativity in teaching.

http://www.creativeteachingsite.com/
http://www.pbs.org/wnet/americanmasters/database/database_visual_arts.html
http://invention.smithsonion.org/centerpieces/iap/
http://www.decordova.org/decordova/exhibit/stories/Default.htm

Answer the following questions about the site:
What is the purpose? How could I use the materials or ideas provided here to add more variety to my teaching?

B. Now review one of these bilingual Web sites or discover your own:

http://www.storyplace.org
http://www.colorincolorado.org/homepage.php
http://babelfish.altavista.com/babelfish/

Describe the site and explain how you can use it or another Web site to involve English-language learners in classroom discussions.

Application Experiences for Your Course

A. *Literacy Teacher Vocabulary: A List of Terms.* With a small group or a partner, devise a way of helping each other master the chapter terms.

intuitive learning	Piaget
explicit learning	Vygotsky
implicit learning	role player
constructivist	Torrance

B. *What's Your Opinion?* Discuss *why* you agree or disagree with the following opinions:

1. Lev Vygotsky's research demonstrated that children learn best when they work alone without any major abstractions.
2. Letting children learn to read and write without being told the correct way is a terrible waste of time for teachers and children alike.
3. Jean Piaget's research demonstrated that young children learn best through concrete language and experiences.
4. Children need to become highly conscious of what they are learning. Therefore, most learning should be teacher-directed and highly explicit.
5. Self-correction of miscues should be taught as a vital way to improve students' ability to learn, read, and write on their own.
6. Creative thinking requires flexibility, originality, but not fluency.

C. *Causes of Early Reading:* Which Can Transition to Classroom Teaching?

1. Parents read to children daily—sometimes many times per day.
2. Parents read to themselves, and their children imitate them by reading by themselves.
3. Parents have books and magazines or other reading materials in more than one place in the house.
4. Parents write letters or e-mail messages to their friends and let their children watch.
5. Parents listen to their children and answer their questions.
6. Parents allow their children to have their own books, paper, and pencils and pens.
7. Parents accept their children's funny spelling as honest attempts to communicate.
8. Parents allow their children to read or try to read without correcting them.

Creativity Training Session

A. Make a list of all the things you can do with the following:

1. A single wooden pencil
2. One dozen wooden pencils with erasers
3. One dozen soup spoons

B. Using each letter of the word *creative*, make an eight-word motto or statement emphasizing the need to teach reading, writing, and spelling in interesting and original ways.

C. Develop a character for a story who is the kind of teacher you would like to be. Describe this character in creative detail, complete with a name. Share your character with others in a small group.

Field Experiences

A. *Mini–Case Study 1:* Carefully observe a 3- or 4-year-old and then a 6- or 7-year-old. Get samples of their writing and reading behavior. Talk to them individually, very informally, about reading and writing. Ask questions that Piaget and Vygotsky might have asked. Record your observations shortly afterward (or during if you can do it without disturbing the learning environment). Be sure to record the child's exact age in years and months. Then share your study with others who have done a similar study.

B. *Mini–Case Study 2:* Carefully observe a child who is between the ages of 10 and 14. Go through the same procedures used in Mini–Case Study 1.

References

California Department of Education. (1999). *Reading and language arts frameworks for California Public Schools: kindergarten through grade twelve.* Sacramento, CA: Author.

California Department of Education. (2003). *Science frameworks for the California public schools: Kindergarten through grade twelve.* Sacramento, CA: Author.

Clay, M. M. (1991). *Becoming literate: The construction of inner control.* Portsmouth, NH: Heinemann.

Clay, M. M. (2001). *Change over time in children's literacy development.* Portsmouth, NH: Heinemann.

Clay, Y. (2002). *An observation survey of early literacy achievement.* Portsmouth, NH: Heinemann.

Davis, G., & Rimm, S. (1998). *Education of the gifted and talented.* Upper Saddle Creek, NJ: Prentice Hall.

Davis, W. E., & McCaul, E. J. (1990). *At risk children and youth: A crisis in our schools and society.* Orono: University of Maine.

Doake, D. B. (1986). Learning to read: It starts in the home. In D. R. Tovey & J. E. Kerber (Eds.), *Roles in literacy learning: A new perspective.* Newark, DE: International Reading Association.

Durkin, D. (1966). *Children who read early.* New York: Teachers College Press.

Ferreiro, E. (1990). Literacy development: Psychogenesis. In Y. M. Goodman (Ed.), *How children construct literacy: Piagetian perspectives.* Newark, DE: International Reading Association.

Forbes, S., Poparad, M. A., & McBride, M. (2004). To err is human; to self-correct is to learn. *The reading teacher, 57,* 566–572.

Goodman, Y. M. (Ed.). (1985a). *How children construct literacy: Piagetian perspectives.* Newark, DE: International Reading Association.

Goodman, Y. M. (1985b). Observing children in their classroom. In A. Jagger & M. T. Smith-Burk (Eds.), *Observing language learners* (pp. 9–18). Newark, DE: International Reading Association and Urbana, IL: National Council of Teachers of English.

Goodman, Y. M. (1990). Forward. In Y. M. Goodman (Ed.), *How children construct literacy: Piagetian perspectives.* Newark, DE: International Reading Association.

Goodman, Y. M., & Goodman, K. S. (1994). To err is human: Learning about language processes by analyzing miscues. In R. B. Ruddell, M. R. Ruddell, & H. Singer (Eds.), *Theoretical models and processes of reading* (4th ed., pp. 104–123). Newark, DE: International Reading Association.

Green, M. (2000). *Releasing the imagination: Essays on education, the arts and social change.* San Francisco: Jossey-Bass.

Grossi, E. P. (1990). Applying psychogenesis principles to the literacy instruction of lower class children in Brazil. In Y. M. Goodman (Ed.), *How children construct literacy: Piagetian perspectives.* Newark, DE: International Reading Association.

Holdaway, D. (1979). *The foundations of literacy.* Sydney, Australia: Ashton Scholastic.

Holdaway, D. (1986). Guiding a natural process. In D. R. Tovey & J. E. Kerber (Eds.), *Roles in literacy learning: A new perspective* (pp. 42–51). Newark, DE: International Reading Association.

Landsman, L. T. (1990). Literacy development and pedagogical implications: Evidence from the Hebrew system of writing. In Y. M. Goodman (ed.) *How children construct literacy: Piagetien perspectives.* Newark, DE: International Reading Association.

Piaget, J. (1974, January 30). *Manas.*

Rogoff, B. (1986). Adult assistance of children's learning. In T. E. Raphael (Ed.), *The contexts of school-based literacy* (pp. 27–40). New York: Random House.

Rogoff, B. (1990). *Apprenticeship in thinking: Cognitive development in social context.* New York: Oxford University Press.

Rorty, R. (2000, March 10). Being that can be understood is language. *The London Review of Books,* p. 23.

Schwartz, R. M. (1997). Self-monitoring in beginning reading. *The Reading Teacher, 51,* 40–48.

Schwartz, R. M. (2005). Decisions, decisions: Responding to primary students during guided reading. *The Reading Teacher, 58*(5), 446–453.

Spencer, M. M. (1986). Nourishing and sustaining reading. In D. R. Tovey & J. E. Kerber (Eds.), *Roles in literacy learning: A new perspective.* Newark, DE: International Reading Association.

Spencer, M. M. (2003, July 29). *What more needs saying about imagination?* International Reading Association World Congress, Edinburgh, Scotland.

Spencer, M. M. (2003). What more needs saying about imagination? *The Reading Teacher, 57*(1), 105–111.

Sternberg, R., Grigorenko, E., & Jarvin, L. (2001). Improving reading instruction: The triarchic model. *Educational Leadership, 59*(6), 48–52.

Sternberg, R., Troff, B., & Grigorenko, E. (1998). Teaching for successful intelligence raises school achievement. *Phi Delta Kappan, 79*(9), 667–669.

Sulzby, E. (1985). Children's emergent reading of favorite storybooks: A developmental study. *Reading Research Quarterly, 20,* 458–481.

Teale, W. H. (1986). Home background and young children's literacy learning. In W. H. Teale & E. Sulzby (Eds.), *Emergent literacy: Writing and reading.* Norwood, NJ: Ablex.

Torrance, P. (1995). Insights into creativity: Questions asked, ridiculed and ignored. *Eucational Psychology Review, 7*(3), 313–322.

Tovey, D. R., & Kerber, J. E. (Eds.) (1986). *Roles in literacy learning: A new perspective* (pp. 66–72). Newark, DE: International Reading Association.

Vygotsky, L. S. (1978). *Mind and society.* Cambridge, MA: Harvard University Press.

Vygotsky, L. S. (1986). *Thought and language.* Cambridge, MA: Harvard University Press.

Other Suggested Readings

Arizpe, E., & Styles, M. (2003). *Children reading pictures: Interpreting visual texts.* London: Routledge Falmer.

Forester, A. D. (1986). Apprenticeship in the art of literacy. In D. R. Tovey & J. E. Kerber (Eds.), *Roles in literacy learning: A new perspective* (pp. 66–72). Newark, DE: International Reading Association.

Hall, M. H. (1986). Teaching and language-centered programs. In D. R. Tovey & J. E. Kerber (Eds.), *Roles in literacy learning: A new perspective* (pp. 34–41). Newark, DE: International Reading Association.

Heany, I. (1995). *The redress of poetry* (p. 15). London: Faber.

Levy, Y. (1999). Early metalinguistic competence: Speech monitoring and repair behavior. *Developmental Psychology, 35,* 822–834.

Mason, J. M., Peterman, C. L., & Kerr, B. M. (1989). Reading to kindergarten children. In D. S. Strickland & L. M. Morrow (Eds.), *Emerging literacy: Young children learn to read and write* (pp. 52–62). Newark, DE: International Reading Association.

Piaget, J. (1955). *The language and thought of the child.* New York: Meridian.

Pressley, M., Allington, R., Wharton-McDonald, R., Block, C. C., & Morrow, L. M. (2001). *Learning to read: Lessons from exemplary first-grade classrooms.* New York: Guilford.

Ruddell, M. R., Ruddell, R. B., & Singer, H. (Eds.). (2000). *Theoretical models and processes of reading* (4th ed., pp. 104–123). Newark, DE: International Reading Association.

Ruddell, R. B., & Ruddell, M. R. (1995). *Teaching children to read and write: Becoming an influential teacher.* Boston: Allyn & Bacon.

Sippola, Arne. (1994). Literacy education in kindergarten classes. *Reading Horizons, 35*(1), 52–61.

Tovey, D. R. (1986). Overview of the role. In D. R. Tovey & J. E. Kerber (Eds.), *Roles in literacy learning: A new perspective* (p. 65). Newark, DE: International Reading Association.

Vygotsky, L. S. (1978). *Mind in society: The development of higher psychological processes* (M. Cole, V. John-Steiner, S. Scribner, & E. Souberman, Eds.). Cambridge, MA: Harvard University Press.

Wood, D. (1998). *How children think and learn.* Oxford, England: Blackwell.

Chapter Two

The Nature of Reading, Writing, and Creativity

Second Objective for Your Teaching Success:

Teach students the processes of reading, writing, and creative thinking

---

Many thousands of years ago reading and writing did not exist. Communication was dependent on speaking and listening (or smoke signals, perhaps). About 5,500 years ago writing was invented by the Persians, and communication gradually came to be less concrete and direct—far more distant, magical, and abstract. Communication between people far apart became possible through the use of runners and boats carrying messages.

The Connection Between Reading and Writing and Listening and Speaking

Professional Standard: Understands the interrelation of reading and writing and listening and speaking

The nature of reading and writing is based on the nature of listening and speaking. The practical benefit of this knowledge is the realization that speaking and listening interacted in the same way that writing and reading did. People used to speak and listen to each other; now they can also write to each other and read what has been written.

This concept is not amazing to adults, but it is intriguing and important information for 6 to 9-year-old struggling readers who are discouraged by their slow progress as they try to learn to read and write well. Once children realize how speaking and listening, as well as writing and reading, are all related, the frightening mystery that many children experience when learning to read seems to disappear. Thus, there is a need to teach about the roots of writing and reading so that children do not see reading and writing as mysterious and abstract.

Communication is what happens when a child or adult reads, not to meet a requirement but to grasp what an author has to say. The reward is either entertainment or information or both. Communication also happens when a child or adult writes, not to meet a requirement but to provide other human beings with entertainment or information. And communication happens when someone speaks or listens with that same desire to entertain or inform or to be entertained or informed.

Five Magical Clues for Understanding What an Author Means

Professional Standard: Recognizes that reading should be taught as a process

Fortunately, both the writer and the reader use the same types of clues.

First Clue: Phonemes

Phonemes are the smallest language sounds, and your lucky students have already learned many of those sounds from past experiences of speaking and listening. Phonemes are those miniature sounds that Pat learned long ago from hearing them over and over in her name. Consequently she subconsciously memorized those sounds—/p/+/a/+/t/.

In kindergarten, at home, and in other places, Pat gradually mastered other tiny language sounds just from listening to cheerful rhyming books, rhyming songs, and Dr. Seuss, of course. (Many children are not so lucky, as you'll see in Chapter 3.) So the good news for Pat? On a 100-yard football field she's already on the 20-yard line. Her phonemic awareness is one of the major reasons she is rapidly acquiring literacy (Goswami, 2001; Harvey, Story, & Buker, 2002).

This same phonemic awareness is partly responsible for her rapid vocabulary development (Metsala, 1999). Without this awareness she probably would not be able to progress rapidly in learning how to read and write (Juel, 1988). Pat has it made: Not only does she have abundant phonemic awareness, she also has parents who engage in storybook reading and caregiver teaching—the best possible way to produce a lover of reading and writing (LeFevre & Senechal, 2001).

Second Clue: Graphemes

Graphemes are the written symbols for phonemes. They're the tough guys in our language. They put your spoken phonemes into writing, almost magically.

Each grapheme usually takes the form of one or two letters, sometimes more. When you write the word *shack*, you will need to write the grapheme, *SH* or *sh*, to represent the /sh/ sound. What grapheme would you write to represent the /th/ sound in *thin?* Yes, you would write the two-letter grapheme *TH* or *th*.

How many phonemes do you hear in the spoken word *tin?* That's right, three phonemes. So you need three graphemes to match them. You can represent the sounds of the three phonemes—/t/ + /i/ + /n/—by writing *tin* or *TIN.* As you can see, a grapheme is nothing more than a letter, like the *a* in *shack,* or a pair of letters, like the *sh* in *shack.*

To sum this up, you can *write* a grapheme, you can *hear* a phoneme. We human beings have always had phonemes in our lives, but only in the last 5,500 years or so have we had graphemes. Thanks again to the people of Sumeria, who invented the writing of messages and records with funny marks we now call letters and numbers.

Fortunately for all of us, our extremely complex brains guide our nervous system in such a way that when we read, we can see the graphemes and change them into phonemes. This magical change from graphemes to phonemes is what *phonics* is all about. And phonics, along with our search for meaning, helps us to decode, or decipher, a word or a whole message.

Third Clue: Syntax

Authors don't just throw words at you all at once, like a handful of sharp rocks. They put them on a string like pearls and pull them by your eyes one at a time. The order of the words, or *syntax,* gives you important clues about what the authors are talking about. For example, if an author puts the words in this order—*John ate the lion*—you know that John was the lucky one. If the author puts the words in this order—*The lion ate John*—you know the lion was the lucky one.

Fourth Clue: Semantics

A box of *semantic clues* makes a great gift from the author, especially at dinner time. These attractive, picture-like meaning clues provide solid meat for the dinner; they tell things like who, when, where, and what (four condiments for the dinner). For instance, in this message from the author—*John greedily ate the mean, ferocious lion right after shooting it with his rifle and cooking it over the fire*—the author gives you bite after bite of delicious, picturesque meaning.

Fifth Clue: Memories and Minitheories from Prior Experiences

When you read, an author is giving you four gifts, and you're giving the author one. If the author tells you that John is about to have a feast and eat the lion, she may not tell you everything you want to know about the feast. You may have to guess about the things that were left out. To help you understand what the author is telling you, you'll have to remember and think about your own past experiences.

When you think about a feast, for instance, you might get pictures in your mind of John cooking the lion on a spit, basting it with its own juices, smelling the beeflike aroma, and perhaps sharing with you the task of carving the meat. What a gift you're giving the author!

Reading is like a potluck dinner that includes the past experiences of both author and reader and the other four magical clues: the graphemes we see in print that stimulate the creation of phonemes inside our heads; the syntax clues that provide us with the order or structure of a sentence; and the descriptive images that help create meaning. All five elements work together and keep right on influencing each other while we're reading.

The Importance of Prediction

Does reading include predicting what the writer is going to write next? Absolutely!

Predicting as We Read

Prediction made, prediction checked, that's the way to do it when you read (Goodman & Goodman, 1994). Reading is simply an extension of what we humans do during our nonreading times: constantly predicting and checking, predicting and checking. What's the general message going to be? What's the author going to say next? Was I right? What word is coming next? Was I right? What's the main character in the story going to do next? Was I right?

Just watch what you do as you read right now. What word do you think goes at the end of the next sentence?

Tarzan swam across the current and climbed out on the other side of the _____.

Pretty easy to predict, right? Now try this one.

The dog lifted his _____ and watered the fire hydrant.

Another easy one, I dare say. All right, try a harder one.

It was a very cold day in winter. On the pond three ducks _____ across the _____.

Even though your prediction might not have been exactly the same as mine (*skidded across the ice*), it probably made as much sense.

Checking Our Predictions

We do check our predictions (Goodman & Goodman, 1994): (1) we notice the author's meaning (e.g., something like *a glass*), and (2) we see letters grouped into graphemes (g + l + a + ss) that we hear as phonemes (/g/ + /l/ + /a/ + /s/). *Caution:* Don't try to memorize this stuff yet. Just aim for awareness and understanding.

Watch what happens when you try to read this sentence:

> Tarzan swam against the current and got out on the other side of the _____ .

Did you predict the word *river?* Better check the grapheme clusters: r a p + id + s. This time your first prediction, based only on meaningful context, wasn't quite right. So you checked the graphemes, changed your mind, and read the word as *rapids.*

When we read, we predict . . . check . . . change our prediction . . . check again—all the time paying attention to the author's meaning and all the time paying attention to the graphemes. Our brain—even a child's brain—is capable of such simultaneous, interactive thinking (Adams, 1990, 1991)—provided the subject is fairly easy to understand. But let me give you one or two more examples—to get you a bit more ready to *teach* reading rather than *misteach* it. See if you can predict what words go in the blanks:

> The b_____ sailed over the _____ .

Here's how my friend Phil predicted the words.

Phil: The first word is obviously *boat.*

Frank: Why do you say that?

Phil: Because of the word *sailed.* I don't know about you, Frank, but whenever I sail, I use a boat.

Frank: So do I, but suppose I told you that the first word isn't *boat.*

Phil: Then I'd say you're playing tricks on me.

Frank: No tricks, honestly. The first word isn't *boat.*

Phil: OK, so what is it? I know it starts with *b*, but nothing else starts with *b* that sails over something.

Frank: What about a ball?

Phil: A ball?

Frank: Sure. I hit the ball and it sailed over the _____ .

Phil (smiling): You're a rat. You know that, don't you?

Frank: Yeah. So what's the last word in the sentence?

Phil: Obviously the word is *net.*

Frank: How can you be so sure? You were wrong with the first word.

Phil: I'm just sure, that's all. The only thing a ball's going to sail over is a tennis net—or maybe a volleyball net.

Frank: Umm, what about a baseball?

Like I said a few sentences ago, reading is predicting . . . checking . . . changing predictions . . . checking again. But how do we know what to predict? And how do we know how to check that prediction? There will be more about this as we go through the remaining chapters. But just listening to Phil and Frank suggests something else about reading that we didn't talk about before. Reading is not simply devouring words held loosely together. Reading is looking inside your own understanding. It's allowing the words to stimulate and stir up your own memories. It's letting yourself interact with the author by thinking about past experiences—with boats and balls and nets and things that go sailing across something. Reading is hitting the ball back to your communication partner, the author.

Reading Without Correct Schemas

Reading is also matching your schema with the author's. A *schema* is a theory or a hunch or a belief that you and I create as we experience life. Schemas, also called *minitheories*, get stored in our minds and help us survive and learn. Have you ever had the experience of trying to read something that made no sense at all? Probably no more than 95 times, right? When that happens, it's usually the fault of the writer, who simply doesn't realize how much information has been left out. I tell you about this because teachers are sometimes guilty of asking questions or giving information that is outrageously inadequate.

So I'd like you to have an emotional experience that will help you remember the importance of having accurate schemas. Once you finish this experience, you'll know nearly all of the things that reading is really composed of.

> This operation is really not that difficult. First you remove them from the room you've just used and take them into the other room. Next you remove the material you no longer want and place each piece in the appropriate place. Don't worry if this sometimes seems difficult. In time you'll get used to all the possibilities that are available to you. After you're satisfied with the arrangement, just follow the directions on the front and you'll be finished for a while. Later, when you have a need for them again, you can use them directly or put them away and use them some other time. It's true that you have to repeat the operation many times in the course of living, but I'm sure you'll agree that it's worth it.

What? You didn't understand my meaning? You say there's something lacking? In that case please read it again. It's very important that you read it again, but not before you realize that I was merely trying to describe how to use a simple dishwasher during the course of a normal day. Good teachers would have told you this before you tried reading the passage, right? Yes, but I wanted to play the role of bad teacher this time. In fact, I wanted to prove to you that reading is truly a process of matching schemas between writer and reader (Rumelhart, 1976). Please do read the selection again and see how much easier it is to communicate with the author now that you have a mutual understanding.

An Illusive Ingredient of Reading Imagination

As you probably know so well, skillful reading requires students to create pictures in their minds. My virtual colleagues Arizpe and Styles (2003) and Wood and Endres (2005) agree wholeheartedly. This piece of knowledge is so important that I hope you will remind your students every time they are about to read a book or a chapter or a page. Give it a catchy name that they can remember, like Imagination Time or Time for Pictures or just Picture Time. I'm sure you can come up with something better.

To help you remember this vital ingredient, let me tell you a short story about a farmer's son I taught in my fifth-grade class in Pullman, Washington. James was not only my student; he was my neighbor down the road, when we lived out in the country. In my class James was always quiet and dutiful and enjoyable. He worked very hard to read the books and materials that the rest of the class read, but he seldom understood what he was reading. His peers thought he was a good reader because he never mispronounced a single word. But what good did it do him—he wasn't learning anything the books' authors were trying to teach him.

When I talked to his dad, who was gathering his large flock of sheep, he said, "Oh, don't worry about it, Frank. He doesn't like to read like his sister does. I guess boys aren't so good at that kind of thing."

A month later school was over, and I was feeling really disappointed. I'd failed this sweet, thoughtful boy, and I vowed I would keep on trying to teach him to read well, if he was willing to meet with me every day for the month of June. To my surprise he was excited about learning to read that way: "Just me and you, Mr. May!"

It took only 2 weeks for James to turn himself into a much better reader. A casual remark by me had started the change: "Do you see anything inside your head when you're reading, James?"

His mouth dropped, and he stared at me like I was someone from outer space. "I din' know I was spose'ta!"

End of story, until the moment when James's dad came driving down the road, carrying a medium size sheep just for me. "You're a miracle man, Frank. That boy reads as good as his sister now. Keeps us awake at night, reading book after book together. You musta attached his brain to a 'lectric wire."

Before I could respond, he held up the sheep and said with grim determination, "I'm taking this one to the slaughterhouse. You and your family are gonna have one heck of a feast!"

I don't like killing animals, but all I could do was grin. If a sheep had to be sacrificed so this wonderful lad could learn to read, so be it.

By this time I'm hoping you have seen that reading is still one more thing. Have you guessed it? You're right—reading is playing. And playful literacy is what it's all about. This time five of my colleagues agree fervently: Padak & Rasinski (2000); Saracho (1994); and Scully & Roberts (2002). Playfulness and literacy belong together, whether we are teaching or reading or writing.

And now let me summarize this process called reading. If I leave something out, I hope you'll tell me what it is.

1. Predicting the graphemes, word, idea, or action that's coming.

2. Checking your predictions and changing them if necessary, by thinking about the letters and the content.

3. Communicating with the author by actively making sense out of the printed words and ideas being expressed.

4. Allowing the author's words to stimulate memories, imagination, and pictures of your own experiences.

It's just that amazing!

Why Kids Make Mistakes

Professional Standard: Understands the nature of reading and writing difficulties

Reading is only as difficult as we make it for children, and it becomes more difficult when we correct them for the wrong things. Our ancestors believed that to teach children to read well, you had to correct them every time they made a mistake. That way they wouldn't make the same mistake over and over again. And that way they'd learn to read carefully, word by word, and not guess. To guess was to be uncertain, and to be uncertain of your next move was a first cousin to sinning. My own great-grandmother, bless her, believed that all mistakes were the work of the devil.

All right, I'll stop picking on those well-intentioned parents and teachers way back then. I really do understand that they were doing the best they could. After all, no one had done any research yet to see if their assumptions were correct, so how were they to know that they weren't? No one had told them, for instance, that the way good readers read is to make intelligent guesses called predictions. No one had explained that good readers don't plod along letter by letter, word by word. Good readers are those who have learned to communicate with authors like zestful listeners, as equals, not like timid little mice carefully nibbling each bit of cheese laid out in a row by a frightful giant called an Author.

A Mini–Case Study of a Skillful Reader

Let me give you an example of what I mean. Belinda is a good reader who reads with gusto and scores well on comprehension tests, which require her to read a passage silently, then check the best answers to the questions. She almost always understands the author's message. Notice how she reads a passage out loud.

Author's Version

Jimmy rode his bike into the street. The driver of an automobile slammed on his brakes to keep from hitting the boy. Then the driver got out and scolded Jimmy.

Belinda's Version

Jimmy rode his bike into a busy street. The driver of a car screeched on his brakes to keep from hitting Jimmy. Then the driver got out and scared . . . and scolded him.

How many errors did this skillful reader make? If you believe what your great-great-grandma was taught, Belinda made nine serious errors, and therefore she's a poor reader. In the first sentence she substituted *a* for *the* and inserted the word *busy*. In the second sentence she substituted *a* for *an, car* for *automobile*, and *screeched* for *slammed*. She omitted *the* and then substituted *Jimmy* for *boy*. In the third sentence she first substituted *scared* for *scolded* but then self-corrected herself. She went on to substitute *him* for *Jimmy*.

Nine errors—and only one of them corrected! Belinda is definitely full of the devil. And she couldn't possibly be a skillful reader, could she? She's certainly no good at reading out loud. Hurrumph!

In actuality Belinda is a budding skillful reader if you accept two observations: (1) Over 90% of all reading done by adults is silent rather than aloud (Rogoff, 1990), and (2) from a practical standpoint, reading is an act of understanding rather than just pronouncing what the author has to say. When we are reading silently, and even when reading out loud, we must concentrate on understanding the author in order to be successful.

So, does Belinda read with understanding? You can actually tell by the errors she makes. Instead of saying that Jimmy rode his bike into the street, she says that Jimmy rode his bike into a *busy* street. Now that's understanding! She communicated with the author by thinking of her own experiences with bicycles and streets. And instead of the driver slamming on his brakes, he *screeches* them on. That's definitely comprehension. Belinda is right there on the scene, seeing and hearing the action. She even gets carried away for a moment and imagines that the driver *scares* Jimmy instead of just scolding him. But then she corrects that "error." (Wouldn't a kid be scared of a big guy scolding him?) Belinda's not only an understanding reader, she's also a self-corrective one. Normally she corrects only those errors that truly change the author's message.

Belinda would verify the theories of Vygotsky (1978, 1986) and Piaget (1955, 1974): Children often teach themselves, although Rogoff (1990) found that it is often satisfying to have an adult overlooking their learning strategies.

Why Skillful Readers Keep Looking Ahead

Why in the world *did* Belinda substitute the word *car* for the word *automobile*? Couldn't she see that one word started with the letter *c* and the other with the letter *a*? Here again Belinda demonstrated one of the characteristics of a skillful reader. Even though she was reading out loud to people who might have judged her, she didn't cautiously read word by word. Nor does she seem to do that when she reads silently. She does something trickier.

By the time Belinda was ready to pronounce the word *automobile* out loud, she had already looked ahead and read *automobile* silently. In fact, using her past experiences, her eyes and brain had raced ahead to think about the driver's brakes and how they must be causing the tires to screech.

In order to read ahead like that, Belinde's brain had to store what she had already read silently: "The driver of the automobile . . . " When she then wanted to retrieve what she had stored, her brain remarkably translated the word *automobile* to the more familiar word *car*. As you can see, Belinda was interacting intensely with the author by subconsciously translating his language into her own language. And that is why her comprehension is so good.

Does your brain do the same thing when you're listening instead of reading? Yes, that's exactly what it does when you are listening to someone speak. Imagine that John says, "Yeah, Jimmy was almost killed by a big ol' automobile that ran into him when he was riding his bike." How would you then tell that story to someone else? Probably something like this: "Jimmy was hit by a car! Yeah, he was riding his bike, and he got clobbered!" The word *automobile* would have been transformed in your translation.

The good news is this: When you subconsciously translate an idea into your own language, you understand it much better. The next time you silently read a book or a magazine article, notice those times when you've made word "errors" in order to predict what the author is going to say next or those times when you've read ahead and translated a word or two into your own language. I think you'll be amazed at how many harmless mistakes we adults make when we read. Actually, they're not only harmless; they're usually quite useful in helping us dig deeper to understand what we read.

A Mini–Case Study of a Struggling Reader

Now let's listen to Micah as he reads the same passage aloud. He's got a cold, so you'll hear him read the word *street* as *streed*, but this is not a reading error. Once again, please read all of the author's version before you read Micah's version.

> **Author's Version**
>
> Jimmy rode his bike into the street. The driver of an automobile slammed on his brakes to keep from hitting the boy. Then the driver got out and scolded Jimmy.

> **Micah's Version**
>
> Jimmy rode his bike into the streed the diver of an . . . out-o-byle slammed on his brakes to keep from hiding the boy then the diver got out and . . . (What's that word?) . . . scolded Jimmy.

Hey, wait a minute. Micah made only four errors and Belinda made nine. Doesn't that make Micah the good reader and Belinda the poor one? You're right; it does *not*. Belinda's goal was to thoroughly understand the author's message. Micah's goal was to get through the passage and get on with something other than reading (perhaps riding his bike).

Micah, a struggling reader, has the wrong concept of what reading really is. To Micah, reading is knocking off those silly words quickly, one at a time, until they're done for. They're dead. They're history.

How Struggling Readers Approach Reading

A poor reader often reminds me of a window scraper I once knew. A window scraper? Yes, this is a real occupation. A window scraper is a painter's apprentice, the one who comes around after your house or apartment has been painted and he scrapes the excess paint off your windows with a razor blade. The window scraper I knew, whose name was Barry, had a very definite strategy for scraping off the paint. Left-handed Barry would start at the upper left-hand corner, scrape toward the right, then lift his razor blade and move back to the left edge again, exactly like an old typewriter moves—or the eyes of a person reading a book in English. As he scraped, the peeled paint fell to the ground like discarded curls.

Are Some of Your Students Using Barry's Method?

Barry's method worked fine for window scraping. Later, though I realized to my horror that many poor readers also use Barry's method. They start reading a page at the upper left-hand side and move to the right, scraping off streaks of words and letting them fall to the floor like discarded curls of paint.

Micah was using Barry's method. When he came to *driver* in the second sentence, he opted for the easier word *diver* despite the fact that he had just read about Jimmy riding his bike into the street. If Micah had had the correct concept of reading, his mind would have been digging up past experiences related to streets and bicycles, and he would have known that the word *driver* fit the author's context much better than *diver* did.

Micah's concept of reading is that it is strictly a pronouncing act rather than an act of understanding or communicating with someone. Therefore, his strategy is to scan the letters quickly and come up with something that sounds like a word. Or in Barry's terminology, "Keep scrapin' to the right till the words get out of your way." When his reading "razor" encountered a tough spot in *automobile* (Micah did understand the word—I asked him about it later), he simply saw a stubborn streak of "paint." Rather than think about what Jimmy might have seen in the street, Micah came up with a nice long nonsense word—*out-o-byle*. Good enough. Down came that nasty, long word.

Micah's final miscue was the word *scolded*. He did not attack the word by using context clues or searching for the phonic patterns, like *old* and *cold*. Instead, he chose the struggling reader's favorite device—asking someone else for the word. ("What's that word?" he said.)

Did you also notice that Micah bypassed all punctuation? Sort of like a speed demon on the road, bypassing the stop signs and other "obstacles." Many struggling readers do this, seeing no purpose for the author's punctuation.

Do Your Struggling Readers Know What Reading Is?

Micah didn't choose to read this way because he's lazy or stubborn. He chose it because the poor lad didn't understand the nature of reading. He really thought that reading was some kind of job—you know, like a paint scraping job. Or maybe like a dusting-chairs-for-your-mom job. You dust one chair, then the next, and so on till they're all done. Then your mom says, "Good job."

If you had listened to as many teachers as I've listened to, you would recognize that phrase as well as your name—"Good job." To the struggling reader, the one who has just huffed and puffed his way through a whole page of print, "Good job" means "You're all finished now. You made a noise for each word. So run along and do something you'd really like to do."

How Successful Teachers Think and Teach Creatively

Professional Standard: Gives learners opportunities as readers, writers, thinkers, reactors, and responders

To be truly successful, you need to be a model of good thinking, speaking, listening, reading, and writing—as well as a good demonstrator of what makes this world tick. It's a very tough job, as I remember so well. I'm still teaching a little and writing a lot, and in both cases I have to think creatively, but never as much as I have to when I'm teaching. Reading and writing, plus listening and speaking—all need the assistance of inventive, creative thinking by you and your students.

You know what imagination is, but what is creativity? Nothing more and nothing less than the ability to imagine and think thoughts you haven't thought before. Creative thoughts are either new or at least slightly new to you. But what else is creativity? More than anything else, it's a positive attitude about change. You and I are being creative whenever we accept change or do something in an original way—or even when we simply admire something that's new. An admiration of newness shows an open mind.

You and I are being creative when we have fun playing with our ideas, whether they're crazy like mine or semipractical like yours. More than anything else, you and I are creative when we're as flexible as a strong rubber band, instead of being as rigid as a steel rod. Without flexibility it's very difficult to think creatively or with a sense of excited inventiveness. Just think about it. Most teachers I've known, including me, do not stay in the teaching world very long unless they are flexible and optimistic. To put this another way, teachers are almost forced to think creatively in order to survive as teachers.

Robert Harris (2004) has done a beautiful and critical job of temporarily isolating five major methods of engaging in creative thoughts and actions: evolution, synthesis, revolution, reapplication, and changing direction—all categories that help us understand creativity in depth.

The Evolution Method of Creative Thinking and Teaching

With the *evolution method* we make improvements very gradually, with things like automobiles, washing machines, refrigerators, computers, and airplanes. These gradual improvements have occurred because people like you and me imagine how those things could become better. Lucky for us, imagination is the mother of our thinking abilities.

All creatures on this Earth (including us human beings) rely on creating images in our minds. Before we hit a baseball, for instance, we first imagine ourselves swinging the bat, hitting the ball, and watching it fly way over the fence. For less active humans creative thinking leads to imagining how to improve things like toaster ovens and refrigerators. For most other Earth creatures it means something more serious, namely, improving their survival strategies for living in the forests, in the waters, and on the extra-dangerous streets.

In addition to inch-by-inch improvement over time, the evolution method of creativity includes the action of taking one idea and letting it spark another one. Let's take peanut butter as an example. I don't know about you, but I've always had to combine peanut butter with something else—you know, like blueberry jam. However, as a camp counselor in northern New York, I learned that peanut butter simply *must* be combined with sweet pickles. What an exciting and creative improvement that was!

More recently, from my creative wife and best friend, Louise, I learned that peanut butter and a banana make the most ingenious and yummy combination ever generated in the history of the universe. When I discussed this matter with my friend Bogglestar from the Planet Xania, he agreed with me wholeheartedly and immediately sent a message to Xania. What a tasty creative evolution I have experienced in my life, and how splendid this bit-by-bit method of inventing and creating has become.

You may be wondering how to teach the evolution form of creative thinking and behaving. That's easy—by letting your students brainstorm together. Ask them how they would like to improve the common pencil, for example. Have somebody write down the many ideas they produce, but remember, with brainstorming every idea is accepted without criticism. The following day ask them how they would like to improve something else in the classroom, and make a list of those ideas. As a bonus just think how many words they're going to learn from this playful but powerful experience.

After that, gradually use the brainstorming method to help your students write and read, speak and listen. Let them brainstorm the meaning of new and difficult words, for example. Let them brainstorm the way those words should be spelled; then have them write their choices on the board. There are a zillion ways to use brainstorming, an experience that automatically and gradually improves their ability to think quickly, creatively, and critically.

After—and I do mean *after*—they have generated a long list of ideas, have them evaluate what's good and not so good about each one. Thus, critical thinking can be learned at the same time. If you wish, you can actually vote on which idea or combined ideas they want to use—but not "Whose idea is the best?" please.

The Synthesis Method of Creative Thinking and Teaching

Have you ever gone to a dinner theater? If no, save up your money—an astonishing experience is awaiting you. Instead of going to a restaurant for dinner on your birthday and then going to another place to see a musical, why not experience the inventive combination that the dinner theater provides? Whoever first thought of the dinner theater was doing some good creative thinking.

Of course, every time you drive your car and listen to your radio at the same time, you're giving another example of the *synthesis method* of creative entertainment and behavior. And what about a trio: driving your car, listening to your radio, and talking on your cell phone—all at once? That's a touch *too* creative for me, but you're probably younger than I am and think nothing of it. Here's a creative sample for your students.

> First review some of the compound words they have already learned, like *drugstore, breadbox, bookcase, blackboard, backpack,* and *catnap.* Then provide them with a list of compound words that are broken in two and mixed up helter-skelter. Show them how to create new compound words with any two of the words that they choose. Then have one child at a time go to the board, circle two words that fit together, and write that new compound. Then tell them to create brand new compound words that they would like to see in the dictionary, such as *softman* or *ringcatcher* or *newdog.* As they imagine and think of them, let them go up to the board and write them—with reasonable spelling.

And there you have a sample of the synthesis method of creative thinking. In the Application Experiences at the end of each chapter, you'll have other examples of the five methods of creative thinking for yourself and your students.

The Revolution Method of Creative Thinking and Teaching

The *revolution method* is not as complicated as a revolutionary war, but the concept of a major change is right there—front and center. A truly revolutionary creative idea might be something like this one:

> Mr. Fishbait was quite upset. The termites were eating up his house. Everything he tried—to get rid of the termites—did not work. But he was a creative thinker, and he had a revolutionary idea. He decided to change his tactics. Always before, he had used pesticide sprays. But this time, he said to himself, why not use liquid nitrogen? It should freeze the termites to death!

As you can see, the revolution method requires you to get rid of old ideas and try brand new ways of problem solving. Or try this experience with your students: Instead of letting them ask you how to spell a word while they're composing or journaling or editing, show them how to use inventive spelling for the first draft. Instead of "Sylvester caught the rabbit without touching him," let them use inventive spelling: "Sillvessdur cawt the rabbit withzowt tucheen him."

After students revise their composition with a buddy and are satisfied with how well they communicated, have them write the final draft for the class book, using only standard spelling approved by a team of skillful peer editors. The revolution method can be the most popular because it's exciting to bring novelty into your students' life.

The Reapplication Method of Creative Thinking and Teaching

I learned this creative method when I was putting a new roof on my house. The asphalt tiles I was nailing down were very easy to work with in the nice hot sun. But suddenly I came to the far edge of the roof and realized that I needed to use a tile cutter—an expensive tool designed to cut the tiles with great precision. With a lot of groaning and moaning, I remembered that I hadn't bought such a tool, and now I would have to drive into the city at a very busy time. Climbing down the ladder with a minor curse or two, I suddenly had an image in my mind of a pair of metal cutters—similar to the scissors you have in your kitchen, but bigger. I marched to the garage, grabbed the metal cutter, and headed back to the ladder.

My father-in-law, who was eating a sandwich while sitting on the grass, called out with an unearthly bellow. "Whatcha doin' with that metal cutter?" I gave him a smile, thinking he would praise me for such creativity and flexibility. No such luck. "Are you crazy?" he added, his brow furrowed, his eyes glaring like headlights. All I could come up with was a more feeble smile as I proceeded to cut the tiles with the metal cutter, happy as can be.

Reapplication involves looking at something old in a new way, going beyond labels, removing prejudices, getting rid of old assumptions and expectations. Keep your eyes open for things and ideas that can be reapplied. After all, a paper clip can become a tiny screwdriver, and paint can become glue to make lightweight wallpaper stick back on the wall.

When one of your students bogs down on a book, should you make her finish the book or else? No! Simply help her pick out a book that is more interesting to her and that she can read with ease. This is a good example of an idea that should be reapplied. Why make a child hate what she is reading? The creative way is the reapplication way.

The Changing-Direction Method of Creative Thinking and Teaching

This method is probably the one most needed in this world of ours. Have you ever been on a committee that gets bogged down because one person is convinced that he has *the* solution. He's had that solution before the chairperson opened the meeting. He's had it even before coming to the committee meeting. He's had it before the Earth was created! Unfortunately, most people on the committee don't like his solution. They don't know what the solution should be, but they do know they do not want his solution.

So what's the problem? The problem is this: The committee has jumped to solutions before they have defined what their problem really is. So what's the creative thing to do at this point? Whether you're adults or fifth graders just list the possible problems on the board. Spend as much time as necessary to creatively list the things that might be wrong. Once this happens, spend the rest of your time boiling down those things to only one or two major problems. And then you're ready to engage in brainstorming solutions, following the rules for brainstorming.

Without any discussion of individual solutions suggested, write them on the chalkboard or newsprint. Remind everyone that no negative comments are allowed while the brainstorming is going on. The solutions can be as creative or as wild as you wish. When you've brainstormed long enough, begin the critical thinking phase. Talk about the pluses and minuses of each idea—without arguing, only listening. Once everyone has been heard, begin the debate. Praise each other for the thoughtful suggestions offered. If some don't like a suggestion, encourage them to find something in the suggestion that might work *if* the suggestion is modified. Aim for a consensus; vote only if absolutely necessary. This approach works quite well with children in fifth through eighth grades as long as they work in small groups of three or four instead of the entire class.

Let me close with this reminder: Creative thinking is dependent on critical thinking. Start with critical thinking, move to creative thinking (let's make it better); and finish off with conclusive thinking (now this way's going to work). You can see how real learning is taking place with this method, which requires your students to engage in talking, listening, writing, and reading. All of those literacy skills are developed with this method.

The Ingredients for Thinking and Teaching Creatively

Characteristics of Creative Adults and Children

I guarantee that you'll see yourself in some or all of these personality traits. This self-examination is appropriate for both adults and children from fifth grade on up.

Autonomous: These adults or children are comfortably independent. They like to make their own decisions and judgments without relying too much on the opinions of others. They have a high degree of self-confidence. They're willing to go against the crowd in the interest of trying to determine what is true or beautiful or fair or right. As a teacher you probably see yourself to some extent in this description. How autonomous are you now or do you soon want to be—a little, an average amount, quite a bit, very much?

Visionary: These adults or children aren't afraid of changes and often desire them. They perceive important changes as possible when others may not. Visionary individuals feel consciously or subconsciously that they are agents of change for the better. They're emotionally and intellectually far sighted. How visionary are you now or do you soon want to be—a little, an average amount, quite a bit, very much?

Goal-oriented: These adults or children have numerous ideas for keeping themselves occupied. They apply considerable effort toward projects that interest them. They have both short-range and long-range goals, and they seldom give up on their goals. How goal-oriented are you now or do you soon want to be?

Flexible: These adults or children show a high degree of adaptability in problem situations. They also use language flexibly and humorously. Give-and-take is their middle name. How flexible are you now or do you soon want to be?

Open: These adults or children demonstrate abundant curiosity and are reluctant to make judgments too quickly. They tolerate and seek new ideas and are willing to have closure or conclusions delayed. How open are you now or do you soon want to be?

Adventurous: These adults or children enjoy taking risks. They like to try new things. They enjoy the challenge of complex stimuli. How adventurous are you now or soon want to be?

Children who are highly creative tend to enjoy helping make important decisions, choosing their own books to read, planning their own schedule of work, making comparisons between or among books. They tend to be curious, optimistic, and able to suspend judgment. However, they don't thrive on working alone all the time. In fact, Johnson and Johnson (1991) found the following to be true:

In a number of studies, highly creative students at various ages did better in heterogeneous, cooperative groups than they did alone . . . they have more positive attitudes about the learning situation, are more motivated, and tend to feel better about themselves. They practice . . . leadership skills and conflict-resolution skills . . . they are accepted by their peers and are seen as resources rather than as competitors to be feared and stereotyped (p. 40).

Experiences That Can Lead to Greater Creativity

Students who are usually goal oriented tend to enjoy projects, both individual and small-group, particularly if they get to choose what they will work on. So have an index-card box on your desk with ideas for extra projects in it, such as creating a new spelling game, writing a history of the school, or reporting on the most inexpensive and effective materials for teaching first graders about fractions. Most students enjoy book projects like those in Appendix E. Be sure to encourage them to make up their own project ideas as well.

Here are some ways to encourage creative thinking in your literacy program.

1. **To encourage flexibility**—provide students with problems that require adaptability and offer more than one answer. For a journal experience or a language experience chart, have students engage in an imaginary adventure: for example, lost in a huge city with no money—only a watch, a bag of lemons, and clothes—how do you get home? Or try this one: stuck in a stalled elevator with your little brother, who is crying, decide how to entertain him until help arrives. All you have in your pocket is a paper clip, a handkerchief, three pennies, and a pencil with no point. Have students share their stories, orally or in writing.

   Also provide students with opportunities to use language flexibly. If they make a pun with your words, try to enjoy their humor with them. (If the puns are too disruptive to share orally, have them make a book of them for others to enjoy.) Help students play with words by recommending books by Fred Gwynne (*The King Who Rained* and *A Chocolate Moose for Dinner*) and also by Marvin Terban (*Eight Ate: A Feast of Homonym Riddles, In a Pickle and Other Funny Idioms, Too Hot to Hoot*).

2. **To encourage open-mindedness**—give students 5 minutes to list as many things as they can think of that they want to find out about. Have them use the hot water method when they make their list. (The hot water of ideas is the only faucet turned on; they should not turn on the cold water of criticism while the hot water is on.) Have them write down every idea they have, no matter how silly it might seem. Then have them select the one they're most curious about. Collaborate with them on a plan for doing the research that will help them find out what they want to know.

Another idea is to have two or more children read the same book and then compare their ideas about the book. Let the not-so-creative students participate, too. Who was the most important character? Why do they agree or disagree? How would they have done something differently from the way the main character did it? Could this story have taken place in any other setting? Why was the setting the author chose important or not important? If this story could have taken place in another setting, how would that setting have affected what happened in the story? Could the main character have been different in age or personality? If the children agree with each other too readily, you should try disagreeing with them, cheerfully challenging their ideas.

3. **To encourage adventurousness**—remember that highly creative children often like to take risks, trying something new and even dangerous; and they often enjoy things that are complex. Recommend books such as *Island of the Blue Dolphins, Call It Courage, Exploring the Bismark: The Real-Life Quest to Find Hitler's Greatest Battleship, My Side of the Mountain*, and of course, *The Hobbit*. Encourage students to try a book project that no one has ever tried before. Help them use books as starting points for writing their own adventures and then reading them to others. Let them use a tape recorder to add a variety of sound effects to their stories.

When accelerated readers are provided the same basic reading instruction as other students in a class, [they] may . . . perform at a level similar to that of less advanced readers. . . . Young gifted students with advanced abilities may have as great a need for . . . instruction—but at their own level of performance—as other students. (Burns, Collins, & Paulsell, 1991)

Let me describe one research study of accelerated and nonreading children in which this regression was demonstrated. When the study began, the children were 4 years old. The gifted children were already reading between first- and fifth-grade levels; they were also quite advanced at invented spelling. The nonreaders could not read a word, and they had a very limited degree of phonemic awareness or awareness of phonic patterns.

During the next 4 years, these children had the same type of basal instruction in spite of the large differences in their prior knowledge. When they were tested 4 years later, "no significant differences were found on subtests measuring word recognition or comprehension" (Burns, Collins, & Paulsell, 1991, p. 118). Evidently, without the special stimulation they needed, the gifted children simply slid toward the lowest common denominator.

Focus on Students with Special Needs: Comments by Louise Fulton

Peer Mediated Learning

"When we practiced math and reading together, we both learned." These words from a fifth grader who had participated in the Peer Education Partners (PEP) Program at Hillside School tell a story about the effectiveness of a peer mediated learning. Peer-to-peer instructional intervention offers one way to get special needs students actively engaged in the reading process.

Small groups and one-on-one instruction are especially important for students with special needs, who need more time than the average student to sort out words and make sense of what they are reading. In addition, they need confidence-building success experiences, they thrive on frequent and positive feedback, and they need to be reminded to apply their learning strategies. One solution is to use all available resources, and students are a golden resource.

A few years ago, my former student Chris and I set out to develop a peer-to-peer program to promote interaction between special and general students at his school. In order for this idea to sell, we needed to find a way to convince teachers and parents that typical students would benefit, too. After spending months talking with parents and teachers about their ideas and concerns, we knew that we needed a real "carrot." Thus, a career development component was devised, and the peer education program was born (Fulton, LeRoy, Pinkney, & Weekley, 1994).

To participate in PEP, students must read about job vacancies posted on the school bulletin board and then complete a job application. Examples of jobs include reading pal, computer buddy, library friend, and math mentor. After an interview with the teacher, a student is hired for a 6-week period. Two training periods are then scheduled, in which students learn about specific job requirements. Once trained, the PEP students participate in accountability procedures, such as sign-in-/-out cards, weekly self- and teacher evaluations, and daily journal writing.

To our surprise, several students with special needs applied and were hired. Their behavioral problems seemed to disappear. In PEP they had many opportunities to practice such skills as journal writing, staying on task, reading silently, reading along with a peer, and listening while another student read aloud.

The principal was so supportive of PEP that she initiated an awards assembly at which each PEP graduate received a PEP leadership cap in front of the student body. After 2 years I surveyed parents and teachers and conducted interviews with the students. It was clear to all that PEP had resulted in academic and social gains for both special-needs and general-education students. The parents were especially enthusiastic about the development of leadership and career skills for their children. As one parent put it, "Now Gracie is talking about a career in teaching!"

Summary of Main Ideas

- The writer and reader use the same type of cues or clues: phonemes, graphemes, syntax, semantics, images, and schemas.
- Predicting and checking are vital reading strategies.
- Successful readers understand the nature of reading and use specific strategies for getting the author's meanings. Struggling readers do not.
- Reading and readers are often dependent on creative thinking, an ability that can be learned.
- Successful teachers model creative thinking.
- Successful teachers encourage creative behaviors such as autonomous, visionary, goal oriented, flexible, open minded, and adventurous.

Literacy Through Technology

A. Working with a partner, go to the PBS Web site at http://www.pbs.org/circleofstories/ and investigate film, artwork, and music honoring authentic Native American storytelling. What did you learn from this site to make your storytelling more interesting and authentic?

B. In the same way, visit the American Academy of American Poets Web site at http://www.poets.org to see how you might incorporate more poetry from across the world in read-alouds to your students. Be sure to notice the audio recordings of poems as a possible resource.

Application Experiences for Your Course

A. *Literacy Teacher Vocabulary: A List of Terms.:* With a small group help each other master the professional terms:

semantic cues   syntactic cues   schematic cues   schemas   creative thinking

miscues   decoding   phonemes   graphemes   struggling reader

B. *What's Your Opinion?:* Discuss why you agree or disagree with the following opinions. Support your point of view specifically, using your own experiences and the textbook.

1. In a natural, rather than a forced, learning environment, human beings don't cut a new skill into little pieces in order to learn it.
2. Reading is much more the process of predicting and checking than it is the process of simultaneous decoding and comprehending.
3. Struggling readers suffer primarily from erroneous concepts and strategies of reading.
4. The evolution method of creative thinking is inferior to other methods.

C. Turn to Appendix B at the back of this book and read "The Sam Trap," a short story written in an alternative alphabet called Applebet. Your experience will be somewhat similar to that of young children when they're first learning to read. You'll have fun and gain some understanding at the same time.

Creativity Training Session

A. Try a creative thinking activity that makes you get out of your rut and opens your mind to new possibilities. With others, determine the real meanings of a sports car. Come up with at least six ideas—funny, serious, or ridiculous. Then determine the real meanings of a pair of jeans that has been almost destroyed—six ideas minimum.

B. With a small group of classmates, create a new alphabet, complete with symbols that stand for letters. Feel free to vary the number of letters in your new alphabet. Then create words that use only those letters and write a few short sentences with the new alphabet. Finally, make up a code sheet and ask another person to read your sentences as fast as they can, using the code sheet of course.

Field Experiences

A. Informally interview several children, one at a time, to see if you can determine what their concepts of reading and writing are. Create a question list before the interview, and be sure to make your questions interesting. You may want to start with questions like these:

1. What do you think reading is? What is writing?
2. Why do people read?
3. Is reading mainly pronouncing words or do you have to understand the words?
4. Do you think that silent reading is like listening to someone tell you a story?
5. When you read a story, do you ever feel like you are the one *telling* the story?

B. Compare successful versus struggling readers. Listen to a child read who is a level above grade level in reading, then one who is a level below grade level. Do the high-level readers produce self-corrections as well as substitutions that fit the meaning of the author? Explain how they differ. What kinds of substitutions do the low-level readers produce? Do they often ask for help with words? If possible, use a tape recorder for this experience so you can easily write it up or have others listen to your results.

References

Adams, M. J. (1990). *Beginning to read: Thinking and learning about print.* Cambridge, MA: MIT Press.

Adams, M. J. (1991). Beginning to read: A critique by literacy professionals and a response by Marilyn Jager Adams. *The Reading Teacher, 44,* 370–395.

Arizpe, E., & Styles, M. (2003). *Children reading pictures: Interpreting visual texts.* London: Routledge Falmer.

Burns, J. M., Collins, M. D., & Paulsell, J. C. (1991). A comparison of intellectually superior preschool accelerated readers and nonreaders: Four years later. *Gifted Child Quarterly, 35*(3), 118–124.

Fulton, L., LeRoy, C., Pinkney, M., & Weekley, T. (1994). Peer education partners. *Teaching Exceptional Children, 26*(4), 6–11.

Goodman, Y. M., & Goodman, K. S. (1994). To err is human: Learning about language processes by analyzing miscues. In R. B. Ruddell, M. R. Ruddell, & H. Singer (Eds.), *Theoretical models and processes of reading* (4th ed., pp. 104–123). Newark, DE: International Reading Association.

Goswami, U. (2001). Early phonological development and the acquisition of literacy. In S. Newman & D. Dickinson (Eds.), *Handbook on early literacy* (pp. 111–25), New York: Guilford.

Harris, R. (2004). *Five forms of creative thinking.* Unpublished document.

Harvey, J. M., Story, N., & Buker, K. (2002). Convergent and concurrent validity of two measures of phonological processing. *Psychology in the Schools, 39*(5), 507–514.

Johnson, D. W., & Johnson, R. (1989). *Cooperation and competition: Theory and research.* Edina, MN: Interaction.

Juel, C. (1988). Learning to read and write: A longitudinal study of 54 children from first through fourth grades. *Journal of Educational Psychology, 80,* 437–447.

LeFevre, J., & Senechal, M. (2001). Storybook reading and parent teaching: Links to language and literacy development. *New Directions for Child and Adolescent Development, 92,* 39–52.

Metsala, J. L. (1999). Young children's phonological awareness and non-word repetition as a function of vocabulary development. *Journal of Educational Psychology, 91*(1), 2–19.

Piaget, J. (1955). *The language and thought of the child.* New York: Meridian.

Piaget, J. (1974, January 30). *Manas.*

Rogoff, B. (1990). *Apprenticeship in thinking: Cognitive development in social context.* New York: Oxford University Press.

Rumelhart, D. (1976). *Toward an interactive model of reading* (Tech. Rep. No. 56). San Diego: Center for Human Information Processing.

Scully, P., & Roberts, D. (2002). Phonics, expository writing, and reading aloud: Playful literacy in the primary grades. *Early Childhood Education Journal, 30*(2), 93–99.

Vygotsky, L. S. (1978). *Mind and society.* Cambridge, MA: Harvard University Press.

Vygotsky, L. S. (1986). *Thought and language.* Cambridge, MA: Harvard University Press.

Wood, K. D., & Endres, C. (2005). Motivating student interest with the imagine, elaborate, predict, and confirm (IEPC) strategy. *The Reading Teacher, 58*(4). 346–357.

Other Suggested Readings

Beebe, M. T. J. (1980). The effect of different types of substitution miscues on reading. *Reading Research Quarterly, 15,* 124–136.

Clay, M. M. (2001). *Change over time in children's literacy development.* Portsmouth, NH: Heinemann.

Clay, M. M. (2002). *An observation survey of early literacy achievement* (2nd ed.). Portsmouth, NH: Heinemann.

D'Angelo, K., & Mahlios, M. (1983). Insertion and omission miscues of good and poor readers. *The Reading Teacher, 36,* 778–782.

Fielding, L. (2002, December). *Interventions* [Iowa Communications Network broadcast and recording]. Iowa City, IA: Iowa Department of Education.

Forbes, S., Poparad, M. A., & McBride, M. (2004). To err is human; to self-correct is to learn. *The Reading Teacher, 57*(6), 566–572.

Fountas, I. C., & Pinnell, G. S. (1999). Matching books to readers: Using leveled books in guided reading K–3. Portsmouth, NH: Heinemann.

Johnston, P. L., Jiron, H. W., & Day, J. P. (2001). Teaching and learning literate epistemologies. *Journal of Educational Psychology, 93*(1), 223–233.

Levy, U. (1999). Early metalinguistic competence: Speech monitoring and repair behavior. *Developmental Psychology, 35,* 822–834.

McNaughton, S. (1988). A history of errors in the analysis of oral reading behaviour. *International Journal of Experimental Educational Psychology, 1,* 21–30.

Schwartz, R. M. (1997). Self-monitoring in beginning reading. *The Reading Teacher, 50*(1), 40–48.

Spencer, M. M. (2002, July 29). What more needs saying about imagination? International Reading Association, World Congress, Edinburgh, Scotland.

Chapter Three

Phonemic Awareness and Other Avenues to Phonics

All roads lead to Rome; all words lead to phonemes.

—*Frank May (2005)*

On Earth, my dear Xanian offspring, the hills are alive with the sounds of music . . . but also the sounds of language and phonemes—and scratchy scribbling on paper.

—*The Letters of Bogglestar*

In our print-based culture, few will contest the notion that literacy is a way of life. Few also are inclined to challenge the belief that early childhood experiences have a profound effect on a person's development.

—*Kevin Feldman (2003)*

Third Objective for Your Teaching Success:

Help your students develop their phonemic awareness and other avenues to phonics.

The Power of Phonemic Awareness

The *bad* news is this: Research studies strongly indicate that children who finish kindergarten and first grade without developing phonemic awareness have little chance of becoming effective readers. This is true of children in later grades as well (Beach, 1990; Griffith & Olson, 1992; Goswami, 2001).

The *good* news is this: Researchers Kamhi and Catts (1999) Juel (1999), and Juel and Minden-Cupp (2000) found that proper instruction enhances the development of phonemic awareness. And this is where *you* come in, of course, no matter what grade level you're teaching. Unless you promote phonemic awareness, about 25% or more of your students may become struggling readers, kids who can't understand why their friends are doing so much better than they are (Juel & Minden-Cupp, 2000).

Phonemic awareness is the ability to hear individual language sounds in spoken words. As you recall, those sounds are called phonemes, the smallest language units. Ask this question of one of your students, "If your name was Shana, how many phonemes would that represent?" That's right—there are five letters but only four phonemes: /Sh/ + /a/ + /n/ + /a/.

Helping children develop phonemic awareness has become a major responsibility of teachers. The International Reading Association's standards for teachers include an understanding of the phonemic and morphemic systems of language. (See Appendix A for those standards.)

Phonemes are essential for both reading and writing. When we read, we change the written graphemes (i.e., letters) into phonemes we can hear inside our heads. When we write, we change the words we are thinking of inside our heads into phonemes, which are transformed into written letters and words. In essence, the writer is speaking nonvocally to a silent reader. And that silent reader is "listening" to the writer "speak."

What would happen if you lost your awareness of phonemes? A silly question but a good one! Straightforward, my dear Watson. If you lost your awareness of the tiny sounds that make up a spoken word, you would not be able to spell new words in your head, and you wouldn't understand the messy blob of sound you'd hear with a new word. But worst of all, you might be put back to first grade!

This lack of phoneme awareness will likely be a major problem for some of your students throughout your career. In an average classroom of 5- to 8-year-olds, one out of four children will have negative learning experiences because of a lack of phonemic awareness (Juel & Minden-Cupp, 2000). When you're teaching phonemic-awareness lessons or any other language-based lesson, these students will probably need much more practice.

My experience and training have shown me that phonemic awareness is a skill that should first be taught orally, preferably a short while before phonics is taught. Researchers differ a bit on this matter, with some saying that children should go right into phonics and phonemic awareness at the same time—or worse yet, go right into phonics, period. My experience, my common sense, and the research of Armbruster, Lehr, and Osborn (2001) have led me to prevent my beginners from experiencing the complexity of two processes at the same time. Other researchers—Hohn and Ehri (1983), Yopp (1992) and Ericson and Juliebo (1998)—agree wholeheartedly.

By teaching or confirming your students phonemic awareness skills first, you prepare them to move comfortably to phonics and more sophisticated reading. Whatever you do to develop their phonemic awareness gives them more self-confidence. Actually, it also seems to give them a greater boldness in attacking new words. In fact, In my experience, children who first developed phonemic awareness learned their letters faster. Shoot me if I'm wrong. (I've been waiting a long time to say something like that!)

Teaching Phonological Awareness

Professional Standard: Understands phonemic and other language systems as they relate to reading and writing

Phonemic awareness is part of a broader *phonological awareness,* which focuses on phonemes, syllables, compound words, alliteration, and sentences. To put it more vividly, phonological awareness includes a keen awareness of those bright or sleepy bossy syllables, as in *al-pha-bet.*

I'm now modeling a way to teach this to your students: "Those bossy labels make us think twice or thrice, instead of only once like we do with a short, friendly word like cake. In addition, phonological awareness includes the awareness of those chummy *buddy words*, the compound words like *riverside* and *basketball.* And there's good old alliteration like this: *Aunty Agnus ate an awful angry ape, poor ape.* All right, but let's not forget awareness of those long snake-like things we call sentences – like the one you're reading right now."

No more modeling. To become good readers, writers, and communicators, children have to become aware of those language units.

The following activities can help develop phonological awareness and will be discussed further as appropriate throughout the chapter. With most of them you're already familiar, and most are perfect for professional or parental assistants. But the list should help you see the wide variety of activities you can incorporate into your teaching—with beginners in kindergarten or first grade or with older struggling readers as well. *Above all, have fun with your students.*

1. In a 5-year longitudinal study, LeFevre and Senechal (2001) discovered that children who had the highest exposure to reading aloud at home were ahead of their peers in spelling and decoding all the way through third grade. So why not read out loud several times a day to your beginners, all the way up to your "enders"? In other words, don't stop. I have taught from kindergarten to Grade 12—they all love to be read to, provided you read with enthusiasm.

2. Read to and with small groups one or more of those big books that teachers like—be close up and involved each day. Read other books to the total class. Reading children's literature out loud is the best practice possible for developing phonemic awareness. Whether fiction or nonfiction, just think of all the old and new phonemes being injected into their eager ears. And think of all the speedy phonemes being blended into real words.

3. Guide students each day as they play the roles of writer and reader, sender, receiver, and responder. Use primitive messages to and from you and their peers. Be sure that students understand and feel the purpose of writing and reading—to exchange written words with each other. "Without purpose no good reading and writing are done" (Bogglestar, 2005).

4. Enjoy listening to rhyming words and learning to actually create rhyming words together. Generously treat yourself and your students to Mother Goose and Dr. Seuss (and any other "oose" or "ouss" you can snare).

5. Help students gradually learn to use rhymes, for they become a powerful phonics tool. Help them write their own Mother Goose and Dr. Seuss verses—then chant the verses together. The more practice with clear, sharp language sounds, the better. You probably remember this one:
   A dillar, a dollar,
   A ten o'clock scholar,
   What makes you come so soon?
   You used to come at ten o'clock,
   But now you come at noon.

   Here's my adaptation:
   A dollar, a dillar,
   An eleven p.m. driller,
   A hat makes you such a fool.
   You used to drill at sleepy time,
   And now you just act cool.

Adapting Mother Goose *together* is great fun and teaches rhyming well.

6. Enjoy an intriguing experience with alliteration each day. Alliteration is a fantastic, subconscious process for learning more about the nature of language, and kids love it. ("The brown-bag boys better be bringing Bob's berries to my building.")

7. Teach students how to blend phonemes into words. For example, "Here are three phonemes: /c/+/u/+/p/. Blend them together and what word do you get?"

8. Help students segment the word *cup* by separating it into its three phonemes. (i.e., phonemes). When segmented, its /c/ + /u/ + /p/.

9. Use games to introduce the oral and written names of all letters of the alphabet. Begin in preschool if at all possible.

10. Help your students polish their knowledge of the oral alphabet. For example, have them sing the alphabet song "until you're blue in the face, nose, and ears too".

11. Help students playfully polish their knowledge of the printed alphabet. For example, "Show me the letter *B, F . . .* " and so on. Also play games like Go Fish, Memory, Loss of Memory, and a zillion others you can find in toy stores.

12. Teach students the difference between words and letters, words and sentences, words and messages, syllables and phonemes, loud sounds and soft sounds, silent reading and reading out loud, speaking and listening. *But right now lets move on to some real teaching.*

Teaching Sentences, Compound Words, and Syllables

I used to have my graduate students teach phoneme blending and segmentation first thing. But I learned the hard way that it's best to start young children with easier language units—sentences, compound words, and syllables.

Modeling Sentence Awareness

Here is a script for your teaching:

Say, "How many sentences do you hear?" Then read these sentences slowly with a slight pause between the sentences: *Jack Sprat liked to eat. His wife liked to eat, too.* Do this at least three times while your students listen to decide how many sentences they're hearing. After each reading ask, "How many sentences did you hear this time?"

Then say, "Listen while I read the first sentence again. Clap once for each word you hear in the first sentence: *Jack Sprat liked to eat.* How many words did you hear? [Pause.] Yes, five words. So we can say, 'That sentence has five words in it,' can't we?"

"Now listen to the second sentence to see how many words it has: *His wife liked to eat, too.* [Read this two or three times.] How many words did you hear this time? [Pause.] Yes, six words. This time clap while you count. [Read it once more.] Again, we heard six words. So now we can safely say: That sentence has six words in it, doesn't it?'" What's the first word? The second word . . . etc.

When you're teaching them about sentences, be sure to model speaking sentences that sound like you're just talking smoothly.

Say, "Now listen again for how many sentences you can hear: *Paula walked over to Jose's house. She saw a bowl of strawberries. Paula ate them all up!* Teach these in the same way as the first example.

For more practice make up your own sentences for the next day. Or better yet have the children help you create the sentences.

Compound-Word Awareness

Instead of clapping for every word, this time have students clap for each half of the compound words. This will be easy for them, since there are normally only two big sounds in compound words. Here are some compound words for you to choose from:

Spiderman, Superman, downstairs, upstairs, popcorn, sunshine, weekend, scarecrow, fairground, hallway, ballpark, heartache, bedroom, hotdog, noontime, piggyback, fairway, postman, postcard, barnyard

Syllable Awareness

Before you rush on with bated breath and flopping hair to teach the segmentation of phonemes, teach your students to separate words into their syllables. Teaching the separation of syllables is easy; teaching the separation, or segmentation, of phonemes is a bit harder. By teaching syllable awareness first, you'll find your job and your students' job easier when it's time to segment phonemes.

Tell your neophytes to listen to a word. Then say *candy,* but accent both syllables. "I heard two syllables in that word, did you? Let's say it again to see it you hear two sounds. [Repeat.] Now clap your hands on each sound when you say it."

Tell them to listen to another word and tell how many sounds they hear. Pronounce the word *apple,* but again accent both syllables. "How many sounds do you hear when you say the word *apple?* [Pause.] Now clap your hands on each sound when you say it. [Repeat.] Say it three more times, clapping on each sound."

"You're doing very well, but don't let me trick you this time. How many big sounds do you hear in this word: *man?* [Pause.] That's right. There is only one big sound in the word *man.* Now let's play a word game. See whether you can tell me how many sounds you hear in each word that I call out. Show me how many sounds you hear by putting up that number of fingers."

"Let's practice with this word: *hap-py.* Good, you're showing two fingers. OK, let's start the finger game." Make each syllable loud and sharp enough to be counted.

1. go (1)	8. spaghetti (3)
2. doctor (2)	9. octopus (3)
3. cucumber (3)	10. popcorn (2)
4. Easter (2)	11. banana (3)
5. October (3)	12. Cinderella (4)
6. bite (1)	13. kindergarten (4)
7. winter (2)	14. Saturday (3)

"Would you like to know what grown-ups call the sounds that you and I have been listening to? They call them *syllables.* Say the word slowly with me: *sylla-bles.* Say it again slowly and loudly: *syl-la-bles.* Isn't that a silly name? Let's go back to our list of words and count the number of syllables in each word." Let them tell you how many syllables there are in each word. (For example, "The word *go* has how many syllables?")

"How many big sounds are in the word *syllables?* Who can tell me how many? [Pause,] That's right. There are three big sounds in *syllables.* Now don't let me trick you—how many syllables are in the word *syllables?* You're just too smart to be fooled." For some peculiar reason young children love to count syllables, particularly when a word seems to go on forever, like the 14 syllables in *supercalifragilisticexpialidocious.*

Teaching Phonemic Awareness

A Lesson on Blending

Now we're ready for the big time. In this sample, your goal is to teach the students to vocally blend several phonemes into a single word. In this way students can bet-

ter understand the nature of multipart words and thereby come closer to achieving phonemic awareness. Children who can blend the phonemes in words are subconsciously aware that words are made up of phonemes, the smallest form of language sounds. The teacher here, Margaret Selfton, decides to have the children play a simple game called Guess What Word I Am Saying. Like this:

"All right, people, the game works this way: First you listen to all of the little sounds that are in the word. Then you put the little sounds together in your head and tell me what the word is. Let's do a sample one first.

What word am I saying to you: /c/+/a/+/t/? Say those three sounds with me: /c/+/a/+/t/. Say those three sounds with me again: /c/+/a/+/t/. Let's say the three sounds faster: /c/+/a/+/t/. Now very fast: /c/+/a/+/t/. What word am I saying to you? Yes, the word is *cat,* and it has three little sounds in it: /c/+/a/+/t/. Let's say those three little sounds once again and then say the word.

"All right, new game. Do you remember what the king's men tried to do for Humpty Dumpty? That's correct. They tried to put Humpty Dumpty together again. And that is what you have to do in this game. Each word has already been taken apart. Your job is to put each word back together again. Are you ready for the second word?"

Here are the phonemes that the teacher used on this particular day:

/c/ + /u/ + /p/
/s/ + /i/ + /t/
/b/ + /a/ + /g/
/m/ + /a/ + /n/
/l/ + /e/ + /g/

Other words you can use for this game are *mom, cut, sun, dog, pet, fed, mud.* Use your imagination. There's no limit.

Lesson on Segmenting

The teacher's goal this time is to teach the students to vocally *break apart* a word into its phonemes. Again, this helps students better understand the nature of multi-part words and thereby come closer to achieving phonemic awareness. The teacher, Margaret Selfton, decides on *sat* as a good word for teaching the phonemic nature of words.

First she tells the students they're going to take the word *sat* and break it apart. She has everybody say the word *sat.* Then with her lips parted and her teeth close together, she loudly produces the first little sound in *sat,* holding the *s* sound, /s/, for only a second or so.

Next she loudly produces the second sound in *sat,* /a/. Finally, she produces the last sound, /t/, and asks, "Who can say the three little sounds that are in the word *sat?* OK, Janice, what are the three little sounds in the word *sat?*"

Janice says, "The three little sounds are /s/, /a/, /t/."

Margaret says, "That's exactly right, Janice. Now tell me something else. We started out with the word *sat,* but what would we have if you threw away the first little sound in the word *sat?*"

Janice quickly says, "We would have only /a/, /t/."

Margaret then asks, "If we put /a/ and /t/ together, what word would we have instead of *sat?*" Most of the children excitedly say *at* and seem pleased that they have made another word.

A Switch from Segmenting to Blending

The teacher is also pleased but then asks the children to repeatedly do what the king's men tried to do for poor Humpty Dumpty. They all shout, "Put Humpty Dumpty together again!" She then asks them to put the word *sat* back together again, which they do, of course, by blending the /s/, /a/, /t/ together again.

But Margaret decides to do just a little bit more blending with her neophytes. So she asks Janice to say those three little sounds slowly, then faster, then very fast. When Janice does it well, Margaret asks the entire group to say them slowly, then faster, then very fast, and she then asks them to say the word in unison: *sat!* Thus, they succeed in blending the three sounds together again "into a real word".

Helpful Hints

It's a good idea to use just *spoken* words during the first week of phonemic-awareness instruction; even longer for those who have trouble blending or segmenting. Rushing them on to phonics too soon would be problematic.

Another reason to use just spoken words during the first several days is that your students can stay focused on language sounds rather than paying attention to both sounds and print right away. Instruction usually begins with playing language games and listening to the teacher read books that are full of precise phonemes and rhymes.

Be sure to choose your stories carefully. For kindergarten and first-grade children story-listening experiences help them pay close attention to spoken words and provide them with abundant opportunities to listen to meaningful words that are repeated with zest. The word *called,* for example, is powerfully used in "Old King Cole" three times in a row. Talk about the fiddle and how it's been used for thousands of years. Show them a fiddle or a picture. "It's like a violin." Talk about other words. Dramatize this story.

The part of that poem that children like the most and want to say with you again and again is near the end: "Twee tweedle dee, tweedle dee, went the fiddlers."

> *Old King Cole*
> *Was a merry old soul,*
> *And a merry old soul was he.*
> *He called for his pipe,*
> *And he called for his bowl,*
> *And he called for his fiddlers three!*
> *And every fiddler he had a fiddle,*
> *And a very fine fiddle had he.*
> *Twee tweedle dee tweedle dee, went the fiddlers.*
> *Oh, there's none so rare,*
> *As can compare*
> *With King Cole and his fiddlers three.*

My father told me this nursery rhyme about fiddlers well over a hundred times, I'm sure, and each time he would say. "Some day you'll be playing the *violin.*" His prediction didn't come true, but I thoroughly loved him for reading and talking to me. Just as I loved my teachers who did the same.

A Supportive Environment

The learning environment for developing phonemic awareness should be pretty much the opposite of what used to be common in kindergarten classrooms. The research done in the 1970s and 1980s by Durkin (1984), Anderson and colleagues (1985), and Adams (1990) found 5-year-old budding readers wasting their time and eagerness on phonics worksheets. Worksheets were shown by Anderson (1985) to be very time consuming and to produce negative results. The more whole texts children read, the more their reading improved. As a result of these findings, the Anderson Commission recommended that children be provided with at least 2 hours per week of uninterrupted silent reading of literature in the school environment.

An effective environment at any age or grade should be highly enjoyable and very relaxed. Lessons and games should be easy to understand, and an abundance of children's books should reside in different nooks and crannies. Phonemic awareness and reading itself is best brought about through an attitude of pleasant surprise and a sense of playfulness with language. Segmenting words into phonemes and larger units like syllables should be something to laugh and clap about.

Trusting Researchers' Recommendations

Professional Standard: Knows relevant reading research

Having mastered the basic ideas of teaching phonemic awareness, segmentation, and blending, you're now ready to understand a valuable collection of research reports—along with ideas on how to use those reports to improve your teaching of phonemic awareness, phonological awareness, reading and writing and *Teaching Exceptional Children.*

Because medical doctors are expected to keep up with the latest research in various medical fields, they read the medical journals that arrive every month. As professional teachers, you and I are also expected to keep up with the latest research, particularly as it applies to reading and writing. However, school teachers may decide that they don't have the time to study the research reports. What's the solution?

By all means get a subscription to one or more journals, particularly *The Reading Teacher.* Another solution is to keep reading inexpensive paperback books on teaching reading, which are available from the International Reading Association (IRA) or from many regular bookstores. And for a real picnic, go to IRA meetings in the local district.

Research is your best friend for helping students, as the contributions of the following researchers should make clear:

David Cooper (2002): wanted to know whether young children who had abundant daily experiences with oral language communication would do well in developing their phonological awareness (i.e., phonemic, syllable, and the other forms of language awareness). What he discovered was that abundant oral language experiences did influence the development of phonological awareness and usually contributed to the development of early reading. Why? Because of the necessity for both phonemic awareness and of phonological awareness. In other words, building up a child's phonemic awareness and other simple forms of language awareness can have an effect on the child's ability to read and write.

David Dickinson and Allyssa McCabe (2001): found in their study that the act of learning vocabulary successfully is at least modestly related to phonological awareness. This makes common sense: Awareness of phonemes as you pronounce a whole sentence of words should automatically improve your ability to read those words.

Maureen Dixon, Jackie Masterson and Morag Stuart (2002): found that children who were ready to perform phoneme segmentation learned new vocabulary faster than those who were less able to handle phoneme awareness tasks: This is significant in showing how important phonemic awareness can be to reading success in general.

Linnea C. Erhi, Simone R. Nunes, Dale M. Willows, Barbara V. Schuster, Zohren Yaghoub-Zaden, and Timothy Shanahan (2001): produced their study for the National Reading Panel after investigating 52 controlled studies published in officially accepted journals. Their goal was to evaluate the effects of phonemic awareness instruction on learning to read and spell. Here are their results:

- Both word reading and reading comprehension benefited from the teaching of phonemic awareness (PA).
- The effect of PA teaching was greater when children were taught in small groups rather than by themselves or in entire classrooms. Group size can make a great deal of difference in reading success.
- PA teaching assisted numerous types of children, including normally developing readers, high-risk and disabled readers, preschoolers, kindergartners, first graders, and both low-and high-socioeconomic-status kids. This is perhaps the most important finding.

D. Fuchs, L. S. Fuchs, A. Thompson, J. A. Otaiba, L. Yen, N. J. Yang, M. Braun, and R. E. O'Connor (2001): conducted a well-developed study to determine the effectiveness of phonological-awareness training. In their study 33 teachers in eight urban schools were randomly assigned within their schools to three groups: control, phonological-awareness training, and phonological-awareness training with some beginning decoding instruction. After a 20-week treatment both treatment groups outperformed the control group, confirming the value of directly teaching phonemic awareness.

U. Goswami (2001): researched early phonological development and demonstrated that the size of a child's vocabulary may play a role in building phonolgical awareness. The more books or pages children read successfully, the more they have relied on their awareness of phonemes in every word. In other words, practice leads to success.

C. Hulme (2002): found in comparative measurements of children's onset-rime skills and their phonemic-level skills that phonemic-level skills are better predictors of early *reading* skills, [In the word *train* the onset is *tr* and the rime is *ain*.] Once again we see the importance of developing phonemic awareness before and during the learning of phonics. [Both are better].

Claire Wood (2002): studied a set of home programs for parent-child preschool activities. After an entire year children who were involved in these preschool programs, as compared to those who were not involved, showed the "best achievement in reading" (p. 256).

Hallie Kay Yopp (1988): discovered that phonemic awareness can best be assessed with 10 measures: (1) sound-to-word matching (Is there a /g/ in /dog/?); (2) word-to-word matching (Do *bat* and *ball* begin the same?); (3) recognition of rhyme; (4) isolation of a sound; (5) phoneme segmentation; (6) phoneme counting; (7) phonemic blending; (8) phonemic deletion; (9) specifying deleted phonemes; and (10) phoneme segmentation. [Dr. Yopp is probably the most knowledgeable person today when it comes to phonemic awareness. Her Test for Assessing Phonemic Awareness in Young Children is widely used and can be found in *The Reading Teacher, 45,* pp. 696–703.]

Hallie Yopp (1992): recommends that children be limited to oral activities until they have developed phonemic awareness, followed by learning the alphabetic letters.

Hallie Yopp (1995a): offered an annotated bibliography of read-aloud books for developing phonemic awareness. [Her text offers guidelines for the use of nursery rhymes, alliteration, nonsense sounds, poems, games, songs, and stories with rhymes.]

Hallie Yopp (1995b): found that phonological awareness does a better job of predicting reading ability than do measures of general intelligence or reading readiness.

Connie Juel and Joanne Meier (1999): found that, in addition to phonemic awareness, K–2 children need to master the terms that teachers use. Learning activities should focus on the following concepts:

- ■ **Print** carries a message. [Let me add: Have your children writing from Day 1. Without Writing We Have No Reading should become a motto. Have students writing to you and to each other and then responding in writing. Start with two-word sentences and gradually move up to three-, four-, five-, and six-word sentences according to students' skills and awareness.]

- **Words** —*what are they?* [After you use them as oral language for a week or so, begin showing them in written form as you work in small groups reading out loud. Count the number of words in each sentence. Speak the sentence slowly enough to accent each word. Then speak it as the author might have written it.]
- **Letters** match the sounds we make when we speak. Words are composed of letters. Without letters we could not write. Letters help us say exactly what we want.
- **Message** is carried in print. [We speak and write messages to other people. A message can be something we get and something we give. Bogglestar says, "On Earth a message is like a car that carries you to your destination—and then returns with a brand new message."]

Conne Juel and Cecilia Minden-Cupp (2000): discovered that children who entered first grade with minimum reading skills seemed to have greatest success with the following four practices:

1. Teachers modeled word recognition strategies by (a) chunking words into component units such as syllables, onset/rimes, or finding little words in big ones; (b) sounding and blending individual phonemes; and (c) considering known letter-sounds and what makes contextual sense.
2. Children were encouraged to point to words as text was read.
3. Children used manipulative materials to actively compare and contrast words (e.g., pocket charts for sorting picture cards by sounds and word cards by spelling pattern).
4. Instruction groups were small and with lesson plans designed to meet the specific needs of each child within the group.

These four teaching techniques are excellent and should not be limited to children entering first grade with minimum reading skills. These techniques are essential tools for teaching struggling and Ell students.

Moving Boldly Toward Phonics

Use Creative Approaches

Professional Standard: Creates an environment that fosters interest and growth in all aspects of literacy

- At odd times of the day, use guessing games that encourage the blending and segmenting of phonemes. "What word am I thinking of? I'll take it apart, and you put it back together: /f/ /a/ /n/.
- Take turns exaggerating the names of things in the classroom: *p-p-p-paper, ch-ch-ch-chalk, s-s-s-scissors.*

- Listen for the oddball: *big, dig, dog, pig* (right, *dog* is the oddball. Let them explain, in their own inimitable way, what makes it odd. Then let them help you create more oddballs. Lots of creative fun, lots of thinking, lots of excitement and laughter.
- More easy oddballs: *run, red, rat, bat* and *sap, soap, slap, trap* Some hard ones: *big, ball, kick, bad* and *sit, cat, call, hot*
- Have an awfully alluring alliteration adventure by reading these books to your students; they're available in most public libraries.
  All About Arthur, E. Carle
  Dinosaur Chase, C. Otto
  Dr. Seuss's ABCs, Dr. Seuss
  Zoophabets, R. Tallon
  Children's librarians will be happy to find more.
- Read some rhyming books for the sake of laughter, rhythm, and phonics!
  A Giraffe and a Half, S. Silverstein
  I Can Fly, R. Krauss
  Miss Mary Mack and Other Children's Street Rhymes, The Random House Book of Poetry for Children

Test Assumptions

Let's talk about a common teaching problem. I dare not tell you how many times I have assumed that my students were already knowledgeable about a particular skill or concept and then double-assumed that they were ready to learn something more difficult about that skill or concept. I tried to teach them phonics, for instance as if they already knew what comes before phonics.

I even made that kind of assumption when I was teaching something as simple as learning to hear rhyming words. Everybody can hear rhymes, can't they? No, not everybody can. Some kids don't even notice the rhyming part—not without abundant help from others. Nor can all youngsters (or all adults) create their own rhyming words. Look at what happened to Betsy:

"What word rhymes with *mop,* Betsy?"

"Uhm, *map?*"

"Try again, Betsy."

"Uh . . . *mom?*"

"No, but give me a word that rhymes with *mop* and *slop.*"

"Uhhhh . . . *slap?*"

You see what I mean? I made an assumption about what Betsy had already learned. I assumed she already knew something she didn't know. And that led me to test her rather than teach her—a problem most teachers today experience all too often. Before asking any test-like questions, I should have taught or reviewed something.

It's no wonder many kids are graded as C − instead of A+. We lead them to the slaughter when we make assumptions like that. I apologize profusely, dear Betsy. I hope you had a smarter teacher in your next grade. As for me, Betsy, you taught me something very well—not to make assumptions, or at least to check out my assumptions.

With Betsy's teaching in my mind, I carefully avoided making assumptions about my sixth-grade class. To my astonishment I discovered three children with reading and writing difficulties. What did I do? What I had to do! I taught them how to combine phonemes, segment phonemes, and create rhymes. What a sad waste of self-confidence they had gone through for 5 or 6 years!

Explore Rhymes, Alliteration, and More Rhymes

Start the movement toward phonics by reading rhymes of all sorts to your children. The contrasts among rhyming words (e.g., *cat, sat, hat*) provide abundant experiences in mentally segmenting beginning phonemes from the rest of the word (e.g., *c-at, s-at, h-at*)—a skill that's necessary when your students move into phonics. You can even make such separations explicit by talking about the rhyming words after you've read a poem or a patterned, predictable book. For example, "Let's make up some words that belong to the *at* family."

Here's an example of a teacher introducing the concept of family words.

Teacher: Look at the two words I have written: *cap* and *lap*. OK, Jackson, you had your hand up first. What are the two words?

Jackson: *Cap* and *lap*.

Teacher: Yes. What two letters do they both end with?

Jackson: Uhhh . . . *a-p.*

Teacher: Right. Can you think of other rhyming words ending with *a-p?*

Jackson: Uhh, uhh. I can't, ma'am.

Teacher: [Writes *nap.*] How about *nap?*

Jackson: Oh yeah. I get it now. How about *map* . . . and *tap?*

Teacher: [Adds them to the list.] Would the word *slap* work?

Jackson: [Excited] Yeah!

Teacher: [Adds *slap* to the list.] What else?

Jackson: *Flap* . . . and . . . *trap!*

In this way Jackson and most of the other students learned how powerful rhyming words can be. They all end in the same way—they all end with *a-p!* Here's what the kids eventually came up with a major ingredient in phonics:

c-ap sl-ap
l-ap tr-ap
n-ap fl-ap
m-ap cl-ap
t-ap

Thus the class learned to notice the *phonogram ap* at the end of a short, one-syllable word. And in turn this allowed Jackson later to tackle longer words like *hap-py* and *ap-ple*.

In a similar situation many years ago, I remember how my youngest son proudly picked up the Rice Krispies box and said "/Sn/ . . . /ap/ . . . yeah, it's *snap*." Then he guessed the other two words from the context of the cereal box: "Are these two words *crackle* and *pop*?!" It may be hard for some of us to remember the joy that kind of discovery can bring.

As you work with children at this stage be sure that you say the sound rather than concentrating on the letters. Working on letters, of course, should be an ongoing thing, but my advice again is to spend a week or so strictly on the awareness of phonemes. Mixing the two right away is not good for beginners—especially those who are already struggling. Just be patient.

Have Fun Creating Your Own Rhymes

It's easy to make up your own rhymes and alliteration. Here are some examples that I made up just for you—and your students. Use them as is or make creative changes. For example, in the first one you might change the cat to a *snake* and find words that rhyme with *cake*.

> **A VERY JEALOUS CAT**
> *My best friend is a cat.*
> *Well, well, imagine that.*
> *With Kitty I love to chat*
> *About Brenda, Robert, and Pat,*
> *But Kitty's so jealous, oh drat.*
> *She only wants me and my hat!*

> **SOME FROG-LIKE HOGS**
> *Diggety doggety hogs,*
> *I think I heard two frogs.*
> *One frog said gul-ink!*
> *The other frog said gul-unk!!*
> *And diggity doggety hogs*
> *Growled kul-unk! kul-unk!! kul-ink!!!*

> **A HAPPY SAPPY SONG**
> *Silly, sappy, sad songs,*
> *Sung by Sarah Stoody,*
> *Can make me mumble madly,*
> *But mom can make me moody.*

> **AWFULLY AWESOME ALLITERATION**
> *Peaper Piker packed a pocketful of peppered pickles.*
> *Nancy Nipper never knew her nasty naughty neighbors.*
> *Mr. May might make more moldy messy mops on Monday.*

After you and your students have played with my measly mess of meager moldy rhymes, help them create some of their own together. Or you can give them rhymes or alliterations that are just begun and let them finish them with a partner. By the second or third time they'll probably be chanting them with you. You might let them repeat each line after you or say the rhymes in choral fashion with a big group and then small groups. Do this kind of repetition as long as needed. Also talk about the occasional meaning of each verse, and be sure to talk about which words rhyme.

Let Young Detectives Hunt for Clues

This is a well-loved game you can play with both new and experienced detectives. *It's* a great way to have students become more certain about the nature of rhymes. *It* can take place in the classroom or outside later if you wish. You might want to bring along extra items to combine with the normal schoolroom items.

Scatter the items around the classroom without actually hiding them. Then have the kids become detective partners. When the first pair finds the rhyming item, the next pair becomes the detectives. This list is just to get you started. The second time you play the game, allow only 10 seconds for each item. Writing them on the board will spoil the fun.

1. Find something in the room that rhymes with *sock* and *rock*. [clock]

2. Search for something that rhymes with *hen* and *ten*. [pen]

3. Search for something that rhymes with *boat* and *goat*. [coat]

4. Search for something that rhymes with *two* and *you*. [shoe]

5. Find something that rhymes with *night* and *fight*. [light]

6. Find something that rhymes with *man* and *pan*. [fan]

7. Find something that rhymes with *look* and *hook*. [book]

8. Find something that rhymes with *joy* and *toy*. [boy]

9. Search for something that rhymes with *curl* and *twirl*. [girl]

10. Search for something that rhymes with *talk* and *walk*. [chalk]

11. Search for something that rhymes with *floor* and *more*. [door]

12. Search for something that rhymes with *ants* and *dance*. [pants]

13. Find something that rhymes with *hurt* and *flirt*. [shirt]

14. Find something that rhymes with *mad* and *sad*. [pad]

15. Find something that rhymes with *bring* and *ring*. [string]

Try Some Advanced Challenges

Phonics requires the separation and rejoining of word parts.

1. What happens to my cat when I take away its /cuh/ sound? What sound is left? [/at/]

2. What happens to my dog when I take away its /d/ sound? What sound is left? [/og/]

3. What happens to my tiger when I take away its /t/? What sound is left? [/iger/]

4. What happens to my rabbit when I take away its /r/? What sound is left? [/abbit/]

5. What happens to my bird when I take away its /b/? What sound is left? [/ird/]

6. What happens to my *at* when I give it back its /cuh/? What do I have now? [/cat/]

7. What happens to my *og* when I give it back its /d/? What do I have now? [/dog/]

8. What happens to my *iger* when I give it back its /t/? What do I have now? [/tiger/]

9. What happens to my *abbit* when I give it back its /r/? What do I have now? [/rabbit/]

10. What happens to my *ird* when I give it back its /b/? What do I have now? [/bird/]

Segment Phonemes Differently

This is a review: Once your beginners know how to segment a word into its phonemes, they are ready to take a big step closer to phonics. How? Simply by learning to segment, or separate, only the first one or two phonemes. You see they've already learned from your teaching that words are made up of phonemes, but in order to prepare them for important items like onsets and rimes (*rimes* are also known as *phonograms*), you will need to show them a more advanced form of segmenting.

Here's an example of what I'm talking about. After they've segmented the word *fat* into /f/ /a/ /t/, have them segment it this way: /f/ /at/. Likewise have them change /c/ /a/ /t/ into /c/ /at/. Each time you play this little game with your trainees, have them make the new sounds they have learned.

For *fat,* instead of saying /f/ /a/ /t/, say /f/ /at/.
For *cat,* instead of saying /c/ /a/ /t/, say /c/ /at/.
For *rack* instead of saying /r/ /a/ /ck/, say /r/ /ack/.

For *sip* say /s/ /ip/.　　For *sap* say _____.
For *pot* say /p/ /ot/.　　For *mop* say _____.
For *shop* say /sh/ /op/.　For *tail* say _____.

For *pill* say /p/ /ill/.   For *pain* say _____.
For *bad* say /b/ /ad/.   For *train* say /tr/ /ain/.
For *dog* say /d/ /og/.   For *lump* say _____.
For *lob* say _____.   For *thump* say _____.
For *cob* say _____.   For *sick* say _____.
For *cap* say _____.   For *stick* say /st/ /ick/.

And now you have your students ready for the phonics procedure of onsets and rimes. For example, with /h-at/ or /ch-at/ *at* is the rime and /h/ or /ch/ is the onset.

Teach the Alphabetic Principle

Professional Standard: Understands the phonological system as it relates to the alphabetic principle

The **alphabetic principle** is simply this: Speech sounds should be represented by one or more letters. The alphabetic principle requires, for instance, that the first phoneme you hear in the words *Randy, rubber,* and *road*—the /r/ sound—be represented by the alphabet letter *r*. Likewise the alphabetic principle requires that the first phoneme you hear in the words *this, that,* and *those*—the /th/ sound—be represented by the alphabet digraph *th*. Learning how to match an alphabet letter or letter combination to speech sounds is not only a vital precursor to the development of phonics decoding in reading (Stahl, Duffy, & Stahl, 1998), it is also essential for developing spelling and writing skills.

Leslie Morrow (1993) suggests ways children can learn the alphabetic principle by playing games. The games center on letter naming, letter sounds, and the connection between letter names and sounds. Some of the materials needed include alphabet puzzles, magnetic letters, sandpaper letters, alphabet games, letter stencils, letter flash cards, alphabet charts, dry-erase boards, clay trays, paper, pencils, markers, painting easels, alphabet logos, cereals and foods, and commercially published alphabet books. These supplies can be found at teaching supply stores or garage sales or can be made by parental volunteers.

You might want to have an alphabet center stocked with many of these materials when you are teaching kindergarten or first grade. Children can write, trace, or copy alphabet letters in that center. Individual-sized chalkboards, dry-erase boards, clay trays, tracing paper, and painting easels also draw children into copying, tracing, and experimenting with letters.

Dry alphabet pasta and alphabet cereal are fun for letter play, as well as Scrabble, bingo, magnet alphabet and computer games. Children should be encouraged to sort the letters into alphabet letter categories. You might seat students in pairs or small groups to show which letters they have been given. If you are using cereal letters, allow the kids to eat the letters after the game is done. (The trick is to keep them from gobbling up your teaching tools before they have learned from the lesson!) This kind of playful interaction can increase children's awareness of letters, sounds, and alphabetical order.

Environmental print logos can be used to create alphabet books. These books are often patterned after well-known alphabet books such as *The Z Was Zapped* by Van Allsburg or *On Market Street* by Lobel. The idea is for children to select one or more products to represent each sound. For example, labels from Cocoa Puffs cereal and Capt'n Crunch cereal could go on a page dedicated to the letter *c*. Because children select logos they can already read, these books are easily read by every child—a source of confidence building and enjoyment.

Assess Print Concepts That Beginners Need to Learn

The conventions of writing in English are arbitrary and not necessarily logical. I'm referring to such things as print moving from left to right and from the top of the left-hand page downward. *Print concepts* is a term that refers to the conventions that govern written English, including such abstractions as a letter, a word, a sentence, punctuation symbols, and so on.

Marie Clay (1985) suggests these key print concepts for teachers to assess using easy-to-read predictable books:

1. Can return sweep to the left

2. Can do word-by-word matching

3. Understands first and last concept

4. Understands bottom of the picture

5. Looks at left page before right

6. Notices one change in word order

7. Notices one change in letter order

8. Knows the meaning of a question mark

9. Knows the meaning of a period

10. Knows the meaning of a comma

11. Knows the meaning of quotation marks

12. Can identify the first and last letter of a word

13. Can identify one letter and two letters

14. Can identify capital letters

Now your students probably are ready for learning or reviewing phonics and the process of *decoding*, the alphabetic essence of reading and the second half of reading for meaning.

Focus on Students with Special Needs: Comments by Louise Fulton

Caring Teachers Help All Students Learn

During my ever-fulfilling career of teaching typical and not-so-typical students and working with thousands of teachers, I have come to believe certain things about teaching special needs students. Caring teachers who are interested in helping all students learn are a principal's dream come true. Their classrooms are magical. They have an insatiable curiosity and enjoy determining what makes each student tick. These teachers get a huge thrill out of their students' successes, and they see each of their students as a real learner. They never use demeaning labels such as handicapped or slow learners. And their students respond beautifully to a mutually respectful classroom community.

The problem is that some teachers have come to believe that special needs students don't belong in typical classrooms but can be better served in a special class or resource room. "After all, they'll be in a smaller class and get much more individual attention."

There is ample evidence to blast this notion into the stratosphere. The reality is that resource rooms, or pull-out programs, often don't work. **Moody, Vaughn, Smith, and Fisher (2000)** found that the resource room experience failed to result in significant gains in reading fluency and comprehension. In a comprehensive review of research on effective practices in special education, **Lloyd, Forness, and Kravale (1998)** found that special class interventions often result in negative rather than positive outcomes.

Typical resource teachers have a caseload of 30 to 50 students, with varying ages, grade levels, and disabilities. They need to work with parents, other teachers, and professionals to implement each child's individual education plan (IEP). A typical special day class teacher spends most of the day in a classroom filled with special needs students, usually covering at least three grade levels. These special day classes are often crowded, many with 35 or more students.

On a positive note, I recently observed an elementary school in an economically impacted region of Southern California. The school was using a procedure that was working well: Resource teachers spent most of the day team teaching by working with individuals and small groups of students in regular classrooms. I noticed that when the resource teacher entered a regular classroom, several eager hands went up, but few of those in need of help were actually special needs students.

However, in this school at least one special needs teacher is always scheduled in the resource room, where students can go to get individual help with their classroom materials—usually reading. This way, regular and special education teachers can understand students and communicate frequently with conversations or short notes. These collaborating teachers are caring and helpful, and the students know it. Everybody wins in this kind of environment.

Summary of Main Ideas

- Phonemic awareness and phonics are not the same thing. Phonemic awareness is the ability to hear individual sounds in spoken words.
- When you read the word *shack,* you see five letters, but you hear only three phonemes: /sh/ + /a/ + /k/.
- Those children who finish kindergarten and first grade without developing phonemic awareness have less chance of becoming effective readers by the end of first grade. Children in later grades also have similar problems of becoming effective readers.
- The good news is this: Researchers have found that proper instruction enhances the development of phonemic awareness.
- There are over 30 skills or concepts that children should learn before teachers attempt to teach them phonics.
- Playful activities are needed before phonics.
- Phonological awareness includes awareness of phonemes, syllables, compound words, alliteration, and sentences.
- Phoneme blending and segmenting are the two most important concepts for children to learn. Without them it can be very difficult for children to learn to read and write at competent levels.

Literacy Through Technology

A. With one or two partners, conduct an Internet search for ideas on teaching phonemic awareness to your students. Try www.eduplace.com, a free online service designed to help elementary-school teachers integrate Internet resources into their curriculum. Find computer practice activities.

B. With a partner, learn about useful Web sites for publishing poetry created by your students. Try a search on your own or start with one of these;

http://www.poetryforge.org
http://www.poetrysociety.org
http://www.poetryteachers.com
http://www.publishingstudents.com

Application Experiences for Your Course

A. *Literacy Teacher Vocabulary: A List of Terms.:* Test each other on how well you have mastered these professional terms. Think of examples for each one.

phoneme	phonemic awareness	onset
phonological awareness	phonogram	rhyme
blending	segmenting	alphabet
sentence awareness	syllable awareness	principle
compound-words awareness	rime	

B. *What's Your Opinion:*

1. There's no real difference between phonics and phonemic awareness.
2. Oral language activities should precede written ones.
3. Children who don't have a strong sense of phonemic awareness are likely to become struggling readers.

C. Plan with peers a new lesson involving blending or segmenting. Share it with the rest of the class.
D. Since rhyming experiences are essential for learning phonics and since children love funny poems with a steady rhythm and rhyme, create your own poem with a partner and present it in the class you're teaching.
E. Search for one or more books in the list of "Rhymes and Poetry" at the back of the book in Appendix N. Use this with your students and report your results at your next universiity class session.

Creativity Training Session

A. Submit the original poem you created in Application Experiences to one of the poetry Web sites focused on teacher and student online publishing.
B. In a small group, create some off-the-wall, crazy poetry. First generate a list of words that rhyme. Be sure to have at least six words for each rhyme, such as *hat, bat, mat, flat, drat,* and *that.* Then create a poem together, using those rhymes at the ends of lines. You can add rhyming words to your list as you go. Let yourself go. Silly and meaningless poems can be fun.
C. Decide how you might use this poetry-writing activity in your own classroom.

Field Experiences

A. Interview two teachers about their use of technology to teach literacy. Use the following questions to start. Add other questions, based on your curiosity and interests.

1. Is your classroom set up for Internet access?
2. Do students use a computer for reading, writing, or classroom activities?
3. Do the students use the Internet for research?
4. What is the primary use of technology in your classroom?
5. How do you feel about using technology to enhance student literacy skills?

References

Adams, M. J. (1990). *Beginning to read: Thinking and learning about print.* Cambridge, MA: MIT Press.

Anderson, R. C., Hiebert, E. H., Scott, J. A., & Wilkinson, I. A. G. (1985). *Becoming a nation of readers: The report of the Commission on Reading.* Urbana: University of Illinois, Commission for the Study of Reading.

Armbruster, R. B., Leir, F., & Osborn, J. (2001). *Put reading first: The research building blocks of teaching children to read.* Jusup, MD: National Institute for Literacy.

Beach, S. A. (1990). *The interrelationship of phonemic segmentation, auditor of abstraction, and word recognition.* Paper presented at the annual meeting of the International Reading Association, Atlanta CA.

Bogglestar. (2005). *The letters of Bogglestar.* Xania: Planet XYZ.

Clay, M. M. (1985). *The early detection of reading difficulties.* Portsmouth, NH: Heinemann.

Cooper, D. (2002). The contribution of oral language skills to the development of phonological awareness. *Applied Psycholinguistics, 23*(3), 399–416.

Dickinson, D., & McCabe, A. (2001). Bringing it all together: The multiple origins, skills, and environmental supports of early literacy. *Learning Disabilities Research and Practice, 16*(4), 186–202.

Dixon, M., Masterson, J. & Stuart, M. (2002). The relationship between phonological awareness and the development of orthographic representations. *Reading and Writing: An Interdisciplinary Journal, 15*(3), 295–316.

Durkin, D. (1984). Is there a match between what elementary teachers do and what basal manuals recommend? *The Reading Teacher, 37,* 734–744.

Erhi, L. C., Nunes, S. R., Willows, D. M., Schuster, B. V., Yaghoub-Zaden, Z., & Shanchan, T. (2001). Phonemic awareness instruction helps children read: Evidence from the National Reading Panel's meta-analysis. *Reading Research Quarterly, 36*(3), 256–287.

Ericson, L., & Juliebo, M. F. (1998). *The phonological awareness handbook for kindergarten and primary teachers.* Newark, DE: International Reading Association.

Feldman, K. (2003, Summer). Literacy: Prekindergarten and beyond. *The Special Edge.* Sacramento, CA: California Department of Education.

Fuchs, D. Fucks, L. S, Thomson, A. Otaiba, S. A., Yen, L. Yang, N. J., Braun, M. & O'Connor, R. E. (2001). Is reading important in reading-readiness programs? A randomized field trial with teachers as program implementers. *Journal of Educational Psychology, 93*(2), 251–267.

Goswami, U. (2001). Early phonological development and the acquisition of literacy. In S. Neuman & D. Dickinson (Eds.), *Handbook on early literacy,* (pp. 111–125). New York: Guilford.

Griffith, P. L., & Olson, M. W. (1992). Phonemic awareness helps beginning readers break the code. *The Reading Teacher, 45,* 516–525.

Hohn, W., & Ehri, L. (1983). Do alphabet letters help preschoolers acquire phonemic segmentation skills? *Journal of Educational Psychology, 75,* 752–762.

Hulme, C. (2002). Phonemes, rimes, and the mechanism of early reading development. *Journal of Experimental Psychology, 82*(1), 58–65.

Juel, C., & Meier, J. (1999). Teaching content and form through balanced instruction. *Teaching and Change, 6*(2), 182–196.

Juel, C., & Minden-Cupp, C. (2000). One down and 80,000 to go: Word recognition instruction in the primary grades. *The Reading Teacher, 53*(4), 332–335.

Kamhi, A. G., & Catts, H. W. (1999). Language and reading: Convergence and divergence. In H. W. Catts & A. G. Kamhi (Eds.), *Language and learning disabilities* (pp. 1–24). Needham Heights, MA: Allyn & Bacon.

LeFevre, J., & Senechal, M. (2001). Storybook reading and parent teaching: Links to language and literacy development. *New Directions for Child and Adolescent Development, 92,* 39–52.

Lloyd, J. Forness, S., & Kravale, K. (1998). Some methods are more effective than others. *Intervention in School and Curriculum, 33*(4), 195–200.

Moody, S., Vaughn, S., Smith, M., & Fisher, M. (2000). Reading instruction in the resource room: Set up for failure. *Exceptional Children, 66*(37), 305–316.

Morrow, L. M. (1993). *Literacy development in the early years: Helping children read and write.* Boston: Allyn & Bacon.

Savacho, O. N. (1994). The relationship of preschool children's cognitive style to their play preferences. *Early Child Development and Care, 97,* 21–33.

Stahl, S. A., Duffy, A. M., & Stahl, R. A. D. (1998). Everything you wanted to know about phonics (but were afraid to ask). *Reading Research Quarterly, 33*(3), 338–355.

Wood, C. (2002). Parent-child pre-school activities can affect the development of literacy skills. *Journal of Research on Reading, 25*(3), 241–258.

Yopp, H. (1988). The validity and reliability of phonemic awareness testing. *Reading Research Quarterly, 23,* 159–177.

Yopp, H. (1992). Developing phonemic awareness in young children. *The Reading Teacher, 45,* 696–703.

Yopp, H. (1995a). Read-aloud books for developing phonemic awareness: An annotated bibliography. *The Reading Teacher, 48*(6), 538–543.

Yopp, H. (1995b). A test for assessing phonemic awareness in young children. *The Reading Teacher, 29,* 20–29.

Other Suggested Readings

Harvey, J. M., Story, N., & Buker, K. (2002). Convergent and concurrent validity of two measures of phonological processing. *Psychology in the Schools, 39*(5), 507–514.

Johnson, F. (1999). The timing and teaching of word families. *The Reading Teacher, 53*(1), 64–75.

Juel, C. (1988). Learning to read and write: A longitudinal study of 54 children from first grade through fourth grade. *Journal of Educational Psychology, 80*(4), 437–447.

Juel, C. (1995). The messenger may be wrong but the message is right. *Journal of Research in Reading, 18*(2), 146–153.

Metsala, J. L. (1999) Young children's phonological awareness and nonword repetition as a function of a vocabulary development. *Journal of Educational Psychology, 91*(1), 2–19.

Rolanda, E. (2001). Is reading important in reading readiness programs? *Journal of Educational Psychology, 93*(2), 251–267.

Saracho, O. (2002). Teachers' role in promoting literacy in the context of play. *Early Child Development and Care, 172*(1), 23–34.

Smith, F. (1988). *Joining the literacy club.* Portsmouth, NH: Heinemann.

Stanovich, K., & Cunningham, Q. (1993). Where does knowledge come from? Specific associations between print exposure and information acquisition. *Journal of Educational Psychology, 85,* 211–220.

Chapter Four

Phonics, Decoding, Vowel Patterns, and Spelling Go Together

Learning to read should be a joyous adventure, as exciting for youngsters, their families, and their teachers as when children learned to walk and talk.

—*Margaret Moustafa*

According to the National Reading Panel (2000), phonics instruction is a way of teaching reading that stresses the acquisition of letter-sound correspondences and their use in reading and spelling (p. 8).

Fourth Objective for Your Teaching Success:

Teach students phonics, decoding, and spelling the analogy and vowel pattern ways.

Lets sneak into the Phonics Club like we already belong. Now that we're here let's listen to some phonics jazz:

One: The famous educator Margaret Moustafa was telling the absolute truth in her chapter-opening statement about learning to read being a joyous adventure. Let me recommend that you make that your creative modus operandi. In other words, have fun with phonics—it can be almost ambrosia for your students. In fact, playing during literacy instruction is crucial for your teaching success (Scully & Roberts, 2002).

Two: Moving from a focus on phonemic awareness and natural oral language to a focus on written symbolic letters that stand for phonemes is a dramatic change. However, giving your students a week or so of devoting themselves almost entirely to the oral language sounds should encourage a pleasant transition (Armbruster, Lehr, & Osborn 2001; Ericson & Juliebo, 1998; and Yopp, 1992). But don't rush into full-scale phonics before you see that your young students have truly gained phonemic awareness. Have they mastered the activities in Chapter 3?

Three: The results of a study by Schneider, Roth, and Ennemoser (2000) and confirmed by McQuillan (1998) and Smith (2003) demonstrate that phonological-awareness training alone yields stronger effects than letter-sound training alone. Continue to teach phonological awareness as you see that your students benefit from it.

Four: There's a notion that a primary emphasis on skills and phonics *instruction* produces superior results with children's reading, writing, and spelling. Not quite. Reading programs that provide children with a lot of interesting and understandable texts are also needed for those results to occur.

Five: Remember that reading is simultaneous decoding and comprehending, involving the interaction of these cues: (1) phonics, (2) the reader's schemas (from previous experiences), (3) the author's syntax (the order and the types of words presented), (4) semantics (the descriptions and the meaning the author gives), and (5) the images the reader gets in response.

Six: You're not the only teacher of a particular student, of course. If you can get the parents or others to assist you, your success rate will probably soar (Padak & Rasinski, 2000). Family assistance programs really work: (a) Children's school achievement and social skills improve; (b) parents' or other caregivers' reading, writing, and parenting skills increase; and (c) families learn to value education and become more involved.

Seven: To ignore phonics might be close to a serious sin. As Nicholson (1999) puts it, the problems experienced by "low-progress readers" are due to a lack of explicit attention to phonemic awareness and phonics. Even though that's only half-way true, let's move on to the teaching of phonics.

Using Both Sides of the Brain: A Fabulous High

The left and right sides of your brain have different jobs. The right side is usually responsible for recognizing or producing patterns. The left side is usually responsible for explaining those patterns—as well as explaining your unusual emotions or your occasional moments of chaos. As we both know, those two jobs require a gigantic amount of problem solving. I myself am problem solving right now—as I try to create an intelligent pattern of connected sentences, hoping they'll hang together and make sense to both of us.

There seems to be little doubt that human beings have survived and thrived as pattern-seeking and pattern-producing beings. That's why I propose that it's wise for us teachers to take advantage of this natural pattern-izing inclination, especially when teaching phonics, word recognition, spelling, and vowel patterns—and especially when teaching students how to use strategies to decode difficult words.

What Really Happens When a Person Decodes a Word

Decoding is the mother of phonics. The varied phonics methods have all been developed to deal with the difficulty of decoding language-type messages. I know I have yet to tell you exactly what phonics is. It's not what most people think. *Phonics* is actually a shortcut term for what really should be called graph-o-phonics. Whenever you need to decode a word, you're "required by law" to examine both its graphic (i.e., written) features and its phonic (i.e., sound) features—thus, the word *graphophonics.*

As you attempt to read the word *splash*, you automatically note the graphic features of the six letters: *s, p, l, a, s,* and *h.* At the same time that you're eyeing the letters, something fantastic is happening inside your head. You are translating each of the

letters *s*, *p*, *l*, and *a* and the digraph *s-h* into the five little phonemes that we whispered about in chapter three—/s/-/p/-/l/-/a/-/sh/. As you make this translation from print to sound, you also blend the five phonemes into the single word *splash*. If that word fits your prediction of the meaning you were expecting, you're entitled to keep on reading.

But what does an excellent reader like you actually decode? You *decode*, or translate, the author's printed graphemes into your own spoken or imagined phonemes. In short, the printed word *splash* leads the reader to both see the graphemes and simultaneously transmit them into phonemes. Your marvelous brain is well equipped to handle this multitasking challenge. In fact, when you're reading, you're actually multitasking all of the cues we talked about earlier: phonics, syntax, semantics, and schemas.

Common Methods of Teaching Phonics

This chapter presents the most common methods of teaching phonics to your students: (1) analytic, (2) synthetic, (3) phonogram (or onset rime), and (4) vowel pattern. The phonogram, or rime, method is by far my favorite and the favorite of children and teachers I have taught. Why? Because of the healthy side effects and its playful approach. However, for some children the phonogram/rime method has to be supplemented by one of two other methods: the analytic or the synthetic method. Oh well, the best teaching needs to be different for different children, I suppose (please say yes).

The Difference Between Analytic and Synthetic Phonics

Both the analytic and synthetic methods require teachers to use the direct-teaching approach. Picture yourself face to faces, with *you* running the show. You will demonstrate in person, and you will check with each student to see if what you're teaching is understood. The direct-teaching method does not depend at all on the use of worksheets, activity-type booklets, or constant minitests. Instead, it depends on a complete understanding of what you're doing as you teach.

Both the analytic and the synthetic methods are gentle and direct forms of teaching phonics to children. They are learning modes that teachers often need to use with children who are not yet getting it. They are also often used as the chief method of teaching phonics. The main difference between the two methods is this: The analytic method emphasizes the *visual* mode of learning, and the synthetic method emphasizes the *auditory* mode. You'll understand what this really means as you learn about each of them. These two methods are the most traditional choices and seem to have dominated commercial reading instruction and materials off and on for over 50 years.

A Carefully Planned Lesson Using the Analytic Method

Suppose some of your students are having trouble decoding the digraph *sh*, as in *shell* or *dash*. (A *digraph* is a combination of two letters standing for only one sound, such as the *th* in *thin* or the *oa* in *boat*.) Decoding simply means changing the graphemes into phonemes; for example, the digraph *sh* becomes the phoneme /sh/). Here are some steps to follow when you use the analytic method:

1. Make a list of easy words that include the single grapheme *sh*. Words ending with *a-s-h* would give you a start: *cash, dash, gash, hash, lash, mash, crash*, and so on. Those ending with *i-s-h* can also be listed (e.g., *dish, fish, wish*), and with advanced students you can use some that *begin* with *sh* (e.g., *shell, shut, should, shake, ship*).

2. Write one or two sentences for each of the target words you plan to use in your lesson. Usually four or five words are enough.

3. To provide even more context for the target words, you may want to weave the four or five sentences together to make a very short story.

   > "I like *hash*," Dan said.
   > "I like *fish*," Nan said.
   > "What *should* we do?" he asked.
   > "I know what we can do" *she* said.
   > "Let's go eat *fish hash*!"

   Notice that the context words that *surround* the target words (like *said, what,* and *know*) are purposely not more difficult to understand than the target words. [*Tip*: To save this kind of lesson for use with other children, put your story and other important features in a manila folder and file it away.]

4. Find other *sh* words in the children's anthology or another book they use in common. Write down the pages where the children can discover and practice the words in whole text (i.e., real books, real stories, real nonfiction explanations).

5. Create a simple reading game that will provide the students with even more practice. (Practice being creative and think of simple games from childhood.)

A Modeled Lesson on Decoding the Sh Digraph Analytic Method

"OK, listen carefully. I'm going to read these five sentences on the board." Read smoothly and informally, as if you were speaking rather than just reading out loud. Have five students act out the story.

"I like *hash*," Dan said.

"I like *fish*," Nan said.

"What *should* we do?" he asked.

"I know what we can do," *she* said.

"Let's go eat *fish hash!*"

"Now let's read one sentence at a time. I'll read it first, and you repeat it after I read it. Are you ready? Here comes the first sentence: '*I like hash,*' *Dan said.* Now you say it. [Pause.] That's good. Now do the same thing after the other sentences." Read the remaining sentences with them.

"Now say each word that I point to. We'll say them together." Point to each underlined target word, moving from left to right, and say the word together. Accent the /sh/ sound: *hash . . . fish . . . should . . . she . . . fish . . . hash.*

"Now as I say all the special words again, I want you to discover what letter or letters are the same in each word. [This part they like because of the mild challenge.] As I say all the target words to you again, I want you to decide what sound is the same in each word." Repeat the words.

"I like *hash*," Dan said.

"I like *fish*," Nan said.

"What *should* we do?" he asked.

"I know what we can do," *she* said.

"Let's go eat *fish hash!*"

"Ginger, what two letters do you see in each of the words that I point to? . . . Brad, what sound do you hear in each of the words that I point to?" Then ask them all, "What *sound* should you think of when you see the *s* and the *h* together?"

"Jose, give me another word that has the /sh/ sound at the end of the word." This challenge can lead to writing some of the words that end with the /sh/ sound. *Warning*: Don't ask for the /sh/ at the beginning of the word it. If one of your kids thinks of *sh_t* the rest of your beautiful lesson may be lost in giggles for 20 minutes straight.

Return to the five sentences, and have the children first read them all together and then take turns reading each sentence. End with a game you create if you wish.

Advantages and Disadvantages of the Analytic Method

The analytic method uses the phonics cues and moderately involves the syntactic, semantic, and schematic cues. The analytic method also allows for children to discover rather than always be told, which can be highly motivating to your eager learners. Its disadvantages are that many children in the group wait for others to do the discovering. With the analytic method the visual mode of learning and remembering is emphasized. The problem is that some children rely more on the auditory mode. Do you know which mode *you* tend to use the most when you're learning or remembering?

Easy Planning Steps for Using the Synthetic Method

With the synthetic method children first learn to decode, or transfer, isolated graphemes into phonemes. For example, children learn to read *sh* as a sound, /sh/. Then they learn how to put the phonemes together to make either silent or audible words. This is similar to the activity in chapter 3 that used only phonemes. Now, though, your students have advanced to using both graphemes and phonemes.

Here's a mnemonic device for remembering the synthetic method:

say . . . write . . . blend . . . write, or SWBW for short

The children say the new letter sound. Then they write it. Next they practice blending it orally with other known letter sounds. And finally they write the new letter sounds as parts of whole words. This will become more clear as you read the modeled examples that follow.

When planning a lesson using the synthetic method, make a list of one-syllable words that include the grapheme *sh* and other graphemes students have already learned. Useful words would be *shack, ash, bash, cash,* and so on. Than you're ready to begin your lesson using the synthetic approach and remembering that graphemes are written forms of phonemes.

A Step-by-Step Lesson

1. Write *sh* on the board. Point to this grapheme and tell the children explicitly what sound they are to make when they see it. [I refer to the letters as "standing for the /sh/ sound," but most programs simply call the letter or letters a sound.]

2. Have the children make the /sh/ sound whenever you point to the letters. Make sure each person in the group says it.

3. Review the sounds related to the graphemes *a*, *b*, *h*, *m*, and *ck* in the same way, using Steps 1 and 2.

4. Have each child write the grapheme *sh*, first on the board and then on paper. Have them point to what they've written on the board and say the sound (not the letters).

5. Remind them how to blend sounds together by using a reminder word that they already know, such as *mess*. Write it on the board and have them say it slowly: *mmmeeesss*. Then have them say it fast: *mess*. [This is the same thing you learned in Chapter 3 when we talked about blending phonemes.]

6. Point to the isolated graphemes that you've put on the board (*sh*, *a*, *b*, *h*, *m*, *ck*). Tell students they are now going to blend these together to make some words. Say: "Whenever I point to one of them, you make the right sound."

7. Point to three graphemes that will produce a word, such as *b*, *a*, and *sh*, and have students make the appropriate sounds as you point to them: /b/ + /a/ + /sh/. Point to this same sequence of three graphemes several times, each time faster than the previous time. Finally, tell them to say it fast.

8. Write the word you've just produced—in this case *bash*. Have each child say the separated phonemes slowly and then fast. Then have them write the word. [Writing is what makes this program work so well.]

9. Repeat this sequence with other words: *hash*, *mash*, *shack*, *crack*.

10. You may wish to extend the lesson by (a) writing some of the words in sentences, (b) finding the words in other reading materials, and/or (c) playing a word game that you create.

Advantages and Disadvantages of the Synthetic Method

On the plus side, the synthetic method is much more explicit than the analytic method. Children are told which sound is associated with which letter or letter pair. They don't have to discover this association on their own, as they do with the analytic method. And this seems to fit the learning style of some individuals, but definitely not all. Those who have trouble learning to decode through the analytic method often are able to learn to decode with the synthetic method (Anderson, Hiebert, Scott, & Wilkinson, 1985).

Unfortunately, by learning to decode letters that are isolated from a word, the student may not be learning to use phonics in the most efficient way. Many letters do not stand for sounds when they're all by themselves. They must be seen in a spelling pattern before they can be properly decoded. The letter *a*, for example, stands for a different phoneme in *can* and *cane*. It's the spelling pattern that makes the difference.

Despite the disadvantages of the synthetic phonics method, research shows that it works well for many children (Anderson et al., 1985). For those having trouble with the analytic method, the synthetic method may work better. Classroom reading teachers should become familiar with the synthetic method so they can use it with children whose mode of learning demands a more auditory approach. Again, some people learn and remember better through the ears; some learn and remember better through the eyes. The phonogram method that you and I will discuss next requires a very different mode of learning phonics—through the eyes and ears plus an awareness of language patterns.

Using the Phonogram Method

Professional Standard: Uses phonics to teach students letter/sound correspondence

The *phonogram* approach to phonics is based on one-syllable rhyming words like *cat, fat, sat,* and *that.* All of these have endings that not only rhyme but also spell exactly the same way. The ending *at* is an example of a phonogram—now often called a *rime.* What is the phonogram, or rime, for the words listed vertically here?

cop

top

stop

mop

slop

chop

hop

pop

The phonogram method has been around for a long, long time, disguised as little words in bigger words or as family words (*at, bat, cat, fat,* etc.) or just as rhyming words. More recently the phonogram method has been given different labels, such as the analogy strategy (Fox, 1996) or simply rime. Do you remember the terms *onset/rime?* In the word *slap* the onset is *sl*; the rime is *ap.* In the word *rug* the letter *r* is the onset; the rime is *ug,* as in *bug, tug, lug, drug, thug.* "A number of studies have suggested that there is a special link between early onset-rime awareness and reading development" (Goswami, 2000, p. 254).

Right now, we'll use both terms—*phonograms* and *rimes*—until we get to a more thorough explanation. Phonograms, or rimes, are not rhyming words; they are not family words. All by themselves, they are not words at all. They're like the second half of a one-syllable word. In words like *fat, flat, hat,* and *that,* the phonogram, or rime, is simply the rhyming part of the word—/at/.

Use the right side of your brain to intuitively discover just what a phonogram, or rime, looks like. The *at* in *cat* is a phonogram or rime. The *ab* in *cab* is a phonogram or rime. The *ab* in *scab* is a phonogram or rime. The *ed* in *fed* is a phonogram or rime. What about the *en* in *ten* and *hen* and *men?* Yes, it is, too. What about words with more than one syllable? The *ap* in *apple* is a phonogram. The *en* in *renter* is a phonogram—a sneaky one hiding in the middle of a word.

As you can see, a phonogram or rime always has at least one vowel and one consonant at the end of a one-syllable word—or at the end of a syllable, like the *ap* in *capture.* So let us hereafter praise the phonogram, now going by the name of *rime,* for after all it's the rhyming part of a rhyming word. Funny, isn't it, that rimes are what make rhymes rhyme? Without rhymes we'd have no songs or rap; without rimes our onsets would have no meaning. Take *flab* or *blab*, for instance. Without *ab*, we've got only *fl* and *bl*—how embarrassing! How can we communicate without our funny little rimes?

> *No songs, no rap*
> *No gongs, no flap*
> *No reason to jump.*
> *No season for a bump.*

The Famous Wylie-Durrell Study

Wylie and Durrell's report on an extremely important piece of research was proudly published by *The Reading Teacher,* once in 1970 and then, because of its extreme importance, again in 1995. The subject of the research was the advantages of the phonogram method of teaching phonics. This research passed almost unnoticed by the publishers of instructional materials until Marilyn Adams praised it in her 1990 report 20 years later.

In this now-famous study, carried out with 900 children, Wylie and Durrell found that only 37 phonograms were necessary to generate 500 words used frequently by children in Grades 1 through 3. Each of these particular phonograms appeared in 10 or more one-syllable words used frequently by children and adults.

Powerful Phonograms Discovered by Wylie and Durrell

ack, ail, ain, ake, ale, ame, an, ank, ap, ash, at, ate, aw, ay, eat, ell, est, ice, ick, ide, ight, ill, in, ine, ing, ink, ip, it, ock, oke, op, ore, ot, uck, ug, ump, unk

A Modeled Lesson Teaching Phonics via Onsets and Rimes: Part A

Professional Standard: Understands that spelling is based on the knowledge of letter names

As teacher and model, I've chosen the responsible *op* rime because of its ability to just say stop. My actual teaching words appear in quotation marks. Please note that this sample lesson has been designed to inspire children to intuitively understand the connections between onsets and rimes.

Your students will not need this dramatic experience every time you're introducing a new rime family. It would definitely be a waste of instructional time to use this technique for each rime or phonogram. Rather than having your students master every single phonogram, you can rely on the human brain to generalize from the samples you offer.

Written on the Chalkboard or Permanent Chart

top

flop

drop

"All right, people, to play this time we have to count to ten backwards. Are you ready? Ten, nine, eight, seven, six, five, four, three, two, one. OK, it's time for us to build that pretend tower I promised you. Have you ever seen a tower? . . . Have you ever been inside a tower? . . . Here's a photograph [or a large sketch on the chalkboard or chart] of what a tower looks like.

"Do you know why kings built so many towers—hundreds of years ago? . . . The towers were used for protecting the king and his guards from their enemies. And . . . for putting their enemies in prison or jail! The prisoners were forced to go downstairs into the cold wet basement called a dungeon and wait for food and water that might or might not be brought down to them.

"Today we're going to pretend to build a tower ten floors high. Do you see those three words way up there? What is the word on top? Yes, that word is *top*, and do you know why it's called *top*? [After they guess, tell them it's also because Prince Top lives there.]

"Because this tower is a magic tower, we have to build it from the top to the bottom—instead of building it from the bottom to the top. Isn't it strange that we can start building it way up there, instead of starting to build the tower way down here?

"Prince Top's real name is just Top, because he lives on the top floor—on Floor Ten. Do you all see the top floor up there [on the board or chart paper]? What does the word say? Yes, it really does say . . . *top*.

"Now then, right below Floor Ten is Floor Nine, where Prince Flop lives. Most people just call him Flop. What do you think of that name? Yes, I agree. His name is very funny. Who can show me what it means to flop? [if not, you do it.]

"But what does *flop* mean? Yes, it's what you do when you fall on the couch–you just flop on the couch. Or you flop on the bed. Or you flop on the floor, like this! [Laugh and flop with them.]

Do laugh "OK, if we don't hurry, we won't be able to build the whole tower. Do you know what? The word *flop* rhymes with *top*. So I wonder who lives on Floor Eight? It must be someone whose name rhymes with *flop* and *top*.

"OK, let's go down one floor to Floor Eight. Who lives on Floor Eight? Can you read the word up there? Yes, the person on Floor Eight is called Drop. That's because Mr. Drop lives there, and [softly] he will often drop things. [More loudly] He will drop his pencil. He will drop his keys. He will drop his glasses. He will drop his watch. And worst of all, he will drop his ice cream cone!

"But just look at that word *drop*. It really does rhyme with *top* and *flop*. . . . So what are those three words that rhyme together? That's right, *top, flop,* and *drop*. Say it with me. The top three floors on our brand new tower all rhyme with each other. Isn't that a little bit scary? Or is it just magic? What do you think?

"Hurry now . . . Since our tower is truly a magic tower, it has to have exactly ten floors. And the floors have to be built upside down, from the tenth floor down to the first floor. We have seven more floors to build. We have to build Floor Seven, [together] Floor Six, Floor Five, and what next? That's right, Floor Four, Floor Three, Floor Two, Floor One. [Write *floor* on the board.]

"We already have rhyming words for Floor Ten, Floor Nine, and Floor Eight, and those rhyming words are *top, flop,* and *drop*. Who can think of another word that rhymes with *top, flop,* and *drop?* . . . OK, I'll write that one on Floor Seven of our tower. Watch how I spell the new word. Make sure I don't make a mistake.

"Do the same thing quickly with Floor Six, Five, Four, Three, Two, and One, but let the brightest ones catch your spelling mistake on one or two of them. To speed them along, toss in your own idea every other one. Also remind them, "If we don't get ten floors filled, the Wild Heads will be released from the dungeon and come after us.

A Modeled Lesson: Part B

[Look worried] "We have made a very good tower with exactly ten floors—just like the King wanted us to do. But . . . something terrible has happened! Someone let the Wild Heads get out of the dungeon. And they're searching for their tails. [Write "The Wild Heads want their tails!" on the board or chart.] They all want their tails back to fasten to their heads.

"But what do they mean by heads and tails? Does anyone know? [Discuss with them for a moment or two. Then pretend to call up the King.] Hello? Is this the King? (Oh good [softly to your students] we have reached the King.)

"Dear King, what should we do? The Heads have escaped from the dungeon, and they all want their tails back. Yes, that's right—the head and tail monsters that live in that cold, wet, deep, deep dungeon. They are creatures that have only a head and a tail. . . . (Oh, he says that the wise men told him that some very mean boys and girls took the monsters' tails away, and now they want them back . . . right now.) . . . All right, I'll tell the girls and boys what they have to do.

"There are ten of the head and tail creatures trying to get in our door! I need ten of you to go quickly to the board [or chart] and print the letters that I tell you to.

"Each of you print *op*, which rhymes with *top*. Print *op* exactly where I tell you to. The first person should put his *op* way up high. The second person should put her *op* exactly under the first one. The third person should put his *op* under the second one . . . [and so on].

"The king told me exactly what the tail really is. Just like a real tail, he said. And it's right there in the tower that we built. It's *op,* the tail—the same tail we put on each floor of the tower, the same *op* you each put on the board [or chart]. It's the same *op* that Mr. Top owns.

"But where *is* the head for each *op* tail? Well, I have printed the head on these ten cards. Those people who are standing by one of the *ops* will each print the letter or letters from the card. Please print the letter or letters right in front of the *op*. Here's your head, Mr. Top. Please print your *t* right in front of *op*. Now I'll pass out one card to each of the writers. The *t* card for *top*, the *fl* card for *flop*, the *dr* card for *drop*, and a card for each of the *seven* other rhyming words that we already put in our tower [e.g., *cop, crop, hop, lop, mop, pop, plop, slop, sop, stop*—in addition to residents *top, flop,* and *drop*.].

"And now I would like each one of you ten people to tell us five things: (a) What rhyming word do you have? [e.g., *top*], (b) What is the tail for that rhyming word? [e.g., *op*], (c) What is the head for that rhyming word? [e.g., *t*], (d) How do you say the head? (e) How do you say the tail? Put them together and what do you say? [e.g., *top*]."

Talk over the experience, making sure they all know that the tail of the word was the rhyming part, *op.* You can tell them that this part of the word is called the rime or the phonograph, depending on what they would like to call it as their friend.

Quickly build another tower the following day, without pretending this time, so they can intensively learn the principle of rimes, or phonograms. From that time on, building a tower each day (or twice a day) is advisable until they have learned all of the 37 phonograms from Wylie and Durrell's study. After they have mastered those phonograms, you may wish to use a more thorough list of phonograms, which is shown in Figure 4.1.

The VC (Vowel-Consonant) Phonograms (26)

Short A:	ab, ad, ag, am, an, ap, at	(as in *cab* and *mad*)
Short E:	ed, en, et	(as in *bed* and *ten*)
Short I:	id, ig, im, in, ip, it	(as in *lid* and *big*)
Short O:	ob, od, og, op, ot	(as in *Bob* and *God*)
Short U:	ub, ug, um, un, ut	(as in *tub* and *rug*)

Example: Phonogram *ab.* Rhyming words: *cab, dab, gab, jab, lab, tab, crab, drab, grab, slab, stab*

The VCC (Vowel-Consonant-Consonant) Phonograms (23)

Short A:	ack, amp, and, ang, ank, ash	(as in *sack* and *lamp*)
Short E:	ell, end, ent, est	(as in *bell* and *send*)
Short I:	ick, ill, ing, ink, int	(as in *sick* and *pill*)
Short O:	ock, ong	(as in *sock* and *long*)
Short U:	uck, uff, ump, ung, unk, ush	(as in *luck* and *buff*)

Example: Phonogram *ack.* Rhyming words: *back, hack, Jack, lack, pack, rack, sack, tack, black, crack, flack, knack, quack, slack, stack, whack*

The VCE (Vowel-Consonant-Final E) Phonograms (16)

Long A:	ace, ade, ake, ale, ame, ane, ate, ave	(as in *lace* and *save*)
Long E:	VCE is an uncommon way of spelling the long /e/ sound	
Long I:	ice, ide, ime, ine, ive	(as in *mice* and *hive*)
Long O:	oke, one, ope	(as in *poke* and *bone*)
Long U:	VCE is an uncommon way of spelling the long /u/ sound	

Example: Phonogram *ace.* Rhyming words: *ace, face, lace, mace, pace, race, brace, grace, place, trace*

VVC (Vowel-Vowel-Consonant) Phonograms (8)

Long A:	ail, ain	(as in *pail* and *rain*)
Long E:	eak, eal, eam, eat, eed, eep	(as in *beak* and *peal*)
Long I:	VVC is an uncommon way of spelling the long /i/ sound	
Long O:	VVC uncommon except with oa, as in *goat* (none with 10)	
Long U:	several with fewer than 10: *cool, room, moon, loop, boot*	

Example: Phonogram *ail.* Rhyming words: *ail, bail, fail, hail, jail, mail, nail, pail, rail, sail, tail, vail, wail, frail, quail*

Oddball Phonograms (14)

ay, all, ar, are (*dare*), ark, aw, ear, ew, ight, ind (*find*), ow (*low*), ow (*cow*), ore, orn

---

FIGURE 4.1   Essential phonograms (with 10 or more rhyming words).

Advantages of the Phonogram Method

Researchers (Adams, 1990; Wylie & Durrell, 1970, 1995) have found the phonogram (onset/rime) method to be the easiest for most children. Onsets and rimes, or phonograms, have distinct advantages as a teaching device (Anderson et al., 1985). Marilyn Adams, cognitive psychologist, in her report to the U.S. Department of Education (1990), argued enthusiastically for this method. In her opinion single vowels or consonants are far more difficult for young students than onsets and rimes. "As coherent psychological units in themselves, the onset and rime are relatively easy to remember and to splice back together . . . and this, as we have seen, is in marked contrast to the slowness with which words can be developed through individual letter-sound correspondences" (p. 324).

Eleven years after her major report on the teaching of reading, Adams is still providing research reports related to phonics and alphabetic instruction (Adams, 2002). Research over the past 15 years has demonstrated that students are more successful at breaking apart the onset and rime in a word (e.g., than in breaking the word into individual phonemes (e.g., *t-o-p*) or breaking the word at another place e.g., *to-p* (Johnson, 1999). A structured phonics curriculum that includes both onsets and rimes and the sounding and blending of phonemes within rimes appears to be the most effective (Juel & Minden-Cupp, 2000). Combining the onset-rime method of learning with the sounding and blending of phonemes is highly creative.

Helpful Hints

There are many creative ways of helping beginning or struggling readers to recognize those tag-along phonograms—along with their forthright onsets, of course. For fun, call them rime tails, phony grams, or funny grams—whatever kids like. Once children get used to them, they're constantly pointing them out in their own writing, in group stories, in Big Books that are read to a group or the whole class, in the literature selections they read themselves, and in environmental print.

The Important Principles Discovered by Wylie and Durrell

Professional Standard: Teaches students to recognize and use various spelling patterns

Wylie and Durrell (1995) discovered other important things from their research with 900 first grade children:

1. Is it easier for children to identify separate vowel sounds or whole phonograms? Definitely phonograms.

2. Are short-vowel phonograms (*ap, op, ug*) easier to learn than long-vowel phonograms (*ail, ine, oke*)? No, they are equally easy to learn.

3. Are long-vowel phonograms spelled with a silent *e* (*ate, oke*) easier to learn than those with vowel digraphs (*ail, eat*)? (Vowel digraphs are two-vowel letters standing for one vowel sound.) The answer is . . . no difference. They are equally easy to learn.

4. Should phonograms containing vowel sounds that are neither long or short (*ark, ool, ound*) be taught later than those with definite long or short sounds? The difference in difficulty is too small to be significant.

5. Are phonograms that generate over 10 words easier to learn than those that generate fewer than 10? The researchers found that as long as you have 5 or more, there's not enough of a difference to worry about it.

6. Are short-vowel phonograms ending with a single consonant (*an, ip, ug*) easier to learn than those ending with a consonant digraph (*ask, ack*) or a consonant blend (*est, ump*)? Well, yes, somewhat. Because of this I recommend that you first teach many single-consonant phonograms like *fat* and *not* before introducing the dual or trio consonants like *flat* and *splat*. Remember that *f, fl*, and *spl* are all called onsets and the phonograms are often called rimes.

Create Family-Word Charts as a Quick Learning Game

It will be easy for you and your students to make one or more family-word charts every day. These charts take no more than 5 to 10 minutes to produce on an 8 1/2 × 11 sheet of paper (instead of the tower shape we produced earlier). It's important that you display each new family-word chart on a major wall that can be easily seen from the students' seats. This is a crucial way for your students to master all of them.

I recommend starting with the *ack* phonogram because it produces at least 20 words. Select a student who wishes to propose the first rhyming word, then a student to propose the second, and so on—up to the tenth word. Whoever proposes a rhyming word should print it carefully.

Then each day, pick one new phonogram, or rime. Be careful not to push this process—do it every day for 3 or 4 days, then skip a day. They need to feel successful, highly motivated and very proud of themselves. If students seem to be losing interest after 3 or 4 days, change to a friendly but timed competition between two halves of the classroom, with plenty of distance between each half if possible. Then see which side can write down 10 family words first. They'll have to learn to talk softly so the other team cannot steal their words.

Use Picture Charts of Family Words

Many teachers use picture charts of the family words that students generate (see Figure 4.2). The pictures demonstrating the *ail* phonogram—as in *jail, nail, pail, tail*, and *trail*—can help children remember not only the pronunciation of the *ail* phonogram itself but also the pronunciation of the onsets—*j, n, p, t*, and *tr*. These picture charts can be produced by the teacher, an aide, the children in the class or their older buddies, or even your talented spouse or significant other. The pictures can be drawn, photographed, or cut out of magazines. They can also probably be obtained from an educational materials store or even from the Internet.

Be sure to put the picture charts on the wall, too, along with the family-word charts.

FIGURE 4.2 A picture chart of family words for *ail*.

Keep the Learning Going

Once you've creatively led the way and helped your students start one family-word chart after another, they'll be happy to keep adding "just one more word" to them. And creating new family-word charts is a perfect enterprise for children who enjoy learning together—with their peers, their teacher, and even their own families. Best of all, while learning phonograms, your students will be making surprising improvements in their spelling, word recognition, writing composition, and that all-important self-confidence.

Once your students have mastered the 37 basic phonograms (and the 370 family words that go with them), it may be time to shift to the list in Figure 4.1. Depending on your students' age and stage, start with the vowel-consonant (VC) phonograms that weren't part of Wylie and Durrell's list, and let your students generate 10 meaningful words (for *more* reading and *more* spelling practice). Keep the words on the wall, and you'll find that they are easily learned—thanks to the power of repetition and rhyming that children love so well.

Using the Vowel-Pattern Method of Advanced Phonics

To use the vowel-pattern phonics method, you'll need to modify your family-word charts using a simple T-frame, like the ones shown in Figure 4.3. The family-word charts using a T-frame will then need to be put on the wall in such a way that students are continually reminded of the different vowel patterns—and the sample words that fit each pattern.

When children ask you what *VC* means, simply say "a vowel letter and a consonant letter." If they haven't yet learned the difference between consonant and vowel letters, tell them the ugly truth: Vowel letters are *a, e, i, o, u,* and sometimes *y;* the consonant letters are all the rest. Keep it simple for now. VCC stands for vowel, consonant, consonant; VCE stands for vowel, consonant, and silent *e.* If you use such frames faithfully for your revised family-word charts, your students will be ready to learn the vowel-pattern phonics method—usually sometime during third grade and normally for me no later than the fourth grade.

	VC		VCC		VCE
	in		ink		ine
p	in	m	ink	d	ine
t	in	p	ink	f	ine
w	in	s	ink	l	ine
ch	in	bl	ink	m	ine
gr	in	dr	ink	sh	ine
				sp	ine

FIGURE 4.3 Family-word charts using a T-frame.

It's important for you to know that children definitely like using the letters *VC* better than saying *vowel and consonant*. They *greatly* prefer *VCE* to *vowel, consonant, and final e*. And abbreviations do make the teaching of vowel patterns easier because your tongue doesn't get tied up in knots.

Teaching Steps for Vowel-Pattern Words

A large part of the effectiveness of teaching vowel patterns depends, of course, on how you teach them. The steps I'm going to describe are those that my master students and I have found to be the most enjoyable and productive. As you were teaching phonograms, you were already beginning to teach vowel patterns. When you used the *et* phonogram with words like *bet*, *let*, and *met*, you were already informally demonstrating the VC vowel pattern.

All you have to do now is to place a *VC* above the column of phonograms on a family-word chart, just the way you see it in Figure 4.3. Help your students see that with VC all of the words end with a vowel letter followed by a consonant letter. By this time your students will already have learned a great many phonograms and will have begun to grasp the meaning of vowel patterns intuitively.

1. Using Figure 4.4, read the first eight VC words to the children, and point out that each word ends with a vowel followed by a consonant. Tell them that these words are all VC words. [Think of this as a right-brain intuitive learning experience rather than one requiring left-brain verbal analysis.]

Short VC		Short VCC	Long VCE	Long VVC	Long CV
	in	ink	ape	eat	he
p	in	sink	cape	heat	she
	at	ill	ate	aid	go
c	at	pill	plate	paid	me
th	at	spill	note	mail	by
d	ot	blank	lake	soak	fly
c	up	dash	like	boat	try
ch	ip	bell	five	feet	no
	top	send	came	road	Hi
	not	lamp	rope	train	my
	bud	best	nine	green	be
	fun	sick	flame	jail	we
	bed	bang	time	beak	so
	sad	spring	poke	pain	pro
	spin	hint	bone	mean	sky
	pet	sock	kite	clean	spy

FIGURE 4.4 Words for teaching vowel patterns.

2. Hand each of the children five cards, each of which has one word from each of the five columns on it. For example, you might hand Bernice these five cards: *top, send, came, road,* and *Hi.* Ask the students to find the one card that is like the VC words you just read. Bernice would choose the word *top.*

3. Have them all show you their chosen cards at the same time. Ask them to check to see if the word ends with a vowel letter followed by a consonant letter. If necessary, remind them of what the six vowel letters are. Have them hold up their chosen cards again. Help those who have the wrong pattern to find the right one.

4. When all students have the correct pattern, have them read their chosen words (with your help, if necessary) and place the cards on the chalkboard railing. As each child brings a card forward, ask what kind of word it shows (a VC word), and ask the child to point first to the vowel letter and then to the final consonant letter.

5. If you have time, now or later, let the children play a game with the VC words. For example, divide the class into pairs to play a game of concentration. Each pair can first prepare two identical cards for each of 10 words in the VC column. They should place the cards on a flat surface, completely mixed up, and face down. The rules are simple. Player A picks up a card, player A and B both look at it, and then player A picks up another card, hoping it will be a perfect match. If it is, player A puts both of the cards in a special pile and repeats the process. If the cards are not a perfect match, Player A puts both of them back exactly where they were. Player B does the same thing. Whoever builds the largest personal pile wins. This is superb practice.

6. Later, have students search for VC words in their "little books" while they're reading a story or a nonfiction piece together.

Moving on to the More Complicated Vowel Patterns

After the children have thoroughly learned the VC pattern, you're ready to teach or review the VCC pattern (like *back* or *slack*). As soon as you think they're ready, have them work with both patterns simultaneously. Instead of finding a VC word in their stack of five cards, have them find both a VC and a VCC card. If you want to make this more challenging later, give them more than five cards to deal with.

After your students have mastered the VC and VCC patterns, gradually teach them the VCE, VVC, and CV patterns, in that order. You may find that the activities and games become increasingly interesting and challenging to them as you increase the number of patterns they must deal with.

But what should you do about sneaky *diphthongs,* such as the /oi/ sound in *toy* or *boil?* Just treat them like the single phonemes that they are—one sound instead of two. But also treat words like *toy* as a special CV sound, a little like *go*, and words like *boil* as a special VVC sound, somewhat like *meat*. For reading and writing, concentrate on the /oi/ and /oy/ and the /ow/ and /ou/ sounds and spelling.

Most second term third-graders that my graduate students have worked with have been able to handle the first three patterns, but only if they first had considerable experience with onsets and rimes. By the time children reach the first half of fourth grade, most can handle all five patterns if they are introduced after previous vowel patterns have been mastered.

The Value of Patterns

Patterns Versus Rules   Research tells us that implicit awareness works better than memorized rules (Adams, 1990; Greif, 1988; Rosso & Emans, 1981; Tovey, 1980). My own experience and that of my graduate students support the research. It seems to me that children are not exactly crazy about rules, unless they've made them up themselves. And many children do make up their own phonics rules. Then they try them out, find them wanting, and either modify them or throw them away. What's not terribly natural is for teachers to provide language rules that children must memorize. This doesn't work very well at all.

When Tovey (1980) administered a phonics test consisting of nonsense words to children in Grades 2 through 6, he found they did quite well in pronouncing the words correctly, with scores ranging from 55% to 83%. When the students were asked to verbalize their phonics knowledge, however, very few of them were able to do that.

A study by Rosso and Emans (1981) was even more revealing. These researchers also gave children a phonics test, this one consisting of 14 words that represented 14 phonics rules. The students were asked to give a rule for each word they had pronounced correctly. An average of 75% of the children pronounced each word correctly, but fewer than 15% could explain the rule for their correct pronunciation.

We seem to be talking about an implicit, intuitive behavior that some of us abstract-thinking adults have tried to make analytical and explicit. As Adams (1990) says,

> It is automatic, frequency-based pattern recognition that is responsible for the speed and reliability with which skillful readers process the spellings, sounds, and meanings of words. . . . Rules that are acquired only as abstract principles must live in another part of the head—the part in charge of conscious interpretation, not the part in charge of automatic, frequency-based responding (p. 211).

My own opinion is that teacher-imposed phonics rules are a great example of Piaget ignored: Children tend to be more *concrete* than abstract in their thinking.

Predictive Power   How powerful are the five vowel patterns in predicting the correct pronunciation of the vowel sounds? I decided to find out by checking the five patterns against Fry's list of the 1000 most frequently used words in the English language (Fry, Fountoukidis, & Polk, 1995). For example, if a VCE pattern is supposed to predict a long vowel sound, then I wouldn't count any VCE word in Fry's list that didn't have a long vowel sound—even though researchers have consistently found that even an imperfect pattern often gives children enough of a clue to figure out a word with an assist from context (Adams, 1990; Groff, 1986; Wylie & Durrell, 1970, 1995). But for the sake of research, I set tougher standards and did not count words that were poor examples of a pattern—like the words *love* and *gone*, which are poor examples of the long-vowel VCE pattern.

Here are my results on how well the five vowel patterns predict the pronunciation of the 1000 most frequent words in the English language.

VC (short-vowel) pattern: 86% reliability
VCC (short-vowel) pattern: 89% reliability
VCE (long-vowel) pattern: 81% reliability
VVC (long-vowel) pattern: 77% reliability
CV (long-vowel) pattern: 77% reliability

Clearly, the predictive power of these five patterns is much better than mere chance. Consequently, teaching children these patterns can make a difference in their fluency, comprehension, and recognition of words.

Using Phonograms and Vowel Patterns to Attack Multisyllable Words

One of the most important advantages of teaching phonograms and vowel patterns is the contribution they make to determining the pronunciation of words with more than one syllable. In examining the several hundred miscues generated by ineffective or inexperienced readers, I've often noticed the paralysis that sets in for these children whenever they come upon big words. Sometimes it's a frantic display of bravado, tossing out any big word that starts with the same letter.

Text: The car was speeding down the boulevard.
Nervous student: The car was speeding down the bulletin.

At other times a young reader may just invent a new word right on the spot—for example, *billycopy* for *helicopter*.

How can a knowledge of phonograms and vowel patterns help? Let's assume that the words *rabbit, basket,* and *robin* are not part of Randy's sight vocabulary. One glance at the word rabbit identifies a familiar phonogram and vowel pattern, *ab,* which young children who have been taught phonograms will associate with *cab, grab,* and other *ab* words. Advanced youngsters from fourth grade on can be taught to use the more expansive vowel-pattern method. For instance, the word *rabbit* would be seen by them as a VC pattern (*rab*) followed by another VC pattern (*bit*).

So what makes the vowel-pattern method better than the phonogram method? The phonogram method is the first step, and many teachers and children will stop right there. I don't blame them: The phonogram approach is fairly concrete, whereas the vowel-pattern approach is more abstract and may be too difficult for some children.

The advantage of the vowel-pattern approach, though, is that you don't have to memorize all those phonograms, or rimes. Instead, all you have to do is recognize a vowel pattern. Without worrying about whether we have an *at, ap, ad,* or *ag* phonogram, we can instantly see that we have a VC vowel pattern, which handles any phonogram within that pattern. Thus, instead of all those hundreds of phonograms to remember, we have just five vowel patterns: VC (or CVC as some people like to call it), VCC, VCE, VVC, and CV—and that's it.

It's quite true that the second syllable in *rabbit* contains a schwa vowel sound rather than a short *i* sound, but research has shown that this is really not a problem. Wylie and Durrell (1970), for example, found that 95% of the phonograms in the words used in primary-grade books can be read with understanding by ignoring the less accurate schwa sound and using a short or long vowel instead. Groff's research (1986) agrees.

Syllables & Structures: Friends of Phonograms and Vowel Patterns

Looking at the word *basket,* Randy will find not only the high-frequency phonogram *et,* but also the phonogram *ask*—one with considerably lower frequency. If Randy has learned vowel patterns, he will intuitively see that *basket* can be broken up into two VC patterns, *bas* and *ket;* or it can be broken into a VCC pattern, *bask,* and a VC pattern, *et.* Either form of syllabication will work fine; the point is that with *both* phonogram and vowel-pattern knowledge, Randy has an excellent chance of decoding the word with minimal challenge.

What about a harder word, like *robin* or *robot?* Using a rule once taught to me by a friendly teacher, I would divide before the consonant. Whoops! It works with *robot* but not with *robin.* Whatever rule you might have learned, the fact is this: If you examine the top 1000 words, you'll find that dividing *before* the consonant letter works 50% of the time, and dividing *after* the consonant letter also works 50% of the time: a fascinatingly fickle fate for former experts on syllabication rules.

With words like *robin* and *robot* we can encourage students to try pronouncing the word both ways (see Figure 4.5). Whichever sound rings a bell or seems right in context is the one to use. Arm your students with knowledge of phonograms and vowel patterns, but teach them to keep using other major types of cues as well.

Adding Context Clues to Syllabication and Vowel Pattern Clues

If you want children to more thoroughly understand this concept of combining syllabication with vowel patterns, it's time to bring in the context clues shown in Figure 4.6.

VC	CV	VC	CV
Try r o b/i n and r o/b i n.		Try r o b/o t and r o/b o t.	

FIGURE 4.5 Syllabication patterns in *robin* and *robot.*

VC min/er	CV mi/ner	The miner is in the pit digging coal.
VC ced/ar	CV ce/dar	The blankets are in the cedar chest.
VC Chin/a	CV Chi/na	China is a country in Asia.
VC stap/ler	CV sta/pler	Use a stapler to put the pages together.

FIGURE 4.6   Combining three types of clues.

Have them read each word out loud both ways and then tell you which one sounds right in the sentences.

Syllabication becomes a thoughtful, flexible tool for the reader who is searching for meaning—searching for the message the author is presenting. Syllabication should not be a busy-work exercise of merely drawing lines between syllables according to secretarial rules.

Cooling Our Debate: Teaching Phonics Using Whole Text

When your students are not catching on to what you're teaching them about phonics, more phonics is not necessarily better. Just as more aspirin is not necessarily better when you're feeling bad. Adams (2002) puts this in a way that makes sense to me: "Like arithmetic without application, phonics without connected reading amounts to useless mechanics" (p. 147).

So whether a graphophonic pattern is introduced through a phonogram chart, a direct lesson, a literature experience, or a writing experience, the concept of immediate applicability needs to be a dominating force. You have intuitively understood this concept since you first learned new words from your parents, since you were first taught how to drive a car, since you were first shown how to appear cool in front of the opposite sex. Immediate application is a basic law of learning. Here's a good example.

A Teacher in Action

Benny: [Reading] The man aimed his rifle and shot the deer with the broken leg.

Teacher: [For the benefit of the group] We know why the man had to shoot it before it was killed by the mountain lion. But how did Benny know that last word was *deer* and not *desk?*

Martha: [Chuckling] Because *deer* doesn't end with *s-k.*

Teacher: Good, you noticed one of the clues. Now what's another clue? George, do you know why that last word couldn't be *desk?*

George: Because . . . uhh . . .

Teacher: Why don't you read Benny's last sentence again, but this time use the word *desk* instead of *deer.*

George: The man . . . the man aimed his rifle and shot the desk. [Laughs out loud] You can't shoot a desk.

Martha: Yes, you could. You could shoot a desk.

George: Yeah, but it would be silly, and . . . and besides, there wouldn't be any desk in the woods!

Teacher: Good work, both of you. You paid attention to the letter clues, but you also paid attention to what you already know. Lucilla, why don't you read the next page.

Lucilla: When the man reached the dead deer, he looked at the an . . .

Teacher: [After several seconds] Try that trick I showed you.

Lucilla: With a blank?

Teacher: Yes, the blank trick.

Lucilla: When the man reached the dead deer, he looked at the blank and saw that he had killed a five-point buck. His family would eat well this winter.

Teacher: Now go back to your blank; see if you can fill it in.

Lucilla: [After a few seconds] Antelope?

Teacher: Try it out.

Lucilla: When the man reached the dead deer, he looked at the antelope and . . . no, that wouldn't make sense.

Teacher: [Smiling encouragement] How about the last part of that sentence? What does it say after your blank?

Lucilla: And saw that he had killed a five-point buck.

Teacher: Do you remember what we said a buck is?

Lucilla: A male deer.

Teacher: That's right. And what part of a male deer would have five points on it?

Lucilla: Oh, I know. That thing on top of his head. His horns.

Teacher: That's right. And those horns have a special name.

Gwen: I know what they are.

Teacher: Lucilla, would you like Gwen to tell you?

Lucilla: [Smiling] Yes.

Gwen: They're antlers.

Lucilla: Oh yeah, antlers.

Teacher: All right, Lucilla, try your sentence again and fill in the blank.

Lucilla: When the man reached the dead deer, he looked at the antlers and saw that he had killed a five-point buck.

Teacher: Did it make sense this time?

Lucilla: Yes.

Teacher: So your guess is a good one. But what should you check to make sure?

Lucilla: Check the letters.

Teacher: Right. How do we know that word is really *antlers?* Do you see any group of letters that you recognize?

Lucilla: I see *a-n-t.*

Teacher: Good. So how do you say that part of the word?

Lucilla: *Ant.*

Teacher: Yes, and what about the second part?

Lucilla: *Lers.*

Teacher: Fine. That was good checking. Now, why don't I read the next page to you, and then Judd can share the one after that.

This teacher was not in a hurry to finish the story so she could do the next thing in her planning book. The story, she knew, would be finished by the children later if they didn't finish it now. What was important to her was the quality of their learning time together. Because of her patience they were beginning to understand the story, and she knew they would enjoy what was going to happen next. And because of her willingness to model good interactive reading for them, she sensed they were getting much better at using what they knew: graphophonic patterns, sight words, making and checking predictions, and using their own background of experiences to communicate with an author. (Read about another teacher on next page.)

Those Teachable Moments

After 3 years of teaching regular third-grade students, I moved to a classroom of 5- to 6-years-olds who were either deaf or semideaf. As you can imagine, getting their attention required lots of stimulation and novelty. Children with hearing handicaps lag in language development but not necessarily cognitive ability, so my priority was to help them develop literacy skills.

Even though my students had difficulty hearing, they responded well to things you know about—good teaching, including good planning, relevance, explicit and frequent feedback, repetition, and practice. Therefore, I taught them numerous direct-instruction lessons, an approach that is effective with special-needs learners (Lloyd, Forness, & Kraval, 1998).

But it was those teachable moments—the unplanned lessons—that really kept me going. One day James brought to class an unopened package from his grandma, with a note to me about sharing it in class. James had no trouble garnering the attention of his curious classmates, and I seized the moment to create an adventure that would stimulate spontaneous language. Placing the package on a shelf beyond their reach, I used sign language, gestures, and vocalizations with enthusiasm: "Surprise!" "Party!" and "James!"

The children tried in vain to reach the package but soon came up with several problem-solving strategies. First they tried to push my arm up toward the package. But I couldn't seem to manage. They signed and verbalized "help," "come," "package," and "get." I extended the experience by reaching toward the package without success, using every possible opportunity to stimulate language and problem solving. Eventually they solved the problem by getting a broom and a tall chair and using teamwork to knock down the package. What a thrill for all of us!

The package contained homemade cookies, party hats, and big red balloons, all of which provided a playful and functional way for me to teach the children new vocabulary. This form of functional teaching is much more likely to make the words stick in their memories than vocabulary drill would. However, following up the next day with a playful drill is an excellent way to make the words stick even more. Try it for yourself if you haven't already, first using an indirect approach like a party, game, or outing and then following up with an enjoyable review taught in a very direct way.

During our party I tried to reinforce not only the new vocabulary, but social transition skills as well—sharing responsibility for passing out cookies and napkins, making choices about what to eat or drink, cleaning up after the party, and most of all, cooperating in ways that were fair to each of the participants. While they weren't looking, I took photographs of each stage of the action.

In the next few days the students got more reinforcement for mastering both the vocabulary and the social transition skills. We wrote the new words on the board, put the party photographs in sequential order, read "The Big Red Balloon" together, dramatized it, made cookies, and wrote a story for their parents. Why all the writing? These children have to rely more on vision rather than hearing.

Summary of Main Ideas

- The analytic method of teaching phonics uses the visual mode of learning and allows children to discover rather than be told; however, many childen rely more on the auditory mode.
- With the synthetic method, students are told directly what the language sounds are as they relate to graphemes, but learning each letter sound in isolation deprives students of the basic cue of context.
- With the phonogram method children can be gradually introduced to phonics by starting with phonemic awareness and the concept and practice of rhyming.
- Learning phonograms helps students with spelling, word recognition, writing, and self-confidence.
- Vowel patterns normally are very reliable in predicting pronunciation.
- Immediate application is important for learning graphophonic patterns.

Literacy Through Technology

A. With one or more partners conduct an Internet search for ideas on teaching phonics (i.e., graphophonic patterns) to your students. You might start by doing a search under "teaching phonics" or try one of these websites.

http://surfnetkids.com/quiz/phonics
http://pbskids.org/lions/games
http://www.nelsonthornes.com/primary/phonics/games

B. Try out one of the phonics teaching ideas that you found on the Internet in the previous activity. Establish goals and methods that coincide with what you have gained from Chapter 4. Ask a colleague to give you feedback on your plan before you try it with your students. After trying it, write a self-evaluation, reflecting in depth on ways to improve your planning and teaching.

Application Experiences for Your Course

A. *Literacy Teacher Vocabulary: List of Terms:* Help yourself and others master these terms so you can communicate accurately with other professionals:

phonogram onset	onset
phoneme	analytic method
grapheme	synthetic method
rime	phonogram method
vowel-patterns phonics	phonics

One way to assure your knowledge of these terms is to *make up several examples of each one.* Share your examples with your colleagues.

B. *What's Your Opinion?:* Discuss why you agree or disagree with the following statements. Use *both* the textbook and your own experiences to justify your opinions.

   1. When children don't know a word, you should just tell them to sound it out.
   2. With phonics, direct instruction is always better than indirect instruction.
   3. The synthetic method is superior to the analytic method.

C. *Individual Teaching Plans:* Using Figures 4.1 and 4.4, decide on some of the phonograms or rimes, you should probably have your students learn before helping them learn the difference between the VC and VCE vowel patterns. What procedures will you use to help your students learn those phonograms, or rimes? Discuss your plan with someone else before you try it with third, fourth, all the way to struggling eighth graders. Report back to your colleagues.

D. *Teaching and Reflecting with Peers:* With a small group, use the Teaching Steps for Vowel-Pattern Words in this chapter to help your "students" (i.e., peers) master the difference between the VC and VCE patterns from Figure 4.4. Then let another peer help *you* master the difference between the VC and CV patterns. Reflect on your procedures and goals to decide how you might creatively improve this teaching/learning situation.

E. *Team Planning:* Plan with your peers how you will provide learning experiences related to phonograms with the short-*e* sound, a difficult vowel for some children. See Figure 4.1 for the seven phonograms that are worth special attention because of their high frequency.

F. *Role-Playing:* In small groups role-play the teacher and the students debating the virtues of the analytic method versus the synthetic method. Use your own creative talents during your role-playing.

Creativity Training Session

A. Imagine that you are finally retiring after many successful years of teaching and serving as the literacy specialist for your school. You are being honored by having the school renamed after you. Make notes to use for the speech you will be making at your retirement banquet. After teaching all those years, what do you think you would be saying? Share it out loud if you can.

B. In a small group, create a new flag for America. It cannot have stripes and stars and cannot be made of cloth, nor can it be rectangular. Draw a sketch of the flag.

C. Tell a story about a seed you found on the way home. Imagine that you planted it and something very strange grew from it. Let your imagination go freely to the unimaginable. How can this experience, or a similar experience, be used to help your students create original stories? How would you adjust the same activity for English-language learners in your classroom?

Field Experiences

A. *Teach from Your Plan:* Using the plan you made in Application C in this chapter, help two or more children learn several phonograms that have the VC and the VCE vowel patterns. For a follow-up mini-lesson help them learn the difference between the VC and VCE patterns. Be sure to have them apply this knowledge to a selection of whole text for a short while during your second session and then more intensively in a third session. *Note:* This series of learning sessions would not be appropriate for most first graders. For first and even many second graders, you may wish to concentrate on having them learn only the phonograms, or you might use only the VC *at* and the VCC *ash* frames.

B. *Teach from Your Team Plans:* (1). Using the plans made by your team for Application D, "Teaching and Reflecting with Peers," teach one of the contrasting pairs of vowel patterns discussed in that application experience. If you're working with kindergarteners or first graders, concentrate on contrasting phonograms instead of vowel patterns.

C. *Teach from Your Team Plans:* (2). Using the plans made by your team for Application E, "Team Planning," assist children in learning several phonograms that include the short-*e* sound. If your students are reading, use the VC or VCC T-frames.

D. *Provide Additional Practice with Learning Games:* Teach five different phonograms with the same vowel pattern from Figure 4.1, the Essential Phonograms List. Use T-frames to help the children learn the vowel pattern while they're learning the phonograms. For a follow-up session, play a game of Steal the Words (see Appendix B), using one-syllable words that have one of those five phonograms as endings.

References

Adams, M. J. (1990). *Beginning to read: Thinking and learning about print.* Cambridge, MA: MIT Press.

Adams. M. J. (2002). Alphabetic anxiety and explicit, systematic phonics instruction. In S. Newman & D. K. Dickinson (Eds.), *Handbook on early literacy.* NY: Guilford Press.

Anderson, R. C., Hiebert, E. H., Scott, J. A., & Wilkinson, I. A. G. (1985). *Becoming a nation of readers: The report of the commission on reading.* Urbana: University of Illinois, Center for the Study of Reading.

Armbruster, B. B., Lehr, F., & Osborn, J. (2001). *Put reading first: The building blocks for teaching children to read, kindergarten through grade three.* Washington, DC: National Institute for Literacy.

Ericson, L., & Juliebo, M. F. (1998). *The phonological awareness handbook for kindergarten and primary teachers.* Newark, DE: International Reading Association.

Fox, B. J. (1996). *Strategies for word identification: Phonics from a new perspective.* Upper Saddle River, NJ: Merrill.

Fry, E. B, Fountoukidis, D. L., & Polk, J. K. (1995). *The new reading teachers' book of lists.* Upper Saddle River, NJ: Merrill.

Goswami, U. J. (2000). Phonological and lexical processes. In M. L. Kamil, P. B. Mosenthal, P. D. Pearson, & R. B. Mahaw (Eds.), *Handbook of Reading Research* (Vol. 3, pp. 251–267). Mahwah, NJ: Erlbaum.

Greif, I. P. (1988). *The usefulness of six phonics rules in producing the correct pronunciation of words in trade books and reading, science, and social studies textbooks used in the third, fourth, fifth, and sixth grades: A research report* [Abstract from ERIC Document Reproduction Service].

Groff, P. (1986). The maturing of phonics instruction. *The Reading Teacher, 39,* 919–923.

Johnson, F. (1999). The timing and teaching of word families. *The Reading Teacher, 53*(1), 64–75.

Juels, C., & Minden-Cupp, C. (2000). Learning to read words, linguistic units and instructional strategies. *Reading Research Quarterly, 35*(4), 458–492.

Lloyd, J., Forness, S., & Kravale, K. (1998). Some methods are more effective than others. *Intervention in School and Curriculum, 33*(4), 195–200.

McQuillan, J. (1998). *The literacy crisis.* Portsmouth, NH: Heinemann.

Moustafa, M. (1997). *Beyond traditional phonics.* Portsmouth, NH: Heinemann.

National Reading Panel. (2000). *Report of the National Reading Panel.* Washington, DC: U.S. Department of Health and Human Services.

Nicholson, T. (1999). Literacy in the family and society. In G. B. Thompson & T. Nicholson (Eds.), *Learning to read: Beyond phonics and whole language* (pp. 1–22). New York: Teachers College Press.

Padak, N., & Rasinski, T. (2000). *Family literacy programs: Who Benefits* (Available at ED438470).

Rosso, B. R., & Emans, R. (1981). Children's use of phonic generalizations. *The Reading Teacher, 34,* 653–658.

Schneider, W., Roth, E., & Ennemoser, M. (2000). Training phonological skills and letter knowledge in children at risk for dyslexia: A comparison of three kindergarten intervention programs. *Journal of Educational Psychology, 92*(2), 284–295.

Scully, P., & Roberts, N. (2002). Phonics, expository writing, and reading aloud: Playful literacy in the primary grades. *Early Childhood Education Journal, 30*(2), 93–99.

Smith, F. (2003). *Unspeakable acts, unnatural practices.* Portsmouth, NH: Heinemann.

Taylor, B. M., Pressley, M., & Pearson, P. D. (2002). Research-supported characteristics of teachers and schools that promote reading achievement. In B. M. Taylor & P. D. Pearson (Eds.), *Teaching reading: Effective schools, accomplished teachers* (pp. 361–373). Mahwah, NJ: Erlbaum.

Tovey, D. R. (1980). Children's grasp of phonics terms vs. sound-symbol relationships. *The Reading Teacher, 33,* 431–437.

Wylie, R. E., & Durrell, D. D. (1970). Teaching vowels through phonograms. *Elementary English, 47,* 787–791.

Wylie, R. E., & Durrell, D. D. (1995). Teaching vowels through phonograms. *The Reading Teacher, 48,* 429–433.

Yopp, H. (1992). Developing phonemic awareness in young children. *The Reading Teacher, 45,* 696–703.

Other Suggested Readings

Beach, S. A. (1990, May). *The interrelationship of phonemic segmentation, auditory abstraction, and word recognition.* Paper presented at the annual meeting of the International Reading Association, Atlanta, GA.

Coles, G. (2000). *Misreading reading.* Portsmouth, NH: Heinemann.

Fountas, I., & Pinnell, G. (1996). *Guided reading.* Portsmouth, NH: Heinemann.

Gaskins, I. W., Donner, M. A., Anderson, R. C., Cunningham, P. M., Gaskins, R. W., Schomner, M., & teachers of Benchmark School. (1988). A metacognitive approach to phonics: Using what you know to decode what you don't know. *Remedial and Special Education, 9,* 36–41.

Griffith, P. L., & Olson, M. W. (1992). Phonemic awareness helps beginning readers break the code. *The Reading Teacher, 45,* 516–525.

Hulme, C. (2000). Phonemes, rimes and mechanisms of early development. *Journal of Experimental Psychology, 82*(1), 658–664.

Knafle, J. D. (1978). Word perception: Cues aiding structure detection. *Reading Research Quarterly, 8,* 502–523.

Lobel, A. (1981). *On Market Street.* New York: Scholastic.

Lyon, G. R. (1998). Why reading is not a natural process. *Educational Leadership, 55*(6), 14–18.

Morrow, L. M. (1993). *Literacy development in the early years: Helping children read and write.* Boston: Allyn & Bacon.

Stahl, K. A. D. (2004). Proof, practice, and promise: Comprehension strategy instruction in the primary grades. *The Reading Teacher, 57*(7), 598–609.

Stahl, S. A., Duffy, A. M., & Stahl, K. A. D. (1998). Everything you wanted to know about phonics (but were afraid to ask). *Reading Research Quarterly, 33*(3), 338–355.

Van Allsburg, C. (1987). *The z was zapped.* Boston: Houghton Mifflin.

Zinna, D. R., Lieberman, I. Y., & Shankweiler, D. (1986). Children's sensitivity to factors influencing vowel reading. *Reading Research Quarterly, 21,* 465–478.

Chapter Five

The Recognition and Spelling of the Most Frequent Words

From what I can see up here, it looks like those things on Earth they call sight words. They're some kind of clue that makes it possible for them to communicate.

—*Bogglestar*

Children who arrive in first grade with more knowledge of letters, deeper phonological awareness, greater familiarity with environmental print, the ability to recognize sight words with great speed and accuracy and with larger vocabularies are more likely to learn to read without difficulty.

—*Jordan, Snow, and Porche (2000)*

Recognition? Eye, me lad, I recognized the word, elaborate, by the word, labor, hiding inside like me boss always does. Eye, the recognition of things is me specialty, ya know. I'm also the best speller in all of Ireland!

—*An unknown Irish laborer*

Fifth Objective For Your Teaching Success:

Teach a variety of ways for all students to recognize, read, and spell words.

But What Are Sight Words?

Sight words are the ones you use so much you get bored with your own voice—words like *stop, help, go away, no, come back. Instant sight words* are those words you recognize in one second—max. They are considered the 100 most frequently used words that we read, write, speak, and listen to.

I define instant sight words a bit more rigorously: An instant sight word is a word that can be both read and spelled within 2 seconds. Go ahead, try it. Read and spell this instant sight word silently within 2 seconds:

> come

Now try the same word, *speaking* it and spelling it out loud. What happened this time? A bit more difficult? That's to be expected. So have your students keep practicing the instant sight words with the goal of speaking and spelling them in 2 seconds. But slow down a bit at first so they won't get discouraged.

In this chapter we'll concentrate on teaching instant recognition of words whose meanings are usually understood and whose frequency of use is extremely high—words like *is, you, that, he, or, and, them.* On the other hand, if you're traveling in Europe or Asia, there's an even more important sight word. Take your choice: *toilette, cabinet, gabinetto, tearai, damas,* or *caballeros.* It's amazing how quickly some words become sight words.

How Sight Words Help You Think and Read

Many of the instant sight words that we all need for reading and writing are function words like these:

Personal pronouns—*us, they, I*
Articles—*a, the*
Relative pronouns—*this, those*
Prepositions—*over, in, out, on*

Many of these instant sight words are hard to define, yet they are crucial for reading fluently—and for grasping the complete message of an author. For instance, what message do you get from this sentence?

> Quickly grabbed pair tongs threw smoldering liner sink.

All right now let's slip in those special sight words called function words and see what happens to the meaning of the message:

> Quickly *he* grabbed *a* pair *of* tongs *and* threw *the* smoldering liner *into the* sink.
> What a difference those six little sight words make! Learning to recognize simple function words by sight can help children predict what word is coming next, enhance their reading fluency, and grasp the total message of an author.

Pressley (2000) gets straight to the heart of it: "When less effort can be put into decoding during reading, there is more short-term capacity for comprehension of text. . . . When words are recommended automatically, this maximizes the capacity available for understanding. . . ." (p. 552).

Sight Words and Vocabulary

Instant sight words also help us predict the meaning of unknown words. Watch what happens in this difficult sentence:

> His foin was wide of the mark.

What in the world is the author talking about? What's a foin? Staring at a strange word gets us nowhere, but if we study the functional sight words that surround it, we might get somewhere.

We know from the sight word *his* that a boy or man is involved. The sight word *was* tells us that we're talking about the past, and it also connects *foin* to the word *wide*, which might be remembered as a measurement. The sight words *of the* relate *wide* to *mark*, meaning the foin was too far away from where he wanted it to be.

Wait a minute. By using our own past experiences, we can guess that this foin might have something to do with a game—something like golf, maybe. And on and on we go, relying on those functional sight words—*his, was, of, the.*

Despite its importance, vocabulary should be only one feature of your reading show. The U.S. government's National Reading Panel (2002) rightfully insists that we include all five features in our *show:* phonemic awareness, phonics, fluency, vocabulary, and comprehension, all of which interact to make a learning program suitable for teaching children to read and write.

Sight Words and Spelling

A child who learns the instant sight words learns the spelling of those words in a natural way. A positive side effect of this learning is being able to spell easily while composing a written document—provided the child has largely mastered phonemic awareness. As you probably remember from Chapter 3, when you and I write something, we spell the words we need by subconsciously listening to the phonemes we silently create. Steffler (2001) calls this "implicit memory and implicit learning." The

writer is unaware of learning phonemic awareness and mastering those wonderful instant sight words.

Having children learn to recognize and spell the instant sight words is one of the very best ways to teach spelling. By having them learn to rapidly recognize and spell those high-frequency words, you will be giving them a tremendous advantage. If you also have them memorize families of onsets and rimes, you are nearly guaranteeing their success.

As Lenski and Nierstheimer (2004) have discovered, "When children are taught the spelling patterns of word families, they are empowered to read and spell many more words" (p. 186). And as Johnston (1999) said earlier, "The ability to hear, see, and use the rime as a reliable cue for reading new words and spelling words that sound alike, offers students a powerful insight into how English spelling works" (p. 64). A similar message is found in the International Reading Association's Standard 6.5: Teach students to recognize and use various spelling patterns in the English language as an aid to word identification. (See Appendix A for further examination of the professional standards.)

Which Sight Words to Teach First

It makes sense to start with the words children really *want* to know by sight. Having learned the words they want, it seems easier to learn words that are other words common to their speaking vocabulary and most frequently encountered in print. But how can the classroom teacher determine which words are most frequently encountered in print? Fortunately, this job has already been done by various educators, such as Dolch (1936), Johnston (1999), and Fry, Kress, and Fountoukidis (1993). Fry's list, which seems to be the most used today, appears in Figure 5.1.

Depending on the age of your students, I recommend that you teach the first 50 to 200 instant sight words on Fry's list (Fry et al., 1993). Fry's list was selected through an extensive process of examining 500-word samples from 1,045 books in 12 subject areas in Grades 3 through 9. Samples were also taken from library books and magazines.

I have selected the top 240 words from Fry's list rather than the usual top 100, in order to include more of the popular high-frequency irregular words that "God didn't spell correctly," as one of my second graders told me. Words such as *of, one, some, would, two, could,* and *come* can best be learned through the left side of the brain, the side that deals with words and explanations. Why? Because these word spellings don't fit into the phonogram patterns that you and I studied in Chapter 4. Irregular words require a child's visual capacity more than an auditory capacity. Memorizing is the only way to master them.

the	of	and	a	to	in	1–6
is	you	that	it	he	was	7–12
for	on	are	as	with	his	13–18
they	I	at	be	this	have	19–24
from	or	one	had	by	words	25–30
but	not	what	all	were	we	31–36
when	your	can	said	there	use	37–42
an	each	which	she	do	how	43–48
their	if	will	up	other	about	49–54
out	many	then	them	these	so	55–60
some	her	would	make	like	him	61–66
into	time	has	look	two	more	67–72
write	go	see	number	no	way	73–78
could	people	my	than	first	water	79–84
been	called	who	oil	its	now	85–90
find	long	down	day	did	get	91–96
come	made	may	part	over	new	97–102
sound	take	only	little	work	know	103–108
place	years	live	me	back	give	109–114
most	very	after	things	our	just	115–120
name	good	sentence	man	think	say	121–126
great	where	help	through	much	before	127–132
line	right	too	means	old	any	133–138
same	tell	boy	following	came	want	139–144
show	also	around	form	three	small	145–150
set	put	end	does	another	well	151–156
large	must	big	even	such	because	157–162
turned	here	why	asked	went	men	163–168
read	need	land	different	home	us	169–174
move	try	kind	hand	picture	again	175–180
change	off	play	spell	air	away	181–186
animals	house	point	page	letters	mother	187–192
answer	found	study	still	learn	should	193–198
American	world	high	every	near	add	199–204
food	between	own	below	country	plants	205–210
last	school	father	keep	trees	never	211–216
started	city	earth	eyes	light	thought	217–222
head	under	story	saw	left	don't	223–228
few	while	along	might	close	something	229–234
seemed	next	hard	open	example	beginning	235–240

FIGURE 5.1 The top 240 instant words.

Note. From "The Reading Teachers' Book of Lists" (3rd ed.) by E. B. Fry, J. E. Kress, and D. L. Fountoukidis, 1993, Englewood Cliffs, NJ: Prentice Hall. Copyright 1993 by Prentice Hall. Reprinted with permission.

How Important Are the Top 100 Words?

Let's take a look at how important the 100 most frequent words can be for our students. Fry, Kress, and Fountoukidis (1993) discovered that children who have learned the top 100 instant sight words are halfway to understanding whatever they read through Grade 12. How amazing! We have well over a half-million words in English, but half of everything we write and read from age 6 to 17 depends on the 100 most frequent ones.

Take a special look at the top 10 most frequent words—they account for 24% of the words used during that same time frame. Try writing or speaking a paragraph without at least one of these 10 words:

THE	OF	AND	A	TO	IN	IS	YOU	THAT	IT

How Many Instant Words Should Students Master?

Professional Standard: Guides students to refine their spelling through reading and writing

You and I have already talked about this a little, but based on research by Robert Leibert (1991), I would recommend that students master at least the first 80 words by the end of first grade; the first 160 by the end of second grade; and the total 240 by the end of third grade. More advanced children may master 120 by the end of first grade and the second 120 by the end of second grade. In schools that are in operation 160 or more days a year, either of those schedules would require fewer than one instant sight word per day.

Challenge your students by telling them something like this: "You can get in the Instant Sight Word Club after you have learned 10 sight words. But you must say each word first and then spell it out loud in 2 seconds." Those who learn and retain 10 sight words that way can join the Instant Sight Word Club—and be called the Smart Beginners or whatever inspires them. Those who learn 20 instant sight words can be the Wonderful Twenties; 30 sight words, the Fabulous Thirties; 40 sight words, the Fantastic Forties. This incentive should continue throughout the first year until students have learned at least the first 80 words.

How to Help Students Master Sight Words

For many decades 'basal readers', or level-book stories, served as a major medium for gradually teaching new words in print. Because basal readers were designed to control the difficulty of the selections—stories, poems, and articles—the publishers introduced new words in practically every selection. So without teachers even trying, many of the high-frequency instant words were gradually introduced. Alas, however, the stories were not written by highly skilled authors, and they were required to use specific new words.

Naturally, both teachers and students were turned off—to put it mildly. Here's a sample: "Oh look, Jane, see Dick run. Oh, look. See Spot. See Spot run." The dedicated educators who created those books were doing their best to make the stories easy for young children to read. But companies stopped publishing those basal readers, now called anthologies.

Instead, the companies began publishing works by successful authors like Margaret Wise Brown, Eric Carle, Beatrice de Regniers, Bill Martin, Dr. Seuss, and Judith Viorst. Thus, control over the words in a book or anthology was no longer tight, but children could read the books they thoroughly enjoyed.

Unfortunately, those days may be over. Books similar to basal readers are back again, now called level books and under tighter government persuasion than ever. Today's anthologies include many stories written by unpublished authors who evidently do what they're told. The main goal of publishers today seems to be to include high-frequency words that are repeated.

From past experience I am sure some children can learn the instant words strictly from the practice provided by this type of anthology, but many children need more *meaningful* practice. Merely repeating a word 20 or 30 times may not work, especially if the book is too difficult or uninteresting or if the teacher does not supplement the selections with interesting word activities (Rasinski & Padak, 2000). More is needed. More books by famous authors are needed.

Fortunately, many teachers are making sure that their "extra" books, those written by successful authors for children, are being read. My hat's off to them. Most schools today do have silent reading time, as well as a time for reading aloud. And nothing is stopping teachers from reading really good books to their students. After all, it's been known for a century or more that reading aloud to students is often the best way to motivate and teach, no matter what the age. In addition, we can still take our kids to the school library—even though we might not have as much time for that any more.

Research on Predictable Patterned Books

One of the best forms of additional practice can be found in predictable patterned books like *Brown Bear, Brown Bear, Who Do You See?* Researchers have found that patterned books can work even better than basal readers in teaching essential sight words.

In a study by Bridge, Winograd, and Haley (1983), experimental and control groups of first graders were taught to read the same 77 words, with the experimental group using patterned books and the control group using basal readers with very few patterned stories in them. Both the control and the experimental groups consisted of below-average learners. The teaching occurred for 25 minutes a day, 5 days a week, for 4 weeks. The results are shown here:

Group	Pretest	Posttest	Words Gained
Patterned books	15 words	52 words	37
Basal readers	23 words	35 words	12

Do you see what I see? The patterned-book group was hot, wouldn't you say? The basal-reader group was just sort of tepid. What made the difference?

Many of the children who had the benefit of using patterned books changed their strategy from slowly sounding out each word to relying more on context clues as well. Furthermore, when asked how they felt about reading out loud in their reading group, these children were much more positive than the basal-reader group.

Look at the list of more than 200 predictable patterned books in Appendix M at the end of this book. And don't forget that there are children's book sections in every single public library in the United States, and they don't cost a penny. Go on. Be a creative professional and enjoy what you teach. Those patterned books are great bedtime reading for adults, they soothe you and take you away from your troubles. And they make you popular with your students.

Steps for Teaching Instant Sight Words

These are the steps followed by the teachers in the study.

1. Select an enjoyable patterned book that emphasizes the target words.

2. Read the book out loud.

3. Read the book again, with the children joining in whenever they can predict what comes next.

4. Have the children take turns with echo reading (rereading sentences after you read them) and choral reading (rereading that alternates between two groups, also called antiphonal reading).

5. Read the text from teacher-made charts (e.g., flip charts, overhead transparencies, or dry erase boards) with no picture clues. Ask the children to echo-read and/or choral-read.

6. Have the children place matching sentence strips on the charts. (Create the charts so that a sentence strip can be taped under a sentence.)

7. Have the children place matching word strips on the charts, saying the word as they match it. Ask the children to match the words in the correct order at first, then in random order.

8. Join the children in chorally rereading the entire story.

9. Finally, place word strips in random order at the bottom of the chart, and have the children come up and match the strips to words in the story, saying each word as they match it.

The only step I would add to this set of procedures is to have the children write the target words as well as read them. Experience has shown me that writing helps children remember words.

Do You Need Books Fitting the Instant Sight Words?

When using patterned books in this way, it might seem a bit tricky to find books that contain the exact words you want to teach. This is less of a problem than you might imagine, because the list of instant sight words is composed of high-frequency words. You can count on most patterned books to include many of the words from the instant sight word list. To provide practice with most of the words on the list, you can gather a collection of patterned books from libraries or little books which Menon and Hiebert (2005) recommended.

You may also want to create your own patterned stories to emphasize particular words. You can do this by adapting a patterned story that already exists. For instance, I adapted the following story from Bill Martin's book *Brown Bear, Brown Bear, What Do You See?* It features a dozen words from the instant word list, as well as three repetitions of several two-word phrases. My adapted story is called "Little Bug, Little Bug, What Do You Fear?"

> *Little bug, little bug, what do you fear?*
> *A hungry bird might come for me. That's what I fear. Hungry bird, hungry bird, what do you fear?*
> *A stalking cat might come for me. That's what I fear.*

Stalking cat, stalking cat, what do you fear?
A barking dog might come for me. That's what I fear.
Barking dog, barking dog, what do you fear?
A teasing child might come for me. That's what I fear.
Teasing child, teasing child, what do you fear?
My angry brother might come for me. That's what I fear.
Angry brother, angry brother, what do you fear?
A scary night might come for me. That's what I fear.
Scary night, scary night, what do you fear?
A friendly sun might come for me. That's what I fear.
Friendly sun, friendly sun, what do you fear?
NOTHING!

Easy Literature

The more easy books children read, the more practice they have in using words from the instant word list. Therefore, if at all possible, these books should be readily available in the classroom.

In 1975 the first "Children's Choices" was published in *The Reading Teacher*, a journal of the International Reading Association. Since that time teachers, librarians, and parents have looked forward each fall to the appearance of a new list, both in *The Reading Teacher* and on the Web site for the International Reading Association. The idea behind the list is simple: If children are to learn about the joy of reading and become proficient lifelong readers, they need to know that books are fun (Children's Choices, 2003).

How are the Children's Choices books selected? Each year approximately 500 new children's books are sent to each of five test sites across the United States. At each of these sites, about 2,000 children participate in reading and evaluating the books. The votes from all five sites are tabulated, and the most popular books (usually just over 100 titles) are selected to appear as the year's Children's Choices.

Children's literature experts at each site then place the favorites in several categories, such as beginning independent reading, younger readers, middle grades, and older readers. By selecting the categories of beginning independent reading and younger readers, you can expect the books to be at least moderately easy and contain many repetitions of instant sight words. Before you read any further, turn back to Appendix N and look at the list of 2001–2004 Children's Choices for Beginning Readers Ages 5–8. That's a great list, don't you think? And it should give you plenty to choose from.

Games Versus Worksheets

Teachers often use games for teaching or practicing instant sight words, but there's always a fear that maybe the children aren't really learning anything important when they play games. "Aren't they just having fun?" one teacher asked me. And another asked, "Don't the games distract them from real learning?" I can understand fears like this, because I've had them, too.

	Active Games		Passive Games		Worksheets	
	Boys	Girls	Boys	Girls	Boys	Girls
Pretest	4	4	4	3	2	3
Posttest	35	34	30	27	21	21
Gain	31	30	26	24	19	18
One week later	32	31	27	25	20	20

FIGURE 5.2   Sight words learned via three methods.

Some Research on Using Games

Research shows that the use of games to reinforce sight vocabulary can work quite well—in fact, much better than traditional workbooks, worksheets, or activity books. One of the best-designed studies on the use of games in teaching sight words was conducted by Dolores Dickerson (1982), who compared the effectiveness of games with worksheets, using 274 first graders from 30 classrooms in a large urban school system. Those children who knew more than 25% of the words before the experiment began were eliminated from the study. The results *looked like those* shown in Figure 5.2.

After 6 weeks, the passive-games approach brought about a 30% greater gain than the worksheet approach; the active-games approach, a 57% greater gain. Those are pretty impressive differences. What made the difference?

The worksheets involved isolated individuals completing some matching exercises and some sentence-completion exercises, whereas the games involved two or more individuals in a cooperative learning situation. Psychologists have known since the late 1950s that even monkeys can learn faster and more thoroughly when learning with a partner or two. Psychologists have also known for decades about the effect of feedback on learning: frequent and specific feedback usually results in greater learning. The games group received abundant feedback of an instantaneous and highly specific type. (Example: "No, that's not *thought*; that's *through*. You have to go back a step.")

What were the active games that helped to cause that 57% greater gain? They included Word Toss, Words in a Circle, See the Same, Word Point, and Stepword from *Teaching Slow Learners Through Active Games* (Humphrey & Sullivan, 1970). Another active game was a variation on the commercial game Twister from Milton Bradley. The passive games, which helped to create a 30% greater gain than the worksheets, were Go Fish, Word Checkers, The Snoopy Game, Concentration, Word Rummy, and Word Dominoes (Dickerson, 1982, p. 47).

Some Advice on Using Games

Dickerson's advice might prove valuable: "Incorporating games into regular lessons and not as adjunct activities increases the value of the game, since its objective reinforces the lesson" (1982, p. 49). Dickerson believes that using games as part of direct (i.e., teacher-directed) instruction can increase the value of the game.

That idea does not negate the value of games as an indirect form of learning, as in classroom learning centers. A balanced approach using both indirect and direct forms of gaming can have great benefits in vocabulary instruction.

If you use games indirectly (i.e., without direct supervision by an adult), I would advise you to arrange it so that each child plays a particular game only a few times before moving on to another game or activity. Some children tend to keep returning to the same game again and again because of their familiarity and success with it. You might consider having a rotating monitor for the games corner, or you might simply put a different game in your literacy center.

I would introduce each game by playing it with a child in front of the other children. Then have two children play it while the others watch and ask questions: What happens if he gets the word wrong? Is it cheating if you don't play a card that's in your hand?

Because games can become somewhat competitive (and even unproductive in the heat of competition), I recommend these criteria for selecting competitive games:

1. Select games with a strong chance factor so that anyone can win.

2. Offer no extrinsic rewards to the winners. Let the reward for all the children be the fun of learning new words in an enjoyable way.

3. Emphasize cooperation while playing the game. You may wish to choose, modify, or create some games so that children can work with a partner or a small group.

Direct Teaching of Spelling

I recommend direct as well as indirect teaching of sight words for two reasons: (1) Some children don't seem to learn sight words indirectly as well as others do, and (2) some teachers prefer to introduce sight words directly, saving the indirect methods for later practice. In both cases a series of spelling lessons directed by the teacher can work well.

Having children spell a word out loud helps their auditory memory of the word; they learn "in fewer sessions and with lower error percentages" (Wollery, Ault, Gast, Doyle, & Mills, 1990, p. 47). In addition, it is well known among literacy educators that having children write a word can help their visual memory of it and thus increase their ability to recognize it instantly in print. Apparently, it's the best way to lower error percentages (Wollery et al., 1990, p. 47). And according to Ehrlich, Oakhill, Seigneuric, and Yuill (2000), writing was a good predictor of their reading comprehension. Memory, after all, is the center of our attempts to learn almost anything and will certainly it will apply to the learning of instant sight words.

A Step-by-Step Spelling Experience

For this activity you can work with either a small group of children or the entire class.

1. **Introduce new sight words in context.**   Learning words in context seems to work better than learning them in isolation (Adams, 1990). Select no more than three to five words.

    A. Write sentences containing the words on the chalkboard, using only one target word in each sentence. Underline the target words: "*Who* has my ball?" Jim asked. "I *want* it back." "*There* it is," Janet said. "*Your* coat is on top of it."
    B. Read the entire story or isolated sentences to your students.
    C. Have the children echo-read each sentence the second and third time through.
    D. List the target words on the board. If you do teach these words to a large group, you would want to use an overhead projector or use your computer program.
    E. Point to one of the words, pronounce it, and then ask a child to spell it out loud and pronounce it. Have a different child do the same with each word. (With students whose native language is not English, be sure they understand word meanings too.)

2. **Insert sight words into students' auditory and visual memory.**   By having students spell a word out loud from a written prompt, you are enhancing both their auditory and their visual memory of the letters in the word.

    A. Have students look at one of the new words in printed form and spell it to themselves.
    B. Have them close their eyes and imagine themselves writing the word on their papers.
    C. Ask them to look at the chalkboard to see if they have it correctly spelled.

3. **Ask students to write the same word from memory.**

    A. Have them look at the same word again and spell it to themselves.
    B. Cover the word on the chalkboard and ask students to write the word from memory.
    C. Uncover the word and ask them to check to see if they have it correctly spelled.
    D. Move through the group quickly to be sure each child has the word correctly spelled.
    E. Repeat Steps 2 and 3 for each underlined word.

4. **Practice the new words in isolation.**

   A. With words on flash cards (5″ × 8″) or computer screen, reveal each one for no longer than a second and ask the group to say it out loud together.
   B. Reveal each one again to one child at a time. Do this two or three times.
   C. Repeat Step 4 with the first letter of each word capitalized.

5. **Practice the words in context.**   To ensure that the words are learned, arrange for the children to practice the words in context.

   A. Go back to the sentences you displayed at the beginning of the lesson, and ask the children to read them without your help—first chorally for each sentence, then solo.
   B. Have the children search for the words in their library books, basal anthologies, or other reading material; give them page numbers for their search. This kind of transfer from direct instruction to application is crucial.

6. **Practice using games.**   Practice with games and activities over several days and weeks. There are a variety of ways to make the practice sessions different each time.

   A. Play the number-line game.

      (1) Draw a number line from 0 to 10 for each child who will be playing the game (see Figure 5.3).
      (2) Prepare a stack of about 30 word cards (3″ × 5″) and a stack of about 30 number cards (some with +1, some with +2, and some with +3 written on them). Place both stacks face down.
      (3) Flash a word card for 1 second to each child in turn, who must read the word before drawing a number card off the top of the number stack. (A child who can't say the word within 3 seconds after you've flashed the card misses a turn. But kids will seldom miss if you have provided massed practice during direct instruction and a quick review before the game.)
      (4) The child shows the number card and places an X above the appropriate number on the number line.
      (5) The first child to get to 10 wins.

   B. Before the children get to go somewhere—lunch, recess, or home— have them tell you the password, which is simply a word on one of the flash cards.

Betty	0	1	2	3	4	5	6	7	8	9	10
John	0	1	2	3	4	5	6	7	8	9	10
Sam	0	1	2	3	4	5	6	7	8	9	10

FIGURE 5.3   Number lists for sight-word games.

Use of Flash Cards

Connected Flash Cards

My favorite way of using flash cards is to use five or more cards, depending on the child's age, as a connected sentence. You simply flash them one at a time in the exact order of the sentence, as shown in Figure 5.4.

There are several advantages in using connected flash cards.

1. The connected sentences can include mostly essential sight words, thus giving children more practice learning words from the instant sight word list.

2. It is easier and more like real reading to learn basic sight words in context, rather than in complete and unrelated isolation (Goodman, 1965).

3. Once the children have learned the particular words in context, you can challenge them by mixing up the cards and presenting them in an unrelated order, thus assuring yourself that they've learned the words and not just the sentence.

4. There are numerous opportunities during a school day to use connected sight words: as a morning greeting, as a message before they go home, as a quick reminder about a classroom procedure, as a beginning to a discussion.

5. You can adapt this procedure to any sight words you want them to learn—not just those on the instant sight word list.

Unconnected Flash Cards

Unconnected flash cards are fine, too, because you want your students to learn to recognize sight words instantly regardless of the context. Just be sure to make the

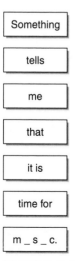

FIGURE 5.4 A sample of connected flash cards.

cards a pleasant experience rather than a threat. You can use them as a necessary ingredient for a game; tell your students that they have to read a flash card correctly before they get their turn. You can even use them as a way of letting children get in line for a room exit; each child who reads a word correctly gets into line.

The best of all is Race the Clock, which my elementary-school children became addicted to. For this game you should hold a pack of 30 or more flash cards, all with instant sight words that are read to the children slowly the first time, and then faster and faster until they beg for a "break."

This type of practice has been studied by Tan and Nicholson (1997), who claim that better results are obtained when the practice is run like a military drill—drilling until the words are recognized without any hesitation. Naturally, the drill works better when you have other students to compete with.

A similar practice program has been described by Hiebert and Taylor (2000). It would allow children to learn instant sight vocabulary as well as more difficult vocabulary in a 15-week program with a very specific design.

1. Children get 15 weeks of 30 minutes a day in one-on-one tutoring.

2. The time is evenly split between text reading and word-recognition activities—15 minutes each.

3. Activities include practicing sight words and working on phonemic awareness, the alphabetic principle, and decoding and writing.

From my experience, embedding sight words with other skills is best after simpler activities have served their purposes.

Personal Key Words

Aren't there some other words besides the instant words that we should be encouraging children to learn by sight? Absolutely. In the early 1960s Sylvia Ashton-Warner labeled as key words those words kids really want to learn, and others have strongly advocated their importance as well, especially Jeannette Veatch (1996) and Veatch, Sawricki, Elliott, Falke, and Blakey (1979).

Ashton-Warner (1963) noticed that children find it very easy to learn some sight words of very high interest. In fact, she referred to key vocabulary words as one-look words because that seemed to be all it took for some new words to be permanently learned. The key words that were easiest to learn fell into several distinct groups: affection words (e.g., *love, kiss, sing, daddy*); fear words (e.g., *skeleton, knife, yell, hit*); locomotion words (e.g., *airplane, truck, car*); and miscellaneous regional words that children would immediately know (e.g., in Southern California: *Disneyland, taco, surf, Lakers*).

The use of key words in a classroom of 30 children is somewhat complicated and needs to be more structured, so that a lot of learning can occur as a result of a moment or two of the teacher's time. Here are the steps I recommend to use this approach—not as a substitute for learning the high-frequency instant words, but as a highly meaningful supplement.

1. Each child is given the opportunity to tell a new special word to the teacher (e.g., *ghost, mama, motorcycle, dinosaur*).

2. The teacher prints the word on a card, saying each letter as it is written.

3. The teacher asks the child what should be done with the new special word. The child could write it on paper or the chalkboard; could use it, along with other key-word cards, to create a sentence train with a friend; or could use it, along with a set of instant words, to create a sentence train—whatever the teacher and child agree on.

4. Every few days each child should bring a set of key words to the teacher or to another adult in the room—or even to an older buddy.

You can turn this into a game by having the children read their own special cards as quickly as they can. The ones they can decode in 1 to 3 seconds (depending on their experience), they get to keep. Those they miss are set aside. After missing a word three times on three different days, a child has to turn in the card. If children miss them three times, they're probably not very interested in them; but do keep them just in case.

You can encourage the children to use their key words in a variety of ways, especially in their writing. This, of course, also provides more practice in reading the words, and their sight vocabularies continue to expand.

Environmental Print: Another Writing Experience

Have you ever noticed how readily you read signs as you wend your way home in your car or on a bus or a subway? In a boring situation your eyes and brain crave intellectual stimulation; and as inferior as advertisements are, they may be all you have. Most children have a similar experience inside the confines of the normal classroom. Whenever there's a dull moment, their eyes roam around the room, landing on a familiar word here and there, a familiar picture—anything!

You can use the walls and objects in your classroom as a superior bus ride. Let the students help you decide what goes on the walls—involvement is the key (Strickland & Morrow, 1988, p. 156). Here are some ways to involve your students in creating environmental print.

- Ask your students what things will be used a lot that should be labeled. Print the ideas on the chalkboard.
- If you have students who can print reasonably well, let them create the labels and tape them up.
- Let students label their own desks, both by name and by place—for example, "Tom Jones" and "Rocket Man Hideaway" or just "Harrison Street." If the children also have cubbies, they might want to label those, too. All of these labels will provide endless environmental print and even conversation starters.
- If you're using learning centers in the classroom, many things in each center and the center itself can be labeled. Learning centers often need directions, which again provide reading practice.

- Let children bring in pictures or photographs and label them. Change these at least once a month.
- Gradually create lists of special words: animal words, tree words, space-travel words, words related to whatever you're using as a topic for science or social studies or sheer enjoyment. Also consider measurement terms, computer terms, map words, dinosaurs, lists of things to take on a field trip, favorite TV shows, or worst TV shows.
- Let your imagination run wild. Environmental print should express the personalities of the people living in the environment.

Creating Your Own Sight Words as You Write

The more meaningful, purposeful writing students do, the more they will have to learn how to write additional sight words—both the basic type and the more personal type. By its very nature writing causes us to pay attention to the smallest units of language sound, phonemes, and the smallest units of written language, graphemes.

Special Help for Special Students

Rivera, Koorland, and Fueyo (2002) recommend that kids with learning disabilities create a picture for each word. For the word *girl*, for example, they can draw a picture of a girl and write the word *girl* underneath. They can then place the picture in their portfolio or on the word wall or on a large piece of butcher paper so that they can look at the drawing whenever they need it as a crutch. I can remember my own first-grade teacher doing something like this; she probably knew that drawing not only increases the memory, but also motivates kids to get involved.

Lenters (2003) recommends cutting up printed sentences—from newspapers, for example—and building a bank of sight words. Lenter explains that using cut-up sentences provides scaffolding for those students who try to memorize text without really focusing on it. Basically, any kind of keenly involved movement activates the brain and memories and causes us all to focus better.

Sight Words and Spanish Words in Diverse Classrooms

Professional Standard: Recognizes how learners' differences influence their literacy development

What you've learned about teaching sight words in English through the use of language games and predictable books can be used in teaching your students who speak Spanish as their first language. I'm using Spanish only as my teaching model. So you and I need to talk about the differences between the Spanish language and the English language and the reasons Spanish-speaking students often have trouble communicating with English-speaking students and teachers. If you have already mastered Spanish, you can send me a critique every now and then, since my Spanish has a coat of rust on it. But have no fear—each of the tables I'm giving you is the gift of an expert, Lori Helman, from her very informative 2004 article in *The Reading Teacher.*

Differences That Cause Confusion

If you have not mastered Spanish, let me share with you the differences that can cause confusion in a diverse classroom.

- English and Spanish share many of the same phonemes (like the smallest language sounds in /p/ /a/ /t/, which, when decoded, become *Pat*). But here's the rub: Some of the English and Spanish language sounds are not recognized in the other language.
- Spanish and English have many of the same consonant sounds. The English consonant sounds that also exist in Spanish are these: /b/, /ch/, /d/, /f/, /g/, /k/, /l/, /m/, /n/, /p/, /s/, /t/, /w/, /y/. That's 14 out of the 20 consonant sounds that we have in the English language. What are the separate consonants Spanish doesn't use? The *c* is used only with *h*. The *h* is used only with *c*. The *j* is used to represent the *h* sound, *qu* is spelled more intelligently as *kw*, and *z* is used only when *zero*, the tough guy, is around.
- Goldstein (2001) has found that the sounds shared between English and Spanish are sufficient for communicating between the two languages. Helman (2004) has found that the letters that represent the consonant sounds are sufficient for teaching Spanish speakers the English letter-sound correspondences. So there you are. Have heart, ye English-speaking teacher (and I'm speaking to myself as well—for a moment there I was losing hope).
- Many consonant clusters are shared between English-speaking and Spanish-speaking people. According to Goldstein (2000), those 10 consonant blends include *bl, br, cl, cr, fl, fr, gl, gr, pl,* and *pr.* . . a fact that cheers me up all the more. There isn't a single one that I haven't used dozens of times. The Spanish-speaking and English-speaking students are getting closer and closer together. But stop the press, I've just been informed that English has many more possibilities for consonant blends than Spanish does. Without weeping, I will stare at Table 5.1 and observe 15 of the English consonant blends that are *not* in the Spanish language.
- Oh my, none of those are found in the Spanish language: st, sp, sk, sc, sm, sl, sn, sw, tw, qu, scr, spl, spr, str, and squ. Are you beginning to appreciate some of the difficulties that Spanish-speaking students have as they bravely and gradually learn this thing called English?
- It's true that my favorite *r* sound sounds different in Spanish, but it bothers me not at all. I'm thoroughly heartened by the fact that I can call grass *gris* when I'm speaking the Spanish tongue (pardon my humor).

TABLE 5.1 English consonant blends that are not in Spanish.

English consonant blend	Sample word
st	star
sp	spirit
sk/sc	scar
sm	small
sl	sleep
sn	snack
sw	swim
tw	twice
qu (kw)	quick
scr	scrap
spl	splash
spr	spray
str	straight
squ (sqw)	square

Note. From "Building on the Sound System of Spanish: Insights from the Alphabetic Spellings of English Language Learners" by L. A. Hellman, 2004, *The Reading Teacher, 57*(5), p. 455. Copyright 2004 by *The Reading Teacher.* Reprinted with permission.

■ Seriously, we need to be very considerate when our Spanish-speaking students have trouble writing or reading what they have the right to call foreign sounds and letters.

Spanish Speaking Errors Caused by English Sounds

Take a look at the linguistic problem in Table 5.2. Now you can understand how difficult English can be for Spanish-speaking students when it comes to pronouncing the sounds represented by the letters *d, j, r, v, z, sh, th* and the impossible word

TABLE 5.2 Possible errors caused by distinct English sounds.

Distinct English sound	May be pronounced	Example of a spelling error
/d/ as in *den*	then	dem (for them)
/j/ as in *joke*	choke	gob (job)
/r/ as in *rope*	(rolled r) rope, wope	waipen (ripen)
/v/ as in *van*	ban	surbing (serving)
/z/ as in *zipper*	sipper	sivalais (civilize)
/sh/ as in *shell*	chell	ched (shed)
/th/ as in *thick*	tick	tenk (think)
/zh/ as in *treasure*	treachure	chesher (treasure)

Note. From "Building on the Sound System of Spanish: Insights from the Alphabetic Spellings of English Language Learners" by L. A. Hellman, 2004, *The Reading Teacher, 57*(5), p. 455. Copyright 2004 by *The Reading Teacher.* Reprinted with permission.

treasure. The Spanish language simply does not have the sound of the English *j* or the sounds of the *v, z, sh,* and *th* (as in *thick*). And notice what can happen when it comes to spelling. The Spanish-speaking student is likely to spell the word *them* as *dem, job* as *gob, ripen* as *waipen, serving* as *surbing, civilize* as *sivalais, shed* as *ched, think* as *tenk,* and *treasure* as *chesher*. All in all, Spanish and English each contain several consonant sounds that do not occur in the other language (Dalbor, 1997; Goldstein, 2001).

I'm sure you can see that Spanish-speaking students will need to learn many words through visual memory instead of auditory memory. Not that those of us who are English speaking don't have the same problems with words like *knight, people, heard, brought,* and *should* staring us in the face, which incidentally will be passed on to our Spanish-speaking students. How brave our students of both linguistic forms! But do not despair. Students who speak English as a second language are getting degrees by the thousands every year—thanks to good teachers like you.

Now Let's Look at Vowel Sounds

The Spanish system of vowel sounds is much simpler than that of English (Foster, Altamiranda, & Urioste, 1999), but this couldn't possibly be comforting to our Spanish-speaking students. Once again, visual learning of words is their best hope for a good spelling record. Let's start, though, with the common vowel sounds between the two languages (see Table 5.3). As you can see in the table, the first line demonstrates our similar long *a* sound. The second line demonstrates our similar long *e* sound, the third, our similar long *i* sound; the fourth, our similar long *o* sound; the fifth, our similar short *o* sound; and the sixth, our similar long *u* sound.

Let's look now at the problems your Spanish-speaking students may have by substituting Spanish vowels for English vowels (see Table 5.4). To make it even more difficult for our Spanish-speaking students, Spanish does not contain four of the short-vowel sounds in English (*man, pen, tip, up*) and also *r*-controlled vowels such as *her*.

TABLE 5.3 Vowel sounds common to English and Spanish.

English vowels	Similar vowel sounds used in a Spanish word	Example of a spelling error
a as in *cake*	e as in *hecho*	shek (shake)
e as in *bean*	i as in *ido*	spic (speak)
i as in *like*	ai as in *aire*	nait (night)
o as in *hope*	o as in *ocho*	flout (float)
o as in *top*	a as in *ajo*	jab (job)
u as in *June*	u as in *Usted*	flut (flute)

Note. From "Building on the Sound System of Spanish: Insights from the Alphabetic Spellings of English Language Learners" by L. A. Hellman, 2004, *The Reading Teacher,* *57*(5), p. 456. Copyright 2004 by *The Reading Teacher*. Reprinted with permission.

TABLE 5.4   Spanish speakers' possible vowel substitutions.

Vowel sound as in the following	Closest Spanish vowel sound	May be pronounced
man	a	"mahn" for *man*
pen	e	"pain" for *pen*
tip	i	"teep" for *tip*
up	a	"op" for *up*
her	u	"who" for *her*
could	u	"cooed" for *could*
away	a	"ahway" for *away*
caught	a	"cot" for *caught*

Note. From "Building on the Sound System of Spanish: Insights from the Alphabetic Spellings of English Language Learners" by L. A. Hellman, 2004, *The Reading Teacher,* 57(5), p. 457. Copyright 2004 by *The Reading Teacher.* Reprinted with permission.

Teaching Spanish- and English-Speaking Students at the Same Time

Professional Standard: Respects and values cultural and linguistic diversity

1. Rely on the commonalities between Spanish and English that we recently talked about: the common consonant sounds—/b/, /ch/, /d/, /f/, /g/, /k/, /l/, /m/, /n/, /p/, /s/, /t/, /w/, /y/—realizing that *c, h, j, q, r, v, z* are either not used or used in a different way from English.

2. Rely on the commonalities of the consonant blends—*bl, br, cl, cr, dr, fl, fr, gl, gr, pl, pr,* although the *r* will be pronounced differently in English.

3. Realize that there are many consonant blends in English that are not used in Spanish: *st, sp, sk/sc, sm, sl, sn, sw, tw, scr, spl, spr, str, sku.* You will need to help your Spanish-speaking students learn these blends, using some of the games and activities discussed earlier.

4. The vowels are similar in both languages, but words are spelled differently (see Table 5.3 for a reminder). Make a game of spelling both in Spanish and English. It's a great cultural experience for all.

5. Use sight word games and exercises similar to those you learned in this chapter. For instance, try the number-line game referenced in Figure 5.3.

6. Create either student-made bilingual dictionaries or classroom word walls. Color code them for easy recognition. In this way you can provide vivid demonstrations of the similarities and differences between the two languages. Choose your words from the 100 most frequent words, since they're largely meaningful in both cultures. Assist Ell, English language learners.

Focus on Students with Special Needs: Comments by Louise Fulton

Help Students Make Successful Transitions

As you learned in Chapter 1, when children play the role of readers and writers, they are continually making transitions from one level of knowledge to the next. More specifically, they are making growth transitions from one concept, skill, or attitude to the next. And in the case of students with special needs, they may be transitioning from special education programs to regular education programs.

Transition skills are those that are needed for living, playing, and working in current and future environments. They are skills that allow students to move successfully from elementary school to middle school, from inside school life to outside social life, from childhood to adolescence, from formal to informal behavior, and from purely self-centered objectives to a mixture of self- and group-centered objectives.

Students learn and desire transition skills when they've had an abundance of functional teaching and learning experiences. Functional and other motivational experiences propel a learner forward. As the famous educator John Dewey said many decades ago, children should be taught those skills that drive them to want to learn more and more at a higher and higher level.

Summary of Main Ideas

- Vocabulary development is probably most assured in a classroom environment that is balanced between learner-centered and teacher-centered experiences.
- Teachers must help children recognize words in print that they already understand from their listening and speaking experiences. For instructional purposes these are usually referred to as sight words, or sight vocabulary.
- Instant sight words are those that are high in frequency and are often used in children's writing, reading, and speech.
- Key words are personal sight words that children ask to learn because they are important to them and/or carry intense meaning (i.e., they are captions for powerful events in children's lives).
- Sight vocabulary can be enhanced through a variety of learning experiences: word walls, word activities, direct spelling lessons, games, writing, patterned books, connected flashcards, and more.
- There are commonalities between Spanish and English, but many consonant blends in English are not used in Spanish.
- Students can use bilingual dictionaries and classroom word walls that compare English and Spanish words.

Literacy Through Technology

A. With one or more partners, learn about educational resources found on the Internet. Begin your own annotated bibliography of the Web sites you find useful and add them to your computer's Favorites list. Because Web sites appear and disappear frequently, you'll want to update your list regularly. Start with one or more of the following:

http://wordsmith.org/awad/
Introduction to a new word each day, with interesting information on its derivation

http://www.vocabulary.com
Vocabulary University—word puzzles galore

http://www.virtualflashcards.com/
An easy way to print creative flash cards

http://www.manythings.org
Vocabulary quizzes with pictures for English-language learners

http://www.vocabulary.co.il
Word-search game for students

http://www.funbrain.com/vocab/
Reading and vocabulary game—matching words to pictures

http://www.eduplace.com/fakeout/
Word game for learning definitions (K–2)

B. Go to one of the following Web sites to examine materials for word walls. Think about how you can use this resource for your classroom.

http://teacher.scholastic.com/teachingstrategies
http://www.theschoolbell.com/Links/word_walls/
http://www.teachnet.com/lesson/langarts/index.html

C. Your television set has built-in circuits that decode and display *closed-captioned* programming, programs that can be read with subtitles. (Just push the button that accesses the closed captions, but be sure to use programs in a local television guide that have a *cc* next to them.) View a cc child's program, and take some notes on its potential for teaching sight words and other vocabulary. Share your thoughts with the class.

Application Experiences for Your Course

A. *Literacy Teacher Vocabulary: A List of Terms:* Help yourself and others master these terms:

instant sight words	high-frequency words
sight words	personal pronouns
functional words	anthology
top 10 words	patterned books
Ell and cc	predictable books

B. *What's Your Opinion?:* Discuss why you agree or disagree with the following statements. Use both the textbook and your own experiences to justify your opinions.

1. To teach essential sight vocabulary, worksheets and basal readers are the most effective.
2. Games are too distracting for learning sight words. They teach the wrong thing.
3. Sight word instruction should be direct rather than indirect.
4. Key words are more important to learn than the so-called instant sight words.

C. *Creative Problem Solving:* Creative thinking is the most important ability for success. Think creatively about this problem: By edict, boys over 14 must be initiated into society by having their right little finger cut off. List 10 things that might happen—serious or funny. When you finish, try this one: What are all the things that might happen if school boards all over the country decided to save money by eliminating the principal? Exercises like this enable students to loosen up their minds and think without fear. Bored students are usually turned on by these kinds of challenges. Feel free to create your own—or let the students create them.

D. *Miscue Analysis:* In the following dialogue, study Matt's miscues, and decide how his essential sight vocabulary helped him use the four interacting cues to comprehend the author's message. Also, decide whether his miscues are caused by a lack of knowledge of certain essential sight words or by the failure to follow the normal process of predicting and checking, or by both.

Text: The man and woman went out to the country and dug up edible plants. Then they went back home and cooked them.

Jamie: The man and wuh-woman went to the city—country and dug up some eatable plants. The-they-then- they went home and ate— cooked them.

E. *Instant Words:* With a partner or small group, make a list of the nouns from the instant words in Figure 5.1. Why are these nouns of such high frequency in our language? How might they be important to children in their writing?

Creativity Training Session

A. Since the Spanish language does not use the short sounds of *a* (*man*), *e* (*pen*), *i* (*tip*), and *u* (*cup*), create a spelling test of 10 words that do not use these vowel sounds. How can you use this experience to be more aware of spelling errors made by English-language learners?

B. Each group of three is given five items. The assignment is for each group to use all five items and no others to create a new object. The product must be original, and the group must describe its use, after asking others to guess. Enough items can usually be gathered from the people present. Examples of items to use include a pencil, paper clip, hair clip, pen, stapler, rubberband, eraser, stick, balloon, notebook, book, hat, and whatever other interesting things are offered from class members' pockets, backpacks, purses, hair, and so on. Discuss the process used in the groups as well as the creativity of the products.

Field Experiences

A. *Direct Teaching of Sight Words:* With two or more children, try out the direct spelling approach to teaching three or four sight words from the instant word list in Figure 5.1.

B. *Teaching Sight Words Through Patterned Books:* Use a patterned book to teach one or more children several sight words from the instant word list in Figure 5.1. Be sure to bring an extra patterned book or two in case the children don't care for the one you have chosen.

C. *Teaching Sight Words Through Other Means:* Help children learn new sight words through one of these methods:

1. Word walls
2. Creating words
3. Key words
4. Connected flash cards
5. Environmental print

D. *Learning Words on the Internet:* Teach a group of students (Grade 3 or above) to use one of the Internet resources you located in the technology activity in this chapter. Later have them locate their own Web sites for word learning. Help students create a classroom wall chart of their different Web sites.

References

Adams, M. J. (1990). *Beginning to read: Thinking and learning about print.* Cambridge, MA: MIT Press.

Ashton-Warner, S. (1963). *Teacher.* New York: Simon & Schuster.

Bridge, C. A., Winograd, P. N., & Haley, D. (1983). Using predictable materials vs. preprimers to teach beginning sight words. *The Reading Teacher, 36,* 884–891.

Children's Choices. (2003). *The Reading Teacher, 56*(10). (See http://www.reading.org/choices/cc2003.html

Dalbor, J. B. (1997). *Spanish pronunciation: Theory and practice.* Fort Worth, TX: Harcourt Brace College.

Dickerson, D. P. (1982). A study of the use of games to reinforce sight vocabulary. *The Reading Teacher, 36,* 46–49.

Dolch, E. W. (1936). A basic sight vocabulary. *Elementary School Journal, 36,* 456–460.

Ehrlich, M. F., Oakhill, J. V., Seigneuric, A., Yuill, N. M. (2000, September). Working memory resources and children's reading comprehension. *Reading and Writing: An Interdisciplinary Journal, 13,* 1–2, 81–103.

Foster, D. W., Altamiranda, D., & Urioste, C. (1999). *The writer's reference guide to Spanish.* Austin: University of Texas Press.

Fry, E. B., Kress, J. E., & Fountoukidis, D. L. (1993). *The reading teachers' book of lists* (3rd ed.). Englewood Cliffs, NJ: Prentice Hall.

Goldstein, B. (2000). *Resource guide on cultural and linguistic diversity.* San Diego, CA: Singular.

Goldstein, B. (2001). Transcription of Spanish and Spanish-influenced English. *Communication Disorders Quarterly, 23*(1), 54–60.

Goodman, K. S. (1965, October). A linguistic study of cues and miscues in reading. *Elementary English,* 639–643.

Goswami, U. (2000). Phonological and lexical processes. In M. L. Kamil, P. B. Mosenthal, P. D. Pearson, & R. Barr (Eds.), *Handbook of reading research* (Vol. 3). Mahwah, NJ: Erlbaum.

Helman, L. A. (2004). *Building on the sound system of Spanish: Insights from the alphabetic spellings of English-language learners, The Reading Teacher, 57*(5), 452–460.

Hiebert, H., & Taylor, B. M. (2000). Beginning reading instruction: Research on early interventions. In M. L. Kamil, P. B. Mosenthal, P. D. Pearson, & R. Barr (Eds.), *Handbook of reading research* (Vol. 3, pp. 463–464). Mahwah, NJ: Erlbaum.

Humphrey, J. H., & Sullivan, D. D. (1970). *Teaching slow learners through active games.* Springfield, IL: Charles C. Thomas.

Johnston, F. R. (1999). The timing and teaching of word families. *The Reading Teacher, 53,* 64–75.

Jordan, G. E., Snow, C. E., & Porche, M. V. (2000). Project EASE: The effect of a family literacy project on kindergarten students' early literacy skills. *Reading Research Quarterly, 35*(4), 524–546.

Leibert, R. E. (1991). The Dolch list revisited—An analysis of pupil responses then and now. *Reading Horizons, 31,* 217–227.

Lenski, S. D., & Nierstheimer, S. L. (2004). *Becoming a teacher of reading,* Upper Saddle River, NJ: Pearson/Merrill/Prentice Hall.

Lenters, K. (2003). The many lives of the cut-up sentences. *The Reading Teacher, 56*(6), 535–536.

Menor, S. & Hiebert, E. (2005). A comparison of first graders' reading with little book or literature-based basal anthologies. *Reading Research Quarterly, 40*(1), 12–38.

National Reading Panel. (2002). *Scientific research base: Put reading first.* (ERIC No. ED468696)

Pressley, M. (2000). What should comprehension instruction be the instruction of? In M. L. Kamil, P. B. Mosenthal, P. D. Pearson, & R. Barr (Eds.), *Handbook of Reading Research* (Vol. 3). Mahwah, NJ: Erlbaum.

Rasinski, T. V., & Padak, N. D. (2000). *From phonics to fluency.* New York: Longman.

Rivera, M. O., Koorland, M. A., & Fueyo, V. (2002). Pupil-made pictorial prompts and fading for teaching sight words to a student with learning disabilities. *Education and Treatment of Children, 25*(2), 197–207.

Steffler, D. J. (2001, June). Implicit cognition and spelling development. *Developmental Review, 21*(2), 168–204.

Strickland, D. S., & Morrow, L. M. (1988). Creating a print rich environment. *The Reading Teacher, 42*, 156–157.

Tan, A., & Nicholson, T. (1997). Flashcards revisited: Training poor readers to read words faster improves their comprehension. *Journal of Educational Psychology, 89*, 276–288.

Veatch, J. (1996). From the vantage of retirement. *The Reading Teacher, 49*, 510.

Veatch, J., Sawricki, F., Elliott, G., Falke, E., & Blakey, J. (1979). *Key words to reading.* Columbus, OH: Merrill.

Wollery, M., Ault, M. J., Gast, D. L., Doyle, P. M., & Mills, B. M. (1990). Use of choral and individual attentional responses with constant time delay when teaching sight word reading. *Remedial and Special Education, 11*(5), 47–58.

Other Suggested Readings

Bear, D. R., Invernizzi, M., Templeton, S., & Johnston, F. (1996). *Words their way: Word study for phonics, vocabulary, and spelling instruction.* Upper Saddle River, NJ: Merrill.

Cunningham, P. M., & Cunningham, J. W. (1992). Making words: Enhancing the invented spelling-decoding connection. *The Reading Teacher, 46*, 106–115.

Macmillan, B. M. (2002, February). Rhyme and reading: A critical review of the research methodology. *Journal of Research in Reading, 25*, 4–42.

Nagy, W. E. (1988). *Teaching vocabulary to improve reading comprehension.* Urbana, IL: National Council of Teachers of English.

Rasinski, T. (1999). *Making and writing words.* Unpublished manuscript.

Wyley, R. E., & Durell, D. D. (1970). Teaching vowels through phonograms. *Elementary English, 47*, 787–791.

Wyley, R. E., & Durell, D. D. (1995). Teaching vowels through phonograms. *The Reading Teacher, 48*, 429–433.

Chapter Six

Creating Vocabularies with Concept-Laden Words

There is the danger of treating . . . new words simply as new labels rather than new concepts. Teachers can fall into the trap of thinking that hard words are only fancy ways of saying things that can be said with short, familiar words.

—*W. E. Nagy (1988, p. 21)*

It's funny how people on Earth respect words more than they respect what the words stand for. Maybe that's why they get into so much trouble.

—*Bogglestar*

Our concepts nervously hide in words
Little *Book* worms, just acting like nerds
Didja *Book* 'im? Yeah, chief. I Booked 'em.
But I need a *Book* of stamps.
Didja *Book* a table for six?
But your favorite *Book* was "Bambi"!

—*Bogglestar's Bad Dream*

Sixth Objective for Your Teaching Success:

Teach words by modeling, scaffolding, semantic mapping, and direct and indirect ways

Abstract Words and Hidden Concepts

Professional Standard: Teaches students to connect prior knowledge with new information

Do you remember those little kids in Chapter 1 who were capable of understanding concrete things like rocks and snakes? They were also good at handling concrete experiences like digging in the mud or throwing the mud at each other. But those young kids weren't so good at handling abstract things like written words and sentences.

Have you noticed that the reverse is true for you and me—and for our older students? We're now expected to deal *mostly* with abstract things, like depositing a check in a bank or watching TV. Almost everything we do is more symbolic than real.

This kind of abstract thinking we now depend on is very important when we're reading and writing. We've been taught that a written word is a concrete thing, when in fact the real thing is actually hiding abstractly inside the word—which, in turn, is hiding inside our marvelous brains. Is it any wonder that a great many children, many teenagers, and some adults are struggling to fully understand how to read? Is it any surprise that you are desperately needed as a teacher?

Most students comprehend sight words the moment they decode them. But what about words that stand for more sophisticated concepts? I'm referring to concept-laden words like *coward* or *crafty*. Do you remember seeing reruns of old western and gangster movies—the ones in which a coward was always called "a dirty coward"? Let's abstractly "cogitate" on the subject of concept-laden words like these:

> *coward* Does this mean someone who's always dirty?
> *crafty* Does this mean people who make arts & crafts?

A rule on words: When words stand for sophisticated concepts, the concepts themselves must be learned before the words can truly become part of your students' vocabularies. This is the most important rule for teaching words.

When do we really know the meaning of a word? For an example of what we just talked about, let's use the made-up word *nambol.* I'll lead you through the steps that will help you comprehend it.

- First, you can look at the spelling of the word and decode it. That is, you can study the grapheme print and decode it into your own phonemes inside your head.
- From the spelling pattern you can expect two distinct syllables when you pronounce the word: /nam/ and /bol/.
- By noticing the phonogram *am,* you can tell that *nam* will rhyme with *ham.*
- Now let's introduce a bit of syntax. Let's say "THE nambol" instead of just *nambol.* When the target word is surrounded by other words, we can begin to understand its meaning.
- By placing the word *the* in front of *nambol,* we've given *nambol* a position. It's no longer an isolated word. Its position tells us that *nambol* is probably a nounlike word (e.g., "The nambol is here"). Or it could be an adjective-type word (e.g., "The nambol bogitt is here").
- Now let's get closer to understanding the word by introducing a semantic cue. Let's insert a word that adds *meaning* to nambol's position—maybe "the muddy nambol."
- At this point most readers are ready to make a hypothesis about nambol's meaning because the word muddy means "wet, squishy dirt." But most people don't think like a dictionary and stop with "wet squishy dirt." Instead, they use their personal schemas about mud—"*Nambol* is something I found near a river" or "*Nambol* is that stuff that pigs roll in" or "*Nambol* is the stuff I scraped from my boots."
- Experienced readers may come up with a theory—perhaps a *nambol* is a river—but as they read further, they change their theory. If they read, "The muddy nambol licked . . . ," they may quickly decide that a *nambol* is not a river; it's probably a creature of some sort, a creature with a tongue. And based on schemas from past experiences, readers probably suspect that a nambol is a muddy dog or cat—or something similar. Only with the complete sentence does the meaning become clear. "The muddy nambol licked its feet and purred."

Teaching Difficult Words

What words should be taught before you have your students read a certain book, chapter, or difficult passage? In general, you should teach the words the author has chosen to describe the main person, problem, place, event, or behavior—seldom more than three or four words. Let your students begin to learn other words while reading, by relying on their own experiences and being aware of the particular circumstance or situation, context, or content, all provided by the author.

A Teaching Example of Choosing the Best Difficult Words

For our example let's look at the word *demolish*. We need to decide whether to treat it like a major concept, a minor concept, or a simple synonym of an easier word. To make that decision, we need to consider the big picture—the story or the problem in the story, don't you think?

Let's say that the main idea of the story (or explanation or description) is that the demolishing of historical buildings can be very damaging to the morale of people with fond memories of those buildings. In this case the word *demolish* becomes a major concept for students to learn. Having them merely come up with another label, like the synonym *destroy,* wouldn't help them get at either the deep meaning of the author or the deep meaning of the word.

In this case you'll need to have a more involved discussion with your students, during which, questions like these would be debated:

"What do you think *demolish* means to people who are about to see their favorite buildings destroyed?"

"Have you ever had a favorite house demolished . . . or places where you played demolished . . . or toys demolished . . . or other objects that were very important to you demolished?"

"How did you feel or act when that happened?"

"What do you think the people in the story are going to do when they realize their favorite buildings are about to be demolished?"

Do you see that this kind of teaching—paying attention to both facts and emotions—leads to a more complete understanding?

Using Dale's Cone to Teach the Meaning of Concept-Laden Words

Edgar Dale (1969) developed a model for teachers to use when planning vocabulary-building experiences. That model—called the cone of experience and shown in Figure 6.1—is still highly useful today for guiding the instruction of conceptual vocabulary. Dale's theory goes like this: Children learn best through direct, purposeful experiences—the concrete base of Dale's cone. They learn least well through verbal experiences—the abstract tip of the cone. In between the base and the tip of the

FIGURE 6.1 Dale's cone of experience.
Note. From *Audiovisual Methods in Teaching* by Edgar Dale, 1969, New York: Holt, Rinehart and Winston. Copyright 1969 by Holt, Rinehart and Winston. Reprinted with permission.

cone are various experiences that provide different depths and intensities of learning. Next to the direct experience of driving a car, for example, the deepest and most intense experience would be that of a contrived experience with a simulated car, which could simulate a road, other cars, a crash, and so on.

Students usually retain the information they receive at the verbal level (including new words) just long enough to pass a test. Information they receive at the direct level of experience (such as the word *hot* the moment they touch a hot stove) stays with them longer and becomes part of their readily available supply of words or concepts.

The Rozaga Hunt

Professional Standard: Teaches students to use context clues to identify unfamiliar words

Let's take the words *rozaga hunt* as an example. Suppose you are teaching a social studies unit on the rozaga hunters of North Borneo. You want to show how these people have adapted to their environment, and since rozaga hunting is their chief means of survival, it is important that your students understand the words *rozaga hunt*. You plan to discuss these people on and off for the next few weeks, so your

students need to make the words *rozaga hunt* part of their vocabulary. What should you do?

The best way to teach your students about a rozaga hunt would be to take them on one. Let them get up with you in the middle of the night, carry a flashlight in one hand and a sharpened spear in the other, and stumble through the woods toward the swamp. Let them listen to the hurrumping of the bullfrogs, the hooting of the owls, and that eerie low whistle of the rozaga. Let them shiver with fright as they unexpectedly come face to face with one, its fangs and yellow eyes highlighting the swanlike neck covered with dark, leathery scales and its snakelike tongue darting in and out of its mouth just 3 feet away from them. Let them hear you shout a warning and watch your spear go through the rozaga's vital spot, right through the middle of its neck. Do you have any doubt that these students would remember the word *rozaga?*

Unless you're very rich, you probably can't provide your students with the direct experience of a rozaga hunt. Even a contrived experience might be out of the question because of the time and expense (although taking apart and putting together a plastic model of a rozaga would be one type of contrived experience). What about a dramatized experience of a rozaga hunt? This would be excellent after children have acquired enough information about rozagas and the way a rozaga hunt is carried out. Telling the students that they will eventually get to enact a rozaga hunt would spur them on to learn about it.

The next layers of the cone of experience suggest the use of demonstrations, field trips, and exhibits. Having someone such as the teacher who has seen a movie of a rozaga hunt provide a demonstration of the hunt would help the children get a deeper understanding of the concept. A field trip in this case would be impractical, unless you were able to take them to a museum with exhibits related to the rozaga hunt. At an exhibit they would be able to see the weapon and perhaps a stuffed rozaga close at hand.

If those options aren't possible, a movie or a videotaped documentary, although not providing the close-at-hand experience of an exhibit, would provide the emotional impact. And if nothing else is available, perhaps you'll at least have some still pictures showing the rozaga and the hunters and perhaps a recording of someone describing the actual hunt.

Any doubt

that students

will remember

the word *ROZAGA?*

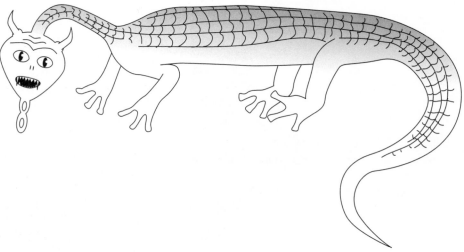

FIGURE 6.2 A rozaga.

Beyond those possibilities there's nothing left but visual symbols (such as diagrams or maps) and verbal symbols (i.e., words and definitions). You could simply write the word *rozaga* on the board and say, "A rozaga is an amphibian with dark leathery scales and a swanlike neck that lives in the swamps of North Borneo." That would certainly take a lot less time than all the vicarious experiences we've been discussing. And there are times when that's all a word deserves. At other times a picture will do (see Figure 6.2) or a quick discussion.

But on all occasions when you truly want your students to make a word a part of their meaningful vocabulary, you'll want to combine the verbal experience with one or more nonverbal ones. Depending just on the verbal medium is seldom the most effective way. In Chapter One you learned the need for concrete learning—not so much of the abstract, right?

Knowing Words in Context

When words are used for communication, they are known or understood in context. Many years ago Ken Goodman showed with 100 first, second, and third graders that children can miss many words on a list but can correctly read three-fourths of those same words in a story (in Eeds & Cockrum 1985). When the children in Goodman's study had all four types of cues available to them, they could read the words quite well.

As teachers we always have to ask ourselves, "What's the goal?" The reading process is an intelligent, active process of observing, predicting, and confirming, with a personal purpose in mind—not a passive or mindless spouting of words and synonyms for a cookie or a grade. *So when* is a word really known to a reader? Whenever that reader purposefully and successfully makes use of that word and its concept(s) to understand the written message presented by the author.

Vocabulary as Seen from the Perspective of Communication

The notion that a large vocabulary demonstrates superior intelligence still lingers in our society. People are apt to be impressed by those who use big words, rather than those who communicate clearly and meaningfully. Unfortunately, the tendency to make the goal a large vocabulary is encouraged by the fact that vocabulary growth is much easier to measure than communication growth. We may still be too primitive in our assessment procedures. But we must remember that (1) a message is infinitely more than the sum of its words and (2) a word is useful and powerful only when it helps to communicate the author's or speaker's message.

Let's watch Alma as she tries to understand the following passage:

Jake was beating the batter happily. The muffins were going to be great! Suddenly he smelled something. One of the *liners* was smoking. Quickly he grabbed a pair of *tongs* and threw the *smoldering* liner into the sink. He had left the rear burner on underneath the muffin pan!

The three italicized words are unfamiliar to Alma. She can use the graphophonic cues to help her pronounce them, but she doesn't know their meanings. When she first reads that one of the liners is smoking, she imagines a liner to be some type of person who smokes.

But when Jake throws the liner into the sink, she knows that her prediction was wrong. She quickly tries out another schema related to her experience watching her mother bake muffins. She remembers the "paper things" her mother put in the muffin pans.

Now Alma makes another prediction and checks it by rereading part of the passage. This time her prediction is confirmed. The semantic and syntactic cues that the author provides (plus the easier words that Alma recognizes) help her realize that the liners must be those paper things and the tongs must be something to hold the liners so Jake won't get burned. And the word *smoldering?* Judging from what Jake is doing, it must mean about the same as *smoking*.

Without those wonderful schema cues that Alma brought to the text, all of her own word bank wouldn't have helped her comprehend the author's message. Vocabulary and schemas must interact for comprehension to take place. Do you see the possibility of making reading seem fun, like a mystery game? If you try this, you'll find the possibility becomes a probability rather than a possibility. A message is indeed much more than the sum of its words. A message is a drop of the author's life that merges with your own.

Scaffolding: Helping Students Become Independent Vocabulary Learners

If a house painter wanted his apprentices to paint areas that were higher than they could reach, what could he do? He could have them use a ladder, of course, like most of us amateurs use. But he wouldn't. Instead, he would help them build a strong and comfortable scaffold. Then if one of his apprentices—let's call her Alicia—was brand new to the job, the painter would do some *symbolic scaffolding* for her.

First he would model how he wanted Alicia to paint, thinking out loud for her as his brush slid swiftly and artistically over the wooden siding. Next he might paint alongside her for awhile, patiently answering her questions and respecting her anxieties about doing it right. Then he would allow her to paint alone while he prompted her from below. And from that point on, the only additional scaffold he might offer would be professional reminders now and then.

This same spirit can pervade the classroom of a skillful teacher, who acts as an expert with a child who needs help, but also as a warm and supportive collaborator. Learning is something to do together, with the teacher serving as a stimulus for increasing a student's awareness and knowledge. Gradually, though, the teacher pulls away the symbolic scaffolds that are no longer needed and encourages the child to become the independent learner that she needs to be. This is very similar to interactional reading, recommended by Green-Brabham and Lynch-Brown (2002).

Let's watch a teacher in action use the principles of scaffolding to help her students learn vocabulary on their own. Her goal is to help them learn a strategy for learning new words on their own. Let's see what she does to help them understand the book they have chosen to read.

It's Monday and a small group of children are discussing and sharing the book they've been reading. Alvin is having trouble with a page that he wanted to read to the rest of the group, and the teacher takes this opportunity to create a symbolic scaffold for the entire group. She apologizes for interrupting them and asks permission to do some modeling for them. They like it when she models because she makes it fun, so they give permission immediately.

Level 1: Modeling a Strategy

In this case the teacher needs to model how to solve a reading problem—that is, how to read the word *furniture* in the following sentence: "Moving furniture from one house to another is hard work."

"OK," she says with a twinkle in her eyes, hinting that the fun is about to begin, "Let me show you how I use my world-famous trick called fill-in-the-blank. Today my name is Alvin, and I don't know this hard word, so I'll just say *blank* instead of the hard word and read the rest of the sentence: 'Moving blank from one house to another is hard work.'

"Well," she continues with a big frown, "I still don't know what the author is talking about, so because my real name is Alvin the Wise One, I will now look at the picture to see if this helps me. Ah ha! The picture shows a very sad boy sitting on the steps of his house. I wonder why he's sad. Oh, I know. The author is talking about moving from one house to another, so maybe the boy is sad because he's moving away from his home."

With a smaller frown she says, "I'm still not sure, though, so I'm going to look at the first letter of the hard word. Being Alvin the Wise One, who can see through solid steel, I find that this hard word starts with the letter *f*. So I'll ask myself what word might make sense that could fit in the blank and starts with *f*. What about moving *families* from one house to another? That would make sense.

"But I am wise and *not* reckless," she continues. "I will first check the rest of the letters in the word. It starts with *f-u-r*, so that says /fur/. This means the unknown word can't be *families*, can it? Then, after *f-u-r* it has *n-i-t*, which rhymes with *bit* and *sit*, so it must say /nit/. *Fur-nit*. Then it says *u-r-e*, but I'm not sure. So I'm going to try filling in the blank: 'Moving *fur-nit-your* from one house to another is hard work.' Moving *fur-nit-your?* I wonder what those people are moving, don't you? Oh, I get it. They're moving stuff from one house to another, so they must be moving *furniture*."

Level 2: Engaging a Child in One-on-One Guided Practice

On Tuesday the teacher observes Alvin reading by himself, and he's frowning. The teacher moves from modeling to the next level of scaffolding, providing him with a little more independence but still plenty of support.

Teacher: [Sees that Alvin is having trouble with the word *reforested* in the sentence "That whole hillside was reforested by our Boy Scout troop." Teacher points to *reforested*.] Is this a word you would like me to help you with?

Alvin: Unh-huh.

Teacher: Let's try what we did yesterday. Do you remember what we called it?

Alvin: (Smiling) Fill-in-the-blank.

Teacher: That's right. Do you remember what we did first when we were stuck on *furniture?*

Alvin: I don't remember.

Teacher: That's all right. The first thing we did was say *blank* and finish . . . [She pauses.]

Alvin: . . . the sentence.

Teacher: Right. Give it a try.

Alvin: That whole hillside was *blank* by our Boy Scout troop.

Teacher: Fine. Do you remember another thing we did?

Alvin: Look at the picture?

Teacher: Yes. What do you see?

Alvin: Looks like kids planting trees.

Teacher: Can you fill in the blank yet?

Alvin: [Impishly] No, but you can do it for me.

Teacher: [Laughs] What should we do next?

Alvin: I don't remember.

Teacher: OK, this is a tough word, but we'll break it apart. What are the first two letters?

Alvin: *R-e.*

Teacher: And that says . . .

Alvin: /ree/.

Teacher: And the next three letters say . . .

Alvin: /for/.

Teacher: And the next three?

Alvin: /est/.

Teacher: And what about the last two letters?

Alvin: /ed/.

Teacher: Now put those four parts together.

Alvin: [Slowly] Re-for-est-ed.

Teacher: Put the two middle parts together.

Alvin: Forest?

Teacher: Good. Now put the first three parts together.

Alvin: Reforest?

Teacher: Right again. Put all four parts together.

Alvin: Reforested.

Teacher: Perfect. Do you know what that word means?

Alvin: No.

Teacher: What does it mean to re-do something—like if I tell you to re-do the story you wrote?

Alvin: [Smiling] Do it again.

Teacher: Yes. So what does *re-forest* mean?

Alvin: Forest again?

Teacher: Yes, make a forest again. Look at the picture and see if they are reforesting that hillside.

Alvin: [Grins] Yeah!

After that, the teacher was gradually able to provide Alvin with more independence. The process actually occurred over 3 or 4 weeks, but let's condense it here into 3 days so we can illustrate the last three levels of scaffolding.

Level 3: Prompting the Child's Problem Solving

On Wednesday Alvin needs help with *retold* in the sentence "The children begged him so much he retold the story." The teacher asks him to use the first step of fill-in-the-blank, and he quickly reads the hard word as a blank. Then without commenting, he looks at the picture of the storyteller and the children. "I can't fill in the blank," he says (unconsciously following two more steps of the fill-in-the-blank strategy). The teacher says, "Try taking the word apart," which he does successfully. "I know! It means *told again!*"

Level 4: Suggesting a Strategy

On Thursday when Alvin asks for help with a word, the teacher merely reminds him to use fill-in-the-blank, which he does successfully.

Level 5: Asking What Should Be Done

On Friday the teacher says, "You're having a problem with that word. What do you think you could do to solve that problem?" Alvin grins and says, "Fill-in-the-blank."

I have just demonstrated the five levels of scaffolding recommended by Beed, Hawkins, and Roller (1991). I agree with Allen (2003), who tells us that these kinds of scaffolding experiences help students become more independent readers.

Moving On to Direct Instruction: What Does Research Say?

Even though scaffolding is a wonderful way to help your students learn to teach themselves, many educators believe that direct instruction is the only way to be sure children learn. Can you and I come to grips with this debate?

One important study (McKeown, Beck, Omanson, & Pople, 1985) showed that to have any lasting effect on the learning of concept-laden words, you would need to spend as much as 20 minutes per word. Not only that, but you would need to have about 24 encounters with each word. Now, how many words are we talking about? Nagy and Herman (1987) determined that the reading vocabulary encountered in student reading materials between Grades 3 and 9 adds up to about 88,500 words. They further calculated that learning those words through direct instruction would require learning 12,600 words per year. Hmm. If you and I provide 20 minutes per word and 24 encounters for each concept-laden word, we would have to spend over 24 hours per day just teaching vocabulary! Now, I know you're a superior teacher, and I'm pretty good myself, but I don't think we could accomplish that.

But let's look at this from another angle. How many new words does the average child acquire each year? About 3000 according to the study by McKeown et al. (1985). And yet, "few vocabulary programs cover more than several *hundred* words in the course of a year" (Nagy, 1988, p. 30). Somehow, the average child is sneaking around, picking up well over 2,000 words a year without our direct instruction. Do they learn them by watching television? Some of them. By having scintillating conversations with friends and relatives? Some of them. By writing the words? Probably some more. But most words appear to be learned through *free-time reading*.

Nagy and Herman (1987) have demonstrated that the number of words children learn through context during periods of sustained silent reading far outnumbers the words they learn from direct instruction. In another study, Anderson, Wilson, and Fielding (1988) found that the number of free-reading minutes was the best predictor of vocabulary growth between Grades 2 and 5. So it appears that we've identified the most important reason for having children expand their vocabulary through reading: It's frequently the best way to get the job done.

I was interested to find a similar message in the International Reading Association's Standard 6.6, which urges teachers to employ effective techniques and strategies for the ongoing development of independent vocabulary information. See Appendix A for more.

Nonetheless, there are times when you want your students to learn a few words in a fast and efficient way; it's true that learning words and building vocabulary just through reading is a long-term solution. Learning through direct teaching can be the quickest solution for reading and analyzing something like a single book. This is also true for reading within a group meeting, class project, theme, or unit.

What does this mean in practice? Children require frequent reading opportunities—both at school and at home. And don't forget—to learn a word in this direct way, students normally must experience it many times and in many different contexts. And direct teaching of vocabulary usually works only when teachers have learned how to do it well, when they have developed a depth of knowledge about each word.

Finding a quick definition or asking a student to use the word in a sentence doesn't work—the knowledge of that word doesn't last. In short, hurried teaching simply takes time away from later reading of real stories or articles or books that your students really want to read. It takes time away from teaching your students to predict what will happen on the next page. Hurried teaching can easily present a double jeopardy (Novick, 2000), something the ancient Chinese knew over 2,000 years ago.

Using Effective Strategies to Build Vocabulary

Read to Your Students

From your own life experiences you probably already know that young children can build a larger vocabulary if they are read to frequently—both at home and at school. Research demonstrates this idea (Elley, 1989; Jennings, 1990; Maher, 1991; Vygotsky, 1986). Joan Jennings (1990) puts it succinctly: "You can't afford *not* to

read aloud" (p. 568), and many researchers and teachers agree (Green-Brabham & Lynch-Brown, 2002; Hall & Moats, 2000; and Hickman, Pollard-Durodola, & Vaughn, 2004).

Reading aloud to students of *various ages* teaches vocabulary in one of the most natural ways possible. Most of the questions come from them rather than the teacher—a much more natural, *constructivist* mode of learning. And words that are puzzling can be quickly explained in the context of the story. In addition, the atmosphere is relaxed and provides a great environment for learning, according to superlearning research (Ostrander, Schroeder, & Ostrander, 1975).

Reading aloud to children of all ages also fits constructivist beliefs. It makes sense, doesn't it? In a teacher read-aloud environment, children can construct new meanings, learn from errors without fear, become passionately interested and involved, and connect new knowledge to old.

But what about older children? Does reading to them work as well as it does with younger children? My own experience confirms it, and so does research. In one 8-week study conducted by Edward Maher (1991), two groups of randomly selected fifth graders were compared on vocabulary gains. For both groups the new words were listed on the board before a story was read. The control group was given the traditional assignment of using the dictionary before reading the selection silently and alone. The experimental group had the selection read to them by the teacher.

Eight different selections were used from a regular basal series. The experimental teacher asked the children for the meaning of each new word after it appeared in a sentence. If they could not come up with the meaning, the teacher told it to them. Then the teacher would again read the sentence in which the new word appeared and would go on with the story. For both the control and the experimental groups, a brief vocabulary test was given shortly before and after the selection was read.

What were the results of this 8-week experiment? For the pretest on all of the words, the two groups averaged the same score. For the post test the experimental group retained over 90% of the words; the control group, less than 50%. The subjects of Maher's study were all average students from an urban school in Florida, with students representing 41 countries.

According to Green-Brabham and Lynch-Brown (2002); Hall and Moats, (2000); and Hickman, Pollard-Durodola, and Vaughn (2004), if you read aloud to your students, no matter what their age, and informally talk together about what they're learning, you can truly help children build their word bank and their store of important concepts that match the words. Just remember that what they read should be a balance of both nonfiction and fiction.

To summarize, reading aloud to students (1) exposes them to a fluent model of reading, (2) corrects the pronunciation of new words, (3) ensures meaningful context for those new words, and (4) provides an opportunity for students to question and clarify meanings. In addition, it's a social affair that can bring the entire class together—physically, intellectually, emotionally—and perhaps spiritually.

Teach Semantic Mapping

Nagy (1988) suggests a standard for teaching vocabulary that he calls meaningful use, or purposeful involvement. One way to achieve this kind of involvement is to help your students construct a webbing device called a *semantic map.* Probably the best way for you to understand the concept of semantic mapping is to complete the map shown in Figure 6.3. All you have to do for this particular map is mentally fill in the blanks. Please complete it before you read any further.

While you completed the map, you probably noticed that semantic mapping is a procedure for extending the meaning of a word by showing the categories of words that relate to it. Semantic mapping is based on the premise that everything we learn must be related to something else that we already understand.

If I want to teach the meaning of *demolish,* for instance, I may relate it to old buildings, tearing down, breaking up, and other terms and experiences that come to mind. The advantage of the semantic-mapping process is that it enables a child not

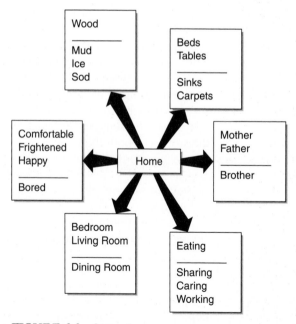

FIGURE 6.3 Semantic map.

only to visualize relationships, but also to categorize them. Such categorization re-inforces both the understanding of the target word and the child's ability to perceive similarities and differences in words.

Normally you wouldn't want to start with a nearly completed map; the process of constructing the map is more important than the map itself. Here are some steps you can follow:

1. Select a word that represents a concept you want students to understand in greater depth.

2. Use pictures, drama, miming, and/or other vivid experiences related to the word.

3. Have children work with partners to write down as many words as they can think of that relate to the target word. Make this a thoughtful experience rather than a race, which would distract them and lead their emotions away from the lesson.

4. Share the word associations of the different pairs while guiding the categorizing and mapping of the words on the chalkboard. This can lead to the excitement of learning something new rather than the disappointment of losing a race.

5. Have the children create a title for each category. Together have fun adding more words to each category.

A study by Stahl and Vancil (1986) demonstrated that it is important for teachers to have a discussion with students while they are producing a semantic map. This discussion should help the children use their own experiences to expand the map and put their words in categories. I recommend that you first do one or two maps with the whole class. Then follow with one or two maps students can make in a small group as a cooperative learning experience.

Model Context Cue Awareness

Professional Standard: Helps Students Develop Independent Vocabulary

Researchers Blachowicz et al. (1990) studied learning events occurring in six differ-ent classrooms. This is what they found:

1. The strategy of using context cues to learn new words while reading was not taught 55% of the time. The difficult words in the selection were treated in isolation.

2. When context was used, it was usually only a single sentence, and the sentence was usually unrelated to the selection the students were about to read.

3. Most of the time vocabulary was taught orally. The words and sentences were not put into written form for the students to see.

4. Teacher modeling of the use of context was not observed at all.

5. "The major vocabulary goal . . . was to develop discrete word meanings rather than develop vocabulary related to the conceptual framework of the selection . . . " (p. 135).

The teachers being observed were probably not negligent. They were most likely experiencing what many teachers have often experienced: goal confusion. In this case the confusion over what should be taught and why probably led to methods confusion, as it usually does. Not really understanding why good readers rely on context cues can lead to not bothering to teach the use of context cues, thereby depriving students of *one of the most important strategies for learning new words.*

The Need for Modeling the Use of Context Cues

It is essential to keep our major goal in mind: to improve our students' communication skills—that is, reading, writing, speaking, and listening. Helping students learn how to use context cues as a vocabulary-learning strategy is well-suited to our goal because people rarely communicate successfully without using words in context.

Right here teachers can step into the breech using a gentle form of direct instruction, and modeling the way we ourselves use context cues. This can be a major step for some teachers and may explain why very little modeling is done in the schools. Few educators have taught teachers how to model.

Let me give you two examples of modeling adapted from observations by Duffy, Roehler, and Hermann (1988). The first example demonstrates how to flexibly use context cues during the reading act. The second example will show a teacher who tries to model but reverts to her old ways of teaching her methods of doing something right.

An Effective Modeling Procedure

"I want to show you what I do when I come across a word I don't know the meaning of. I'll talk out loud to show you how I figure it out.

[The teacher reads.] 'The cocoa steamed fragrantly.' Hmm. I've heard that word *fragrantly* before, but I don't really know what it means here. I know the word that comes before *fragrantly*. Yes, I know the word *steamed*. I have often watched a pot of boiling water, and there is always steam coming from it. That boiling water was hot, so this must have something to do with the cocoa being hot.

"OK, what do I know so far? I know the pan of hot cocoa is steaming on the stove. That means steam is coming up and out, but that still doesn't explain what *fragrantly* means. Let me think again about the hot cocoa on the stove. I'll think about what I already know about cocoa: Hot cocoa bubbles. It steams. And what else? It smells! Hot cocoa smells good. 'The cocoa steamed fragrantly.' That must mean it smelled good.

[Now addressing the students.] "So by thinking about what I already knew about hot cocoa, I was able to figure out what *fragrantly* means."

An Ineffective Modeling Procedure

"The first thing you do is try to guess from your own experience what the word is. If you can guess what the word is, then fit the word into the sentence to see if it makes sense.

"Second, if you can't guess, ask yourself this: Is the word explained in the passage? Look before and after the word. If it is explained, then see if the word makes sense now.

"Third, ask yourself this: Is there a synonym for the word before or after the word? Do you know what a synonym is? It's when the words have the same meaning, like *big* and *large*.

"Fourth, ask yourself if you can guess what the word is by the general mood or feeling of the passage. By using these four steps you will probably be able to guess what the word means, and it's faster than going to a dictionary."

These examples demonstrate the difference between modeling and teaching favorite steps. Both are useful techniques, but to make children aware of how flexible a reader has to be, modeling seems to work much better (Duffy, Roehler, & Hermann, 1988). The first teacher conveyed a sense of flexibility by using the author's context cues and her own background experiences to demonstrate how to think when one reads. The second teacher reverted to *telling* students how to read with understanding. Consequently, she ended up lecturing to them on her favorite steps.

Is the Dictionary a Good Way to Learn Words?

Most of us, at one time or another, have relied on a dictionary for teaching words to others—a tradition that began even before Noah Webster. My question for you is this: What should we teach children about the best ways to use a dictionary in learning new vocabulary and concepts?

Perhaps we'd better begin by learning the limits of dictionaries as learning tools. Research demonstrates that a dictionary is best used by students and writers who have already learned hundreds or thousands of words and merely need a dictionary as a reference tool, to refresh their memories or verify a meaning. Frankly, the dictionary is not always a very good teaching tool.

Miller and Gildea (1987) examined the results of having children look up definitions of new words and write them in their own sentences. The researchers concluded that the errors the children made were so serious and frequent as to make the task instructionally futile. When another group of teachers studied this teaching practice, they were astonished at how poorly even the good readers did at retaining what they had supposedly learned from this procedure (Blachowicz et al., 1990).

In my experience, dictionaries are designed as memory refreshers and meaning clarifiers. They list various meanings of words so that the reader can pick the appropriate one. But as Nagy (1988) reminds us, this vast list, which sometimes contains many words harder than the one the student is looking up, can work against an inexperienced reader trying to use a sophisticated adult tool—even if the dictionary is adapted for elementary students (Scott & Nagy, 1991).

Trying to use a dictionary is a pretty complicated task. Let's watch a student named Eduardo and see what he must do when we tell him to look up a word. Suppose we asked Eduardo to look up the word *fatigue* and tell the class how to pronounce it. What knowledge would he need to do this task quickly and correctly? Let's do a little task analysis and find out.

1. First of all, he needs to know that, because the word starts with *f,* he should open the dictionary somewhere in the first part of the book.

2. If he opens it to words beginning with *i,* he must know that he should now go toward the front of the book rather than toward the back.

3. As soon as he finds the *f* pages, he shouldn't look randomly for the word *fatigue;* he should head toward the first *f* pages, because the second letter in *fatigue* is *a.* To put it another way, he should know alphabetical order perfectly.

4. As Eduardo continues his search, his eyes should be scanning only the top of each page rather than the whole page, because at the top he will find two guide words that indicate the first and last entries for the page.

5. When he finally finds the word, he should study the re-spelling in parentheses. In the case of *fatigue,* the first syllable is shown as *f* followed by a schwa; the second syllable is shown as *teg* with a macron over the *e.* (Can't you just see little Eduardo beginning to wilt?)

6. Suppose he's thrown by the pronunciation of the first syllable with its *f* followed by a schwa. Then poor sweet Eduardo, who's already exhausted, has to go to the bottom of the page to study the Concise Pronunciation Key, where, if he's lucky, he will find that a schwa has the sound of the *a* in *alone.*

7. Now, by paying attention to the diacritical mark (the macron) over the *e* in *teg,* by noticing the syllabication and the accent mark, and by employing his phonics knowledge, he is ready to tell the class how to pronounce *fatigue.*

Suppose we had also asked Eduardo to find the *meaning* of the word. Now he would have to go through each of the definitions to find the one that matches the context of the sentence in which the word is embedded. Not very easy (the word *run* has about 50!). So you are probably asking, What *is* the appropriate role of dictionaries in vocabulary and concept learning?

The Constructivist View of Dictionary Use

Carl Smith said it well: Elementary students learn vocabulary more effectively when they are directly involved in *constructing* meaning rather than memorizing definitions or synonyms (Smith, 1988, p. 238). I wholeheartedly agree with Carl—and maybe you do, too. We can't fully understand something unless we reinvent it for ourselves. Each of us must, in a sense, mold our own meanings, based on the interaction between the author's message and our own knowledge of the world around us. Your students must construct their own meanings if they are to learn in depth. Simply copying down adult meanings does not empower that form of mental transformation. Poplin (1988) nicely sums up this constructivist view of vocabulary and concept learning:

> *All* people are learners . . . always actively searching for and constructing new meanings. . . . *Errors* are critical to learning . . . . *Learners* learn best from experiences about which they are passionately interested and involved. . . . *Experiences* connected to the learner's present knowledge and interest are learned best (p. 405).

Consider the Researchers' Results

"Libraries Called Key" (2004)
> "Numerous research studies conducted during the past decade indicate that well-stocked, professionally staffed school libraries contribute to improved student achievement on standardized tests. . . . Research findings from more than 4,000 schools in more than a dozen U.S. states indicate links between academic achievement and strong school libraries. . . . Indeed, schools with stronger school library programs average between 10% and 20% higher test scores on standardized tests. . . . (p. 1)

J. Allen (2003)

"Explaining, modeling, and supporting transfer to independence [as done with scaffolding] help students recognize and use words to support comprehension." (p. 68) [My experience indicates that modeling is by far the most important teaching strategy.]

E. Green-Brabham and C. Lynch-Brown (2002)

"Vocabulary acquisition was facilitated more by interactional reading than performance reading. Both verbally mediated styles resulted in greater vocabulary learning than just reading." (p. 466)

W. Nagy, V. Beringer, R. Abbott, K. Vaughan, and K. Bermeulen (2003)

These researchers evaluated the contribution of phonological, orthographic (spelling), morphological (inflection, derivation, compound words), and oral vocabulary factors to the ability to read, spell, and comprehend what was read. The population of the study was 98 second graders at risk of failing state requirements in reading and 97 fourth graders at risk of failing state standards. For the second graders a moderate mastery of oral vocabulary and spelling contributed to their reading ability. For the fourth graders their reading ability was helped by their knowledge of spelling and phonology. [The moral of all this is to keep your reading program in balance by developing your students' spelling abilities and their increased phonological awareness.]

E. S. Menon and E. Heber (2005)

These researchers found that first graders reading in "little books" with only a modicum of scaffolding became capable of reading second grade books in 15 weeks. One third of the comparison group did not reach the first grade level. Only 10% of the "little book" readers failed to reach it.

N. Padak, T. Rasinski, and M. Mraz (2002)

These researchers found that activities effective in improving comprehension include writing response journals, retelling and evaluating texts, and holding discussions.

U. Goswami (2001)

"Among young children evidence is beginning to indicate that the size of a child's vocabulary may play a role in bolstering phonological awareness."

S. L. Hall and L. C. Moats (2000)

The most important activity for encouraging reading success is reading aloud. This is especially true during the preschool years.

R. Novick (2000)

To encourage children's language use, Novick recommends (1) creating an unhurried atmosphere, (2) responding to cultural differences, and (3) including a mix of planned and child-initiated activities.

C. Ehri, S. R. Nunes, D. M. Willows, B. V. Schuster, Z. Yaghoub-Zaden, and T. Shanahan (2001)

A quantitative meta-analysis evaluating the effects of phonemic awareness instruction on learning to read and spell was conducted by the National Reading Panel. There were 52 studies published in peer-reviewed journals, and those contributed to 96 cases for comparing the outcomes of control groups. Not only word reading but also reading comprehension benefited from phonemic awareness instruction, which, in turn, impacted reading under all of the conditions examined.

A. C. Hargrove and M. Senechal, (2000)

These wise souls experimented with two types of storybook reading experiences. One was the standard shared reading experience, normally with a small group. The other experience was the so-called dialogic method, which simply means having a dialogue between two people—two peers or one student and the teacher. *The point is to interact with another reader,* rather than always taking turns or just reading in a choral fashion. Children using the dialogic reading method made significantly larger gains in both reading and speaking vocabulary. Please pay more attention to *these* results than to any others.

D. K. Dickenson and A. McCabe (2001)

Even before children commence formal instruction in reading and writing, they display differences that mirror some of the divisions in our society. This occurs with children from less advantaged and non–English-speaking homes. These early differences are remarkably stable and have consistently been found in cross-sectional examinations of children. Longitudinal studies also provide evidence of considerable consistency within individual children from first grade to the later elementary grades. (p. 186)

C. L. Z. Blachowicz and P. Fisher (2000)

When students in fourth grade were allowed to choose their own words for vocabulary and spelling instruction, they learned the words more effectively and remembered their meanings longer than they did with words chosen by the teacher.

Four main principles should influence instruction:

1. Students should be active [i.e., involved] in developing their understanding of words and ways to learn them.
2. Students should personalize word learning.
3. Students should be immersed in words.
4. Students should build on multiple sources of information to learn words through repeated exposures. (p. 504)

"Teaching vocabulary becomes not a simple process of teaching words but one of teaching particular words to particular students for a particular purpose." (p. 517)

F. P. Roth, D. L. Speece, and D. H. Cooper (2002)

The phonological awareness measured in kindergarten predicted the quality of word and pseudo-word reading in first and second grades. However, it did not predict reading comprehension in those grades. This simply shows that phonological awareness has to do with auditory matters, but remember that reading comprehension has to do with *total understanding* through syntax, schemas, grapheme/phonemes, and meanings.

P. Hickman, S. Pollard-Durodola, and S. Vaughn (2004)
Teacher read-alouds are perhaps the most consistent activity used by classroom teachers that provides frequent, if not daily, opportunities to enhance the literacy of English-language learners by integrating effective vocabulary-development practices.

I. L. Beck, M. G. McKeown, and L. Kucan (2002)
Words can be learned best with *robust instruction* of vocabulary.

Building Vocabulary in a Diverse Classroom

According to August and Hakuta (1997),

Researchers in the field of second-language acquisition have repeatedly stressed the need for instruction that addresses not only the social language needs of English language learners, but also the academic, cognitive, and language development that is critical to success in schools, especially in light of current accountability standards and standardized assessments. (p. 3)

Grabe (1991) adds that "a student's level of vocabulary knowledge has been shown to be an important predictor of reading ability (fluency) and reading comprehension for English-language learners" (p. 381). This need to increase students' vocabulary prompts me to suggest a number of functional experiences for both Spanish-speaking and English-speaking students.

Functional Experiences

■ Consider having pairs of students, one English speaking and the other Spanish speaking, listen to the same poem in Spanish and then in English. Have them do this several times and then help each other write the poem first in English and then in Spanish. Try to use many of the 100 most frequent words in English.

■ Morrow (2001) and Perez and Torres-Guzman (2002) recommend the use of onomatopoeia with both young Spanish-speaking students and young English-speaking students. They can imitate or act out the sounds the words represent, such as *meow, cock-a-doodle-doo,* or any sound that can be recognized in both cultures. The advantage of this experience is that both cultures are taught at the same time. (By the way, my Hispanic friends assure me that roosters do not say *cock-a-doodle-doo*. They say *kikiriki* (kick-er-eek-ee).) Sing some long words like you sing cock-a-doodle-do: ir-*rec*-on-*cil*-a-ble.

- Manuela Gonzalez-Bueno (2003) recommends the use of the environment for both English-speaking and Spanish-speaking students to learn the English alphabet. You can use trade names and advertising posters that can be seen in the streets to help students learn all 26 of the letters in the English language. Choose brand names that appear frequently in the areas where the children live or that are used widely in their everyday lives.

- Morrow (2001) recommends that you have your mixed Spanish- and English-speaking students use illustrations in books to recognize that words have meaning and to be able to decode written words.

- Because children use illustrations to decode written words (Morrow, 2001), you can double your effectiveness by combining illustrations with books of songs (plus audiocassettes) in which each song represents a letter of the alphabet. The songbook *Abecedario de los animals* (Ada & Escriva, 1990) is a good example. Its design superimposes an image on the lyrics of a song, which normally include an endless number of words that begin with the letter at issue. In this way the children, already familiar with the song from listening to the cassette, get used to seeing the image of the object at the same time that they see the word that represents that image. Later, present children with the lyrics of the song without the image and ask them to place cutouts of the image (or stickers) over the corresponding words. This forces learners to sight read the target words. The same procedure can be followed with songbooks in English. (Gonzalez-Bueno, 2003, p. 191)

Functional Vocabulary

Based on numerous intensive experiences of both Louise Fulton and me—traveling, teaching, and living in Europe, Asia, and South America—we highly recommend that you teach both Spanish-speaking and English-speaking students the names and the spellings of various foods, first in English and then in Spanish. Do the same with other languages represented in your classroom. These words in English are highly meaningful and should be mastered rather than merely introduced. The experience of mastering words will ensure that your students' memories will assist them—in school and out. At your direction, they will be frequently examining, touching, and eating samples of common ethnic foods, mastery will come rather quickly. I say this because of my living and Dr. Fulton's living long enough in various parts of the world to become used to the names and spellings of the foods.

Please don't ignore this procedure because of rigid adherence to state standards and expectations. Gradually studying different foods does not take that much time and is far more interesting and effective in developing vocabulary and spelling writing abilities than any other method I have seen or used.

One of the best approaches is to create a food wall, using one column for major foods in English and one column for major foods in Spanish. To organize the lists, use subheadings: fruits, vegetables, meats, breads, cereals, flavorings, snacks, drinks. Let your students place a colored drawing next to each food item to serve as an abstract reminder.

However, the real foods should gradually be brought to your classroom by you and your students or their parents and other caregivers. Your students need the opportunity to use most of their five senses in understanding and remembering the names and spellings of the foods. A papaya felt, smelled, heard about, and tasted is far more memorable than the abstract word *papaya*. Remember that young children and older students need concrete experiences.

After you've completed and used your food wall, create a clothes wall. Help your students learn functional clothing words in the same way—this time with items brought to school or worn. Set up your clothes wall with sections: shirts, pants, dresses, shoes, jackets, hats, socks/stockings, scarves (forget the underwear—they get too silly). Again use one column for English words and one for Spanish words, and if needed for another language. These names and spellings can be learned and gradually mastered, contributing to a highly useful vocabulary and an excellent gain in spelling and writing skills.

A final word wall of living spaces should probably be taught in the last half or last quarter of the academic year. This wall project is more sophisticated because of students' limited experience in seeing, living, or working in a large variety of living spaces. Rather than telling the types of shelters, let your students take pride in scouting, investigating, and finally coming up with their careful organization of the data. This will cause them to do more research, be intrigued by the differences, and extend the abilities developed in the first half of the year. It will also cause them to experience the excitement and fun of doing research on the internet and in the library.

Summary of Main Ideas

- When words stand for sophisticated concepts, the concepts themselves must be understood before those words can become part of children's conceptual vocabulary.
- A word is seldom known in isolation. When words are used for communication, they are known or understood in context. Developing students' context awareness helps them find the true meaning of words.
- Dale's cone of experience provides an excellent model for planning vocabulary instruction.
- Scaffolding is highly appropriate for helping children learn vocabulary—as long as the teacher doesn't forget to relinquish control in favor of independent learning.
- Teachers should help students fall in love with their special words.

Focus on Students with Special Needs: Comments by Louise Fulton

A Creative Teacher at Work with Words

Professional Standard: Intervenes to help those students in greatest need

How can you help your students with special needs develop their vocabulary? Let me tell you about a teacher who gets kids to construct their own meaning of words. Julian Quarles teaches a class of 25 seventh-grade students at a school in Apple Valley, CA. At any given time there are usually three or four special-needs students in his regular education classroom. But Julian doesn't see a need to single out any students as special. He treats all of his students as unique learners and wants them to feel comfortable.

At times some of his students require more time before they respond to his questions. Other students need to have him move closer to their desks. Still others become more involved when he personalizes his comments ("That's a good word for describing your shirt, Kevin"). Like other students, students with special needs require a stimulating classroom where they can develop a passion for what they are doing with words.

After hearing about Julian, I had to visit his classroom to see for myself. The first thing he did, without warning his students, was to walk over to the window: "It looks like spring is incipient," he announced. Then he paused and moved closer to one of his students. "What a lovely word, *incipient.* Just listen to the sound—it has an exciting, dramatic sound. Listen to the sound again: *in-SIP-ee-ent.*" All eyes focused on Julian as he drama-tized the word with his face and hands. "The grass is growing and spring is incipient. What do you think *incipient* means?"

As his students playfully tossed around different ideas, I watched them fall in love with the word. Later Julian said, "When we read the passage that contains the word *incipient,* we will see if our invented definitions are in the ballpark. My students are delighted when they come close to one of its meanings."

All students, including those with special needs, can participate in and learn new words through constructive invention and drama. Julian encourages his students to dramatize each word that is new to them. Starting with interesting verbs like *deliberate* and later moving to adjectives like *incipient,* students produce 30-second skits for their classmates. "Learning new words is not a study," Julian says. "It is enjoyable. I want all my students to develop a natural interest in words and sounds. I don't like to present words for their literal meaning only, but for their dramatic potential as well. After we go a few times around a word that way, it sticks. The new word then makes a transition from being a 'school word' to being a word the students use informally in their everyday vocabulary."

What you can observe from Julian's example is that all students, including those with special needs, enjoy and respond well to drama and enthusiasm. When we make it possible for them to fall in love with words, we have given them a gift for life.

Literacy Through Technology

A. With the entire teacher-education class, create the beginning of a conceptual vocabulary database for a social studies or science topic, such as worldwide communication. First, spend 10 minutes brainstorming words that come to mind when you think about worldwide communication. This process should arouse your creativity.

Next, follow these steps:

1. Build temporary categories.
2. Use the computer thesaurus to provide more synonyms and word clusters.
3. Separate the synonyms and mere associations into two columns (a process that creates a much sharper idea of word meanings).
4. Decide on the exact organization of your database (which requires identification of purpose and use).
5. Create the database itself.

As you continue to study the topic, more categories will need to be invented, and old categories will need to be revised.

B. Review the database in A for indications that you and your peers considered diversity in developing it. Spend at least 15 minutes discussing how you could modify the database to better reflect the diversity in our country. Make at least five creative and innovative adaptations to evidence your diversity awareness.

C. Evaluate the usability of two Web sites designed to build vocabulary. Critique their consideration of diversity. Use examples to back up your critique. Determine whether and how you would use these Web sites.

http://www.vocabulary.com/
http://travlang.com/wordofday/
http://www.m-w.com/
http://www.seussville.com/

Application Experiences for Your Course

A. *Literacy Teacher Vocabulary: List of Terms:* Use cooperative learning procedures to own these terms:

concept	context awareness
constructivist	scaffolding
diversity	semantic mapping
Dale's cone	context cues
functional vocabulary	

B. *What's Your Opinion?* Rewrite these in any way you wish, as long as you can justify your reconstruction of each idea with textbook and experiential authority.

1. Children should learn to use the final authority on word meanings—a dictionary.
2. The best way to really learn a word is in isolation. Context merely adds to the confusion; it's not that important.
3. It's important for you to understand the differences between the English and the Spanish languages.
4. The difficulty of a word depends primarily on the number of its syllables. For example, *Saturday, saturate,* and *saturnine* can be of equal difficulty for different people.

C. *Team Planning and Peer Teaching:* In small groups think of a word that represents an abstract concept (e.g., *courage* or *justice*). Plan three creative ways to help your peers learn this word in considerable depth. One of the ways must be through direct teaching of one or more of the other small groups. The other two must be indirect methods that you simply report to the other groups. Establish a plan that you can use later in a particular classroom.

D. *Preparing Children for Reading:* Decide with a small group of your peers how you might use information in this chapter (include Dale's cone of experience and other ideas) to help you enhance children's vocabularies and/or schemas before they read a selection about living on a farm in 1880. Three of the words in the story are *plow, oxen,* and *yoke.* Allow no more than 6 minutes to prepare the students for reading the selection. One sentence in the selection might help you create a plan: "Jake attached the yoke to one of the oxen, but the other ox started to move away."

Creativity Training Session

A. Create a human machine made up of 5 to 6 people. One person begins by coming to the front of the room and making a repetitive movement, similar to one of a large machine. Each of the other human machine parts enters one at a time, as a complementary and cooperative repetitive moving part. No talking or verbal planning is allowed. This is all spontaneous. When the entire machine has been working for at least 1 minute, their work is complete.

B. The next group can add sounds to each part of their machine.

C. The third group can give their machine a name and a function.

D. Describe the cooperative group process that occurred. How can this be used or modified for classroom use with children? How can it be used to stimulate language or to write a descriptive narrative?

Field Experiences

A. *Use the Plan Created by Your Team:* In Application Experience C you worked with a team to develop a plan to teach a particular word in depth. Carry out that plan with two or more children.

B. *Use the Preparation Ideas Developed by Your Team:* See if you can apply what you learned in Application Experience D to teach a group of elementary-school children. Spend 5 to 10 minutes enhancing children's schemas before they read a selection. This prereading activity should involve conceptual vocabulary; select one to three concept-laden words and prepare the children for the major ideas or behavior described in the selection.

C. *Semantic Mapping:* Use ideas from this chapter to help a student develop a semantic map. Be sure you choose a word that represents a multifaceted concept and therefore has several categories of associations. If possible, choose a word that ties in with an important concept in one of the curriculum areas presently being studied by the student.

D. *Teach a Comprehension Strategy with the Scaffolding Method:* Use the five scaffolding steps described in this chapter to teach the fill-in-the-blank strategy (or a different strategy).

References

Ada, A. F., & Escriva, V. (1990). *Abecedario de los animals.* Madrid: Espasa Calpe.

Allen, J. (2003). "I can comprehend . . . I just can't read big words." *Voices From the Middle, 11*(1), 60–61.

Anderson, R. C., Wilson, P. T., & Fielding, L. (1988). Growth in reading and how children spend their time outside of school. *Reading Research Quarterly, 23,* 285–303.

August, A., & Hakuta, K. (Eds.) (1997). *Improving schooling for language-minority children: A research agenda.* Washington, DC: National Academy Press.

Beck, I. L. McKeown, M. G., & Kucan, L. (2002). *Bringing words to life: Robust vocabulary instruction.* New York: Guilford.

Beed, P. L., Hawkins, E. M., & Roller, C. M. (1991). Moving learners toward independence: The power of scaffolded instruction. *The Reading Teacher, 44,* 648–655.

Blachowicz, C. L. Z., & Fisher, P. (2000). Vocabulary instruction. In M. L. Kamil, P. B. Mosenthal, P. D. Pearson, & R. Barr (Eds.), *Handbook of reading research* (Vol. 3, p. 507). Mahwah, NJ: Erlbaum.

Blachowicz, C. L. Z., et al. (1990, April). *Teachers look at fourth grade students.* Paper presented at the annual meeting of the American Educational Research Association, Boston, MA.

Dale, E. (1969). *Audiovisual methods in teaching*. New York: Holt, Rinehart & Winston.

Dickenson, D. K., & McCabe, A. (2001). Bringing it all together: The multiple origins, skills, and environmental supports of early literacy. *Learning Disabilities Research & Practice, 16*(4) 186–202.

Duffy, G. G., Roehler, L. R., & Hermann, B. A. (1988). Monitoring mental processes helps poor readers become strategic readers. *The Reading Teacher, 41,* 762–767.

Eeds, M., & Cockrum, W. A. (1985). Teaching word meanings by expanding schemata vs. dictionary work vs. reading in context. *Journal of Reading, 28,* 492–497.

Elley, W. B. (1989). Vocabulary acquisition from listening to stories. *Reading Research Quarterly, 24,* 174–187.

Ehri, L. C., Nunes, S. R., Willows, D. M., Schuster, B. V., Yaghoub-Zaden, Z., & Shanahan, T. (2001). Phonemic awareness instruction helps children read: Evidence from the National Reading Panel's meta-analysis. *Reading Research Quarterly, 36*(3), 256–287.

Gonzalez-Bueno, M. (2003). Literacy activities for Spanish-English bilingual children, *The Reading Teacher, 57*(2), 189–192.

Goswami, U. (2001). Early phonological development and the acquisition of literacy. In S. Neuman & D. Dickenson (Eds.), *Handbook of early literacy research* (pp. 111–125). New York: Guilford.

Grabe, W. (1991). Current developments in second language reading research *TESOL Quarterly, 25,* 375–406.

Green-Brabham, E., & Lynch-Brown, C. (2002). Effects of teachers' reading-aloud styles on vocabulary acquisition and comprehension of students in the early elementary grades. *Journal of Educational Psychology, 94*(3), 465–473.

Hall, S. L., & Moats, L. C. (2000). Why reading to children is important. *American Educator, 24*(1), 26–33.

Hargrove, A. C., & Senechal, M. (2000). A book reading intervention with preschool children who have limited vocabularies: The benefits of regular reading and dialogic reading. *Early Childhood Research Quarterly, 15*(1), 75–90.

Hickman, P., Pollard-Durodola, S., & Vaughn, S. (2004). Storybook reading: Improving vocabulary and comprehension for English-language learners. *The Reading Teacher, 57*(8), 720–730.

Jennings, J. (1990). You can't afford not to read aloud. *Phi Delta Kappan, 72,* 568–571.

Libraries called key. (2004, Feb/Mar). *Reading Today, 21*(4), 1 & 4.

Maher, E. B. (1991). *The effect of reading aloud to fifth grade students on the acquisition of vocabulary* (Report No. 143). Miami: Florida International University.

McKeown, M., Beck, I., Omanson, R., & Pople, M. (1985). Some effects of the nature and frequency of vocabulary instruction on the knowledge and use of words. *Reading Research Quarterly, 20,* 522–535.

Menon, S. & Hiebert, E. (2005). A comparison of first graders reading with little books or literature-based basal anthologies. *Reading Research Quarterly, 40*(1), 12–38.

Miller, G. A., & Gildea, P. M. (1987). How children learn words. *Scientific American, 257,* 94–99.

Morrow, L. M. (2001). *Literacy development* (4th ed.). Needham Heights, MA: Allyn & Bacon.

Nagy, W. E. (1988). *Teaching vocabulary to improve reading comprehension.* Urbana, IL: National Council for Teachers of English.

Nagy, W., Beringer, V., Abbott, R., Vaughan, K., & Bermeulen, K. (2003). Relationship of morphology and other language skills to literacy skills in at-risk second-grade readers and at-risk fourth-grade writers. *Journal of Educational Psychology, 95*(4), 730–742.

Nagy, W. E., & Herman, P. (1987). Breadth and depth of vocabulary knowledge: Implications for acquisition and instruction. In M. McKeown & M. Curtis (Eds.), *The nature of vocabulary acquisition.* Hillsdale, NJ: Erlbaum.

Novick, R. (2000). Supporting early literacy development: Doing things with words in a real world. *Childhood Education, 76*(2), 70–75.

Ostrander, S., Schroeder, L., & Ostrander, N. (1975). *Superlearning.* New York: Holt.

Padak, N., Rasinski, T., & Mraz, M. (2002). *Scientifically-based reading research: A primer for adult and family literacy educators* (ED469865). Kent State Universiity, Ohio Literacy Resource Center.

Perez, B., & Torres-Guzman, M. (2002). *Learning in two worlds* (3rd ed.). Boston: Allyn & Bacon.

Poplin, M. S. (1988). Holistic/constructivist principles of the teaching/learning process: Implications for the field of learning disabilities. *Journal of Learning Disabilities, 21,* 401–416.

Roth, F. P., Speece, D. L., & Cooper, D. H. (2002). A longitudinal analysis of the connection between oral language and early reading. *Journal of Educational Research, 95,* 274–295.

Scott, J. A., & Nagy, W. E. (1991, April). *Understanding definitions* (Report No. 528). Urbana: University of Illinois, Center for the Study of Reading.

Smith, C. B. (1988). Building a better vocabulary. *The Reading Teacher, 42,* 238.

Stahl, S. A., & Vancil, S. J. (1986). Discussion is what makes semantic maps work in vocabulary instruction. *The Reading Teacher, 40,* 62–67.

Vygotsky, L. (1986). *Thought and language* (Ed. and rev., A. Kozulin). Cambridge, MA: MIT Press.

Other Suggested Readings

May, F. B. (2001). *Unraveling the seven myths of reading: Assessment and intervention practices for counteracting their effects.* Boston: Allyn & Bacon.

McFalls, E. L. (1996). Influence of word meaning on the acquisition of a reading vocabulary in second grade children. *Reading and Writing: An Interdisciplinary Journal, 8*(3), 235–250.

Mezynski, K. (1983). Issues concerning the acquisition of knowledge: Effects of vocabulary training on reading comprehension. *Review of Educational Research, 53,* 253–279.

Thorndike, R. L. (1973). *Reading comprehension education of fifteen countries.* New York: Wiley.

Chapter Seven

Creative and Intriguing Comprehension Strategies

Strategy: A plan or method for achieving a specific goal.
Strategem: A scheme or trick for deceiving an enemy.

—Take Your Pick

To grasp what humans on earth are thinking, you must select
the very finest of strategies.

—Bogglestar

Seventh Objective for your Teaching Success:

Personally model specific strategies for understanding authors

---

Back in Chapter 2 you were reminded that there are four communication cues, or clues, and not just one. In addition to phonics, good readers also search for syntax cues, meaning cues, and their past-experience cues. But even if your students master the use of all of those cues, you will still have to deal with this particular reality: your students will still need strategies at times in order to really understand what message an author is truly sending. And this strong need, in turn, demands that they learn comprehension strategies—which in simple words means they must figure out ways of understanding the author.

As Katherine Stahl (2004) says:

> Comprehension strategies can be important to a reader because they have the potential to provide access to knowledge that is removed from personal experience. . . . Children who actively engage in particular cognitive strategies . . . are likely to understand and recall more of what they read. (p. 598)

For the past four decades classroom teachers have been creating their own methods of helping students understand *in depth* what authors are trying to communicate. In this chapter you'll find a potpourri of good teaching ideas that will make it easy for you to pick and choose the ideas that best fit you and your students. But don't forget to keep creating your own ideas—or better yet, work with your students to create new and enjoyable methods for digging way down deep into an author's basket of interesting, intriguing meanings.

What Are Strategies and How Can They Be Learned?

Lapin (2003) identified a variety of general comprehension strategies like these:

1. Activating prior knowledge

2. Building vocabulary

3. Determining importance

Forbes, Poparad, and McBride (2004) just ask simple questions or make comments like these—"How else can you do this?" "Did you read the sentence again?" "I like the way you read the sentence again to make more sense." These kinds of questions and comments can help your apprentices develop a sense of satisfaction and self-esteem as they move forward toward successful reading. Such an approach can lead to a greater sense of independence and responsibility.

Comprehension strategies can be simple or elaborate, general or specific. What's important is that they work—and help your kids read with understanding. Here are my favorites.

Strategy: Help Students Create Mental Images

Proficient readers form images in their minds as they read, and teachers can guide young readers to do the same. To help students visualize as they read, a teacher can start with simple sentences and ask students questions that help create images. Guiding students with detailed questions that lead to open-ended answers helps them create a visual interpretation of the sentence. This activity not only encourages students to create images but also encourages them to think about questioning and to become question-askers themselves.

Strategy Use: Poetry to Help Students Learn

So you want to find a strategy that will teach kids what it's like to fall in love with words—especially worded messages. Do you remember the fun of making up new or modified Mother Goose Rhymes in Chapter 3? The same kind of thing can become a strategy for getting older students, 8 to 13, turned on to learning and comprehending words.

Instead of giving your students dry, barely alive stories and books, why not give them poems and books of poetry? Not right away—first you need to woo them for a while until they're simply begging to hear more. Then read more . . . and write more poetry together . . . and have them write and read more of their own poetry . . . and then rush home after school to show their poem to mom, dad, sis, or bro, whoever truly wants to hear and read it. At that point they're reading with enthusiasm, and they're learning more words without memorizing them.

Many teachers have learned the power of rhythm, rhyme, haiku, and all the other poetic-sounding ways to speak, write, read, and listen. Some poems have to rhyme; many others do not. All you have to do is communicate poetic feelings and language in a way that intrigues the listener or reader.

Poetry dominates regular popular music, it dominates rap music, and best of all, it dominates love letters. Without poetry Shakespeare would never have been heard of, nor would those who created the Greek pageants and plays. So why do we worship poetry like that, but often deny the value of poetry for teaching reading? After all, it's pretty difficult to remember the lines in a song without relying on poetic rhymes.

Here's what Kurkjian, Livingston, Young, and Hopkins (2004) have to say about this matter:

> Because poetry is so multisensory and evocative, it often lingers with us, eliciting visual images, remembered lines, and powerful emotional responses. It can encourage a love of language in all of its forms. . . . The music of poetry, along with its sensory detail and visual imagery, invites us to experience poetry intensely, and thus it stays with us.

Oh, the details that we so easily miss or forget while reading regular text. And yet with poetry, as described by Ryan (2001) in his children's book *Hello Ocean*, we don't just learn about the physical aspects of the beach; we feel what it's like to taste salty lips contributed by the sea: "Sandy grains in a salty drink are best for fish and whales I think. I lick the drops still on my face; I love the way the ocean tastes."

Dr. Louise Fulton told me about how she used haiku several years ago with children with special needs who were having comprehension problems and a lackluster interest in vocabulary and words. I've asked her to share her experience with you.

Louise Fulton's Experience with Haiku

I had recently returned from my year in Japan, and I was especially excited to be teaching elementary-grade children again. I had designed a nifty word-study lesson on the Japanese culture, which I was going to center around the teaching of poetry called haiku. My students and I were going to enjoy Japanese culture while playfully creating our own original poetry. "This is just the thing my students need," I said to myself—successful reading and writing experiences to expand their vocabulary, build their confidence, and provide them with a simple strategy or two. I couldn't wait to get started.

I noticed my hands shaking just a bit and smiled at my nervousness as I began to read two haiku poems, written and illustrated by children and found on the Children's

Haiku Garden Web site (http://www.tecnet.or.jp/). Zoe, a second-grade student in Georgia, had written:

lying on the ground
i wished on a falling star,
i wished for a dog

Charlie, a second-grade student in Minnesota, had written:

butterflies are cute
fluttering their scaly wings
very, very fast

The children were so interested in this simple format that I decided to read one that I had written the day before:

bending in the wind
trees dance to the sound of waves
crashing on the beach

I asked the students to close their eyes while I read it and to imagine that they were right there. Then I asked them to tell what they could see and hear. This method really got them involved and enhanced their excitement.

The next two haiku poems that I read had been written by two children in the class, Keiko and Tim. I had told all the children the day before that we would be writing Japanese poems called haiku, and those two kids went ahead on their own. The whole class learned quickly that haiku had a simple pattern of five syllables on top, seven syllables in the middle, and five syllables on the bottom to finish the poem. So that day those two poets had an audience all primed to close their eyes and imagine they were right there. And this time when I read, the other children were very excited indeed. Seven-year-old Keiko, a fourth-grade student with learning problems, had written this poetic haiku with a perfect 5-7-5 pattern that was very picturesque to her peers, some of whom actually clapped.

funny turtles walk
across a rocky dirt road
looking for safety

Tim, a very bright lad who was also struggling with various learning problems, practically knocked me on my derriere with his metaphor and simile:

rocks hide in the sand
like sleeping bears in winter
waiting for springtime

Excitedly we conferred with each other as to what each author was telling us and how it feels to walk on a dirt road and climb barefoot on rocks. Then we closed our eyes and called out what we had learned about turtles and described the things that we saw through our mind's eye. Then we opened our eyes and looked around for 10 seconds and then closed them again to see what we could remember. Quite a bit, we proudly boasted.

As we sat in our chairs, I demonstrated the format of haiku poetry again. We clapped out the rhythm of the two poems that I had now put on the board, and to their amazement and mine, they were hooked.

I then went to the board and modeled the creation of an original haiku right on the spot. I stopped to count out the rhythm and paused to ponder what the next line would be, talking aloud as I played with words that fit the message and the rhythm. My most eager students were beginning to suggest words of their own—just the interaction I was hoping for.

Next, I asked them to work together to create a poem of our own. I wrote the first line on the board but then presented myself as being stumped. Could anyone please think of a second line? I had lots of eager volunteers, and we played around with several ideas, checking for rhythm and words that would work. We discovered that there could be many ways to take the outdoor theme into a second line. We spent more time on that line than I had expected, but it was time well spent on rich, ripe discussion. We finished our poem together by adding a final five-beat line.

running through raindrops
drinking like we are thirsty
dirty skin so clean

The next poem we created together was easier, so after the second line was created, I stopped and let students think of their own last lines and write them at their desks as best they could. After reading their own lines, with repeated choral reading of Lines 1 and 2 from the board, these dear students who had struggled so much with reading were having no trouble at all. They were motivated, confi-

dent, and successful readers of the most sophisticated form of language—poetry.

A few days later I listened to some of them arguing about how many syllables there were in certain words—a major learning feat for them. The next day they were trying to see who could write a word that had the most "sullables"—until I wrote the word *syllable* on the board and had them appropriately divide it into three syllables. Shortly after that they excitedly discovered that compound words had syllables in them, too—*classroom, baseball, basketball,* and a very sophisticated *outcome.* Anyway, the way I see it, motivating energetic lessons are good for us all.

Sets of Poems for Teachers to Use

Thank you Louise, for such a vivid inspiration. Let me recommend a book by George Sloan (2003) called *Give Them Poetry: A Guide for Sharing Poetry with Children K–8.* I also recommend books of poetry scattered around the classroom.

Leap into Poetry by Avis Harley—lively poems about insects

Put Your Eyes Up Here and Other School Poems by Kalli Dakos—all-too-funny familiar events in the classroom

A Fury of Motion: Poems for Boys by Charles Ghigna—a world of base-full dreams, boxing lessons, and other almost truths

In the Spin of Things: Poetry in Motion by Rebecca Kai Dotlich—word-play things that shake, slap, whoosh, whirl, swirl, or spill

Little Dog and Duncan by Kristine O'Connell George—a big dog and a little dog discovering how similar they are

Autumnblings by Dougles Florian—a follow-up to *Winter Eyes* and *Summersaults* and much fun

Giant Children by Brod Bagert—a collection of irresistible poems, fun for choral reading

Plum by Tony Mitton—a wise and silly book of hefty hedgehogs, mermaids, and a zap machine

Knock on Wood, Poems About Superstitions by Janet Wong—black cats, ladders, and much, much more

The Blood Hungry Spleen & Other Poems About Our Parts by Allan Wolf

Strategy: Use Open-Ended Discussion More Than Oral Testing

The concept-laden word *discussion,* in some teaching circles, may mean nothing more than recitation—a chance for the teacher to ask quick questions and get quick answers from the children. One study conducted in the 1980s found that the average teacher allowed only 1 or 2 seconds for a child to respond to a question (Gambrell, 1983). This is not what I mean by *discussion.* Instead, the ideas we discuss and savor with our students—before, during, and after they read—should really be the most important part of reading instruction.

Discussions for Wide Open Thinking Together

The inquisition method doesn't teach children the true long-term purpose of reading; in real life we don't read so we can answer the teacher's questions. Instead, the process of comprehension should be perceived by students as a highly purposeful and personal act: "I'm looking for two things when I read—(1) information or

(2) entertainment." The inquisition method doesn't even relate to those two benefits. Nor does it allow for the *diversity* of children's minds and experiences—or their
cultural backgrounds or various opinions or biases.

Reading comprehension should not be seen as a multiple-choice test. But what
happens so often in this test-giving world is that answering questions on one reading selection leads abruptly to answering questions on the *next* selection, and the
next. It's as if children are working on an assembly line producing frothy answers—
ones that quickly evaporate and leave the mind as vacant as before.

But How Practical Is Time on Discussion?

After students read, is it practical to spend time on discussion? Flood and Lapp (1990)
answer yes. According to their extensive research, discussion is a major ingredient of
any functional comprehension instruction. Gall's (1984) survey of several research
studies shows that children who experience discussions learn more than those who
don't. And Kelly (1990) found that regular discussions gradually increased children's
awareness of the complexity of authors' ideas. As I remember what Vygotsky said,
children learn to think mainly by communicating with adults and peers.

My conclusion? Use a variety of discussion methods to increase the four communication abilities—reading, writing, speaking, listening—particularly since these
four abilities interact and assist each other. *They're like a family that sticks together
and supports each other.*

Effective Discussion Webs

Professional Standard: Models questioning strategies

Lucky for all of us teachers, Donna Alvermann (1991) developed a simple but powerful graphic device called the *discussion web* for helping children aged 8 to 12 participate fully in discussions. Here's her advice:

> A problem with most discussions is the tendency for teachers and a few
> highly verbal students to monopolize classroom talk. When this happens . . .
> other students soon become inhibited, self-conscious, and unwilling to
> voice their opinions. One way to counteract [this] tendency . . . is to
> provide all children with the opportunity to assume their own voices in
> these discussions. The discussion web gives students this opportunity
> (pp. 92–93).

How Does the Discussion Web Work?

Professional Standard: Teaches students strategies for monitoring their own comprehension

Suppose your students are about to read the story of *Stone Fox* by Gardiner. This
story is about a dogsled race between Little Willy and Stone Fox for $500 in prize

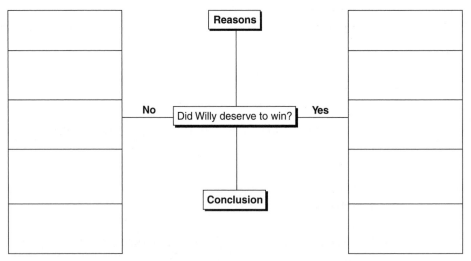

FIGURE 7.1   A discussion web for *Stone Fox. Note.* Adapted from "The Discussion Web" by D. E. Alvermann, 1991, *The Reading Teacher, 45*, pp. 92–99.

money. Stone Fox has won this race before and always uses the prize money to purchase land that was taken over by white settlers. "Ah-ha!" you might be thinking. "The motives of Stone Fox are so noble, he should be the one who wins again." But let me tell you about Little Willy. If he doesn't win the $500, his sick grandfather will lose his farm. So who are you rooting for?

Look at the discussion web format shown in Figure 7.1 and the completed web in Figure 7.2.

Here are some steps to follow to create discussion webs with your students:

Step 1: Strengthen your students' schemas and related vocabulary. In the case of *Stone Fox*, you would carefully strengthen their theories about dog races, contestants, and the meaning of being disqualified before they even begin reading. Have them remember what they have already learned about those concepts and share ideas.

Step 2: Help your students establish purposes for reading. For example, "Who do you hope will win the race? Let's all read to find out *where* the race will be run, which one is expected to win the race, *why* he needs to win the race, and *when* you realized who probably would win it."

Step 3: Have students read the selection to satisfy their reading purposes.

Step 4: Introduce the discussion web question. A good discussion web question is normally a highly controversial one that leads to critical thinking about both perspectives. In the case of *Stone Fox*, this question might be, Did Willy really deserve to win?

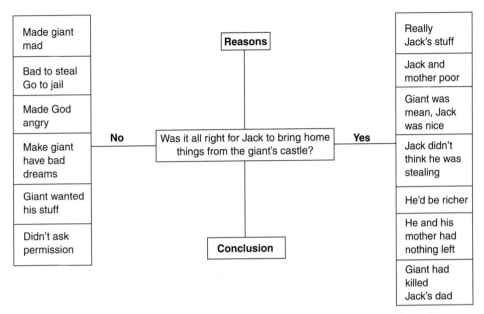

FIGURE 7.2 A discussion web for *Jack and the Beanstalk. Note.* Adapted from "The Discussion Web" by D. E. Alvermann, 1991, *The Reading Teacher, 45,* pp. 92–99.

Step 5: Have students work in teams of two. They should take turns writing approximately the same number of key words or phrases in both the yes and no columns.

Step 6: Before the partners have had enough time to fill up all the blanks, have two pairs form a new group of four and compare their reasons. Urge each group of four to work on staying open-minded and reaching a consensus rather than a victory.

Step 7: Choose a student from each group to explain the group's best idea to the entire class. Give the small groups about 3 minutes to decide on their best idea.

Step 8: Let the leaders compare their best ideas and also mention any dissenting ideas from their own small groups.

Step 9: Have the students each write a paragraph, explaining their individual opinions on the discussion web question.

Step 10: Post the individual paragraphs for all students to read.

The Advantages of Discussion Webs

The key advantage of discussion webs is good communication. You and your students should often work in small cooperative learning groups, which promote purposeful speaking, listening, writing, reading, and working together, fostered and supervised by you. There should be intense, natural, and highly interesting practice through critical and creative thinking. The rule needs to be total involvement by every member of the class, with these consequences:

1. There will be excellent motivation to understand what is read.

2. Children will be more likely to read for the purpose of understanding the author.

3. Discussions will no longer be dominated by a few people who do all the learning.

These kinds of discussions also give us teachers the opportunity to demonstrate that we must all respect one another's answers and questions during discussion. For example, if a student is always struggling to think of questions or answers or to read with confidence or to pronounce difficult words, we must help other students to respond with encouragement rather than ridicule.

This is particularly true of students who are learning a second language and are still trying to decipher and interpret a question while fluent readers are quickly forming an answer. We need to model ways for students to participate in making those less skilled feel good about whatever progress they have made—and at the same time discover that where they are is OK. Every student needs to feel that everyone progresses at a different rate.

Strategy: Help Students Learn the K-W-L Method Matching Through Self-Questioning

Lucky for us again, Donna Ogle (1986) developed a teaching approach that gets young readers even closer to independent reading comprehension. It also honors nonfiction as an important form of literature. The idea behind her method is this: To comprehend a topic that we are reading about, we must actively and continuously access what we already know about that topic. In Chapter 2, I referred to this as schema matching. Ogle's *K-W-L method* (i.e., know-want-learn) is a form of schema matching that teaches children to ask two specific questions before they read informational material: What do I know about this topic, and what do I want to find out? And it teaches children to ask two other questions right after reading: What did I actually learn, and what do I still need to learn?

Here are the three K-W-L steps:

Step K: Brainstorm with the total group ("What do I know or think I know?"), using the chalkboard, overhead, or PowerPoint projector—a highly creative procedure. Use a very specific topic—for example, "sea turtles" rather than "animals that live in the sea." If there is insufficient student response to "sea turtles," use something better known-like "turtles." Then categorize the responses you get—for example, apearance, food, caring for young, enemies. This will aid students' thinking as they read and will also give them more ideas to add to the brainstorming. A sample K-W-L chart is shown in Figure 7.3.

Topic: Sea turtles		
K *What I know . . .*	**W** *What I want to know . . .*	**L** *What I learned after reading . . .*
Live in water They can come on land Most are a green color (I think)	What do they eat? Are they warm-blooded? How old do they get? What are their enemies? What is their coloring?	

FIGURE 7.3   A K-W-L chart (prior to reading).

Step W: Brainstorm together what they want to learn. Then emphasize the gaps in their knowledge before they read—to provide real purpose for their reading. Also ask students to write down the question each most wants to have answered. Then have them read the selection aloud.

Step L: Students write down individually what they learned and then have the chance to discuss (either with the teacher or with at least one peer) whether their special question was answered.

After trying the K-W-L method with many teachers and children, Ogle (1986) concluded that there were *real improvements for students in the quality of their thinking,* their involvement in learning, and their enthusiasm for reading nonfiction. In fact, she says, it "goes from lukewarm to really keen" (p. 570).

Strategy: Encourage Students to Use a Variety of Individual Comprehension Techniques

The discussion web and the K-W-L technique give us a "little bit of bloomin' luck." Now we've created other comprehension strategies that can be used independently by students. Here are some ways of creative problem solving that readers can use individually to better understand authors and to remember important ideas.

- Trying fill-in-the-blank strategy discussed earlier in which a student says *blank* for a difficult word and completes the sentence before going back to the blank and using context clues to determine the word's meaning (see Figure 7.4).
- Asking questions of the author as the student reads—for example, Why did he do that? or What's the point? or How is this going to be solved?
- Paying attention to the framework of a story—the setting, the conflict, attempts to solve the conflict, the outcome—so that the reader's predictive power is improved.

All of these strategies can help readers comprehend better—*and stay alert.*

Strategy: Engage Students in Repeated Reading

Repeated reading is recommended highly by Ruth and Hallie Yopp (2003), who remind us that this strategy is appropriate for elementary, middle, and high-school students. Repeated reading is simple. A student working alone or preferably with a partner rereads a short, meaningful passage until reaching a high level of fluency—that is, smooth, ex-

FIGURE 7.4 The fill-in-the-blank strategy. *Note.* Adapted from "Amazing Underground City" by Edward Hymoff, August 1963, *Boy's Life.*

pressive language that sounds as though the author is doing the talking. When a student has been reasonably successful, it's time to move on to a new selection.

The partners can encourage each other, comment on the quality of the performance, or even time the reading. One way of making this activity more fun and more effective is to use the readers-theater method. Readers theater provides students with an opportunity to perform for peers after reading a selection several times. No props are needed, and usually the reading is a script rather than a book, but either way works fine. (There will be more details about this in Chapter 8.)

Researchers Martinez, Roser, and Strecker (1999) worked with two classes of second-grade students for 30 minutes a day, using the readers-theater method of reading. After 10 weeks the researchers found that the students had made a dramatic gain in their reading rates. Their motivation tended to be high, especially since most students supported each other. In other words, this method can bring about both better reading and better self-confidence.

Strategy: Consider the Directed Reading-Thinking Activity

We're now going to watch a teacher using a venerable discussion method labeled by Stauffer (1975) as the *directed reading-thinking activity (DRTA)*. The teacher will then turn this approach into a comprehension strategy for the children to use on their own. With this method children are first asked to predict what each page or two might be about. According to Cleveland, Connors, Conors, Dauphin, Hashey, and Wolf (2001) this reinforces the value of picture and word clues, allows students of varying skill levels to participate, provides a reason for reading, and promotes equity in discussions. Students are then directed to read silently to check their predictions and are finally asked to prove their interpretations of what the author said. Using a variety of questioning techniques, the teacher asks her students these three questions:

What do you think?
Why do you think so?
Can you prove it?

Now here is the passage to be read, followed by a model of the DRTA method:

Magic Doors

Johnny's mother asked him to go to the big new store at the corner. His little brother Howie said, "I want to go, too! I want to go, too! I'll be good."

So Johnny took his little brother to the big new store.

There were two big doors. One door had the word *IN* on it. The other door had the word *OUT*. Johnny and Howie went to the IN door. Whish! The door opened all by itself. Howie said, "Look at that. It's magic!"

"You are silly!" said Johnny. "It isn't magic. The new doors work by electricity."

Mrs. S:	[Before the children read] Look at the title of this story please, and tell us what you think the story is going to be about.
Janie:	Maybe about some doors that open by magic when you say "Open Sesame," and inside the doors you find gold and jewelry and things like that.
Mrs. S:	That's an interesting idea, Janie. What makes you say that?
Janie:	Well . . . I remember this story my daddy read to me once, and that's what happened.
Mrs. S:	All right. Who has another idea?
Sergio:	I think it's going to be about some doors in a closet that lead into another land with witches and elves and things.
Mrs. S:	OK, that sounds possible. Why do you think your idea is right?
Sergio:	Umm, I heard a story like that once.
Mrs. S:	I'll bet you did. There's a story like that called *The Lion, the Witch, and the Wardrobe.*
Sergio:	[Excitedly] That's the one!
Mrs. S:	Let's turn the page and look at the picture on the next page. Maybe that will give you another idea of what this story is going to be about.
David:	Oooh, I know.
Mrs. S:	David?
David:	It's a picture of a supermarket. I'll bet the magic doors are, you know, those doors that open all by themselves.
Mrs. S:	Does anyone see anything else in the picture that makes you think that David is right?
Sandra:	There's a lady walking through one of the doors, and she's not pushing on it or anything.
Mrs. S:	Yes, you did some careful looking, Sandra.
Roland:	Maybe she already pushed the door and it's just staying open for a while.
Mrs. S:	That's quite possible, Roland. Well, why don't you all read the first two pages to yourselves and see if you can find out why the author called the story "Magic Doors."
Mrs. S:	[Two minutes later] Were you right, Janie? Are they going to find gold and jewelry behind those magic doors?
Janie:	[Shaking her head] No, but they'll find ice cream.
Mrs. S:	[Laughing] How do you know?
Janie:	Because those doors go inside a supermarket, and that's where we buy our ice cream.
Mrs. S:	You can tell it's going to be a supermarket by the picture. Is that how you knew?

Janie:	Yes.
Mrs. S:	Can you find something the author tells you that makes you sure?
Janie:	[Looking] Oh, here it is. It says, "One door had the word *IN* on it. The other door had the word *OUT.*"
Mrs. S:	Good. Can you find another clue from the author, Sergio?
Sergio:	[Long hesitation] . . .
Mrs. S:	What about the first sentence? Why don't you read it to us.
Sergio:	[Reading] "Johnny. . . his mother asked him to go to the big new store at the corner."
Mrs. S:	Does that sentence give you an idea of where Johnny will be going?
Sergio:	[Smiling] To the grocery store.
Mrs. S:	Why do you say that?
Sergio:	Because that's where my mother always wants me to go.
Mrs. S:	Good. You used your own experience to help you think about this, didn't you?
Sergio:	Yeah!
Mrs. S:	Let's see . . . David? Why don't you tell us what the magic doors were.
David:	[Proudly] Just what I said. They're doors that open by themselves.
Mrs. S:	You were right, David. But what really makes the doors open? Is it magic, Roland?
Roland:	No. It's an electric motor or something.
Mrs. S:	Can you find a sentence that proves it?
Roland:	The last sentence says, "The new doors work by electricity."
Mrs. S:	But how in the world did you read that big word?
Roland:	[Smiling] I thought it was *energy* the first time. But then I saw it was *electricity.*
Mrs. S:	How did you know it wasn't something like *electronically?*
Roland:	[Says nothing and smiles].
Mrs. S:	Suppose I read the last sentence this way: "The new doors work by electronically."
Roland:	[Laughs] That sounds funny!
Mrs. S:	You're right, it does. But how did you know it was *electricity* and not *energy?*
Roland:	[Shrugs] I don't know.
Janie:	I know. Because you can see the word *city* at the end of it.
Mrs. S:	Janie, what else can you see that makes you sure it's *electricity* and not *energy?*
Janie:	[Studies the page but makes no response].

Mrs. S:	What two letters does electricity start with?
Janie:	It starts with *e–l.*
Mrs. S:	And what would *energy* start with?
Janie:	With *e–n.*
Mrs. S:	Yes, that's right. So, David, do you agree with Johnny in the story? Was it electricity that made the doors open?
David:	[Smiling] Sure. It's electricity. It's not magic.
Mrs. S:	[Nods and smiles] Now, before you read the next two pages, I would like you to do the Prove-It Exercise with your partner. Who can tell me how to do that? Janie?
Janie:	First whisper to your partner what you think is going to happen next. And then . . . oh, and why you think so. And then read the next, uh, two pages. And after you're both finished reading, you tell each other what really happened—and you prove it!
Mrs. S:	That's fine. Work with your partner, and I'll stop you in about 2 minutes.

Several studies have shown that the DRTA method results in higher levels of comprehension than methods that simply test the children's memory at the end of their reading (Stauffer, 1975). One probable reason for this success is that the DRTA method recognizes that each student differs in ability and development. "Children differ not only in motivation, attitude, and purpose but in the ability to grasp, assimilate, retain, and use information as well" (p. 3).

Because of these differences, you should definitely *not* expect all students to give the same answers to the same questions. Teachers who use the DRTA discussion method properly *don't even ask the same question of each student.* Their interaction with their students is dynamic, rather than static. They may have the students use the prove-it strategy by themselves, but not every time they read on their own—just often.

Students may also be given a prompt to help with this strategy—something like the one shown in Figure 7.5. A prompt sheet can be used for discussion after the story has been read; as a point of comparison with a partner or small cooperative group; for a comparison of viewpoints for a bulletin board; or as a reading record for portfolios or other writings.

Other forms of DRTA include Pearson's (1985) and Nessel's (1987) versions, but all three forms emphasize the same basic features: (1) *the importance of predictions before reading,* (2) *the use of personal schemas or text information* to justify predictions or statements, and (3) *the importance of having children get actively* involved by proving their predictions. It's no wonder this type of strategy leads to greater involvement and comprehension (Nessel, 1987). Predict, justify, prove—that's DRTA. I recommend this process heartily. It gives children the feeling of power that they need and a simple but effective tool for comprehending what they're reading. DRTA teaches kids to look for answers in depth.

Name _____

Pages to _____

BEFORE YOU READ: What do you think this will be about?

Why?

AFTER YOU READ: Prove you were right or wrong.

Pages to _____

BEFORE YOU READ: What do you think will come next?

Why?

AFTER YOU READ: Prove you were right or wrong.

FIGURE 7.5   A prove-it prompt.

Strategy: Help Students Use Story Grammar as a Comprehension Strategy

We all carry around a set of concepts, or schemas, that help us know what to expect as we read certain types of writing: stories, informational text, persuasive writing, and so on. Once we know that a text is going to be a story, our brains shift to the schema for stories, which tells us that we should expect such things as characters, a setting, and a plot with a series of conflicts and resolutions. These elements, called *story grammar*, refer to the system or rules governing the construction of a story. As we read a story, we expect to see those elements. Our expectation, if fulfilled, helps us comprehend the story.

An author normally follows an intuitive story grammar—the set of rules that the text must include to comprise a cogent story. For example, there is always a *main character* and usually other support characters—e.g., Goldilocks and the three bears.

There must be a *setting*—the forest. And there is an *initiating event or conflict* that gets the story going—the three bears go for a walk and leave their house unguarded.

There is also a *response* by the main character, who is attempting to resolve the conflict—she sneaks into the bears' house. The response may lead to further problems or a new conflict—she makes the bears very upset. But there is a *resolution* to the conflict—Goldilocks manages to escape rather than being thrown in jail for trespassing.

Sometimes there's a *theme* or even a moral to the story—bears are only human after all or . . . look what happens when you leave your front door unlocked or . . . bears are very fussy about who sleeps in their beds.

A Direct or Indirect Approach

Two approaches to story grammar can enhance your students' ability to write and read stories with better comprehension. One indirect approach is advocated by Muriel Rand (1983), and that is "having many experiences with well-formed stories" (p. 331). In other words, children will develop an intuitive framework for writing and reading stories if they have many stories read to them and are given many to read.

But what about the kids who do not respond very well to indirect learning? Remember that in a balanced literacy program teachers include both direct and indirect methods. As Adelise Harris, a gifted reading teacher, once said to me, "We want to marinate children in essential reading knowledge so that it becomes part of them." One way to provide kids with direct support in learning story grammar is suggested by Reggie Routman (1988) and Berk and Winsler (1995). It's called a *story map*. Like the K-W-L chart discussed earlier, a story map is a learning aid we introduce with a great deal of teacher modeling and guided practice. The student completes the story map after reading and uses it as a discussion tool with a peer. The story map can also be quite useful as an assessment tool to gauge student learning. An example of a story map is provided in Figure 7.6.

Story Map

Name _____ Date _____

Story _____

Where does this story take place? (SETTING)

Who are the characters in the story? (CHARACTERS)
◆ Main character-

◆ Other characters-

What happened first in the story? Was there a problem the main character had to solve? (INITIATING EVENT or PROBLEM)

What did the character or characters do to try and solve the problem? (RESPONSE)

How did the story end? (RESOLUTION)

What do you think was the author's message? (THEME)

FIGURE 7.6 A story map.

A Framework for Discussion Questions

Another approach is to use story grammar as a structure for *shaping the questions* you ask children before, during, and after a story they read. Based on my own experiences and on suggestions by Sadow (1982) and Marshall (1984), I'd recommend using the following types of questions during a guided reading and discussion of a story. These questions should not necessarily be used in this order, nor do they all need to be used. They are simply suggested ideas to weave into a discussion to help children think more about a story.

Setting: Where do you think this is taking place? When? If it happened in another place, would it make a difference? What about another time?

Character: What kind of person is the main character? What makes you think so? What feelings do you think the character was having that prompted him or her to act that way in this situation?

Conflict: What problem does the character face now? What might have caused this problem to occur? How do you think the character will solve it?

Response: What did the character do about the problem first? What do you think he or she will do next? Why did the first attempt fail?

Resolution: How was the problem finally solved? How did the character feel about the way it was solved? What are some other ways it might have been solved? What do you think the character will do now that the problem has been solved?

Questions like these can provide a framework not only to help students understand a particular story, but also to guide their writing and reading of other stories. By emphasizing story grammar in *both* reading and writing, you will be able to improve your students' reading comprehension and make their writing of stories a more successful experience.

Strategy: Try Reciprocal Teaching

Should the teacher always be the one asking questions? Absolutely not! A primary comprehension goal is to get students to eventually ask themselves questions as they read. The teacher's role, at first, is to stimulate thinking by asking questions. But that role shifts gradually to show children how they can understand a writer better by asking questions of themselves. This technique is similar to Clark's and Grave's (2005) "verbal scaffolding".

An Important Study

Nolte and Singer (1985) conducted an unusual study of the effects of story-grammar instruction on children's comprehension. Ruth Nolte, a teacher of fourth- and fifth-grade students at the time of the study, planned her approach with Harry Singer, an educational researcher. One of their research goals was to see whether training children to ask their own story-grammar questions would result in comprehension superior to that of a control group that did not receive this training. The other goal was to see whether this training would transfer to new reading material. They called this procedure *reciprocal teaching* (Lubliner, 2000).

On the first day Nolte explained story grammar to the whole class and gave them a pep talk on the importance of asking themselves good questions when they read. Then she guided their silent reading of the first half of a story by explicitly modeling story-grammar questions after every paragraph or two. During the last half of the 40-minute period students finished the story, asking their own story-grammar questions as they read. Then the students took a 15-item, multiple-choice comprehension test.

On each of the next 3 days, Nolte guided the whole class through a new story, asking students questions that gave *them* practice in phrasing story-grammar questions. For example she might have asked, "What would you like to know about what happens next?" And a student's response might have been, "How does she solve this new problem?" Students were encouraged to ask only those questions that were central to the story. Then at the end of each session, the students took a comprehension test.

For the following 3 days, the students worked in cooperative learning settings— groups of five or six with one student obtaining story-grammar questions from the others in the group. Then for the next 2 days, the students worked in pairs, and for the final 2 days of the study, they read by themselves, asking themselves the questions.

For the control group the teacher wrote difficult words on the board each day and pronounced them; then she asked a question about the story. The children read the story on their own and took a written comprehension test on it.

On the final day of the study, both control and experimental groups were given a brand new story, with 30 minutes to read it and take a test. The average score for the experimental group was 12.3; the average score for the control group was 9.9. (It was estimated that a difference this great would occur by chance only once in 100 times.) Thus, not only did they learn to ask their own questions, but their comprehension also increased considerably.

Other Ways to Use Reciprocal Teaching

Here are some variations on reciprocal teaching for you to try out in your classroom.

Peer-Led Discussions

Having students take charge of asking the questions about a story or soliciting questions from others is one type of reciprocal teaching that can encourage students to ask themselves questions as they read. Peer-led discussions (after initial guidance by the teacher) can be a very powerful learning mode. Janice Almasi (1995) was given an award for the best doctoral dissertation of 1994; her findings suggest that peer-led discussions can produce richer and more complex interactions than teacher-led discussions. Also, students in peer-led groups can experience greater retention of the thinking processes engaged in during the discussions.

Self-Questioning with Nonfiction

Teaching children how to ask story-grammar questions works only with stories, of course. But what about informational text? Can't they ask their own questions there, too? Hahn (1985) found that fifth- and sixth-grade remedial students could be taught to ask themselves questions while reading textbooks and other expository text. Their success was probably due to the fact that they had borrowed the role of reciprocal teaching expert from the teacher (Hashey & Conners, 2003). The students were also reminding their peers to get completely involved. And after the teacher modeled question-asking several times, the students gradually learned to *write* their own questions and ask peers for answers. They also learned that there are three places to find answers: (1) the author's words, (2) between the lines (i.e., inferences), and (3) their own experiences.

Combining Reciprocal Teaching with Drama

Shoop (1986) cites several studies demonstrating that comprehension improves when students ask each other questions. She describes an activity done in an elementary classroom when the teacher is reading a story aloud. At an important point in the story, the teacher interrupts the oral reading and assigns some children to be reporters and others to be characters from the story. For the reporters the teacher models how to ask good questions, ones that lead the character actors to interpret rather than just tell the major events. For the characters she models how to stay in character and think on their feet. More details of this interesting technique are available in the Shoop reference at the end of the chapter.

Four-Part Reciprocal Teaching

Annemarie Palincsar and her colleagues (Palinscar 1987; Palincsar, David, Winn, & Stevens, 1991; Palincsar, Ransom, & Derber, 1989) have developed a four-part form of reciprocal teaching that seems to work well even with children in first grade, although it is also quite suitable for the upper grades. In their version of reciprocal teaching, teachers and students take turns leading a dialogue about the meaning of the text with which they are working. The discussion focuses on four activities: *generating questions* from the text before and after reading, *summarizing* the text, *clarifying* portions that impair understanding, and *predicting* upcoming content.

When the dialogues begin, the teacher assumes principal responsibility for leading and sustaining the discussion, modeling skilled use of the comprehension strategies. Even from the first day of instruction, however, the students are encouraged to participate in the discussion by generating their own questions, elaborating on or revising the summary, or suggesting additional predictions (Palincsar et al., 1991, p. 46).

Some Evaluative Comments

How do the creators and users of reciprocol teaching feel about it? Babigian (2002) is impressed with this back-and-forth process that integrates the four substrategies of predicting, generating questions, clarifying, and summarizing: "For the teacher, reciprocal teaching is a lot like stepping out of his or her skin and showing students what a good reader thinks and does" (p. 232).

Buehl (2001) has a different form of praise for reciprocal teaching: "[It] provides a window into the thinking of proficient readers as they problem-solve their way toward meaning. Students are conditioned to approach reading as an active and strategic process and to learn behaviors that will help them become more independent readers, capable of handling increasingly sophisticated material" (p. 225).

Hashey and Connors (2003) found that one of the outcomes of their reciprocal-teaching program was richer discussion in both literature circles and Socratic seminars:

> Prior to reciprocal teaching, we had varying success with these activities. Because we had relinquished the role of "reciprocal teaching expert" from the teacher to the students, they were able to remind one another to implement strategies and to ask for full participation from every group member. (p. 232)

Rosenshine, Meister, and Chapman (1996) conducted an intensive review on the importance of students asking each other questions, as done with reciprocal teaching.

1. The studies of reciprocal-teaching programs show that children spent three-fourths of the time in the questioning mode.

2. The other three strategies of clarifying, summarizing, and predicting added very little to what the children learned.

3. Self-generated questioning was very successful.

4. Mutual question-asking was considered by the National Reading Panel (National Institute of Child Health and Human Development, 2000) to be a powerful strategy.

Strategy: Teach Inferential Thinking and Reading

Professional Standard: Ensures that students can use various aspects of text to gain comprehension

A major concern of literacy teachers is how to help students infer what the author has left out. Authors do leave out a lot of words, but don't get me wrong—to make reading more interesting to you, we leave out many things that would bore you. Who wants to read every thought the main character has? Who wants to read what toothpaste he's using? The point is that the good reader reads between the lines, using stored schemas.

This brings us to the fascinating problem of teaching children important ways of thinking: inferential thinking, creative thinking, and critical thinking.

Every decade or so there's a new rush toward teaching critical thinking and other higher-level abilities. As Bracey (1987) puts it, critical thinking becomes a "hot topic." What I would like to show you is that higher-order thinking can be taught in the context of a balanced literacy program that emphasizes comprehension. This context satisfies many of the goals for a critical-thinking curriculum advocated by experts such as Ennis (1985) and Hudgins and Edelman (1986). In my opinion, critical thinking shouldn't be a fad; it should be part of every curriculum every year.

A Demonstration Teaching Episode on Thinking

The best way of understanding those various types of thinking is to watch a teacher use all of them and pass them on to the students. Watch as a teacher enriches the discussion of a reading selection by bringing up points that encourage inferential, critical, and creative thinking rather than just literal thinking. The teacher's questions often urge the students to go beyond the literal—what color did the author say the bus was? You can tell that the teacher is responding to the students and to the actual text.

For your convenience in analyzing this teacher's high level of skill let me first describe four types of questions that literacy teachers often use in developing children's thinking:

- *Literal*—questions calling for answers that reflect sheer memory of what the author said
- *Inferential*—questions calling for answers that reflect the use of personal schemas to read between the lines
- *Evaluative*—questions calling for careful analysis and judgments that require the use of criteria
- *Creative*—Questions calling for new-to-you, inventive uses, interpretations, improvements, or solutions

If you watch this teacher like a child watching a new puppy, you'll learn how to teach those thinking processes with ease.

This particular teacher is working with a small group of fourth graders who are going to read an article about a snowstorm that hit New York City. Watch how the teacher provides practice in all four types of questions. You'll want to read the first page of the article so you can see how the teacher prepares the students for it, guides them through it, and encourages thinking and comprehension along the way rather than merely testing later for memory.

The Beginning of New York's Underground City

In 1888 a terrible snowstorm hit New York City. Tall poles snapped, and electric wires fell into the street. People were killed by electric shock. Some were killed by the falling poles. And nearly a thousand died in the fires that broke out.

The mayor saw that he must do something to make his city a safe place to live. He asked electricians to put electric wires safely underground. Then the mayor sent men out to take down the wooden poles.

These electric wires were the beginning of America's amazing underground city in New York. Today the narrow streets and the sidewalks hide more than 4 million miles of wire. In some places there are so many wires and pipes that two fingers cannot be pushed between them.

Teacher: [Before the students read] Do you know what kinds of things you can find underneath the streets here in New York City? [Fosters literal thinking—memory of details—and inferential thinking based on personal schemas]

Juana: Oh, I know. Subways!

Teacher: That's true. Can anyone think of something else you might find underneath the streets? [Urges more literal and inferential thought, as well as creative thoughts]

Donald: There are all kinds of pipes under the streets. I know, because my dad told me. And they're full of water.

Janet: [Sheepishly] Somebody told me there are monsters under there.

Teacher: Well, I hope that's not true, but I'm sure there are people who think there are. [Encourages courageous and creative thinking] What do you think, Ramon? Do you think there are monsters down there? [Encourages critical judgment]

Ramon: I don't think so.

Teacher: Why not? [Fosters critical thinking by requiring the selection of criteria for judgment]

Ramon: Well, I don't know anyone who has ever *seen* monsters down there.

Ken: And there's probably no place for them to live down there.

Teacher: OK, what you and Ramon are saying is that monsters could be down there only if people have seen them and if there's enough space for them to live. Can anyone think of anything else you'd have to have before you would believe that there are monsters down there? [Helping them build criteria for making critical judgments]

Bill: [After several ideas are offered and discussed] Besides, aren't there wires and things like that down there anyway?

Teacher: Yes, that's true. I just read in here [touches a closed teacher's guide] that there are over 4 million miles of wire under our streets. Make a quick guess: How many times do you think that much wire would go around the world? [Urges creative imagery]

Teacher: [After several different guesses] In math today would you like us to figure that out together?

Students: Yes!

Teacher: All right, but for right now can you predict why that wire is down there? [Urging inferential thinking based on personal schemas]

Ken: For sending messages?

Bill: Maybe for telephones.

Teacher: What do you think it might be for, Janet?

Janet: Electricity?

Juana: Uh-huh, electricity.

Teacher: Well, I'll tell you what. I'd like you to find out why some of that wire was put down there in the first place. Read the first page of this article to yourself and then let's stop and talk about it.

Teacher: [A few moments later] Well, now you know why they first put the wire under the streets. What do you think it looks like under the streets? Can you get a picture in your mind? [Fosters creative imagery]

Bill: I think it looks like spaghetti.

Teacher: [Joining in the laughter] You may be right, Bill. What do you think it looks like, Barbara?

Juana: I don't know, but I know it doesn't look like spaghetti.

Teacher: Who can find a sentence on this page that tells what it looks like? [Requires proof for their literal and critical thinking]

Ken: Oh, I know. It's the last sentence. It says, "In some places there are so many wires and pipes that two fingers cannot be pushed between them."

Teacher: Yes—maybe that's why Bill said it must look like spaghetti down there.

Bill: Yeah, like a whole bunch of spaghetti all squished together.

Teacher:	Would it be like uncooked spaghetti that comes out of the box all straight, or would it be like cooked spaghetti that's all piled up on your plate? [Asks for inferential thinking based on personal schemas]
Janet:	Oh, I know. It would be like uncooked spaghetti when it comes out of the box.
Teacher:	[Nodding] Why do you think so, Janet?
Janet:	Because that's what they do with wires and pipes.
Teacher:	They lay them out straight?
Janet:	Yes.
Teacher:	Have you seen people do it that way? [Suggests another criterion for critical judgment; fosters use of personal schemas]
Janet:	Yes, that's the way they do it. They don't bunch it all up like cooked spaghetti.
Teacher:	[Laughing] I'm sure you're right, but has anyone actually watched people put in wires and pipes anywhere?
Bill:	Yeah, I have. My uncle does that kind of thing for his job. He puts wires in buildings.
Teacher:	He's an electrician? [Helps them develop the critical-thinking criterion of expert opinion]
Bill:	Yeah.
Teacher:	All right. Now let me ask all of you something else. Did they take down the wooden poles before or after they put the wires under the street? [Encourages literal memory for sequence]
Ken:	They took 'em down first, and then they put the wires under the street.
Teacher:	Well, Ken, let's pretend you were the mayor of New York at that time. If you had told them to take down the poles and then put the wires under the street, wouldn't you have made people angry with you? [Requires an integrated use of inferential, critical, and creative thinking]
Ken:	[Laughing] Oh, yeah. They wouldn't have had any electricity if I'd had 'em take down the poles first.
Teacher:	[Smiling] So what do you think would be the smart thing to do, as mayor of New York? [Requires critical judgment]
Ken:	I'd put the wires under the streets, and then when they're all fixed up and the lights and everything work, then I'd do it.
Teacher:	Do what?
Ken:	Have 'em take down the poles.
Teacher:	Does that make sense to everyone else? [Offers opportunity for others to use critical judgment]
Teacher:	[Seeing all pleased with Ken's plan] Well, I was wondering what they used all those poles for. Do you have any idea, Donald? [Encourages creative thinking in applying prior knowledge to a new situation]

Donald: I don't know. Maybe they built log cabins with them.

Teacher: [Looking at others] That would work, wouldn't it? Any other ideas?

Juana: They could use them for firewood!

Teacher: What do you think of that idea, Ken? [Asking for critical judgment]

Ken: That would work, too . . . because they could cut them up and sell them to people. You know, make money for the city.

Teacher: [Nodding to Ken] Well, we have only a minute or two left. Why don't we see how many ideas for using those poles we can think of in that time. Can we come up with 10 ideas? [Lets them practice creative thinking with an emphasis on rapid production of new ideas]

Strategy: Help Students Search for the Main Idea

For many years a goal in our schools has been to emphasize something we call main ideas. And yet teachers who wish to teach main ideas don't always agree on what they are. According to research (Cunningham & Moore, 1986; Duffelmeyer & Duffelmeyer, 1987), many teachers and other educators think that main ideas are nothing more than topics. For example, if a selection is about *how bears live in the woods,* then the main idea is how bears live in the woods. Cunningham and Moore found that teaching manuals and teachers have at least nine notions of what a main idea is: theme, title, gist, interpretation, key word, selective summary, topic, topic issue, and topic sentence.

Is the main idea of a passage something that all readers must agree on, as most teachers have said in the past? With the continued movement toward literature and writing as the foundations of literacy programs, things seem to be changing for the better, and many teachers no longer seek just one right interpretation of a main idea. Instead, they analyze responses carefully, ask students to clarify as necessary, and then *coach them* into higher levels of understanding.

You might want to begin by asking your students to share the main ideas they each got from the reading selection. Show enthusiasm for the variety of perceptions that your students have. This will not only bring them closer to the truth about how human beings differ, but will also get them much more involved in literature discussions and discussions about peer writings. If they seem to be a little off the mark in their interpretation of the text, try to draw them to other understandings through questioning rather than telling.

In analyzing the needs of struggling upper-grade elementary readers, Lubliner (2000) concluded that questioning was the most powerful, practical strategy to provide them with the help they needed. Specifically, Lubliner (2004) discovered that *teaching children to create their own main-idea questions essentially forced them to comprehend as they were reading.* And that, in turn, caused them to become good readers. Thus, a short-term teaching intervention that requires self-created main-idea questions may be called for. It makes sense to me: What we're after is finding ways for our students to really focus on what they're reading.

By letting your students read with their own purposes in mind, they will unfalteringly find main ideas. And by encouraging them to discuss both fiction and nonfiction, they will learn from other students that we all get something different from what we read.

Student *writings* are another avenue for learning to appreciate big ideas, important ideas, deep ideas—or as I used to say when I was 8, "Oh, I've got the greatest idea in the whole world!" Give your neophytes the chance to write big important ideas whenever they write. As others appreciate the main ideas they're producing, these students are more likely to recognize what other writers perceive to be *their* main ideas.

Strategy: Teach Comprehension Monitoring

Professional Standard: Teaches students strategies to organize and remember information

Good reading, like good dancing or good sailing, is something that happens only if you're really into it and practice. There's not only a connection between the writer and you, there's a connection to your own being, your own feelings, and your own thoughts. There's a keen awareness of your own skill and an ability to monitor that skill so that you get more meaning and delight out of the experience. Comprehension monitoring is *metacognitive*, the process of monitoring your own understanding, making sure that you are communicating with the author while you're reading. These monitoring activities need to be modeled out loud by the teacher in front of the students:

- Making sure you know what your purposes are for reading a particular text

    Comprehension-monitoring questions to model for students:
        What's my goal in reading this?
        Am I really reading this with my goal in mind?
- Modifying your reading rate and strategies to match your purpose

    Comprehension-monitoring questions to model for students:
        Should I be scanning this for certain details rather than reading the whole thing?
        Should I just skim this quickly to get the general idea, or should I make sure I understand every detail?
        Should I follow the plot quickly, or should I slow down enough to understand the characters?
- Paying attention to the sequence of events, steps, or logic

    Comprehension-monitoring questions to model for students:
        What step (or event) comes next?
        Why does this step (or event) follow the last one?
        Does this point really follow from the last one? (Or is this author selling me a used car?)
        Can I picture the steps (or events) the author wants me to follow?

Variations in Students' Metacognitive Abilities

The ability to monitor reading comprehension develops slowly with some students. Children in Grades K through 2 often can't explain why they're having trouble understanding something. By the time they reach third or fourth grade, though, skilled readers can begin to verbalize the problem: "I don't know what that word means" or "I've never heard about this stuff before" or "I don't know how to pronounce that word" (Baker & Brown, 1984). Less skilled readers, however, even in the intermediate grades, need considerable help in developing their metacognitive awareness.

Research suggests that the metacognitive process of comprehension monitoring can be taught, even to low-skilled readers (Baker & Brown, 1984). I'd like to show you an example of comprehension monitoring based on a study by Jane Hansen (1984). Note how the teacher in this example tries to make these fourth-grade low-skilled readers conscious of the need to use their own past experiences to understand what the author is describing. Studies consistently demonstrate that many children don't even realize they're *supposed* to engage in this most basic form of thinking (Baker & Brown, 1984).

Teacher:	For many weeks now we've been doing something special before you read each new story. Do you remember what it is?
Sally:	Talking.
Teacher:	Yes. What special kind of talking?
Johnny:	Comparing.
Teacher:	Yes, that's the word we've been using.
Phyllis:	Comparing what's happened in our lives to what will happen in the story.
Teacher:	You're absolutely right. And why have we been doing this?
Jay:	So we'd . . . so we'd get an idea of what the story's going to be about.
Sally:	To help us understand the story better.
Teacher:	Uh-huh.
Phyllis:	So we'd remember it better.
Teacher:	Those are all good reasons. Now, last time we met I had you imagine the kind of comparing you would do if you were going to read about some children flying kites. Remember?
Children:	Yes.
Teacher:	Well, today let's imagine that you're going to read in your social studies book about some schools in Japan.
Phyllis:	Awesome!
Teacher:	[Smiling] OK, what might you think about *before* you read and as you're reading? What comparisons would you make?
Johnny:	I'd think about our class.
Jay:	I'd think about this school, and about my old school, too.
Phyllis:	We could see if their school is like ours.
Johnny:	It'd be different, I'll bet.

Not bad for struggling 9 and 10 year old kids! Let's look at others.

Focus on Students with Special Needs: Comments by Louise Fulton

Comprehension Strategies for Students with Learning Difficulties

Children with learning difficulties, as you probably know, often experience a greater struggle with fluency and comprehension than general students do. Not only may they not have the background experiences of the author, they may also have physical and emotional problems that distract them from concentrating on an author's message or description. Let me tell you what recent research studies have shown about the specific problems of children with learning difficulties and the teacher interventions that can help them reduce those problems.

An exhaustive study by Vaughn, Gersten, and Chard (2000) demonstrates that in spite of the problems facing students with learning disabilities, there are several procedures you can use to help them learn to concentrate on their reading and determine the message of the author. The study also shows that your special efforts to help students with learning disabilities will cause equal or greater results with the other students in your class.

1. Work with individuals with learning disabilities in small, interactive groups—the smaller the better with young children. Working with only one student works well, too, but often not as well as with one or two peers.

2. Control the task difficulty. To help these students understand what they read, for example, keep the reading samples small and very easy at first. Then gradually and humanely increase the difficulty of the samples. No matter what their age is, don't assume that these students have already mastered a reading level equal to their grade level. And by all means, *build their self-confidence with plenty of simple reading before increasing the difficulty level.*

3. Teach students to create questions as they read. For example, What is this about? What do I already know about this subject, object, or person?

4. Whatever procedure you use, be sure to have students think and question aloud as they read. This will allow you to model how to answer their questions by thinking aloud about the same passage. Don't assume that individuals with learning disabilities (or any students for that matter) will automatically be able to use a new procedure successfully with new reading material. Automatic transfer of the procedure may be months away.

5. Teach them the strategies discussed in this book, such as fill-in-the-blank, predicting ahead, checking false guesses, tell what you've learned, and check with your peer.

6. Provide specific and frequent feedback (more than "Good job").

7. Have your students work with a partner, taking turns as tutor and tutee. Watch their spirits rise with this responsibility.

When students with disabilities act as a tutor for a partner, cross-age or same-age, you'll most likely find that the role of tutor creates greater improvements than would be found in a whole-class situation where they simply served as tutee. And by the way, age is not a factor, nor are these ideas limited to students with learning disabilities.

Summary of Main Ideas

■ Modeling comprehension monitoring can be a major factor in helping children become better readers.

■ The time before and after reading may be as important as the actual reading experience.

■ Developing appropriate schemas for students before they are asked to read allows them to increase their skill in both reading and thinking.

■ DRTA, story grammar, and other teaching methods must be transformed into comprehension strategies for children to use independently.

■ Scaffolding is a necessary procedure for helping children learn comprehension strategies.

■ Reciprocal teaching is one way of using the scaffolding technique.

■ Critical and creative thinking and other types of higher-order thinking can be encouraged through reading experiences.

■ Students can be helped to recognize main ideas through skillful coaching by the teacher and by constructing their own important or exciting ideas in their writing.

Literacy Through Technology

A. Examine some of the many online lesson plans at one of these sites:

http://www.atozteacherstuff.com
http://www.folger.edu/
http://www.pbs.org/teachersource/arts_lit.htm

Identify some innovative ways other teachers have taught vocabulary in some of these lesson plans.

How would you use these lesson plans, units, or thematic units to teach vocabulary and achieve a high level of comprehension?

B. Check out the American Dreams educational Web site http://www.bay-breeze.com/americandreams/ Look for interdisciplinary materials focusing on diversity. How can you use some of these materials to strengthen the vocabulary of students in grades 4 and above?

C. For another thought-enhancing experience go to Starfall at http://www.starfall.com/ to examine interactive books and rhyming games that teach phonemic awareness and vocabulary. How do you see yourself using Web sites such as this in your classroom?

Application Experiences for Your Course

A. *Literacy Teacher Vocabulary: List of Terms:* In a small group quiz and question each other on the meaning and use of each word listed here. After 10 minutes certify that every member has a thorough understanding of each of these concepts by writing and signing a statement to that effect.

comprehension strategies	DRTA	metacognition	story maps
story grammar	repeated reading	modeled reading	
higher-order thinking	reciprocal teaching	main ideas	

B. *Analysis of DRTA:* With a small group, examine the teaching/learning episode that demonstrates first the DRTA teaching method and then the procedures for changing DRTA into a comprehension strategy. Go through it line by line, dividing up the lines, and decide what the teacher's purpose is. In this way you'll learn in each exchange how to use the method yourself. Discuss the procedure in your small group, decide why you would or would not use this strategy, and then report the findings of your group to the entire class.

C. *Development of a Story-Grammar-Map Lesson Plan:* Choose a chapter book at about the fourth- or fifth-grade level—or one of the books in the Harry Potter series. Develop a lesson plan in which you introduce and model the story map concept as a scaffolding tool. Present this lesson to a group of several peers, and ask them to discuss the strengths and needs of your plan.

D. *Development of Higher-Order Thinking:* With a small group examine the demonstration lesson on thinking. Go through it line by line and decide what the teacher's changing purposes are. How successful do you think the teacher is in creating an environment for higher-level thinking? Then see if you can convert this teaching method into a personal comprehension strategy. You'll need to think first about the other comprehension strategies you've already seen and read about in other chapters. What do they have in common? What information or skills will your students have to gain in order to use a comprehension strategy related to higher-level thinking?

Creativity Training Session

A. *Creative Teaching:* With partners, create an innovative new strategy for children to use when reading difficult passages or words. Give your new strategy a catchy name. Try it out on each other before demonstrating it to the class.

B. *Creative Problem Solving:* In small groups, develop a list of at least five creative problem-solving topics around which you might develop lessons. Select two of these topics and discuss several teaching-learning activities that would actively involve every student in a very diverse classroom.

Field Experiences

A. *DRTA Method and Prove-It Strategy:* Use the DRTA method with three or more children. After using this method two or three times with the same students, see if you can help them learn the prove-it strategy that derives from the DRTA method.

B. *Story-Grammar and Reciprocal-Teaching Methods:* Use the story-grammar method to discuss a story with three or more children. After using this method two or three times with the same kids, see if you can help them learn the reciprocal-teaching procedure so they can gain an independent comprehension strategy. Try using the stages that Nolte and Singer used.

C. *Awareness of Main Ideas:* Using what you've learned in this chapter, help a group of children learn to write text that contains main ideas. Have them use what they've learned to discuss important or exciting ideas that they discover in other texts. Discuss the students' differing perceptions of what is important.

References

Almasi, J. (1995). The nature of fourth graders' sociocognitive conflicts in peer-led and teacher-led discussions of literature. *Reading Research Quarterly, 30,* 314–351.

Alvermann, D. E. (1991). The discussion web: A graphic aid for learning across the curriculum. *The Reading Teacher, 45,* 92–99.

Babigian, K. (2002). *Comprehension reciprocal teaching: An effective pathway to reading.* Retrieved July 8, 2002, from http://www.cascd.org/

Baker, L., & Brown, A. L. (1984). Cognitive monitoring in reading. In J. Flood (Ed.), *Understanding reading comprehension* (pp. 21–44). Newark, DE: International Reading Association.

Berk, L. E., & Winsler, A. (1995). *Scaffolding children's learning: Vygotsky and early childhood education.* Washington, DC: National Association for the Education of Young Children.

Bracey, G. W. (1987). If not golden, silence may be helpful. *Phi Delta Kappan, 68,* 398–399.

Buehl, D. (2001). Reciprocal teaching builds reading comprehension. Retrieved July 8, 2002, from http://www.weac.org/news/2000-01/may01/read-print.htm

Clark, K. & Graves, M. (2005). Scaffolding students' comprehension of text. *The Reading Teacher, 58*(6), 570–580.

Cleveland, L., Connors, D., Conors, D., Dauphin, T., Hashey, J., & Wolf, M. (2001). *Action research on reciprocal teaching.* Vestal, NY: Vestal Central Schools.

Cunningham, J. W., & Moore, D. W. (1986). The confused world of main ideas. In J. F. Baumann (Ed.), *Teaching main idea comprehension* (pp. 1–17). Newark, DE: International Reading Association.

Duffelmeyer, F. A., & Duffelmeyer, B. B. (1987). Main idea questions on informal reading inventories. *The Reading Teacher, 41,* 162–166.

Ennis, R. H. (1985). Goals for a critical thinking curriculum. In A. L. Cosa (Ed.), *Developing minds: A resource book for teaching thinking.* Association for Supervision and Curriculum Development.

Flood, J., & Lapp, D. (1990). Reading comprehension instruction for at-risk students: Research-based practices that can make a difference. *Journal of Reading, 33,* 490–496.

Forbes, S., Poparad, M. A., & McBride, M. (2004). To err is human; to self-correct is to learn. *The Reading Teacher, 57*(6), 566–572.

Gall, M. (1984). Synthesis of research on teachers' questioning. *Educational Leadership, 42*(3), 40–47.

Gambrell, L. B. (1983). The occurrence of think-time during reading comprehension instruction. *Journal of Educational Research, 77*, 77–80.

Hahn, A. L. (1985). Teaching remedial students to be strategic readers and better comprehenders. *The Reading Teacher, 39*, 732–737.

Hansen, J. (1984). Poor readers can draw inferences. *The Reading Teacher, 37*, 586–589.

Hashey, J. M., & Connors, D. J. (2003). Learn from our journey: Reciprocal teaching action research. *The Reading Teacher, 57*(3), 224–232.

Hudgins, B. B., & Edelman, S. (1986). Teaching critical thinking to fourth and fifth graders through teacher-led small group discussions. *Journal of Educational Research, 79*, 333–342.

Kelly, P. R. (1990). Guiding young students' response to literature. *The Reading Teacher, 43*, 464–470.

Kurkjian, C., Livingston, N., Young, T., & Hopkins, L. B. (2004). Poetry: A feast for the senses. *The Reading Teacher, 57*(7), 694–702.

Lapin, G. (2003, May). Get that brain reading. Annual Meeting of the International Reading Association, Orlando, FL.

Lubliner, S. (2000). *A practical guide to reciprocal teaching*. Bothell, WA: Wright Group/McGraw-Hill.

Lubliner, S. (2004). Help for struggling upper-grade elementary readers. *The Reading Teacher, 57*(5), 430–438.

Mandeville, T. F. (1994). KWL: Linking the affective and cognitive domains. *The Reading Teacher, 47*, 679–680.

Marshall, N. (1984). Discourse analysis as a guide for informal assessment of comprehension. In J. Flood (Ed.), *Promoting reading comprehension* (pp. 79–96). Newark, DE: International Reading Association.

Martinez, M., Roser, N., & Strecker, S. (1999). "I never thought I could be a star": A readers theatre ticket to fluency. *The Reading Teacher, 52*, 326–334.

Moustafa, B. M. (1999). *Content area reading: Summary of reference papers* (ED 427297).

National Institute of Child Health and Human Development. (2000). *The report of the National Reading Plan: Teaching children to read: An evidence-based assessment of the scientific research literature on reading and its implications for reading instruction*. Washington, DC: U.S. Government Printing Office.

Nessel, D. (1987). The new face of comprehension instruction: A closer look at questions. *The Reading Teacher, 40*, 604–606.

Nolte, R. Y., & Singer, H. (1985). Active comprehension: Teaching a process of reading comprehension and its effects on reading achievement. *The Reading Teacher, 39*, 24–31.

Ogle, D. (1986). K-W-L: A teaching model that develops active reading of expository text. *The Reading Teacher, 39*, 564–571.

Palincsar, A. S. (1987, April). *Collaborating for collaborative learning of text comprehension*. Paper presented at the annual meeting of the American Educational Research Association, Washington, DC.

Palincsar, A. S., David, Y. M., Winn, J. A., & Stevens, D. D. (1991). Examining the context of strategy instruction. *Remedial and Special Education, 12*(3), 44–53.

Palincsar, A. S., Ransom, K., & Derber, S. (1989). Collaborative research and development of reciprocal teaching. *Educational Leadership, 46*(4), 37–40.

Pearson, P. D. (1985). Changing the face of reading comprehension instruction. *The Reading Teacher, 38,* 724–738.

Rand, M. K. (1983). Story schema: Theory, research and practice. *The Reading Teacher, 37,* 337–342.

Rosenshine, B., Meister, C., & Chapman, S. (1996). Teaching students to generate questions: A review of the intervention studies. *Review of Educational Research, 66,* 181–221.

Routman, R. (1988). *Transitions: From literature to literacy.* Portsmouth, NH: Heinemann.

Ryan, P. M. (2001). *Hello ocean.* Watertown, MA: Charlesbridge.

Sadow, M. W. (1982). The use of story grammar in the design of questions. *The Reading Teacher, 35,* 518–523.

Shoop, M. (1986). Inquest: A listening and reading comprehension strategy. *The Reading Teacher, 39,* 670–675.

Sloan, G. (2003). *Give them poetry: A guide for sharing poetry with children K–8.* New York: Teachers College Press.

Stahl, K. A. D. (2004). Proof, practice, and promise: Comprehension strategy instruction in the primary grades. *The Reading Teacher, 57*(7), 598–609.

Stauffer, R. G. (1975). *Directing the reading-thinking process.* New York: Harper & Row.

Vaughn, S., Gersten, R., & Chard, D. J. (2000). The underlying message in LD intervention research: Findings from research syntheses. *Exceptional Children, 67*(1), 99–114.

Yopp, R. H., & Yopp, H. K. (2003). Time spent reading. *The California Reader, 36*(4), 22–30.

Other Suggested Readings

Beed, P. L., Hawkins, E. M., & Roller, C. M. (1991). Moving learners toward independence: The power of scaffolded instruction. *The Reading Teacher, 44,* 648–655.

Belmont, J. M. (1989). Cognitive strategies and strategic learning. *American Psychologist, 44,* 142–148.

Carbo, M. (1987). Deprogramming reading failure: Giving unequal learners an equal chance. *Phi Delta Kappan, 69,* 197–202.

Harvey, S., & Goudvis, A. (2000). *Strategies that work: Teaching comprehension to enhance understanding.* New York: Stenhouse.

Keene, E. O., & Zimmermann, S. (1997). *Mosaic of thought: Teaching comprehension in a reader's workshop.* Portsmouth, NH: Heinemann.

McAllister, P. J. (1994). Using K-W-L for informal assessment. *The Reading Teacher, 47,* 510–511.

Pearson, P. D. (Ed.). (2000). *Teaching comprehension* (2nd ed.). New York: HBJ College & School Division.

Rosenblatt, L. (1982). The literacy transaction: Evocation and response. *Theory into Practice, 21,* 268–277.

Rosenshine, B., & Meister, C. (1992). The use of scaffolds for teaching higher-level cognitive strategies. *Educational Leadership, 49*(7), 26–33.

Chapter Eight

The Importance of Fluency in Reading

Oral reading fluency is a strong predictor of silent reading.

—*Timothy Rasinski*

In skating o'r thin ice, our safety is in our speed.

—*Emerson*

In reading through thick text, our safety is comprehension.

—*Guess who*

The combination of choric reading and Readers' Theater does wonders for students who are just learning English.

—*Sam Sebesta*

Eighth Objective for Your Teaching Success:

Guide your students through imaging, oral reading, and predictable and expository text.

Have you ever noticed that when you're understanding and appreciating an author, your reading speed keeps gently increasing? And have you ever noticed that when you speed up your reading a bit and allow the author's message to flow, your comprehension goes up, too? There's nothing mysterious about this, of course. It's just that comprehension and fluency are in love, they can't do without each other. The more you comprehend what the author's message is, the more fluently you can read that message.

On the other hand, the more slowly you read a message, the less you might comprehend that message. By the time you get to the end of the sentence, you may have lost the message. Our students who think that reading is just pronouncing one word after another may have been *misled* and usually are frustrated and disappointed (Rasinski, 2000).

Reading with fluency doesn't mean to read real real fast. It doesn't mean you have to read as fast as an auction dealer speaks. Hoffman (2003) says, "Fluency is not just about rate. Faster is not always better" (p. 5). Reading fluently simply means to *communicate* smoothly, easily, and freely with an author—just as *you* do with your favorite novelist. Or just as *you* do when you're talking with your best friend on the telephone. A fluent reader is also a flexible one, *changing* the speed of reading with the difficulty of the text—just like you do, I would imagine.

The Important Characteristics of Fluent Readers

The important thing to remember about fluent readers is their continuous use of all four interacting cues: (1) the phonics of the words, (2) the order and arrangement of the words, (3) the meaning of the words, and (4) the reader's prior knowledge schemas, or theories. Those four interacting cues allow good readers to fluently pronounce and comprehend an author's message, whether fiction or nonfiction—just like making noise.

When musicians are making music, they have the habit of making constant *predictions* about the next notes coming up. Like the clarinet player, fluent readers also leap ahead—making predictions about the author's next thought. At the same time the words they have *already* read, silently or aloud, have been instantly inserted into their brain's short-term memory, waiting for a split second to connect with the total message (Smith, 2003). In short, fluent readers constantly try to match their own schemas with those of the author. What do fluent readers not do? They don't read word by word by word. Instead, they read total messages from a writer—fluently, of course.

If the author and the reader have had similar experiences or have learned similar information or have even imagined similar things, schema matches can be easily created. The skillful writer and the skillful reader can laugh at *the same imagined events,* or they can share the same *true* events, the same intriguing information, the same famous ball game, the same shocks and delights. In this way, real communication takes place . . . fluently.

Modeling Fluent Reading

Professional Standard: Teaches students to vary reading rate according to their purposes

If students are to become fluent readers, they need a good model from you of what fluent reading sounds like. Research by Rasinski and Padak (2001) demonstrates that your frequent reading to children helps accomplish this goal, especially if you occasionally point out what you're doing to make the reading sound so fluent. My own experience in teaching all of the grades from 1 through 12 confirms what the research says.

Both my high-school students and my elementary students could see the value of my reading aloud the first chapter of a novel they were assigned to read. "It really gets me into the book," they told me. And from others, "Please read a little bit of this chapter, OK?" or "When you read it to us, I get used to the characters real quick-like." And still others, "The way you read it, I feel like I'm right there" or "It feels like the author is reading to me" or "I really dig this book" or "I can read much faster after you read the first chapter." These are the kinds of emotions you want to encourage before you ask them to read a book they did not choose for themselves.

If you feel uncomfortable about reading out loud, let me assure you that kids will listen to any voice on the face of the Earth as long as you choose a good book. As philosopher John Dewey said long ago, human beings are story people. For thousands of years people have been educating young and old alike by telling or reading stories. Just look at all the stories Americans consume in movies and on television. We're story freaks! So take advantage of that when you're teaching.

Encourage Fluent Reading with Predictable Text

There's a certain kind of text that is ideal for teaching students to read with fluency, meaning, and considerable pleasure. It's called predictable text, as you recall. Text of this sort is often so plainly written that fluent reading can probably occur even on the first day of first grade, using choral reading.

Predictable books are those in which the authors use familiar language and language patterns, common background knowledge, and other devices that help readers *anticipate* what comes next. For example, here's a familiar language pattern that will help you predict the missing word:

Johnny pulled his pretty _____ wagon over to Maria's house.

Did you predict red? The notion of what color a wagon might be is based on common experiences that most of us have had. Thus, we can predict.

The most abundant source of predictable text is the school and local public library. For the teacher interested in helping students develop a feel for real and fluent reading, there is no shortage of books that can be used. Hundreds of patterned stories in picture-book form are available to choose from. Hundreds of detective stories—and wait a minute, how about folktales? They're about as predictable and patterned as they come.

The most important step in using predictable books is choosing the one that's just right for your *students.* The book itself is usually the major source of motivation for them—more important than tokens, progress graphs, or stickers. So if you find that the book doesn't excite your students on the first reading, put it aside and try your next choice—until you find one that produces a glow of enjoyment.

Patterned Books

Predictable literature starting in kindergarten often comes in the form of picture books, which some of us call *patterned books*. They're called that because of their simple but enjoyable patterns of speech, language, rhythm, and plots. Patterned books became so popular in the mid-1970s that many publishers started including highly predictable patterned stories in their reading textbooks.

Patterned books and stories follow a highly repetitive style that children can easily learn. The repetition is very effective in building their *memory of words* and consequently building their reading fluency. Patterned books that you may have already read include the series written by Bill Martin, the most simple being *Brown Bear, Brown Bear, What Do You See?*

Here are a few more samples, but don't forget that there are more than 200 patterned books listed in the back of this book (see Appendix N).

Monkey Face by Frank Asch
Seven Little Rabbits by John Becker
The Important Book (and many more) by Margaret Wise Brown
The Very Busy Spider (and many more) by Eric Carle
May I Bring a Friend? (and many more) by Beatrice De Regniers
Six Creepy Sheep by Judith Ross Enderle
Ask Mr. Bear by Marjorie Flack
The King Who Rained by Fred Gwynne
Fire, Fire, Said Mrs. McGuire (and many more) by Bill Martin

Here are three more patterned books for students in upper grades:

Where the Wild Things Are by Maurice Sendak
Alexander and the Terrible, Horrible, No Good, Very Bad Day by Judith Viorst
What Do You Do, Dear? by Sesyle Joslin

These patterned books have been written for the explicit purpose of enjoyment and getting kids to read with fluency rather than one . . . slow . . . word . . . at . . . a . . . time. But this method works only when teachers read the books playfully, choral-read and echo-read the books, have the kids copycat each other's reading of the books, and finally involve those marvelous young actors in a *readers theater* performance. That's your job, and it's great fun.

But What About Mother Goose and Fluency?

For the real beginners in K–2, who could build more fluency than Mother Goose—and Father Crow, a pretend look alike? Mother Goose says, "I can foster your fluency, too, just watch.":

> *Hickory dickory dock*
> *The mouse ran up the clock*
> *The clock struck one*
> *And down he run*
> *Hickory dickory dock*

Mother Goose also says:

> *Georgie Porgy*
> *Pudding and Pie*
> *Kissed the girls*
> *And made them cry.*
> *When the girls*
> *Came out to play*
> *Georgy Porgy*
> *Ran away.*

Father Crow (a.k.a. Bogglestar) says he can really inspire fluency, too.

> *Flockerie, Flickerie, Fleck*
> *You're stomping on my neck*
> *My clock struck one*
> *And it weighed a ton*
> *Flockerie, Flickerie, Fleck*

And for his encore, Father Crow says:

> *Gorgeous porky*
> *Bacon and pie*
> *Kissed the pigs*
> *And made them sigh*
> *When the piglets*
> *Came out to shop*
> *Mean ol' porky*
> *Forced them to stop.*

The *frequent repetition* of Mother Goose-type books and all those other patterned books we've been talking about has been noted for many years as one of the best ways to quickly teach the first 100 sight words—and to encourage students to read picture books with fluency from the word go. Fortunately, nursery rhymes are making a come back (Roush, 2005).

Books without Rhyme

Authors who use rhyme can make text very predictable, but there are other devices for making stories predictable. My favorite predictable book, *Can I Keep Him?* by Steven Kellogg, has no rhyme but has pleasant repetition and a very intriguing plot. Books like his are suitable for children in Grades 1 to 6 and beyond.

In this storybook a little boy with a vivid imagination keeps bringing home a different kind of pet to show his mother. "Can I keep him?" he asks each time. And each time his mother gives him a new excuse, like "Your grandmother is allergic to cat fur." The story is touching and humorous, with insights into both children and mothers, and it contains words and language patterns that are similar throughout. It's a delightful book that children can enjoy reading or even pretend reading—"one more time." And it's a great one to read out loud to your students and then, together as a group, extend the story with your own creative ideas.

In Marjorie Flack's *Ask Mr. Bear*, Danny keeps asking a new animal, "Can you give me something for my mother's birthday?" In the case of the goat, the predictable exchange goes this way:

"Maa, maa," said the goat. "I can give you milk for making cheese."

"Thank you," said Danny, "but she has some cheese."

"Let's see what we can find then," said the goat.

No matter what the animal is, the language pattern is very much the same: I can give you something. . . . Thank you, but she has some. . . . Let's see what we can find then. No rhyming is necessary, but what is necessary in most predictable or patterned books is a sense of rhythm and repetition—the very ingredients most children like.

Other examples are found in predictable, repetitive folktales, like "Sody Sallyraytus" by Richard Chase, which appears in his book *Grandfather Tales*. The wicked bear in the story keeps gobbling up members of a family as they travel one by one to the country store. First to be swallowed is the little boy, then the little girl, then the grandpa, then the grandma, until the only one left is their pet squirrel.

Each time the bear crawls out of his hiding place to gobble up a family member, he says and does exactly the same thing. After the pattern of the language and the plot have occurred twice, most children grasp the concept and easily predict much of the *language* as the story progresses. Recurring language, recurring themes, and recurring actions all combine to make this story quite predictable and therefore easy to read fluently.

Finally, Judith Viorst's *Alexander and the Terrible, Horrible, No Good, Very Bad Day* is a famous example of a patterned book for all ages. It has a highly predictable plot pattern and moderately predictable language patterns. As you may recall, Alexander has one of those days when everything goes wrong— "one of those terrible, horrible, no good, very bad days." He doesn't get a window seat in the car, he doesn't get an easy question from the teacher, and even his best friend doesn't want to play with him. Although the language is not the same from episode to episode, many of the words and sentence structures are repeated—especially his forlorn complaint about his terrible, horrible, no good, very bad day.

Predictable Books for Older Students

For older students (9–13) predictable books and stories come in various styles: the detective story is a good model. In detective stories you have seven highly predictable features: (1) a murderer or a thief; (2) clues that the murderer or thief leaves behind; (3) a smart detective who uses his or her noodle and makes good use of those clues; (4) several suspects to observe; (5) a reader who suspects and an author who tries to fool; (6) often an interrogation of the suspects; and finally (7) an exciting conclusion that has you eager to read another detective mystery.

You can see the patterns, of course. And probably you can see why this type of book, if enough of them are read, can lead your students to a high level of fluent reading. You can see the abundant practice in comprehending all of those plot variables, the interesting words that are used, and the new words that are acquired. And best of all, you can see a happy reader.

Research on Predictable Books

Research on the use of predictable books has been highly encouraging. Several researchers have found that predictable books tend to increase children's success more rapidly than school-bought anthologies (Bridge, 1979). McCormick and Mason (1986) also found that when predictable stories were given to an experimental group of children of preschool and kindergarten age and their parents, these children later scored significantly higher than control children on three variables: story reading, word reading, and spelling. The rhythm and the repetition that are so abundant in predictable books and stories probably led the children to:

- greater confidence in predicting the plots and language patterns of stories.
- greater awareness of familiar words.
- greater awareness of the letter patterns in words.

Check Out This Teaching Plan for Young Students

The following is a list of steps for using predictable books to develop fluent, natural reading with beginners—and *also with older students having problems*. I have "packaged" it in a 3-day format, but feel free to reorganize the plan as you wish. The same ideas for beginners have been used very successfully with older readers who need to change their concept of reading. Many of them have been thinking of reading as a slow, tedious process of decoding letters and words. The following 8-step method should change their perception to reading as a fluent process of searching for meaning and enjoyment.

- **First day:**
  1. After reading the title of the book to your students and showing them the picture on the cover, ask them to predict what the book will be about.
  2. After you have read three or four pages, ask students what they think will happen next—or what they think a certain character will do or say next. This causes them to use their background knowledge, syntax, vocabulary knowledge, and any other cues the author has supplied to help make the text predictable.

3. Let the children briefly *explain their reasons* whenever they make a prediction. For example ask "Why do you think that might happen?" "Why do you think those words may come next? Have you seen those words before in this book?" "Is that the kind of thing he would say? Why do you think so?" I use words like *may* or *might* or *could* instead of *will* in questions like "What do you think *might* happen next?" This helps to avoid instilling that useless notion of looking for the one right answer to the teacher's questions. As long as the response makes sense within the context of the story, treat it as a minor victory.

4. Follow each set of predictions and explanations by checking the actual text.

5. As you read the rest of the story, at a reasonable speed, ask students to join in whenever they think they know the words. I call this *sing-along reading*.

■ **Second day:**

6. Read the story to students again, allowing them plenty of opportunities to join in and say the next line before you read it.

7. Then use either a large wall chart or a big-book version of the same story. Point to the words as you read some of the lines. Let the students take turns pointing to the words.

■ **Third day:**

8. After they have had enough time following along, ask for volunteers to read parts of the story from the big-book or your charts.

Predictable Student Writing

Where else can you and your students find text that is predictable? We're talking about predictable text that is (1) on an appropriate reading level for the readers, (2) is appealing to their interests, and (3) that flows in some kind of repetitive way. Now that's predictable.

Normally, students of all ages like to read each other's stories and articles. The motivation is keen, and the fluency is usually swift and smooth. Why? Because kids speak and write kids' language.

And nothing is *more predictable to read than your own language.*

When children have just written (or dictated) a sentence, it's pretty easy for them to read it. That's why the *language-experience approach* hasn't died—it has children dictate or write their own reading materials.

So if students have had insufficient success with other methods, try changing them temporarily from readers into writers. Have them each dictate a real or a fictional story or description to you. Then type it up and give it back to them to read—either alone or with a partner or with you. If it sounds good, have the student read it to the class and receive peer praise. Do the same thing for several weeks and then gradually wean the students author-written to real books.

Encourage Fluent Reading of Expository Text

By the time they reach third grade, most children appear to be quite good at predicting what's going to happen next in a story. Their past experience provides them with a story schema: There's going to be a setting, a main character, some conflicts along the way, and some resolutions to those conflicts. Expository, or explanatory, writings though, usually give readers none of those things. Instead of leading readers along familiar and predictable paths, these writers (and the teacher) have a challenge. They must go through a complicated tangle of information, which may sometimes seem like a veritable jungle, full of strange and threatening beings.

Instead of encountering a main character or two, readers encounter a series of twisting and turning abstract ideas. Instead of watching a character bravely face a series of conflicts, they must cautiously confront a series of strange beasts—those slithery, elusive comparisons and contrasts, those domineering Siamese twins called cause and effect, or most hideous of all, the nine-headed water serpents hissingly referred to as *lists*. No, the schema that children might have developed for stories is not adequate to protect them from what I lovingly call the monsters of exposition.

What Are the Patterns of Explanation?

Research shows that our apprentices comprehend content-area information and other nonfiction better when we explain to them exactly how authors organize and present their explanations (Hayes, 1998; Paratore & Indrisano, 1987). Children need to learn that informational writing requires certain types of expository structures, or patterns of explanation. Let me list those six patterns for you in the order of difficulty that most children seem to have with them (Piccolo, 1987).

- **Sequence:** The author is usually telling the reader how something happened or how to do or make something—and in the right order. "Now pull up close to the car in front of the parking space, put the car in reverse, turn the wheel to the right, accelerate with a light foot, straighten out the wheel. . . . "
- **Lists:** The author enumerates details to support a main idea or simply to provide a set of elements or ideas. Notice that you're trapped by one of those lists right now. You feel almost compelled to keep going until you reach the end.
- **Cause and effect:** The author presents one or more effects or results and provides the reader with one or more causes. "The world is experiencing global warming because of greenhouse gases."
- **Description:** The author wants to tell the reader what is happening or what something looks like. Authors often do this in more detail than readers wish to receive. "Her hair was long, smooth, and black, shimmering in the August moonlight like a swarm of flickering fireflies, making every man in her

presence dream of making her his own but doubt that he could ever afford to buy such a beautiful horse." (Ha! Tricked you.)

■ **Problem and solution:**   The author presents a problem or two and suggests a solution. "The economy is heating up much too fast, so it's time to raise interest rates on mortgages" (right after I finish buying my house).

■ **Comparison/contrast:**   The author tells the reader how things are alike and different. "Whereas a butterfly is usually diurnal and brightly colored with club-shaped antennae, a moth is usually nocturnal and duller in color with feather antennae."

A DRTA Approach to Explanation Patterns

You probably remember the Directed Reading and Thinking Activity (DRTA) demonstrated in Chapter 7. With this approach the teacher guides students' reading with these three questions: What do you think? Why? Can you prove it? Then the teacher helps the students turn this process into a reading strategy in which they ask themselves those same three questions.

The DRTA can be a very useful method for explanation and content-area reading. David Hayes (1998) suggests combining DRTA with direct instruction on the ways of explaining things. Let me recommend, though, that you first teach two or three of the six patterns in isolation, using a dozen or so pure examples until students get used to calling the patterns by name. Then you can integrate your instruction of the patterns with content-area concepts you're discussing in science, social studies, or some other area of the curriculum.

Here's a Modeled Lesson Using DRTA

Teacher: Prepares students for the list method used in the first paragraph of the text they are about to read together] In the early 1800s many women had to work for a living, just as they do today. Where do you think they worked back then? [Students offer suggestions.] OK, now read the first paragraph to see how good your predictions were.

> Life for American women greatly changed with the growth of factories. Growing numbers of women took paying jobs. Some went to work in factories. A few went to work in offices. A large number began sewing clothes for money in their homes.

Teacher: Which of your predictions were correct? [Students answer.] Can you read us a sentence that proves it? [Students read.] OK, what way of explaining things did the author use in that paragraph? Was it cause and effect, problem and solution, or the list method? [Students answer.] That's right, the author used the list method to explain the main idea.

The author also used the method we worked on last week. Do you remember how you wrote some main-idea paragraphs with supporting details? What do you think is the most important idea in the paragraph we just read? [Listens to several different ideas from the students and encourages each of them to express the ideas in their own words. Prepares the students for the cause-and-effect method coming up in the next two paragraphs.]

What kind of working conditions do you think the women had in those days? [Students answer.] All right, check your predictions by reading the next paragraph on the next page.

> In looking for jobs, women found they were not allowed to do certain kinds of work. Most of the jobs that women could get paid low wages. None of them offered much hope for the future. A poor boy could hope to be a rich businessman when he grew up. But in the 1800s a poor girl had no hopes like these. State laws worked against women. They said that if a woman married, her husband controlled all she earned.

Teacher: Which of your predictions fit what the author wrote? [Students answer.] Can you find a sentence that would prove it? [Students read.] Good. [Prepares them for the *effect* portion of the *cause-and-effect* pattern] Many women thought those working conditions were unfair. What do you think they did about it? [Students answer.] OK, check your predictions by reading the next paragraph.

> Beginning in the 1840s, women formed groups to work for more rights. One woman, who wanted to be a printer, explained why in this way: "We women did more than keep house, cook, sew, wash, spin, and weave, and garden. Many of us had to earn money besides. . . . " (Hayes, 1989, pp. 54–55)

[When the students discussed this last paragraph, two of them realized that the author had blended the cause and effect in the same paragraph, starting with the effect (i.e., groups were formed to demand more rights) and sliding back into the main cause (i.e., wanting to earn money in a way that suited them.) The teacher reassured the students that when they did their own writing the next day, they could try this way of explaining things in writing.]

The DRTA is an excellent way of transitioning between fiction and nonfiction of the most difficult kind—expository text. I believe the DRTA is by far the most likely way for students to achieve fluent reading of difficult material. In Chapter 10 you will see how students can write their own expository patterns, thus increasing their chances of reading this kind of material fluently.

Question Patterns for Both Reading and Writing

Here is a reminder of prereading and guided reading questions appropriate to these exposition structures, a.k.a. explanation patterns.

- **Lists:** Before you read this, what things do you think are necessary for the health of plants? Let's make a list of them.
- **Cause and effect:** Why do you think plants turn brown?
- **Problem and solution:** If so many trees are being removed to make way for housing, what can people do to replenish the oxygen lost to the atmosphere?
- **Comparison/contrast:** How do evergreens differ from deciduous trees? How are they the same?

After discussing *each* of these kinds of explanation questions, raise this question: "What type of explanation would you probably need to use if you were *writing* your answer?" For example, after asking, "Why do you think plants turn brown?" and discussing students' answers, ask what explanation method they would use to *write* their answers. ("That's right, cause and effect.")

Increase Students' Use of Mental Imaging

There are several ways to increase students' imaging power, and thus fluency, as they read content-area materials.

- **Provide schema-building experiences prior to reading.** In science, for example, this means that students should usually read *after* numerous firsthand observations and hands-on experimentation. It also means that you should give students opportunities to draw a diagram or picture of their observations rather than merely discuss them. Then compare those sketches with pictures in their textbooks and other sources. In *math* this means dramatizing story problems and equations. *In social studies* it means using discussions, pictures, films, videotapes, interviews, and artifacts *before* students read and using dramatizations while they read or after they have read.
- **Use creative drama often.** For many hundreds of years the children in Great Britain have been learning to speak, think, listen, write, and read through the process of drama. Unfortunately in U.S. schools, drama has been all too often seen as an extracurricular activity. However, the ideas presented to children in social studies texts can often be made more visual and meaningful through creative dramatizations. Consider this example:

> Mr. Novick and his pupils were studying European exploration of the Americas. The class was divided into five groups, one that chose to study Coronado, one Columbus, and so on. Each group was given help in finding information from li-

brary sources and a textbook. Each group then planned a skit to present their major ideas about their explorer.

Each small group presented its plans to Mr. Novick, who praised the students for specific aspects of their work and also asked questions to show them where they needed to do more research. After further research, the groups modified their plans for their skits and again presented their ideas to Mr. Novick. When Mr. Novick approved their plans, they were free to rehearse their skits in earnest.

After all five groups had their skits ready, they presented them in a theater-in-the-round fashion: actors in the middle of the room, audience in a circle surrounding them. After each skit, the audience provided praise and specific suggestions for improvement. Further rehearsals prepared the groups for presenting their skits to another class.

Mr. Novick's approach was very well structured and certainly made the social studies reading more visual and real to the students. However, not all drama experiences related to content areas need to be this elaborate. Once the children have become used to giving spontaneous skits, they can be invited at any time to dramatize something they've been reading. After one small group has tried it, another group can be asked to give its interpretation. Inviting another class into the room (or another group in a team teaching situation) can be reserved for special occasions when the children have decided with you to polish a skit for a larger audience.

- **Use modeling and discussion.**   Help your students realize that their ability to create images while they read has a major impact on their understanding of what they're reading. Model this process for them, explaining the images you are creating as you read. Then have them practice often with a partner. When I worked with sixth graders, I had them listen to my reading and raise their hands whenever they noticed that they were forming images of what I was reading.

- **Help students realize what they can do when they can't come up with their own images for what they're reading.**   Model the use of prior knowledge, textbook pictures, maps, encyclopedias, and other visual resources such as graphs and tables. Encourage students to study pictures related to the topic being studied. The same goes for maps of wherever a story or article takes place. And don't forget to have them use the Internet, along with a pictorial encyclopedia.

- **Rely on cooperative learning.**   *Encourage your students to ask each other to provide images.* Your students have diverse backgrounds, and what one student doesn't know from experience, another one often does.

Let me give you some examples: a child who has had the experience of living in an adobe house; one who knows how to eat with chopsticks; one who can explain what a pigsty is; one who has lived in a rainforest; one who has lived in a rural mountain village; one who can pump water from a well; one who has ridden on a subway; one who can walk safely across the street in a busy city like Houston, TX; one who knows the difference between a temple, a shrine, or a church; one who knows what it's like to fish for a living; one who has helped to break open a pinata; and one who can dance hora.

By letting partners read content material together (a fluent reader with a less fluent one), you can provide more cooperative practice in image making. Make sure the partners check each other's images after each paragraph or two and take turns being the "image checker". Above all, have your students share their images. Make it an exciting and friendly group discussion that leads to creative action.

■ **Engage children in writing that requires image making.** Encourage descriptive writing:

1. Give students a chance to silently imagine the scene you are reading to them, and then discuss the different perceptions they have.
2. Provide abundant images for students to write about. These include objects and pictures you bring in and cooperative experiences they can talk about and then write about. Also use journals of their own experiences and feelings. Vividly descriptive nonfiction books can be read to them and used as a basis for imagery discussion followed by writing.
3. Read children's writing out loud and have students listen for good images; encourage specific comments on *why* the images are clear and interesting. Ask, "What did the writer do to make them clear and interesting?"
4. Encourage effective readers to write clear, image-provoking minibooks for other students. Next year these minibooks can be recommended to struggling students who are having trouble reading content-area material with understanding.

Why Not Use Graphic Materials?

Now that you're an expert in using your imaging power, imagine the wealth of images that can be obtained just by using graphics. When students see a graph or a table in a content-area selection, they often think they have less to read and can skip it. I can remember my own joy in doing this as a student. But one day the textbook was so dull, I found myself trying to figure out a graph just to keep myself awake. It was on that day that I discovered a secret—creating information from a graph or a table can be a lot more fun than reading page after page of text.

Look at the table in Figure 8.1, for example. See how much information you can create by examining it right now.

Do you see what I mean? Without reading a lot of text, you can figure out for yourself that twice as many boys as girls have trouble when it comes to reading.

Maps can also be a fascinating way for children to gain information—witness the enthusiasm of children reading the map related to the journey of Bilbo Baggins in Tolkien's *The Hobbit*. And so can diagrams and pictures, as shown in the eagerness of students following diagrams to build model airplanes or studying pictures of dinosaurs.

Grade	Boys	Girls
2	10%	4%
3	15%	7%
4	24%	12%
5	26%	12%

FIGURE 8.1   A table showing the percentages of boys and girls reading 1 year or more below grade level.

If graphs, tables, maps, diagrams, and pictures can be so interesting, why are they often given only the briefest glance? There are probably numerous reasons, including the possibility that they take more energy to read than simple explanations. But perhaps the biggest reason is that children have had too few opportunities to discover that reading graphics can be fairly easy and enjoyable.

Let Students Create Their Own Graphics

One way to help students discover graphics is by having them *create* graphs, maps, tables, and diagrams of their own. To start, have them use simple information that you provide—such as average winter temperatures in various parts of the world or other such statistical data found in almanacs. But quickly get them involved in gathering their *own* information and translating that information into graphic or tabular form.
Here are some ideas for original graphics:

A graph of kids' choices of different flavors of ice cream
A map of the classroom, the school, or the neighborhood
Annotated diagrams of their dream house or a simple glider
A table showing school enrollment during the past 10 years
A mural of village life in the Middle Ages
An annotated photographic essay

All of these projects can be displayed for other children to read and discuss, thereby providing some of the guided practice necessary to learn to appreciate and understand visuals. By constructing their own, students will discover for themselves the need for some type of scale or key on maps, graphs, and diagrams; symbols such as color or special lines; and accurate titles and labels.

Use Trade Books to Improve Information

Today's libraries are full of trade books that can be used to supplement inadequate textbooks—and there are plenty of *those*. "Trade books to support content learning are proliferating so quickly that it is difficult to keep up with them" (Armbruster, 1991). Here are some examples:

- Fifth and sixth graders can learn a great deal about medieval life by reading a funny book called *Harold the Herald: A Book About Heraldry*.
- Most students will enjoy having a rhyming book read to them about the voyage of Christopher Columbus. It is called *In 1492* and was written by Jean Marzollo.
- Other students can find much to learn in *A 19th Century Railway Station* by Fiona Macdonald, who explains how railroads changed our world.
- Books by Alvin and Virginia Silverstein can help students to develop a better understanding of humans and animals. Their series, *All About Them* and *Systems of the Body*, provide several books that are highly readable and informative.
- Another science author, Seymour Simon, has written more than 50 books designed to help young children understand, in everyday language, interesting facts and principles concerning the earth, space, and animals. *Meet the Giant Snakes* and *Danger from Below: Earthquakes, Past, Present, and Future* are just two examples.
- The National Council of Teachers of English recommends nonfiction books like these:
  > *When Marian Sang: The True Recital of Marian Andersen* by Pam Ryan
  > *A Gruesome But True Story About Human Brain Science* by John Fleischman
  > *Hurry Freedom: African Americans in the California Gold Rush* by Jerry Stanley
  > *Voices of the Alamo* by Sherry Garland

Thousands of fiction and nonfiction trade books are now available for students in content areas. Updated annotated lists can help you select new books for integrated thematic units or for units in specific curricular areas.

Sources of Intriguing Nonfiction Stories

1. *The Childen's Book Council (CBC)* is a nonprofit trade association whose membership consists of publishers, packagers of trade books for children and young adults, and other producers of related literary materials. The CBC promotes the use and enjoyment of children's trade books and related materials and disseminates information about trade book publishing. The CBC also sponsors Young People's Poetry Week and Children's Book Week. CBC works with the American Library Association and the International Reading Association on joint projects. For more information go to http://www.cbcbooks.org

2. *The National Science Teachers Association (NSTA)* is committed to promoting excellence in teaching and learning. One of NSTA's initiatives, SciLinks, brings pages of science textbooks to life by linking them to resources on the Internet. The links transport teachers, students, and others to Web sites related to lessons in science textbooks. Publications, books, posters, and other educational tools are available through the NSTA. It also publishes a list of

outstanding children's science trade books each year for Grades K–12. For more information go to http://www.nsta.org

3. *Book Links* is a magazine designed for teachers and others interested in connecting children with high-quality books. Each issue of *Book Links* focuses on a core curriculum area, including science, social studies, language arts, history, geography, and multicultural literature. On the *Book Links* Web site you will find highlights of the current issue, including descriptions of recently published trade books. Visit the Web site at http://www.ala.org/ala/productsandpublications

4. "*Children's Books*" is a journal section appearing in *The Reading Teacher*. It frequently provides a special annotated list of new social studies, humanities, and science trade books, as well as fiction. If you'd like to develop a unit on good books of the past, for example, you can find a list in each September issue through a university library.

5. *Teacher's and Children's Choices* is an annual list of outstanding trade books published for children and adolescents and found by teachers to be exceptional for use across the curriculum. About 200 to 500 new books are read—each by a minimum of six teachers in each of seven regions of the country. Ratings are collated to generate the list for the United States, which is usually grouped by grade levels. The list can be obtained through the International Reading Association, or from http://www.reading.org

Develop Fluency Through Oral Reading

Oral reading, instead of silent reading, is making a big comeback (Rasinski, 2003). I've been amazed at how many teachers, administrators, professors, and researchers have been emphasizing oral reading learning experiences. These experiences include read-aloud, modeled reading, repeated reading, paired reading, choral reading, echo reading, poetry reading, and—my favorite—readers theater. Before I describe these various forms of oral reading, let me tell you *why* oral reading activities are so very important and share a personal experience. Oral reading activities:

- develop students' vocabulary and love of reading.
- develop students' comprehension (Pinnell, Pikulski, Wixson, Campbell, Gough, & Beatty, 1995).
- develop students' fluency.
- develop students' self-confidence.
- develop students' motivation to read quality literature.
- develop students' desire to learn.

Let's get a cup of java and talk more about this.

When I was teaching a fifth-grade class and then a sixth-grade class in Pullman, Washington, things were going OK, but I was suddenly aware that my students weren't getting the chance to choose their own projects. So I grabbed a pack of 3 × 5 cards and marched to my typewriter (I was afraid of computers back then). I tried to stay very open and let the ideas pour in. My teacher guilt kept me at it for several hours over several nights—dreaming up 21 oral projects, 12 drama projects, 22 writing projects, 16 arts-and-crafts projects, and 3 demonstration projects.

At first it was only a handful of eager students who walked up to my desk and fingered through the cards, choosing just the right project for their "extra time." But the choosers grew rapidly after that. And which group of projects do you think they chose the most? To my pleasure, the oral projects attracted them the most, with the drama projects a close second. (All five sets of projects are in Appendix F at the end of the book.)

Here's the point: In the 1800s most teaching and learning was based on speaking and oral reading. By 1920, though, educators had decided that silent reading was much more important because *that was what adults used.* Starting in the 1980s and 1990s more and more educators were beginning to see the light, and they discovered, among other things, that oral reading can be fun (Rasinski, 2003).

1. **Oral reading can be a lot of fun.**   Gay Ivey and Karen Broaddus (2001) found in their survey of 2000 sixth graders that 62% loved to be read to by their teachers. Their number one choice was free-reading time, but close behind that was read-aloud time. What a perfect balance for your reading program!

2. **Oral reading is not symbolic; it's real reading.**   We use oral reading almost every day: reading stories to our children; reading stories to our significant others; reading articles and newspaper accounts to each other; giving speeches of all sorts; reading jokes out loud; reporting news out loud; singing songs using written words; reading menus out loud; and so on.

3. **Oral reading experiences give students confidence to read and write.** (Martinez, Roser, & Strecker, 1999). You will see this clearly when we talk about readers theater.

4. **Oral reading brings your students together in a friendly community.** This is particularly true when your students engage in choral reading or readers theater, but also whenever you read a wonderful book out loud to your students.

5. **Oral reading can improve decoding skills.**   Children can best decode a word by engaging their senses: Look at the word, say it, hear it, touch it, and trace it. Oral reading requires looking at the text, saying it, and hearing it and thus provides excellent practice in decoding.

6. **Oral reading unites spoken and written language.**   This uniting action is what I've tried to explain to my students when I've told them that speaking and writing are almost twins. *They can send the same message.* Only recently

have I completely realized that speaking and writing are united by oral reading. Thank you, Tim Rasinski (2003), for making this clear to me.

Cunningham and Stanovich (1998) add that oral reading, or being read to, expands the mind and raises the level of intelligence. No more excuses!

Echo Reading: A Natural Way to Learn

With *echo reading* the teacher or a student leader reads a sentence, and the rest of the group repeats what has been read, trying to use the same intonation. The advantage of this approach is that the students can hear the correct words and intonation before they read. Thus, there is real potential for reading more fluently.

Echo reading is an excellent way to build confidence and fluency. Simply have your students follow along in their own copy or on the large copy you have for them, repeating each sentence you read. If you're using some type of big book or chart, it's a good idea to point to the words as you and they read them. This can help in the development of sight vocabulary, and it will help young or struggling readers understand what adults mean by *words*. If you're having students read from their own books, permit them to point with their fingers as they follow along.

After they have echoed a portion as a group, you may wish to have the eager ones take turns repeating each sentence in solo fashion. (More experienced readers can repeat an entire paragraph.) My teacher friends, graduate students, and I have found that this works with both young children and older ones, as long as the text content is age appropriate. It also works when more experienced students echo-read with inexperienced readers.

Mathes, Torgesen, and Allor (2001) found a way for low-achieving students to make major gains in reading ability after only 16 weeks of intervention. The main ingredients of the program were echo reading and peer assistance.

Choral Reading: A Joyful Way to Learn to Read

With *choral reading* the students read out loud together, in a relaxed but alert fashion, sometimes breaking into small groups or even soloing on occasion. Any type of choral reading has the advantage of taking the pressure off the individual reader, because there's a sense of security in numbers—and a chance to learn from others.

Some teachers who don't like using large groups for choral reading have found that having two buddies read out loud at the same time provides them with sufficient security. Solo reading should generally be reserved for those who actually wish to solo or for a reading conference between the teacher and one student. Putting kids in the spotlight when they don't want to be there can cause them to develop a negative attitude toward reading and learning in general.

Choral reading has many advocates among reading experts, all of whom point out the special values of this procedure—for instance, greater interest in and enjoyment of reading (Miccinati, 1985). Some believe that it leads to greater self-confidence

(Harste, Short, & Burke, 1988). Some found that it increases fluency while decreasing anxiety (Bradley & Talgott, 1987), and still others note that it is useful for expanding vocabulary (Sampson, Allen, & Sampson, 1991; Templeton, 1991).

Choral reading provides a much safer environment for inexperienced or struggling readers; no one makes fun of you because they're too busy reading. Joyce and Daniel McCauley (1992) also found, while working with children on the island of Guam, that choral reading promotes language learning for students learning English.

Simple patterned and humorous books provide excellent material for choral reading. You can have the children read the entire story or divide it up so that they can perform for each other in small groups. With Kellogg's *Can I Keep Him?* for example, half of the class can read the justification the boy uses each time he brings home a different kind of pet. The other half can read the different response the mother gives him each time. Older children enjoy using humorous poems, such as Jack Prelutsky's deliciously sarcastic "I'm Thankful." McCauley and McCauley (1992) recommend Prelutsky's "Dainty Dottie Dee" or Shel Silverstein's "Captain Hook"—good for English language learners.

Repeated Reading: A Wonderful Partnership

Repeated reading typically requires two students working as encouragement partners. They read and reread a short, meaningful passage until each one individually reaches a high level of fluency—smooth, expressive language that sounds as though the author was doing the talking (Dowhower, 1987; Samuels, 1979). In one of Samuels's experimental studies, he found that a group that used the repeated-reading method of developing fluency did better than a control group using comprehension and speed tests.

In another study, repeated readings produced higher achievement than a method focused strictly on automatic word recognition (Dahl & Samuels, 1974). And practice with whole texts worked better than practice with isolated words alone. No attempt was made to discover what would happen if they tried both methods together.

Dowhower (1987) also found with second graders that repeated reading of only six different stories resulted in significant improvement in reading rate, accuracy, and comprehension. The average reading rate doubled, word-recognition accuracy increased from 89% to 95%, and the percentage of comprehension questions answered correctly rose from 66% to 81%. Furthermore, the reading gains carried over to new but similar selections.

Does repeated reading (or repeated listening) work with both low-success and high-success readers? With learning disabled children? Rasinski's (1990) study and one by Sindelar, Monda, and O'Shea (1990) demonstrated that the answer to both questions is *yes*.

Paired Reading: Readers Helping Readers

Paired reading involves two students, one who is reading well and one who is reading poorly. Using an easy book or story, the two of them read together at the speed of the struggling reader. Whenever the struggling reader miscues on a word, the advanced reader pronounces it correctly and moves right on. When the less advanced reader wishes to carry on alone, a simple touch on the other's hand signals "I think I can do it myself for awhile." This procedure works well with parent and child, two siblings, two students, and teacher aide and student.

A period of 5 or 6 weeks, 15 minutes a day, has brought miracles to some children, although this is not guaranteed. Li and Nes (2001) found that paired reading caused English language learners to read with greater fluency and accuracy.

Modeled Reading: A Bond Between Teacher and Students

Modeled reading is what the teacher does in reading aloud to students and pretending to struggle with words or meanings. During this struggle the teacher solves the problems by using the many strategies described in Chapter 7. Modeled reading is probably the most powerful of all reading strategies.

The Read-Aloud: Classroom Clue

The *read-aloud* is usually performed by the teacher but heck, this doesn't have to be. Since the purpose of the read-aloud is to inspire students to want to read more and more, what is read during the read-aloud must be very interesting and hopefully exciting. If you'll look at the list of titles in Appendix O at the back of the book, you'll have a great chance of choosing the right books for reading aloud.

If you are the teacher in charge of the read-aloud, try to read as if you are the author speaking. In this way the author's meaning will come quickly to the listening students. Furthermore, the students will gradually realize, with your assistance, that this way of reading provides the most fun—and the most information. In addition, if you read out loud every day, you will find your students coming together as friends—friends who can talk about, and laugh about, the same characters in a book. More about this in Chapter 9.

Poetry Reading in an Old-Time Coffee House

One of the best ways to have your students read poetry out loud is to tell them about the 1950s and 1960s. At that time there were coffee houses all over town, as there are today, but in *those* coffee houses musicians would play and poets would read their newest poems. The lights were soft and the coffee drinkers were keen on actually listening to the poets.

So why not play a game with your class of Going to the Poetry Coffee House? Students can pour a cup of cocoa or tea or decaf coffee as they step into the coffee house, where the shades are drawn and the seats are just pillows on the floor. Posters, curios, knickknacks, bric-a-brac, ornaments, clothes, antique junk, and other stuff from the fifties and sixties enhances the atmosphere. Soon you will be treated to the fabulous poetry of several class members reading poems they have either selected or written. Instrumental, not verbal, music from the fifties and sixties play in the background, just barely heard, so as not to distract the audience from the poetry. And now the poetry reading begins . . .

Readers' Theater: Everybody's Favorite

Let's start with a sample of a readers theater experience. This sample was written by Timothy Rasinsky (2003), an ever creative educator.

> Six students stand in front of their classmates, about to perform "The Three Billy Goats Gruff." They wear no costumes but have signs around their necks identifying the characters they are portraying. Three students are the goats, one is the mean old troll, and two share the role of the narrator. There are no scenery and props, except for six music stands holding copies of a script version of the

beloved tale. The narrators stand off to one side. The three goats stand together in the middle of the so-called stage, with the troll only slightly away from them. The students read the script with as much expression and gusto as possible. When the troll is banished and the performance ends, the audience bursts into honest, appreciative applause.

Here are some procedures you might want to follow to help your students enjoy and succeed in performing in front of their peers:

1. Work with the students to select the script—the written text from a skit, play, or movie; pages copied from a book; or passages obtained from some basal readers or classroom newspapers.

2. You might select the first set of scripts and let students make the selection the next time. Try visiting the Internet, searching under one of these phrases: *children's scripts, children's readers' theater,* OR *readers' theater.*

3. When you become skilled in this total process, help students write their own skit or miniplay.

4. Make sure your students really understand the what, where, when, and who of the script.

5. Be sure to tell them the purposes of readers theater, such as having lots of fun, learning how to act like a movie star, learning how to speak like a stage star, learning how to make people laugh or shudder or gasp or whatever emotion you want them to portray.

6. Have students volunteer for individual parts at first. After three or four performances let them audition for a part they want.

7. For the first time, you should randomly divide the class—for a class of 28 try four acting groups of seven each. Have each group follow the same script so that they can see how others handle that script. Tell them not to forget sound effects.

8. The roles can be selected by the teacher or the students and can rotate so that everyone eventually acts three or more parts. Another option is to go on to a new script.

9. Make sure students practice their parts with one or more peers, under your gentle guidance, and also with adults at home.

10. Let students perform for an audience of classmates at first, but as confidence builds, invite the principal and the parents. But don't rush it. Let's take a break and listen to the story of Rudolpho.

Focus on Students with Special Needs: Comments by Louise Fulton

Special Needs Kids can Benefit from Technology

Professional Standard: Provides opportunities to use a variety of print and non-print electronic sources

Help your students with special needs succeed by using current technology. Don't forget about the possibilities technology has to offer when you're looking for ways to assist your students with special needs. Technology has been a boon for teachers of students with disabilities for several years.

For example, students with vision problems can read and write with their Braille keyboards, Braille embossers and translators, talking computers, talking and large-print word processors, screen-enlargement programs, and screen readers. Students with mental retardation, or those students who are overly active, can enjoy success when the computer program is self-paced, exciting, and interactive.

Students with hearing deficits have learned to make use of many forms of electronic communication, including e-mail, teletypewriters, relayed voice mail, and messaging cell phones. And many more adaptive devices are now being developed that will further enhance communication possibilities.

As a teacher, I've had a lot of success using such technology—especially to get my students with autism interested in reading by using touch screens on their computer monitors. Voice synthesizers, electronic pointing devices, alternate keyboards, and other computer adaptations have made it possible for many students with physical disabilities to communicate with little difficulty. The possibilities are endless.

But let me tell you about Rudolpho, a 13-year-old student in Ms. Ng's class. After several weeks of being a compliant student, Rudolpho refused to read aloud or write on the board in front of his peers. And Ms. Ng knew why. Rudolpho had normal intelligence but wore a hearing aid and had lesser communication skills than his classmates. As an adolescent, Rudolpho keenly felt that he was different.

Not only was he different, but his technological equipment was definitely not cool. For example, at home he had a teletypewriter, or TTY, which enables deaf people to telephone each other and type conversations. But none of his peers in the general education class had ever seen anything so weird.

Ms. Ng had an idea. What about finding a popular communication device to level the playing field! So she spoke to Rudolpho's mother, who went shopping for an up-to-date vibrating pager that could receive e-mail and also convert voice mail into e-mail. That would allow Rudolpho to type e-mail messages to his peers, keep in touch with Mom and others, and—best of all—be considered cool by the local teenagers.

As for Ms. Ng, she was happy with what Mom purchased Why? Because not only was Rudolpho feeling more connected to his peers, he was also more eager to learn how to read, write, and spell. After all, that would be cool, too. It was not long before Rudolpho was considered the coolest kid in the class. Now he could feel motivated to improve his reading and writing skills, communicate with friends, and keep up with the local gossip.

For more information on technology, you can check out the Alliance for Technology Access at www.ATAccess.org

Summary of Main Ideas

- Fluency refers to reading that's smooth, fluid, and moderately flowing.
- Fluency can be learned by using predictable text.
- Predictable text has familiar words, common language patterns, and a common plot.
- Expository patterns occur when authors explain their messages via lists, cause and effect, comparisons and contrasts.
- The well-known DRTA method can be used to help students understand content information and explanation patterns.
- Mental imaging can cause readers to comprehend an author better, learn new words, predict new text, and solve problems.
- Oral reading fosters fluency.
- Oral reading also strengthens decoding skills.
- Readers theater provides the most enjoyable and effective practice in reading, writing, listening, and speaking.
- Fluency can also be developed through the reading of graphic materials.

Literacy Through Technology

Professional Standard: Uses instruction and information technologies to support literacy

A. With a partner, conduct a search for scripts you might use in your classroom. Search *children's theater* or *children's theater scripts*, and see what you can find. Or go to *Funtastic Kids Theater Scripts* at http://www.angelfire.com/scifi/theaterscripts/ Identify several royalty-free scripts that interest you.

B. Download a royalty-free script from the Internet to share with the class. Be sure to give credit to the author. Explain how this script could be used to develop fluency. What other things could you do to make script reading even more exciting? You may want to follow up by e-mailing the author to get more ideas.

Application Experiences for Your Course

A. *Literacy Teacher Vocabulary: List of Terms.* Teach each other these professional words and concepts:

read-aloud	repeated reading	choral reading
paired reading	echo reading	fluency
expository structures	readers theater	DRTA

B. *What's Your Opinion?* Discuss why you agree or disagree with the following statements:

1. Choral reading does not teach as well as paired reading.
2. Oral reading can build a classroom community.

3. Fluency is far more important than comprehension because comprehension is just understanding.
4. Repeated reading is great for first graders but not for fifth.

Creativity Training Session

A. Develop a creative way of showing or diagramming how fluency, oral reading, and comprehension contribute to each other and to the ability to read.

B. A creativity challenge: Take five 7-year-old children to the end of the other side of the Earth and leave them with only 5 gallons of Gator ade. *Exactly how many of the five children* will likely cry within the first 24 hours? Your job is to answer this challenge with a highly intellectual and creative answer, one that will please your professor and at least five of your peers.

Field Experiences

A. Select a patterned picture book and try out the 3-day procedures described in this chapter. Discuss your experiences with the class.

B. Engage a small group of five children (Group 1) in choral reading with whatever you give them to read. Then add five more children and engage all ten of them (Group 2) in choral reading the same piece. Then write a brief report on which group seemed to be more comfortable with the choral reading and very specifically why.

C. Do a quick survey of students, asking them, "Which of the following two activities in school do you like more?" Also ask them, "Which activities have taught you more? The activities are these: (1) having the teacher read to them and (2) allowing them to have free reading time. Explain your results.

D. Ask teachers who are teaching reading to English language learners, "How is your teaching different from teaching other students?"

References

Armbruster, B. B. (1991). Using literature in the content areas. *The Reading Teacher, 45,* 324–525.

Bradley, J. M., & Talgott, M. R. (1987). Reducing reading anxiety. *Academic Therapy, 22,* 349–358.

Bridge, C. A. (1979). Predictable materials for beginning readers. *Language Arts, 56,* 503–507.

Cunningham, A. E., & Stanovich, K. E. (1998). What reading does for the mind. *American Educator, 22,* 8–15.

Dahl, P. R., & Samuels, S. J. (1974). *A mastery-based experimental program for teaching poor readers high-speed word recognition skills.* Unpublished paper, University of Minneapolis.

Dowhower, S. L. (1987). Effects of repeated reading on second-grade transitional readers' fluency and comprehension. *Reading Research Quarterly, 22,* 389–406.

Harste, J. C., Short, K. G., & Burke, C. (1988). *Creating classrooms for authors.* Portsmouth, NH: Heinemann.

Hayes, D. (1989). Expository text structure and study learning. *Reading Horizons, 30*(1), 52–61.

Hoffman, J. V. (2003). Forward. In Timothy V. Rasinski, *The Fluent Reader.* New York: Scholastic Professional Books.

Ivey, G., & Broaddus, K. (2001). Just plain reading: a survey of what makes students want to read in middle school classrooms. *Reading Research Quarterly, 36*(4), 350–377.

Li, D., & Nes, S. L. (2001). Using paired reading to help ESL students become fluent and accurate readers. *Reading Improvement, 38*(2), 50–61.

Martinez, M., Roser, N., & Strecker, S. (1999). "I never thought I could be a star": A readers theatre ticket to reading fluency. *The Reading Teacher, 52,* 326–334.

Mathes, P. G., Torgesen, J. K., & Allor, J. H. (2001). The effects of peer-assisted literacy strategies for first-grade readers with and without additional computer-assisted instruction in phonological awareness. *American Educational Research Journal, 38,* 371–410.

McCauley, J. K., & McCauley, D. S. (1992). Using choral reading to promote language learning for ESL students. *The Reading Teacher, 45,* 526–533.

McCormick, C., & Mason, J. M. (1986). *Use of little books at home: A minimal intervention strategy that fosters early reading* (Technical Report No. 388). Urbana: Illinois University, Center for the Study of Reading.

Miccinati, J. L. (1985). Using prosodic cues to teach oral reading fluency. *The Reading Teacher, 39,* 206–212.

National Institute of Child Health and Human Development. (2001). *Report of the National Reading Panel: Teaching children to read.* Washington, DC: Author.

Paratore, J. R., & Indrisano, R. (1987). Intervention assessment of reading comprehension. *The Reading Teacher, 40,* 778–785.

Piccolo J. A. (1987). Expository text structure: Teaching and learning strategies. *The Reading Teacher, 40,* 838–847.

Pinnell, G. S., Pikulski, J. J., Wixon, K. K., Campbell, J. R., Gough, P. B., & Beatty, A. S. (1995). *Listening to children read aloud.* Washington, DC: U.S. Department of Education, office of Educational Research and Improvement.

Rasinski, T. V. (1990). Effects of repeated reading and listening-while-reading on reading fluency. *Journal of Educational Research, 83*(3), 147–150.

Rasinski, T. V. (2000). Speed does matter. *The Reading Teacher, 54,* 146–151.

Rasinski, T. V. (2003). *The fluent reader.* New York: Scholastic Professional Books.

Rasinski, T., & Padak, N. (2001). *From phonics to fluency: Effective teaching of decoding and reading fluency in the elementary school.* New York: Longman.

Roush, B. E. (2005). Drama rhymes: An instructional strategy. *The Reading Teacher, 58*(6), 584–587.

Sampson, M. R., Allen, R. V., & Sampson, M. B. (1991). *Pathways to literacy.* Chicago: Holt, Rinehart & Winston.

Samuels, S. J. (1979). The method of repeated readings. *The Reading Teacher, 32,* 403–408.

Sindelar, P. T., Monda, L. E., & O'Shea, L. J. (1990). Effects of repeated readings on instructional- and mastery-level readers. *Journal of Educational Research, 83*(4), 220–226.

Smith, F. (1994). *Understanding reading* (5th ed.). Hillsdale, NJ: Erlbaum.

Smith, F. (2003). *Unspeakable acts, unnatural practices.* Portsmouth, NH: Heinemann.

Templeton, S. (1991). *Teaching the integrated language arts.* Boston: Houghton Mifflin.

Other Suggested Readings

Burns, M. S., Snow, C., Griffin, P., & Alberts, B. (Eds.). (1999). *Starting out right: A guide to promoting children's reading success.* Washington, DC: National Academy Press.

Clay, M. M. (1991). *Becoming literate: The construction of inner control.* Portsmouth, NH: Heinemann.

Clay, M. M. (1993). *Reading Recovery: A guidebook for teachers in training.* Portsmouth, NH: Heinemann.

Fountas, I. C., & Pinnell, G. S. (1996). *Guided reading: Good first teaching for all children.* Portsmouth, NH: Heinemann.

Fulton, L., LeRoy, C., Pinkney, M., & Weekley, T. (1994). Peer education partners. *Teaching Exceptional Children, 26*(4).

Heckelman, R. G. (1966). Using the neurological impress remedial reading technique. *Academic Therapy, 1,* 235–239, 250.

Heckelman, R. G. (1969). A neurological impress method of remedial reading instruction. *Academic Therapy, 4,* 277, 282.

Henk, W. A. (1983). Adapting the NIM to improve comprehension. *Academic Therapy, 19,* 97–101.

Hoffman, J. V. (1987). Rethinking the role of oral reading in basal instruction. *Elementary School Journal, 87*(3), 367–373.

Holdaway, D. (1979). *The foundations of literacy.* Sydney, Australia: Ashton Scholastic.

Rayner, K. (1998). Eye movements in reading and information processing: 20 years of research. *Psychological Bulletin, 124*(3), 372–422.

Reutzel, D. R., & Cooter, R. B. (1999). *Balanced reading strategies and practices.* Upper Saddle River, NJ: Merrill Education/Prentice Hall.

Chapter Nine

Teach Reading Through Literature

It is the supreme art of the teacher to awaken joy in creative expression and knowledge.

—*Albert Einstein*

The man who does not read good books has no advantage over the man who can't read them.

—*Mark Twain*

Ninth Objective for Your Teaching Success:

Use literature, book clubs, technology, and parents to motivate reading.

What does *literature* include? Besides joy? A vast volume of worthwhile, high-quality literature available to children and adults alike. What else? Stories, poems, humorous novels, serious novels, easy books, studious books, biographies, books on science, and history, sports stories, picture books, folk tales, mysteries, animal stories, realism, fantasy, information, outdoor adventures, teenage romances and plays. What else? Textbooks. They're included in the term *literature*. What we're talking about is the reading of *connected meaningful language,* rather than the bits and pieces of language found on worksheets and activity booklets.

The most effective kind of reading practice is the reading of *whole-text literature*. That's why the National Reading Panel strongly recommends that school children be provided with at least 2 hours per week of uninterrupted silent reading of literature in the school environment (National Institute of Child Health and Human Development, 2000).

Allowing students to read an author's entire book of fiction or nonfiction is what we are after, and this can best be accomplished through a bona fide literature program. You already know that children's literature can provide a variety of benefits, but I'm asking that we study those benefits like you and I study the clothes we buy— you know, like holding them up to our tired bodies, frowning at the unfriendly mirror, trying them on, and finally seeing the exciting advantage of the sixteenth item.

The Astonishing Advantages of Literature

Professional Standard: Models reading and writing as valuable lifelong activities

Literature Provides Meaningful Reading Practice for Different Students

People learn at different speeds and in different ways. How easy that is to say, and yet how difficult it can be to do anything about it. Attending to individual differences can be especially challenging when it comes to reading instruction. We know that teachers working in self-contained classrooms usually have students whose general reading abilities vary by several grade levels. For instance, a fifth-grade teacher may have to work with children whose grade-level reading-achievement scores range from 1.0 to 8.0. And don't forget the variations in reading interests among students.

Here is a chance for literature to come to the rescue—for both the teacher's and the child's benefit. Literature can, in the hands of a knowledgeable teacher, provide very nicely for individual differences, offering adequate practice that is enjoyable and highly motivated.

Literature Offers Abundant Models with Whom Children Can Identify

Psychologists tell us that one of the chief ways people develop values, ambitions, and that all-important self-concept is through emotional identification with another person—by imagining themselves to be that person or by becoming like that person. Literature, particularly biographies and fiction, provides infinite opportunities for such identification. A single book, of course, is not likely to provide as powerful a model as a likable teacher or an admired parent. But if you think about your own experience with books, you'll probably remember times that books made a difference—in how you felt about yourself, about human behavior, or about your beliefs.

Literature Is an Important Supplement for Textbooks

Without literature it would be nearly impossible to achieve some of the objectives of social studies and science programs—as well as music, physical education, art, health, and math programs. Suppose you want to help your students identify with the problems, values, and lifestyles of different people. Simply having them read about these people in a textbook will not accomplish your objective. Social studies textbooks, for instance, don't provide enough of a deep understanding; abstract information goes right through our students' heads and leaves them hankering for something concrete. But if you have ever read any of the *Little House* books by Laura Ingalls Wilder, you know firsthand how she breathed life into the history of the 19th century and made it possible for thousands of children to understand what times were like back then.

As a model and inspiration for children's own writing, literature is hard to beat. My students have always been highly motivated to write following the conclusion of a book I've read aloud to them. And other teachers I've talked to have had the same experience. If the teacher has helped the children become aware of an author's use of words, the personalities of the characters, and the subtleties of the plot, children will be bursting with ideas—to extend the story, change its ending, or write a sequel. Similar enthusiasm follows the conclusion of a book kids have read all by themselves, especially if they've had a chance to discuss the book with others in the class.

Literature Can Send Thrills Down Your Spine

Some of the best writing and graphic art today is found between the covers of children's books. My absolute favorite, Marguerite Henry's classic *King of the Wind,* is rich in beautiful prose, sensitive characterization, subtlety of plot development, and deep layers of meaning. By achieving an intangible sense of beauty and wonder, the author provides us with an aesthetic experience, and the book is worth reading for that reason alone. Other similar aesthetic experiences that come to mind are found in the marvelous oldies—Speare's *Witch of Blackbird Pond,* Hunt's *Up a Road Slowly,* Paterson's *Bridge to Terabithia,* Fleischman's *Joyful Noise,* Rylant's *Missing May,* J. R. R. Tolkien's *The Hobbit* and *The Lord of the Rings.* (Sorry . . . Harry Potter books can't yet be considered oldies, but wow!

Literature Brings the Social Cohesion So Desperately Needed

Literature often is the glue that makes us a society rather than a mere collection of unrelated individuals—for example, the luscious glue provided by J. K. Rowling. Okay, I'll admit that some of our cohesion comes from watching the same television programs—*David Letterman, Oprah Winfrey, Saturday Night Live,* the newest of the sitcoms, or maybe even *Monday Night Football.* But schools do have more than an equal opportunity to build cohesion in our society. As William Boly (1987) said.

> The public schools are potentially one of the most meaningful forces for social cohesion. They are the modern equivalent of the village square—a forum for identifying the shared ethos of our diverse and cosmopolitan society; a place where all our children can come together and discover what it is that unites us as people. Well-taught literature is an essential part of that consensus building (p. 12).

Literature Can Be a Great Teacher of Ethical and Moral Responsibility

Boly (1987) believes that the greatest value of literature is that it can help each young person feel responsible for self and others. As he puts it:

> Literature asks the big questions such as: "What is the relationship of the individual to society? What gives meaning to a woman or man's life?" In

providing answers to these questions [most] authors do not sermonize. Instead they show plausible characters grappling with the force of circumstance and the consequences of their own acts. (p. 9)

In short, if read often enough, literature can play a vital role in character development-exploring concepts like caring, sharing, honesty, politeness, sensitivity, and friendly kindness, not to ignore the opposites of those virtues.

Reminder: Exposition Is Literature, Too

Did you know that between third and ninth grades, a student is expected to read at least 12,600 nonfiction words from content-area textbooks each year, particularly in the areas of science, social studies, and mathematics? That's a total of 88,200 words. If you include Grades 10 through 12, the total is 126,000. That's a lot of reading, don't you think?

Unfortunately, the schema that children develop for stories is not adequate to protect them from the "monsters of exposition". Kids from kindergarten to grade 6 need years of guidance to build explanation schema, preferably beginning with some of their earliest books in the home and the classroom. Two good examples of such books include Eric Carle's *Draw Me a Star,* in which he explains for children's benefit how one type of story can be developed, and *Cactus Hotel* by Brenda Guiberson, in which she verbally and pictorially illustrates the growth of a giant saguaro cactus. Fortunately more and more research is being focused on the values of expository text in early literacy development (Gambrell, 2005).

Protect Your Students from the Monsters of Exposition

You can help by patiently and playfully guiding your students step by step through books in which the author is explaining rather than telling a story. You can *show* them how to separate cause from effect, how to separate problems from solutions, how to draw images of things that are named in lists. The right environment for understanding nonfiction authors requires much more talking about informational things in the classroom and the home. For example, during show-and-tell time or during news-sharing time, you can pose questions that gently introduce the explanation patterns: "How would you compare those two things? How are they alike? How would you say they're different? What causes this difference, do you think?"

Through *listening, talking,* and *writing* about informational matters, children can get a much better feel for the informational language they are expected to read. And this is true for children of all ages. As Bill Harp (1989) explained, "The old saying that 'children learn to read in the primary grades and read to learn in the intermediate grades' is not true" (p. 726). As was mentioned earlier, children comprehend content-area materials much better when we explain to them exactly how authors organize and present their explanations (Hayes, 1989; Paratore & Indrisano, 1987)—using sequence, lists, cause/effect, description, problem/solution, and comparison/contrast.

The Challenge of Content Area Vocabulary

The specialized vocabulary of content areas can also be challenging—words like *culture* or *energy* or *dividends* or *divisors.* But what really makes these specialized words so difficult? As Nagy (1988) reminds us again from Chapter 6, these words are difficult not because of their length or even their spelling, but because the *concepts* they represent are difficult. So don't waste your time and your students' time by simply writing them on the board or spelling them out loud. This is where your creativity can shine. Go back to Chapter 6 if necessary and review the ways to teach concept-laden words.

Reap the Benefits of a Good Classroom Library

Professional Standard: Uses a variety of trade books to stimulate an appreciation of the written word

If we truly believe that skilled reading is a major asset in the modern world, if we believe that teaching children to read well is one of our major responsibilities as teachers, and if we want our students to *practice* reading, then we had better provide time and space for that practice in school. (Outside school there's a real monster called television that craves your students' attention.)

And where should they carry on such practice? As Bissett's research (1969) determined many years ago, when a classroom has its own literature collection, children read 50% more books than they do in classrooms without such a collection. However, to freely translate a strong reminder from Fractor, Woodruff, Martinez, and Teale (1993), children are like cats—they're very picky when it comes to choosing what they want to do (or consume): "A classroom library must be well designed to entice children to read when given the opportunity of selecting from a variety of classroom activities" (p. 476).

Fractor, Woodruff, Martinez, and Teale are two elementary school teachers and two professors of education who observed the libraries in 183 classrooms, rating those as excellent that met these criteria:

- at least 8 books per child
- a procedure for keeping books organized
- a special classroom area that is given a name
- a space large enough to accommodate five children

Four Excellent Classroom Libraries

Out of those 183 classrooms *only four* libraries met all of the criteria.

- **Cynthia Sloan's kindergarten classroom library.** In a suburban, largely middle-class school, this library is set in one corner of the classroom and occupies approximately 15% of the total available floor space in the room. Approximately 400 books are available. The library was named The Book Nook by the children and also contains a listening center, props that students use to recreate stories, a rocking chair, class-published books, videotapes, and puppets. This library is exactly what our four researchers were looking for.

- **Marjorie Woodruff's Grade 2 classroom library.** The children in this room are all considered to be at risk because they have experienced problems in learning to read. One of the first priorities for Ms. Woodruff was to develop, in concert with the students, a classroom library. There were no bookshelves and few books in the classroom since this was a newly added second grade. Consequently this teacher brought her own hand-built open-faced shelves to school, purchased two other shelves, and stocked the library with 170 books from her personal library. The students named their library Kids' Corner Library. Classroom collections with multiple copies of appropriate trade books were ordered through the school. Many features of this library lure happy youngsters to find a favorite book and relax: a bulletin board with book jackets and author information, comfortable pillows, a basket of stuffed animals, a designated shelf of puppets, and an adjacent listening center.

- **Jann Fractor's Grade 5 classroom library.** This suburban, ethnically mixed school opened just 3 weeks before the researchers' visit. No bookshelves were yet provided for teachers, and no provisions were in place for making trade books or other materials available to teachers for their rooms. Yet, because she is committed to the importance of a classroom library, Ms. Fractor had already gathered together a range of quality books. She displayed the books attractively, provided a comfortable and interesting reading space, and had the children develop a literature-related display.

■ **Laura Barrera's classroom library.** This school is located in the midst of a housing project in an intercity area. Almost 98% of the students at this school qualify for free or reduced lunch, and over 98% of the students are Latino. The school has been working on developing literature-based reading instruction, with a special emphasis on the use of multicultural literature. Ms. Barrera's library—its name is Tierra de Fantasia—is a cornerstone of this classroom project. In addition to promoting voluntary reading with a good selection of quality books, comfortable seating, and movable bulletin boards for privacy, the library also reflects the teacher's emphasis on the integration of reading and writing. Writing materials and activities are part of the library, with one bulletin board being used as a message board where children can leave all kinds of notes for each other, including messages about the books they have been reading.

Laura Barrera's classroom library is similar to what educators Koskinen, Blum, Bisson, Phillips, Creamer, and Baker (2003) have been promoting and what they refer to as a book-rich classroom environment. These children take their books home and reread them to one or more adults; at home they also have audio models to read along with. In their study of 16 teachers and their 162 first-grade students, these researchers found that (1) there was significantly enhanced comprehension, with or without the home contributions; (2) the home-based rereading increased students' reading motivation and promoted more parent involvement; and (3) the audio models were highly beneficial for students learning to speak English.

Know Children's Literature Intimately

In many community libraries, juvenile books account for at least one half of the total circulation. Part of this increase is the result of the vast growth in the publication of books for children—from 852 new titles in 1940 to over 4,000 annually in recent years. And along with this quantitative growth has come an increase in the variety of juvenile books. The ever-popular mysteries and fantasies must compete for shelf space with fictional stories of a dozen other genres, with informational books on nearly every conceivable subject, and with books that portray life as it is. Whether you teach in a push-pull-click-click type of school or a flexible, creative learning environment, knowing and showing "children's books" is the most important skill you can develop, don't you think? Reading them yourself is a great way to wind down

after a hectic day—and knowledge of the books your students like can provide you with enormous prestige in their eyes.

In selecting the books for your classroom library, look for challenging ones for better readers, but also search for a large quantity of easy books—those that are interesting to your students but a snap to read. These books are often referred to as high-interest / low-vocabulary books. Children (and adults) can easily become discouraged if one book after another offers them little more than frustration. Teachers who make it a habit to read children's books themselves have little trouble offering children guidance in selecting books.

The International Reading Association (IRA) occasionally puts out an annotated list of high-interest/low-vocabulary books. One of these, *Easy Reading* by Ryder, Graves, and Graves (1989), describes a variety of book series and periodicals for struggling readers. This inexpensive paperback can be ordered through the Internet; be sure to ask for the newest edition.

A large number of teachers encourage their students to purchase their own paperback books at a reasonable price from one or more of the commercial book clubs like Scholastic or Troll. My own students couldn't wait to buy their very own paperbacks. Also, several anthology publishers have fairly large classroom collections of paperbacks designed for their programs. You can check the reviews of "children's books" in each issue of *The Reading Teacher,* as well as the list of Children's Choices Awards in each October issue. Through school libraries, municipal libraries, book clubs, bookstores, and publishers, a resourceful teacher can always find ways to provide students with a wide choice of well-written literature.

Provide Plenty of Time to Read

As Jane Hansen (1987) says, readers need long blocks of uninterrupted time: time to choose books, to think, to interact with other readers, to show their excitement. And Hansen's belief is backed up by the report of the National Reading Panel (National Institute of Child Health and Human Development, 2000).

Note that Hansen says what *readers* need, not just what children need. If you reflect on your own reading, I think you'll agree that she's right. I don't like being interrupted, I really like to choose my own books, and I do like to share things *I've chosen* and am reading all by myself. And the kids I've worked with at various grade levels seem to feel the same way.

The modern classroom is often a better place in which to read than the home. At home, remember reading must frequently compete with the omnipresent television and its tempting tidbits of instant culture, instant mirth, and instant action. That's why Anderson, Wilson, and Fielding (1988) wanted to find out how much time children spend voluntarily reading outside school. They used fifth graders as their sample population because children at this age should be able to concentrate for long periods of time. How long do you think the kids voluntarily read outside school? Would you guess 60 minutes a day, 40 minutes, or 20? Try 4 minutes—or less! But that's only for 50% of the children. The rest read for even fewer minutes. Is it any better now? Only because of Harry Potter.

There are many reasons for this miserable showing, but one reason was discovered in a consumer research study: 60% of American households did not buy a single book during a 1-year time period (NPD Group, 1991). And are things any better today? Except for those parents who buy those wonderful Harry Potter books, I don't think so. Would you like a good way to make a difference? Try sending home a short list each month of recommended books from the new book list in *The Reading Teacher*, which is available from the International Reading Association (http://www.reading.org).

The SSR and DEAR Approaches

Many years ago Fader and McNeil (1968) provided one answer to the time problem in *Hooked on Books: Program and Proof*. They recommended a timed approach in which, during the first week, only 5 minutes a day is set aside for intensive silent reading. This time is gradually increased until the students are reading for 30 minutes or more a day. Fader and McNeil claimed considerable success, even with kids who were reluctant to read. Their name for this approach was sustained silent reading (SSR). Many teachers prefer the name, drop-everything-and-read (DEAR) time.

Research on SSR provides mixed reviews. However, as Spiegel (1983) points out, most researchers have tried the approach for only a month or two before administering achievement tests and closing up shop. When a new football coach is hired, the fans usually give him 2 or 3 *years* to shape up the team. Yet when a new idea is tried in a classroom, the teacher is expected to produce results in 2 or 3 months! Kaisen (1987) studied the effects of DEAR time on very young children and found that it works even with *first graders,* as long as certain conditions are met:

1. Teachers themselves read.

2. Each child has more than one book readily available.

3. Wordless picture books are available.

4. Books read to the children at home are available.

5. Preprimers are available.

Flaspeter (1995) reviewed several other studies and found that long-term SSR consistently has a positive effect on attitudes and reading achievement, regardless of whether children use English as a first or a second language. Ozburn (1995) found the same thing to be true of at-risk ninth graders, who improved an average of 3.9 grade levels when engaging in DEAR time. Cash and Young (1991) also found positive effects on elementary-grade children's attitudes toward reading.

Why SSR May Not Always Work

As much as I want to encourage the use of an SSR program, I must caution that SSR is not a panacea. In fact, the National Reading Panel (National Institute, 2000) reviewed research on the effects of SSR/DEAR time on student reading achievement and concluded that SSR may or may not work.

There are obvious reasons that SSR doesn't always work very well. McCracken and McCracken (1978) investigated several SSR programs that were doing poorly and found the following common characteristics. This list provides an excellent checklist for teachers who wish to check the quality of their SSR programs.

- The teacher did not read during the SSR period.
- The troublemakers did not read during the SSR period.
- Visiting adult aides did not read during the SSR period.
- The SSR period was too long for the particular students involved.
- There were not enough books available.
- The teacher didn't want to give the program time to work.

I have found several other reasons for poor results:

- Students are reading at the frustration rather than the independent level.
- No help has been given to students to find interesting and easy books.
- Teachers have been given no help in learning precise procedures.
- Teachers have been given no help in understanding the value of SSR.
- Teachers have not taken the time to assist struggling readers.

Struggling readers need a great deal of guidance before independent reading begins. The teacher should be directly involved in helping struggling readers establish a purpose for reading. SSR or DEAR time for independent reading must be *successful* time—just having students read is not enough. The kid who is asked to read unsuccessfully for 30 minutes learns that reading should be avoided. The best solution for students struggling with reading is to provide them with *supported* one-on-one reading time.

Get Students to Respond to Literature

Teachers today are encouraging their students to *respond* to literature. How involved a person is in responding emotionally and intellectually to a writer's story or ideas makes the difference in the reader's understanding. *Involvement is nearly always a key factor in learning* (Pratten & Hales, 1986). Let me give you an example of how important involvement is. Twice in my university teaching career, I have taken a leave of absence and gone back to teaching kids again, as a refresher course. *Children are a teacher's best teacher.*

Book Projects: The Power of Choice

I signed a contract to teach a group of fifth graders for a year. During the first day I was trying to get the students used to the idea of a literature program rather than a basal-reader program. They were dubious, of course; reading couldn't possibly be that much fun. To them, reading had been basal readers, worksheets, and formal book reports. And here I was telling them that they could read any book they wanted to and that I would be much too bored to read mere book reports.

I wanted them to do book projects instead—projects that would interest their classmates and me and sell us on the idea of reading another book. There was a visible change in their faces as I told them about projects in which they could perform a skit about one of the events in their book, create a bright and colorful advertisement for it, write a newspaper report on one of the scenes, or do one of dozens of other things. I was lucky—that one discussion did it.

The book projects began slowly, modeled first by me and then by three of the bravest kids in the class. These were shared during my designated Friday-before-reading time. The next Friday *six* projects were shared; the third Friday, ten; and so it went. Their favorite project became Twenty Questions, a very good thinking game. They enjoyed it so much that by November I had to change the rules: We would share book projects twice a week instead of once, and a particular style of book project could be done only twice during the year by each child. In February the rule had to be changed again: Book projects could be shared for only 10 minutes a day—but every single day.

These book projects started with 40 ideas that I had gathered or invented. As the school year continued, however, the children began to get in on the act, inventing new book projects individually and later brainstorming with me for more of them. We read an incredible number of books that year. The range per child was 15 to 58 books, with an average of 34.

Part of the credit for all of that reading was a cooperative project to see how many books the entire class could read by the end of the school year. We created "book ends" of many colors made of simple 8½; × 11 sheets of paper. Each sheet of paper made 16 tickets that were 1 × 5½; the colors represented different genres. When a student had read a book and done a book project on it, he or she would print the title and author on the ticket and tape it to the rail close to the ceiling on the longest wall. They were allowed to put their names on their tickets but only on the back. Competition was out and cooperation was in. And so was learning.

Tips for Success

The guidance you offer students on individual projects is probably the key factor in making the projects interesting and worthwhile. Simply passing out a list of projects is not very motivating. The most effective form of guidance is to read juvenile books yourself and model some of the projects yourself. For instance, one of the recommended oral reading projects is to put on a puppet play about one part of the book. You can inspire your class by sharing your book in this way and letting them share their books in a similar fashion. Don't make your presentation so awe-inspiring that they'll be afraid to emulate you. Do use a simple cardboard stage and puppets that they can easily make themselves.

Along with the more creative approaches, just chatting about a book you have read will usually encourage many in the class to read it or to use the same approach with another book. This is sometimes called a book talk. Besides guiding through modeling, you can provide classroom discussion time to talk about different ways class members are thinking about sharing their books. This is usually inspiring to those who are having trouble deciding on a project for a particular book.

Reading Workshops: Learning from Each Other

Teachers engaged in literature-based programs have invented several other formats, including *reading workshops, literature circles,* and *book clubs.* There are similarities among these, but also some important differences you should be aware of to derive the special benefits of each. Also, you should be aware that these terms do not mean exactly the same thing to any two teachers, even in the same school building.

To Ann, a fourth-grade teacher described by Vacca and Rasinski (1992), a *reading workshop* is a period of 45 to 60 minutes during the school day in which reading is *king*. Her students spend part of this time in practice reading (SSR). While they are reading, Ann is not engaged in any form of direct teaching but is modeling what she preaches by reading an enjoyable book in front of them and then talking about it later.

When students are *not* reading during the workshop, they are usually doing things such as *skimming* books in the classroom library, in search of a new book; *writing* notes or letters in their reading journals; *responding* to a previous e-mail message about a book they have finished reading; and *writing* a response to a letter they've received.

Sometimes at the beginning of a reading workshop the neophytes give book talks to convince someone else to read "their" book next. Often at the beginning or end Ann presents a mini lesson on a literacy-related skill or strategy.

There are reading-workshop rules up on the wall which have been read several times to show how serious this activity is. Nearly all of the class have figured out that they can't do homework or read textbooks or comic books during this time. Yes, they should go to the bathroom before the workshop begins. And yes, they can sit wherever they wish as long as they disturb *no one* and feet do not go up on furniture. Ann does not believe in *laissez-faire* education; learning is serious but enjoyable business.

Here are the key elements you should include in a reading workshop, including very approximate time lines.

- Part I:
  Teacher read-alouds of new books — 5 minutes
  Teacher-led mini lessons on critical reading skills and strategies — 10–15 minutes
  Student self-selection of books — 5 minutes
- Part II:
  Sustained silent reading — 20 minutes
  Responding to literature (often group work) — 20 minutes
  Teacher assessment of individual readers or small groups
  (during previous two segments) — 10 minutes
- Part III:
  Student sharing of literature response projects — 5–10 minutes

Literature Circles: Book Clubs for Kids

Literature circles are like those great-books clubs that many adults belong to—clubs in which you voluntarily discuss books everyone is reading at the same time, sharing chapter by chapter until it's time to put the book in the room library. It's a book you really want to read, and you gain meaning from the blend of several people's interpretations. Literature circles fit the general nature of *book clubs*, according to Raphael and McMahon (1994): "a program that integrates reading, writing, student-led discussion groups, whole-class discussions, and instruction" (p. 102). Literature circles seem to be useful for Grades 4 and up and can be creatively modified to fit younger students as well.

Harvey Daniels (1994, 2002) describes the literature-circle routine:

Literature circles are small temporary discussion groups that have chosen to read the same story . . . While reading each group-determined portion of the text, each member prepares to take specific responsibilities in the upcoming discussion, and everyone comes to the group with the notes needed to help perform that job. The circles have regular meetings, with discussion roles rotating each session. . . . Once readers can successfully conduct their own wide-ranging, self-sustaining discussions, formal discussion roles may be dropped. (p. 13)

Long and Gove (2004) recommend literature circles for two reasons: (1) They encourage students to self-select what they want to read and talk about, and (2) they encourage students to interpret, in cooperative groups, what they have been reading. Vacca, Vacca, and Gove (2000) also like literature circles because they are formed *not according to the students' reading abilities* or cultures, but by their choice of book to read. Consequently, the size of each literature circle can vary, and students are encouraged to take an interest in each other's opinions and discuss each other's ideas. The motivations and beliefs of main characters are usually hot items.

Jill Scott's Experience

Jill Scott (1994), a teacher in Henry, Illinois, tells about her particular experimentation with literature circles:

Literature circles are groups of three to eight students who have read the same story or novel and have gathered to discuss their reading. Usually the students have self-selected their books, and the literature circle members change as books are completed and new ones chosen. These discussions are teacher supported but student led. . . . Literature circles meet on a regular basis, and students agree on how much to read independently by the next circle meeting .. . . Students learn various ways to respond to the literature and to prepare for a literature circle discussion. . . . (p. 37)

Scott based her decision to use literature circles on Knoeller's (1994) discovery that at least 90% of students will voluntarily participate in student-led discussions— a much better rate than most teacher-led discussions enjoy. Scott also based her decision on the eagerness of her students to share book ideas with others. As one student put it: "The meaning of the book isn't complete until it is shared." And as Scott herself put it: "Peers are so important to school students—let them talk, argue, debate, agree, and disagree over books" (p. 37).

Scott also chose the literature-circle approach because it doesn't require that students be grouped as fast, average, and struggling readers. Instead, the literature circle idea is built on the principle of appreciation for other people's ideas and perceptions. Thus, building a sense of self-esteem for everyone in the group is a key feature of this type of literature study and is accomplished only in a classroom environment that already fosters those same principles.

A Combination of Reading Workshop and Literature Circle

Scott (1994) engages her students in a reading-workshop format for 3 or 4 weeks and then switches to literature circles for the same amount of time. These two formats seem to "balance and complement each other and ensure that . . . students are reading more text than ever before" (p. 38). When she has her students begin a new cycle of literature circles, she gives book chats related to the topic for the next cycle (e.g., historical fiction, a theme, or an author study).

Before students meet in their group, they are expected to respond in writing to the portion they have been reading. At first their response is highly structured by Scott's assignment of each student to a role to carry out in the group. For instance, a student assigned to be Character Captain would concentrate on writing down responses to the behavior of the characters. A student assigned to be Discussion Director would concentrate on developing meaningful questions to be discussed during literature-circle time. Other roles include these:

- Word Wizard—learns the meanings of interesting or confusing words
- Summarizer—keeps track of key points
- Passage Master—finds important passages to share
- Connector—thinks of ways that the book applies to real life
- Illustrator—decides on an important part to illustrate and share
- Scene Setter—determines the nature of each scene and describes it to the rest of the group

According to Scott, these roles are intended "to teach students to build on each other's comments, make connections, reflect, and evaluate the story instead of simply reporting on the book" (p. 39). The roles are taught to the students in two ways: (1) by having students play the role while the teacher is reading books out loud to them and (2) by having students take notes on only one character in preparation for literature-circle time. Scott gradually increases the roles that the students write about and discuss. Their notes are personal, rather than specific answers to specific questions asked by the teacher. Eventually the students are able to use the roles intuitively as they read books and discuss them.

Scott also uses mini lessons to discuss such processes as listening to each other, creating interesting discussion topics, taking useful notes, and learning a procedure such as *graphic webbing*. Another role Scot plays is to observe the effectiveness and ineffectiveness of the different groups so that she can provide suggestions to the entire class. She usually circulates while the groups get started and then joins one of the groups for more intensive observation.

Literature circles, or book clubs, last from 15 to 40 minutes, depending on the depth of the book or topic. Such variation in time requires the teacher to circulate again as circles gradually disband and students return to independent reading. Students are guided to take more and more responsibility for keeping the reading, writing, and discussions organized.

Scott (1994) offers some advice:

> There are times when I am facilitating literature circles in my classroom and things are simply not working well .. . . This happens in every classroom, in every subject area, and we must not be tempted to look only at a certain day's product and take the responsibility back from the students. After seeing the power of literature circles in my classroom . . . I am confident the process . . . is extremely valuable. (p. 41)

So what's the real purpose of having book clubs? According to Lois Brandts (Frank, Dixon, & Brandts, (2001), it's for the advancement of thinking:

> My whole purpose, doing Book Clubs, is to get them to learn how to have civilized conversations about good books. You can structure that through Book Club, but there is so much more to it. I mean, that's the part that you see. All the parts that you don't see are the questions they start to ask themselves. The way they start to think about authors. The way they start to think ahead. The chess moves in their mind. (p. 449)

Engagement Strategies for Literature Circles

Professional Standard: Provides opportunities for creative and personal responses to literature circle discussions

Long and Gove (2004) have created three engagement strategies that can be blended effectively with literature circles:

1. Ask open-ended questions; listen to, honor, and respond to students; and encourage students to read between the lines of the text.

2. Invite students to investigate and find out about explicit or implicit text information—in order to dig deeper into the text's meaning.

3. Encourage students to pose and solve problems related to important text events. (p. 352)

There's one major difference between Long and Gove's form of literature circle and the form described by Scott. Whereas Scott's appoach is in line with Daniels's (1994, 2002) form of literature circle, Long and Gove's approach is adapted from Edmiston and Long (1999), Davis (1997), Edmiston (1998), Long (2001), Manley and O'Neill (1997), O'Neill (1995), Taylor (1996, 1998), and Wilhelm and Edmiston (1998).

To explain what I just said, with Scott's approach, groups of three to eight students read the same story or novel and then *meet afterwards to talk about it.* With the approach of Long and Gove, teachers and *students stay together as they read,* creating their respective individual meanings as they read. As you can imagine, the teacher is heavily involved in developing questions ahead of time that will make the students think more at each step of the way through the book.

My own experience tells me that students would feel safer and more interested if Scott's approach (small groups) was used with the first two or three books. This would take advantage of the fact that students generally prefer two ways to be taught: (1) The teacher reads out loud to the students and occasionally stops to get their reactions and to ask a question or two to keep them alert and involved, or (2) Students get to choose books that interest them and time to read them by themselves. To start directly with the approach of Long and Gove might be too challenging: We don't want to bombard them with teacher-type questions that demand a quick answer, and them can make many children nervous, embarrassed, and even resistant to learning.

My recommendation is to use the Long and Gove teaching approach on the fourth book for fourth graders and students who are struggling readers; roughly the third book for fifth graders; the second book for sixth graders; and the first book for seventh graders. However, later it would be wise to *interchange* the two methods of teaching throughout the school year.

Try a Theme Approach for a Different Learning Experience

Perhaps for your next unit or focus, you and your students might decide to center attention on a *theme;* that is, "an underlying idea that ties the characters, the setting, and the plot together . . . " (Sippola, 1993, p. 222). A theme is "what remains after the details of the characters, the plot, and the setting have faded away" (p. 217). You might arrive at a theme as a result of your awareness of children's books and the fact that several books have the same theme. Or you might arrive at it by brainstorming with your students or deciding to integrate art, music, and literature.

Rather than a theme, you and your students might choose a topical unit that "focuses on a specific concrete phenomenon in nature" (Sippola, 1993, p. 218). The goal of these units is usually to learn more about something that interests both teacher and students—for example, monsters, dinosaurs, how things work, fantasy lands, journeys, famous people, dogs, or horses.

Another type of unit would be a genre unit, which explores a particular type of book, such as historical fiction, science fiction, or biography. Still another *type* would allow students to explore a contemporary issue, such as race relations or religious persecution.

Later you might decide to focus on writing techniques, or literary elements (Eeds & Peterson, 1995), such as the development of plot through the creation of conflicts; the development of characters; or, with older students, the development of different characters through variations in dialogue and mannerisms. The unit of focus can be most anything that inspires your students to read, write, and learn.

Combining Literature and Content Areas

Another focus for your units can be created by combining literacy development through literature with a content area like social studies or science. In this way the teacher's instructional program is not broken into discrete subjects. Also, the students' learning activities have more coherence, and it is more likely that one area of the curriculum will inspire the study of another. For instance, the study of storms can be enhanced by knowledge gained from science reading. It can be enlivened through social studies, reading about famous storms in history—ones that changed the results of a battle or the status of rich and poor. Through literature, storms can be understood in greater depth. Rather than learning only how storms begin and how large they get, students can read about the effects on individuals, e.g., a Tsunami.

Or you and your students might sometimes choose not to concentrate on anything at all. As Tompkins and McGee (1993) point out,

> [It is] not always necessary to have students focus on a single book, a unit, or a theme cycle .... Much of the time students should have the freedom to select and read the books they are interested in, without having to read books the teacher or other students have selected. (p. 312)

It is also possible to have both a unit and individual choices at the same time— particularly for avid readers who think nothing of reading two or three books per week.

Let Technology Motivate Reading

Professional Standard: Provides opportunities to use a variety of electronic reference sources

Here are some questions and answers about technology and reading that might be useful.

Question One: Is it a good idea to encourage my students to use the Internet instead of those wonderful trade books we just talked about?

Answer: No, but it's a great idea to have them use *both*. And don't feel bad if you're unsure of yourself. At least 50% of all teachers consider themselves to be computer novices, and only 42% of new teachers feel well prepared to teach with technological media (Labbo, Leu, Kinzer, Teale, Cammack, Kara-Soteriou, & Sanny, 2003).

Question Two: What are the benefits of technological reading for me and my students?

Answer: Let me list just some of them for you:

- You can keep up with the age we live in—and with your students.
- Students who don't like to read books are often turned on to reading at their own rate at the computer, without being critiqued.
- Students get lots of immediate feedback, a powerful teaching tool.
- They can write a multitude of organizations for information via e-mail.
- Students can play educational games without bothering classmates.

Question Three: Will computers and the Internet eventually take over my role as a professional teacher?

Answer: Computers will never replace teachers in the classroom. Technology is a tool, not the teacher, While computers are becoming more interactive and use immediate reinforcements . . . they pale in comparison to one-on-one teaching correspondence with a living, breathing person with whom a student can converse about word-attack strategies and the author's meaning. Technology should be used . . . as a supplement to, rather than replacement of, literacy instruction by the teacher. (Labbo et al., 2003, p. 304)

Question Four: How do I reach the National Educational Technology Standards for Students—I have questions?

Answer: Go to http://www.ncrel.org or e-mail iste@iste.org

Question Five: What exciting and educational literature experiences are provided through the Internet for my students?

Answer: Virtual tours.

- **Virtual Tour A** is a collection of 300 tours of countries, cities, museums, exhibits, and the U.S. government. Right in the classroom you and your students can vividly see as well as read about persons, places, and things. (http://www.virtualfreesites.com/tours.html).
- **Virtual Tour B** is a set of tours designed to make you feel as if you are right there, traveling among the Chinese people (http://www.chinavista.com/travel/virtualtours.html).
- **Virtual Tour C** lets you see the Tower of London, Britain's crown jewels, and other historical things and places (http://www.toweroflondontour.com/).

■ **Virtual Tour D**   is a virtual marching tour of the American Revolutionary War—"The Philadelphia Campaign 1777, From Rebels to Mature Army" (http://www.ushistory.org/march/).

■ **Virtual Tour E**   lets you visit a total of 45 museums at little or no cost to you. Are you ready?
(http://www.virtualfreesites.com/museums.museums.html)

1. Virtual Altair Museum (First Personal Computer)
2. American Museum of Natural History
3. American Museum of Photography (Guided Tour)
4. American Red Cross Virtual Museum
5. American Treasures—Library of Congress
6. Ancient Olympic Games Virtual Museum
7. Ancient Roman Villa
8. Andy Warhol Museum
9. Canadian Museum of Civilization
10. Catherine Palace of Tsarskoye Selo
11. Collection at the National Gallery of Art
12. DeCordova 35-acre Sculpture Park
13. Drop Zone Virtual Museum (WW II Airborne)
14. Durham Cathedral
15. Ellis Island, NY 1900–1920 Photographic Exhibit
16. Institute and Museum of History of Science—Florence, Italy
17. German Leather Museum
18. Greek and Roman Art Collection
19. Henry Ford Museum and Greenfield Village
20. Holocaust Museum
21. International Museum of Horses
22. Jimmy Stewart Museum
23. Museum of HP Calculators
24. Museum of Unnatural Mystery
25. Metropolitan Museum of Art
26. First Virtual Mousepad Museum
27. Historic Mount Vernon, home of George Washington
28. National Museum of Women in the Arts
29. Natural History Museum in London
30. Olympic Museum
31. Orchard House, home of the Alcotts
32. Museum of Promotional Pens
33. Tokugawa Family Art Museum—Nagoya, Japan
34. U.C. Berkeley Museum of Paleontology
35. Museum of the Rockies (rich in natural and human history)
36. Rock & Roll Hall of Fame and Museum
37. Samurai Asian Museum
38. International Surfing Museum

39. Virtual Egyptian Museum
40. Smithsonian, The World's Largest Museum
41. Toyota Automobile Museum—Tokyo, Japan
42. Ueberseemuseum—Bremen, Germany (in German)
43. Williamsburg, a tour through the pages of Colonial America
44. National Museum of Women's History
45. World Art Treasures

Hopefully this will provide you with many rich and exciting experiences.

Family: The Originating Source of Literacy

Research consistently points to parents as the originating source of literacy experiences for their children (Darling & Lee, 2004). According to Shonkoff and Phillips (2000),

> A vast store of research . . . has confirmed that what young children learn, how they react to the events and people around them, and what they expect from themselves and others are deeply affected by their relationships with parents, the behavior of parents and the environment of the homes in which they live. Even when young children spend most of their waking hours in child care, parents remain the most influential adults in their lives. (p. 226)

Children are immensely influenced by their parents' intelligence and the way their parents pass on their wisdom. Unfortunately, because of a multitude of life's misfortunes, some parents need assistance in fulfilling this role. A teacher's job, then, is to help those parents learn with their children in a way that is satisfying to the parents as well as the kids. And yet the successful assistance we provide can be based only on the capability, background, and drive of the parents.

For example, Denton and Germino-Hausken (2000) revealed that as the mother's education goes up, the child's reading and math scores go up. More specifically, Britto and Brooks-Gunn (2001) showed that as the educational level of the mother goes up, so do her child's vocabulary skills. And from a more practical standpoint, Primavera (2000) demonstrated that when there are numerous home activities that involve parent-child literacy, such as helping the child with writing and reading homework, the child's language skills and interest in books go up.

Another major home activity is meal-time conversation. Starting with the preschool years, the more that parents use story and explanation-type talking during meals, the higher the scores are at age 5 on measurements of vocabulary, definitions, and listening comprehension (Beals, 2002, p. 90). So how can teachers foster this kind of success?

Let Social Scientists "Talk" to Parents

A brief letter can be sent home explaining what research has shown. The letter needs to be sensitive to the language of the home.

I thought you might be interested in what the social scientists are saying about children's success in school. They have found that the more parents and children talk together at meals, the more their children will succeed in learning words and the meaning of those words. If they are already in school, children will do better in understanding what they are listening to.

The scientists have created a list of things that you and your children can talk about at meals so that they can become successful in talking to their teachers and other adults. Here is that list, but I recommend that you break it into three or four letters:

Take time each day to have extended discussions with your children.
Allow them to choose their own topics and children's books.
Answer your children's questions, particularly those about why things happen.
Discuss people's reasons for what they say or do.
Talk about special objects, places, or events that you are interested in or that you want to know more about.
Expose your children to new words and talk about what they mean.
Tell your children about something interesting that happened to you—at work, at the store, or anywhere.
Ask your children to tell you about things that have happened to them. Try not to be critical, so they will continue to tell you things.
If they begin to tell about something, allow them to tell it all by themselves.
Discuss future events and plans, real or just desired.

Involve Parents in Teaching Their Children

Several studies have shown that parents' involvement in their children's education has a rather direct effect on reading achievement. In one study, for example, 150 third through fifth graders who were behind in reading by at least two grade levels were placed in a parent tutoring program. Moderately trained volunteer parents worked with their children at home by helping them read books, do homework, practice word lists, and play reading games. This experimental group of students ended the year with an average grade-equivalency score in reading of 3.8 as contrasted to 2.8 for the control group that was not in the parent tutoring program (Shuck, Ulsh, & Platt, 1983). Tutoring, though, is just one of many ways parents can get involved. Here are some others:

■ **Create a parent read-aloud collection**—This collection can be in your classroom or in the school library. Students, parents, and grandparents can check out the books and take them home. You may wish to use *The Read Aloud Handbook* by Jim Trelease to help you select books for this purpose. His book is normally revised every few years.

■ **Train volunteer parents as aides**—These aides can be invaluable in helping children write group stories, responding to children's journals, conferring with children during reading or writing workshops, providing one-on-one sharing of a book, helping problem-solving groups process their difficulties, discussing books during a literature circle, and much more. Retired teachers are often willing and eager to help in these ways.

■ **Ask parents to produce a collection of skinny books**—Ask parents or grandparents to cut out single, interesting, but easy-to-read stories from old reading materials in the school. Have them attach a cardboard cover to each one and place it in a special classroom library collection. Skinny books are excellent for enticing reluctant readers. Parents or children can also check them out for read-aloud experiences at home. And parent aides can use them for easy one-on-one book sharing with children who need special encouragement.

■ **Provide a center for language and reading games**—Provide a center in your classroom for language and reading games for parents, grandparents, and older students to play with your students during rainy lunch periods or when children need special practice. Encourage parents to check out these games to use at home with their children.

■ **Provide a selection of parent brochures**—Helpful brochures are available in three languages from the International Reading Association (www.reading.org) for special connections to parents and grandparents. Here are just a few examples:
"You Can Encourage Your Child to Read"
"Summer Reading Is Important"
"Use TV to Stimulate Your Child's Reading Habits"
"Studying: A Key to Success—Ways Parents Can Help"
"Gifted and Talented Children: Help from Parents"
Another source of brochures for parents is Reading Is Fundamental at
http://www.rif.org/educators/advicetips/

The Homeless Child: An Extreme Need for Literacy and Literature

In 2001 there were about 1.35 million homeless children in the United States (Duffield, 2001), and over 40% were under the age of 5 (Burt & Aron, 2000). That's bad enough, of course, but the number keeps growing each year. (Noll & Watkins, 2003). Homelessness affects all races but is most clearly linked to poverty, according to Dail (2000) and Nunez and Fox (1999). And this homelessness doesn't just occur in the cities; it is also in the suburbs and rural areas. Sadly, the rate of grade retention for homeless students is twice the rate of those children living in a home (Better Homes Fund, 1999).

This situation has been problematic in the public schools of Albuquerque, New Mexico, but is being addressed through a Title One homeless migrant program in a manner that should give us all ideas for helping these children. (For more information contact Sam Ornelas at 505–827–6527 or sornelas@sde.state.nm.us)

Good literature for these New Mexico children is a very small piece of the solution pie. For the past several years a project has been established to provide after-school tutoring, a summer day camp, and a summer math program for these homeless children. And each year more than 2,000 backpacks filled with notebooks, pens, pencils, and other grade-appropriate supplies are distributed to this growing population of school children. My question is, Why can't all school districts in our country provide these simple but powerful signs of kindness and intelligence?

Homeless children across the nation are moving in and out of our schools and are losing whatever they learn because of insufficient repetition and explanation. When these kids first come to a school, they often don't know what Mother Goose is all about, for example, or what rhyming words are all about, what writing has to do with learning, what onsets and rimes are all about, exactly how the alphabet principle works, and they're not likely to be on top of phonemic awareness. Consequently, they need to be treated according to their actual learning background.

But lest I give you the wrong impression of these children and their parents, let me share the incorrect assumptions I held for many years. I often assumed that homeless students were so far behind academically that they were incapable of anything difficult like critical or analytical or creative thinking. Ha! What was I thinking! Many of these children have lived in the steets, so to speak. And over half of them are older children who became homeless by fleeing from an abusive household (Nunez & Fox, 1999). As Noll and Watkins (2003) tell us,

> We have been surprised by their ability to interpret what is written "between the lines." . . . There are gaps in their knowledge, but in class discussions their interpretive skills are sometimes remarkable. When discussing inferences or engaging in comparative studies of literature, these children reveal more insight than we had expected. This may be due at least in part to their living in a world where they constantly have to solve problems just to survive. (p. 364)

Ways to Help

According to Owoki and Goodman (2002), teachers should keep in mind the high rate of transience among the homeless and should not wait until they have time to administer formal assessments before making their own observational and anecdotal notes about what children know and where they need help. The following questions are helpful for teachers taking such notes (and are appropriate for all children):

What is the child's language background?
What is the child's cultural background?
What topics/content/genres are of interest to the child?
What language and literacy practices does the child lean toward when given a choice?

How would I characterize the child's language and literacy identity?

What discourse patterns seem familiar to the child?

How is the child applying familiar language and literacy practices to new context and settings?

What themes and roles does the child explore in play?

How are language and literacy used in play?

Would that we could all find the time to do this, of course, but nevertheless, these guidelines might help us realize how little we know about our students much of the time. And let me boldly add even more questions to the list we just looked at:

What kinds of books does the child like to read?

In a simple, informal reading inventory, what level of reading can this child handle with comfort?

Did the parents read to this child?

Do I have the right books in the right language to get this child going?

Cultural Differences in Diverse Classrooms

It's well known that teachers today have challenges not only with homeless children but also with children whose culture and language are different from the teacher's. As stated by the National Center for Education Statistics (2000), almost 40% of the total U.S. public school population is made up of nonmajority students, many of whom have linguistic or behavioral styles that can make it difficult to communicate effectively with the average teacher in the average U.S. school. Many of us educators are searching for ways to close this gap.

Part of the challenge also comes from the fact that many of these kids have not learned to think of books as attractive and exciting.

If books are not compelling to children, then no amount of time spent on rhyming games, phonemic awareness exercises, or any other kind of literacy activity will result in their becoming proficient and empowered readers. . . . the sooner children forge a deep and authentic connection to books—the likelier it is that they will be successful in school. There is no more essential task for teachers in preschool and kindergarten classrooms than to help make books meaningful in children's lives. (Meier, 2003, p. 246)

So what can you do? Choose books that relate to your young students' lives. Remember these words of Candy Dawson Boyd (1997) as you make your selections:

As an African American female child, I never saw my face or the lives of my family, friends, and neighbors in the books I read. . . . The characters were always white, nice, safe, and perfect, in their own distant way. I realized that I was invisible, excluded, disaffirmed, spurned, discarded, scorned, and rejected in the white world of children's literature. (p. 107)

Let's you and I promise that no student of ours will ever need to experience those feelings.

Abundant Resources Are Available

Fortunately, today's libraries and book stores are full of trade books that can be used to satisfy your students' needs.

But to help with your search, let me point you to a wonderful literature collection that targets different ages and grade levels. That collection is in the amazing—and I do mean amazing—Appendix O in the back of the book. Enjoy it. Take a bath in it. The books recommended are tried and true, mostly new but some old and blue. Used copies of recommended books can be located via the internet.

After you've marveled at all of those possibilities, take a look at the collection of Web sites that comes next. You'll find fiction and nonfiction, cultural and multicultural, informational and entertaining. Step right up!

Internet Sources of Fiction and Nonfiction Books

http://www.ala.org
The American Library Association (ALA) awards the Caldecott Medal for the previous year's most distinguished American picture book for children. The Newbery Medal is awarded to the author of the most distinguished contribution to American literature for children. This Web site includes lists of both Caldecott and Newbery Medal winners and honor books. ALA also publishes *Book Links* magazine; each issue focuses on a core curriculum area, including science, social studies, language arts, history, geography, and multicultural literature.

http://www.cbcbooks.org
The Children's Book Council identifies books and other materials to encourage reading. The Council is the official sponsor of Children's Book Week and Young People's Poetry Week. It holds joint projects with the International Reading Association and the American Library Association.

http://www.nsta.org/ostbc
The National Science Teachers Association recommends outstanding science trade books.

http://superkids.com
http://www.CreativeThink.com
These are two sources for books, games, puzzles, and vocabulary builders in Spanish, French, and English—and other resources to encourage critical and creative thinking and imagination building.

http://www.aft.org/american_educator
The American Educator provides a list of diverse resources, including multicultural books to inspire young readers.

http://www.afb.org/
http://www.nbp.og/
These are two sources for books in Braille and large print for children with visual disabilities.

http://teacher.scholastic.com
http://www.troll.com
These sites identify inexpensive paperback books for readers with a variety of interests, cultural backgrounds, and levels of reading skill.

http://www.reading.org
Children's Choices, an exciting list of outstanding trade books, is published yearly for children from kindergarten through age 13 and young adults. Ten thousand school children from across the United States read and vote on newly published children's and young adults' trade books they like best.

http://www.ncss.org
The National Council for the Social Studies provides for young people an annotated list of notable social studies trade books across the curriculum, with human relations and diversity being their main theme. Their goal is to give fresh slants to traditional topics. Their recommendations for books are incredibly accurate and rich with cultural beauty.

http://www.ncte.org
The National Council of Teachers of English gives the Orbis Pictus Nonfiction Award every November to the author of the most outstanding nonfiction book for children. Five honor books are also recognized yearly.

http://www.reading.org
Teachers' Choices is an interesting yearly list of outstanding trade books for children and youth that teachers across the United States find to be exceptional for teaching across the curriculum.

Focus on Students with Special Needs: Comments from Louise Fulton

Children's Literature Once More to the Rescue

"We can take any book and make our special needs students successful in some way," said Rich Frederick, a teacher at Kimberly School in Redlands, California. He went on to explain that the hardest things he struggles with are the preemergent skills of rhyming, phonemic awareness, and antonyms. "But," he said, "my students can read anyway. Take 7-year-old Kevin, for instance. He loves books and likes to talk about the pictures in books. So, when he comes to a word he can't read, I ask him to find something in the picture that 'might be that word.' He's thrilled to succeed and can't wait to read some more."

The same is true when Rich team-teaches with the regular classroom teacher each morning. "The special needs students may not be as fluent as some of the other students," he says, "but they can succeed at many of the literacy activities."

I asked Rich to show me some of the books his students enjoy. Here are a few of his favorites, along with his comments:

- *The Little Old Lady Who Was Not Afraid of Anything* by Linda Williams: "While reading this book, my students can get involved in it by clapping, stomping, wiggling, or knocking. The sounds and actions keep them keenly focused as I read aloud. They love it."
- *Brown Bear, Brown Bear, What Do You See?* by Bill Martin: "We follow up by having the students work together to dictate their own 6–8 page books, using Bill Martin's pattern. Other similar books are about things we see when we take walks, things we see or do in our classroom, and parties and celebrations

that mean something to us. The students read their books over and over, eventually taking them home to read to their parents."
- *Jamberry* by Bruce Degan: "The make believe and rhyming in this book make it fun to read together."
- *The Day Jimmy's Boa Ate the Wash* by Trinka Hakes Noble: "When I read this book, I put my students' names into the story. They listen intensely, waiting to hear their names called!"
- *The Little Red Hen* by Lucinda McQueen: "My students love the pictures in this big book."
- *The Very Hungry Caterpillar* by Eric Carle, *One Gorilla* by Atsuko Morozumi, and *One Fish, Two Fish* by Dr. Seuss "are some of the books I like for reinforcing numeral, calendar and color concepts."

Rich went on to tell me that it's the books he and his students make together that best teach them the joy of reading. I flipped through several of their original books myself: *Snowman, Snowman, What Do You See?, What I See at Thanksgiving, Santa's Walk, What I Want for Christmas, We Went for a Walk, We Like to Play, My Alphabet,* and *Valentine, Valentine, What Do You See?* There were dozens—some written in crayon, some with personal artwork, some with photographs, and some with cutout pictures pasted haphazardly onto each page. These original books came in all sizes, and all of them were well worn.

(continued)

Focus on Students with Special Needs *(cont.)*

How do I know Rich's students have learned to love books? When I started looking at their books, the students could not stay away from me. One student, Jamie, pulled up a chair and began reading *What I Want for Christmas*. When I dared to look over at another student, Jamie reached over and jerked my face back toward the book he was reading. Another student, Roberto, impatiently stood with his arm across my shoulder. He then learned forward, pointing to the words and clammering to have his turn to read. Such enthusiasm about books! Rich summed it up this way: "If my students write something themselves—or even think of it—they are more motivated. It's always easier for them to read their own words."

Summary of Main Ideas

- Literature is a far more effective medium for reading instruction than workbooks and worksheets.
- Literature has multiple advantages, providing for individual differences, personal growth, aesthetic experiences, enriched curricula, a positive effect on character development, and the social cohesion that every society needs.
- Teachers can make literature a powerful medium of learning by encouraging active responses to literature, by becoming highly knowledgeable about children's books, and by providing sufficient time and books for both independent and guided reading in the school environment.
- Sustained silent reading can be highly effective in providing whole-text practice. Ineffective readers need considerable extra help in selecting books.
- Reading workshops, webbing literature circles, book projects, and other forms of active involvement can provide structure and greater depth for literature study.
- Readers of informational material need to understand the different expository structures and vocabularies used by authors in different fields of knowledge.

Literacy Through Technology

A. From the list provided in this chapter, select one of the literary awards (Caldecott or Newbery) or a list of books recommended by an organization focused on literacy (National Council of Social Studies Teachers, International

Reading Association, or the National Council of Teachers of English), review the recommended book list, and answer the following questions:

Are these books divided by any particular age or grade category?
Do the lists include books specifically focused on the interests of ethnically, culturally, and linguistically diverse readers? Which are those titles?
Which books do you see that you, as a teacher, will use? How?

Application Experiences for Your Course

A. *Literacy Teacher Vocabulary: List of Terms:* Make these terms your own.

literature trade books expository writing book clubs
multicultural literature literature circles

B. *What's Your Opinion?* Defend your reactions to these statements with both textbook quotes and your own experiences:

1. Fictional literature doesn't provide for individual differences any more than any other medium of instruction.
2. Encouraging children to engage in active responses to literature is really not that important. Just let the kids enjoy reading and forget about the so-called responses.
3. Once you teach children the basic skills and subskills of reading, they should be able to read *anything*—a science text, a math text, you name it.
4. Children should learn to read standard textbooks rather than rely on library books, particularly fiction.
5. Leave the children alone during SSR Time.

Creativity Training Session

A. *Drama.* Think of ways your students can use creative dramatics or some other creative process to understand what they are presently reading. Demonstrate your decisions for your peers. Have fun with this.

B. *Problem-Solving Experiences.*

1. A Spanish-speaking mother comes to you at school and shyly asks for help. She would like you to help her learn English by allowing her to read simple books with her child. She feels as if she's falling behind her own child. Create three solutions to this problem.
2. Imagine that you have only $200 to develop a beginning library for your new classroom. What will you do to meet the criteria of a highly effective classroom library?

Field Experiences

A. Identify a person who is responsible for a school library. Set up an appointment and interview that person on site. Develop a list of questions before you go.

B. Invite a knowledgeable educator to talk with the class about the need for more cultural and ethnic sensitivity in the books children read. Ask what you can do to improve the situation.

C. Go to the Fulton-May Library in Appendix O. Examine this list for books that appeal to you to read aloud with a class of students in Grades K–3, 4–6, or 7–8. Then check a school library for availability of the books you have selected. Share your findings with your peers.

References

Anderson, R. C., Wilson, P. T., & Fielding, L. G. (1988). Growth in reading and how children spend their time outside of school. *Reading Research Quarterly, 23,* 285–303.

Armbruster, B. B. (1991). Using literature in the content areas. *The Reading Teacher, 45,* 324–325.

Beals, D. (2002). Eating and reading: Links between family conversations with preschoolers and later language literacy. In D. Dickenson & P. Tabors (Eds.), *Beginning literacy with language* (pp. 75–92). Baltimore: Brooks.

Better Homes Fund. (1999). *Homeless Children: America's new outcasts.* Retrieved from *http://homelessed.net/newspage1.htm*

Bissett, D. (1969). *The amount and effect of recreational reading in selected fifth grade classes.* Unpublished doctoral dissertation, Syracuse University, Syracuse, NY.

Boly, W. (1987). *The handbook for planning an effective literature program.* Sacramento: California State Department of Education.

Boyd, C. D. (1997). I see myself in there: Experiencing self and others in multiethnic children's literature. In D. Muse (Ed.), *The New Press guide to multicultural resources for young readers* (pp. 106–114). New York: New Press.

Britto, P. R., & Brooks-Gunn, J. B. (2001). Beyond shared book reading: Dimensions of home literacy and low-income African American preschoolers' skills. *New Directions for Child and Adolescent Development, 92,* 73–90.

Burt, M., & Aron, L. (2000). *America's homeless: Populations and services.* Washington, DC: Urban Institute.

Cash, J. C., & Young, T. A. (1991). Sustained silent reading: Learning to read by reading. *Arizona Reading Journal, 19*(2), 52–53.

Dail, P. W. (2000). Introduction to the symposium on homelessness. *Policy Studies, 28,* 331–337.

Daniels, H. (1994). *Literature circles: Voice and choice in one student-centered classroom.* Portland, ME: Stenhouse.

Daniels, H. (2002). *Literature circles: Voice and choice in book clubs and reading groups* (2nd ed.). Portland, ME: Stenhouse.

Darling, S., & Lee, J. (2004). Linking parents to reading instructions. *The Reading Teacher, 57*(4), 382–384.

Davis, D. (1997). *Interactive research in drama in education.* Oakhill, England: Trentham Books.

Denton, K., & Germino-Hausken, E. (2000). *America's kindergartners* (NCES 2000–070). Washington, DC: U.S. Department of Education, National Center for Education Statistics.

Duffield, B. (2001). The educational rights of homeless children: Policies and practices. *Educational Studies, 32,* 323–336.

Edmiston, B. (1998). The A,B,C's of drama. *Drama matters: The journal of the Ohio Drama Exchange, 3,* 49–59.

Edmiston, B., & Long, T. W. (1999). *Reading texts inside out: Engagement and interpretation with drama.* Unpublished manuscript, The Ohio State University, Columbus.

Eeds, M., & Peterson, R. L. (1995). What teachers need to know about the literary craft. In N. L. Roser & M. G. Martinez (Eds.), *Book talk and beyond: Children and teachers respond to literature.* Newark, DE: International Reading Association.

Fader, D. N., & McNeil, E. B. (1968). *Hooked on books: Program and proof.* New York: Putnam.

Flaspeter, R. (1995, September). Sustained silent reading: Implementation in the LEP classroom based on research results. TESOL Annual Meeting, Jacksonville, FL.

Fractor, J. S., Woodruff, M. C., Martinez, M. G., & Teale, W. H. (1993). Let's not miss opportunities to promote voluntary reading: Classroom libraries in the elementary school. *The Reading Teacher, 46,* 476–478.

Frank, C. R., Dixon, C. N., & Brandts, L. R. (2001). Bears, trolls, and pagemasters: Learning about learners in book clubs. *The Reading Teacher, 54*(5), 448–462.

Gambrell, L. B. (2005). Reading literature, reading text, reading the Internet: The times they are a'changing. *The Reading Teacher, 58*(6), 588–591.

Hansen, J. (1987). *When writers read.* Portsmouth, NH: Heinemann.

Harp, B. (1989). How are we using what we know about literacy processes in the content areas. *The Reading Teacher, 42,* 726–727.

Hayes, D. (1989). Expository text structure and study learning. *Reading Horizons, 30*(1), 52–61.

Kaisen, J. (1987). SSR/Booktime: Kindergarten and first grade sustained silent reading. *The Reading Teacher, 40,* 532–536.

Knoeller, C. P. (1994). Negotiating interpretations of text: The role of student-led discussions in understanding literature. *Journal of Reading, 37,* 572–580.

Koskinen, P. S., Blum, I. H., Bisson, S. A., Phillips, S. M., Creamer, T. S., & Baker, T. K. (2003). Book access, shared reading, and audio models: The effects of supporting the literacy learning of linguistically diverse students in school and at home. *Journal of Educational Psychology, 92*(1), 23–36.

Labbo, L., Leu, D., Kinser, C., Teale, W., Cammack, D., Kara-Soteriou, J., & Sanny, R. (2003). Teacher wisdom stories: Cautions and recommendations for using computer-related technology for literacy instruction. *The Reading Teacher, 57*(3), 300–304.

Long, T. W. (2001). *How to use engagement strategies in the urban classroom.* Unpublished manuscript, Cleveland State University, Cleveland, OH.

Long, T. W., & Gove, M. K. (2004). How engagement strategies and literature circles promote critical response in a fourth grade, urban classroom. *The Reading Teacher, 57*(4), 350–361.

Manley, A., & O'Neill, C. (Eds.). (1997). *Dreamseekers: Creative approaches to the African American heritage.* Portsmouth, NH: Heinemann.

McCracken, R. A., & McCracken, M. J. (1978). Modeling is the key to sustained silent reading. *The Reading Teacher, 31,* 406–408.

Meier, T. (2003). "Why can't she remember that?" The importance of storybook reading in multilingual, multicultural classrooms. *The Reading Teacher, 57*(3), 242–252.

Nagy, W. E. (1988). *Teaching vocabulary to improve reading comprehension.* Newark, DE: International Reading Association.

National Center for Education Statistics. (2000). *The condition of education.* Washington, DC: U.S. Department of Education, Office of Education Research & Improvement.

National Institute of Child Health & Human Development. (2000). *Report of the National Reading Panel: Teaching children to read.* Washington, DC: NICHD Publications Clearinghouse.

Noll, E., & Watkins, R. (2003). The impact of homelessness on children's literacy experiences. *The Reading Teacher, 57*(4), 362–371.

NPD Group. (1991). *1990–1991 consumer research study on book purchasing.* New York: Book Industry Study Group.

Nunez, R., & Fox, C. (1999). A snapshot of family homelessness across America. *Political Science Quarterly, 114,* 289–307.

O'Neill, C. (1995). *Drama worlds: A framework for processing drama.* Portsmouth, NH: Heinemann.

Owoki, G., & Goodman, Y. (2002). *Kidwatching: Documenting children's literacy development.* Portsmouth, NH: Heinemann.

Ozburn, M. S. (1995). A successful high school sustained silent reading program. *English in Texas, 26*(3), 4–5.

Paratore, J. R., & Indrisano, R. (1987). Intervention assessment of reading comprehension. *The Reading Teacher, 40,* 778–783.

Pratten. J., & Hales, L. W. (1986). The effects of active participation on student learning. *Journal of Educational Research, 79,* 210–215.

Primavera, J. (2000). Enhancing family literacy competence through literacy activities. *Journal of Prevention and Intervention in the Community, 20,* 85–101.

Ryder, R. J., Graves, B. B., & Graves, M. F. (1989). *Easy reading: Book series and periodicals for less able readers.* Newark, DE: International Reading Association.

Scott, J. E. (1994). Literature circles in the middle school classroom: Developing reading, responding, and responsibility. *Middle School Journal, 26,* 37–41.

Shonkoff, J. P., & Phillips, D. A. (Eds.). (2000). *From neurons to neighborhoods: The science of early childhood development.* Washington, DC: National Academy Press.

Shuck, A., Ulsh, F., & Platt, J. S. (1983). Parents encourage pupils (PEP): An inner-city parent involvement reading project. *The Reading Teacher, 36,* 524–528.

Sippola, A. E. (1993). When thematic units are not thematic units. *Reading Horizons, 33*(3), 217–223.

Spiegel, D. L. (1983). *Reading for pleasure: Guidelines.* Newark, DE: International Reading Association.

Taylor, P. (Ed.). (1996). *Researching drama and arts education.* London: Falmer.

Taylor, P. (1998). *Redcoats and patriots: Reflective practice in drama and social studies.* Portsmouth, NH: Heinemann.

Tompkins, G., & McGee, L. (1993). *Teaching reading with literature: Case studies to action plans.* New York: Richard C. Owen.

Vacca, J., Vacca, R., & Gove, M. (2000). *Reading and learning to read* (4th ed.). New York: Longman-Addison Wesley.

Vacca, R. T., & Rasinski, T. V. (1992). *Case studies in whole language.* New York: Harcourt Brace Jovanovich.

Veatch, J. (1996). From the vantage of retirement. *The Reading Teacher, 49,* 510.

Wilhelm, J. D., & Edmiston, B. (1998). *Imagining to learn: Inquiry, ethics, and integration through drama.* Portsmouth, NH: Heinemann.

Other Suggested Readings

Dixon, C. N., Frank, C. R., & Brandts, L. R. (1997). Teacher in writer's workshop: Understanding the complexity. *CliPs: A Journal of the California Literature Project, 3*(1), 31–36.

Frose, V., & Kurushima, S. (1979). The effects of sentence expansion practice on the reading comprehension and writing ability of third graders. In M. L. Kamil & A. J. Moe (Eds.), *Reading research: Studies and applications.* Twenty-eighth yearbook of the National Reading Conference, Rochester, NY.

Maher, E. B. (1991). *The effect of reading aloud to fifth grade students on the acquisition of vocabulary* (Report No. 143). Miami: Florida International University.

McGee, L. M., & Richgels, D. J. (1985). Teaching expository text structure to elementary students. *The Reading Teacher, 38,* 739–748.

Neville, D., & Searles, E. (1985). The effect of sentence combining and kernel identification training on the syntactic component of reading comprehension. *Research in the Teaching of English, 19,* 37–61.

Noyce, R. N., & Christie, J. F. (1981). Using literature to develop children's grasp of syntax. *The Reading Teacher, 35,* 298–302.

Odegaard, J. M., & May, F. B. (1972). Creative grammar and the writing of third graders. *Elementary School Journal, 73,* 156–161.

Olson, M. W., & Gee, T. C. (1991). Content reading instruction in the primary grades: Perceptions and Strategies. *The Reading Teacher, 45,* 298–307.

Piccolo, J. A. (1987). Expository text structure: Teaching and learning strategies. *The Reading Teacher, 40,* 838–847.

Scott, J. H. (1998). Official language, unofficial reality: Acquiring bilingual/bicultural fluency in a segregated Southern community. In T. Perry & L. Delpit (Eds.), *The real Ebonics debate: Power, language, and the education of African-American children* (pp. 189–195). Boston: Beacon Press.

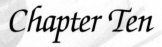

Chapter Ten

Writing as a Critical Connection to Literacy

Human beings have a deep need to represent their experiences through writing. We need to make our truths beautiful . . . we write because we want to understand our lives.

—*Lucy Calkins*

Tenth Objective for Your Teaching Success:

Teach writing and reading as equal partners in communication

Writing is an essential ingredient in any good reading program. At the same time writing needs no such justification for its existence. It is important in its own right. For without the ability to write our thoughts, we are far less human.

> Human beings have a deep need to represent their experience through writing. We need to make our truths beautiful. . . . We write because we want to understand our lives. (Calkins, 1986, p. 3)

> Writing was invented on Earth about 5,500 years ago in Persia. Only after that invention came along was reading needed. Nothing has changed today. For Earthlings, writing is a busier activity than reading. (Bogglestar, 2005)

Introduce the Art of Writing with the Wonder of Poetry

Mrs. Friedman read several poems to her fourth-grade class that day. "It was just one of those poetry days," she said later. The sun hadn't been out for 3 days straight, Billie Jean had thrown up in the cloakroom, and Mrs. Friedman had forgotten to turn in her lunch count, prompting a mild reprimand over the public address system. "If ever humorous poetry was called for," she said, "it was that day."

Shel Silverstein came to the rescue with his poem about Peggy Ann McKay, who was able to find 16 chicken pox on her body, along with a sunken belly button, and 25 other ailments that were sure to keep her from going to school. Then there was his poem about the peanut butter sandwich that locked the jaws of a silly young king. And, of course, the one called "Stone Telling," in which the poet insists that throwing a stone at a window is the only way to determine whether it's open or closed.

The last poem read that day was my own opinionated verse proclaiming that "Waffles Are Better" (see Figure 10.1). The students in Mrs. Friedman's class enjoyed the poem, and there was quite a discussion about the virtues of pancakes versus waffles. While the children were engaged in debate, she decided that this poem would be a useful model for their own writing.

Mrs. Friedman and I had pretty much the same opinions about poetry: Many different kinds should be introduced to children, especially free-flowing unrhymed verse. However, we both agreed that for teaching reading and writing at the same time, rhymed verse was very effective. So the very next day, when things were running smoothly once more, Mrs. Friedman showed students the

---

Waffles Are Better

Some favor pancakes
Fried in a pan,
Then piled high,
Slathered in butter,
Drowned in syrup!
But not I.

I favor waffles.
Waffles are something
You never fry.
You pour in the batter,
You put down the lid,
And my oh my!

You wait and you wait,
Your patience so thin,
Your hopes in the sky,
While the magic takes place,
While waffle elves work,
And eternity goes by.

You watch and you stare
Through mystical steam
At the little red eye.
"Will it ever go off?
Will it ever turn dark?"
You cry . . . then sigh.

But at last the aroma!
And the steam disappears.
The red light does die.
You open the lid
And the magic is done.
It's time to pry.

Out pops the disk
As gold as the sun,
As round as a pie.
On goes the butter
Like molten lava
From mountains high.

Then on with the syrup
Into valleys so deep
You try and you try
To fill every one . . .
And not miss a peak:
A feast for the eye!

Now gobble that moonscape,
Demolish that city,
Let no building lie.
You could have had pancakes
So flat and so smooth
And delicious—but why?

FIGURE 10.1 The Poem "Waffles Are Better."

waffle poem, now written on a large chart. She invited them to join her in a choral reading of the poem; she read every other stanza by herself (to provide modeling), and the children read the alternating stanzas as a group. Then she asked them to talk about how the poem had been written. Through skillful questioning, she helped them discover the poem's characteristics, which she wrote on the chalkboard:

1. Two favorite things were compared.

2. Every third line rhymed.

3. The rhyming sound was the same throughout the poem.

4. One of the favorite things was shown to be better.

5. The rhythm throughout the poem was the same.

The children then attempted to write a similar poem as a group. Janet suggested that they compare eggs and bacon, but Alex thought they were too different and suggested chicken and steak. Nancy waved her hand wildly and said, "Let's compare an ice cream cone with a candy bar!"

This idea met with approval from the entire class, but then they had a bigger problem to solve: Which one would they show to be better? The vote was close, but the ice cream cone won. To diminish the candy lovers' disappointment, Mrs. Friedman told those students they could write the parts of the poem in praise of the candy bar.

Next they had to select a rhyming sound that would be the same on every third line. Mrs. Friedman asked, "What are some words that rhyme?" and Dennis came up with *cat, bat,* and *sat.* The list of *at* words on the board grew from 3 to 18, and they decided that /at/ was a great sound. With enough words for their poem, Mrs. Friedman wrote the first line—"Some like candy bars"—and invited the candy bar lovers to describe a candy bar in such a way that everyone in the room would want one.

She waited for a response. Robin said, "Filled with nuts and covered with chocolate." So Mrs. Friedman wrote:

> *Some like candy bars,*
> *Filled with nuts*
> *And covered with chocolate.*

This version met with strenuous protest, since the third line didn't end with the exact rhyming sound of /at/. Mrs. Friedman asked for another third line.

"Pat, pat, pat," Cindy said, smiling and patting her hand on her desk.

Mrs. Friedman smiled back. "You mean as if someone were patting the nuts into the candy bar?" Cindy assured her that this was exactly what she had in mind. So Mrs. Friedman changed the third line by drawing lightly through it and writing the new third line off to the side. In this way she knew she wouldn't lose the

---

Ice Cream Cones Are Better

Some like candy bars,
Crammed with nuts
Pat, pat, pat.

Some like candy bars
Mooshed with cream,
Fat, fat, fat.

Most like candy bars
Smothered with chocolate,
Imagine that!

With so much sugar
It can sweeten up
The meanest brat.

But I like ice cream cones,
So smooth and round
Not bumpy and flat.

You stand at the counter
With noses pressed to the glass,
You and Shelly and Nat.

And you wait and you wait
As she scoops it up,
Pat, pat, pat.

Finally yours is ready
And you take a secret nibble,
Feeling like a rat.

You know you should wait
For your friends to get theirs.
So you anxiously chat

About weather and school,
About cabbages and kings,
About zit, zoom, and zat.

And finally you've got them
Enclosed in your fists,
The ball and upside-down hat.

Only one more choice to make:
To lick, lip, or bite.
Oh, drat!

FIGURE 10.2 The Poem "Ice Cream Cones Are Better."

contribution that had been made earlier about the candy bar being covered with chocolate. The poem now read:

> *Some like candy bars,*
> *Filled with nuts.*
> *Pat, pat, pat.*

Mrs. Friedman said, "Since we're putting all those nuts into the candy bar, perhaps we need a word that's stronger than *filled.*"

> *"Smashed,"* said David.
> *"Mooshed,"* Diane said.
> *"Crammed,"* Bobbie said.

And on through their poem they plunged and weaved and slashed, with Mrs. Friedman contributing a line now and then to keep them going, until 35 minutes later the tired poets rested. Their poem is shown in Figure 10.2. What would we do without poetry? We teachers must preserve the learning of poetry for the future. (Linaberger, 2005)

Examine the Writing/Reading Connection

Professional Standard: Helps students integrate their reading and writing

You've just seen an example of a teacher, using rhymed poetry to combine writing and reading instruction. But why combine them? What are the advantages?

What Research Shows

Much of the support for combining writing and reading instruction comes from our knowledge of early readers, those who learn to read and write before they even enter school. Durkin (1966), you may remember from Chapter 1, studied early readers for 6 years in California and 3 years in New York City. One of her conclusions was that the scribbling and writing done before they started formal schooling made an important contribution to their success in learning to read at an earlier age than most children. One implication she drew was that writing and reading should be taught together.

> Purcell (2001) also advocates a balanced literacy approach, thus avoiding the long debate between phonics and whole language . . . putting literacy at the center by involving both reading and writing to develop students' lifelong interest in both. The reading and writing process are central to the balanced program . . . tied directly to reading and writing activities rather than tests. (pp. 13–14)

Other researchers have come to the same conclusion from their own research (Graves, 1983; Hansen, 1987; Shanahan, 1988; Wilkinson & Sillman (2000). Writing can have a positive effect on children's *reading* comprehension as well as on their critical-thinking abilities (Qian, 1990). In his synthesis of research on the reading/writing connection, Holbrook (1987) found that "almost all studies that used writing activities specifically to improve reading comprehension or retention of information found significant gains" (p. 216). In another synthesis of research results, Harp (1987) reported that scores on the Standford Reading Test were considerably higher for those children involved in an authorship program, writing their own stories.

Writing can have a powerful motivational effect as well. Dionisio (1983) found that teaching reading through writing was the best approach for her sixth-grade re-medial readers, who were turned off to reading. By modeling both writing and revising behavior with the students and giving them plenty of opportunity to read each other's work (as well as their own), she was able to help them become readers abilities without using formal reading instruction.

One Unified Process: Writing and Reading

Such results are not too surprising. Any author, including a child writer, has the opportunity to feel mildly godlike in creating a title or a topic, a plot or an organization, a well-developed character or a well-developed argument. *Most* children can learn to truly enjoy writing in a school setting. (Witness this enjoyment by reading a book called *They All Want to Write* by Burrows, Jackson, & Saunders, 1985.)

The important thing for you to realize is that your students' concept of writing greatly *influences* their concept of reading; as they learn to write, they gradually learn what reading is all about. It originates with someone creating a written document, followed by a reader interpreting what has been communicated.

Since writing is a somewhat more personal, more creative, more original, and more involving process, it is an excellent medium for understanding authors and the relationship between authors and readers. When we make separate subjects of reading and writing, as we often have done in schools, we create an unnatural, nonlinguistic division. It is very important for children to learn that reading and writing are two parts of the same communication process.

Teach Writing Creatively

A Literate Environment

When researchers examine classrooms that are literacy oriented, they nearly always find a physically literate *environment* (Taylor, Blum, & Logsdon, 1986). There will be *some* place in the classroom where children can easily find things: pencils, paper of various types, a three-hole punch, a stapler, washable colored markers, blank books made of inexpensive material, a computer or two or six, an extra chalkboard, and other things to write *with* and *on*. Children are not handed these things by a busy, harried teacher or parent; they choose them themselves, usually following a class discussion about how not to abuse this privilege.

A literate environment has firm surfaces to write on—desks, tables, a large smooth floor space in the writing center, clipboards. There are written materials everywhere that can serve as private tutors to those who don't like to invent their own spellings for odd words like *diapers, fragile, Pepsi,* and *cucumber.* There are birthday announcements and announcements about lunch menus, after-school sports, a child's cat that was lost at the beach but might miraculously show up at the school, and a newspaper headline telling that the space shuttle has been stolen by terrorists from Mars. There are books, magazines, songs, and actual restaurant menus to serve as examples of good writing. And don't forget the computers.

Research shows that increased reading tends to result in better writing (Cox, Shanahan, & Sulzby, 1990). That's why there are also books and other writings that *children* have created and lists of color words, animal words, weather words, and words that no one can spell. There are mailboxes, places to read, a safe for keeping treasured documents, and separate containers for your students' personal belongings like keys, barrettes, and a mummified rat tail. In a nutshell, the environment inspires the classroom occupants to think, talk, laugh, listen, read, write, laugh, and think some more.

The Importance of Teachers' Beliefs

Vivian Colvin (1991) was a classroom teacher until she became the head of the gifted-and-talented program for a large city in the West. She tells of a study she did of the second-grade teachers of two children she knew personally. We'll call the children Melissa and Cassandra. Colvin wanted to see whether and how their two teachers differed. She suspected they did since, nearly every day Melissa proudly brought home the stories she had written at school. But Cassandra wouldn't show her family anything she had done at school.

Some of the teachers' comments may seem a little hard to believe, even though I transcribed them exactly as they were tape-recorded. As you eavesdrop on the two interviews, you should be able to guess which teacher taught which student.

Colvin: What are your basic assumptions about children and writing?

Teacher A: I believe that writing is a good way for children to practice their letter-sound relationships. Handwriting is important, too; kids are getting sloppier and sloppier all the time. I have them copy a few things off the board each week so they can totally focus on the handwriting without having to think about the content. I have some fun ditto sheets where the children are able to fill in their own words to make the little stories more interesting.

I don't have them write many original stories because I don't have the time to get around to help each child. They become so frustrated if they have to wait a long time just to ask me how to spell a word. I know it's so important for children to learn to write in this day and age, but I think third or fourth grade is a much better place to emphasize it. There are just too many principles of writing that second graders don't know.

Colvin: What types of material do you think are important for the children to have access to?

Teacher A: I always have the children use pencils because their work looks so sloppy if they use pens. I have tried to teach them how to use a dictionary, but very few children are ready to use this tool.

Colvin: How do you prefer the children to function—in groups, in teams, as a total class, or as individuals?

Teacher A: Most of the introductory writing lessons I give to the whole group. When they are working, I sometimes have the children choose a partner to work with.

Colvin: How is the children's progress evaluated?

Teacher A: I rate the neatness of each paper on a scale of 1 to 10 . . . I grade for whatever rule we were focusing on for the day. These children are too young for me to grade the whole paper. Some of the children really take off with their writing, but for the most part second graders are just working on foundations of writing.

Colvin: What are your basic assumptions about children and writing?

Teacher B: I believe children want to explore the world of print, and I believe my role is to provide a wonderful environment that will encourage the children to explore writing. I sit down with them, and we talk together about what they are writing, even though technically it may only be drawing and invented spelling. I like to take dictation from the children. That way they get to watch me writing.

    I believe that all my students are learning to write by having lots of opportunity to write in a risk-free environment. The children all consider themselves as authors, and they are! They desire to have others read their writing. And this desire becomes a major impetus to learn more about spelling and punctuation. All the children have wonderful stories to tell.

    I encourage note writing between the children as this is one of the strongest motivators toward careful and neat writing. I encourage the children to construct their own spelling. Waiting to find out the correct way to spell a word slows down the flow of their thoughts. I help the children create word banks where they deposit the correct spellings of their favorite words. My greatest goal for my writing program is that it helps each child believe in his own ability as a writer.

Colvin: What types of material do you think are important for the children to have access to?

Teacher B: I have large quantities of many different kinds of paper. Each child has his or her own journal to write in as well as book-making supplies. I provide the children with marking pens, crayons, a typewriter, and letter stamps, as well as the computer with a word-processing program and printer. I provide the children with posters of their favorite songs and poems as well as cereal boxes, magazines, and other kinds of print.

Colvin: How do you prefer the children to function—in groups, in teams, as a total class, or as individuals?

Teacher B: When the children are writing, they have the choice of whether they want to work by themselves or with friends. I encourage them to talk with each other, as well as to me or another adult, about what it is they are writing about. They really enjoy reading their own writing to a friend or small group of classmates.

Colvin: How is the children's progress evaluated?

Teacher B: I believe it's very important for me to keep track of each child's progress. I use the skills list from our basal reader. Even though I don't teach from the basal, I find the checklist of skills helpful for me to keep aware of where each child is.

I feel that the students' attitudes toward writing are as important as their writing, and so I keep track of how often and for what reasons each child chooses to write. I also keep folders for each child with samples of work from throughout the year. The children and their families love looking through the folders, and it keeps a perfect running record of how the children are progressing with their work.

I'm sure you already know who taught Cassandra, the reluctant writer, and who taught Melissa, the joyful writer. You can learn a great deal about the importance of beliefs and attitudes by observing these two teachers. Some of the ideas and examples that follow can help you produce joyful writers.

Try a Kindergarten Writing Workshop

Angela Behymer (2003) has developed an interesting form of writing workshop, which she and her very young students carry on *together.* Their interactive writing means that when the neophytes write a message or whatever, they are supported by the wisdom of the teacher as the writing proceeds. "The students," Behymer says, "are able to take the supported writing and carry what they have learned over into their independent writing." The writing workshop is in operation every school day, whenever the children feel like writing to express their thoughts and ideas. Behymer gives them advice on their spelling until they are ready to work more independently via phonetic spelling.

Step 1: The children draw what they want to write about later. A cool move, don't you think? That way they can do a lot of their thinking and planning ahead of the writing. So many of us good teachers first had our students write something and *then* illustrate it. What a difference Behymer's approach makes. Notice how this group responded to "What would *you* do with $1000?"

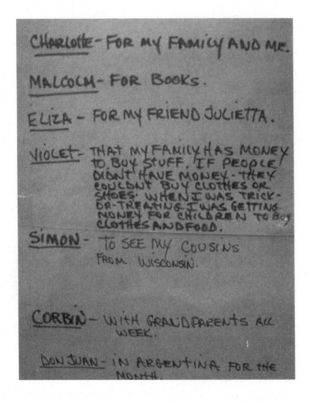

CHARLOTTE- FOR MY FAMILY AND ME.

MALCOLM- FOR BOOKs.

ELIZA - FOR MY FRIEND JULIETTA.

VIOLET- THAT MY FAMILY HAS MONEY TO BUY STUFF. IF PEOPLE DIDN'T HAVE MONEY- THEY COULDN'T BUY CLOTHES OR SHOES. WHEN I WAS TRICK-OR-TREATING I WAS GETTING MONEY FOR CHILDREN TO BUY CLOTHES AND FOOD.

SIMON - TO SEE MY COUSINS FROM WISCONSIN.

CORBIN - WITH GRANDPARENTS ALL WEEK.

DON JUAN - IN ARGENTINA FOR THE MONTH.

Step 2: Students concentrate on the phonics of the words. The teacher helps them listen together for the sounds of the words. Later she challenges them to listen to more difficult sounds and to write the sounds they hear.

Step 3: The adult underwrites what the child is trying to say in the written word—similar to scaffolding. The third step also includes mini lessons and praise for what the children have done so far.

Step 4: A large group gets ready to read or tell their journal stories in the Author's Chair. Other kids ask questions and make positive comments for the sake of reinforcement and feedback.

Step 5: Children choose partners, share journals, and share the writing that each child has created.

Step 6: The children revise, edit, and publish their work. It's show time, and they love it.

Listen to Behymer's winning philosophy:

I have high expectations when it comes to writing. We work through all of the writing stages. In the beginning, my students wrote only one or two of the easiest letters. Then they added the vowels and the more difficult consonants. Now they use their knowledge of digraphs and blends, remember those tricky sounds that I taught them, and use environmental print (e.g., word wall, charts, interactive writing) to support their writing. . . . There's an enormous amount of early childhood research that says: Read, read, read. What they say for reading is just as true for writing: Write, write, write (p. 87–88).

Use Patterned Books

A Case Study of Students with Learning Disabilities

One way to take advantage of this strong learning relationship is to engage students in reading and writing various types of patterned literature. Let's listen to a teacher in Vancouver, Washington, who used a patterned picture book to teach both writing and reading to first graders considered to have a learning disability. The teacher, Brenda Louthan, chose Steven Kellogg's book *Can I Keep Him?*, which I described in Chapter 8.

Day 1: I read Kellogg's book to the children. I then read it again and asked them if they had noticed anything that had happened over and over in the story. They were able to see the pattern in which Arnold tries to bring home pet after pet and his mom always tells him, "No, dear. You can't keep him."

Day 2: I read the book again, and we made a list on the board of all the animals that Arnold brought home. We went back through the book and checked to see if we had found all of them.

Day 3: I read the book a third time, and we made a list of all the other animals that Arnold could have brought home. They really enjoyed this and came up with a long list.

Day 4: I read the book again, and we made a list of all the reasons Arnold's mom gave him for not keeping the pets. We also looked closely at the illustrations this time, as they showed clearly what Arnold's mom was talking about.

Day 5: At this time I told the children to choose three animals from our long list that they would like as a pet. They chose a hippo, a bald eagle, and a worm. We then made a list, for each animal, of reasons a mother might give for not keeping these pets.

Day 6: I read the story a fifth time, and we made a list of all the reasons Arnold gave his mom for keeping the animals. We then made a list for each of our three animals. We also made a list of all the places these animals might be found, and the children each got to choose one to be their own animal.

Day 7: I read the book again and discussed the pattern of the mother's replies to Arnold. We looked back at the list we had made on Day 5 (reasons for not keeping the animals) and chose three of them for each of our three animals. We then put these reasons into sentences, using the pattern of the mother's words. We also chose our main character, who turned out to be a boy named Fred.

Day 8: I read Kellogg's book for the seventh and final time, and this time we discussed the pattern of Arnold's words. We then looked back at the list we had made on Day 6 (reasons for keeping the animals) and chose three of those for each of our animals. We then put their reasons into sentences, using the pattern of Arnold's words and including where our animals had been found.

Day 9: On separate pages the children and I wrote out each sentence we had developed. We read these together, and the children illustrated the pages.

Day 10: We talked about the ending of the story, where Arnold tries one more time to bring home a pet. There is only a picture of this event, so the children each drew a picture of what animal they thought Fred might bring home. We then made a cover for our book, and each child drew a picture of one of our three animals on it.

Day 11: We made photocopies of our book and read it together. The children then colored the pictures and took the book back to their homeroom to share. They were really thrilled that they could write and read a book! I felt it was a very positive learning experience.

On several occasions I, too, have used Kellogg's *Can I Keep Him?* and with second through sixth graders as well. With regular students I've used 5 to 8 days rather than 11 and 5 to 8 animals rather than 3. Students have been asked to prepare their copy for a younger sibling or friend, and they've enjoyed being a real author preparing a real book for someone else.

Tips for Success

I have had the pleasure of working with hundreds of students and teachers in the creation of patterned books. Here are some of the things other teachers and I have found to be important in producing patterned books in the classroom:

1. Be sure to work only with a model book toward which your students show considerable enthusiasm.

2. Don't rush it. The process usually takes 5 to 10 days to do well, no matter what the grade level. But spend only 20 to 30 minutes a day on the process to avoid fatigue and to increase excitement.

3. Read the book to your students several times, but read for a different purpose each time. Brenda Louthan read the book to her students seven times, but each time targeted a new list or description. The students were not bored with that many readings because each was on a different day and they had a specific goal for listening to it again. They understood that they were writing a new book similar to Kellogg's book and that lists and descriptions were necessary for that process.

4. Make lists related to the model book and then to the new book. This helps the students focus on descriptions, plot patterns, and language patterns in both the model book and the new book. Listing also provides ample practice in meaningful writing and reading.

5. Be sure each student gets a copy of the book to read to others, including those at home, who are generally very impressed.

6. Provide encouragement to those students who decide to make their own new book, even though it might be quite similar to the group-made one.

Inspire Students with Other Types of Literature

Many other types of literature, including wordless picture books (Cairney, 1987), can serve as models as they learn to write and read. One of my favorite experiences, for example, is inspiring children (from third grade on up) to write detective stories. (See the mystery and detective section appendix for a list of good model books.) Detective stories tend to have a predictable pattern, as do myths, folktales, tall tales, and even love stories. All of them, when read in abundance before children try to write their own and again as they share their own with others, become excellent models for practicing the writing/reading connection.

If you're interested in teaching writing through literature, and particularly if you're teaching fourth through eighth graders, you'll probably find John Stewig's (1990) third edition helpful. It's called *Read to Write: Using Children's Literature as a Springboard for Teaching Writing,* and it contains a variety of good ideas for helping students develop better plots, characters, and settings. With each idea he suggests books that you can read to give them a feel for good writing.

Let Your Students Write a Movie

Hoffner's (2003) writing-a-movie activity is similar to readers theater, which we talked about in Chapter 8. In readers theater the student chooses a brief story, play, or poetry to read and, after numerous practice sessions, reads skillfully, dramatically, and proudly to peers and others in the classroom audience. The goal of the performers is to cause their peers to vividly visualize the action, setting, and related emotions (Martinez, Roser, & Strecker, 1999).

The opposite occurs with writing-a-movie. Why? Because the children have been studying a *section* of a movie, and thus they've already been absorbing the action, setting, and emotions related to the action.

> To "Write a Movie," students view a short film segment (5 to 10 minutes) and write a script in which they describe the scene. The exciting music of the film's sound track can play in the background as the students read their script expressively. (p. 78)

This sounds like fun and results in some impressive benefits for students:

- They used repeated readings meaningfully after writing their script for the movie segment.
- The repeated readings led to improved word recognition, comprehension, and good old fluency.
- The numerous practices of the actual script led to improved vocabulary because of the precise words needed to describe the movie segment.

If I were in your shoes, I'd probably want to give this creative approach a try. Kids from age 9 up would probably beg to participate.

Try Informational Text, Too

Don't let your students be stumped by nonfiction. Learning to read authors' explanation patterns—like cause and effect or problem and solution—can best be learned by *writing* informational text. *Warning:* Many people in the education field like to use the phrase *exposition structures,* but you'll communicate much better with your students if you simply use the words *explanation patterns*. They're what you use when you're trying to describe and explain things when you're writing. (*Exposition* is simply a synonym for *explanation,* and *structure* is a form of organization.)

But back to my real point: By using explanation patterns while your students write, they can more quickly learn how to read those authors who use the same explanation patterns. For example, an author might write the following: "The ancient Romans had a habit of eating from clay pots containing lead, which caused impotency." In this case the *effect* was impotency, and the *cause* was the leaded pots. The student author who frequently uses the cause-and-effect pattern in writing can more easily recognize this pattern when *reading* informational nonfiction. Obviously, this kind of learning can lead to a deeper level of reading.

Writing About Their Community History

According to Allen et al. (2002), writing narrative stories about themselves and their neighbors helps children make personal, social, and cultural connections with people today and in the historical past. And developing real-life stories can bring students a sense of direction, esteem, and purpose (Muley-Meissner, 2002). Dorothy Leal (2003) and a second-grade teacher in Coaltown, Ohio, saw the writing of the history of the community as a chance to improve both the literacy of the kids in the town and community fellowship. "Believing that writing goes hand in hand with reading, and that writing always includes some reading during production," the two teachers planned to produce a 20-page spiral-bound "The Story of Coaltown."

Here are the steps they followed:

Step 1: Got the students excited by using the K-W-L exercise (discussed in Chapter 7) and generated questions to ask of two experts who were coming to talk about Coaltown in the past.
Step 2: Watched a 1930s film about the community, had a lively discussion, and generated more questions.
Step 3: Did a semantic web of things the students learned about Coaltown in the past. Taught them how to show and not just tell when writing about Coaltown.
Step 4: Had the first guest expert answer the students' questions. Wrote down the answers given. Audiotaped the guest's talk about Coaltown's history.
Step 5: Brainstormed for the book's first chapter. Decided on "The History of the Coaltown Coal Mines" as a name for the project. Broke students into five groups, each of which selected a topic and dictated their information and emotions.
Step 6: Edited and polished the first chapter, with both teacher and students using a computer. (Students entered their drawings related to each chapter.)
Step 7: Using the semantic web, decided on other chapter topics the students would like.
Step 8: During their journaling came up with new and creative ideas and questions for the next guest.

Step 9: Had the next guest answer their new and creative questions, as well as some of the former questions, just to clarify or check memories.

Step 10: Worked 2 mornings a week for an hour for many weeks. Had students author their chapters and edit them. Also created more illustrations.

Step 11: Had older students help enter the available text on the computer, thus making the project schoolwide.

Step 12: Debated book titles and chose "The Story of Coaltown." Had students draw more book covers and discuss their virtues.

Step 13: Planned ways to evaluate the quality of the work and the soon-to-be-finished book. Ended up approving it highly.

Step 14: Copied and spiral bound the books. Sent them home with an invitation for a party.

Step 15: Had an authors' party. Had the students read their chapters aloud, show their pictures to parents, and later give all teachers in the school and community friends a copy of the 20-page creation. What a success for all, including the small community! (Leal, 2003)

Model and Teach Good Writing

Professional Standard: Ensures students understand the conventions of standard written English

As a neophyte teacher I made the mistake of *testing* children on writing rather than teaching them. I gave them things to write about and then evaluated their writing. Only years later did I begin to realize that this procedure was just testing rather than teaching. You may know teachers who still do the same thing, essentially asking their students to produce a written composition to be evaluated rather than first showing their students how to write—with pleasure.

It's true, children do teach *themselves* how to write—as we discussed in chapter 1. But we also discussed Vygotsky's notion that children's intellectual abilities can be *expanded* with *encouragement* from adults. So we can help them write *better*—and consequently achieve more satisfaction from their writing. And we can do this by providing models of good writing and having them attempt to emulate those models. In one example we talked about earlier, we used patterned writing as a model. In other words, we let *authors serve as models* and then show the children how to *reconstruct* the patterns in slightly different ways in books they write themselves.

Help Students Learn What Good Writers Do

But how can you help your students discover what good writers actually do? By sponsoring discussions that encourage children to think intuitively about writers, for one thing. By having writers visit the classroom. But equally important, by following the procedures that Burrows, Jackson, and Saunders (1985) and three other elementary teachers pursued with their students:

- They encouraged all children to write if they had the slightest inclination.
- They read children's work out loud anonymously with plenty of dramatic emphasis.
- They asked for specific peer comments (praise only) and added *their* own specific praise.
- They acknowledged the real author.

In this way the children learned from their peers and their teacher the characteristics that made their writing come alive.

When I used the approach of Burrows and colleagues with my own elementary-school students, I found these eight characteristics being important again and again:

1. *Imagery*—describing a situation or subject in vivid, colorful, concrete language

2. *Naturalness*—using informal language when appropriate, maintaining personal contact with readers, expressing one's own personality

3. *Inventiveness*—creating fresh analogies, characters, settings, plots, or words and playing with homonyms, alliteration, and other humorous devices

4. *Insight*—portraying human strengths and weaknesses by means of satire, humorous incongruity, philosophical generalization, and realistic description

5. *Sincerity*—demonstrating keen interest in or feeling for one's subject, story, or characters

6. *Flexible style*—avoiding monotony by altering sentence length, clause position, sentence type, and other elements of style

7. *Conciseness*—expressing the essence of an idea or situation, avoiding words and details that distract from the main idea or impression to be conveyed

8. *Clarity*—avoiding pronouns with hazy referents, dangling participles, slang or jargon, mystical phrases, and other elements that are likely to confuse listeners or readers

When Robin Bright (1995) asked children, themselves, what good writers do, he found that their intuitions were surprisingly mature. As one child wrote, "I guess they put a lot of effort into it, and they practice at it. They write a lot of different kinds, too." And according to another child, "If you've read a book about, say, whales, then if you have to write a piece on whales, it comes easy because you know information and you can think up a story" (p. 83). To these children good writers do at least four things: apply considerable effort, spend time practicing their craft, experiment with variations, and gather information for a story background. Children's intuitions can be exceedingly accurate.

Another important way of modeling the writing process is to actually show students how writers *think* as they write. If you want them to engage in journal writing, for instance, you might model the way you think as you prepare to write in your own journal.

"I want to write about my car breaking down. Let's see, how did I feel when that happened? No, I'll write about that later, after I first tell exactly what happened . . . "

Or you might show them how you *think and write* when you create a letter to a friend.

"Let's see, now. What does Mary need to hear about? She's interested in skiing, so I'll tell her about my ski trip first . . . I'll try to write it so she can feel like she was there. Then I'll ask her if she's done any skiing, so she can tell me about it in her next letter."

The same kind of modeling can be done for other forms of writing: dialogues, narratives, arguments, advertisements, shopping lists. Modeling is essential; mere testing does not teach students enough, not even when you have conferences afterward. What is needed more than anything else is direct modeling of a writer at work—not just a finished product.

What About the Basic Steps of Writing?

Since the early 1970s, when writing instruction experts such as Donald Graves (1983) began their efforts to improve writing in the schools, teachers have been busy teaching children the five steps to follow when they are writing—*prewriting, drafting, revising, editing,* and *publishing.*

I have no quarrel with this idea. And yet a friend of mine who writes both fiction and nonfiction books chuckled more than a little when I read those five steps to him. "Don't I wish it were that easy," he said. And when I checked further with other writer friends, one of them, Phil Margolin, a well-known writer of suspense novels and a successful lawyer, grinned and said something like, "I don't use five steps, Frank. I use exactly 365, one for every day in the year."

Starting students off with five basic steps is probably a good idea, provided teachers don't treat those steps as sacred or always sequential. When I am writing a new scene in a fiction work, for instance, I often find that my subconscious mind has done much of the presorting for me. And student writers will learn in time that they, too, have many side steps to add to those five, depending on their own ways of prewriting, drafting, revising, editing, and publishing. Writing is simply too much like thinking to be limited to a standard five-step process.

Setting of Goals and Purposes for their Writing

Professional Standard: Teaches planning strategies for particular kinds of writing

There are many decisions to make as one problem-solves during the prewriting phase. Bright (1995) found that "students whose teachers stressed writing as a communicating tool *only* did not necessarily make the leap . . . to understand that writing can be personally relevant and valuable to their lives" (p. 89). Therefore, it is important in your modeling that you voice what you are personally planning on getting out of your writing experience. Then remind students of the importance of doing the same thing before *they* begin to write. You might ask questions such as these: "What is my real purpose for writing this?" "Do I want to *entertain* my readers?" "Do I want to inform them of something I know?" "Do I simply want to express myself without having anyone read it?"

It's very important that you model this kind of thinking. *Bright's study showed that most students did not know why they were writing.* He concluded that "teachers can make explicit their own reasons for assigning certain writing tasks, but students should [also] be allowed to develop their own goals and purposes for writing" (p. 85).

Establishing Internal and External Audiences

Closely related to the purpose for writing is the discovery that experienced writers generally establish *two* kinds of audiences for their work: (1) They decide, consciously or unconsciously, how they wish to please themselves, and (2) they decide, consciously or unconsciously, what person(s) they would like to have read their work. The entire work then speaks to those two audiences at the same time.

Let me suggest some ways you can encourage this kind of decision making:

■ Modeling aloud the process of making those two decisions about audience: "All right, what things would I like to accomplish as I write that would please me very much?" "Who would like to read this when I'm finished?"
■ Discussing with your students what they learned from the modeling
■ Brainstorming with them about topics, themes, story ideas, characters, story conflicts, or story events
■ Then immediately having them engage in silent decision making just before they write

Of course, the questions don't end with the audience—they're actually just starting. Depending on the kind of writing, "Do I need to gather any information before I begin?" "What do I know already?" "Maybe I could make some quick notes on this." If it's going to be a story, "What do I need to decide about the setting and the characters?" "What are two or three conflicts that the main character might go through?" Your modeling helps students see the importance of this first step.

Engaging Your Students in Group Writing Experiences

Professional Standard: Teaches students to draft, revise, and edit their writing

For the next three steps—drafting, revising, and editing—I recommend a group writing experience. Why group writing? My own experience has demonstrated that group writing is an excellent way to help students learn the steps. Besides, if you should get carried away with one-on-one instruction and spend too much time with a student, you risk the chance of getting in the way. Too much *drafting* with one individual, for example, can have the same effect as having an art teacher take the brush out of your hand and paint the painting for you.

The same is true with editing and revising. The words your students have produced during the drafting, editing, and revising stages can be seen as very precious by the writer. So it's better to have young writers do *most* of the actual drafting, revising, and editing by themselves. How best, then, to first learn these three steps? The answer lies in a safe and comfortable group-writing experience.

Some Specific Suggestions

Earlier in this chapter I gave you examples of group drafting, revising and editing in the waffle-versus-pancake lesson and in the episode of the boy wanting to keep every stray animal that crossed his path. For more examples and ideas on this topic, as well as other ideas for teaching writing, be sure to see the small book edited by Bernice Cullinan (1993) called *Pen in Hand: Children Become Writers*. Let me tempt you with a few ideas from one of the five articles in the book. This one was written by two team teachers, Virginia Schroeder and Ann Lovett (1993), who attended a Nancie Atwell conference on writing and then experimented with her ideas and their own in their classrooms. Here are just a few of their ideas:

Step 1: Prewriting
If we want children to write freely, they need to understand that their choice of topic is in no way limited by their control of the conventions and mechanics of writing; they also need the stimulation of sharing potential topics with one another. . . . (p. 40)
Step 2: Drafting
When we model the drafting stage, we use very rough versions of our pieces, in which we deliberately leave holes. With a little prompting the child will ask questions about the missing information. In this way we demonstrate how information can be added or deleted from a draft. . . . (p. 42)
Step 3: Revising
One way we encourage revision is to allow children to confer with peers as they are drafting their pieces, rather than waiting until after the first draft is finished. This way they can think about revising before the piece becomes too long, thereby making the task less onerous. . . . (p. 44)

Step 4: Editing

From the beginning, we deliberately misspell words, omit proper punctuation, and make grammatical errors. . . . They are often the first things the children point out. . . . When this happens, we remind students that in the drafting stage the mechanics of writing are not as important as concentrating on getting thoughts and information on paper. . . . Later . . . comes the editing stage. . . . (pp. 46–47)

Step 5: Publishing

Some pieces are shared within the classroom and then filed into portfolios. Others are "bound" between simple covers and displayed in a classroom collection or in the hallway. Whatever the form or format, final copies are celebrated. . . . (p. 47)

Help Students See Themselves as Writers

What causes students to begin seeing themselves as writers rather than as students following orders from the teacher? The ones Bright (1995) observed seemed to see themselves as writers. Why? Because the teacher engaged in a considerable amount of one-on-one instruction. This enabled them to apply that advice immediately to their own writing, rather than applying general principles discussed *only* with the total group.

In addition, the teacher encouraged them to express themselves personally rather than writing only what they thought the teacher wanted to read; the teacher encouraged them to write about feelings they couldn't express verbally. The teacher also helped them develop a feeling that writing was relevant and valuable and then helped them become competent writers.

Use One-on-One Writing Conferences

What are writing conferences anyway? They're probably not what most adults think of. They're often only an informal way for the teacher to move from desk to desk, assisting Benito and Luisa, who seem to need help right away because they can't get started, or commenting on Brad's topic about dinosaurs, or providing Amelia with positive feedback on the paper she gave the teacher to read the night before.

Student-initiated conferences are often only an informal way of responding to a friend's softly spoken question, "Hey, man. How's this look to you?" Teacher-initiated conferences may be teacher-student meetings or peer meetings. They work pretty well as long as the *content* of the child's composition is the focus of the conference and the child's spelling and mechanics are discussed later, in reference to publication. Writing conferences are a way to generate greater learning, as well as to cement the community of literacy learners. They provide one avenue for your students to communicate about their real problems with language.

Bring Spelling into Writing

Allow Invented Spelling

Invented spelling should be the modus operandi for your student's first drafts. You and I talked in Chapter 1 about the way invented spelling can encourage children's natural problem-solving tendencies. Another benefit is that of helping children learn to read. In a study by Robinson (1991), "Children's invented spelling was found to provide the best prediction of subsequent reading success." One possible reason is that the use of invented spelling helps strengthen phonemic awareness, the learning of letter names and sounds, and confidence in an ability to figure out what authors are saying.

Indeed, Ehri (1987) concluded from her study of invented spelling that this developmental process "draws learners' attention to sounds in words and to letters that might symbolize those sounds. This . . . makes learners more interested in the spellings of specific words as well as how the general spelling system works" (p. 8). And as we saw in Chapter 5, learning to spell common words makes it easier for children to bring those words into their bulging vocabulary reservoir.

Use the Phonogram Method

Sometimes people have asked me why I don't help teachers teach spelling. But you see, I did teach spelling way back in Chapter 4, when we were talking about phonics, onsets and rimes, and vowel patterns. You may be thinking about the times when there were spelling tests every week, but the phonogram method provides much more meaning and repetition for kids.

Please look again at Figure 4.2, the essential phonograms list: Phonograms With Ten or More Rhyming Words. Do you remember building towers of words, each with the same phonogram, or rime? For example, the phonogram *ad* can help children learn the spelling of 16 meaningful rhyming words: *ad, bad, Brad, cad, clad, dad, fad, gad, grad, glad, had, lad, mad, pad, sad,* and *tad.* And since there are 87 very common phonograms on that chart, you can see how the spelling of hundreds of simple words can be learned while children are happily learning phonogram phonics. Actually, each phonogram on the list creates at least 10 common rhyming words, so 87 phonograms give 870 spelling words. Voila!

Encourage Children to Create Their Own Spelling Strategies

Do you want to know another way that children learn how to spell? A study by Dahl et al. (2003), involving 18 teachers in Solon and Columbus, Ohio, demonstrated that children develop their own spelling strategies. This mammoth quantity of strategies can be boiled down to five *major* ones. The spelling strategies that young children are inventing are these, according to Dahl:

1. **Strategies for *visualizing* the spelling:**

    Remember words from books
    Picture the words
    Visualize alternative spellings

2. **Strategies for *making connections*:**
    Use word families and analogies
    Start with known patterns and add on
    Build words by starting with a root or base word

3. **Strategies for focusing on sounds:**

    Sound out letters from left to right
    Chunk groups of letters and match sounds to the groups (e.g., *Aus tra lia*)

4. **Strategies for reflecting (looking back):**

    Verify the spelling
    Correct the errors
    Check with resources like a dictionary

5. **Strategies for combining information:**

    Weave together the information from several strategies
    Create a fixed routine (e.g., first sound it out, then look it up in a dictionary)

What can teachers do to assist? We can reinforce whatever strategies we discover by modeling them for students. We can also encourage students to share their own strategies with a partner or in front of the entire class. Since "children have their own ways of thinking about spellings as they revisit writing drafts, . . . teachers . . . need to consider that information from children and use it to reshape instruction" (Dahl et al., 2003, p. 319).

Develop Literacy Through Journal Writing

One of the most common literacy activities used in elementary-school classrooms today is journal writing, which occurs at all grade levels and with a variety of literacy programs, including literature-based and basal-reader programs. Journal writing opportunities usually begin in first grade and in enlightened kindergartens. However, I've also observed 2- and 3-year-olds in many preschool centers using a journal to experiment with writing. They were inventing their way through the levels of awareness, differentiating between drawing and writing, writing their own name, inventing theories about what letters stand for and even intuitively applying what they're learning through songs and games.

I've even been watching my 18-month-old grandson, Connor, and his preschool-center buddies get ready for journaling—scribbling on the sidewalks, drawing on an easel, or illegally writing on the wall. Children can't be stopped from imitating those they admire—at least temporarily—and they certainly do see people writing. Connor watched his dad write on an envelope, put a letter in it, seal it, and toss it on the bed. He then tried his best to imitate all of those exciting moves but lost interest after "writing" all over the envelope. He then became more fascinated with removing and replacing the cap on the pen. And within another month, he was happily scribbling lines and circles with his sidewalk chalk.

Connor and the rest of his playmates may well enter kindergarten or first grade as established "authors." But many kids will not come to school with such experiences dancing in their heads. And thus we teachers handle the amazing diversity by day and the long planning sessions by night.

Start with Dictation from Child to Adult

Many kindergarten and first-grade teachers start out with several weeks of dictation, from child to adult. Usually that motivates children to try their own hand at writing.

Gunderson and Shapiro (1988) collected writing samples from two multiethnic first-grade classes for a year and found that half of the children needed to dictate to the teacher for a short while. (The other half were writing letter strings like *BVTHGT* or another exotic concoction of letter strings, conventionally spelled words, and invented spellings.) Within only 4 weeks the "dictators" had gradually switched to invented spellings, spacing between words, and identifiable sentence strings. Encouraging, don't you think?

How did this amazing transformation take place? Well, ask yourself what would happen if you were suddenly placed in a country in which English wasn't spoken (or was spoken even more poorly than it often is in the United States). Imagine that you've been settled for the year in Outer Monslavia, and naturally you have to communicate in order to survive in that environment. Wouldn't you ask your neighbors how to say something? How to write it perhaps? Wouldn't you pay very close attention to how adults spoke or wrote? Wouldn't you study any type of environmental print you could find? And wouldn't you seek out someone who would respond to your attempts to speak or write the language?

Create a Positive Classroom Environment

Those same *kinds* of behaviors were noticed by Gunderson and Shapiro in their 1988 study. Here's what they found in those classrooms:

1. Much interaction among the members of the community

2. Lots of helping and caring, as modeled by the teacher (much like a large family of 6 to 10 children might do it, at least on television)

3. Everyone helping one another get into the literacy club

4. Plenty of environmental print all around the room and the school (e.g., labels for coats and jackets and scissors and written questions such as "What will we do first today?")

5. Plenty of time for journal writing every day

6. Time for a writing conference every day, either with the teacher or with a peer

7. Numerous written and oral responses from the teacher or a peer about each child's writing

What were some other things that Gunderson and Shapiro discovered? With an amazing computer program that ranks the frequency of words in students' writing, they noticed that these students did learn important high-frequency words, even though they were not exposed to the words through a traditional word-oriented reading program. The researchers also discovered that the children's invented spelling revealed considerable growth in awareness of the letters needed for describing phonic patterns. (Give part of the credit to the inspiring physical and emotional classroom environment.)

Three other researchers (Manning, Manning, & Hughes, 1987) analyzed the contents of journals written by 20 first graders during their first school year. The researchers found that the writing ranged widely: scribbling, random letters, descriptions of pictures, lists, informational "articles," imaginative stories, retelling of stories, you name it.

All of these first graders wrote in their journals from the very beginning of the year and did not seem to lose interest during the entire year. Most of them wrote several times a week and shared what they had written with their teacher and peers. (p. 311)

Include Older Students, Too

Older students learn just as much from using journals as first graders do. Here's what one researcher had to say after observing journal writers for their first 4 years of school:

The most outstanding development at Springside during the four years of dedication to journal writing is the abundance of eager authors. Students write fluently and easily. They take risks with paper and pencil because they have years of experience in building confidence. (Kintisch, 1986, p. 168)

In Chapter 9, I showed you an example of Ann, a fourth-grade teacher, helping children learn to respond to literature in their reading journals. Here is how Vacca and Rasinski (1992) describe Ann working with children and their journals during a writing workshop:

For approximately 35 minutes each day, [often] following the reading workshop, the children engage in process writing. . . . Some students may elect to continue letters they are writing in the reading journals. Others might be in the middle of a research report they are composing as part of a thematic unit. In addition, all of the students have writing folders [portfolios]. The folders contain current work in progress on topics that are generated by the students. . . . [As with] the reading workshop, the children make decisions as to how to use their time during writing. At any given time, students may be planning, drafting, revising, editing, or preparing a final draft for publication. . . . During the writing workshop Ann either writes with the children, circulates around the room to confer with individuals, or holds a conference at the listening table. When the occasion calls for it, she will begin a workshop with a mini-lesson. . . . (p. 187)

Respond Skillfully to Children's Journals

Perhaps the most difficult skill for some teachers to develop is that of responding to what children write in their journals. Some teachers tend to write evaluative comments instead of responding to the actual content of what the child has said. Sumitra Unia (1985) gives us an example of this difference:

Child: I saw my mom. I want four a walk with my "clase." I like my teacher. I saw some machines and they were "picing up rokse." My friend came to my hose and we played dolls and it "wass" fun. I wore a dress today "Im" invited to "Melanie" Birthday she is going to be 7.

Evaluative comment: You are doing your journal very nicely. I am very pleased.

Content-oriented comment: Your dress is very pretty. I hope you have fun at Melanie's birthday party. Do you like wearing dresses? It is nice to be able to wear different kinds of clothes. I am glad I don't have to wear dresses to work all the time now. In cold or rainy weather, I prefer to wear pants. How about you? (p. 68)

The content-oriented comment provides motivation for practice in *actual communication*. The evaluative comment makes journal writing just another test—another search for good grades or pats on the head. *Children tend to write more freely and more often if teachers save the evaluative comments for helping students with their final drafts for a classroom publication* (Burrows, Jackson, & Saunders, 1985).

Let's look at another example from Unia (1985):

Child: Dear cjch I am going to the contest and it's going to be fun. I want to the vair and it was fun. I want to the Falie to pike some apples and pirs. And then we want to a plaes to eat awer lunch and It was fun.

Contrived response: How many pears and apples did you pick at the fair? I would like you to tell me more about your weekend. (p. 68)

This response is a step in the right direction, but as Unia points out, this sort of message from the teacher may be merely an attempt to demonstrate the correct spelling of misspelled words (in this case *pears* and *pick*). One wonders if the teacher was truly interested in how many pears and apples the child had picked. The message also implies that the teacher was dissatisfied with the *amount* that the student had produced. This kind of pretense at communication, in which the adult *conceals a judgment,* has led sadly, in my own experience, to drying up children's enthusiasm for using writing as a means of *true* communication.

But on to another issue: Do teachers who use journal writing respond to every child's entry each day? Not at all. Most teachers seem to have time to respond only once a week or so. Remember that children can respond to each other's journals, and many of them don't always *want* a response each time. Much communication that we do in journals and diaries, after all, is with ourselves.

Inspire Writing Through Activities

Integrated Projects

Children often need an adventure or a memorable experience to inspire them to write; they can't always get excited about books and family life. Consequently, there needs to be some flexibility in the schedule that allows for adventuring together. Let me give you an example.

With the help of their teacher, a group of fourth graders decided to find out why their city ran out of water during the summer. No one in the city had been allowed to water their grass, and the shower and sink fixtures in hotels and motels had been fitted with water-restriction devices. Newspapers and television stations pleaded with people not to use the usual 2 gallons of water to brush their teeth.

The fourth graders' teacher, Phil Peterson, helped them develop a battle plan for scouting out the enemy—the water hogs. First, they had to learn a bit about city water and where it came from. The librarians in the area agreed with Phil to help his students find books on the subject, as did several parents, and they all divided into neighborhood teams for hunting-and-gathering expeditions.

When the books were all collected, Phil helped the children divide themselves into project teams. The projects revolved around institutions and groups of people they would eventually interview after they had learned enough from reading. One group was the children in the school; another group was the teachers; a third was the parents. The institutions included schools, hospitals, and hotels. There were about four children on each project team.

For several days Phil taught about water and water supplies, along with learning how to take simple notes and "stuffing the data bank" (Phil mixed his metaphors freely). Each project team insisted on reporting its findings. Math time was taken over temporarily by the need to understand water volume and just what 5 gallons, 50 gallons, and 500 gallons looked like.

When they found out that city reservoirs were measured in *billions* of gallons, they had to find out about a billion and what *billion* meant. And naturally, they had to see a reservoir for themselves. Thus, the famous field trip to Bald Mountain Reservoir, in which Phil lost his shoe in the mud, trying to get one of his students out of a security area. By the time Phil took care of the cut on Jimmy's finger and got back to the security area to get his shoe, the area had been filled with a *billion* or more gallons of water. (Jimmy was allowed to write up this story for the classroom newspaper.)

After the reading, writing, internet searching, and field tripping, the project teams practiced their interview techniques, made their phone calls (Phil had already obtained permission), and the interviews began in earnest. Needless to say, they were amazed at how much water human beings consume. And needless to say, they had plenty of things to write about, including some factual newspaper reports, private journal mutterings, and imaginative adventure stories in which the main adult character always seemed to lose his shoe.

Language-Experience Activities

Adventuring together is a form of motivation for writing that obviously can't occur every day. A simpler, everyday form of motivation can be generated through a *language-experience activity*. Language-experience approaches have been around for a long time and will probably always be useful as supplements or as programs in their own right. Rather than relying on literature, anthology selections or little books as the sole medium of instruction, these activities rely on the language of the students. Peregoy and Boyle (2001) refer to language-experience activity as "the most frequently recommended approach for the beginning second-language readers. . . . It is tailored to the learner's own interest, background, knowledge, and language proficiency" (p. 268).

Language-experience projects use oral language to stimulate ideas and discussion, which lead to written experience and reading. Students see their own language in print, read it, and become increasingly motivated to read from other sources, like books and magazines (Norton, 2004).

Here is one small example of language experience in operation, with the teacher developing interest and leading a stimulating discussion before the students create an experience chart together. For a much more detailed explanation of language-experience activities, look at the classic book by Mary Anne Hall (1981) called *Teaching Reading as a Language Experience*.

The second-grade teacher you're about to observe was tape-recorded several years ago. The teacher had brought in a caged animal and began by asking an open-ended question about it. Research by Burrows, Jackson, and Saunders (1985) shows that this type of verbal stimulation before composing can produce longer and more creative compositions.

Teacher: What do you think this hamster feels about your looking at him?

Jerry: I think he's happy.

Teacher: Why, Jerry?

Jerry: Because he has someone to play with.

Teacher: [Nodding appreciatively] He doesn't seem very frightened, does he?

Mona: He's got long whiskers.

Teacher: Yes, they're quite long. How long would you say they are? Are they as long as this pencil?

Ming-Hsiu: [Laughing] They're not that long. They're as long as . . . as long as my little finger.

Teacher: Yes, I think you're right, Ming-Hsiu. What else do you notice about this little hamster . . . Stephen?

Stephen: He's got real sharp teeth.

Teacher: How can you tell?

Stephen: Because . . . because they're pointed and because he can chew up those little round things real fast.

Teacher: Yes, he can, can't he? Those little round things are called pellets, and they're what he likes to eat. Do you know what they're made of?

Stephen: I don't know. Nuts maybe.

Teacher: Well, in a way, you're right! They're made from the seeds of wheat and barley and other grains like that. Since nuts are a kind of seed, Stephen, you were right!

Stephen: [Smiling] Yeah.

Teacher: What else would you like to know about our hamster?

After the discussion (and hamster observation) continued for a while, the teacher began the dictation period by moving to a tagboard chart.

Teacher: Who would like to begin today? We need a sentence at the top that will remind us what we've been doing just now . . . Julie?

Julie: We've been lookin' at a funny little hamster.

Teacher: All right, let's write that down. I'll start way at the top and way over on the left side. I'll start with a capital letter. [The teacher writes, "Julie says, 'We've been looking at a funny little hamster,'" then points to each word and reads the sentence out loud.] Who would like to have the next turn? Stephen?

Stephen: He has real sharp pointed teeth . . .

The dictation continues until everyone has had a turn or until the group feels that the story is complete. Here's an example of what a finished chart in first or second grade might look like.

Julie says, "We've been looking at a funny little hamster."
Stephen says, "He has real sharp pointed teeth."
Ming-Hsiu says, "He has whiskers as long as my little finger."
Mona says, "He lives in a wire cage, and he keeps looking at us when he eats."
Marilyn says, "The funny little hamster runs races with himself."
David says, "The funny little hamster ain't got a friend to live with."
Francis says, "But we can be his friends. We'll feed him and give him water and play with him."

With language experience, *children either dictate or write their own reading selections,* thereby learning in a natural and practical way that reading is a form of communication and that writers and readers are truly communicators. Literature is also used, but teachers rely most (at first) on reading selections created by their students. The purposes of this dictating/writing/reading process are (1) to provide children with opportunities to search for new ideas about the world and (2) to search for an understanding of how adults use language. Teachers keep track of children's progress through the same means used by literature-based programs: careful observation, observation checklists, portfolios, and other ways that are described in Chapter 11.

Language-Experience Applications

Kindergarten Many kindergarten teachers have used language experience part of the day to get children ready for more formal instruction in first grade. Children in small or large groups dictate their ideas or experiences to the teacher, who immediately prints them, exactly as dictated, on the chalkboard or on tagboard charts. The teacher reads the ideas back to the children and then encourages them to read or say the ideas all together, thus confirming to kindergartners that printed words can represent spoken words. A left-to-right reading orientation is developed; letter names are taught or reviewed; uppercase and lowercase letters are identified and used; simple vowel patterns are played with; and phonemic awareness is reinforced—all through the use of meaningful experience charts or group stories.

First Grade First graders do more personal, individual writing than they did in kindergarten, now writing and speaking in coherent sentences. They learn from dictation and writing experiences to recognize more words by sight and to write common suffixes and graphophonic patterns. As the year progresses, they can read not only more of their peers' written accounts, but more stories and descriptions by adult authors as well. They also write brief narratives and expository descriptions. Library books or selections from basal anthologies provide opportunities to practice the communication skills they have gained through language-experience activities.

Other first-grade teachers use language-experience activities right along with a basic reading program from the very beginning, using anthologies prescribed by the school district. For the development of skills or concepts they rely on a general program. For developing the understanding that reading is a communication process, they rely on language experience—especially through the use of group charts.

Older Students In the later grades language-experience charts can be used to describe what students already know about a topic they are about to study—the K-W-L procedure is one example of this. Language-experience charts can be used to summarize what has been learned so far. They can be used as part of the process of creating class magazines, newspapers, journals, and books—all of these designed to keep track of what students are learning, experiencing, and feeling. In short, group-experience charts provide a natural, social-developmental mode (or a social constructivist mode) for learning.

Students with Reading Difficulties Students who need special instruction at any grade level can be helped through language experiences, too. This is especially true of those students in Grades 3 through 7 who have been turned off by too many worksheets and language drills. For many reluctant readers a language-experience approach can provide a first glimpse into the real meaning of reading.

Tyrone, for example, was a leader of a small group of third-grade boys who hated reading and going to school. Their teacher asked me for help, so together we came up with a plan. At that particular time in my midlife crisis, I was driving a red hot sports car. So according to plan, I drove to their school the next day and gave Tyrone's team, one boy at a time, an exhilarating ride in my sports car.

When we got back to her classroom, the teacher skillfully took dictation while the boys excitedly took turns telling her about their adventure. When their story was finished, they read it with the teacher several times and then proudly to the entire class. For the first time, reading made sense!

Tyrone's teacher duplicated their story so that the boys could take it home to read to their parents. She then formed a special writers' group, appropriately called Tyrone's Team, which created numerous experience stories and gained both reading skill and self-confidence by reading their own compositions out loud. By the end of third grade, both Tyrone and his teacher had made sure that every member of the team was a bona fide member of the literacy club.

The Rationale for Language-Experience Activities

By now you could probably write your own rationale for the use of language-experience approaches. Because they use the child's present language, rather than language created by adults, the translation of print back into speech (i.e., subvocal thought) is natural, *predictable,* and meaningful. Furthermore, children quickly learn the most important concepts about the reading process: (1) Reading involves communication with a person who wrote down his or her thoughts; (2) reading is *not* a subject in school, a torturous process of sounding out words or an endless conveyor belt of worksheets and workbook pages; and (3) reading is just one of four avenues of communication, along with speaking, listening, and writing.

The vast majority of research studies on language-experience approaches have demonstrated that the language-experience method is as effective as basal-reader programs and may even have special advantages (Hall, 1981). Perhaps the greatest fear educators and parents have about the use of a language-experience approach is that children will not learn as many words or graphophonic patterns as they would through other approaches. However, research demonstrates that this fear is unfounded (Hall, 1981). Again, for more details on how to use language experience, be sure to see the book by Mary Anne Hall. Language experience is a classic method that has outlived dozens of less meaningful approaches to teaching literacy.

An Innovative Approach   Let's enjoy one more sample of the versatility of language experience. Wright and Laminack (1982) describe an innovative practice in which a first-grade teacher used a language-experience approach to teach students about television commercials. The children learned a great many "commercial words," such as *fresh, new, better, product,* and other favorites of advertisers. They also wrote many language-experience charts to describe how they tested the advertisers' claims. Like this one:

> We listened to a cat food commercial.
> They say that it is sealed in a pouch.
> On TV when the man opens the pouch,
> A voice says, "Fresh!"
> Cammie tried this at home.
> Her cat food did not say, "Fresh!"

> We put water into two small cups.
> Next, we put a Mounty paper towel in one cup
> And a plain paper towel in the other cup . . .
> We could lift a cup with a wet Mounty.
> The plain paper towel fell apart.

> Z-soap will make you feel awake.
> Meredith tried Z-soap.
> She said that she did not feel any better.
> We did not see her jump up and down.

Involve Budding Authors with Technological Sites

There are a variety of free and creative Internet links for getting your students involved in writing projects. Students can work with you to identify the ones most appropriate and exciting for your classroom. These resources can be used to access information needed for writing projects or to connect with other students and classrooms around the world. Students can also publish their materials through many of these sites. It's important to guide your students in their research and communications and to secure their help in identifying ways to evaluate and screen sources of information or contacts and ensure privacy of personal identification. Here are a few sites you might want to start with, but have fun finding your own.

http://www.gsn.org
Formerly FrEdMail, Global SchoolNet is a groovy online site developed by teachers to involve students in meaningful exchange with people around the world and to improve communication, literacy skills, and multicultural understanding. With over 900 online projects organized by topic and grade, students find partners or join writing projects around the globe.

http://www.factmonster.com
Fact Monster provides information students might need for developing creative writing projects and reports under such categories as World & News, U.S., People, Science, Sports, and Homework Center.

http://www.ajkids.com
Ask Jeeves Kids is a place where students can get answers to specific questions that will help them get started on their writing projects. For example, What kind of food

do children eat in the Congo? How can I make a model of an adobe house? How many years do children in Saudi Arabia have to go to school? There is also an authors reading segment in the main menu, where you can actually set up a Web page for your classroom to publish students' creative writing.

http://kotn.nta.ac.uk
At Kids on the Net students can submit their own writing and read the published writings of other students around the world. The menu includes stories, poetry, tall tales and offers advice from authors and illustrators. Students can also add a new chapter to an ongoing book being written by other students like them.

http://www.rcls.org/ksearch.htm
Rampo Catskill Internet Guides provides kids search tools for conducting research. This page is adapted from InFoPeople's best search tools page. Here you can find a great variety of Web sites for kids to use for their writing activities.

http://sunsite, berkeley.edu/KidsClick!
Kids Click is a database of over 6,000 sites compiled by librarians. Students can conduct searches of over 600 subjects.

http://www.kidpub.com
Kidpub is another possibility for setting up a Web page for your classroom where students can read and publish their own written work. Their database holds over 43,000 stories written for and by students. There is a small one-time fee.

Excite Your Students with the Author's Computer Chair

In the 1980s researchers like Calkins (1983), Graves (1983), and Graves and Hansen (1983) insisted on making children proud of their writing, instead of ashamed and sometimes hostile. The Author's Chair that Graves and Calkins promoted was to get students to admire *each other* by helping them produce an interesting piece of work. In the Author's Chair a student could sit like a king and request feedback from peers on what they liked and what they suggested at any stage in the writing process.

Today, writing has become the true king, allowing us to communicate in thousands of ways using abundant software and the speedy Internet. Why not try an Author's Computer Chair, recommended by Labbo (2004)? After all, computers are frequently equipped with kid-friendly word processors, presentation software, and multimedia authoring programs. Now commonplace fixtures in the modern classroom, computers have become readily available for use in most elementary schools (Jerald & Galofsky, 1999).

Guidelines for the Author's Computer Chair

Labbo gives us five key guidelines for using the Author's Computer Chair method.

1. Foster peer collaboration and a sense of community. Think of this experience as one that truly fits our society.

   > Most employers do not expect people to sit in rows and compete with colleagues without interacting with them. The heart of most jobs, especially the higher-paying, more interesting jobs, is teamwork, which involves getting others to cooperate, leading others, coping with complex power and influence issues, and helping solve people's problems in working with each other. Teamwork, communication, effective coordination, and divisions of labor characterize most real life settings. It is time for schools to . . . realistically reflect the realities of adult life. (Johnson & Johnson, 1989, p. 79)

2. Conduct mini lessons to guide the total class efficiently, frequently modeling by asking questions of the student sitting in the Author's Computer Chair and then letting his or her peers do the asking. There should be questions about helpful Web sites, Internet sources, e-mail possibilities, ways for students to focus more closely on a specific topic, a possible commercial company online, ways to use Google or some other popular search engine, and most of all, What will be your steps?

3. Make sure to schedule time for the Author's Computer Chair and encourage sharing of whatever is on the monitor. Don't let kids hog it. They need to learn from each other and assist each other—just like they're on a job.

4. Have students share the equipment. There are three distinct uses of the Author's Computer Chair: seeking help or feedback, sharing knowledge and experience, and showcasing a student's work.

5. Allow for abundant discussion of different problems.

   Try this approach. You may be pleasantly surprised.

 ## Summary of Main Ideas

- Although writing is an important ingredient in any successful reading program, it is important in its own right.
- Writing and reading assist each other throughout the grades as a child gradually develops adult literacy.
- Patterned books, detective stories, verse, and other predictable literature serve as excellent models for children's writing.

- Motivation for children to write is influenced by many factors, including the teacher's attitude toward writing, the physical literacy environment of the classroom, and the degree of acceptance of invented spelling.
- Learning to write includes determining what good writers do, establishing both an internal and an external audience, setting goals and purposes, perceiving oneself as a writer, and practicing the overlapping and interacting stages of prewriting, drafting, revising, editing, and publishing.
- Language-experience approaches can be used effectively by any teacher who wishes to use children's own writing as one medium for developing literacy.

Focus on Students with Special Needs: Comments by Louise Fulton

Teaching Writing to Students with Special Needs

What do teachers know about the most effective strategies for teaching writing to students with special needs? Students with learning disabilities often have difficulty recognizing letters, even after your best teaching efforts. In addition, these students make many capitalization, spelling, and punctuation errors. When you see these problems, you might assume that the students are unable to conceptualize. But don't let their performance in those specific areas fool you. Yes, students with learning disabilities do make more of those kinds of errors, but they are quite capable of writing complex ideas (Goldman & Hasselbring, 1997).

What can you do to help these students? Vaughn, Gersten, and Chard (2000) summarized research on the best practices in expressive writing instruction.

1. Use highly explicit instruction in the critical steps of the writing process: prewriting, drafting, revising, editing, and publishing.
2. Model how to use these critical steps by writing several samples.
3. Use mnemonics (i.e., memory aids), think sheets, and prompt cards extensively to support the writing process.
4. Use highly explicit teaching of the different text structures, such as persuasive essay, personal narrative, comparing and contrasting, and highly descriptive works.
5. Give frequent feedback to students on the qualities of their work and the elements that can be improved.
6. Provide access for special-needs students to the general education curriculum.
7. Provide opportunities to write not only persuasive essays but also interpretation of personal experiences.
8. Help students understand the all-important links between reading and writing.

Perhaps the most important conclusion that the researchers came to was that students with learning disabilities often demonstrate conceptual-thinking processes that far exceed what teachers would have predicted.

Literacy Through Technology

A. Go to http://www.gsn.org and find out how you could use Global SchoolNet to develop writing activities that would foster multicultural understanding among your students. Then try out one of GSN's writing and thinking projects. Here are a few examples:

    1. *Noon Day:* Students all over the world measured shadows at noon and communicated by e-mail to collaboratively calculate the circumference of the earth.

    2. *GALA:* Students exchanged compositions, some of which were then published in a global anthology.

    3. *GeoGame:* Students attempted to guess the locations of participants through scrambled geographical clues.

B. Take a look at these Web sites to examine some of the many resources available to enhance awareness of the rich cultural heritage represented in our diverse classrooms.

    1. Go to the Underground Railway to start an interactive journey with Harriet Tubman.
http://www.nationalgeographic.com/features/99/railroad/index.html

    2. Kids Web Japan provides information on the Japanese language, folktales, and customs. http://www.jinjapan.org/kidsweb/index.html

    3. Distinguished Women of the Past and Present includes biographies of women who have contributed to our culture in many ways.
http://www.distinguishedwomen.com/

    4. Documenting the American South follows the lives of African American slaves through their narratives. http://docsouth.unc.edu/neh/

Application Experiences for Your Course

A. *Becoming a Model for the Writing Processes.* Decide with one or more partners whether you can engage in enough writing of your own to be a model for your students. What kind of writing do you normally do now that could serve as *process* examples? What kind of writing have you wanted to do but never or seldom have done? Would you be willing to experiment with this kind of writing in front of your students? Would you be willing to model the prewriting, drafting, revising, editing, and publishing stages, even if it meant admitting your uncertainties and fears—which is just what they need to hear?

B. *Experiencing Language Experience as Students.* Use an actual event that has affected everyone in the class to create a group-experience chart. Or substitute an extraterrestrial activity like this one: Divide up the class into several groups, and have the instructor secretly give each group a different Earth object, such as a paper clip or a felt-tip pen. The members of each group are to imagine themselves as people from a faraway planet who are studying Earth. They should then creatively write a report on the strange and mysterious object they have found. Each group will need to appoint one person as the teacher-recorder.

Each group should go through the five stages of development for an experience chart: (1) *Stimulate* each other's interest in the project, making sure everyone understands what your goals are and what you might gain from the experience. (2) *Discuss* the mysterious item, its nature, and the possible uses earthlings might have for it (but don't include its actual use). (3) *Write* a brief list of ideas about your strange item, with one person as chart recorder. (4) *Read* your report to the rest of the class, allowing them to read along silently and guess what object you had. (5) *Teach* something from the chart: an idea, some common sight words, some common phonograms, whatever.

C. *More Practice in Creating and Using an Experience Chart.* As a total group or a small group, create a What Do We Know chart (on tagboard, butcher paper, or the chalkboard) about the importance of teaching reading and writing together. Use both textbook ideas and your own experiences.

Creativity Training Session

A Hilarious Interview Experience. In this imagination-stretching experience, let your imagination go far and wide. Two people are needed. The person being interviewed sits in a chair in the front of the room, assuming a thoughtful position about the story he or she will be telling about an imaginary experience. The second person, the interpreter, stands behind and to the side of the interviewee. The seated interviewee begins to tell about an imaginary experience, making one statement and then pausing. But the interviewee is speaking gibberish (i.e., nonsense sounds) that sound like oral communication but are not; the rhythm, sounds, pauses, voice changes, and emotion of speech are there, but there are no recognizable words. The standing person interprets the gibberish statement as if it makes sense. The seated person, the interviewee, then makes another statement. The session continues this way for several minutes. No laughing—stay in your story and character and let the story unfold, even if the audience is cracking up. A story will unfold, bit by bit, as the interpreter describes what he or she imagines the interviewee is saying. Repeat this activity. Discuss how this idea could be used or modified to stimulate more creative writing with a class of 9- to 12-year-olds.

Field Experiences

A. *Model the Writing Steps.* Model the first four writing steps in front of a small group of children—or a large group if you wish. Try to do this without notes. Spontaneously voice your thoughts as you work on each step. See Application Experience A for ideas.

B. *Create and Use a Language-Experience Chart.* Show something intriguing to a group of children as the first step of *stimulation.* Then either lead a *discussion* on the item yourself or, in fourth grade or above, select a student to lead the discussion. You can use the five *w*'s (*what, who, where, when,* and *why*) to get the discussion started. Follow the discussion with *writing.* You can take dictation or let someone else take the dictation, or you can allow the children to write their own brief compositions on the item. Follow that with the *reading* step. Help students if necessary, or let them read each other's. For the *teaching* step discuss ideas learned, common sight words, phonic patterns, or whatever you feel this particular group needs.

C. *Interview Children on Writing.* Interview several children independently or in a group as to what good writers do. Also ask this question: "When you write, who do you write for?" Tape-record and/or write down the responses, along with your tentative conclusions, to analyze with your colleagues later.

References

Allen, J., et al. (2002). PhOLKS lore: Learning from photographs, families, and children. *Language Arts, 79,* 312–322.

Behymer, A. (2003). Kindergarten writing workshop. *The Reading Teacher, 57*(1), 85–88.

Bright, R. (1995). *Writing instruction in the intermediate grades.* Newark, DE: International Reading Association.

Burrows, A. T., Jackson, D. C., & Saunders, D. O. (1985). *They all want to write.* Newark, DE: International Reading Association.

Cairney, T. H. (1987). Collaborative stories. *The Reading Teacher, 41,* 116–117.

Calkins, L. M. (1983). *Lessons from a child.* Portsmouth, NH: Hienemann.

Calkins, L. M. (1986). *The art of teaching writing.* Portsmouth, NH: Heinemann.

Colvin, V. (1991). *The effects of two teachers' views on their students' writing.* Unpublished manuscript. Portland State University, Portland, OR.

Cox, B. E., Shanahan, T., & Sulzby, E. (1990). Good and poor elementary readers' use of cohesion in writing. *Reading Research Quarterly, 25,* 47–65.

Cullinan, B. E. (Ed.). (1993). *Pen in hand: Children become writers.* Newark, DE: International Reading Association.

Dahl, K. L., Barto, A., Bonfils, M., Carasello, J., Christopher, R., Davis, N. E., et al. (2003). Connecting developmental word study with classroom writing: Children's descriptions of spelling strategies. *The Reading Teacher, 57*(4), 310–319.

Dionisio, M. (1983). Write? Isn't this reading class? *The Reading Teacher, 36,* 746–750.

Durkin, D. (1966). *Children who read early: Two longitudinal studies.* New York: Teachers College Press.

Ehri, L. C. (1987). *Movement in word reading and spelling: How spelling contributes to reading* (Report No. 408). Urbana: Illinois University, Center for the Study of Reading.

Goldman, S. R., & Hasselbring, T. S. (1997). Achieving meaningful mathematics literacy for students with learning disabilities. *Journal of Learning Disabilities, 30,* 198–208.

Graves, D. H. (1983). *Writing: Teachers and children at work.* Portsmouth, NH: Heinemann.

Graves, D., & Hansen, J. (1983). The author's chair. *Language Arts, 60,* 176–183.

Gunderson, L., & Shapiro, J. (1988). Whole language instruction: Writing in first grade. *The Reading Teacher, 41,* 420–437.

Hall, M. A. (1981). *Teaching reading as a language experience.* Columbus, OH: Merrill.

Hansen, J. (1987). *When writers read.* Portsmouth, NH: Heinemann.

Harp, B. (1987). Why are your kids writing during reading time? *The Reading Teacher, 41,* 88–90.

Hoffner, H. (2003). Writing a movie. *The Reading Teacher, 57*(1), 78–81.

Holbrook, H. T. (1987). Writing to learn in the social studies. *The Reading Teacher, 41,* 216–219.

Jerald, C. D., & Galofsky, G. F. (1999). Raising the bar on school technology. *Education Week, 24*(4), 58–69.

Johnson, D. W., and Johnson, R. (1989). *Cooperation and competition: Theory and research.* Edina, MN: Interaction.

Kintisch, L. S. (1986). Journal writing: Stages of development. *The Reading Teacher, 40,* 168–172.

Labbo, L. D. (2004). Author's computer chair. *The Reading Teacher, 57*(7), 688–691.

Leal, D. J. (2003). Digging up the past, building the future: Using book authoring to discover and showcase a community's history. *The Reading Teacher, 57*(1), 56–60.

Linaberger, M. (2005). Poetry top 10: A foolproof formula for teaching poetry. *The Reading Teacher, 58*(4), 366–372.

Manning, M., Manning, G., & Hughes, J. (1987). Journals in first grade: What children write. *The Reading Teacher, 41,* 311–315.

Martinez, R., Roser, N., & Strecker, S. (1999). "I never thought I could be a star": A readers' theatre ticket to fluency. *The Reading Teacher, 52,* 326–334.

Muley-Meissner, M. L. (2002). The spirit of a people: Hmong American life stories. *Language Arts, 79,* 323–331.

Norton, D. (2004). *Effective teaching of language arts* (6th ed., p. 506). Upper Saddle River, NJ: Pearson/Merrill/Prentice Hall.

Peregoy, S., & Boyle, O. (2001). *Reading, writing, and learning in ESL* (3rd ed.). New York: Longman.

Purcell, J. (2001). *Creating a literacy club in a first grade classroom: One teacher's balanced approach* (ERIC Document Reproduction Service No. ED454499).

Qian, G. (1990, November). *Review of the interactive model: Reconsideration of reading and writing relationship.* Paper presented at the annual meeting of the College Reading Association, Nashville, TN.

Robinson, S. S. (1991, April). *Reading achievement: Contributions of invented spelling and alphabetic knowledge.* Paper presented at the annual meeting of the American Educational Research Association, Chicago.

Schroeder, V. C., & Lovett, A. K. (1993). Modeling the process approach in the early elementary grades. In B. E. Cullinan (Ed.), *Pen in hand: Children become writers.* Newark, DE: International Reading Association.

Shanahan, T. (1988). The reading-writing relationship: Seven instructional principles. *The Reading Teacher, 41,* 636–647.

Stewig, J. W. (1990). *Read to write: Using children's literature as a springboard for teaching writing.* Katonah, NY: Richard C. Owen.

Taylor, N. E., Blum, I. H., & Logsdon, D. M. (1986). The development of written language awareness: Environmental and program characteristics. *Reading Research Quarterly, 21,* 132–149.

Unia, S. (1985). From sunny days to green onions: On journal writing. In J. Newman (Ed.), *Whole language theory in use.* Portsmouth, NH: Heinemann.

Vacca, R. T., & Rasinski, T. V. (1992). *Case studies in whole language.* New York: Harcourt Brace Jovanovich.

Vaughn, S., Gersten, R., & Chard, D. (2000). The underlying message in LD intervention research: Findings from research synthesis. *Exceptional Children, 67*(1), 99–114.

Wilkinson, L., & Sillman, E. (2000). Classroom language and literacy learning. In M. Kamil, P. Mosenthal, D. Pearson, & R. Barr (Eds.), *Handbook of reading research* (Vol. 3). Mahwah, NJ: Erlbaum.

Wright, J. P., & Laminack, L. (1982). First graders can be critical listeners and readers. *Language Arts, 59,* 133–137.

Other Suggested Readings

Bloem, P. L. (2004). Correspondence journals: Talk that matters. *The Reading Teacher, 58*(1), 54–62.

Henk, W. A., Marinak, B. A., Moore, J. C., & Mallette, M. H. (2003). The writing observation framework: A guide for refining and validating writing instruction. *The Reading Teacher, 57*(4), 322–333.

Linaberger, M. (2005). Poetry top 10: A foolproof formula for teaching poetry. *The Reading Teacher, 58*(4), 366–372.

Parsons, L. (2001). *Response journals revisited: Maximizing learning through reading, writing, viewing, discussing and thinking.* Portland, ME: Stenhouse.

Chapter Eleven

A Performance Point of View in Assessing Literacy

Assess: to evaluate or judge self or others.

—*Webster*

I'm not sure. My culture on Xania is different from theirs, but it looks like assessing on Earth is sticking your nose in other people's business.

—*Bogglestar*

Eleventh Objective for Your Teaching Success:

Use portfolios, observation, miscues and a variety of other assessment tools to monitor progress.

What are the best ways to determine how well your students are learning to read?

1. Check their scores on a yearly state test? It's your duty but . . .

2. Listen to each student read pages of your choice? Sometimes but . . .

3. Notice how often students read *without* your asking? OK, but . . .

4. Notice that a student can repeat everything the author says? Hire him!

Well . . . Number 1 could be useless, as I'll explain later. Number 2 and 3 sound good. And Number 4 tells us that you and I might be losing our jobs.

Experienced teachers have gradually developed convenient and reasonably quick ways to assess how well their students are learning to read. From research and my own experience the most important are these: (1) student's portfolios, (2) teachers' observations of student's learning behavior, and (3) on-task examination of students' miscues. Let's first explore these three forms of assessment and then check out other ways to determine whether your students really comprehend what the author is saying.

Creative Portfolios

Professional Standard: Uses information from portfolios and other indicators of students' progress

> A reliance on multiple-choice tests conveys to students that what's worth learning is bits of knowledge that can be quickly recalled or recognized. Performance assessments, on the other hand, convey to students that educators value in-depth understanding, the ability to apply knowledge in new situations. . . . (Willis, 1996, p. 3).

What is a *portfolio?* It's an assessment device. It's a portable case for carrying paintings, photographs, written documents. It also carries your creative stories, problems you have solved all by yourself, other graphic material, and favorite Web sites. Journalists show their wares by pulling out published articles from their portfolios to impress editors. Short-story authors use them for the same purpose. Investment specialists pull out impressive charts, graphs, and other data. Children and teen-age actors have portfolios of pictures and videotapes evidencing their best work.

Like an artist's portfolio, a *literacy portfolio* must be a durable case containing student work samples. These samples should demonstrate growth in composing, reading, journaling, searching the Internet, and recording of various types of oral language. Throughout the year students are encouraged to select artifacts of their learning experiences to place in their portfolios and then to share what they've learned. Later, if teachers ask to see what students consider to be their best work, they have a variety of things to pick from.

The Importance of Artifacts

An *artifact* is a term used primarily by archaeologists to distinguish natural objects from objects made by human effort. A natural rock would not be considered an artifact, whereas a rock that has been chiseled into a hatchet head would be. Artifacts discovered by archaeologists help them determine what a group of people had learned to do or understand while they were alive. For a teacher an artifact can serve the same function of determining what a student has learned to do or understand. Whether it be a drawing, a math solution, a reading tape, a newspaper astronomy report, a historical document, a poem, a journal entry, a weather chart, a painting or materials from a Web Site—it can all serve the same purpose. A small sample of the variety of artifacts I have actually seen in children's portfolios is shown in Figure 11.1.

---

1. Letters written to teachers, peers, or famous people
2. A child's reading miscues coded simply enough for children to understand and discuss (usually placed in the portfolio by the teacher with the child's consent)
3. Dialogues written for skits or plays
4. An assessment of a composition
5. Record of books read and how they were shared
6. A nonfiction report
7. A better ending for a novel
8. Other book projects that require writing (see Appendix G)
9. Artwork related to literature or a content area
10. An original song (words and music)
11. A web related to a story or to a difficult word
12. A time line
13. An article or story published in a class book
14. A series of documents relating to a writing project in process: the planning notes, first draft, revised draft, and published draft
15. A checklist related to the child's reading goals or writing goals (created in collaboration with the teacher)
16. Two stories written from entirely different points of view—or for two entirely different audiences
17. A response paper related to someone else's book project
18. A journal entry that turns out to be special—or one that the child thinks really shows "how much I've grown"
19. Photographs of cooperatively produced murals or construction projects or exhibits (with comments on procedures and what was learned)
20. A report on a science experiment
21. A map of an invented country
22. A parent-teacher conference report
23. Copies of anecdotal notes kept by the teacher
24. A recipe invented, tried, and evaluated

FIGURE 11.1 Sample of artifacts seen in children's portfolios.

Artifacts are authentic assessments and should not be treated like assignments that can spoil an atmosphere of respect for young people's creative endeavors. When we think of portfolio work, we need to think of *creativity* and *autonomy*. (If *autonomy* is not your favorite word, try *self-determination* or *self-rule*.) What students put into their portfolios and journals is *their* work—something they're excited about, something they can't wait to share with someone else: peers, teacher, or a parent. Assignments, on the other hand, if not creative or interesting, might be treated in the usual way: Students do them, turn them in, and get feedback from the teacher. But beware—creative, individual ways of working can be highly contagious and may spill over into regular assignments.

Tracking Personal Progress

As photographers and other artists choose materials for or from their portfolios, they go through much reflective thinking. That is, they think about their goals for their work and their methods in achieving those goals. Likewise, motivated students spend time choosing, reflecting, establishing goals, and determining methods—essential processes for successful portfolio use.

When photographers develop prints and choose certain ones for their portfolios, they must engage in self-assessment: Did I use too much light? Is the composition right? How did I get such amazing contrasts this time? What should my goals and methods be for the next photo shoot? Individuals gathering information for their portfolios gradually invent specific standards for a superior performance.

Your students would really appreciate your modeling of how you use your portfolio. The best way to do that is to share your own personal portfolio with your creative writing, creative planning, or whatever you do when you're not teaching. Model for them as you decide whether or not to add something to your own personal portfolio. Students usually love that kind of sharing, which shows how human you are (and worth admiring).

A Real-Life Example

My friend Rick Rappaport can illustrate portfolio assessment for us. He was once a newspaper photographer looking for work, so he created a portfolio. When he went in to see a newspaper editor about a cover piece, he relied almost entirely on his portfolio, rather than his charming personality. But he didn't always get a job that way. What he got instead was a chance to assess his own performance as a photographer.

"Tell me what's good about your photographs," one of the editors said.

Rick told her, "They're user-friendly. You know, they've got some kind of universal theme, such as mother and child love . . . as in this one . . . or the battle against the whims of nature . . . as in this one."

The editor asked him what else made his photographs worthy of publication, and Rick gave her a brief explanation. When he finished, she said, "You're very

good at what you've set out to achieve. When we need some photo essays, I'll keep you in mind. But for now we need someone who's more interested in topical shots—pictures that fit into the events that are happening right now but not necessarily a month from now. Do you know what I mean?"

Rick did know what she meant. He thanked her for her critique and made a silent vow: Before he had his next interview, he was going to update his portfolio. The evaluation he had received from the editor had caused him to engage in *reflection*—thinking about his new goals and his means of achieving them. Assessment by a master had led to self-assessment by an apprentice. This same self-assessment can apply to your students.

Like Rick, artists who paint do not see a portfolio as a mere folder or an exotic business file. It's not an object at all to them, it's their work—sometimes their heart and soul. Your students are capable of feeling that same way about their literacy portfolios, as long as teachers treat their efforts with respect.

Both caregivers and teachers need to help children feel ownership of their portfolios by letting *them* decide what goes in it, what comes out of it to show to you or their peers, and what they want to keep in it forever. The decision-making process alone can result in rich and personalized dialogues and social interchange and communication. After all, learning how to make decisions is a skill we can carry with us way beyond the classroom. And the feeling of ownership, as you know from your own personal experience, is highly motivating. Thus, the use of portfolios leads not only to self-assessment, but also to greater effort and learning (Tierney, Carter, & Desai, 1991).

Other Benefits of Literacy Portfolios

In addition to allowing for self-assessment, literacy portfolios and journals have other virtues. In contrast to paper-and-pencil tests, they can represent the range of literacy the student has developed—especially in classrooms that emphasize literature: writing, journaling, "Web-site-ing," self-selected free reading, thematic units, cooperative learning, and abundant exploration of nonfiction texts. Portfolios provide an opportunity for students to *apply* the knowledge they have gained rather than merely giving back the knowledge via tests.

Equally important, literacy portfolios allow teachers, parents, and administrators to get an invited, broad, and concrete view of each child's success in communicating through reading, writing, speaking, thinking, and listening. That view allows a teacher to compare Susie with herself—over time and in different situations.

Tierney and his colleagues (1991) observed the use of literacy portfolios in over 50 classrooms. Here is a summary of their findings:

- There seemed to be a feeling of ownership by most students. In general, they liked to share their portfolios with peers and adults.
- As a result of using portfolios, students showed considerable awareness of their own goals and accomplishments in reading and writing.
- The assessment procedures generally featured collaboration between teachers and students and between students and their peers.
- Parents and caregivers were active in examining portfolios. As one second grader said, "My mom was amazed at how much I learned."
- Teachers reported having a "richer, clearer view" of each individual than they'd had before using portfolios. They felt that they had records of what their students were actually doing.
- Administrators seemed to be pleased with the results of portfolio use, especially because they had a much better way of observing exactly what students were doing. Then they could tell parents, older siblings, and caregivers how well students were doing in particular classrooms.

Tierney et al. (1991) summed it up this way: "Portfolios are likely to be a far richer source of information about a student's literacy achievement, progress, and ongoing development than other, more formal sources" (p. 51).

Reviewing Literacy Portfolios

Although procedures vary with each teacher, in general a teacher regularly reviews work samples (i.e., artifacts) that are provided by students. Some teachers target two or three kids daily to share or brag about the newest artifact derived from their creative thinking. In that way you can assess your students portfolios in about 10 to 15 school days.

Other teachers include student participation in a different way. About every 3 to 4 weeks, they have children sort through their journals and literacy portfolios to find their gems that show what they've accomplished. The usual request goes like this: "Find three or four samples that best show what you have learned—or that you simply like the best—and put them in your literacy portfolio for me to see tomorrow." The limit of three or four is often used (Tierney, Carter, & Desai, 1991) because teachers want to do a quality job of examining these gems and providing verbal or written comments about them.

With my own use of literacy portfolios I've had my students choose one or two artifacts each Friday afternoon to mark with their personal symbol. Then every quarter, they would pick out three to five artifacts and show them to me. These gems were then kept in the portfolio most of the year so that a student's accomplishments could be examined and celebrated by teachers, peers, parents, caregivers, administrators, and especially the individual. With a writing project, though, it's a good idea to make sure that a series of dated drafts are stapled together and put into the portfolio. In this way all concerned can examine with permission, the progress of the student's thinking and learning, rather than only the final product.

Peers are often involved in helping each other select the gems, although I recommend using groups of two for this, rather than larger groups, especially at first. Making these choices is serious business, and you're liable to have fewer problems with hurt feelings when only one empathic friend is assisting. With children in Grade 5 and up, you may wish to have three members in a group. Some teachers also give a parent or a caregiver a chance to help in the choosing, or at least to have input in the process. But the students should make the final decisions by themselves.

Sharing Portfolios

During the selection of materials, to grace the walls of the classroom and corridors, you can teach your students to value their *processes* of learning as well as their *products*. Spend the most time assessing first, second, and third drafts *in the writing process*, showing how thinking became more refined as individuals proceeded from draft to draft. This can also be emphasized by urging your apprentices to put their drafts on the classroom wall so that others can learn from their thinking and from the thinking of peers and adults who have written comments on stick 'em notes attached to their drafts.

Here's a set of useful questions to use during your singular or multiple writing conferences. The questions emphasize process and not just product.

What have you learned recently in your writing?
What would you like to learn next to become a better writer?
How do you intend to go about learning how to do that?
What have you learned recently in your reading?

What would you like to learn next to become a better reader?

How do you intend to go about learning how to do that? (Hansen, 1992, p. 100).

Observation Tools

Professional Standard: Develop assessments that involve multiple indicators of student progress

One of the oldest forms of assessment is observation. In real life we rely on this form—when we help a youngster learn how to drive, when supervisors help a new employee. The need for observation is true of nearly everything we teach and evaluate. As Bill Harp (1991) says, "Evaluation is often best done by watching children perform literacy acts" (p. 28).

Informal Observations

Informal observations can reveal a great deal. When you're reading a story to your students, their questions often tell you how much they comprehend or don't comprehend. Or when they relate personal experiences to the text you're reading, you know that they're doing a good job of relating their own experiences to those of the author. Even when they're selecting their own books to read, you're sometimes a witness to their strategy of making a selection: Are they asking their peers for recommendations? Talking to someone about genres they prefer? Selecting after reading a portion of it? Always choosing the same genre? Randomly grabbing?

In addition, when your kids read out loud to you, you can observe "how well students ask themselves questions, predict what's coming next, and defend their own ideas about the text." Careful listening will also tell you "how well students recognize and reconcile prior knowledge inaccuracies when they encounter them in reading" (Readance & Martin, 1988, p. 78). And don't forget to observe their *behaviors*—for example, a tentative loss of self-confidence, changing facial expressions, a steady and relaxed enjoyment, signs of approval, and inflections in their speech.

Quickly Recording What You Observe

If you're afraid you won't remember what you observe, learn to use anecdotal records and observation forms. The detailed information you can store in them is an invaluable guide to diagnostic teaching, to conferences with students and caregivers, and to filling out progress reports, and other messages to parents and administrators.

Chittenden and Courtney (1989) carried on interviews with many experienced teachers and found that they were frustrated by not having enough detailed records. To get the best results from observations, try using *observation guides,* which are instruments to make your observations more accurate or scientific. They usually take

Student_____

Date_____

Directions: Show the student index cards on each of which is printed one letter of the alphabet in either upper- or lowercase form. Mark here a plus (+) for each letter recognized and a zero for each letter not recognized.

A_____	H_____	O_____	V_____
a_____	h_____	o_____	v_____
B_____	I_____	P_____	W_____
b_____	i_____	p_____	w_____
C_____	J_____	Q_____	X_____
c_____	j_____	q_____	x_____
D_____	K_____	R_____	Y_____
d_____	k_____	r_____	y_____
E_____	L_____	S_____	Z_____
e_____	l_____	s_____	z_____
F_____	M_____	T_____	
f_____	m_____	t_____	
G_____	N_____	U_____	
g_____	n_____	u_____	

FIGURE 11.2 Letter recognition checklist.

the form of a checklist, a scale, or some other organizing rubric. And they're often based on literacy research, thus managing and focusing your observations in valid and reliable ways. Take a look at the examples in Figures 11.2, 11.3, and 11.4, and use or modify them to suit your needs or the needs of individual kids.

Miscue Analysis

The concept and practice of *miscue analysis* was developed mainly by Marie Clay, Ken Goodman, and Y. M. Goodman in the 1960s and 1970s. It has been the most creative and intelligent improvement in the immediate assessment and teaching of children to read. Before miscue analysis was developed, teachers were stuck with an

---

Observation Rating Scale: Writing

Student name:_____

Directions: For each skill below that is being emphasized in daily instruction, note the date on which an observation was made and rate the degree of development (1 = emergent or not in evidence, 3 = developing, 5 = proficient).

Date observed	*Skill being developed*	*Rating*				
	Punctuation					
_____	Uses commas appropriately	1	2	3	4	5
_____	Apostrophe usage (singular versus plural possessive)	1	2	3	4	5
	Spelling/Usage					
_____	Incorporates word wall vocabulary	1	2	3	4	5
_____	Evidence of dictionary usage	1	2	3	4	5
_____	Uses spell check on computer (final drafts)	1	2	3	4	5
	Elements of Style: Narrative Compositions					
_____	Characterization	1	2	3	4	5
_____	Point of view	1	2	3	4	5

Other observations:

FIGURE 11.3 Observational rating scale: writing elements.

unsophisticated, inaccurate assessment procedure. Each reading error was counted as equal to all other errors, and petty things like hesitations were often considered an error. Teachers were expected to give each student a total score, but most teachers were not taught *why* students miscued. Some kids were held back for a year because they miscued too often.

I won't go any further—it's too embarrassing. I'm sure you'll agree that we owe our students much more than simply counting their miscues. Intelligent children, like

Target Skill: Uses Consonants in Decoding Unknown Words in Print
(Prerequisite Skill*: Context Clues)

Student name:_____

Date(s):_____

Directions: After making several observations of the student and recording notes regarding his/her usage of the target skill, determine the student's level of development. If s/he has not yet reached proficiency in the skill, note possible next steps to help the student achieve proficiency.

Proficient

♦ Uses consonant sounds in *beginning, medial, and final positions* consistently in sounding out unknown words.
♦ Attempts decodings that make sense with the context at least 95% to 100% of the time.
♦ Can perform this level of decoding automatically.

Competency

♦ Uses context clues plus *beginning, ending, and medial consonant sounds* to decode unknown words in print.
♦ Attempts decodings that make sense with the context at least 90% of the time.
♦ Can perform this level of decoding in less than 5 seconds.

Developing

♦ Uses context clues plus *beginning and ending consonant sounds* to decode unknown words in print.
♦ Attempts decodings that make sense with the context at least 75% of the time.
♦ Can perform this level of decoding within 5-8 seconds.

Early learning

♦ Uses context clues plus *beginning consonant sounds* consistently in attempting to decode unknown words in print.
♦ Attempts decodings that make sense with the context at least 50% of the time.
♦ Is slow to moderate in attempted decoding (sounding out).

Emergent

♦ Does *not* use consonant sounds in attempting to sound out unknown words in print.
♦ Uses context clues quickly and efficiently to narrow the possibilities when confronting an unknown word in print.

Comments and observations:

Next steps in teaching:

*This skill should have been learned *prior* to teaching the target skill.

FIGURE 11.4   An observational rubric.

intelligent adults, are busy experimenting, *assessing results*, and engaging in problem solving as they read. Children have the same kind of active brains that adults have, and they're eager to discover what adults already know about how things work. Let me give you several good examples, all true, of what I'm talking about.

Consider Three Minicases

Tommy (age 7)

> *Author:* Roy saw a little boat pull a big boat.
> *Tommy:* Roy was a little boat pulled by a big boat.

Hmm, Do you see what I see? Does Tommy not know the word *saw?* No, he had read it to me many times before because *saw* is used constantly in children's early books (e.g., Bobbie saw a bird, Stella saw him coming). This bright little kid is simply trying to make sense out of the author's first sentence. It evidently doesn't make sense to him that a little boat would pull a big boat. Tommy's erroneous but blossoming concept of reading might be this: "Reading is telling a story in a way that makes sense to me."

What strategies does Tommy use to understand that sentence?

Strategy 1: He automatically predicts the familiar and meaningful syntax pattern of "Roy was. . . ." Why? Many sentences in children's books begin with "So-and-So *was*. . . ." Like *saw,* this is a very common language pattern.

Strategy 2: He reads ahead about the little boat pulling a big boat.

Strategy 3: He creates his own meaning by changing "Roy saw a little boat" to "Roy was a big boat." (Ha! Most boats do have a name, after all.)

Strategy 4: This bright but naive child changes the syntax and meaning from "Roy was a little boat pulled by a big boat" There. Now it makes sense, he decides.

Should this be a focus for your teaching and assessing of Tommy? Yes, if this kind of miscue pattern occurs frequently. If so, concentrate on helping him do the following:

1. Always search for the *author's* message or meaning.

2. Use phonics at the same time he's searching for meaning.

3. Try to see in his mind what the author is talking about.

As his teacher, ask him cheerful questions like this one: "The author says 'Roy saw a little boat,' but you said that 'Roy *was* a little boat.' Let's be detectives, Tommy, and look at that sentence again. See if you can find out why you said something that the author didn't say." Help him realize that he's almost right, but "The author's message, is what you're after when you read. So let's try again and tell just what the author said."

As a model for reflecting with him, don't concentrate at first on the spelling difference between *saw* and *was.* Concentrate on the meaning of the author first. In this way you'll help him develop the correct concept of what reading is all about: Reading is understanding an author. Yes, it's communication, but that's usually far too abstract a word for a child this age. Try to keep things concrete, as Piaget (1955) and Vygotsky (1978) advised us. Use words like *understand,* which children hear so often. Don't use the word *communication* until they first grasp the meaning of the familiar words *understand* and *know.*

Sabina (age 8)

> *Author:* A beaver's home, called a lodge, always has a flooded lower room.
> *Sabina:* A beautiful honey calls a loggid away his floor low room.

From looking at the entire sentence, a good assessment question is: What is Sabina's concept of reading?

1. A serious search for the author's meaning?

2. A desperate recall of known words and letters similar to the author's?

3. Just getting through each sentence, one word at a time?

4. A mysterious series of word-beads that you string together till you reach a dot that tells you to stop?

5. A way to get away from assignments?

Look again at the differences between the author's and Sabina's versions. From looking at the entire sentence, what do you think Sabina's strategies of reading are? How does she choose to get through each portion of text safely?

1. Search through each sentence for familiar words?

2. Ignore the author's meanings and total message?

3. Search for the author's story or ideas?

4. Pay attention to every letter in a word?

5. Search for the author's exact message?

6. Read quickly to get it over with?

In our miscue assessment of Sabina, perhaps you would agree with me that she needs quite a bit of guided practice—with a friendly adult like you. That's the best way to help her change her concept of what reading really is. Lots of gentle, contextual questioning and information are usually necessary, like this: "The author who wrote this story was trying to tell you about the home of a beaver. Have you ever seen a beaver, Sabina? Did you know they eat bark for their dinner? Can you imagine eating bark from a tree? Let's read that sentence again and see what else the author wants to tell us about beavers."

Then talk about the meaning of a room that is flooded. And when Sabina reads other stories, be sure to explain the major concepts behind the words, build her schemas based on her own experiences, and finally help her choose easier books to read.

Maxine (age 9)

> *Author:* The man drove his old automobile up to his home and parked.
> *Maxine:* The map . . . the man drove his old car to his house and parked.

Before you read further, answer these two questions: What are Maxine's miscues? Which strategies does she use to get to the author's meaning?

Now that you've tried answering those two questions by yourself let me offer my own analysis and conclusions.

Question One: What are Maxine's miscues called?
The miscue types are as follows:

Miscue	Miscue Type
map . . . man	self-correction (fixes meaning)
car (for *automobile*)	substitution (fits author's meaning)
up (deleted)	omission (fits author's meaning)
house (for *home*)	substitution (fits author's meaning)

No need for correction. Maxine is reading the author's message with real skill and experience, especially when she takes an old-fashioned word, *automobile,* and translates it immediately into the word *car.*

Question Two: Which strategies does she use to get the message in this sentence?
Answer: My answer: This talented young reader reads the sentence in little more than a glance and does exactly what successful readers do—she looks ahead of the words she is speaking. Subconsciously, this gives her the split seconds she needs to translate the author's language into hers.

To determine Maxine's strategies for getting the message, you may need to be reminded about the way the eyes and the brain work together during the reading act. A good reader, reading aloud, focuses on words that are in advance of the words actually being said out loud. Try it yourself, and you'll see that it occurs even when you read silently. How this phenomenon occurs is explained more precisely by three researchers:

> Since there is a distance between pronouncing words and visually taking in words, the information picked up visually is briefly stored in the reader's memory. The words that fluent readers are pronouncing, then, are based on what is stored in memory rather than on the words [now] visually seen (Johnson, Kress, & Pikulski, (1987).

Now examine the sentence Maxine read once more and notice how her four miscues most likely represent good reading and not poor reading. Instead, they represent good natural communication between author and reader. In the old fashioned way, remember, we would just have counted the number of errors and would have naively used that number to tell us whether Maxine is reading well. Now, with miscue analysis we can examine the miscues and see two things right away: (1) Maxine understands that reading is communicating with a writer, and (2) the strategies being used by Maxine have revealed the deep meaning of the author. I say *deep* because she is not just reading the words; she is doing what most teachers require so often— "Tell us in your own words, Dear."

Examine Reading Miscues Together: Teacher with Student

> *Author:* The dog ran over to Sammy and barked and barked at him.
> *Susan:* Then Doug ran other to Sammy and backed and backed at him.

Usually it's best to stop a child whose version doesn't have any clear meaning, doesn't make much sense, or misses the *main* message of the author. Let me model this for you—something like this:

"I didn't understand that sentence, Susan. Would you read it again, please?" This statement allows the child to go back and try again and gives her a chance to correct her own miscues, which is our goal, isn't it?

If that doesn't work, you can ask about the exact miscues, the most important one first: "The author said, 'The dog ran over to Sammy.' Would you please look back and see what *you* said." "Then Doug ran other to Sammy and backed and backed at him."

"Very good, Susan. Now we know that the dog ran over to Sammy, but what did the dog *do* to Sammy?" Susan responds.

"Yes, that's right. It didn't back at him; it barked at him. Now read the whole sentence again and see if it all makes sense." Susan reads.

"All right, let's be detectives for a moment. Why do you think you said "backed and backed at him"? . . . That's right you were listening to the words, but you weren't listening to the . . . ?

"Right on. You weren't listening to the author. That's very good detective work,
   Susan. Go ahead and read the rest of the page by yourself. What things
   happened to Sammy after that?"

Determine Students' Concepts

When you hear several sentences with similar miscues, you'll know you have to
teach the reader and perhaps a small group or the entire class to look for the author's message and not just those lonely little words. In searching for the probable
root of an ineffective reader's behavior, remember to look in two basic areas:

■ *The student's concept of reading.* Does he understand that when he reads, he
   is listening to the author for fun and ideas? Does he understand that he and
   the author are talking with each other?
■ *The student's strategies for reading that help him understand the author's
   message.* Is he guessing wildly or using the author's context clues? Is he
   relying too much on phonics clues and not enough on the author's meaning?
   Is he trying to read without really knowing how to decode a word from letters
   into talking sounds? Is he hestitating just long enough to get you to tell him
   the confusing word? Is he reading just the words or the author's message?
   Does he look up at you with that charming smile and say, "I don't know,"
   hoping you'll forget all about the silly word he substituted for elephant?

Here's the situation: After looking at the picture in the book, Alberto substituted,
"Johnny rode way up huge on the alphabet" for this actual sentence: "Jimmy rode
way up high on the elephant." So what is Alberto's concept of reading? What strategies does he use to determine the author's message? Yes, we know he uses his
charming smile, but what else do you see him trying? Can you help this boy? What
would *you* do in this case? Can you get help from the small group you're working
with—or from the entire class?

Assess Only Two Types of Miscues

Miscue analysis is one of the best means of assessing comprehension (Goodman,
1989; Watson & Henson, 1991). As discussed in Chapter 2, effective readers make
plenty of substitutions, but they're the kind of substitutions that don't really change
the author's essential message. Effective readers also tend to use meaningful
insertions and *omissions* of words. But as Karen D'Angelo and Marc Mahlino (1983)
found in their major study, insertions and omissions rarely distort the meaning of the
author. Furthermore, "insertions increase as a reader gains proficiency" (p. 778). So
should you penalize children for these things? You're right—it would be absurd.

So what do you have to worry about? There are only two miscues you should
lose a minute of sleep over, and those are *defaults* and *substitutions that change the
author's meaning*, such as "He ate the chair" versus "He ate the cherry." By *defaults*
I'm referring to children not reading the word at all while cleverly begging the

teacher to give them the word. A student who keeps asking you for a word is not comprehending the message. So when you help, don't just give the word. Instead, talk about the total message, about what the author is saying. Help the student use past experiences and memories to understand what the author is talking about.

And what if a student keeps substituting words that don't fit the author's message? For example, the author says, "Billy dropped the ball in the toilet," but your student says, "Billy dropped the bell on the table." These are serious miscues that change most of the author's meaning. Your student is not paying enough attention to the author's message or to the spelling of the words. To correct this problem, talk about the spelling of the two words and especially how they change the author's message. If you're working with a group, do the same kind of assessment for each student. This kind of teaching on the spot is a very powerful method of helping children learn together.

Retelling and Storytelling

Professional Standard: Understands that goals, instruction, and assessments should be aligned

Have you ever asked a student to retell a passage from a book? You know, "Tell me in your own words what you just read." Simply by having student retell a selection, you can learn about their comprehension of an author's message. Do they rely on their own experiences, schemas, and memories to determine what message is presented by the author? As Cagney (1988) reminds us, "Readers may fail to comprehend because they do not have appropriate schemas (mini theories), the author may not have provided sufficient clues to suggest a specific schema, or the reader and writer might not share the same schemas" (p. 81).

In addition to well-developed schemas (i.e., mini theories about what's going on in this world), comprehension of a writer's message does depend partly on the strength of a reader's memory. If readers have poor short-term memories, they can't remember enough of what they've just read to help them understand what they're presently reading. And if their long-term memories are weak, they might not recollect the prior knowledge and schemas that would help them make sense of the author's ideas. To make matters more complicated, memory depends a great deal on the *motivation* to remember, which some students may lack. In the next chapter we'll deal with that thorny problem.

If you wish to *assess* how well Sean, a second grader, remembers what he's read, you can simply ask him to tell everything he can remember about it, or you can use the storytelling strategy and ask him to tell the story in his own words. If he leaves out things that you think are important, you can ask him a question on each of them.

Suppose, though, with fifth-grader Marilina you want to assess something more specific: You'd like to find out how well she can use her prior knowledge in reading a passage about electricity. In that case it's a good idea to tell her exactly what you'll be looking for *before* she reads the selection: "As you try to understand what the author is saying about electricity, Marilina, remember to think about what you already know about the topic. Then, when you're finished reading, you can tell me what you already knew about electricity that helped you to understand the passage: Ok?" "Read outloud for me, please."

Use Modeling and Encourage Practice

This may seem to adults to be a clear and specific set of instructions, yet with a group of children who aren't used to the retelling process, you'll probably want to first model retelling for the entire class. Gambrell, Pfeiffer, and Wilson (1985) found that children who have had practice in retelling become better at both understanding and remembering. They also gain in their ability to organize and retain information. Several other researchers have found retelling to be valuable both as an instructional aid and as an *assessment* tool (Morrow, 1988, p. 135).

Morrow (1988) recommends that when children are being taught the art of retelling, for their first few times you should allow them to use props to aid their retelling, "such as feltboard story characters, graphs, or pictures from text" (p. 129). Sebesta (1996) goes a step further by recommending that you have children treat literature as a story to be retold, not as an exercise in memory. I agree wholeheartedly. This makes *literature* rather than the child's nerves the center of attention.

Whenever you decide to use storytelling instead of retelling, be sure to model it for your students. Right in front of them read a selection, plan out loud the things you want to remember in your own version, and then tell it simply in your own words. This can be done with fiction or nonfiction, although it's usually easier to do with fiction. Let students work with partners the first time, and then have the partners split up and tell their versions separately to two other peers.

Think-Alouds

I went to a play many years ago in which the actors' private thoughts were broadcast to the audience from behind the stage, while the actors acted as though they weren't hearing the private thoughts. It was probably the most revealing play I've ever seen. Think-aloud assessment is designed to achieve the same effect, although it's used mainly for understanding a child's reading or writing strategies. For example, a teacher might ask students during individual conferences to read a selection that they have not seen before and share their thoughts as they read. The thoughts can be about what the author is saying or about reading problems they're having. Or the teacher might ask them to write a short new composition and, while writing it, speak their thoughts out loud. In this way the teacher can immediately diagnose problems and provide on-the-spot instruction or modeling.

A positive side effect of the think-aloud strategy is improved comprehension. In a study that Loxterman (1994) and her colleagues published in *Reading Research Quarterly,* they found that comprehension was better for students who thought aloud while reading than it was for students who just read silently. This finding was true even for selections that had been revised and made more coherent for students. In other words, whether the selections were moderate or extreme in difficulty, the read-and-think-aloud method was the most effective teaching procedure.

Perhaps the main advantage of think-alouds is their ability to blend instruction and assessment. Having children think aloud as they read or write provides the teacher with a means of instantly determining strengths and weaknesses, and instruction can follow immediately for those who need to improve their strategies.

Assess Comprehension Strategies

You can assess your students' comprehension strategies by asking them to think aloud as they read aloud. Here's a quick review of some of those strategies described previously:

■ *The prove-it strategy,* developed through the use of Directed Reading-Thinking Activity (DRTA), requires children to ask themselves three reflection questions: What do I think about this? Why do I think that? Can I prove it in the text?

■ *The story-grammar strategy* gets students to ask themselves questions like these: Where is this story taking place? When? Who is the main character? What's he or she like? What seems to be the central problem? What does the main character try to do to solve the problem? How does this end? Does the main character learn something from this?

■ *The main-idea strategy* encourages such questions as What's the big idea the author is trying to get across? Is there a point to this? Which of the ideas are really important?

■ *The comprehension-monitoring strategy* leads to questions such as, Am I reading this slowly enough to understand the author? Am I matching the author's ideas with what I know about this topic? What are the words I really need in order to understand this selection?

Think-alouds can provide an ideal *assessment* device—a chance to look into the mind of each student. And with a combination of teacher and peer modeling, students can learn to ask questions of themselves. They can learn to carry on a silent dialogue with an author; and when writing with a partner, they can "hear how their partner is making sense . . . " (Brown & Lytle, 1988, p. 101).

Standardized State Tests (Only if You "Hafta")

Professional Standard: Understands how contextual factors such as assessment and school programs can influence student learning

There are myths floating through the hallways of our schools, and they refuse to go away. One myth is based on the assumption that every child in fourth grade should be reading at or above the test maker's version of the average score. However, the average score of any norm group is obtained by determining that 50% of the group scored at or below that point.

Go figure. If the norm group is supposed to represent the total population, teachers should *theoretically* expect half of their students to score at or below grade level and half to score at or above grade level. It is completely unrealistic to expect every child taking the test to be at or above grade level. Furthermore, the grade-level score on a standardized achievement test is typically at a student's frustration level, not an instructional level (Reutzel & Cooter, 2000). The student's actual instructional level will be somewhat lower than the grade-level equivalent score from a standardized test.

It is true that standardized tests have greater *reliability* than most other tests. That is, they rank students from high to low pretty consistently from one version of the test to another. On the other hand, standardized tests have some severe weaknesses in *validity,* that is, the degree to which they measure real ability. Here are some reasons related to reading that support that claim:

1. Students may be timed on standardized tests, thus penalizing those who read well but slowly.

2. Standardized tests often present conditions that are not typical of the reading act. For example, they ask children to respond to multiple-choice questions, which require recognition of a correct answer, but reading is a skill that is far more complex. For this reason and others, it is not surprising that standardized tests often overrate or underrate children's reading ability.

3. Some children are good readers but poor test takers, particularly with standardized tests. Special forms are passed out, the right kind of pencil must be used, everyone in the room is nervous, the tension rises to fever pitch as the teacher looks at the clock and says, "Ready. . . begin." For many children, this kind of atmosphere is not conducive to their best

4. Almost two decades ago, Tierney, Carter, & Desai (1991) warned us that standardized tests do not represent the kinds of work that students do daily in the classroom. Today we still face this dilemma..

5. The format for standardized tests were developed for convenience in test construction and scoring rather than for diagnostic information.

6. "Students are not able to demonstrate their ability to pose questions, justify their answers, or anticipate what is coming in the text" (Readance & Martin, 1988, p. 68).

The Negative Effects of Political Agendas

Although legislators, administrators, parents, and educators have been warned repeatedly not to rely on a single measure to make important instructional decisions (Elmore, 2002; Linn, 2003; & Shepard, 2000), scores from state tests still seem to drive the search for programs and approaches that will help students learn and meet state standards. The popular press, educational publications, teacher workshops, and state and school district policies are filled with attempts to find solutions for poor test performance.

> Every year thousands of U.S. students take standardized tests and state reading tests, and every year thousands fail them. With the implementation of the No Child Left Behind legislation . . . which mandates testing all children from Grades 3 to 8 every year, these numbers will grow exponentially, and alarming numbers of schools and students will be targeted for "improvement." (Valencia & Riddle Buly, 2004, p. 520)

Arlington (2002) and Edmondson (2004) agree that ideology rather than research determines the agendas and reports that transfer to U.S. federal literacy policies—especially lately. We're spending all this energy on getting better test performance instead of assessing how well children are learning to read. To have validity, a test must reflect what students are actually doing when they are studying and learning, as in reading, writing, social studies, and science. But when students are taking a test they are not motivated in the same way that they are when they are reading for information or pleasure which after all is what we tell our students they can gain from reading. Of course, the mandated tests are useful for administrators, who deserve to receive information appropriate to their duties. But you and I need to look at other forms of *assessment* to make good decisions about the progress of each student.

It's especially unfortunate that teachers have to spend so much time trying to get their students ready for the tests (Olsen, 2002). Farstrup (2005), executive director of the International Reading Association, warns that "over reliance on standardized tests can have the undesirable effect of narrowing what is taught in favor of preparing for these kinds of tests" (p. 7). Some schools have even thrown out sustained silent reading to make more time for explicit instruction related to the tests (Edmondson & Shannon, 2002; Riddle Buly & Valencia, 2002). Just imagine how many books those students could have read, how many children could have been helped in bursts of one-on-one teaching. A narrow focus on preparing students for specific tests does not translate into real learning (Klein, Hamilton, McCaffrey, & Stecher, 2000; Linn, 2000).

Take heart, though—the contents of this book were created around good and effective practices specified by the International Reading Association and years of experience. If you follow these suggestions, your students should not only learn to read for enjoyment and information, but should also gain the necessary skills to do well on mandated state assessments (see Appendix A for professional standards).

Profiles of Struggling Readers

In contrast to state tests, Lipson and Wixson (2003) conducted *individual reading assessments*, using a one-on-one teaching approach for approximately 2 hours over several days to gather information about children's reading abilities. They administered a series of assessments focusing on word identification, comprehension and meaning, vocabulary, and fluency. They discovered six different profiles of struggling readers. Theirs was a top-notch example of real assessment.

Unwilling to see test takers as homogeneous, Valencia and Riddle Buly (2004) conducted an awe-inspiring study of average children who fail the state tests and discovered that there are six clusters of mildly struggling students.

- **Cluster 1:** Automatic word callers can decode words well but seldom read for meaning.
- **Cluster 2:** Struggling word callers have trouble with both meaning and word identification.
- **Cluster 3:** Word stumblers have trouble identifying words, but their comprehension is quite good.
- **Cluster 4:** Slow comprehenders are fairly good in decoding, comprehension, vocabulary, and writing, but they read quite slowly.

- **Cluster 5:** Slow word callers are fluent in their word calling but slow. Their decoding skills are good, but their slowness causes them trouble with comprehension.
- **Cluster 6:** Disabled readers have problems with word identification, meaning, and fluency. This is the smallest of the six clusters and has the fewest second-language learners. Older kids in this cluster need very simple reading materials and high interest, low difficulty types of books. They also need instruction in word identification at a first- or second-grade level, even though they may be in fifth or sixth grade.

Once identified, struggling readers need a lot of small-group and individual treatments, based on their specific type of difficulty: word identification, meaning, or fluency. It is more difficult for your students to succeed if you don't use frequent small-group instruction. The report titled *Preventing Reading Difficulties in Young Children* includes summaries of research reviews confirming the value of daily small-group instruction. Today's small-group instruction is a classroom management tool that brings students together for a limited amount of time to teach them a particular literacy skill that is their common need.

Equitable Assessment of Latino Students

Jimenez (2004) tells of an upset teacher who came to him holding the reading test scores for her Latino students and explaining that her principal had demanded to know what she was going to do to improve her students' scores. However, she had not been given enough information even to interpret the scores—nothing about how well her students compared with other Latino students or even with mainstream students. This is what I call *unfair assessment* of students. Standardized state tests may be even less useful in the case of Latino students.

Obviously, something has to be done to assess Latino students more equitably (Garcia, 1994; Perez & Torres-Guzmen, 1996; Torres-Guzman & Abbate, 2002). Jimenez recommends that we test students' literacy in both Spanish and English. In this way teachers and administrators can determine the achievement level in Spanish and thus the relative literacy abilities of the Latino students. This kind of compromise on standardized tests might make a significant difference in both our assessment and our perception of Latino children.

Jimenez (2004) also suggests that we treat the language of Latino students as a potential opportunity for other students to become more culturally aware. He also suggests that other students acquire information on how Latino students respond to the process of learning a new language. Understanding this can help us teachers understand how larger forces adversely affect students' performance. (Jimenez, 2004, p. 576)

Let me give you one more idea. As you may know, many Latino kids go home and teach their parents how to speak English. "These students often translate for their parents in a process known as language brokering. Research shows that the more young people broker language, the better they perform in school" (Orellana, Reynolds, Dorner, & Meza, 2003).

My suggestion is to help those Latino students who would like to teach English to other people in their families. You might provide them with children's books that tell a story in both English and Spanish. Or give them extra copies of the page(s) you assign. Let children and parents learn together. And use a re-reading-at-home program; it can benefit both children and families. I do know this is not easy. Working with parents who do not speak the language of the school is one of the most difficult parts of teaching, and I admire your willingness to take it on as a challenge.

Informal Paper-and-Pencil Assessments

There are a few types of test-form assessments that you may sometimes wish to use. Teacher-made tests that allow children to write and to justify their answers can be useful assessments, especially if they contain application-type questions along with the usual knowledge and comprehension questions. Other kinds of informal tests can be used to diagnose specific strengths and weaknesses.

In the appendixes at the back of the book, you'll find specific tests on reading disabilities, phonics, and instant words. These tests are designed to assess the phonics patterns and sight words that your students have not yet mastered. Most teachers I've worked with have found these tests valuable in determining which sight words and phonics patterns to practice, both in context and with games—such as those described in Appendixes C and D.

Self-Correction and Self-Evaluation

Any teacher assessment should make it more likely that children will carry on their own self-assessment. Can you see then why self-correction is a perfect form of assessment? You're right. It's perfect, or complete. Students can't take their teacher along with them after they leave the classroom or the school—they'd have to pay you too much money, I suppose. Self-correction is also highly useful because it builds self-confidence and problem-solving skills.

When beginning readers self-monitor, they use all sources of information available to them to check on the accuracy of their reading. These sources include language structure (syntax) of the phrase or sentence, the meaning of the story, and letter/sound relationships (visual information in the print). When readers notice a miscue, they begin to search for more information to correct it. (Goodman & Goodman, 1994, p. 43)

Forbes, Poparad, and McBride (2004) have rediscovered and confirmed that fact. Self-assessment is crucial for children's progress in reading.

Self-correction in reading may be similar to self-repair in speech, which is widely recognized as an important sign of progress in language development and a way in which children control their learning about spoken language. Preschool children frequently correct or repair errors in speech without prompting from the listener (Levy, 1999; Wood, 1998).

Self-assessment of speech is a model for the way both children and adults self-assess as they read. The miscues that they make while reading silently are simply repaired, often with hardly a glance. This kind of assessment is a natural phenomenon (Levy, 1999; Wood, 1998). Teachers who capitalize on children's ability to repair speech errors make it easier for them to learn how to read. And children who self-correct while reading learn more about reading, just as they learned more about speech and language through self-repair (Forbes, Poparad, & McBride (2004).

The Benefits of Self-Teaching

Children also receive self-encouragement from their self-teaching. As they learn from their own mistakes and self-assessments, they turn into their own teachers. (Wood 1998). In 1999 Wood found that high achievers self-correct their miscues more often than low achievers. I believe this occurs because the high achiever is bravely doing more vigorous predicting about the author's words and message and gets to the message fast enough not to forget what was read a moment ago. In other words, the high achiever is a fluent reader, and fluent readers do a lot of fluent self-assessments.

Teaching a child to expect reading to make sense provides him with an easy-to-learn signal that processing is necessary. At the moment of making an error, a child reading for meaning will notice it. At this moment he is observing his own behavior very closely because he will have to decide which response he should retain and which he should discard. (Clay, 1991, p. 341)

One of the easiest ways to get children started in the process of self assessment is to use predictable patterned books. Since these books so often use rhyming words, the sounds of the rimes, or phonograms, guide readers to simply change the onsets. When they change them, they immediately know whether the rime is the same or whether they have moved out of the pattern. Self-assessment!

Eventually, though, it's a good idea to wean children from the patterned books. As Fountas and Pinnell (1999) explain, "Each kind of text has important implications for the behavior of the reader and the potential to learn" (p. 2). In other words, the child needs to be challenged to use a variety of strategies, not just one. Much of this can be learned in the supportive and instructive environment of a small group, which can reinforce group members (Fielding, 2002).

> The goal of supportive reading is to assist readers in developing independent control in selecting and using appropriate strategies when reading. Often, support can be in the form of questions: "What else could you try? Have you reread the sentence?" Or brief reminders to employ strategies. . . or even in the form of simple praise for a strategy implemented appropriately: "Good! You went back and reread the sentence to see if it made sense." (Cunningham & Allington, 1994, pp. 60–61)

Just remember that teachers can actively teach for self-monitoring, searching, and self-correcting behaviors within the classroom context (Schwartz, 1997).

"Self-correcting behavior probably has a high tutorial value for the reader" (Clay, 2001). As an example, McNaughton (1988) found that good readers who had previously discovered the pronunciation and meaning of new words could later recognize those same words in isolation. So, working hard to master a word as you're reading can be far better than drilling a new word in an isolated manner. To help your students master this self-assessment trick, model how you determine the pronunciation and meaning of a new word. You'll find examples of this modeling procedure back in Chapter 6.

As teachers model self-assessment themselves—not just to teach a strategy but to participate honestly in the classroom community of learners—it becomes much easier for children to self-assess. If teachers never assess their own mistakes or never talk about them, students can feel nervous about making mistakes. If teachers never show joy in accomplishing something themselves, it becomes more difficult for their students to aim for such pleasure.

Evaluation needs to become a natural social experience. Let me quote something from Cousin (1990) that rings with Vygotskian authority:

> Children learn to reflect through communicative engagements with others. All learners must have opportunities to hear others reflect and self-evaluate and then engage in that process socially before they understand how to do it individually. . . . It is through and because of social interactions that we learn how to reflect and self-evaluate . . . [and] students are seriously affected if these opportunities are absent from their school experiences (pp. 192–194).

Coaches

Professional Standard: Knows principles for diagnosing reading difficulties

While you are busy assessing children, coaches are busy assessing teachers and helping them work effectively with students. Coaches are assessors but never critics, they are friends, models, and mentors. Linda Darling-Hammond (2005), an expert on teaching and education, commented on the most important aspects of a teacher preparation program:

> Good teacher education programs have students in the classroom working constantly with expert master teachers while they are also teaching students a variety of ideas about how students learn, about how to assess their learning, about effective teaching strategies that will allow them to build a repertoire.

The International Reading Association (2004) came out with five key criteria for those master teachers who are chosen to be reading coaches:

1. They must be excellent classroom teachers themselves.

2. They should have a deep knowledge of reading processes, acquisition, instruction, and assessment.

3. They must have experience in working with teachers to improve teacher practice.

4. Coaches should be experienced presenters, familiar with presenting to teacher groups in schools and at professional conferences.

5. They must be trained to master the complexities of observing in classrooms and providing feedback to teachers.

Let's listen in on an interview I had with Mary Gaborko, an experienced reading coach from Rialto, California.

Frank: Thanks for coming, Mary.

Mary: My pleasure, Frank. I feel honored for the chance to be in your book.

Frank: Congratulations on your nomination for the Annual Disneyland Teacher Award, honoring creativity. I'll bet you're on pins and needles waiting to see if you're the winner.

Mary: A zillion of them. But I'm not really counting on winning. It's just fun to be nominated. And before I say another thing, Frank, I was really tickled with what you said to me on the phone.

Frank: I was just asking you if I had reached the real Gaborkoland?

Mary: You must have seen that on the calling card I sent you.

Frank: I loved your humor. Your last name is Gaborko, so naturally you deserve to live in Gaborkoland. It sounds enchanting.

Mary: Well, yes and no. Rialto is not necessarily noted as the most enchanting place in the world, but I like where I live, and I love teaching in Boyd Elementary School. It's very challenging there but very exciting—especially now that I'm a reading coach.

Frank: I've studied the criteria for being a coach, and I'm eager to hear what you've been doing to make you a nominee for such a prestigious honor. I would imagine—let me guess—that your own classroom environment was innovative and unique.

Mary: Thank you. I always try to make a warm and welcome place for the students and their parents. Many of the students arrive in the fall, feeling defeated and unable to succeed because of their learning disabilities. As members of the community that we all call Gaborkoland, they are celebrated and affirmed daily.

I make a very big deal when one of my kidlets makes even a little progress. I find that after a short time, the students begin to compliment and applaud each other's accomplishments. I then build on those little successes to encourage and expect more progress. I'm happy to say that it does happen.

Frank: Sounds great to me. You must have special ways to promote literacy. Am I right?

Mary: I sure do. First, I get excited about the literature I read to my students, and my enthusiasm becomes contagious in only a few minutes. Even my most reluctant readers will pretend-read a book that I'm reading with exaggerated expression. Then I take them to the library, and they pick books written by the authors I've been reading to them. They love to know the names of the authors. It seems to make them feel important—an emotion we all need.

Frank: Fabulous! With your energy I'll bet this excitement continues all through the year.

Mary: That's true, and the excitement really culminates on the last day of school. Each student becomes an official member of the Gaborkoland Literacy Club. They pledge to become a lifelong reader and writer, and all of them are awarded a membership certificate. The students and their parents take this pledge very seriously—partly, I hope, because they're aware of how I feel about it.

Frank: What a great finish for the year! Where do you get all your new ideas—besides all of those you must have been creating daily?

Mary: Actually, many of my ideas begin when I find a suggestion in a professional publication. I'll bring it to my classroom, modify it for my students, and add my own touches. Patricia Cunningham, for example, the coauthor of *Classrooms That Work* (2003), gave me a fun way to teach consonant sounds using actions. I put the consonants on paper plates and as I hold up the plate with the consonant on it, I pantomime a verb beginning with that letter. My favorites are *marching* for *Mm, dancing* for *Dd, singing* for *Ss,* and *laughing* for *Ll*. To determine whether they understand, I ask questions that require actions, like this: "Why are you laughing?" to which they reply, "Because *laughing* begins with *Ll*."

Frank: You can't beat action, all right. But tell me, Mary, what basic ways do you use to assess your young students' understanding and growth?

Mary: Most of my evidence of success is within the activity itself. I can obseve and note the students who need a nudge or a reminder to successfully complete the task within the lesson. Although there are times when I assess formally—which gives me a more specific and concrete example of their mastery of the concept.

Frank: I would imagine that other teachers have asked to collaborate with you. Am I right?

Mary: Oh yes, happily so. The most memorable collaboration in my teaching career happened when I was a special education teacher. I was teaching the primary class (K–2) and my partner was teaching the intermediate class (3–6). We also teamed with a sixth-grade teacher to complete an assignment for an English-language-development class. Our objective was to teach our students about other cultures and to have a final product demonstrating their learning. In deciding how to meet our goal, we collaborated and felt we needed to use books and realia to introduce them to many cultures.

Our classes came together every afternoon for the cultural immersion. Each of us chose the cultures we felt comfortable teaching. We gathered materials, set up an instructional schedule, and set to work. We spent 3 weeks studying the cultures—their food, clothing, customs, legends, music, even their fairy tales. We culminated our study by making a class big book entitled *A Cultural ABC Book*. We filled the chalkboard with the alphabet and modeled how to match a cultural fact with a letter. The big book was a resounding hit.

These days, as a reading coach, I'm collaborating with other reading coaches and especially with the other teachers—to continue these kinds of multicultural activities.

Frank: What has been your most memorable event as a teacher?

Mary: My most memorable event was a day in my special education classroom. I had a dear boy who was a drug baby. When he came to me as a second grader, he was functioning at a preschool level, not even recognizing colors. But the good news is: Within a year he was doing things like partner-reading with a sixth-grade struggling reader. They were reading *Brown Bear, Brown Bear,* and the older student read, "I see cute kids looking at me." My little second grader, now third grader, pointed to the words and said, "No, it's I see b-b-b-beautiful ch-ch-ch-children looking at me." What that proved to me is that no matter how low a child is, with encouragement and positive expectations, he can gradually move up the ladder.

Frank: Thank you, Mary, very much. I know for certain that teachers who read my book will be very interested in your career experiences, your new position as a reading coach, and especially your very practical teaching ideas.

Mary: You're more than welcome, Frank. I can't wait to read your new book. Do I get a copy?

Frank: You get two!

A Philosophical View of Assessment

Our beliefs are more powerful than anything else in making powerful changes. What we believe is what we do. After you read this cluster of statements about assessing and evaluating and repairing, try writing your own philosophy for assessing your students' reading development. Let's start with Johnston (2003):

In theory, assessment is about gathering and interpreting data to inform action. In practice, data interpretations are constrained by our views of literacy and students, the assessment conversations that surround us, and the range of "actions" we can imagine. (p. 90)

True, but what does assessment require of us teachers?

Assessment requires uncovering the sense children make of literacy and literacy instruction. (Johnston, Jiron, & Day, 2001, p. 226)

Also true, but can assessment improve the thinking environment?

Our assessments of children, as we engage them in our classrooms are part of the intellectual environment into which they will grow. (Vygotsky, 1978)

Focus on Students with Special Needs: Comments by Louise Fulton

The Teacher as Keen Observer

I love talking with teachers about observing kids. It's one of my favorite topics. Maybe it comes from being raised by a single mom who was busy earning a living for her three kids, leaving lots of time for me to learn from observing others. Or maybe it stems from my 4 years of training and consultation with a federal research project. For that project we developed an observational rating protocol to assess the behaviors and the learning abilities of deaf-blind children.

Focus on Students with Special Needs (cont.)

I discovered very early on that I could learn a lot about behavior or life just by being a keen observer. Today, I always encourage my teachers to make a game out of observing, playing detective with a huge make-believe spy glass. When we use observation as a way to assess students' reading skills and associated reading behaviors, there is so much to learn, especially since some of our students have a great many potential barriers to overcome. But clear and focused observations can reveal important data to guide our teaching of those individual students. Let me share a couple of observation experiences with you.

Tommy, my new third-grade student, really impressed me with his intense attention. When I was speaking to him, he would stop what he was doing and just listen and look at me. How I wished the other children were so attentive. I also began to notice that he stepped closer to me than the others did when we were talking. I thought he had a cute crush on his new teacher. On another day, though, when he was reading, I observed that he was speaking with a voice that was much louder than that of the other children—a bit annoying. Why was he doing that? What was he thinking?

Later, I observed that Tommy didn't always respond to me—especially when I first asked him a question or when I made a comment about his reading. Then I observed more carefully. He was looking back and forth between book and reader while the other children were reading. So I turned around and spoke very softly: "Tommy, please start reading at the top of page 11." No response. Tommy just kept looking at me and then back again at the other children—for clues of course. How could I have missed it! He was having trouble hearing clearly.

The end of this story is a happy one. Tommy was screened by the school nurse and was quickly referred for further testing and medical evaluation. The prognosis was good: Tommy had a moderate bone-conductive hearing loss in both ears. Following surgery, he was back in school fully benefiting from his almost normal hearing. Careful observation had paid off, and I realized once again that assessing children's behavior and learning by observation is a way of life for teachers of children with limited speaking, hearing, or cognitive skills.

Assessment is much like observation which can be especially revealing when a student has significant learning, behavioral, or sensory problems. By observing carefully, I have been able to recognize tiny gains in communication, even by my students who are deaf and blind. And these tiny increments of growth are just as exciting as the huge ones that I sometimes see in other children.

At the time of this next observation, I was working with an open-air school in Peru—way down on the Amazon, where the only means of travel is by foot or boat. The beautiful teachers there wanted me to show them how to work with Salvador, an adorable 4-year-old child who they said couldn't hear anything. How could I resist! I pulled out one of my trusty balloons and got to work. (I always take balloons, pencils and pads, and a few other interesting things like party favors when I volunteer in educationally deprived areas of the world.)

(continued)

Focus on Students with Special Needs *(cont.)*

There I had Salvador's immediate attention. I blew up the balloon a couple of times and watched his face as the balloon slowly deflated. Next I blew it up and turned it loose. He was spellbound. Maybe this was too scary. I blew it up again and squeezed it tight so the air couldn't come out. Then I placed my mouth against it, made a buzzing noise, and held his hand on the balloon so he could feel the vibration. More amazement in his expressive eyes! This kid had a lot going for him, and I wanted to learn more about him.

I inflated the balloon again and let the air out gradually, creating a high pitched squeal while he watched closely. There was no sign that he had heard the sound, but I wasn't convinced. I inflated the balloon again, but this time I distracted his attention momentarily with weird facial expressions. At the same time I held the balloon behind him and let the air out slowly again, creating that squeal once more. Salvador stopped in his tracks and turned to look for the balloon. The teachers clapped excitedly. "Salvador can hear!"

I began to speculate: Perhaps Salvador had enough residual hearing to learn to speak. After all, he was curious, motivated, attentive, highly visual, and ready to learn. I was determined to find a way to help him and his teachers, who were so willing to try anything. We celebrated by sharing bread and cups of warm soda pop. I gave a small pep talk with ideas of how they could help Salvadore and other special needs children. And I answered dozens of questions.

The next week I was able to get in touch with the speech and hearing specialists back in Lima. Since I had already established myself there by bringing boxes of hearing-aid batteries donated by an American doctor, I knew they would help me, and they did. Within a month Salvador had been fitted with a hearing aid, and the teachers had been given in-service training by staff from the center in Lima. I felt good about their desire to teach and left Peru knowing that Salvador would have a chance to learn how to communicate.

Summary of Main Ideas

- Two key purposes of literacy assessment are to chart the progress of learners and inform instructional decisions.
- True learning can be assessed through observation, miscue analysis and artifacts directly related to students' performance.
- Literacy portfolios provide a means of gathering student artifacts and opportunities for student empowerment and ownership of their own learning experiences.
- The best comprehension assessments provide teachers with artifacts of learning and opportunities for performance assessment rather than simple test-taking assessment.

- Miscue analysis provides teachers, children, and parents with evidence of the children's reading strategies, strengths, and weaknesses, as well as a view of what they perceive reading to be.
- Think-alouds, retelling and storytelling experiences, and informal checklists all provide teachers with a means of structuring their observations to get more information.

Literacy Through Technology

Here are some of my favorite Web sites on portfolios and other forms of assessment. Take a careful look at three of them and decide whether you agree with my choice.

1. http://www.essdack.org   An electronic portfolio Web site set up by a teacher in Kansas.
2. http://www.electronicportfolios.org   For those adventurers who want to get students involved in setting up their own electronic portfolios.
3. http://www.eduplace.com   An authentic classroom assessment in action: Ms. Rodriguez's classroom.
4. http://jonathan.mueller.faculty.noctrl.edu/toolbox/whydoit.htm   Expert advice on authentic assessment from the North Carolina Regional Educational Lab.
5. http://www.teachervision.fen.com   Great teacher resources on authentic assessment.
6. http://www.teachervision.fen.com/lesson-plans   Assessments and lesson plans for your classroom that encourage students to use higher-order thinking skills.

Application Experiences for Your Course

A. *Literacy Teacher Vocabulary: List of Terms.* In small groups define and give two examples of each term:

literacy portfolios	artifacts observations	think-alouds
miscue assessments	miscue analysis	defaults
ineffective substitution	self-corrected substitution	authentic assessments

B. *What's Your Opinion?* Justify your opinion about each of these statements with both textbook ideas and your own experiences:

1. Literacy portfolios are better than tests under any conditions.
2. Retelling assesses memory but not comprehension.
3. Miscue analysis provides the most valid information.
4. We're probably stuck with mandated state testing of literacy, but we can also rely on several authentic measures to make more valid assessments.

C. *A Combined Miscue Analysis and Retelling Experience.*

1. Do a miscue analysis by categorizing Victor's miscues in his reading of the Harriet Tubman story (see Figure 11.5).

Word omission	Complete circle around the word
Self-correction	A large *C* aound one or more words
Insertion	A caret below a word above
Default	A *d* above the word
Repeat	The letter *R* over one or more words
Ineffective substitution	One that does change the author's meaning
Effective substitution	One that doesn't change the author's meaning

Share your miscue results with others in your class.

2. After you finish the miscue analysis, compare the original version of the story and Victor's retelling of it (see Figure 11.6).

Create your own criteria for assessing first his memory and then his understanding, or comprehension. Use your criteria to give Victor a grade. Evaluate your assessment process with other members of your class.

Harry
(Harriet Tubman never dreamed (that) she would become famous. She had been born a slave and (could (neither) read *couldn't* nor write. When she was ~~thirteen~~ a slave boss struck her *13* *or* (on the) head with a heavy iron weight. For the rest of her *pipe* life she carried an ∧ugly scar. *a very* ∧~~She~~ escaped from slavery and began ∧helping others to *Harriet* *to help* escape. People called her Moses because she would wait *d* outside a slave cabin and sing a little song, "Go down∧ Moses." *slave's* *R* It was a signal to get ready. She had come to help them escape. After a while∧ ~~she~~ was so well known (that) the slave *Harriet Tubman* owners offered a (large reward for her capture. They offered *lot* ~~forty thousand dollars~~ in gold for ~~Harriet Tubman~~ whether *$40,000* *her* dead or alive. One day∧ ~~she~~ was sitting at a railroad station. Two men *when* *Harriet* walked by. She knew ∧they were looking at her. ∧She listened *that* *So* carefully and overheard them talking about the reward. Quietly *telling* she took out a book and pretended to read. They walked by again∧ and she heard one∧ say, "That's not her. That can't be *of them* *R* Moses. ∧Moses can't read." *because*

FIGURE 11.5 A transcription of Victor's miscues.

Harriet Tubman never dreamed that she would become famous. She had been born a slave and could neither read nor write. When she was thirteen a slave boss struck her on the head with a heavy iron weight. For the rest of her life she carried an ugly scar.

She escaped from slavery and began helping others to escape. People called her Moses because she would wait outside a slave cabin and sing a little song, "Go down Moses." It was a signal to get ready. She had come to help them escape.

After a while she was so well known that the slave owners offered a large reward for her capture. They offered forty thousand dollars in gold for Harriet Tubman, whether dead or alive.

One day she was sitting at a railroad station. Two men walked by. She knew they were looking at her. She listened carefully and overheard them talking about the reward. Quietly she took out a book and pretended to read. They walked by again and she heard one say, "That's not her. That can't be Moses. Moses can't read."

FIGURE 11.6 The original story of Harriet Tubman and Victor's retelling of it.

3. Discuss with your group why you think Victor read this well and understood the author's message. Also discuss why there are only two negative miscues that readers make—defaults and bad substitutions. Share your thoughts with the other small groups.

Creativity Training Session

A. Design a creative way for you to use a portfolio. Share it with your colleagues and your students. Use it to model for your students on how to use a portfolio.

B. Find a creative way to solve this problem: Albert has a house high on a hill. Baba has a manure factory on the same hill, but higher than Albert's house. Albert finds the smell of Baba's manure annoying and somewhat sickening when it's time to eat. Baba finds the constant criticism from Albert to be annoying. Before long the two men are throwing rocks at each other's houses and breaking each other's windows. Both men consider moving, but Albert has run out of money and can't afford to move. Baba can't move because his wife and father want to be on the highest place on the highest hill, their self-esteem has never been higher. What to do! More and more windows are being shattered, more and more dinner parties have been ruined. What to do! What to do! Use your creative thinking cap to bring peace to rich Baba and poor Albert.

Field Experiences

A. Use the questions that follow and three others that you think of to create a questionnaire for interviewing three of your teaching colleagues about how they assess and report the progress of their students. Report the results to your university class.

1. What do you use besides tests to assess your students?
2. How do students' scores on mandated statewide tests impact the grades you give your students?
3. What would you like to change about how your students are graded?
4. Do you believe in giving your students grades for language arts?

B. At the same interview ask questions about these specific things:

1. Who has access to the student's portfolios and/or journals?
2. How much do the portfolios and/or journals influence students' grades?
3. How much do you rely on your observations in assessing your students' progress?
4. Do you assess your students by evaluating their miscues?
5. Do you use running records, or do you evaluate their reading during small-group instruction? Do you pay more attention to their correcting their own substitutions or *not* correcting their own substitutions? to students who either refuse to read a hard word or beg you for the word?
6. How would you like to change the way students are assessed?

References

Arlington, R. (2002). *Big brother and the national reading curriculum.* Portsmouth, NH: Heinemann.

Brown, C. S., & Lytle, S. L. (1988). Merging assessment and instruction: Protocols in the classroom. In S. M. Glazer, L. W. Searfoss, & L. M. Gentile (Eds.), *Reexamining reading diagnosis: New trends and procedures.* Newark, DE: International Reading Association.

Cagney, M. A. (1988). Measuring comprehension: Alternative diagnostic approaches. In S. M. Glazer, L. W. Searfoss, & L. M. Gentile (Eds.), *Reexamining reading diagnosis: New trends and procedures.* Newark, DE: International Reading Association.

Chittenden, E., & Courtney, R. (1989). Assessment of young children's reading: Documentation as an alternative to testing. In D. S. Strickland & L. M. Morrow

(Eds.), *Emerging literacy: Young children learn to read and write.* Newark, DE: International Reading Association.

Clay, M. M. (1991). *Becoming literate: The construction of inner control.* Portsmouth, NH: Heinemann.

Clay, M. M. (2001). *Change over time in children's literacy development.* Portsmouth, NH: Heinemann.

Clay, M. M. (2002). *An observational survey of early literacy achievement* (2nd ed.). Portsmouth, NH: Heinemann.

Cousin, P. T. (1990). The role of reflection and self-evaluation in the learning process: Implications for classroom practice. In P. Dryer & M. Poplin (Eds.), *Fifty-fourth yearbook of the Claremont Graduate School.* Claremont, CA.

Cunningham, P., & Allington, R. (1994). *Classrooms that work.* New York: Harper Collins.

Cunningham, P., & Allington, R. (2003). *Classrooms that work: They can all read and write.* Columbus, OH: Pearson.

D'Angelo, K., & Mahlino, M. (1983). Insertion and omission miscues of good and poor readers. *The Reading Teacher, 36,* 778–779, 782.

Darling-Hammond, L. (2005). *What matters most: Linda Darling-Hammond on teacher preparation.* Retrieved from the George Lucas Education Foundation at *www.glef.org/*

Edmondson, J. (2004). Reading policies: Ideologies and strategies for political engagement. *The Reading Teacher, 57*(5), 418–428.

Edmondson, J., & Shannon, P. (2002). The will of the people. *The Reading Teacher, 55,* 452–454.

Elmore, R. F. (2002, Spring) Unwarranted intrusion. *Education Next.* Retrieved March 21, 2003, from *http://www.Educationnext.org.*

Farstrup, A. E. (2005). IRA and No Child Left Behind: Support and shared concerns. *Reading Today, 22*(3), 7.

Fielding, L. (Speaker). (2002, December). *Interventions* [Iowa Communications Network broadcast and recording]. Iowa City: Iowa Department of Education.

Forbes, S., Poparad, M. A., & McBride, M. (2004). To err is human; to self-correct is to learn. *The Reading Teacher, 57*(6), 566–572.

Fountas, C., & Pinnell, G. S. (1999). *Matching books to readers: Using leveled books in guiding reading K–3.* Portsmouth, NH: Heinemann.

Gambrell, L., Pfeiffer, W., & Wilson, R. (1985). The effects of retelling upon reading comprehension and recall of text information. *Journal of Educational Research, 78,* 216–220.

Garcia, G. E. (1994). The literacy assessment of second language learners: A focus on authentic assessment. In K. Spangenberg-Urbschat & R. Pritchard (Eds.), *Kids come in all languages: Reading instruction for second language learners* (pp. 183–208). Newark, DE: International Reading Association.

Goodman, Y. (1989). Evaluating of students. In K. S. Goodman, Y. M. Goodman, & W. J. Hood (Eds). *The whole language evaluation book.* Portsmouth, NH: Hienemann.

Goodman, Y. M., & Goodman, K. S. (1994). To err is human: Learning about language processes by analyzing miscues. In R. B. Ruddell, M. R. Ruddell, & H. Singer (Eds.), *Theoretical models and processes of reading* (4th ed., pp. 104–123). Newark, DE: International Reading Association.

Hansen, J. (1992). Student evaluations bring writing and reading together. *The Reading Teacher, 46,* 100–105.

Harp, B. (1991). Principles of assessment and evaluation in whole language classrooms. In B. Harp (Ed.), *Assessment and evaluation in whole language programs.* Norwood, MA: Christopher-Gordon.

Jimenez, R. T. (2004). More equitable literacy assessments for Latino students. *The Reading Teacher, 57*(6), 576–578.

Johnston, P. (2003). Assessment conversations. *The Reading Teacher, 57*(1), 90–92.

Johnston, P. H., Jiron, H. W., & Day, J. P. (2001). Teaching and learning literate epistemologies. *Journal of Educational Psychology, 93*(1), 223–233.

Klein, S. P., Hamilton, L. S., McCaffrey, D. F., & Stecher, B. M. (2000). What do test scores in Texas tell us? *Education Policy Analysis Archives, 8*(49). Retrieved from *http://epaa.asu.edu/*

Levy, Y. (1999). Early metalinguistic competence: Speech monitoring and repair behavior. *Developmental Psychology, 35,* 822–834.

Linn, R. L. (2000). Assessments and accountability. *Educational Researcher, 29*(2), 4–16.

Linn, R. L. (2003). *Standards-based accountability: Ten suggestions* (CRESST Policy Brief 1). Retrieved from *http://www.cse.ucla.edu*

Lipson, M. Y., & Wixson, K. K. (2003). *Assessment and instruction of reading and writing difficulty: An interactive approach* (3rd ed.). Boston: Allyn & Bacon.

Loxterman, J. A. (1994). The effects of thinking aloud during reading on students' comprehension of more or less coherent text. *Reading Research Quarterly, 29,* 352–367.

McNaughton, S. (1988). A history of errors in the analysis of oral language behavior. *International Journal of Experimental Educational Psychology, 8,* 21–30.

Morrow, L. M. (1988). Retelling stories as a diagnostic tool. In S. M. Glazer, L. W. Searfoss, & L. M. Gentile (Eds.), *Reexamining reading diagnosis: New trends and procedures.* Newark, DE: International Reading Association.

Olsen, L. (2002). Overboard on testing. *Education Week, 20*(17), 23–30.

Orellana, M. F., Reynolds, J., Dorner, L., & Meza, M. (2003). In other words: Translating or "paraphrasing" as a family literacy practice in immigrant households. *Reading Research Quarterly, 38,* 12–34.

Perez, B., & Torres-Guzman, M. E. (1996). *Learning in two worlds.* White Plains, NY: Longman.

Piaget, J. (1955). *The language and thought of the child.* New York: Meridian.

Readance, J. E., & Martin, M. A. (1988). Comprehension assessment: Alternatives to standardized tests. In S. M. Glazer, L. W. Searfoss, & L. M. Gentile (Eds.), *Reexamining reading diagnosis: New trends and procedures.* Newark, DE: International Reading Association.

Reutzel, D. R., & Cooter, R. B. (2000). *Teaching children to read: Putting the pieces together.* Upper Saddle River, NJ: Merrill Education/Prentice Hall.

Riddle Buly, M., & Valencia, S. W. (2002). Below the bar: Profiles of students who fail state reading tests. *Educational Evaluation and Policy Analysis, 24,* 219–239.

Schwartz, R. M. (1997). Self-monitoring in beginning reading. *The Reading Teacher, 51,* 40–48.

Sebesta, S. L. (1996, October 15). A telephone conversation with Frank May.

Shepard, L. A. (2000). The role of assessment in a learning culture. *Educational Researcher, 29,* 4–14.

Tierney, R. J., Carter, M. A., & Desai, L. E. (1991). *Portfolio assessment in the reading-writing classroom.* Norwood, MA: Christopher-Gordon.

Torres-Guzman, M. E., & Abbate, M. E. (2002). Defining and documenting success for bilingual learners: A collective case study. *Bilingual Research Journal, 12*(1), 23–44.

Valencia, S. W., & Riddle Buly, M. (2004). Behind test scores: What struggling readers really need. *The Reading Teacher, 57,* 520–531.

Vygotsky, L. S. (1978). *Mind in society: The development of higher psychological processes.* Harvard, MA: Harvard University Press.

Watson, D., & Henson, J. (1991). Reading evaluation—miscue analysis. In B. Harp (Ed.), *Assessment and evaluation in whole language programs.* Norwood, MA: Christopher-Gordon.

Willis, S. (1996). On the cutting edge of assessment: Testing what students can do with knowledge. *Education Update, 38*(4), 1–7.

Wood, C. (1999). The contribution of analogical problem solving and phonemic awareness to children's ability to make orthographic analogies when reading. *Educational Psychology, 19*(3), 277–286.

Wood, D. (1998). *How children think and learn.* Oxford, UK: Blackwell.

Other Suggested Readings

Clay, M. M. (1985). *The early detection of reading difficulties* (3rd ed.). Portsmouth, NH: Heinemann.

Dean, S. E. (1992). *A study of qualitative running records scoring systems for identification of instructional reading levels.* Unpublished doctoral dissertation, Portland State University, Portland, OR.

Farr, R., & Tone, B. (1994). *Portfolio and performance assessment.* Fort Worth, TX: Harcourt Brace.

Johnson, M. S., Kress, R. A., & Pikulski, J. J. (1987). *Informal reading inventories.* Newark, DE: International Reading Association.

Moje, E. (2000). What will classrooms look like in the new millennium? *Reading Research Quarterly, 35*(1), 128–134.

Phelps, L. A., & Hanley-Maxwell, C. (1997). School-to-work transitions for youth with disabilities: A review of outcomes and practices. *Review of Educational Research, 67*(2), 197–226.

Pressley, M., Allington, R., Wharton-McDonald, R., Block, C. C., & Marrow, L. M. (2001). *Learning to read: Lessons from exemplary first-grade classrooms.* New York: Guilford.

Chapter Twelve

The Nature of Motivation for Reading and Writing

You can lead a horse to water, but you can't make him drink.

—Buffalo Bill's Father?

Self-assessment is nothing more or less than a means of self-motivation.

—Bogglestar's Mother

expectancy × valuing = motivation

—UCLA Department of Psychology (2002)

Twelfth Objective for Your Teaching Success:

Provide numerous ways for students to develop self-motivation.

According to Lumsden (1994) and the Clearinghouse on Educational Policy and Management: the passion for learning that infants and young children first have frequently seems to shrink. My response to this clause: It's certainly not an *automatic* kind of behavior. Nor is it something that has to do very much with our students' hormones, I don't think. And we certainly don't blame children's laziness. By and large they're ready to go! "Pass me the stimulation, please. Toss me that Harry Potter book, I'm getting behind! I'm bored to death, give me something new to learn, would you? Could we please learn about something that's really relevant!" (p. 1)

Morrow (2004), president of the International Reading Association, has this to say about our students' motivation:

> During the past few years, the reading community has talked a lot about the systematic and explicit instruction of reading and writing skills to enhance literacy development. Certainly children must develop skills to become good readers and writers. *However,* if we teach children to read and write, but they have no desire to do so, we will not have achieved much. It is time for us to focus on motivation as well as skills, since motivation to read and write and literacy ability go hand in hand. They must be nurtured simultaneously. (p. 6)

Collins (1996), Carr (1995), and Wallace (1995) urge us to use groups where students can ask questions, dictate stories, listen to oral and recorded reading together, and share both real-life experiences and what they are learning from reading. What's their point? *Learning to read must be a social experience for many students,* whatever their cultural background.

Research on Motivation to Read

Professional Standard: Provides opportunities to select from a variety of written materials for many authentic purposes

Let's begin with two big questions: Which came first, the chicken or the egg? and Which comes first in learning to read, positive achievement or positive attitude? After 50 years of childlike research I have discovered that the chicken came first, but I can't prove it. After 30 years of professional research, I have discovered (and rediscovered) that a positive attitude toward reading and writing comes *before* positive achievement. And a major step toward proof comes from a study by Newman (1982), who had the good sense to do a longitudinal study of children instead of chickens.

Newman's Findings

Newman studied a group of children who had scored low on the Metropolitan Readiness Test when they were about 6 years old. By ninth grade, though, these low scorers were considered to be high achievers in reading. In fact, they were much better readers than a comparison group of children who had scored high on reading readiness. So what made the difference between these slow starters/fast finishers and their counterparts who showed so much promise but didn't do as well by ninth grade? According to Newman's findings, the slow starters/fast finishers had these advantages:

- Good models at home and school
- A stimulating environment
- Interest shown by parents and teachers
- Good expectations expressed by teachers, parents, and other caregivers

And let me add these:

- Low but positive pressure toward achievement
- Just plain conscientiousness (Colquitt & Simmering, 1998)

To put this succinctly, important adults spent time helping these children develop positive attitudes toward reading. I have to conclude that positive attitudes can lead to positive achievement.

The Findings of Alexander, Filler, and Davis

Professional Standard: Increases the motivation of learners to read widely and independently

After examining the research on attitudes and reading, Alexander and Filler (1976) concluded that "a universal goal of reading instruction should be the fostering of positive attitudes toward reading" (p. 34). Similarly, after reviewing 110 research reports from 1900 to 1977 on reading achievement and reading attitudes, Davis (1978) concluded that teachers need to be aware of students' attitudes when planning instruction. She also concluded that careful planning can help learners develop positive attitudes and thus become motivated.

So what can you and I do to help our students become motivated to learn? How can we be sure that both teachers and students have an attitude of relating positively to each other? Let's visit with an expert on this matter.

An Interview with Curriculum Director Rebecca Silva

Frank: Thanks, Becky, for stealing a half-hour from your incredible agenda.

Becky: It's my pleasure, Frank. Thank you for giving me a half-hour away from the madness.

Frank: I'm honored, Becky, you know that. And you know exactly why you're here—to give us your sharp ideas on helping students develop motivation, especially the motivation to read and write, at a high level of enthusiasm.

Becky: Motivation, motivation. It's rapidly becoming the number one issue.

Frank: I agree.

Becky: And very high standards for good teaching and student achievement.

Frank: Yes, but it's not working, is it?

Becky: I don't think so. And it's because motivation is the missing link—the need for children to feel like truly wanting to learn.

Frank: I'm sure we both feel it's about time to think hard about motivation. What was the particular stimulus that motivated you to start training your teachers to deal with this problem?

Becky: (With a big smile) I'm a little embarrassed about this, but I didn't really feel the need to deal with it—until I started to pay much more attention to Alex.

Frank: Your son?

Becky: Yes, the one who was identified as gifted.

Frank: That's a problem?

Becky: No, but his attitude is. He struggles so much in school, he's not passing some of the classes, and . . .

Frank: A motivation problem?

Becky: Yes.

Frank: Why do you think it is?

Becky: In the classes that he's passing, he makes positive comments about the class—he likes the teachers and they like him.

Frank: And in the other classes, where he's failing?

Becky: Well. . . in one of them he says, "The teacher doesn't like me, he's a bad teacher—he doesn't teach, he just hands out papers and tells us to find the information." So now I'm very concerned about my child—and all the other Alexes out there.

Frank: What are you planning to do?

Becky: I've read dozens of articles in journals, especially the ones that describe some impressive research.

Frank: Did you read any that talked about students' sense of relatedness? You know, the need for nurturing from teachers?

Becky: Right! The need to feel a protective atmosphere in class—and a fond attachment to the teacher.

Frank: The need for relatedness in the classroom, am I right?

Becky: Absolutely.

Frank: I suppose then that we're talking about the degree to which students and their teachers feel fondness and respect for each other.

Becky: Yes, those two feelings—fondness and respect—are such critical ingredients. It's very clear to me that children who feel loved and appreciated are those who feel interested in learning through reading. This feeling of relatedness in the classroom is absolutely crucial.

Frank: I confess that I did a little reading before you came, and I was really impressed by the findings of Furrer and Skinner (2003).

Becky: What impressed you the most?

Frank: The concept of engagement, the fact that emotional engagement in learning is intimately linked to how well students feel related to their teachers—as well as their peers, parents, and other caretakers.

Becky: Yes, engagement. That's the key, isn't it? I wasn't surprised to find that girls are better at it than boys. But to me the most intriguing information was the finding that boys need to relate the most to their *teachers* rather than their peers.

Frank: Now there's a study! We're not talking about kindergarten to Grade 2 kids—just third grade through sixth grade, ages 8 through 12—but maybe it's simply because boys don't identify with school as much as girls tend to do.

Becky: I agree. Boys don't feel a sense of belonging to the extent that girls might feel it.

Frank: Do you think it might go even deeper? Have you seen the work on children's perceived control?

Becky: Yes, I have, but it must have been several years ago, before I entered my doctoral program.

Frank: (Impishly) I cheated. I just read about it yesterday via the Internet. It's a study by Skinner, Wellborn, and Connell (1990), and it's about how students' perceptions influence students' achievement in school.

Becky: Is this the famous perceived control study?

Frank: That's the one. It's about our students' anticipation—or nervous prediction—of how well they will be able to control their success in school.

Becky: Oh yes, their predictions about the success of their *strategies* for achieving that control?

Frank: Exactly, and also predictions about their own ability to carry out those strategies.

Becky: There's a lot for these 8- to 12-year-olds to worry about . . . and their emotional survival is often at stake.

Frank: What do you think about all this, Becky? Can you bring this to some kind of conclusive statement, something that will wrap it up for teachers?

Becky: Yes, I can. I feel strongly that a lot of us education people have been blind. Teaching is not so much about the subjects we expect our students to shine in. It's more about relating to the nervous concerns that kids have—you know, what it takes to do well in school, as compared to their own perceived capacity to do well academically.

Frank: These fears about control? They're something that most teachers would be happy to learn about, don't you think?

Becky: Yes, I do. Especially the social factor that makes the biggest difference in the classroom environment—the students' sense of relatedness to their teacher and peers.

Frank: You're so right, Becky. Thanks. I know you have to get back to administrative madness, as you call it. I really appreciate your help. My apologies for taking you away from your work.

Becky: Don't worry, dear friend. Next time, it'll be your turn. You owe me one, you know.

Frank: I do indeed. Call me when I can return the favor.

There are many educators who have come to Becky's same conclusions. For instance, Furrer and Skinner (2003) wrote in the *Journal of Educational Psychology* about the sense of relatedness as a factor in children's academic engagement and performance. They found that children who felt appreciated by their teachers were more likely to report that academic activities were interesting and fun. Furthermore, those students felt happy and comfortable in the classroom.

Winebrenner and Berger (1996) looked at gifted children, 9 to 12-year-olds, who are fast losing their motivation to learn—a sad story, indeed. The authors' article describes a remedy—namely, the use of *contracts*, or written agreements, between teachers and students that outline what the gifted students want to learn, and will learn, and how they will be evaluated. This gives them a chance to take control of their lives again, a chance to think creatively again.

Provide a Variety of Models

Professional Standard: Implements strategies to include parents as partners

Observations and research consistently point out that children who want to learn to read better usually have adult models who like to read—children who feel the opposite about reading generally do not. With that in mind, let me throw you a hypothesis for you to consider: Teachers who spend as much time on the modeling approach to teaching reading as they do on skill instruction will have greater success than those who spend all their time on skill instruction. We humans are emotional as well as rational creatures, and most of us long to be inspired as well as instructed. Most of us, particularly as we grow up, want to imitate others whom we admire. Let's talk, then, about how teachers can promote themselves, parents, other adults, and children's peers as models.

Motivational Modeling

Mrs. Deaver obviously believes in the modeling approach. For one thing, she reads to her students every day, even though they're in the fourth grade. She selects her read-aloud books very carefully—some with male heroes and some with female heroines, but all with literary quality and an exciting plot. She reads a chapter every day just before they go home. "That way," she says, "I can end each day on a positive note, and they're eager to return to school the next morning."

Mrs. Deaver doesn't have a Hollywood voice, but she reads with enjoyment and enough expression to display her excitement without overdramatizing. In other words, she models good, involved reading without putting on a show that most kids can't imitate when reading to themselves.

Mrs. Deaver also shares her own personal reading experiences with her class. Once or twice a week, during her students' daily news time, she talks about something she has read in a newspaper, magazine, or book. Often she brings that newspaper, magazine, or book to hold up while she talks, "not necessarily to show them a picture, but just to show them that here's something I like to read when I'm home."

Furthermore, when the children have their customary 30 minutes on Monday, Wednesday, and Friday for library books, she usually sits right up in the front of the class and reads a book of her own. "It's tempting," Mrs. Deaver says, "to use the time for planning and so on, but most of the time I can resist the temptation, because I know how important it is for children to watch me enjoy the process that I so fervently teach every day. Actually I feel hypocritical if I don't read in front of them. Of course, if I see a child struggling, I'll drop my book for a bit and help the child remember a strategy I've taught him. If necessary, I'll help him find an easier, more interesting, or more motivating book. No sense making him come to hate reading."

Encouraging Parental Models

Miss Weingardt uses herself as a model for her second graders in much the same way. But she also tries to involve the parents in a modeling, book-rich, and re-reading approach (Koskinen, Blum, Bissson, Phillips, Creamer, & Baker (2000). In October, for her second teacher-to-parent newsletter of the year, this is what she said:

Dear Parents and Other Caretakers,

I do know how busy you are, so let me assure you that what I'm going to suggest will take no more than an average of 5 minutes a day. And it's for a very worthy cause: your child. (I know that some of you are already doing the things I'm going to suggest, and to you let me just say thank you!)

From what we know about children, it appears that good readers usually have "models" at home who read themselves. These people enjoy reading and like to share what they read with others. The children they're with evidently like to imitate them. Therefore, what I'm going to ask you to do is this (unless you already do it):

1. Would you read silently something pleasurable to yourself—and in front of your child—at least once a week?
2. Would you read out loud something pleasurable to your child at least twice a week? (It doesn't have to be at bedtime; anytime will do—before the bus comes, right after supper, anytime.)
3. Would you please make sure all television sets, radios, CDs, cell phones, video games, computers, headsets, telephones, and all other electronic devices are turned off for at least 1 hour each evening, so that your child will be tempted to fill the time with pleasurable reading or writing?

If you will do those three things (or continue doing them), I feel confident you will be helping me to help your child. I also feel confident that you will gradually see some real progress. To help you in this process, I have gradually developed a classroom library of 320 books, thanks partly to your wonderful contributions. We now have a book-rich place in which the children can read.

But let me ask you to help the children in just one more way. Let's start a re-reading program. Each time they finish reading a book here at school, they will take the book home to read with *you*. In this way, they will learn words more firmly, they will proudly receive your praise, and most important, they will build the self-confidence they must have to keep learning. After they finish the book at home, they will bring it back for our classroom library. Fair enough? Research shows that the re-reading program really works! Call me at school and leave a message for me if you have any questions about this reading program you and I are developing together!

Sincerely,

Marianne Weingardt

School phone: (413). . .

P.S. If you would like me to send you a list of good books to read aloud to that treasured child, please sign below and return the bottom portion of this sheet.

Yes, I would like you to send me a list of good read-aloud books you can find in your local library.

Miss Weingardt decided this letter was so important that she sent it to each home by mail. "It cost me a few dollars' postage," she said, "but my principal liked the idea so much, he's going to get some funds just for this purpose."

Other School Employees as Models

Encourage other teachers such as the physical education teacher, the music teacher, and the art teacher to mention often, but casually, some information they have gotten from their own reading. Ask them to soft-sell the kinds of books and magazines *they* like. Also ask them to recommend specific children's books or magazines on sports, musicians, artists, science, and so on. And don't forget to ask the principals to get involved in promoting reading by visiting classrooms, talking about things they like to read, and recommending specific books for students.

Some schools have librarians who set aside time to present book chats on new books that have arrived. In the many schools the entire community gets involved, with the lunchroom staff, nurse, secretary, principal, teachers, aides, and children all taking a 20-minute reading break each day. In other schools local celebrities are brought in to talk about topics of interest to students and, with a good bit of fanfare, the kinds of things they enjoy reading.

Students' Book-Club Peers as Models

Mr. Munden is a fifth-grade teacher who likes to use peer modeling as well as adult modeling. Once a week the children in his class meet for 40 minutes in book clubs of five or six children each. These clubs are not developed according to subject interest or already-established friendships. Instead, membership is carefully planned by Mr. Munden. "Each club," he says, "has two good readers, one or two typical readers, and one or two struggling readers. For the first 20 minutes they sit around a table and read whatever interests them. For the last 20 minutes, they tell each other something interesting they've been reading. It's quite simple really, but it seems to motivate all of them to do more reading—especially the typical and struggling readers, who are inspired by the good readers."

Parents as Active Tutors

Children's attitudes toward reading are certainly influenced by the degree of success they have in learning to read but also by the behavior and interests of adults around them. Fantuzzo and McWayne (2002) found in their study of 242 preschool children that motivations and prosocial behavior in the home led to prosocial behavior in the classroom. Several other studies have shown that parental involvement in children's education has a rather direct effect on reading achievement (Niedermeyer, 1970).

In one study, for example (Shuck, Ulsh, & Platt, 1983), 150 students from Grades 3 through 5 who were behind in reading by at least two grade levels were placed in a parent-tutoring program. Trained parents worked with their children at home by helping them read a book, do homework, practice word lists, and play reading games. This experimental group of students ended the year with an average grade-equivalent score in reading of 3.8, as contrasted to 2.8 for the control group that was not in the parent-tutoring program.

John McKinney (1977) found that when 50 parents were trained to tutor their third graders, the tutored children ended the year with an average score of 52 on a standardized reading test; the nontutored children averaged a score of 37. Tutoring, though, is just one of many ways parents and other caregivers can get involved. Here are some other ideas:

- Have a special collection of books in the school library that children can borrow and take home for someone to read with them. These should be carefully selected read-aloud books (Armstrong, 1981).
- Use *The Read-Aloud Handbook* by Jim Trelease (2001) to help you select books for parents and children to read aloud.
- Have a workshop for parents on the values and techniques of reading aloud with kids at home (Lautenschlager & Hertz, 1984).
- Have a learning station in the classroom supervised by a parental volunteer, who can help children with basic sight words, skill lessons, language-experience stories, and so on.
- Engage parents in producing a minilibrary of thin books, which are made by cutting out interesting stories from old basals or other materials. The parents or other caretakers can distribute them to the children, possibly read one aloud, and perhaps discuss them with the children after the children have read them (Criscuolo, 1983).
- If there is an available room in the school building, arrange for parents, volunteers and other caregivers to play educational reading and language games with the children during lunch periods and at other times during the day. Also arrange for somebody to check these games out for the children to use at home (Criscuolo, 1983).
- Start a summer reading program. Parents, grandparents, and caregivers sign a pledge to get their children in the program, take them to the library during the summer, and talk about the books with their children. The children receive a certificate at the end of the program.
- Develop a workshop to teach parents and other caregivers how to make simple but effective reading games to use with their children (Criscuolo, 1974).
- Get more men to volunteer as reading models—fathers, principals, janitors, local businessmen, local athletes, physical education instructors. Get them to talk about a good book they can recommend or the way they use reading on their jobs or the meaning reading has for them. According to a study by Downing and Thomson (1977), in some parts of North America there is a stereotype of reading as a feminine activity, which can influence some boys' attitudes. Downing and Thomson found that when children and adults were asked to decide whether the pictured activity of a person reading was more suitable for a boy or girl, the vast majority said for a girl. Still the same?

Inspire Motivation Through the Use of Learning Principles

Children's motivation to read and write can be greatly influenced by how well teachers employ basic psychological and anthropological principles of motivation. These principles seem to be appropriate regardless of whether a person is teaching reading, mathematics, swimming, cooking, firefighting, soccer, or even pickpocketing (judging from Fagin's success with Oliver and the other boys). Let's look at some of those principles.

According to Maslow's (1970) well-known theory of motivation, human beings have basic types of needs: physiological comfort, physical and psychological safety, belonging and love, esteem from self and others, self-actualization, and knowledge and appreciation. The physiological needs for food, warmth, and sleep are generally dominant until they become at least partially satisfied. However, once they're moderately satisfied, they give way to the need for safety—security, stability, and structure. Having moderately satisfied the physiological needs and the safety needs, human beings are then usually dominated by the need for belonging—love, companionship, friendship, and relatedness.

As each set of needs is reasonably satisfied, the next step in the hierarchy takes over. After love comes the need for esteem—importance, success, self-respect, and recognition. After esteem comes the need for self-actualization—self-fulfillment, satisfying one's potential, meeting one's self-ideal, and doing what one is fitted for. Finally, after self-actualization come the needs that relate most to schooling—knowledge, understanding, and appreciation. This hierarchy of needs is shown graphically in Figure 12.1. Generally speaking, then, the "lower" needs must be at

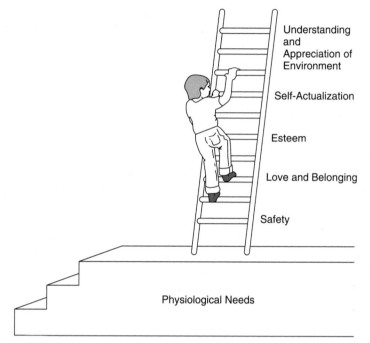

FIGURE 12.1   The ladder of human needs.

least partially met before the "higher" needs of self-actualization and intellectual understanding can be fulfilled.

In a practical sense this hierarchy means that the teacher who ignores children's emergent lower needs will find it rather difficult to motivate them to learn something just to satisfy their intellectual curiosity or their desire to become more skilled readers. Lower needs may be dealt with during the entire school day, of course, but even during a brief lesson a teacher who is conscious of students' needs can be more successful in inspiring motivation.

Principle One: Help Meet Students' Physiological Needs

The physiological need for nourishment, oxygen and exercise is a good example. Teachers may fall short of motivating children simply because the teachers have failed to make sure that everyone has enough nourishment and oxygen. Without a sufficient supply the brain becomes sluggish, curiosity dies, and boredom sets in. Making sure there is plenty of fresh air in the classroom is a help, of course, but it's often not enough. What some teachers have discovered is that some type of invigorating activity at periodic intervals throughout the day is essential for most children. Rather than interfering with learning, such activity actually seems to enhance it.

This doesn't mean your classroom must be conducted like a three-ring circus. It does mean, though, that large-muscle movement should be encouraged frequently.

Even if you do no more than ask students to touch their toes before they sit down for a reading lesson, you stand a better chance of getting their intellectual attention. And during the lesson you can get them up to the board occasionally or have them pantomime a word or sentence.

Which of these times would be best for having a session of dancing, rhythms, or dramatic play:

1. Just before recess so students can take their noise and excitement outside afterwards

2. Between two quiet intellectual sessions so they get the exercise they need

3. Right after recess because they'll be calmer then

Usually it would be a good idea to use the dancing, rhythms, or dramatic play as a time for a physical break between two intellectual activities.

Principle Two: Help Meet Students' Safety and Security Needs

The need for safety or security can be met during your reading instruction in a number of ways—by providing each student with success, by accepting mistakes as natural allies of learning, and by assuring that instruction is carried on under reasonably orderly conditions. Obviously your students are not going to feel safe and secure if a lesson confronts them with a series of failures. To be motivated to engage in an intellectual exercise, students must experience success during that exercise (Ganske, Monroe, & Strickland, 2003). Nor will children feel safe and secure if they perceive an intolerant attitude toward their mistakes. Nor will they feel safe and secure if other children continually misbehave and things seem out of control.

Suppose you ask James to read aloud a page that he has prepared silently for his small group. At one point he reads, "The tried woman couldn't walk another step." What might be your best response?

1. "No, James. You missed the second word in that sentence. Say it again."

2. "Good, Melinda! You corrected him on that second word. You're right. It should be tired and not tried."

3. "James, the second word in the sentence does look like *tried*, but since *tried* doesn't fit the meaning of the author, why don't you look at that second word again."

Which of the three responses would be most conducive to meeting James's needs for security, self-esteem, and belonging? Why do you think so?

Principle Three: Help Meet Students' Need for Love and Belonging

Sarah is a second grader with a minor articulation problem. Her teacher feels that Sarah needs more affection, and a sense of belonging, which has to be considered throughout the school day. But even during a single lesson it can be partially met by letting her know that her teacher and peers are on her side in her efforts to learn to read. To meet both the need for security and the need for a sense of belonging, the teacher should vigorously discourage children from making fun of those who make mistakes. This effort is considerably easier, of course, if the teacher refrains from careless smiles and sarcastic remarks.

When Sarah reads, "I see free cookies on the table" instead of "I see three cookies on the table," what would be the best response for the teacher to make?

1. "Sarah, let me help you make the *th* sound in the word *three*. Watch my mouth."

2. "Sarah, I've told you many times—the *th* digraph is not pronounced / fr"

3. "Free! I didn't know the cookies were free. Did you, boys and girls?"

Principle Four: Help Meet Students' Need for Self-Esteem

You can meet the need for self-esteem by making your students feel important to you and their peers. A child who is rarely called upon, for example, won't feel very important. Yet this can easily happen when a teacher hurries to cover the material or calls on only the brightest and quickest students. This may happen especially when the teacher is tired or wishes he was already home.

Miss Black is developing a whole-language program in which her second-grade children do a great deal of writing and also a lot of reading of literature and each other's writing. From something Samuel has written in his journal, she realizes that he is not feeling very important in the group. Which of these approaches might be appropriate for Samuel?

1. Let him choose the book that the teacher will read to the class at the end of the day. If the children like it, tell them that Samuel selected it (if he hasn't already boasted about this).

2. Read a story anonymously to the class that was written by Samuel (with his secret permission). After giving a good rendition, ask the class to guess the author. After three guesses say, "Will the real author stand up, please."

3. Announce to everyone in the room that Samuel has just written the best story in the whole class.

One of those solutions *stinks*, of course. The other two don't.

When teachers are aware of children's physiological needs and their needs for security, belonging, and importance, their students are much more likely to be motivated toward self-actualization and intellectual understanding. The need for self-actualization, for most children, includes the desire to communicate better. Most children seem to perceive communication, including the act of reading, as adult-like, and something they would like to be able to do as skillfully as adults do.

Children who seem not to want to learn how to communicate better—children from all ethnic and cultural groups, and all economic strata—have frequently been unable to meet their lower needs. Attempts to motivate these children without taking those needs into account will rarely succeed.

Create a Motivational Learning Environment

The learning environment can make or break your students' motivation. The setting in which you and your students work and play should be sparked and checked frequently—sparked to improve self-motivation, checked to find things that cause antimotivation. For instance, when *sparking*, try the recommendations of Intervention Central (2004):

- Actively listen to students and acknowledge their contributions
- Greet students at the classroom door
- Ask students to complete a learning preferences questionnaire
- Train students to be peer editors and/or evaluators
- Hold a weekly micromeeting to make decisions together

When checking, try these recommendations:

- Reduce inappropriate distractions in the room and small groups
- Make sure predictable materials and routines aren't violated
- Avoid isolating students by letting each one have a buddy

All of these recommendations can help to meet the basic needs of your students.

Inspire Motivation Through the Use of Teaching Principles

Principle One: Teach at the Appropriate Level of Difficulty

This first principle is probably violated more often than any other principle of motivation. A learning task that is too easy for children will be boring, and one that is too hard will cause them to withdraw. But how can you select a learning task that will be at just the right level of difficulty for each child? Probably you can't. But to motivate children successfully, you have to come as close as possible to a task that will challenge but not overly frustrate them.

For illustration, let's look at Coach Cassidy, a high-school track coach working with a high jumper named John. Coach Cassidy puts the crossbar down fairly low the first time so that John can clear it with no sweat. Then Coach raises it slightly so that John has to expend a little more effort the next time. Each time Coach raises it a little, not so high that John misses and becomes frustrated, but just high enough to make him put a little more effort into his jump than he did the time before. This gradual increase makes the task hard enough to be challenging but easy enough to be reinforcing—high enough to spur on the jumper to greater achievement but low enough to assure success. *Level of difficulty and success go hand in hand to motivate the learner.*

For the reading teacher the task of finding the right level of difficulty for each student is not so easy. A major step in the right direction is to teach diagnostically rather than with a shotgun approach. This means you find out through kid watching and informal testing procedures what levels individual children are reading on and what reading concepts and strategies they have. Then you'll be able to teach them individually and form small groups of students needing similar assistance.

But suppose the lesson you're teaching is obviously not at the right level: For some children it's too easy, and for some it's too hard. In this case it's best to abbreviate your planned lesson and spend the extra time working with the children who are having trouble, while the rest move on to a follow-up activity or to reading library books. It's seldom advisable to ignore the difficulties some children may be having, thinking they'll get it eventually. Nothing is more dampening to children's motivation than to have one concept after another fly right by and to fall further and further behind.

Imagine that halfway through a lesson on finding the root in words with an *-ed* suffix, you notice that Ronny understands it well and is looking quite bored. Which of these may be the best to do?

1. Challenge him to find the root in some nonsense words such as *ruckled* or some hard words like *investigated.*

2. Do nothing special for him, as extra practice never hurt anyone.

3. Tell him that since he knows so much, perhaps he'd like to take over the lesson.

Principle Two: Provide Frequent and Specific Feedback

The most effective procedure is to help your students learn a small amount of information and follow that with a request for some type of response—answering a question orally, writing a response, circling something on the board, pointing to a place in their books. You then give the students feedback in the form of a nod or the correct answer to compare with their own or whatever will inform them about their understanding.

Which type of written feedback on a child's daily journal would best meet this principle?

1. "Your writing during the past month, Judith, has been excellent!"

2. "What you said about donkeys, Judith, seems to be true. When I had my first ride on one, I had the same trouble getting it to move. Maybe this is why I enjoyed this story the most of all you've written. It sounds so true!"

3. "Your ideas may be fine, but your spelling makes them hard to read."

Principle Three: Add Novelty to Learning Experiences

This principle is so simple that it needn't be discussed. But why then do children in some classrooms suffer the daily tedium of teaching procedures and worksheet workbook formats that never vary? The novelty principle may be simple and obvious, but how often we teachers ignore it!

The novelty principle need not be time and energy consuming for the teacher. Something as simple as having your students occasionally write on butcher paper with a felt pen instead of the usual chalkboard routine can be enough to cause a sharp rise in motivation. Or having them sit on the floor instead of chairs. Or teaching a reading lesson in the afternoon instead of the morning. Or using sign language for part of the lesson. Or using a game for part of the lesson. Or giving a different piece of colored chalk to each student to use at the board. Little things may take a bit of imagination but not much extra energy on the teacher's part.

I should point out that whole-language programs, language-experience approaches, drama baed programs and personalized literature programs normally have considerable novelty built into them. Journal writing, for example, is highly personal, making the chance for novelty considerably greater than it is with worksheets. So, allow your students to choose their literature rather than just their level books. And don't forget to build into your reading program, no matter what type it is, opportunities for personal writing and creative reading adventures.

Principle Four: Pay Attention to Students' Basic Needs

As we discussed earlier, students' basic needs must be satisfied before any teaching can be effective—physiological requirements, security, belonging, self-esteem, and self-actualization. These are prerequisites for motivated learners.

If you'd like to remember these four teaching principles discussed thus far, you may want to make up some type of mnemonic device. Here's one that I like:

Novelty needs level feedback.

By remembering that sentence, I can remember to think about novelty; concern myself with children's basic needs, especially for belonging and importance; teach at a level that is moderately challenging but not frustrating; and provide immediate and specific feedback whenever possible.

Principle Five: Get Everyone Engaged Each Step Along the Way

As Wilkinson and Silliman (2000) recommend, "Adopt the engagement perspective, which emphasizes students' active learning and the integration of language with literacy learning across the curriculum . . . [a perspective that] focuses on the motivation for reading" (p. 352). If you want maximum learning to take place, you should try to get each student engaged in each problem that either you or your student poses and each question that either of you asks—every step along the way.

Which of the following approaches would get the greatest number of students engaged or involved in Mr. Sanchez's class? Pick a first and second choice among the options.

1. "Marcus, would you please go to the board and circle a word in the sentence that gives you an idea of what our target word, *guise*, means."

2. "OK, everyone, write on your card a word that you think helps us understand the meaning of our target word, *guise*. Don't hold up your card until I tell you to. Keep it a secret."

3. "I'd like someone to go to the board and circle a word in the sentence that gives you an idea of what our target word, *guise*, means."

4. "OK, Marcia, go to the board and think out loud about what the sentence and the target word, *guise*, mean to you."

5. "Now, boys and girls, please watch while I circle a word in the sentence that gives me an idea of what our target word in that sentence means."

The last approach requires the involvement of no one but the teacher, although he may hope that all his students will actually watch and think about what they're watching—a vain hope. All his neophytes have to do is tilt their heads in his direction to fool Mr. Sanchez into thinking that understanding is magically transferring from his lips to their brains.

According to Pratton and Hales (1986), active involvement significantly increases motivation, learning, and retention. Getting a student *personally* engaged increases the emotional impact of the instruction, and learning that takes place with feeling generally is retained longer. In addition, personal involvement results in a student's receiving a greater amount of feedback—and encouragement, if you've done your usual excellent job of teaching. Encouragement strengthens the motivation to learn (Hicks & Driscoll, 1988), and feedback provides learners with a check on how well they are doing—another excellent source of motivation.

Differentiate Between Intrinsic and Extrinsic Teaching and Learning

Motivation—that is, being moved into action or thought—comes from many sources: basic needs, incentives, personal interest, or pleasure. The motivation to read is also influenced by memories of emotions associated with prior reading, for example, joy, success, excitement, tranquility. The motivation not to read may be derived from such memories as anxiety, self-disgust, failure, and angry frustration associated with prior reading. Researchers have known for several decades that positive motivations are necessary to get students to read well and to feel a high level of satisfaction while they read.

What does this mean for you and me as teachers? It means that we are each playing the role of orchestra leader. In your classroom, for instance, you're the chosen one to help your students become motivated to create beautiful music—and in this case beautiful reading and writing. Of course as orchestra leader it's your responsibility to know the "music" as well as you do.

I'll help you picture first a teacher (i.e., orchestra leader) who inspires effective *intrinsic motivation* for reading and learning to read; second, a teacher who provides effective *extrinsic motivation* for reading and learning to read; and third, a teacher who uses antimotivational procedures. In each of the cases the students' motivation is significantly influenced by the teacher's beliefs about the importance of motivation in teaching reading.

Intrinsic Motivation for Reading

Professional Standard: Understands the impact of perceptual, emotional, and social factors on reading acquisition

Ray Lubway was my older and more experienced team teacher at the University of Chicago Laboratory School, founded by John Dewey before Ray and I were born. Ray Lubway was a lithe dancer of a man with a slight build and brown eyes that flashed with pleasure whenever his students caught on to an idea, especially when they created their own ideas. It was his belief that learning is a cognitive process, but even more a motivational process, although the processes continuously interact.

Reading and writing well were considered by Ray to be crucial prerequisites to success and pleasure—in school, out of school, and after schooling. But for Ray it was the variety of ways people learn to read and write better that made a difference to his students. To address that variety, Ray attempted to teach in such a way that *all* of his students felt they would survive that day, the next day, and well into the future.

There's something warm about the feeling of survival, isn't there? It's perhaps the most basic kind of feeling, as the heavy learning ball rolls toward the head pin and not the gutter. Many years ago author John Holt demonstrated this for teachers as he portrayed student after student who perceived the educational situation from a survival point of view. And the kids who seemed to be surviving the best were those who believed in themselves. Al Siebert, author of *Survivor Personality*, describes the same perceptions of adults who survived World War II by believing in themselves.

This was the way Ray Lubway perceived his students: More than anything else, Ray wanted his 9 and 10-year-olds to believe in themselves. He wanted them to read well, of course, but not just so they could avoid the loss of respect from elders and peers. He wanted his students to become intrinsically motivated to read for sheer pleasure, for information vital to their own purposes, and for that wonderful, personal feeling of success.

Using Drama and Story Creation

Ray used drama and story creation as two of the most important means of inspiring intrinsic motivation for reading. In story creation his students produced their own group text. He helped them invent their own stories to read silently, then to read out loud in readers-theater style, and finally to tape-record for parents, other caregivers, friends, or themselves. The beginning step was a totally spontaneous event that proceeded in a very inventive way.

Teacher: (Teacher speaks into the tape recorder and then passes it on). OK, let's try this: Once upon a time there was a terrible storm in the land called Mud. Why do you think the people called it Mud?

Albert: Ooh, I know. It was called Mud because it rained a whole lot every single day—and night, too.

Teacher: Yes, and so one day it rained so much, the strong, handsome, and dark King of Mud came out of his castle and spoke to all the people—with a very loud voice. What did he say to them?

Beverly: He said, "People of Mud! Hear what I have to say!"

Tyrone: And he said, "I will give half my kingdom to anyone who will travel to the Rain God and beg him to stop all this rain."

Teacher: And Tyrone, did anyone volunteer to go?

Tyrone: Yes. I volunteered to go!

Teacher: Because you are called Tyrone the Warrior, is that right?

Tyrone: (Nods his head vigorously).

Teacher:	And since Tyrone the Warrior was so big and strong and brave, all the people shouted their approval. "Yes, send Tyrone. We want Tyrone to go." And then what?
Dorothy:	And then Tyrone quickly gathered up his things and marched to the North.
Teacher:	Yes, but halfway to the castle of the Rain God, the rain turned into snow.
Evelyn:	And Tyrone had only his raincoat and nothing else to keep him warm.
Teacher:	What kind of man was this warrior? Was he a man with ideas as well as muscles?
Tyrone:	(Again nods his head vigorously).
Teacher:	Suddenly the warrior got a wonderful idea for keeping warm. What was it?
Frances:	I know! I know! He dug a hole in the snow and went to sleep.

And on they went, improvising right to the end of the story. The next day or so, Ray would bring in copies of the complete and transcribed story for them to read to a partner and to illustrate. Ray Lubway knew that if his students were motivated, they would read and write more often and more successfully with each experience. And the reseach done by Wigfield and Guthrie (1997); Guthrie, Wigfield, and VonSecker (2000); and UCLA's Department of Psychology (2002) confirms his conviction.

The variety of activities that Ray used to inspire his students to read and write seemed endless. He helped them read plays together and then create their own plays. He had them read and study in order to recreate historical events, multicultural customs, and biographies—all of this through spontaneous creative drama. His classroom was always dynamic, with students too busy discovering and creating to realize that they were also learning how to read and write better than ever.

Extrinsic Motivation for Reading

Frances Hopkins, a teacher I observed on several occasions, also believed in emotions and motivation as the "spark plugs for the learning-to-read-and-write engine." She was bright and bouncy, characteristics that enhanced her playful teaching and her businesslike determination to get every student on the reading path. She was such a highly respected teacher in her school that her principal continually begged her to take one more of the "unmotivated kids," as he called them.

Like Ray Lubway, Frances Hopkins was determined to lead her students to the point of reading for intrinsic reasons. However, she knew even then what we've learned through research only recently: Lower achievers tend to be motivated more by extrinsic incentives, and higher achievers tend to be motivated more by intrinsic incentives (Sweet, Guthrie, & Ng, 1998; O'Donnell, 1996). Being a complete realist, she first emphasized extrinsic motivational devices, which she referred to as her bag of tricks. Because most of her students were from families and cultures that emphasized total family involvement, her bag of tricks included several ambitious cooperation projects. My favorite was the combined book projects and bookshelf project.

Using Book Projects and "Bookshelves"

On one wall of Frances's classroom I saw a gigantic vertical thermometer painted on a sheet of butcher paper. Rising from the floor to the ceiling, it was like the thermometers adults use for money drives—you know, "Help Us Get to the Top: One Million Dollars for Cancer Research." In this case Mrs. Hopkins used the vertical thermometer to measure the number of books her entire class had read and recommended to others. The banner at the top of the thermometer looked like this:

Help Us Get to the Top This Year with 300 Books Read

Frances used four procedures for this project.

Step 1: The students were directed to a large illustrated wall chart filled with a variety of interesting book projects, most of which Frances had demonstrated (one each day) before they tried them. For example:

- Read aloud to the class a very exciting part of your library book. Stop reading right in the middle of the action. Ask three people to guess what happens next. Then tell the class, "You'll have to read the book to find out exactly what happens."
- Play Twenty Questions with your classmates. Have them think of the object you have in mind, which was very important in the book you just read. But first tell them whether the object is animal, vegetable, or mineral. The game ends when someone guesses correctly or 20 questions have been asked.
- Plan and present a short skit about a scene in a book that you and a friend have read together. Try to use many of the words that the characters used.
- Write and illustrate a colorful advertisement for the book you have just read. Include the things that would make your classmates want to read the book. Also, write where they can find the book, and place your ad in the best place for others to read it (on the bulletin board or the classroom classified page) or pass it out as a business flyer.
- Write a letter to a friend and try to get your friend to read the book you just read. At sharing time you may read to the class part or all of the letter you received in return.

Step 2: For each book a student read and did a project on, the student received a pseudo book spine (1″ × 6″) made from thin colored cardboard or thick colored paper. The color depended on the genre of the book, for

example, blue for mystery, red for adventure, pink for humor, and so on. The student wrote on this book spine the same information that most actual book spines have—the title, author, and pretend publisher—using gold ink or another shiny color to make it attractive. The student's name went on the other side so that, when the spines were displayed, this project didn't become a race among individuals but a cooperative race against time. ("Let's see how many more we can read before the school year comes to a close.")

Step 3: The pseudo book spine was then attached by the student to the pseudo bookshelf, which can be made of butcher paper or bulletin-board cork. The shelf was prominently displayed in the classroom all year long, resulting in an ever-expanding panorama of color across the top of the chalkboard (or other area of the classroom).

Step 4: At the end of the school year the pseudo book spines were detached and returned to their owners to take home. Note: Some teachers use tangible rewards for each book read, but I have found that this encourages students to cheat, vehemently. And that defeats the purposes of (1) getting them to actually read more books, (2) encouraging them to read a greater variety of genres, and (3) moving them closer to reading for intrinsic purposes.

I have used this idea many times and have found it to be enjoyable and challenging from Grades 2 through 8. (I've never tried it at lower or higher grades.)

Both Frances Hopkins and I have discovered the need to give our students at least two 20-minute periods per week to share their book projects. I have also used those periods as a book-selling game: After a student shares his book, he asks, "Who would like to read this book next?" The number of raised hands gives the student an idea of how successful his communication and selling techniques were. *Warning*: For eager groups of students you'll need a band of butcher paper or cork near the tops of *two* walls!

Anti-motivation for Reading

The teacher I have chosen for this case study is Frank May. That's right—me. Why? Because no one has made more mistakes than I have in my teaching career. My first year of teaching was one I would like to forget, but that wouldn't be fair to you. In my fourth year at Antioch College in Yellow Springs, Ohio, I was asked to teach in a nearby school district. They were desperate for a male teacher to teach boys physical education half a day and a sixth-grade classroom the other half. Because of the work/study arrangement at Antioch, I was free to teach the first and third quarters, and because I was poor and naive, I took the job without any training.

I did all right with the physical education classes, but with the sixth-grade class I bombed an average of twice a minute for the first quarter. Allow me to describe for you just a few of my mistakes. Here is what I first wrote on the board:

"Group 1, read the story starting on page 79 of the blue book; Group 2, read the story starting on page 48 of the red book; Group 3, the story starting on page 31 of the yellow book." I might as well have been a church leader commanding his flock to sing three different hymns at the same time. It doesn't take much talent to call out page numbers.

While my students labored away without any prereading vocabulary or schema enhancement, I methodically copied three sets of questions on the board, which I had dutifully read from the three different teacher's guides. I felt very proud of myself, simply because I was now a teacher and getting paid for it, too. But no teaching was going on; I was merely testing my students on their cognitive comprehension. In essence, *I* was highly motivated, and *they* were antimotivated, a state of being that I was to observe again and again over the years during innumerable observations of teachers, student teachers, and sometimes my own students.

Did we sit down together and discuss the emotional aspects of the literature they had read? Of course not. Did we share our interpretations, our opinions, our feelings, our ideas for exploring further information or further stories by the author? Nonsense. Did we turn the stories into narration and dialogue so we could interpret them in dramatic format? Never. It was far more motivating for *me* to keep those restless, noisy preteenagers quietly scribbling answers at their 35 individual desks. But from the looks on their faces, I'd have to say they were doubly antimotivated.

Using "Discipline"

In time my students grew rebellious, of course. And this meant that I had to "motivate" them by disciplining them. (At that time the word *discipline* referred to punishment rather than its original meaning of "developing the precision of the mind.") And how did I then "motivate" them? Did I teach them more about the discipline called reading by modeling a few comprehension strategies in an interesting way? Did I humorously model how I monitor my own comprehension? Uhn-uhn. That might have been too cognitive for them, and even more so for me.

Instead, I used every single punishment I had observed or experienced during my own schooling. Here's a very abbreviated list, in case you're ever inclined to believe that teachers should be hired to discipline the troops rather than inspire them.

- *Require them to write 200 times*, "I will always read my book quietly without disturbing the reading time of my teacher and his other students." I fooled myself into thinking that this form of motivation worked very well, although I was appalled by their illegible handwriting. For some reason their sentences didn't flow like real sentences; they looked more like piles of different train cars, with all 200 of the *always* cars piled up in one wobbly column and all 200 of the *read* cars piled up in a nearby wobblier column. Naturally the *quietly* cars were so frightened they became impossible to read.
- *Demand their attention.* Of course the most professional way of making them behave was the traditional ruler method: Just demand their attention by slapping a ruler down on the desk. This worked pretty well until I broke my ruler right in front of them.
- *And then there was the corner method*: Make them stand in the corner if they weren't truly reading. This worked for a day or two, but suddenly all of the boys were highly motivated to take their turn in the corner in order to belong to the bad-boy club and to avoid reading. And as you can imagine, we ran out of corners!

Using Rewards

Early in my fourth month I had coffee with one of the other sixth-grade teachers and asked her for suggestions on how to get my kids to read. She was very helpful and said, "I reward them for reading rather than punishing them." That made a lot of sense to me, so I started rewarding them the very next day. For every 5-minute period the whole class read without stopping, I passed out 2 dollars of monopoly money to each and every one of them. (I owned two sets of Monopoly.)

This worked for only the first 5 minutes, and then it fell apart. They rebelled at the pay scale and demanded real money instead. We had a nice little discussion about the matter, during which time I realized I was finally relating to my students. After much fruitful and unfruitful negotiation we agreed that I was just a struggling teacher and could only afford a dime apiece for each of two 20-minute blocks of solid reading. (The dime back then was probably equivalent to 50 cents today.)

Well, as I said to you earlier, it doesn't pay to pay. By the end of the week I was out of dimes and $35 of my grocery budget. Not only that, I felt certain that most of the boys were just staring at the same page for the whole 20-minute period.

Lessons Learned

It took me the full quarter to gradually learn these things about motivation and learning:

1. In order to help students get self-motivated, I really had to inspire rather than hire.

2. What they wanted to learn *through* reading was far more important than what I wanted them to learn *by* reading.

3. Writing independently about their own problems and interests led to much more real reading (through sharing with peers) than lackadaisical reading about book characters' problems and interests.

4. Attempting to solve real problems (like the lack of traffic guides and stoplights near the school) led to much more reading (e.g., newspapers, letters, state laws) and writing (e.g., letters to authorities, legislators, and neighbors) than most of the students had ever done in their lives.

5. Paying attention to students' feelings about reading and writing can be more important than paying strict attention to canned reading assignments plucked out of the teacher's guides and both the district and state manuals.

6. Kids of any age from 1 to 99 enjoy being read to. There's no better way to help children develop their self-motivation to read.

Know the Results of Important Studies Related to Motivation

Whereas the 1980s were the decade of research on reading comprehension strategies, the 1990s might be considered the decade of research on reading motivation. Studies on motivation have been designed to answer a variety of questions, some of which we'll now examine. Each study or research survey will relate to one or more of the following questions:

1. Is reading motivation one-dimensional or multifaceted?

2. What effect does motivation have on reading achievement?

3. What does interest have to do with motivation?

4. What do students' beliefs about their reading competence have to do with their motivation to read?

5. What types of stress or stressors influence a student's motivation to read or not to read?

6. How can reading motivation be assessed?

7. Can nonfiction provide as much pleasure and motivation as fiction?

8. What role does choice have in reading motivation?

9. How can goal setting activate motivation to read?

You are now invited to enter my sacred collection of research studies on motivation—that is, their findings or conclusions. Rather than always listening to other people tell what researchers say, you should try the professional way of finding the information you need. True professionals, perhaps, are those who can make quick use of the library or the Internet to solve some of their teaching problems, especially the teaching of reading. So get out your notebook or highlighter and see what you can learn about motivation and reading. Let's start with the results of the most sophisticated and exciting study by Baker and Wigfield. Most of the studies after this one are considerably smaller and quicker to read.

The Many Dimensions of Motivation

L. Baker and A. Wigfield, "Dimensions of Children's Motivation for Reading and Their Relations to Reading Activity and Reading Achievement"

Results and conclusions:

■ A factor analysis of the Motivation for Reading Questionnaire confirmed an amazing variety of motivations for reading, which included these:
  1. Self-perception as an effective reader
  2. Enjoying the challenge of reading something *difficult*
  3. Curiosity about a new and different topic
  4. Involvement in a story plot or character
  5. Urgent awareness of the importance of learning to read well
  6. Need for recognition by others for skill in reading
  7. Desire for good grades in reading

■ The 10 motivation scales on the Motivation for Reading Questionnaire were endorsed by 300 fifth and sixth-grade students in a highly differential way, with very few students having the same endorsement profiles, or clusters of motivations.

My Comments: As an example of a cluster, a bright student of yours might highly endorse 5, 6, and 7—the *eager-competitor* motivation cluster, which includes an urgent awareness of the importance of learning to read well, a need for recognition by others for skill in reading, and a desire for good grades in reading. Another student might highly endorse 2, 3, and 4—*the book-lover* motivation cluster, which includes enjoying the challenge of reading something difficult, curiosity about a new and different topic, and involvement in a story plot or character. Do you see how they created a profile for each student? This study shows that children, like adults, usually have more than one way to be motivated, and those motivations often operate at the same time.

- Students who feel they are good readers and are intrinsically motivated to read appear to be the ones who read the most, according to self-reports. [Do you have any students like this?]
- Assessment of motivation to read seems to be more accurate when you look at how frequently a child chooses to read rather than looking at the student's reading achievement based on standardized scores.
- No significant relation was found between students' reading motivations and their family income. [How interesting!]
- No significant relation was found between students' reading motivations and their ethnicity. [How do you explain or feel about this finding?]

A Final Comment: Perhaps you are now convinced that the jewel called reading motivation has many sparkling facets. Some researchers, though, feel we have ignored the largest facet of all. If you will examine the next review of research, you'll see what I mean.

T. C. Urdan and M. T. Maehr, "Beyond a Two-Goal Theory of Motivation and Achievement: A Case for Social Goals"

Conclusions:

- "Research on academic achievement motivation has . . . focused on two particular types of achievement goals: task goals and ability goals. A more thorough understanding of motivation and achievement in schools can be developed if we examine *social goals* . . . in addition to task and ability goals" (p. 213).
- One social motivation for academic success is to bring honor to the student's family. Another social motivation is to maintain friendships with those peers who are also successful. The relationship between social motivation and achievement can be highly complex. [How does this relate to your own social-cultural experiences?]

My Last Comments: Highly complex, indeed, and highly individual. Let me add another social motivator, namely, family reading attitudes.

The Importance of Interest and Autonomy

L. Baker, D. Scher, and K. Mackler, "Home and Family Influences on Motivations for Reading"

Conclusions:
- Parents who are interested and entertained by their own reading habit tend to hand on that view to their children.
- Parents who emphasize reading skills rather than enjoyment tend to pass on a less favorable desire to read. [Help children to love to read, and motivation and skills will fall right in place.]
- Early childhood encounters with parents who have an attitude of enjoyment of and interest in reading tend to encourage children to read both frequently and broadly.
- Parents seem to be most attuned to their children's interest or lack of interest in reading, a concept that is "aligned most closely with intrinsic motivation" (p. 70).

My Comments: The conclusions on *interest* as a motivator tie in directly with the conclusions on *choice* as a motivator. Why is this so?

L. M. Morrow, "The Impact of a Literature-Based Program on Literacy Achievement, Use of Literature, and Attitudes of Children from Minority Backgrounds"

Results and conclusions:
- Subjects consisting of 72 Black, 62 White, 23 Asian, and 9 Hispanic second graders from 9 classrooms, 2 schools, and 1 school district were motivated by an intense literature-based program to read an average of 15 books per student between November and April.
- One of the main motivators, as indicated by interviews, was making choices, such as what to read or write and whether to read or write alone or with others. Those choices and other similar choices motivated literacy activities among advanced, slow, and special-needs children alike.
- Other high motivators were (1) being allowed to read a lot; (2) opportunities to tell felt stories, tape stories, and chalk talks; (3) the chance to read in a happy social environment.
- The teachers involved in the study changed their attitudinal stance from fear of taking too much time away from the once-called basal program to wanting literature to become an integral part of their reading program and to allowing students to make choices, thus necessarily allowing them some autonomy.

My Comments: When novelty is available for students and teachers at the very same time, the near-perfect state of motivation has been achieved.

J. T. Guthrie, "Educational Contexts for Engagement in Literacy"

Conclusions:
- Intense collaboration mixed with autonomy while learning about a topic, problem, or theme has proven to be highly motivating.
- Abundant research shows that autonomy can lead to intrinsic motivation.
- When teachers support autonomy by encouraging free expression of opinions, providing a choice of learning tasks, and inviting students to participate in decision making, students increase their commitment to learning.

My Comments: Is it possible that providing students with a daily period of autonomy, which they so desperately need in order to learn, is seen as a threat by many teachers, parents, professors, administrators, and educational publishers? If so, isn't there some way for us concerned people to move beyond this insecurity? It's interesting that the fifth and sixth graders in this study chose periods of collaboration and periods of autonomy. This is exactly the way I am motivated to write. How about you?

The Effects of Attitude and Training

B. D. Payne and B. H. Manning, "Basal Reading Instruction: Effects of Comprehension Monitoring Training on Reading Comprehension, Strategy Use and Attitude"

Conclusion: Average fourth grade readers who received metacognitive skills training had greater reading comprehension, greater knowledge about reading strategies, and more positive attitudes toward reading than children in the control group.

My Comments: *Metacognitive* often means awareness of how well you are learning. We can't generalize these results because the subjects consisted of only 20 students from the experimental classroom and 11 control students from another classroom. They represented only themselves and not a larger population. However, this piece of action research gives us a hint that the teaching of comprehension self-monitoring may lead to greater success in reading and therefore a greater sense of self-effectiveness for a reader. Let's look at more studies of this important motivator—the self-effectiveness that good readers feel. Researchers refer to those feelings as competence beliefs, self-confidence, conceptual change, self-efficacy, or self-effectiveness.

A. Bandura, "Recognition of Cognitive Processes Through Perceived Self-Efficacy"

Conclusions:

- "People who believe strongly in their problem-solving capabilities remain highly efficient in their analytic thinking in complex decision-making situations" (p. 729)—for example, deciding on the author's message.
- "Those who are plagued by self-doubts are erratic in their [motivation and their] analytic thinking. Quality of analytic thinking, in turn, determines the level of performance accomplishments" (p. 729).
- "Those who have a high sense of effectiveness visualize success scenarios that provide positive guides for performance" (p. 729). [This is very likely behavior that all of us experience when we're relaxed or "in the groove" or "in the flow."]

My Comments: Oh, the power of positive thinking—especially about yourself! No confidence, no success. No motivation, no boldness. No boldness, no accomplishments. Help your students to develop their self-confidence. Try drama of any kind. By changing their personalities through drama, kids can gain the boldness that they need. It's just like kids who stutter. If you ask them to sing what they want to say or to speak with a different accent, they do just fine. Help kids with their self-confidence, and their ability to read, write, and contribute can really soar.

A. Wigfield, J. Eccles, K. W. Yoon, R. D. Harold, A. I. A. Arbreton, C. Freedman-Doan, and P. C. Blumenfeld, "Change in Children's Competence Beliefs and Subjective Task Values Across the Elementary School Years: A Three Year Study"

Conclusions:

- The ratings of students' reading competence—based on their parents' and their teachers' perceptions, and their self-perceptions—were increasingly alike over the 3-year period. [Can you figure this out?]
- Students' beliefs in their own competence, as well as their notions of the relevance of the reading task, have a major impact on their motivation and success.
- Their prior performances as a reader, as well as the feedback provided by adults, also have a major impact on their motivation and success.

My Comments: I couldn't agree more with these last two points. Students must see the relevance of what they are asked to learn, and they must be encouraged to believe in their own abilities. We must foster both relevance and self-confidence.

What About Grades?

S. Thomas and P. Oldfather, "Intrinsic Motivations, Literacy, and Assessment Practices: That's My Grade. That's Me"

Conclusions:

- Assessment practices, especially grades, affect students' motivations to read in both a positive and a negative way.
- Grades can have the effect of reducing the self-determination of the learner.

My Comments: I have witnessed the reduction of students' self-determination: (1) having to ignore their own individual ways of learning, (2) being required to read for the purpose of answering the teacher's questions, (3) not being asked to determine what is important and relevant to them and not being able to make their own choices. As a result, they read for the grade and then forget about it.

- "Students perceived that grades shifted their goal orientations away from learning or mastery goals, toward concern with ego or performance goals. . . ." (p. 118).
- Secondary-school students felt that the emphasis on grades rather than on specific feedback made it difficult to improve their knowledge and skills.
- "Although many saw themselves as 'selling out' for grades in high school, they felt that their early experiences in elementary school. . . had some impact in supporting their continuing impulse to learn" (p. 118).

My Comments: Hats off to our wonderful elementary-school teachers!

What About Enjoyment?

Professional Standard: Recognizes the importance of literacy for personal and social growth

I have saved this research topic for last, because enjoyment seems to be so fundamental to motivation. In the long run we're all searching for joy, even those who are more motivated to get out of their present danger or misery.

I came across this last research report through the help of my colleague, Louise Fulton. For over 30 years Dr. Fulton has been involved in teaching and motivating students of great variety: "normal" elementary and high-school students, children who are deaf and blind, children with learning disabilities or behavior disorders, and university students of numerous ethnicities. Dr. Fulton was kind enough to provide me with her brief summary of a research report by a famous psychologist at the University of Chicago, Mihali Csikszentmihali (Cheek-sent-me-high-ee). Dr. Csikszentmihali is the author of several books on education and human development and has spent over 30 years studying the phenomenon of enjoyment, the *source* of motivation. Please note the depth of his research methodology and his insights into the causes of motivation and enjoyment.

M. Csikszentmihali, "Finding Flow: The Psychology of Engagement with Everyday Life"

Procedures: Csikszentmihali first interviewed people directly, face to face, from all over the world, tapping their memories of various experiences and how they felt when they were having the experiences. This provided him with many ideas about enjoyment, but the information was much too general. Consequently, he devised a research method that he called ESM, experience sampling method, which allowed him to obtain information from people at the very moment of their experiences.

Each of his research subjects was equipped with a beeper and a notebook filled with blank response sheets. From 8 to 10 times a day for a full week, he contacted each of his subjects to ask the standard questions—"Where are you now?" "What are you doing?" "Who is with you?" "Specifically, how are you feeling about yourself?" and so on.

Conclusions: There are eight key factors that make up enjoyment, or flow. [Note how similar these eight factors are to the factors of motivation that other researchers have discovered.] Csikszentmihali's eight factors include a clear goal, feedback, challenges that match skills, concentration, focus, control, loss of self-consciousness, and transformation of time.

Louise Fulton's comments:

- *A clear goal.* Why do students often get more involved in a game than in reading? Could it be that they fully understand the procedures involved in the game and know what they must do to win? Do we as teachers provide students with sufficient procedures involved in the game of reading and ways to win that game? Do we model enough to demonstrate how to play the game of learning? Do we learn right in front of them?

- *Feedback.* Why do some students spend so much of their time looking around to see what their peers are doing? Could it be that we as teachers are not arranging for all students, secure and insecure, to receive that vital input from others—that pat on the back that keeps them motivated?

- *Challenges that match skills.* Are we as teachers using our observation skills to notice whether each student is bored or frustrated or moving full-steam ahead?

- *Concentration.* Do we provide a learning environment that permits each student to truly concentrate, or do we allow students' motivation to be dissipated by noise, hostility, embarrassment, or a lack of learning tools?

- *Focus.* How often do our students become so focused on learning or reading that they forget everything else?

- *Control.* Do our students feel that they are in control of their lives in the classroom? Do they get to make enough of their own choices about books, about writing in their journals, about projects they really want to participate in?

- *Loss of self-consciousness.* Do our students feel safe from ridicule—so safe that they can be interested in reading and learning? How much energy do they have to put into being cool?
- *Transformation of time.* Does time fly for our students, or are they so uninvolved in their learning and reading that the hands on the clock seem to be stuck? Perhaps the best assessment of learning is that remark we all long to hear, "Gosh, is this class over already?"

What I've Learned About Motivation

Most students of mine have eventually become motivated learners, but only when I have consistently behaved toward them in certain ways:

1. When I have given my first attention to their basic human need for a sense of belonging and self-esteem in both the classroom and the school community. This has meant taking the time in our community life to

   - celebrate each student's progress and special talents in learning to read, write, think, and live well
   - communicate at least 90% of the time with warm, constructive, positive words and gestures
   - try to make each one of them feel my genuine affection, respect, and concern for them
   - notice their positive characteristics more than their immature characteristics
   - make the importance of each student well known to the rest of the classroom community

2. When I have consistently tried to teach my students at the appropriate level of difficulty. This has meant taking time in your classroom community to

   - check students' ability to take the next step by listening to them read aloud or contribute during discussions and by noticing their frustration or boredom
   - provide extra instruction to those who miscue with ineffective substitutes and defaults
   - help struggling readers find interesting library books at their level of difficulty
   - move students individually and gradually up the cognition scale of Bloom's taxonomy, from knowledge to comprehension to application and maybe even to analysis, synthesis, and evaluation, fully expecting my students to differ from each other in their levels of thinking and responding (much more on this in the next chapter)

3. When I have consistently found ways to provide frequent and specific individual feedback. This has meant taking time in our classroom community to

- respond specifically and promptly to comments in students' journals and portfolios, staying in each student's mode of thinking and feeling and providing all students with responses that are interesting to read
- praise specifically and immediately during discussions or book sharing, rather than relying on "Good job" and other trite forms of approval
- mentor briefly while students are writing, not only after their compositions have been completed to their satisfaction
- provide enough easy but interesting text so that feedback is intrinsically provided by the students' own successful predictions and confirmations
- teach students how to provide positive feedback and then let them work as feedback partners during repeated-reading activities
- provide students with feedback that helps them feel good about their own success rather than their ability to please the teacher

4. When I have consistently found ways to provide novelty in my presentation of ideas and in my adaptations of learning activities. This has meant taking time in our classroom community to

- share reading experiences in different parts of the classroom
- gradually vary the book sharing from groups of two to groups of three, four, and more
- vary my reading aloud to students, for example, using a prop or wearing an item of clothing that fits the style or manner of the main character in the book
- have students learn new words through games, dialogue, and miming
- read varied genres aloud to my students
- consider the interests, needs, primary language, culture, and ethnicity of every child in the classroom, providing a broad array of relevant books, materials, and decor
- let each student have a chance to lead a book discussion, literature circle, or book club
- provide a varied classroom library from which students can choose their own books and allow as much time for reading chosen books as for reading required books

Remember the four most important motivation principles:

Novelty needs level feedback.

Add *novelty* to your students' learning experiences.
Take care of students' basic *needs* for security, belonging, and self-esteem.
Teach at the appropriate *level* of difficulty.
Provide frequent and specific *feedback*.
And don't forget to keep each student involved every step of the way!

Focus-on Students with Special Needs: Comments by Louise Fulton

Prepare Students Early for the Transition to Career and Life

"I now understand the importance of beginning early to prepare students for a future life in the community. In order for this to happen, the learning experiences I provide in my classroom must have a sense of revelance. Relevance leads to motivation." So said Lorna Williams, a special education teacher in Joshua Tree, California, gateway to the beautiful Joshua Tree National Park.

At the time of this statement, Lorna Williams was a student in my graduate course on transition, a required course for every special education major, regardless of the grade level of the children they will be teaching. In this course the students study *The Transitions Curriculum* (Fulton & Silva, 1999 & 2004). This course emphasizes the importance of teaching transition skills to all students, beginning with elementary grades.

As one of the requirements, teachers taking the course must develop a project demonstrating how they are incorporating transition skills into the regular curriculum. Let's listen to more of Lorna Williams's report:

> For my project I decided to plan and implement a Work Program at my elementary school. In my new program, my students could experience what the world of work is really like.
>
> I discussed that matter with my principal and told him that I would take full responsibility for the management and operations of the Work Program. I checked with my colleagues, to see if they needed any "job" assistance in their classrooms. Over the next few days I talked with my students about the importance of learning how to fill out a job application, even if the job is in the school and the job interview is creative role playing. We also discussed how to calculate their "pay" and more important, what to do to work with others. In addition, we talked about being responsible for making choices, getting to work on time, doing a good job, and looking for other jobs which may interest them.
>
> The staff is pleased with the "workers." The students are doing a fine job with the application and interview process. I am especially pleased with the support from the staff, parents and students helping each other to remember their responsibilities. Also I'm pleased that the students cash in their checks on Fridays and exchange their pay for items in my weekly store. Oh yes, during the week, each student is required to be on time for their job, have exemplary behavior, and document their assignment in their journal. I have written the parents and informed them that we continue to have our students blend the work program with our regular academic curriculum, including State Standards: Language Arts 1.0, Listening and Speaking 2.0, Writing Applications and Strategies 1.0, Penmanship 1.0, and Written and Oral Language Conventions 1.0, 1.3, 1.4, 1.6, and 1.7. The students will be learning

(continued)

Focus on Students with Special Needs *(cont.)*

these standards during the application, journaling and interview experiences, as well as when they are on the job.

This program, as you can see, not only begins to prepare students for the real world of work, it also adds sharp relevance and very powerful motivation to the regular school program. As Moje (2000) tells us,

"Students at *all* achievement levels report feeling disconnected from the world in the confines of a school in which learning seems contrived. . . . People in the literacy movement are also concerned about the relevance of the curriculum to the lives of our students."

I guess we have a real job ahead.

Summary of Main Ideas

- Children's attitudes toward reading can greatly affect their reading achievement.
- Parents and other caretakers can have a major influence on a child's feelings about reading.
- Success in reading growth may have as much to do with the models children follow as with the specific instruction they receive.
- Parents, teachers, other caring adults, and peers are all important models for teaching reading and writing.
- Children's feelings toward reading can be influenced by a teacher's use of learning principles and teaching principles.
- Struggling readers are more responsive to extrinsic motivation, whereas successful readers are more responsive to intrinsic motivation.
- The basic needs for safety, belonging, and self-esteem must be at least partially met before academic learning can be successful.

Literacy Through Technology

A. Familiarize yourself with Internet resources you can use to create wordless books and cartoons with your students. Start by trying one of the following Web sites:

http://crayon.net/index
http://dir.yahoo.com/Entertainment/Comics_and_Animation/
http://www.multimedia.lycos.com/

Application Experiences for Your Course

A. *What's Your Opinion?* Use your own background as well as what you've learned from the textbook to defend your responses to these statements:

1. Adults can sometimes be hypocritical with children about the importance of reading.
2. The most important models for children are teachers.
3. Encouraging parents to help teach children is a mistake. They'll abuse the power you give them and create more work for you.
4. Reading out loud to children just interferes with the time they have for reading by themselves.

B. *Learning Principles.* Examine the following case studies with a partner or small group and decide what to do in each case. Determine which learning principle(s) you used in making each decision.

Minicase Study One: You are planning to show a film to your fourth-grade class to prepare them for some social studies reading they will be doing. Which of these procedures would be the most motivational?

1. Show the film without stopping and give a test at the end of it.
2. Stop the film once or twice, ask a question, have students write a brief answer, discuss the answer briefly before proceeding.
3. Show the film without stopping, ask the children if they enjoyed it, tell them that maybe you'll show another film next week.

Minicase Study Two: Which of these written comments by the teacher will lead to the greatest amount of motivation?

1. I like what you've written in your journal, Marianna.
2. You described your cat very well, Marianna. What you said about cats reminds me of my cat. He's also yellow like yours, but he likes cheese the best. I always knew that mice like cheese, but I didn't know that some cats like it.
3. This is good, Marianna, but you might like to know that *meat* is spelled with an *e* and an *a* in the middle.

Creativity Training Session

A. In a small group make a list of ways to get a 7-foot basketball player to date a 4-foot beauty whose father detests him. Make a creative plan to provide the motivation necessary for all three people.

B. Create your own comic section for a Sunday paper. You may want to do a Web search to locate sources for wordless cartoons and images that are not copyrighted. Try one of the Web sites mentioned in the technology section. Or create your own original cartoons.

C. In a small group, use one of the Web sites in the technology section to create a series of wordless cartoons or images that tell a story. After your group has created a story, use your imagination to create different versions of the story with the images. Or for another variation, swap your series of wordless cartoons and images with another group and repeat the activity.

Field Experiences

A. Create your own interview questions to gain insight into why children feel the way they do about reading. Use the questions as a foundation for a frank discussion with your students.

B. Find out the different ways your colleagues use the modeling approach to improve children's attitudes toward reading. What are some other ways you can think of to use the modeling approach?

C. What principles of learning does the teacher you're working with use to motivate children and increase their retention? How does he or she use the principles? Are there some principles to which you would give greater attention?

D. With your small group create five brand new ways to help children become motivated to learn to read better. Don't use any of the ways described in this book, but do use the concepts of motivation that you have learned. Share your ideas with others in the course. Make this a friendly competition if the majority agrees.

E. One more creative thinking project: All of you in your group have happily adopted a beautiful Guatemalan boy whose parents drowned in their attempt to bring him to America. This dear child, who speaks no English, has been here for less than a week. He's about 8 years old, and he's very shy and very frightened. You sincerely want to take care of his needs for safety, belonging, love, and self-esteem. You also want to teach him to read as quickly as possible so that he can fit into the school you have chosen for him. Beyond taking care of his needs, plan your first five steps to teach him to read. Share your plan with the other small groups.

F. Study the equation on the opening page of this chapter: expectancy × valuing = motivation. Then create three new equations about motivation. Use your information from the course but also create brand new ideas. Make it a contest if you wish. Share or defend your equations with the other groups.

References

Alexander, J., & Filler, R. (1976). *Attitudes and reading.* Newark, DE: International Reading Association.

Armstrong, M. K. (1981). Petunia and beyond: Reading. *The Reading Teacher, 35,* 192–195.

Baker, L., Scher, D., & Mackler, K. (1997). Home and family influences on motivations for reading. *Educational Psychologist, 32*(2), 69–82.

Baker, L., & Wigfield, A. (1999). Dimensions of children's motivation for reading and their relations to reading activity and reading achievement. *Reading Research Quarterly, 34*(4), 452–477.

Bandura, A. (1989). Recognition of cognitive processes through perceived self-efficacy. *Developmental Psychology, 25*(5), 729–735.

Carr, D. (1995). *Improving student reading motivation through the use of oral reading strategies* (ERIC Document Reproduction Service No. ED 386 687).

Collins, N. D. (1996). Motivating low-performing adolescent readers. *ERIC Digest.* Bloomington, IN: ERIC Clearinghouse on Reading English and Communication.

Colquitt, J. A., & Simmering, M. J. (1998). Conscientiousness, goal orientation, and motivation to learn during the learning process: A longitudinal study. *Journal of Applied Psychology, 83*(4), 654–665.

Criscuolo, N. P. (1974). Parents: Active partners in the reading program. *Elementary English, 51,* 883–884.

Criscuolo, N. P. (1983). Meaningful parent involvement in reading. *The Reading Teacher, 36,* 446–447.

Csikszentmihali, M. (1998). *Finding flow: The psychology of engagement with everyday life.* New York: Basic Books.

Davis, P. M. (1978). *An evaluation of journal-published research on attitudes in reading.* Unpublished doctoral dissertation. University of Tennessee.

Downing, J., & Thomson, D. (1977). Sex-role stereotypes in learning to read. *Research in the Teaching of English, 11,* 149–155.

Fantuzzo, J., & McWayne, C. (2002). The relationship between peer-play interactions in the family context and dimensions of school readiness for low-income preschool children. *Journal of Educational Psychology, 94*(1), 79–87.

Fulton, L., & Silva, R. (1999, 2004). *The transitions curriculum: Career management.* Santa Barbara, CA: Stanfield.

Fulton, L., & Silva, R. (1999, 2004). *The transitions curriculum: Life management.* Santa Barbara, CA: Stanfield.

Fulton, L., & Silva, R. (1999, 2004). *The transitions curriculum: Personal management.* Santa Barbara, CA: Stanfield.

Furrer, C., & Skinner, E. (2003). Sense of relatedness as a factor in children's academic engagement and performance. *Journal of Educational Psychology, 95*(1), 148–162.

Ganske, K., Monroe, J., & Strickland, D. (2003). Questions teachers ask about struggling readers and writers. *The Reading Teacher, 57*(2), 118–128.

Guthrie, J. T. (1996). Educational contexts for engagement in literacy. *The Reading Teacher, 49*(6), 432–445.

Guthrie, J. T., Wigfield, A., & VonSecker, C. (2000). *Journal of Educational Psychology, 92*(2), 331–341.

Hicks, R., & Driscoll, A. (1988). Praise or encouragement? New insights into praise: Implications for early childhood teachers. *Young Children, 43*, 6–13.

Intervention Central. (2004). *Finding the spark: More tips for building student motivation.* Retrieved from *http://www.interventioncentral.org*

Koskinen, P. S., Blum, I. H., Bisson, S. A., Phillips, S. M., Creamer, T. S., & Baker, T. K. (2000). Book access, shared reading and audio models: The effects of supporting the literacy learning of linguistically diverse students in school and at home. *Journal of Psychology, 93*(1), 23–36.

Lautenschlager, J., & Hertz, K. V. (1984). Inexpensive, worthwhile, educational—parents reading to children. *The Reading Teacher, 38*, 18–20.

Lumsden, L. S. (1994). Student motivation to learn. *ERIC Digest* 92 June.

Maslow, A. H. (1970). *Motivation and personality.* New York: Harper & Row.

McKinney, J. A. (1977). *The development and implementation of a tutorial program for parents to improve the reading and mathematics achievement of their children* (ERIC Document Reproduction Service, ED 113 703).

Moje, E. (2000). What will classrooms look like in the new millennium? *Reading Research Quarterly, 35*(1), 128–134.

Morrow, L. M. (1992). The impact of a literature-based program on literacy achievement, use of literature, and attitudes of children from minority backgrounds. *Reading Research Quarterly, 27*(3), 251–275.

Morrow, L. M. (2004, April-May). Motivation: The forgotten factor [President's message]. *Reading Today,* pp. 1–2.

Newman, A. P. (1982). Twenty lives revisited—a summary of a longitudinal study. *The Reading Teacher, 35*, 814–818.

Niedermeyer, F. C. (1970). Parents teach kindergarten reading at home. *Elementary School Journal, 70*, 438–445.

O'Donnell, A. M. (1996). Effects of explicit incentives on scripted and unscripted cooperation. *Journal of Educational Psychology, 88*(1), 74–86.

Payne, B. D., & Manning, B. H. (1992). Basal reading instruction: Effects of comprehension monitoring training on reading comprehension, strategy use and attitude. *Reading Research and Instruction, 32*(1), 29–38.

Pratton, J., & Hales, L. W. (1986). The effects of active participation on student learning. *Journal of Educational Research, 79*, 210–215.

Shuck, A., Ulsh, F., & Platt, J. S. (1983). Parents encourage pupils (PEP): An inner-city parent involvement reading project. *The Reading Teacher, 36*, 524–528.

Siebert, A. (1996). *Survivor personality.* New York: Perigee.

Skinner, E., Wellborn, J. G., & Connell, J. P. (1990). What it takes to do well in school and whether I've got it: A process model of perceived control and children's engagement and achievement in school. *Journal of Educational Psychology, 82*(1), 22–32.

Sweet, A. P., Guthrie, J. T., & Ng, M. M. (1998). Teacher perceptions and student reading motivation. *Journal of Educational Psychology, 90*(2), 210–223.

Thomas, S., & Oldfather, P. (1997). Intrinsic motivations, literacy, and assessment practices: "That's my grade. That's me." *Educational Psychologist, 32*(2), 107–123.

Trelease, J. (2001). *The read-aloud handbook* (5th ed.). New York: Penguin.

UCLA Department of Psychology. (2002). Re-engaging students in learning at school. *Addressing Barriers to Learning, 7*(1), 1–5.

Urdan, T. C., & Maehr, M. T. (1995). Beyond a two-goal theory of motivation and achievement: A case for social goals. *Review of Educational Research, 65*(3), 213–243.

Wallace, J. (1995). Improving the reading skills of poor achieving students. *Reading Improvement, 32*(2), 102–104.

Wigfield, A., Eccles, J., Yoon, K. W., Harold, R. D., Arbreton, A. I. A., Freedman-Doan, C., & Blumenfeld, P. C. (1997). Change in children's competence beliefs and subjective task values across the elementary school years: A 3-year study. *Journal of Educational Psychology, 89*(3), 451–469.

Wigfield, A., & Guthrie, J. T. (1997). Relations of children's motivation for reading to the amount and breadth of their reading. *Journal of Educational Psychology, 89*(3), 420–432.

Wilkinson, L. C., & Silliman, E. R. (2000). Classroom language and literacy learning. In M. L. Kamil, P. B. Mosenthal, P. D. Pearson, & R. Barr (Eds.), *Handbook of Reading Research* (Vol. 3). Mahwah, NJ: Erlbaum.

Winebrenner, S., & Berger, S. (1996). *Providing curriculum alternatives to motivate gifted students* (ERIC Digest E524. ED372553). Reston, VA: ERIC Clearinghouse on Disabilities and Gifted Education.

Other Suggested Readings

Borton, T. (1985). *The Weekly Reader national survey on education.* Middletown, CT: Field Publications.

Cronbach, L. L. (1977). *Educational psychology.* New York: Harcourt, Brace, & World.

Heathington, B. S., & Alexander, J. E. (1984). Do classroom teachers emphasize attitudes toward reading? *The Reading Teacher, 37,* 484–489.

Neale, D. C., Gill, N., & Tismer, W. (1970). Relationship between attitudes toward school subjects and school achievement. *Journal of Educational Research, 63,* 232–237.

Puryear, C. (1975). *An investigation of the relationship between attitudes toward reading and reading achievement.* Unpublished doctoral dissertation, University of South Carolina.

Quandt, I., & Selznick, R. (1984). *Self-concept and reading.* Newark, DE: International Reading Association.

Wittrock, M. C. (1986). *Handbook of research on teaching* (3rd ed.). New York: Macmillan.

Wood, K. D. and Endres, C. (2005). Motivating student interest with the Imagine, Elaborate, Predict, and Confirm (IEPC) strategy. *The Reading Teacher, 58*(4), 346–357.

Chapter Thirteen

Literacy in a Multi-Cultural Multi-Ability Classroom

The highest result of education is tolerance.

—*Helen Keller*

Never look down on anybody unless you're helping them up.

—*Jesse Jackson*

Animals don't hate, and we're supposed to be better than them.

—*Elvis Presley*

Thirteenth Objective for Your Teaching Success:

Foster an environment of diversity in your classroom

Even before the American Revolution the United States was far more diverse than most countries in the world. Throughout our history we have been a nation of Native Americans, European Americans, African Americans, Latin Americans, Asian Americans, Anglo Americans, and those who are gifted, average, slow, learning disabled, or at risk for various reasons—you name it. Today we live in a diverse environment with more and more categories of cultures, ability levels, and labels. Sometimes it's hard to remember that within each of the many categories there are real individuals with unique talents, highly personal interests, and distinctive ideas about how they want to live their lives.

Our classrooms, of course, are a microcosm of the diversity of the community at large. So here we are, you and I, deeply involved in the process of making sure that all of our students have an equal chance to learn and be accepted and supported. At the same time, all of our students need the opportunity to work and learn with multiple cultures (Seidl & Friend, 2002). My goal right now is to help you feel reasonably comfortable with your complicated teaching responsibilities. I know it's not easy, and that's why my empathy is yours for the taking. However, to tell the truth, I wish I could be there with you. I miss the challenge of solving problems and helping those kids who need us so much—kids like Vincent.

Vincent: An English-Language Learner

When Vincent was 7 years old, he spoke mostly Vietnamese and very little English at home. His father and mother had not been born in the United States, but in Saigon. Vincent, first known as Rang, was born on a boat in the South China Sea as he and his parents and 20 other adults escaped the reprisals of the North Vietnamese army, hoping somehow to reach America across the enormously wide Pacific. Everyone in the boat had sided with the United States and the South Vietnamese government and barely escaped with their lives. But by the time they were picked up by an American ship, three of his parents' friends had died.

Vincent's father had been the vice president of a small bank in Saigon, but when he got to America, he couldn't speak any English and felt fortunate to find work with a Vietnam veteran, who had married a Vietnamese woman while on duty. The work, which was painting cars, paid enough to provide Vincent and his parents with decent food and shelter—they were luckier than most.

When Vincent, age 7, entered public school, he had learned very little English. His mother had stayed home to take care of him and his two younger sisters and had learned only a few English words; and his father always spoke Vietnamese at home. Vincent's first-grade teacher, Mrs. Theophilus, was a loving soul. She liked his shining black hair and his cleanliness, but she had little idea of how to work with him. Most of the time she let him draw or do math, realizing that he learned numbers fast, especially with the use of manipulative aids, but thinking his English would have to be learned "the way other immigrants had learned it—the hard way."

Vincent smiled a lot, and that helped a little. But his teacher interpreted "individual effort" as requiring every child to work alone—no talking, except on the playground. Consequently, there was little opportunity for timid Vincent to learn English, except by listening to the teacher and watching exactly what she did when she said something. He seldom spoke to the teacher for fear of making mistakes with his English. And on the playground he was afraid of not being able to understand the games the other children were playing.

As time passed, Vincent gradually learned a fairly large set of highly useful English words such as *Stop!, boys, girls, McDonald's, eat, noodles, candy, more, sit down,* and *bed*. But his inexperience at stringing words into sentences made it difficult for him to write or read in English. His self-image worsened daily, and yet he was able to bolster himself at times by working hard at his drawing. If it hadn't been for the smiles he received for his pictures, it would have been a very bad year indeed.

The next year Vincent entered second grade because of his age and obvious intelligence. Vera Rubanovick, his teacher, placed him at a table with three other children, all highly verbal and friendly. On the very first day of class she explained why they were all going to be taught to learn in a cooperative way: so they could learn from each other, could work like a team, could provide feedback to each other, and could have a cultural experience.

Vincent didn't know what *cultural* meant, but Mrs. Rubanovick had grouped the children in such a way that kids at each table were truly different from each other in one way or another. According to her, "Kids are all different—and whether the differences are obviously cultural doesn't matter, as long as the children learn to respect and enjoy each other." Mrs. Rubanovick believes that teachers working in culturally diverse classrooms need to know, respect, and empower the students and view them all as capable (Hammerberg, 2004).

For the first time Vincent was provided with actual instruction in reading and writing English. The predictable patterned books that Mrs. Rubanovick used every day helped a great deal. The repetition, rhythm, and humor in those books made it much easier for Vincent to enjoy and hear the music of the language, not just the words. Daily writing in journals helped, too, especially since the teacher usually responded with short written notes that he treasured. The three other kids at his table helped him read the notes. What was even more special, these same three kids competed to have a chance to teach Vincent.

There was no specific English-language-learner program available, but Mrs. Rubanovick took the time to talk privately to Vincent in English, to put words in his mouth that he could repeat and use to communicate. She honored Vincent by learning Vietnamese phrases from him and, in general, was sensitive to his special needs. Second grade was a happy, growing year for Vincent.

Cultural Diversity

Responding to Differences

Whether cultural differences have a positive influence on classroom learning is almost entirely up to us teachers. Let me give you the bad news and then the good news. Two groups of Anglo American teachers (26 in each group) were randomly assigned to listen to one of two sets of tapes. One set consisted of tapes of five African American children whose mother tongue was Standard English. The other group consisted of five African American children whose mother tongue was an African American dialect, often referred to as Ebonics. Both groups of teachers were then asked to predict the intelligence of each student in the new class. In addition, they were asked to anticipate the students' overall academic achievement and their reading ability.

This study by Cecil (1988) indicated that the teachers expected significantly greater academic achievement, reading success, and intelligence from those children who spoke Standard English than from those children who spoke the dialect. These findings indicate a need for teachers to become aware of the negative expectations associated with speakers of nonstandard English (Cecil, 1988; Cazden, 1999).

Yes, there are a lot of differences between one culture and another, but there are often more differences *within* a culture than there are *between* two cultures. In short, we often differ within groups more than between groups, as has been known by social statisticians for decades. But the good news is that having diversity in our classrooms can bring richness, excitement, and more motivated learning.

Communicating Between Cultures

Americans profess to value individuality, yet many of our classrooms are filled with grade-level books, grade-level tests, grade-level expectations for each subject, and materials that require all students to progress through the same sequence of goals. So when some of our students do not respond to requests to write or read faster, we need to remember that their more gentle pace can easily be a cultural difference in the concept of time. And if some of them don't seem to try hard enough to win the gold medal of spelling, reading, or writing, we won't make critical remarks because we know their lack of drive for fame may be closely related to their family identity. Achievement for the family or the extended family group is often more important than self-achievement.

In the traditional Mexican American family, for example, the welfare of siblings has been and still is considered extremely important, and the Good of the Whole usually is the family motto. Parents and elders are typically highly re-

spected and serve as models for the children (Ramirez & Castaneda, 2004). And strong importance is given to family ties and to family and community needs rather than the needs of the individual.

In the traditional Japanese American family, the family, the school, the community, and the nation may all be valued ahead of the individual. In Japan, children attend mandatory school 5 days a week and half a day on Saturday. And homework keeps the children busy until evening. Japanese students are expected to move through the academic program as rapidly as their peers. If they do not keep up in school, it is assumed that they are not trying and are not following good study habits at home. Individuality is actually seen as a problem, as evidenced by a familiar Japanese expression: "The stake that sticks out is hammered down." (Fulton, 1991; Fulton & Dixon, 1993; Fulton & Silva, 1995). Japanese American students in U.S. Classrooms may show varying degrees of these traditional values.

There are many other cultural differences among our students, but to continue itemizing them runs the risk of establishing even more false expectations than already exist. The point I'm trying to make is that differences exist in the classroom because of the fascinating cultures that exist in our society. And these differences can affect the motivation each child brings into the learning environment.

When one motivational approach doesn't work with a student, the temptation is to consider that particular child lazy or deprived or in some other way inferior. If you ever find yourself feeling this way (and it happens to most of us when fatigue gets the best of us). Let me encourage you to keep in mind that it could easily be cultural differences that are interfering with the teaching-learning connection. Let's promise each other that we'll remember that those very differences can be used to enhance rather than interfere with a good learning environment.

There's so much that cultures can learn from each other. According to Grossman (2004), "Cultural pluralism is more and more important. As more and more individuals are coming into American schools from diverse cultural, linguistic, and ethnic groups, we need to respect all and increase our awareness and appreciation" (p. 140). Jiminez (2001) confirm's Grossman's remarks when he says that even though English is the expected language of America, we must take care not to give the impression that those who speak English are superior or that English is better than another native language.

Understanding Language Differences

Census data show that an increasing number of children in American schools speak a language other than English (Choi & Harachi, 2002). Now, roughly 20% of the children aged 5 to 17 speak a language other than English in their homes, an increase of 4 million children since the 1990 census (National Alliance of Literacy Coalition, 2004). And many who do speak English as their primary language don't speak the dialect called Standard English. For those who use English as a second language, educators and government officials once used the label limited-English-proficient (these individuals are now referred to as English-language learners). I hate labels, don't you? I refused to use that earlier label because it offended my beliefs about people in general and non–Anglo speakers in the specific.

On the other hand, I do like what Grant and Gomez (2001) have to say: Don't try to homogenize the current multicultural school or classroom population. Multicultural education today tries to promote *all* students' learning about multiple cultures—teaching *individuals* as well as groups to become truly competent in our diverse society.

From my viewpoint these comments apply to students of all languages—and even dialects. We still hear negative comments about people with dialects different from our own. In my traveling in the United States (all 50 of them), I have found this to be true wherever I go, although fortunately some of the comments have been made with shared humor. Since our students' languages and dialects are at the center of their self-esteem, you and I have a responsibility to model respect for *all* dialects and languages spoken in school—even those fascinating variations that Professor Higgins in *My Fair Lady* didn't like at all (it's "oww" and "gong" that put her in her place).

Are Dialect Differences Important?

An astonishing variety of people in this world use English today—not "limited English," as the labelers once called it, but one of its numerous dialects. Most people know what is meant by a language, but what is a dialect? It's simply a variation of a spoken language, a form of language that includes vocabulary and even rules (Wolfram, Adgen, & Christian, 1999). And to the person who speaks it, it's the mother tongue.

Dialects differ in three ways. First, they differ phonologically, that is, either in the way people produce phonemes or in the particular phonemes that are used. In some parts of the Deep South, for example, native speakers may say /fee-ish/ for *fish,* using a long *e* sound before the short *i* sound. In parts of Texas they might say "guh na-eet" for *good night*. And for the word *iron* my highly educated wife sometimes says "arn"—but not because she's ignorant. It's all because of diversity. Second, dialects differ grammatically, that is, in the way verb tenses, negation, number, and other structural changes are signaled. For instance, someone speaking African American English might angrily say, "'Now on, I don't be playin'!" whereas someone speaking Standard English might angrily say, "From now on, I'm not going to play!"

Third, dialects differ lexically. That is, the actual words or vocabulary may differ from one dialect to another. Someone speaking African American English may say, "Please carry me home," while someone speaking Anglo American English might say, "Please take me home." Someone in America might ask where the restroom is; someone in England might ask why you need to rest. In England and Germany you're supposed to ask for the toilet, although someone in Maine might say, "You want the flush?" Black students are often denigrated for using Black English, which is as natural for them as Standard English is for their White peers and teachers (Sanacore, 2004).

Even though dialect differences are systematic variations of a common language, Americans have spent a great deal of time making fun of each other's dialects—mostly in jest rather than ridicule. But there was so much of that going on, I decided to make fun of those who did the ridiculing. My fake newspaper release (in the Application Experiences at the end of the chapter) may help you and your older students understand something important and silly about our different dialects. And while you're at it, don't forget the Applebet story in Appendix B. It can provide a learning experience for fourth to eighth-grade students, one in which Spanish-speaking and English-speaking students can both shine and can begin to understand what language is all about.

Teaching Students in a Diverse Classroom

Professional Standard: Creates programs to address the strengths and needs of individual learners

Research shows that cooperative learning works the best (Glasser, 1986). Brandt (1988) expands on that idea: "Except for tradition, I don't know why schools use so little cooperative learning. . . . Students still sit and work alone, and are continually told to keep quiet and keep their eyes on their work" (pp. 40–41). According to Keefer, Zeitz, and Resnick (2000), cooperative learning activities are effective in teaching children to collaborate in their thinking and problem solving.

Many children of traditional Mexican descent have already become used to working with others and perceive the process of achieving as a group process rather than an isolated one. For them the learning process is easier in a cooperative setting, working with the teacher and other students rather than working by themselves. For them, learning proceeds more rapidly when peers work together or when older students help younger ones or when the teacher works with small groups that help each other.

Literature study groups and problem-solving groups can also help children and teachers appreciate the diversity of the classroom group—both similar and different viewpoints. Almost any approach to literacy instruction can work better with partners. This way students can discuss or respond to a question the teacher or a peer has posed—or read out loud together in front of a group. It works like two children in the same family at dinner time. Such partnership was found to improve Hawaiian children's reading comprehension, as well as that of Warm Springs Indian children (McGill-Franzen & Allington, 1991).

Important Reminders

Professional Standard: Respects and values cultural, linguistic, and ethnic diversity

Experienced teachers, teacher-coaches like Mary Gaborko, and colleagues like Louise Fulton have provided me with a few basic considerations that should be kept in mind:

1. The teacher needs to be the connection-maker between cultures—not only on the playground but also at times when the author and the reader have different cultural backgrounds. If there isn't a direct relationship between the text and the experience of the culturally diverse child, then it's up to the teacher to draw an analogous relationship between something in the child's life and what will occur in the text (Amalia Mesa-Bains, San Francisco Schools, personal communication).

2. The teacher needs to encourage a variety of learning styles and a variety of cultural values. Kids should be exposed to many different kinds of learning experiences: writing, acting, role-playing, and other active experiences. And lessons should be planned so that a variety of learning styles are encouraged. But even more important, you should examine your own values. Appreciation of diversity requires that you check yourself out first—multicultural bulletin boards won't do it (Susan Arroyo, Portland Public Schools, personal communication).

3. The teacher needs to help provide a common culture for children, one that appreciates diversity. The historic mission of American public schools has been to

help forge a national identity that all Americans share. And the increasing diversity of our population makes it even more imperative that our schools teach children what we as Americans have in common. . . the Thai deli in San Francisco that sells bratwurst, pizza, espresso, and tropical ice cream and the Puerto Rican bakery that makes the best bagels on the upper west side of Manhattan (Ravitz, 1992, p. 9).

A Switching, Bilingual Approach

There's another method I would encourage you to try—allowing children to use a switching approach to communicate. With this method children are encouraged to do what they often learn to do all by themselves—switch back and forth between two dialects or two languages as they communicate. This kind of bilingual communication was discouraged by some teachers in the past and still is in some schools. Children were not allowed to speak Spanish, for instance, while on the school grounds.

Code switching today is more likely to be recognized as a sign of bilingual competence, one that "enhances communication and learning among bilingual students in the classroom" (Quinterro & Huerta-Marcies, 1990, p. 307). Since it's a natural way to develop language, we should encourage code switching, not stifle or discourage attempts to communicate (Garcia, 2000). Students who are learning English as their second language often need to switch back and forth even during short conversations (Berzins & Lopez, 2002).

The Benefits of Technology

The use of technology has made it possible for many students to overcome some of their communication problems in spelling, writing, reading, listening, speaking, thinking, and imagining. Computers today allow them to check their spelling mistakes instantly without any help whatsoever. Instead of constant testing, you can use the computer for drill and practice in spelling, by connecting with one of many Web sites designed for just this purpose. And don't forget the instant availability of a thesaurus and dictionary. The time spent helping students develop some basic computer skills will be time well spent for both you and your diverse students (Castellani & Jeffs, 2001).

Computers with appropriate software can open many other doors, too (Okolo, Cavalier, Ferretti, & MacArthur, 2000). They help youngsters learn to work independently, thereby increasing their feeling of self-esteem. Not only that, students can work at their own speed—their own rate of fluency—thereby eliminating feelings of competitiveness and anxiety. And editing their own work becomes a revealing and consistent routine, providing students with a chance for perfection. Most of all, these students can get that important instant feedback they need to feel successful.

For more experienced students the computer is invaluable for composing creative stories. You can teach the strategies for planning what is to be written and outlining the sequence of the story (Kirk, Gallagher, & Anastasiow, 2003). What joy to erase our mistakes without wearing out the rubber on our pencils!

High-Quality Instruction: Four Techniques

Children who are learning a second language require the same high-quality instruction offered to kids who use English as their first (and probably only) language. Here are some instructional techniques that are particularly useful for both first- and second-language students.

Technique One: Use Predictable Language, Plots, or Explanations

If you've taken any foreign language classes, you already know the value of predictable repetition for a second-language learner. If you took a course in French, for instance, this was the type of repetition and predictability that helped you learn. Notice the frequent use of cognates like *rich* and *riche; attractive* and *attrayantly* (Rodriguez, 2001).

> Robert est francais. [Yes, Robert is French.]
> Il est blond. [You're right—he is blond.]
> Il est intelligent.
> Il est riche.
> Il est attrayant.
> Il est disponible. [Yes, he's available.]

In the same way that you learned a foreign language, children can be taught a second language. Watch as Roberto and a student teacher collaborate in preparing a personal experience chart:

> Roberto likes hot dogs.
> He likes bananas.
> He likes pizza.
> He likes cookies.
> He likes ice cream.
> He likes chocolate ice cream.

I'm not saying that a regular classroom teacher has plenty of time to spend on one-on-one teaching of the English language. I'm just saying that the value of patterned-language learning holds true for many languages. Teachers Owen Boyle and Suzanne Peregoy (1990) believe that patterned reading and writing provide scaffolds for both first and second-language learners: "The predictable patterns allow beginning readers and writers to become immediately involved. . . " (p. 196).

In addition to the predictable books that we've talked about already, you may wish to look at the classic book *Wishes, Lies, and Dreams* by Kenneth Koch (1970). This one is full of sentence patterns written by his English and Spanish-speaking students—patterns that should inspire your own students. Here are examples of similar sentence patterns created by two second graders that Boyle and Peregoy (1990) worked with, using the patterns. "I used to be . . . but now I am . . . " and also "I am the one who . . . ."

Juan:	I used to be a baby.
	But now I am really big.
	I used to be a karate ninja.
	But now I am an orange belt.
Chabela:	I am the one who like my teacher.
	I am the one who gots new shoes.
	I am the one who take care the baby.
	I am the one who plays on the swings.

Technique Two: Use Wordless Picture Books

To understand how wordless picture books can help, consider Collington's wordless picture book called *The Angel and the Soldier Boy.* Here's a description of what the pictures are showing:

> As a little girl falls asleep, her angel and soldier dolls come to life. Suddenly some pirates rob her piggy bank and kidnap the soldier doll. The angel doll eventually frees the soldier doll, and they get back from their adventure before the little girl wakes up.

The use of this wordless picture book caused a group of young English-language learners to generate some rough drafts of what was happening in various parts of the wordless story (Early, 1991, p. 249).

> *From Kenji:* The pirate ship is very big. It has tall sails and many guns. Inside the ship the pirates sleep in hammocks. They sleep with their swords and daggers. They look tough. It is dark and quiet in the ship. It looks scary.

> *From Kehn:* The pirate took the money. The soldier say stop. The pirate got his gun and pointed at the soldier. The pirate said stick up or die. The boy dropped his gun. The pirate kidnapped the soldier. The deck washer got the money. The pirates was gone with the money and the soldier left his sword behind.

Following the rough drafts, the teacher helped the English-language learners merge their various portions of text and edit the composite together. This gave the students practice in reading and rereading their own sections and the sections of others.

As Early (1991) suggests in her article, this approach can lead to many literacy experiences:

1. A class book for all first and second-language members of the class

2. A tape recording to go along with the book for other kids to hear at the listening station

3. A discussion of why different people have different versions of a wordless picture book

4. A dramatization of the book, which gives them oral practice with English

5. A what-if experience caused by changing one of the variables in the story (e.g., What if a pirate woke up while the angel doll was saving the soldier doll?)

6. A search for other wordless and regular picture books

Technique Three: Use Abundant Choral Reading

For English-language learners the use of choral reading can be like standing in the rain with a good wide umbrella over your head. It's still a little scary, but it's safe at the same time. Choral reading is a big hit with most children, and in my experience it leads to more reading and more joy in reading. It even leads to faster reading, better comprehension of text, and a decrease in oral reading miscues. Need I say more?

Technique Four: Use Multicultural Literature

Professional Standard: Recognizes literacy as a means for transmitting cultural values

If you believe in treating student diversity as a valuable experience for *everyone* in the classroom, then you'll want to select multicultural books published since 1990 (Nilsson, 2005).

It is important for you to have a classroom library, as described in Chapter 9, and to include books of appropriate age and experience levels.

A View from Saturday by E. L. Konigsburg
This Newberry Medal children's tale rivals the author's classic *From the Mixed-Up Files of Mrs. Basil E. Frankweiler.* (Ages 8–12)

Number the Stars by Lois Lowry
The evacuation of Jews from Nazi-held Denmark is one of the great untold stories of World War II. (Ages 10–14)

Walk Two Moons by Sharon Creech
The mother of 13-year-old Salamanca has disappeared. By drawing strength from her Native American ancestry, Salamanca is able to face the truth about her mother. (Ages 10–14)

Bud, Not Buddy by Christopher Paul Curtis
This story takes place during the Great Depression in the 1930s. An orphan on the run is trying to escape from abusive foster homes. (Ages 9–12)

A Year Down Under by Richard Peck
Peck is at his best with these hilarious stories that rest solidly within the American literacy tradition of Mark Twain and Bret Hart. (Ages 10–14)

Cuadros de Familia / Family Pictures by Carmen Garza
While relating remembrances of her childhood in Kingsville, Texas, near the Mexican border, the author presents an inspired celebration of American cultural diversity. The book is written in English and Spanish. (Ages 6–9)

Moon Rope/Un Lazo a la Luna by Lois Ehlert
In this imaginative Peruvian tale, Fox persuades Mole to climb with him on a grass rope to the moon. This is a Caldecott Honor winner in both English and Spanish. (Ages 4–8)

El Sombrero del Tio Nacho/Uncle Nacho's Hat by Harriet Romer, Rosalma Zubizarreta, and Mira Reisberg
In these two bilingual folk tales Anansi is rooted in the African American tradition of the Atlantic Coast region of Nicaragua. The book features both Spanish and English. (Ages 4–10)

The Bossy Gallito/El Gallo de Bodas by Lucia Ganzalez and Lulu Delacre
In this traditional Cuban folk tale we travel with Bossy Gallito to his uncle's wedding. The book features both Spanish and English.

Gathering the Sun: An Alphabetic in Spanish and English by Alma Fior Ada
This alphabetic book in Spanish and English includes illustrations and poetry that give voice to the experience of plight and pride of Hispanic agricultural workers. (Ages 4–9)

The Upside Down Boy/El Nino Cabeza by Juan Felipe Herrera and Elizabeth Gomez
Based on his own experiences, the author tells a story of a frightened, shy Hispanic boy's adjustment to an Anglo school. (Ages 4–8)

Cuckoo/Cucu by Lois Elhert
In this bilingual retelling of an old Mexican tale, Cuckoo protects the valuable seeds but loses her voice in all the smoke and soot. (Ages 4–9)

The Magic Dreidels: A Hanukka Story by Eric Kimmel and Katya Krenina
This story involves a boy, a brass dreidel dropped down a well, a goblin who procures magic dreidels that spin out latkes and gelt, and a thieving neighbor. (Ages 4–8)

Hershal and the Hanukkah Goblins by Eric Kimmel and Trina Hyman
Every year the beasties snuff out the menorah candles, destroy the dreidels, and pitch the potato latkes on the floor. (Ages 4–8)

Families Are Different by Nina Pellegrin
This story of a family composed of Anglo parents, their two adopted Korean daughters, and their dog is told in the voice of the younger daughter, Nico. There's a special kind of glue called love. (Ages 4–8)

All the Colors of the Earth by Sheila Hamanaka
This is a poetic picture book and an exemplary work of art. (Ages 4–10)

We're Different, We're the Same by Bobbi Kates
> Who better to teach young children about racial harmony than the colorful crew from Sesame Street? The rhyming text in this Sesame Street picture book celebrates the racial rainbow. (Ages 4–8)

The Color of Us by Karen Katz
> Skin colors are compared to honey, peanut butter, pizza crust, ginger, peaches, chocolate, and more, conjuring up delicious and beautiful comparisons for every tint. (Ages 4–8)

Kite Flying by Grace Lin
> A Chinese girl describes how the members of her family come together to make and fly a dragon kite. (Ages preschool–8)

Dim Sum for Everyone by Grace Lin
> In English *dim sum* means "little hearts" or "touches the heart." To this young girl, on a visit to a bustling dim sum restaurant, *dim sum* means delicious! (Ages 4–9)

For other excellent multicultural books (ages preschool, 5–7, 7–9, and 9–12), check out the list of Multicultural Books Every Child Should Know provided by the University of Wisconsin–Madison and the Colorado Department of Education state library at http://www.cde.state.co.us

Vignette

Ralph: A Student with a Specific Learning Disability

Professional Standard: Knows instructional implications of special education research on treatment of students with reading difficulties

Ralph was a 9-year-old boy who wore many invisible labels. He'd been called a struggling reader, a dyslexic, a disabled reader, a handicapped learner, and a host of other things. Ralph had straight blond hair, blue eyes, and a smile that could melt all but the sternest of teachers. His above-average intelligence was demonstrated daily by his witty remarks and his ingenious ways of getting attention. He had been considered hopeless by his regular classroom teachers and by his former Title One teacher.

Although Ralph was almost 10, he was only in the third grade; he had been held back a year. Until Miss Burnette came along, he had been the number-one troublemaker in the school. Miss Burnette was the new third-grade teacher at Jefferson Elementary School, and Ralph was enamored of her.

"Ralph has been a hyperactive child since birth," according to his mother. "He's always been more interested in fiddling with things or getting into mischief than in looking at books or talking to people. . . . He's not like his sister at all. She's much quieter and likes to read. She's been saying real words since she was 1 year old, but Ralph? Ralph didn't say his first word until he was past 2. And he's always talked so fast and mushy-like. I still have trouble understanding him."

Ralph's particular symptoms caused him to be labeled by his teachers and parents as dyslexic, a label that may not have helped him much since it didn't tell teachers what to do to help. According to Christine Gorman (2003), medical researchers have come to the conclusion that dyslexia is evidenced by an inherent difficulty in making sense of one's own phonemes. And because recognizing words is not automatic for dyslexic students, their reading tends to be slow and labored.

Ralph may or may not have had this problem. He not only read very poorly, but he also spelled atrociously, wrote illegibly, spoke haltingly with weak enunciation, and performed awkwardly in physical education class. Some might have said that Ralph was discombobulated. Others would have said that he might have a specific learning disability—so would Louise Fulton, and so would I since I was the one diagnosing him and working with him.

Ralph was not unusual. Reading problems are the most common academic difficulty experienced by students with learning disabilities. In fact, Schmidt, Rozendal, and Greenman (2002) suggest that as many as 90% of these students have reading disabilities. The specific reading problems vary, but typically these students have difficulty sounding out letters and pronouncing the words. They need specific training and practice, using strategies to help them learn those skills (Lovett, Lacerenza, Borden, Frijters, Steinback, & DePalma, 2000).

Another problem experienced by students with learning disabilities is using context effectively to gain meaning. They need considerable mentoring in using prior knowledge to understand an author's message (Coyne, Kame'enui, & Simmons, 2001). In addition, they frequently attend to small details in what they're reading instead of focusing on main ideas (Hardman, Drew, & Egan, 2005). But again, careful mentoring, scaffolding, and other learning strategies can lead to much more organized learning.

Ralph's Particular Problems

According to the Federal definition, *specific learning disability* means a disorder in one or more of the basic psychological processes involved in understanding or using language, spoken or written. Such a disability manifests itself in an imperfect ability to listen, think, speak, read, write, spell, or calculate. The term includes perceptual handicap, brain injury, minimal brain dysfunction, dyslexia, and developmental aphasia. The term does not include learning problems that are primarily the result of visual, hearing, or motor handicaps, mental retardation, or emotional disturbance.

Thus, Ralph could have a specific learning disability and therefore qualify for special education services. But Ralph would have to be tested extensively before we could refer to him as having a specific learning disability.

Let's review some of Ralph's characteristics. He had average or above-average intelligence, so he didn't have mental retardation. But he did have an imperfect ability to listen, think, speak, read, write, and spell. He didn't have a motor handicap, but he did have awkwardness, poor coordination, and definite signs of hyperactivity. The more I helped and studied Ralph, the more I realized he was practically swimming in energy. His energy was so great he had to constantly keep moving, a sign of severe hyperactivity, and his movements were often awkward and lacking in coordination. From what we could have observed, Ralph might have been considered to have specific learning disabilities, indeed.

Given even average intelligence, there was a great discrepancy between what Ralph should have been doing and what he was doing on measures of reading and writing performance. In October, a month after I met Ralph, I noticed that his grade-equivalent score on a standardized reading achievement test was 2.1, whereas the norm for his age and stage was 4.2. On a standardized diagnostic inventory, his reading score was 1.5. Yet both of these standardized scores, as low as they were, overestimated his reading performance, according to the Title One teacher in his building. On an informal reading inventory, for instance, Ralph had reached frustration level while reading a preprimer passage.

On weekly spelling tests Ralph had been getting 3 or 4 out of 15 words correct, until Miss Burnette decided to give him only 6 words a week. Then he sometimes got 5 or 6 correct. In mathematics he often surprised me and his other teacher with his understanding of operations and his reasoning ability, but he usually made so many silly mistakes on his computations that he scored poorly on assignments and tests. This fact made me feel that he understood the concept of simple multiplication but had little motivation to fiddle with the math operations. Consequently, he made a lot of mistakes and probably lost self-confidence. "In science," Miss Burnette said, "Ralph is a whiz—as long as he can experiment with things rather than read about them." The content of his written compositions showed a degree of creativity, although he had to translate his illegible writing for his teacher.

Figure 13.1 shows a sample of Ralph's writing in response to a field trip he took along with several other children who work with Ms. Benjamin, a new special education teacher. I had previously built a darkroom for her with black plastic so she and her students could develop the photographs she had taken of them. Ralph was excited to assist in the development process but had trouble focusing on the exact procedure. When he wrote about this experience later in the day, he produced what you see in the figure.

We took four pans and we had fun and Mr. May put plastic all over me and a boogie monster was in the black. The boogie monster he hit me and I kicked him and the boogie monster was right beside Terry. The four pans were full of junk and we had a machine and we had a piece of cardboard and there's a magic trick that put it on the cardboard. The end.

In stark contrast here's how another student in Ralph's group interpreted the same field trip:

How We Made Our Pictures in Group 7

Ms. Benjamin took our pictures. Then she opened the film can in the darkroom. She took the film out of the can and wound it on the reel. Then she put it in the tank. Then we put the developer in the tank. We put the cover on the tank and shook it for seven minutes. We took the cap off and poured it out. We then poured in the stop-bath. We shook it for three minutes. Then we poured it out. We took the reel out of the tank and washed all the chemicals out. We hung it up to dry . . .

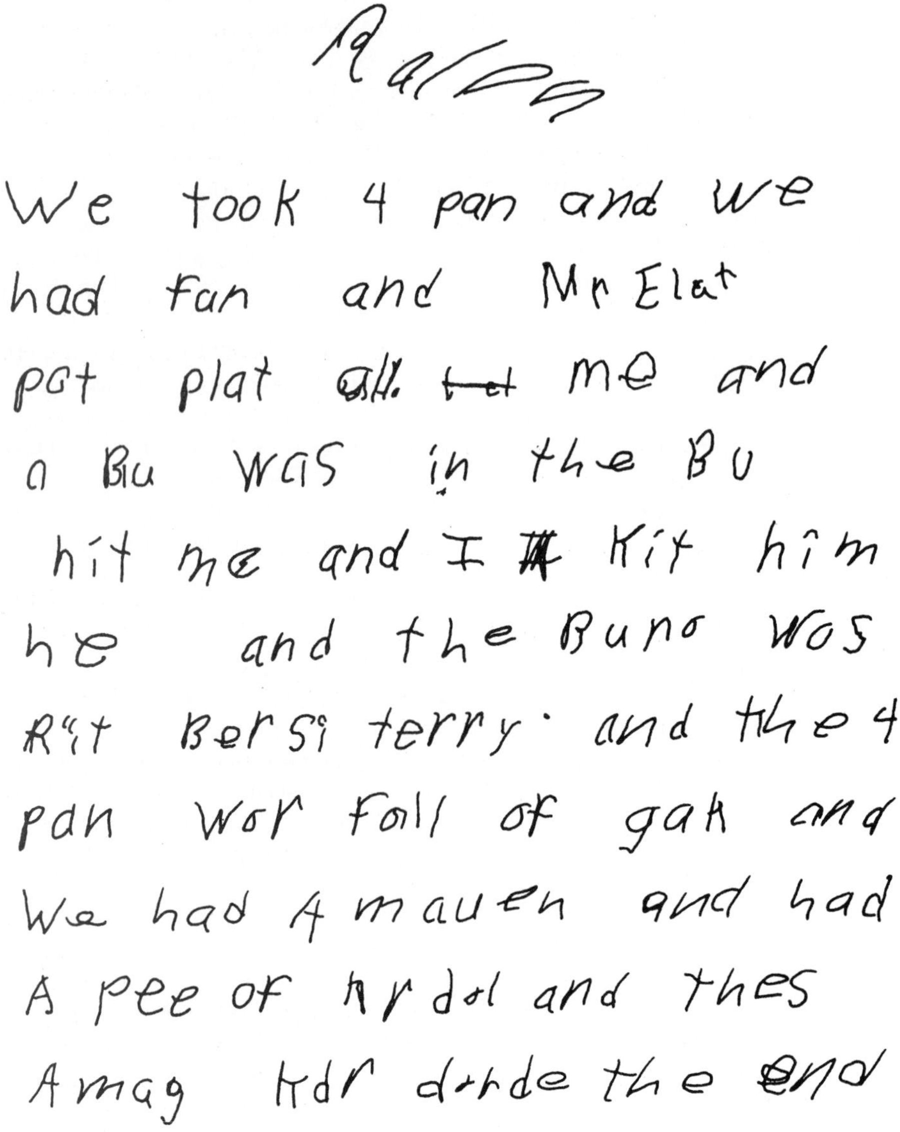

Ralph

We took 4 pan and we
had fan and Mr Elat
pot plat all. tet me and
a Bu was in the Bu
hit me and I # Kit him
he and the Buno was
Rit Bersi terry. and the 4.
pan wor foll of gah and
We had 4 mauen and had
A pee of hrdol and thes
Amag hdr drhde the end

FIGURE 13.1 A language-experience story created by Ralph.

A Question of Concentration? My Findings

At that time in his life, Ralph had difficulty not only with the mechanics of writing but also with writing about his own experiences. His teachers felt that most of the problem came from his inability to concentrate, especially when he was asked to write. Concentrating on the details of developing photographs, for example, may have been an arduous task. When it came time to record his experience in writing, the additional concentration that it required seemed to be too much.

Saying that a student doesn't concentrate might be an old-fashioned excuse for not really understanding the student. The question I had to ask was *why* Ralph didn't concentrate. Let's look at his behavior again and see if we can answer that question. Here are the behaviors I noticed when I was working with Ralph as a reading specialist:

- Very distractable and therefore too eager to go on to another experience
- Couldn't sit still
- Very impulsive
- Loved to make up distracting stories instead of reading or writing
- Short attention span, measured by seconds rather than minutes
- Charming and cheerful
- So full of energy he simply had to keep using it
- Clever
- Awkward in P.E.
- Generally quite excessive in most of his activities

So why was he so reluctant to read and concentrate or focus? Talk about it with your peers. This is a good chance for you to analyze, diagnose, and apply the knowledge gained so far from this book and your experiences.

In November I administered the Slingerland Screening Tests for Identifying Children with Specific Language Disability. This battery of tests seemed to prove to Ralph's teacher that his reading problem was due to poor visual and auditory memory. Such problems with memory are often observed among children with specific learning disabilities who have difficulty with thinking processes. Let's take auditory memory as an example. This sentence was read to Ralph: "He saw this first girl." Ralph wrote: "He scr ther gur feir."

These problems with auditory and visual memory showed up most when I administered my RAD Test (a rapid assessment of disablement), which teachers find easy to use because it's more of a game than a test. In this test Ralph had to write the words rather than select them from among alternatives, as he had to do with the Slingerland Tests. With visual memory, for example, he was shown the word *thundering* for a few seconds and was then told to write it himself after the card was taken away. He wrote *t-h-u-e-n-d-r-o-n-b*. For a 6-year-old this wouldn't have been bad. For a child almost 10, it was below what you and I would have expected.

I would recommend that you now look at the Observation Checklist in Appendix J and the RAD Test in Appendix K, both of which are suitable for a classroom teacher to use quickly without special training. Keep in mind that trying to find out the exact causes of children's language problems has generally not been helpful in directing efforts to improve their reading and writing abilities (Hardman, Drew, & Egan 2005). My suspicion is that you will often be situations where you can't do anything to change the *causes*.

The Problem with Labels

What you can do, though, is accommodate students like Ralph through your caring classroom environment, your skillful teaching procedures, and your refusal to label. As Sternberg and Grigorenko (2001) state, "Too often, labeling is used in place of understanding. We label a child, pretending that somehow the label gives us an understanding when it does no such thing" (p. 336). Ralph was labeled in a variety of ways, but intelligent teachers treated him with respect and understanding, a goal that can be found in the IRA Standards for Reading Professionals (see Appendix A for more information).

In Ralph's case we did talk about the federal guidelines for defining a specific learning disability. But what I hope you'll get from this is the fact that definitions are necessary only for identification purposes—so that students can become eligible for special education services. It is you and I who can see the very specific problems that a student is dealing with. And we can also see that some of the problems are not so different from those of other students who have *not* been labeled.

Ideas to Assist Students with Learning Disabilities

1. Focusing on learning strategies such as organizing, summarizing, using mnemonics, and problem solving can offset some of the difficulties.

2. When the learning disability is severe, such as with dyslexia, teaching compensation skills is important. Modified textbooks can be obtained from Recordings for the Blind and Dyslexic in Princeton, New Jersey.

3. Small-group instruction has been found to be effective with students with learning disabilities.

4. Direct instruction—involving explicit step-by-step instruction, immediate self-correction of errors, gradual fading, practice, and review—can be an effective teaching technique.

5. Cooperation between the designated classroom teacher and the resource room teacher, for specific one-on-one instruction and team teaching, can be of benefit to the student.

6. Demonstration, modeling, and frequent feedback are necessary supports for success.

7. Make directions concrete, specific, short, and easy to understand.

8. Give students frequent breaks to use up excess energy and reduce stress, especially if attention spans are short.

9. Teach from the concrete to the abstract.

10. Provide students with questions to guide reading comprehension.

11. Preview the key vocabulary in reading assignments but concentrate on the concepts behind the words.

12. Adjust the time allocated to assignments, as well as their length. Gradually increase the challenge as students grow more confident.

13. To increase interest and relevance, provide a variety of interesting experiences.

14. Have students work in small cooperative groups and with partners that can support each other.

15. Monitor students' understanding of directions.

16. Demonstrate learning strategies and monitor to make sure students are applying them correctly.

17. Use technology effectively. Although learning to use a computer may be difficult, it will pay off by giving students help with their difficulties (e.g., spell-check, organizing, revising).

18. Have students make their own dictionaries.

Ralph's Gradual Success

Miss Burnette and Ms. Benjamin, both very caring teachers, weren't afraid to try their own ideas with Ralph. After his first successfully written experience story, he proudly read it with ease to his reading teacher, Ms. Benjamin. Ralph was so thrilled by his success and the praise he received, he spruced up his courage and asked his regular classroom teacher, Miss Burnette, if he could read it to the class.

Ralph read his story beautifully, and the children—even those who had once laughed at him—were stunned. Spontaneously, without any signal from the teacher, they clapped loud and long. Some even slapped him on the back and told him what a good reader he was. He was welcomed into the literacy club at last.

Ralph wasn't the same person after that moment of success. He started thinking of himself as a reader. And with the help of caring, affectionate teachers, he eventually became just that.

Children at Risk of Failure

When educators have talked about children at risk, they have often meant economically poor children who have had below-average opportunities to learn what is needed for success in school. However, the term *at risk* has gradually broadened to include a host of other obstacles to children's success in becoming literate. Each year 600,000 children are exposed to alcohol, and 40,000 children are born with some degree of alcohol-associated damage. Each year over 700,000 expectant mothers use one or more illicit drugs during pregnancy—usually cocaine (March of Dimes, 2003). And 500,000 children are homeless in any given year (National Law Center, 1999). Close to 12 million, or 16% of the children in the United States, are now living below the poverty line (U.S. Census Bureau, 2003). In addition, many children are the victims or prejudice of abuse. All of these difficulties can have a negative effect on concentration and the ability to monitor aggressive impulses.

The connection is close between children at risk and those identified as either English-language learners (Ell) or children with learning disabilities. Many Ell children are at risk of failure at school. Many children have been disabled through drugs and alcohol. All of these children are at risk of failure at school and in the community.

Let's spend a little time talking about teaching/learning ideas that apply to all three groups of children—those labeled at risk, Ell, or learning disabled. Your students with those kinds of obstacles have several things in common: They often experience a damaged self-concept. They are nearly always in a position of having to learn something through the medium of a written language that they perceive as confusing (and often meaningless). And they can easily feel left out, or abandoned. Both instruction and the classroom atmosphere need to compensate for these special feelings and learning blocks.

Ways to Help Your Students Improve Their Self-Concepts

Professional Standard: Adapts instruction to meet needs of different learners to accomplish different purposes

Matthew Ignoffo (1988) explains why we need to attend to these issues: "I have discovered that any remedial training that deals solely with content and not with self-confidence improvement is doomed to fail. . . . The student's own inner critic sabotages any possible improvements in content study. . . ." So what can we do about it?

1. *Encourage children to encourage each other.* Praise students specifically for this behavior. In Ruus School in Hayward, California, I watched a child run to the back of the classroom to write a comment on a chart with the heading Things to Praise Our Friends For. This child wrote, "I like the way Bobby kept our group from fiteing today. He was real nise about it."

2. *Avoid comparisons with other students.* Help students see that they are valued not for their reading status but for their status as interesting and worthwhile human beings. As Price (1992) put it:

   > We may argue that instilling self-esteem is no business of the schools, but we are deluding ourselves if we think there isn't a link between self-esteem and achievement. . . . If schools are to succeed for millions of children at-risk who lack adequate support at home and in the community, then educators simply must fill this void in the children's lives. (p. 211)

3. *Use other bases besides reading difficulty for flexibly grouping students.* Also have literature interest groups, integrated-theme teams, and cooperative learning groups.
4. *Help your students observe their own progress.* Use portfolios, individual conferences, self-records of books read, and collaborative miscue analyses.
5. *Help each student become an expert on something.*
6. *Change instructional approaches when one is not working.* Don't expect your students to adjust to your approach.
7. *Give students plenty of time and opportunities to demonstrate to others what they have learned.* Don't just rush on to the next higher level of difficulty. Plateaus are important, even for experienced hikers.
8. *Find materials easy enough for students to feel challenge as well as success.*

9. *Collaborate with parents on strengthening a student's self-concept.* Aim for a consistent uplift from home and school.

10. *Take story dictation from a student occasionally*—by yourself or with an aide, parent, caregiver, student teacher, or older peer. Type up the story, read it to the class, and ask them to guess who the author is. If they don't guess correctly in three tries, say, "Will the real author please stand up?" Let the other students tell three things they liked about the story. Preserve the story in a portfolio for parents or in a class book.

11. *Bring in adults for students to identify with.* Have the adults read a story to the students and talk about how they use reading and writing in their work and play.

12. *Form a strong bond with each student.* Everyone needs to feel a sense of relatedness in the classroom, with both teacher and peers.

13. *Teach students to be proud of their work.* Have high expectations for them and insist on completed assignments of high quality.

14. *Encourage your students to be brave enough to make choices and to take responsibility for those choices.* This will help them develop feelings of self-determination, belonging, and self-esteem.

15. *Urge students to participate in after-school and extracurricular activities and sports.* This keeps them actively communicating and interacting with others and keeps them away from TV.

16. *Present ideas for after-school projects*—particularly those that also relate to the curriculum. For example, they might investigate the kinds of problems they have in their neighborhoods. Or students in two different neighborhoods might count the number of cars, walkers, and bicycles that pass their homes and then report their results to the class.

The Carbo Approach to Literacy

Marie Carbo (1987) discusses the need to give unequal learners an equal chance: "Many poor readers are predominantly global, tactile, and kinesthetic learners" (p. 198). By *global* she means that these children often learn better when they can progress from the whole to the part, just the opposite of many phonics programs. Coles (1985) and Poplin (1998) present a similar argument.

Carbo (1987) recommends teaching strategies for these children that are similar to those you and I have already discussed: Use whole-text selections that inspire high interest and high emotional involvement. In one of the most impoverished at-risk school situations I've seen, the introduction of literature was given credit for a sudden rise in achievement. The 1-year improvement in percentile scores for second graders was 14 percentiles for the literature schools and 3 percentiles for the control schools (Roser, Hoffman, & Farest, 1990.)

Here's what Carbo (1987) recommends for emphasizing the tactile and kinesthetic learning modes: (1) computers, (2) typewriters, (3) active games, (4) drawing, (5) writing, (6) pantomime, (7) verbal drama, (8) puppets, and (9) following written directions for making things. Can you see that good teaching, the kind you use with all kids, is just what is needed by these children with special obstacles to learning?

Making Reading Meaningful

Children of all ages and abilities who are becoming literate need to feel that the process is meaningful.

The Language-Experience Method

One of the best ways to bring meaning into the process is through dictating or journaling about students' own experiences. Nothing is more meaningful to children than their own experiences, their own ways of looking at those experiences, and their own ways of expressing themselves. By capitalizing on events that occur in the classroom, on the playground, and in and out of school, teachers can help children record their own experiences, their own stories, their own ideas—while at the same time developing reading materials that make sense.

Ralph, our potentially able kid, was particularly fond of using the tape recorder to dictate his own stories, having someone transcribe them, and then reading them himself the next day. Like most children, Ralph seemed genuinely thrilled to see

his own creations in print, and he invariably received pleasure from reading them to others. Had the same stories been written by someone else and given to him to read, he would not have been able to read them. But because he had written them himself and because they were based on his own direct or imaginary experiences, he could read them with considerable skill (relative to his normal reading).

I'll admit that much of this reading was based on memory at first, rather than on precise decoding. Nevertheless, Ralph was receiving excellent practice on the type of mature reading that his adult friends wanted him to master. And even more important for Ralph, reading became a purposeful act—it made sense to him.

Adding Meaning Through Writing

For students having difficulty learning to read well, whatever their ages, the writing process can add considerable meaning and awareness. Just as we learn to appreciate pottery making by making it ourselves, we learn to appreciate what writers are saying by writing it ourselves. Wong-Kam and Au (1988) believe that writing is the prime ingredient of a program to help bring struggling readers into the community of readers and writers. What this means, as you no doubt remember from our earlier discussion, is dictating to peers, aides, caregivers, parents, or teachers; share-reading that dictation; and then writing and reading personal compositions. All of these various writing experiences can lead to improved reading and understanding of what authors are saying.

Making Reading Personal

As I said before, many struggling readers feel left out or even abandoned. Their sense of belonging is weak because of numerous failures to communicate, to acquire lasting friendships, and to achieve in the ways their peers are achieving. Perhaps even more than children who are achieving at normal levels, these unequal learners need someone who cares for them and is concerned enough to give them the extra time it takes to help them learn to read and write—someone who will help them stop feeling so inferior.

Their bad luck in being struggling readers in the first place may be exacerbated in school, where they often can't get enough help when they need it. As a result, their self-concept deteriorates, they withdraw rather than risk further failure, and learning to read becomes a meaningless, impersonal, and chaotic experience. This is a major challenge for all of us teachers.

Vignette

Anne Marie: Gifted Learner

Anne Marie was born to loving and bright parents. Added to her genetic inheritance was an early environment ready-made for an eager and curiosity-driven disposition. Some people, of course, would have called that environment impoverished—no bustling city even close, a town of fewer than 3,000 souls, and no readily accessible neighbors or playmates. Furthermore, Anne Marie's parents were not well off financially; her father had lost his job as a teacher, and her mother's part-time work produced "only a few shekels," as she put it.

Anne Marie's playmates were limited to her two younger brothers, but these companions, outgoing and full of I-dare-you-to's, provided stimuli galore, a Caddie Woodlawn experience. And with her adventurous spirit Anne Marie often took those dares and outdid her brothers in feats of courage. They, in turn, with seldom a grudge, made her the unofficial leader of their little gang—her inventive imagination and organizational genius making her a shoo-in for the position. Their very young sister would have voted twice if there'd been an election; instead, she became the perfect student for this natural-born teacher.

Anne Marie's parents and grandparents were avidly interested in the children's education but didn't rely on the local schools alone to provide it. Nor did they rely on a town library—especially since there was no town library. Instead, they filled the house with books of all sorts, used books they could ill afford—12 volumes from *My Book House* series, to give just one example. And they read these books with their children from the time Anne Marie could climb into the nearest adult lap.

Her parents didn't stop with books, though. Trips were important, too. "Educational trips," her mother called them—to the fish hatchery, to the cheese factory, to the huge kitchens of Welch's Grape Corporation. Her parents didn't use the word *schema*, but they knew how to develop such things. Books . . . educational trips . . . and people—lots of people.

When she was still 2, Anne Marie was taught the alphabet by the adults and older children who often crowded into her warm and friendly house. She quickly learned her ABCs by heart—and in the correct order. She learned them verbally, that is. It took her until she was 3 to be able to write them—and to get all the letters correct. The main one she had trouble with was *elemeno*. (Somehow she had convinced herself that *l-m-n-o* was a single letter, and this slowed her down a little.)

Deprived of television and Sesame Street (her parents thought TV was a waste of time and money), Anne Marie taught herself how to write words by pestering

Mother, Dad, Gramma, Grampa, and Uncle Richmond for instant feedback on her paper-and-pen attempts. Well before her fourth birthday she could write her first, middle, and last name. And by age 4 she could read several thin books by herself—not just say the words but read them.

Anne Marie had a lot she wanted to learn, and she waited to get into school like a puppy waits to be fed. There was no kindergarten in the school district budget, but by taking tests and getting her mom to badger the principal, she was able to enter first grade shortly after her fifth birthday.

During the next several years in school Anne Marie often had to compensate for her disillusionment; it wasn't half as exciting as she'd imagined it to be. Yet her active mind didn't allow her to dwell on disappointment or boredom: Even though the school work was often too easy, the group dynamics were always complicated and fascinating to her. In the sixth grade it was especially so as Mr. Jeremiah intrigued her with his amazing strategies for getting the rowdy kids to behave.

In addition to watching a master teacher at work, Anne Marie had another way of dealing with curricular disappointment. When the mobile library van came to school, which it did every 2 weeks, she excitedly selected her six allotted books and dashed back to the classroom. There she proceeded to conceal one of them behind a social studies or science text and to gobble it up whole. By the end of the 2 weeks she would have read each of them at least three times.

Who Are the Gifted?

Because of a federal and state regulation, Anne Marie was classified by her school district as talented and gifted. When speaking to other teachers, Mr. Jeremiah would refer to her fondly as "my TAG kid." But who really are the gifted children? We know that academic ability is certainly not the only indicator of giftedness (Ritchhart, 2001).

With Anne Marie as our prize example, we can observe a high level of personal intelligence and creativity, which seems to continue as long as teachers and other educators encourage these traits. But we can also observe these same qualities in highly diverse situations. What a shame that culturally diverse and economically deprived students are seriously underrepresented in school programs for gifted and talented students (Esquivel & Hotz, 2000).

What Researchers Recommend

Gallagher and Gallagher (2003) suggest four curriculum modifications for students who are gifted:

- **Acceleration**—moving students faster through traditional curriculum
- **Enrichment**—reading biographies of scientists or historical figures, writing short stories, or poetry

- **Sophistication**—mastering the structural properties of a play, debating values, or politics
- **Novelty**—rewriting a play or story by giving it a different ending, writing new words for a familiar song

In addition to acceleration, enrichment, and development of special talents, Davis and Rimm (2004) suggest these best practices for culturally diverse gifted students:

- Celebrate ethnic diversity
- Provide extracurricular cultural enrichment opportunities
- Address and accommodate differences in learning styles
- Encourage parents to participate in support groups
- Provide access to good models (p. 53)

Tips for Success

Since highly creative students seem to be challenging for some teachers to work with, I have asked special education expert Louise Fulton to help me concentrate on special ways of working with them. Consider these suggestions from the two of us:

- Because these children tend to be autonomous in temperament, they usually thrive on opportunities to make important decisions that affect their lives.
- They welcome the chance to choose their own books to read rather than being limited to the next story in the basal anthology.
- They like to choose from a wide variety of ways to share and respond to the books they have read on their own.
- They like to present or write critical evaluations or comparisons of books.
- They want to plan their own schedule of work and, in general, to guide their own ship whenever possible within the school setting.

Dr. Fulton and I have been working on a different way of teaching students of diverse abilities and cultures. Let's let her tell you about it.

Differentiated Instruction

Are you struggling with the problem of meeting the academic needs of every single student in your diverse classroom? Are you also struggling with the problem of meeting all of their literacy needs? Frank and I would like to give you some ideas that have worked for us through the years.

To meet the academic needs of all our students, we need to work on their *intellectual development,* which is what we truly want to do—and our state standards require us to do.

When we use that term, "intellectual development", we're talking about such scholastic things as the ability to read and write, to search for information, to sift and cull that information, to evaluate its worth, and to present it to others, like teachers or peers.

So how are we going to get all of our diverse students to do all of that when many of them are simply not ready for such a daunting, intimidating challenge? Frank and I have solved this problem individually in the past and know that we can help you solve it in the present. We would like to give you three ideas that we call, in jest, the May-Fulton Plan:

- First, use Bloom's Taxonomy of Educational Objectives, which provides you with a structure within your diverse classroom community that allows every child a chance to contribute to the learning projects you set up to meet your students' needs and the state's professional and content standards.
- Second, use Bloom's Taxonomy of Educational Objectives to provide your students with six levels of intellectual development, which they need in order to master your goals and theirs (Anderson & Krathwohl, 2001; Bloom, 1984; Bloom, Englehart, Furst, Hill, & Krathwohl, 1956).
- Third, in order to communicate and function as a diverse learning community, use a cooperative learning process in which children can help each other learn.

A Sample Literacy Project Plan

Let's imagine that you're teaching a second to fourth-grade unit in physical science (although what we're demonstrating is appropriate to almost any grade level). The topic is Five Simple Machines, and the concept you need to teach to meet a content standard is this: Machines are used to apply either pushes or pulls to make things move, and these pushes or pulls are called *forces*. More specifically, you're going to teach about the nature of simple machines so that your students can begin to understand and appreciate how our complex, fabulous machines work. So let's see how you can *engage* every one of your students—of different cultures and academic levels.

Bloom's First Level: Knowledge

Students working at the knowledge level search for information, facts, data, details, and specifics. You can have these students do such things as name, recall, define, label, repeat, record, list, and memorize (see Figure 13.2). The knowledge level is where you might want to have some of your least experienced students learn and work in small groups during this particular project. They can concentrate on finding those small but valuable bits of knowledge, like what the names of the five simple machines are (i.e., the wheel and axle, the wedge, the lever, the pulley, and the inclined plane).

Your students learning at this level will also be asked to learn exactly what those machines look like. So *observation, drawing,* and *finding pictures* will be some of the major skills they will use. How to spell and pronounce the names of the five simple machines will also be of concern, so they can proudly report back to the rest of

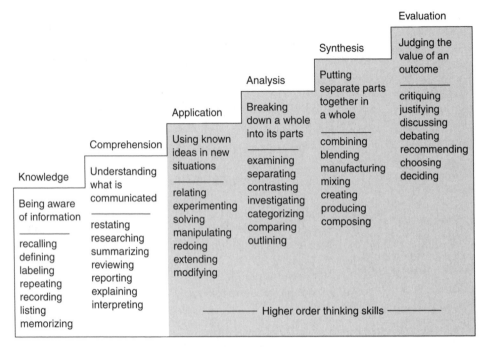

FIGURE 13.2 Six levels of intellectual development.

the class. Be sure to *introduce* each person in each group as students give their brief reports to the "community."

Bloom's Second Level: Comprehension

This group will be responsible for understanding the way each simple machine works. You would want students at this level to read and write about one or more of the simple machines or, if necessary, to dictate what they've learned to you or an aide. You'll want to help this group prepare to give a scientific report about the differences among the simple machines—in their own words if possible.

The pictures and drawings found by students working at the knowledge level are crucial and should be shared as quickly as possible with the comprehension group. In this way the students will have to learn how to meet a project deadline, a word they can then proudly use.

Bloom's Third Level: Application

This level requires *higher order thinking skills* (see Figure 13.2). Application includes things like actually demonstrating the use of one of the simple machines (perhaps a small lever to open a jam jar) or applying a simple machine to a different problem from the one it was made for (maybe a shoe horn?). The students who work at this more advanced level can talk to the class about the use of one or more of the tools, after drawing (or borrowing from the knowledge group) a picture of the tool(s) to help explain how a particular simple machine works. More than anything else, though, this group should actually apply one or more of the simple machines to solving a real or imaginary problem. Then they should write about their efforts and report them to the class after the knowledge and comprehension groups have reported.

Bloom's Fourth Level: Analysis

Words used at the analysis level include *examination, study, discovering, finding cause and effect, breaking down or separating into parts* (e.g., a tool or machine or the beginning, middle, and end of a written report). The use of compound words like *applesauce* (*apple* + *sauce*) or *classroom* (*class* + *room*) and many others described in chapter 3 can help explain the concept of analysis, that is, separating and examining each part. All the work words like *investigate, contrast,* and *investigation* should be learned and shared like jewels of honor. Let the children feel important about their new knowledge.

Students working at this analysis level might want to demonstrate how a doorknob works by taking it apart, showing that it's an example of a wheel and axle, and then handing out their written explanations to their peers to read and edit. Above all, students in this group should analyze exactly how each simple machine seems to work. Question-and-answer sessions can be used to keep the entire classroom community interested.

Advanced students can be given the challenge of analyzing an author's way of writing (e.g., Dr. Seuss). Let them use the word *analyze* in as many ways as they can. Have them think about what other things should or can be analyzed. They might also analyze the table of contents, graphs, and charts in a science book. And what about analyzing a more sophisticated machine that is made up of two or more of the five simple machines?

Bloom's Fifth Level: Synthesis

This level includes the act of *combining, blending, manufacturing, mixing, creating, producing*—all words like this that these students should learn. The advanced group that works at this level can do things like creating a *new* simple machine or combining two or three of the simple machines—and reporting verbally and in writing what they have been doing. Creative producing is the name of the game at this level, so encourage these eager students, starting with the five simple machines and branching off into brand new projects.

Don't forget, though, literacy is always a major ingredient in these learning experiences. At this level there should be an even broader creative use of the four methods of communication: creative writing, creative speaking, creative reading out loud, and creative and intensive listening and responding to the speakers who come to your classroom.

Bloom's Sixth Level: Evaluation

This level of intellectual development includes student determination of the *value* of what they have learned and done—assessing the *quality* of their work and judging the *depth* of their new understandings. The group that is working at this level can concentrate on explaining how the five simple tools have made possible the construction or creation of buildings, cars, better tools, and better kitchen equipment. This will require a good deal of reading and/or listening to tapes and experts.

Students at this level can carry on self-evaluation of their learning progress in reading and writing, in creative and critical thinking, and in whatever else you and your students target. They should also learn to critique each other's work in a professional manner. But be sure to have a celebration at the end of each major classroom project!

Other Applications

This has been just one example of what can be accomplished in a classroom with abundant diversity, using Bloom's levels of intellectual development to differentiate instruction. Another possibility would be to apply the same content-standards approach to a social science unit, such as a study of the major Native American nations in your region of the United States. There are projects galore that could fit right into Bloom's structure e.g., describing the national identities of the American Indian nations (knowledge level) understanding their religious beliefs (comprehension) imitating their customs (application) dividing their government into separate leadership duties (analysis) making a collection of their folklore (synthesis) and critiquing the quality of their government or method of living (evaluation).

And don't hesitate to use Bloom's taxonomy in other discussions and interactions with students. When you ask students questions at their probable levels of success, every student has an equal chance to participate and gain confidence. And active involvement in discussion is critical for you to see how each student is doing—and how well you are teaching.

To encourage each student's success, which is a top priority, we have found that it's a good idea to start with homogeneous groups, each one working at a given level of intellectual development on the same project. However, once students succeed, learn, and feel more confident about working and communicating in groups, you can move them into more heterogeneous groupings. In this way less skilled students can learn from students who are more experienced, and the more experienced students can continue to develop higher cognitive skills by helping a fellow student or learning to see something differently. As a result, heterogeneous groupings can become more accepted by students and teachers alike.

A Community of Cooperation

So now you understand Bloom's taxonomy and the way it allows every student to contribute to learning projects. And we've given you some clear examples of how to use this approach to work on specific content standards in your classroom.

To complete the May-Fulton Plan, you need to combine the Bloom method with plenty of cooperative learning (Johnson & Johnson, 1999). With cooperative group activities your students can learn how to work cooperatively, become fully engaged and involved, and enjoy the support of their peers in either their heterogeneous groups or their homogeneous project groups. Teamwork among changing groups has a strong tendency to build group pride as well as individual pride.

Arrange your project-level groups in such a way that each child can contribute to a particular project group. Try not to have the same project-level groups for every project, but let students move among the six levels depending on their success at the present level or their level of interest in a new project. After their project work, students need to return to their heterogeneous home groups, which can be changed every 2 or 3 months.

Be sure these heterogeneous groups do not have the most experienced kids in one group and the least experienced kids in another. Mix the students so that they can learn from each other and have a chance to relate to their heroes and heroines in the class. These cooperative groups can provide an excellent opportunity to teach respect for differences. And since each student is unique and has something different to offer, everyone can have a chance to shine.

You can organize your students in small heterogeneous groups of three or four, depending on their experience. At the same time you can build a cooperative learning community in your classroom. Plan your cooperative group activities carefully, and continually monitor students' learning. Move from group to group to provide support and encouragement. In this way you not only can teach your students how to work cooperatively but also can be sure that all students are participating and learning.

Tips for Success

Start your cooperative groups with an interesting concrete task, such as making a collage with pictures and text cut from magazine pages or creating the tallest tower with lots of soda straws and marshmallows. Once students have mastered the important skills needed to work cooperatively, you can easily move on to more complex tasks, such as the simple machine project.

With diverse groups of students, you absolutely must build a classroom community. Teach your students to learn together and to praise and respect each other. Most of all, make sure *all* your students feel important and know that they belong. If at all possible, follow Frank's rules for learning: Novelty needs level feedback. And don't forget his extra rule for teaching—get everyone engaged all the time. It's a continuing challenge, but you now have a plan to make it happen. John Blanc, a teacher in Apple Valley, California, comments on the challenge and the reward:

> My greatest challenge is helping every one of my students stay connected with the curriculum, while at the same time making sure that what we are working on is not too easy or too difficult for them. I want all of my students to feel successful. There are days when I feel like I'm in a boat rowing upstream with only one paddle. But there are other days when it all comes together and I feel like the teacher of the year! And those days make it all worth it!

Old and New Teaching Techniques for Diverse Students

Back in Chapter 5 we shared numerous ways to teach the 100 most frequently used words in the English language and ways to relate those teaching techniques to the Spanish language. In Chapter 6 you learned how to develop the vocabulary of both English-speaking students and Spanish-speaking students who are learning English. We planned for your students to learn three sets of functional words related to food, clothing, and living spaces. And in this chapter we've talked about a plan to teach all students in a diverse classroom: utilizing the structure of Bloom's taxonomy of learning, building learning projects around the six levels of intellectual development, and creating a cooperative learning community in which children can help each other learn, in spite of their diversity.

A Final Bundle of Ideas for Teaching in a Diverse Classroom

Before we go our separate ways, I want to provide you with still more ideas for success in your teaching of diverse students. First, let's keep in mind that English-language learners, on the average, can develop conversational skills in about 2 years, but it takes as long as 5 or more years for them to perform as well academically as native English-speaking peers (Collier & Thomas, 1999).

Second, body language is crucial. When you're conversing with Spanish-speaking students or other English-language learners, your body language, facial expressions, gestures, intonations, and many other cues can help them pick up the meaning of what you're saying. If you sit like a block, you'll block their enthusiasm and understanding. And if your facial expression or body language shows displeasure, your message may be misinterpreted.

Third, when you're tempted to speak in academic English, prepare your diverse students by providing them with pictures or other visual images. Motion pictures, of course, help a great deal. But every now and then, stop the film and talk with the whole class about the plot, the characters, and their reactions. This approach can be used with very young children all the way up to high school students.

Fourth, prepare your students for reading with the same care you used in preparing them for a film. Let them know exactly what their purpose should be when they read. If your class is largely bilingual, rely a great deal at first on well-known stories common to both cultures. Common-culture stories can make a great difference in developing your classroom community. And as you probably already know, there are now many books for children that have both Spanish and English text side by side.

Fifth, follow the advice of McCauley and McCauley (1992) and use choral reading. It allows Spanish and English students to learn from each other without becoming embarrassed.

> Choral reading involves the recitation of a poem or other short text, along with motions and gestures that help the students dramatically act out the meaning. The many repetitions of choral reading a selection provide an opportunity to recycle the language. The dramatic gestures and motions students should be encouraged to make provide contextual clues to the meaning of the poem or story. (p. 24)

As you can imagine, choral reading is perfect for kindergartners all the way up to eighth graders.

Sixth, Li and Nes (2001) found that paired reading also works very well. Just pair English-language learners with a skilled reader, who will read a portion of text aloud while the language learner reads along. My own experience and that of my graduate students have shown me that this method works just fine for Grades 3 through 8, but not always so well for younger students in K–2, who may not have enough self-confidence to work together.

Seventh, most students benefit from simultaneously reading and listening to audiotaped stories. Casbergue and Harris (1996), for example, found that audiobooks are very effective in thoroughly engaging students who are not yet hooked on print. And if you can't find exactly what you want for particular students, it's not very difficult to make your own by reading the book into a tape recorder. High school students are often available to make tapes for you (it's cool).

Eighth, don't forget what you learned in Chapter 2 about that thing called *schema,* which refers to the minitheories that children develop because of their experiences. When my daughter, Shauna, was 5, she developed a schema about how her daddy drove a car. I was taking home a plastic swimming pool on the roof of the car and had my left arm out the window, trying to hold on to it. Naturally, a strong wind came along and jerked it out of my grasp. And naturally, I found that to be distracting and ran over a neighbor's tree. Shauna did learn how to drive a car later, but her schema was rather warped for several years.

Ninth, don't ask your English-speaking or Spanish-speaking students to read without first tapping into their schemas, which allows them to understand abstract words. If children come to you without a full set of concrete experiences, you'll need to provide more experiences for them. If you don't, they'll be left to their own resources to get by and will count on memorizing. If you are teaching young Asian children, here are two schema-building folktales for them: *Red Is a Dragon* and *Round Is a Mooncake* by Roseanne Thong.

Tenth, people are more likely to think abstractly when they've had a lot of related experiences (Berk, 2000; Eggen & Kauchak, 2004). For example, if you're having your students read about someone on a boat, make sure you help them conceptualize the particular kind of boat, how someone drives a boat, and what might happen if the story calls for a wreck or some other brand new schema. Remember, also, that students from two different cultures may interpret what they're reading in very different ways.

Eleventh, try interactive writing (McCarrier, Pinnell, & Fountas, 2000), in which you, as teacher, share a pen in writing about a similar experience that you and a student have both had. Here again, you might invite high school students to participate, especially those who are planning on becoming teachers.

> The idea is to help children attend to powerful examples that can enable them to learn something about the writing process that they can incorporate into their own writing. As children gain control of the process, the examples and areas of focus shift. (p. 11)

Twelfth, by all means use the language-experience method. Have your students work together to write a story about an experience they've had either together or separately in the past. They don't actually have to write it; they can just gather around a writing area and dictate it for you to write on butcher paper so they can read it again and again. You can write the first (and later the final) sentence, but let each student take a turn dictating the next sentence. Be sure to write the story in large letters so they can all see it from wherever they are sitting later on. Just think of the written language they can all learn with this method. Think of the spoken language they can all learn or practice. And think of the reading and listening going on every few seconds. (If you don't use this method, I guess I'll just have to fire you.)

Thirteenth and finally, devote yourself to read-alouds. They're one of the answers to help your students develop their vocabulary. Freeman and Freeman (2000) found that when teachers used read-alouds three times a day for a week, the group vocabulary scores rose by 40%. "The key was finding interesting books and coaching teachers to use reading techniques such as pointing to pictures, gesturing, and paraphrasing . . . to be sure students understood the story" (p. 123).

Farewell

Good-bye, dear reader. You would be surprised at how often I've felt like I've really been talking with you, personally. I hope you will put into practice the things we've been talking about. If you do, I'm sure you'll find your students becoming eager learners, and that's what teaching is all about. I wish you success.

Summary of Main Ideas

■ One out of five people in the United States speaks a language other than English at home.

■ Research shows that cooperative learning activities are effective in teaching students to collaborate in their thinking and problem solving.

■ Literature study groups can help students and teachers appreciate the diversity of the classroom group, especially when predictable literature is used.

■ Technology has made it possible for all students, with or without disabilities, to read, write, spell, listen, speak, think, and imagine.

■ It's important to use multicultural literature at times as well as English literature.

■ Learning disabilities are labels more than problems. Teachers should observe much more than they label.

■ Reading problems are the most common academic difficulty experienced by students with learning disabilities, but learning difficulties can sometimes be caused by the teacher.

■ Students should work in small cooperative groups and with partners who support them.

■ Instructional needs common to English-language learners and learning disabled or at-risk students enable teachers to use similar teaching strategies for all three challenges.

■ Global, tactile, and kinesthetically oriented students often learn better when they can progress from the whole to the parts.

■ Writing is the prime ingredient of a program to help struggling readers in a diverse classroom.

■ Gifted learners have an extra drive to make their own choices and decisions.

■ Bloom's Taxonomy of Educational Objectives provides teachers with six flexible, fluent levels of student development to use in a diverse classroom of multicultural and multiability students.

Literacy Through Technology

A. Go to http://www.readwritethink.org and examine the Web Resource Guide developed as a joint project between the International Reading Association and the National Council of Teachers of English. Take the time to become familiar with this very useful resource. Then select five sites of greatest interest to you and be prepared to share them with the class, explaining how you plan to use them in your teaching.

B. Evaluate your technology skills and develop a plan you can share with one of the small groups in your university class about how you will gain more experiences and teaching skills. Use at least two assessment procedures shown in Chapter 11.

Application Experiences for Your Course

A. Take Bloom's six levels of intellectual development and create questions that match each of the levels. The questions should be limited to Grades 4 to 8 and should be related to the dialects story that follows. Let each small group of three or four university students write and speak their questions in a way that also matches the dogalect tale.

Zoologist Says Dog Yaps Make Sense: Making Fun of Dialects
by Frank B. May

LONDON (EPI)—A zoologist from Oxherd University claims to have deciphered the yelps, snarls, and bays of canines. Dr. Feline, who has been studying dog speech for years, says that dogs communicate with each other by means of a very elaborate set of noises, which he has dubbed "fanguage."

After traveling through various parts of the world, Dr. Feline has come to the conclusion that there are at least 3,000 different fanguages. "Furthermore," he states, "most dogs understand only one or two fanguages, resulting in a great deal of confusion, misunderstanding, and dog fights."

Not only are there a great variety of fanguages, but each fanguage has a number of dogalects, or variations within a fanguage. A hound in one part of a large city, says Dr. Feline, may woof a dogalect that differs in many respects from the dogalect woofed in another part of the city. Curs from these two parts of the city can usually communicate to some extent, but they find the experience either irritating or amusing. Dr. Feline has observed, moreover, that each canine acts as though its dogalect is superior to all other dogalects.

Dogalects differ not only among geographical regions, says Dr. Feline, but also between canine classes within a region. The upper-class dogs (i.e., pedigreed animals and those who strive to be like them) woof a different dogalect from that of the lower-class dogs (i.e., mutts, mongrels, and tramps). For example, the upper-class dogs in London woof, "Grr rowlf urr yelp," whereas the lower-class dogs woof "Grr rowlf orr yelp."

According to Dr. Feline, this slight difference is enough to cause frothing of the mouth by upper-class and lower-class dogs alike.

B. Be sure to learn important words as they relate to this chapter: analysis, application, cooperative learning, diversity, learning disability, multicultural, multiability, differentiated instructional, global, tactile, kinesthetic.

Creativity Training Session

Develop a creative problem-solving activity to be used with a small cooperative learning group of your students. Plan who should be in the heterogeneous group of diverse learners. (The diversity arrangement is best when you have diverse cultures *and* abilities.) Also, plan to have your young students discuss how to achieve good communication in the group as equal partners—across cultures, languages, interests, and strengths. Use what you've already learned in this course about communication and working in cooperative learning groups.

Field Experiences

A. Of the 13 chapter objectives presented in this book, select the 3 for which you need the most improvement in your teaching. Use both creative and critical thinking to design an improvement plan. Share your thoughts with people in your small group and/or your professor.

B. Of the 13 chapter objectives presented in this book, select the 3 that you are in the process of mastering as teaching skills right now. Playfully and creatively brag to your small group about what you have mastered as a teacher. Then use your critical thinking abilities to playfully challenge your peers' bragging.

References

Anderson, L., & Krathwohl, D. (2001). *A taxonomy for learning, teaching, and assessing: A revision of Bloom's objectives.* Boston: Allyn & Bacon.

Berk, L. (2000). *Child development* (5th ed). Needham Heights, MA: Allyn & Bacon.

Berzins, W. P., & Lopez, A. E. (2002). Planting the seeds for biliteracy. In M. de la Luz Reyes & J. J. Halcon (Eds.), *The best for our children: Critical perspective on literacy for Latino children* (pp. 81–95). New York: Teachers College Press.

Bloom, B., Englehart, M., Furst, E., Hill, W., & Krathwohl, D. (1956). *A taxonomy of educational objectives: The classification of educational goals: Handbook 1. The cognitive domain.* White Plains, NY: Longman.

Bloom, B. (1984). The search for methods of group instruction as effective as one-to-one tutoring. *Educational Leadership, 47*(8), 4–17.

Boyle, O. F., & Peregoy, S. F. (1990). Literacy scaffolds: Strategies for first and second language readers and writers. *The Reading Teacher, 44,* 194–200.

Brandt, R. (1988, March). On students' needs and team learning: A conversation with William Glasser. *Educational Leadership,* 38–44.

Carbo, M. (1987). Deprogramming reading failure: Giving unequal learners an equal chance. *Phi Delta Kappan, 69,* 197–202.

Casbergue, R. M., & Harris, H. H. (1996). Listening and literacy: Audio-books in the reading program. *Reading Horizons, 37,* 48–59.

Castellani, J., & Jeffs, T. (2001). Emerging reading and writing strategies using technology. *Teaching Exceptional Children, 33*(5), 60–67.

Cazden, C. B. (1999). Forward. In C. Ballenger, *Teaching other people's children: Literacy & learning in a bilingual classroom* (pp. vii–viii). New York: Teachers College Press.

Cecil, N. L. (1988). Black dialect and academic success: A study of teacher expectations. *Reading Improvement, 25*(1), 34–38.

Choi, V., & Harachi, T. W. (2002). The cross-cultural equivalence of the Suinn-Law Asian Self-Identity Acculturation Scale among Vietnamese and Cambodian Americans. *Journal of Social Work Research and Evaluation, 3,* 5–12.

Coles, G. S. (1985). *The learning mystique: A critical look at learning disabilities.* New York: Pantheon.

Collier, V. P., & Thomas, W. P. (1999). Making U.S. schools effective for English language learners (Part 1). *TESOL Matters, 9*(4), 1–6.

Coyne, M. D., Kame'enui, E. J., & Simmons, D. C. (2001). Prevention and intervention in beginning reading: Two complex systems. *Learning Disabilities Research and Practice, 16*(2), 62–73.

Davis, G., & Rimm, S. (2004). *Education of the gifted and talented* (5th ed). San Francisco: Allyn & Bacon.

Early, M. (1991). Using wordless picture books: To promote second language learning. *ELT Journal, 45,* 246–251.

Eggen, P., & Kauchak, D. (2004). *Educational psychology: Windows in classrooms.* Upper Saddle River, NJ: Prentice Hall.

Esquivel, G. B., & Hotz, J. C. (Eds.). (2000). *Creativity and giftedness in culturally diverse students.* Cresskill, NJ: Hampton Press.

Freeman, E. E., & Freeman, Y. S. (2000). *Teaching reading in multilingual classrooms.* Portsmouth, NH: Heinemann.

Fulton, L. (1991). Transition from school to regular lives in the community: A study on rehabilitation trends in Japan [In Japanese]. Tokyo, Japan: Japanese Society for Rehabilitation for the Disabled.

Fulton, L., & Dixon, V. (1993). Interviews with mothers of handicapped school learners in Japan. *Journal of the Division of International Special Education and Services, 3,* 30–34.

Fulton, L., & Silva, R. (1995). *Transition from school to life in the community: Empowering children with special needs around the world.* Madison, WI: Monograph of the International Association of Special Education.

Gallagher, J., & Gallagher, S. (2003). Curriculum modifications for students who are gifted. In S. Kirk, J. Gallagher, & N. Anastasiow, *Educating exceptional children.* Boston: Houghton-Mifflin.

Garcia, G. (2000). Bilingual children reading. In M. L. Kamil, P. B. Mosenthal, P. D. Pearson, & R.Barr (Eds.), *Handbook on reading research* (Vol. 3, pp. 815–834). Mahwah, NJ.: Erlbaum.

Glasser, W. (1986). *Control theory in the classroom.* New York: Harper & Row.

Gorman, C. (2003). The new science of dyslexia. *Time, 162*(4), 52–59.

Grant, C. H., & Gomez, M. E. (2001). *Campus and classroom: Making schooling multicultural* (2nd ed.). Columbus, OH: Merrill/Prentice Hall.

Grossman, H. (2004). Students who are culturally and linguistically diverse. In M. Mastropieri & T. Scruggs, *The inclusive classroom: Strategies for effective instruction.* Columbus, OH: Pearson/Merrill.

Hammerberg, D. D. (2004). Comprehension instruction for socially cultural diverse classrooms: A review of what we know. *The Reading Teacher, 57*(7), 648–650.

Hardman, M., Drew, C., & Egan, M. W. (2005). *Human exceptionality: School, community and family* (8th ed.). Boston: Allyn & Bacon.

Ignoffo, M. (1988). Improve reading by overcoming the "inner critic." *Journal of Reading, 31,* 704–708.

Jimenez, R. T. (2001). Literacy and the identity development of Latina/o students. *American Education Research Journal, 37,* 971–1000.

Johnson, D., & Johnson, R. (1999). The three C's of school and classroom management. In R. Freiberg (Ed.), *Beyond behaviorism* (pp. 119–145). Boston: Allyn & Bacon.

Keefer, M., Zeitz, C., & Resnick, L. (2000). Judging the quality of peer-led student dialogues. *Cognition and Instruction, 18*(1), 53–81.

Kirk, S., Gallagher, J., & Anastasiow, N. (2003). *Educating exceptional children.* Boston: Houghton-Mifflin.

Koch, K. (1970). *Wishes, lies and dreams: Teaching children to write poetry.* New York: Perennial Library.

Li, D., & Nes, S. L. (2001). Using paired reading to help ESL students become fluent and accurate readers. *Reading Improvement, 38*(2), 50–61.

Lovett, M. W., Lacerenza, L., Borden, S., Frijters, J. C., Steinback, K. A., & DePalma, M. (2000). Components of an effective remediation for developmental reading disabilities: Combining strategy-based instruction to improve outcomes. *Journal of Educational Psychology, 92,* 263–283.

March of Dimes Foundation. (2003). Quick reference fact sheets. Retrieved from *http://www.marchofdimes.com*

McCarrier, A., Pinnell, G. S., & Fountas, I. C. (2000). *Interactive writing: How language and literacy come together, K–2.* Portsmouth, NH: Heinemann.

McCauley, J. K., & McCauley, D. S. (1992). Use choral reading to promote language learning for ESL students. *The Reading Teacher, 45,* 526–533.

McGill-Franzen, A., & Allington, R. L. (1991). The gridlock of low reading achievement: Perspectives on practice and policy. *Remedial and Special Education, 12*(3), 20–30.

National Alliance of Literacy Coalition. (2004). *Literacy USA: Statistics.* Retrieved from *http://www.naulc.org/*

National Law Center on Homelessness and Poverty. (1999). *Homelessness in the United States and the human right to housing.* Retrieved from *http://www.nlchp. org/pubs/*

Nilsson, N. L. (2005). How does Hispanic protrayal in children's books measure up after 40 years? *The Reading Teacher, 58*(6), 534–558.

Okolo, C., Cavalier, A., Ferretti, R., & MacArthur, C. (2000). Technology, literacy, and disabilities: A review of the research. In R. Gersten, E. Schiller, & S. P. Vaughn (Eds.), *Contemporary special education research* (pp. 179–250). Mahwah, NJ: Erlbaum.

Poplin, M. S. (1998). The reductionist fallacy in learning disabilities: Replicating the past by reducing the present. *Journal of Learning Disabilities, 21,* 389–400.

Price, H. B. (1992). Multiculturalism: Myths and realities. *Phi Delta Kappan, 74,* 208–213.

Quinterro, E., & Huerta-Marcies, A. (1990). All in the family: Bilingualism and biliteracy. *The Reading Teacher, 44,* 306–312.

Ramirez, M., III, & Castaneda, A. (2004). Values. In D. Norton, *The effective teaching of language arts* (6th ed., pp. 498–499). Upper Saddle River, NJ: Pearson/Merrill/Prentice Hall.

Ravitz, D. (1992). A culture in common. *Educational Leadership, 49*(4), 8–11.

Ritchhart, E. S. (2001). Excellence with justice in identification and programming. In N. Coalangelo & G. A. Davis (Eds.), *Handbook of gifted education* (p. 149). Boston: Pearson Education.

Rodriguez, T. A. (2001). From the known to the unknown: Using cognates to teach English to Spanish speaking literates. *The Reading Teacher, 54,* 744–746.

Roser, N. L., Hoffman, J. V., & Farest, C. (1990). Language, literature, and at-risk children. *The Reading Teacher, 43,* 554–559.

Sanacore, J. (2004). Genuine caring and literacy learning for African American children. *The Reading Teacher, 57*(8), 744–753.

Schmidt, R. J., Rozendal, M. S., & Greenman, G. G. (2002). Reading instruction in the inclusion classroom: Research based practices. *Remedial and Special Education, 23*(3), 130–140.

Seidl, B., & Friend, G. (2002). Learning authority at the door: Equal-status community-based experiences and the preparation of teachers for diverse classrooms. *Teaching and Teacher Education, 18,* 421–433.

Sternberg, R. J., & Grigorenko, E. (2001). Learning disabilities, schooling, and society. *Phi Delta Kappan, 41*(3), 335–338.

U.S. Census Bureau. (2003). *Census 2000 Supplemental Survey.* Retrieved August 25, 2004, from http://www.census.gov

Wolfram, W., Adgen, C. T., & Christian, D. (1999). *Dialects in schools and communities.* Mahwah, NJ: Erlbaum.

Wong-Kam, J. A., & Au, K. H. (1988). Improving a fourth grader's reading and writing: Three principles. *The Reading Teacher, 41,* 768–772.

Other Suggested Readings

Barchers, S. (2004). Judge for yourself: Famous American trials for readers' theatre. Portsmouth NH: Teacher Ideas Press.

Fuchs, L. S., Fuchs, D., & Compton, D. L. (2004). Monitoring early reading development in first grade: Word identification fluency versus nonsense word fluency. *Exceptional Children, 71*(1), 7–21.

Helm, J., & Beneke, S. (Eds.) (2003). *The power of projects: Meeting contemporary challenges in early childhood classrooms—strategies and solutions.* New York: Teachers College Press.

Hui, K., & Yahya, N. (2003). Learning to write in the primary grades: Experiences of English language learners and mainstream students. *TESOL Journal, 12*(1), 25–31.

Jacobs, J., Mitchell, J., & Livingston, N. (2005). 2004 U.S. children's literacy award winners. *The Reading Teacher, 58*(4), 398–406.

Lenters, K. (2005). No half measures: Reading instruction for second language learners. *The Reading Teacher, 58*(4), 328–336.

Livingston, N., & Kurkjian, C. (2004). Literature links: Expanding ways of knowing. *The Reading Teacher, 58*(1), 110–118.

Mohr, K. (2004). English as an accelerated language: A call to action for reading teachers. *The Reading Teacher, 58*(1), 18–26.

Mulholland, R. (2005). Woodshop, technology, and reading! *Teaching Exceptional Children, 37*(3), 16–19.

Sloyer, S. (2003). From the page to the stage: The educator's complete guide to readers' theatre. Portsmouth, NH: Teacher Ideas Press.

Appendixes

Appendix A

International Reading Association Revised Standards for Reading Professionals

Developed by the Professional Standards and Ethics Committee of the International Reading Association

Knowledge and Beliefs About Reading

1 Theoretical Base	Related Chapters in This Text
The reading professional will	
1.1 Recognize that reading should be taught as a process	1, 2, 3, 4, 7, 8, 9, 11
1.2 Understand, respect, and value cultural, linguistic, and ethnic diversity	2, 5, 13
1.3 Recognize the importance of literacy for personal and social growth	1, 2, 4, 12
1.4 Recognize that literacy can be a means for transmitting moral and cultural values	2, 5, 9, 13
1.5 Perceive reading as the process of constructing meaning through interaction of the reader's existing knowledge, the information suggested by the written language, and the context of the reading situation	1, 2, 6, 10
1.6 Understand the major theories of language development, cognition, and learning	1, 2, 3, 4, 7, 8
1.7 Understand the impact of physical, perceptual, emotional, social, cultural, environmental, and intellectual factors on learning, language development, and reading acquisition	1, 2, 7, 9, 12

2 Knowledge Base	**Related Chapters in This Text**
The reading professional will	
2.1 Understand that written language is a symbolic system	1, 2, 3, 4
2.2 Understand the interrelation of language and literacy acquisition	1, 2, 4, 6
2.3 Understand principles of new language acquisition	1, 2, 6, 7
2.4 Understand the phonemic, morphemic, semantic, syntactic, and pragmatic systems of language and their relation to the reading and writing process	3, 4, 10
2.5 Understand the interrelation of reading and writing and listening and speaking	2, 11
2.6 Understand that students need opportunities to integrate their use of literacy through reading, writing, listening, speaking, viewing, and representing visually	2, 4, 10, 11
2.7 Understand emergent literacy and the experiences that support it	2, 3, 4
2.8 Understand the role of metacognition in reading and writing and listening and speaking	7, 10
2.9 Understand how contextual factors in the school can influence student learning and reading (e.g., grouping procedures, school programs, and assessment)	2, 11, 12, 13
2.10 Know past and present literacy leaders and their contributions to the knowledge base	1, 2, 9
2.11 Know relevant reading research from general education and how it has influenced literacy education	All
2.12 Know classic and contemporary children's and young adults' literature and easy-reading fiction and nonfiction for adults, at appropriate levels	3, 6, 8, 9 and Appendix N
2.13 Recognize the importance of giving learners opportunities in all aspects of literacy (e.g., as readers, writers, thinkers, reactors, or responders)	All
2.14 Understand that goals, instruction, and assessment should be aligned	All

3 Individual Differences	**Related Chapters in This Text**

The reading professional will

3.1 Recognize how differences among learners influence their literacy development	2, 5, 6, 7, 11, 12, 13
3.2 Understand, respect, and value cultural, linguistic, and ethnic diversity	5, 6, 7, 13
3.3 Understand that spelling is developed and is based on students' knowledge of the phonological system and of the letter names, their judgments of phonetic similarities and differences, and their ability to abstract phonetic information from letter names	1, 2, 3, 4, 5, 6
3.4 Recognize the importance of creating programs to address the strengths and needs of individual learners	5, 6, 7, 8, 10, 11, 12, 13
3.5 Know federal, state, and local programs designed to help students with reading and writing problems	All

4 Reading Difficulties	**Related Chapters in This Text**

The reading professional will

4.1 Understand the nature and multiple causes of reading and writing difficulties	2, 5, 6, 8, 10, 12, 13
4.2 Know principles for diagnosing reading difficulties	2, 3, 4, 11
4.3 Be well versed on individual and group instructional interventions targeted toward those students in greatest need or at low proficiency levels	6, 7, 8, 11, 12, 13
4.4 Know the instructional implications of research in special education, psychology, and other fields that deal with the treatment of students with reading and learning difficulties	3, 4, 6, 9, 10, 11, 12, 13

5 Creating a Literate Environment	**Related Chapters in This Text**

The reading professional will be able to

5.1 Create a literate environment that fosters interest and growth in all aspects of literacy	3, 4, 5, 6, 7, 8, 9, 11, 12, 13
5.2 Use texts and trade books to stimulate interest, promote reading growth, foster appreciation for the written word, and increase the motivation of learners to read widely and independently for information, pleasure, and personal growth	3, 6, 9, 10

5.3	Model and discuss reading and writing as valuable, lifelong activities	2, 3, 9, 10
5.4	Provide opportunities for learners to select from a variety of written materials, to read extended texts, and to read for many authentic purposes	3, 6, 9, 12, 13
5.5	Provide opportunities for creative and personal responses to literature, including storytelling	3, 6, 9, 12, 13
5.6	Promote the integration of language arts in all content areas	6, 8, 9, 10, 12
5.7	Use instructional and information technologies to support literacy learning	All
5.8	Implement effective strategies to include parents as partners in the literacy development of their children	12, 13

6 Word Identification	**Related Chapters in This Text**

The reading professional will be able to

6.1	Teach students to monitor their own word identification through the use of syntactic, semantic, and graphophonemic relations	2, 3, 6
6.2	Use phonics to teach students to use their own knowledge of letter/sound correspondence to identify sounds in the construction of meaning	2, 3, 4, 6
6.3	Teach students to use context to identify and define unfamiliar words	2, 6, 9
6.4	Guide students to refine their spelling knowledge through reading and writing	4, 5, 6, 9, 10, 13
6.5	Teach students to recognize and use various spelling patterns in the English language as an aid to word identification	3, 4
6.6	Employ effective techniques and strategies for the ongoing development of independent vocabulary acquisition	6, 7, 8

7 Comprehension	**Related Chapters in This Text**

The reading professional will be able to

7.1	Provide direct instruction and model when and how to use multiple comprehension strategies, including retelling	6, 7, 8, 10, 11
7.2	Model questioning strategies	7
7.3	Teach students to connect prior knowledge with new information	2, 6, 7

7.4 Teach students strategies for monitoring their own comprehension	7
7.5 Ensure that students can use various aspects of text structure and genres, figurative language, and intertextual links	2, 3, 4, 6, 7, 9, 10
7.6 Ensure that students gain understanding of the meaning and importance of the conventions of standard written English (e.g., punctuation or usage)	2, 4, 10, 11

8 Study Strategies

Related Chapters in This Text

The reading professional will be able to

8.1 Provide opportunities to locate and use a variety of print, nonprint, and electronic reference sources	8, 9, 10, 12, 13
8.2 Teach students to vary reading rate according to the purpose(s) and difficulty of the material	8 8
8.3 Teach students effective time-management	6, 7, 8
8.4 Teach students strategies to organize and remember information	7, 8
8.5 Teach test-taking strategies	11

9 Writing

Related Chapters in This Text

The reading professional will be able to

9.1 Teach students planning strategies most appropriate for particular kinds of writing	10
9.2 Teach students to draft, revise, and edit their writing	10
9.3 Teach students the conventions of standard written English needed to edit their own compositions	10

10 Assessment

Related Chapters in This Text

The reading professional will be able to

10.1 Develop and conduct assessments that involve multiple indicators of learner progress	2, 11, 12
10.2 Administer and use information from norm-referenced tests, formal and informal inventories, constructed response measures, portfolio-based assessments, student self-evaluations, work/performance samples, observations, anecdotal records, journals, and other indicators of student progress to inform instruction and learning	11

Organizing and Enhancing a Reading Program

11 Communicating Information About Reading	Related Chapters in This Text
The reading professional will be able to	
11.1 Communicate with students about their strengths, areas for improvement, and ways to achieve improvement	11, 12
11.2 Communicate with allied professionals and paraprofessionals in assessing student achievement and planning instruction	11, 12
11.3 Involve parents in cooperative efforts and programs to support students' reading and writing development	3, 11, 12
11.4 Communicate information about literacy and data to administrators, staff members, school-board members, policymakers, the media, parents, and the community	2
11.5 Interpret research findings related to the improvement of instruction to colleagues and the wider community	All

12 Curriculum Development	Related Chapters in This Text
The reading professional will be able to	
12.1 Initiate and participate in ongoing curriculum development and evaluation	6, 7, 8, 11
12.2 Adapt instruction to meet the needs of different learners to accomplish different purposes	3, 4, 7, 8, 9, 10, 13
12.3 Supervise, coordinate, and support all services associated with literacy programs (e.g., needs assessment, program development, budgeting and evaluation, and grant and proposal writing)	11
12.4 Select and evaluate instructional materials for literacy, including those that are technology based	All
12.5 Use multiple indicators to determine effectiveness of the literacy curriculum	2, 4, 11, 12, 13
12.6 Plan and implement programs designed to help students improve their reading and writing, including those supported by federal, state, and local funding	All
12.7 Help develop individual education plans for students with severe learning problems related to literacy	All

13 Professional Development	**Related Chapters in This Text**
The reading professional will be able to	
13.1 Participate in professional-development programs	All
13.2 Initiate, implement, and evaluate professional-development programs	11
13.3 Provide professional-development experiences that emphasize the dynamic interaction among prior knowledge, experience, and the school context, as well as among other aspects of reading development	2

Research	**Related Chapters in This Text**
The reading professional will be able to	
14.1 Apply research for improved literacy	All

Supervision and Paraprofessionals	**Related Chapters in This Text**
The reading professional will be able to	
15.1 Plan lessons for paraprofessionals	All

Professionalism	**Related Chapters in This Text**
The reading professional will be able to	
16.1 Pursue knowledge of literacy by reading professional journals and publications and participating in conferences and other professional activities	All
16.2 Reflect on one's practice to improve instruction and other services to students	2, 11, 13

Appendix B
A Strange but Wonderful Alphabet Exercise

As you begin to read the following story, you'll notice that you can predict many of the unknown words by relying on syntax patterns, semantic clues from the English words provided, and your own schematic clues. After reading the first page or two, look back at the complete Applebet shown in Figure B.1. Then use all four kinds of clues to finish reading the story. Notice how the graphophonic system sometimes allows you to predict the next word and sometimes merely confirms a prediction you've already made with the other cueing systems.

This exercise has many applications. It can be copied and sent home for parents to experience what their young children are going through in learning the standard alphabet. It can also give students with diverse language backgrounds an equalizing opportunity. And it can provide pure fun for students in Grades 4 through 8.

The Sam Trap (a short story in Applebet)

452

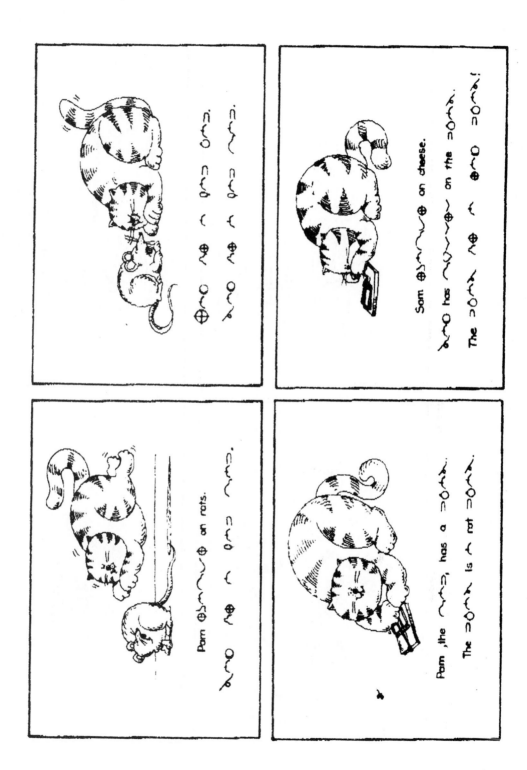

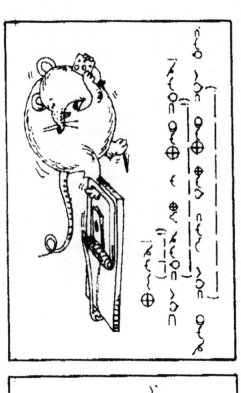

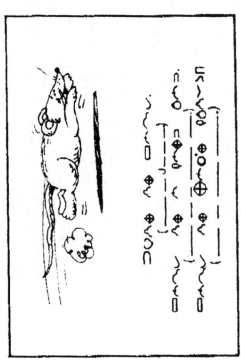

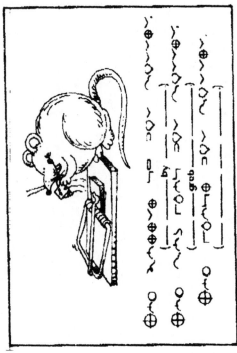

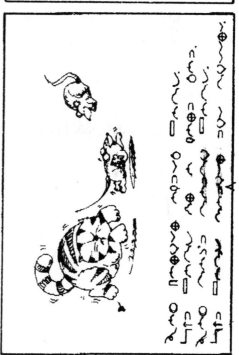

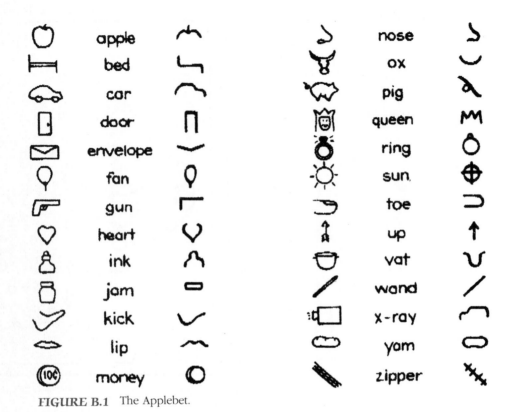

FIGURE B.1 The Applebet.

Appendix C
More Games for Learning Sight Words

Word Chase

Materials

Game board (see Figure C.1); place markers such as plastic cars or buttons; one die. Home spaces should be four different colors (same four colors as markers). You may wish to write the sight words on strips about ³⁄₄″ × 1¹⁄₂″. Glue clear plastic holders on the game board and insert the strips. This allows you to change the sight words whenever you wish. (Or make a new game board from a file holder.)

Object of Game

The first person to get from his home space all around the board and back to his home space wins.

Procedures

Two to four may play.

1. Players roll the die to see who goes first.
2. Each person rolls the die and moves the number of spaces indicated.
3. When a person lands on a space, he must read the word out loud.
4. If a player doesn't read a word correctly (as decided by the other players), he must move back to where he was.
5. The second person on the same space bumps the first person's marker all the way back to that person's home space.

6. After going all the way around, a player must roll the exact number on the die to get back into home space and win.
7. The player must roll a 2, 4, or 6 to get out of the garages.

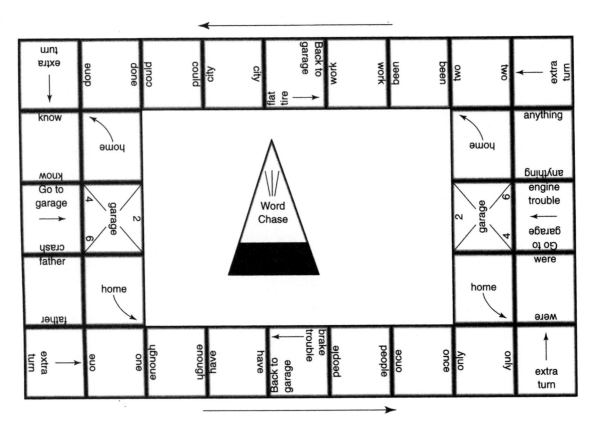

FIGURE C.1 Word Chase game board.

Word Toss

Materials

Four boards, each about 1″ × 6″ × 30″; twelve 2″ to 3″ nails; three rubber or plastic rings (see Figure C.2).

Procedures

This game is best for two to four players.

1. Each person tosses three rings. The person with the highest score goes first.
2. The teacher shows a word on a flashcard (about 2 seconds).
3. If a player reads the word correctly, she gets to throw three rings.
4. The teacher keeps score with tally marks.
5. Whoever has the most points at the end of 10 minutes (or some other designated time) is the winner.

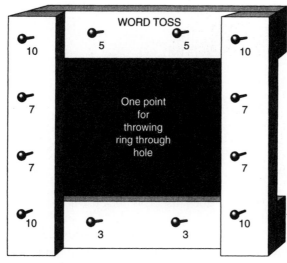

FIGURE C.2 Word Toss playing board.

Steal the Words

Materials

64 cards with 16 different high-frequency irregular words printed on them. Each word is printed twice on four different cards, once right-side up and once upside-down (see Figure C.3). Business cards work well, especially if sprayed with plastic or hair spray after the words are printed. (Check to see whether the print runs after a card is sprayed.)

FIGURE C.3   Steal the Words game cards.

Object of Game

The person with the biggest pile of cards at the end of the game wins.

Procedures

Two to four may play.

1. Draw a card to see who goes first. The person who draws the word with the most letters deals the cards.
2. After shuffling the cards, the dealer gives four cards face down to each person.
3. The dealer then places a row of four cards face up in the middle of the playing area.
4. The person to the left of the dealer goes first.
5. If a player has a card that is the same as a card in the middle of the playing area, he picks it up and places both cards face up in a pile close to him. (This forms the pile of words that others may later steal.) Before picking it up, however, he must read the word on the cards to the satisfaction of the other

players. If there are two cards in the middle that match one in a player's hand, he may pick up only one of them.

6. If a player does not have a card that is the same as one in the middle, he must place one of cards in the middle, thus adding to the selection in the middle.

7. If a player has a card that is the same as the top card of another player's pile, he must first read the word on the card out loud and then say STEAL THE WORDS as he takes the other player's entire pile and places it on top of his own.

8. A person may steal a pile of words only at the time of that person's regular turn.

9. After all players have used up their four cards, the dealer deals out four more cards to each; this time, however, the dealer does *not* place any more in the middle of the playing area.

10. The dealer places any extra cards in the center during the final deal.

11. When the final cards have been dealt and played, the game is over.

12. The last person to take a card with his card gets all the rest of the cards in the middle.

Word Checkers

Materials

Inexpensive or homemade checkerboard; set of checkers; paper labels slightly smaller than the squares on the checkerboard. Print a different word on each label—twice—so that each player can see the word right-side up. All squares should be covered with a paper label.

Object of Game

The first person to get all of the other person's checkers wins, or the person who has the most checkers at the end of a designated time, such as 10 minutes.

Procedures

Two people may play. Follow the same procedures as with regular checkers except

1. Before a person can move her checker, she must say the word(s) that are on her path, including the word she finally lands on.

2. When a person cannot decode (pronounce) a word correctly, she loses her turn.

Boggle

This game combines spelling and decoding using 16 lettered cubes. Purchase from Warren's Educational Supplies, 7715 Garvey Avenue, Rosemead, CA 91770.

Context Clues Game

This game develops vocabularies through the use of context clues. Purchase from Lakeshore Curriculum Materials, 2695 E. Dominguez Street, P.O. Box 6261, Carson, CA 90749.

Appendix D

More Games for Learning Phonic Patterns

e-Boat Adventure

Materials

Game board (see Figure D.1); place markers such as buttons or tiny boats; one die.

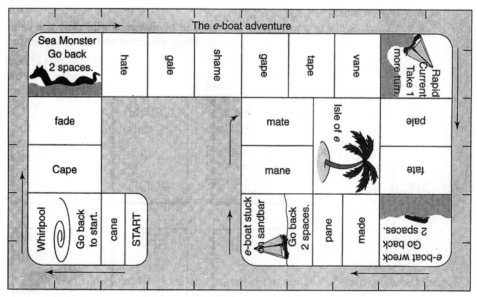

FIGURE D.1   e-Boat Adventure game board.

Object of game

The first one to get into the Isle of *e* wins the game.

Procedures

This game is best for two to four players.

1. Roll the die to see who goes first. The highest number goes first.
2. Each person rolls the die and moves the number of spaces indicated.
3. When a player lands on a word, he must read the word out loud as it is and then cover up the final *e* and read it out loud again (e.g., *tape, tap*).
4. If a player doesn't read the word correctly both ways (and in the correct order), the player must move back to where he was. (Other players decide.)
5. *Optional:* The player must say patterns as well; for example, "VCE, tape; VC, tap."
6. It is all right to have more than one *e*-boat on a space.
7. To land on the Isle of *e*, the player must roll the exact number on the die.

Value of Game

Practice in decoding VC and VCE words.

Adaptations of Game

Use other VC-VCE contrasts such as *pine-pin, bite-bit,* and *ripe-rip;* or *rode-rod, ride-rid,* and *hope-hop.*

Wild Things

Material

Deck of 58 cards with each card containing a one-syllable word. Each word should be an unambiguous example of one of the five major vowel patterns. You will need 10 words for each of these patterns VC, VCE, VCC, VVC, and CV (see Figures 4.2 and 4.5). You will also need eight Wild Things cards. (Do not use any word that ends in *r.*) See Figure D.2.

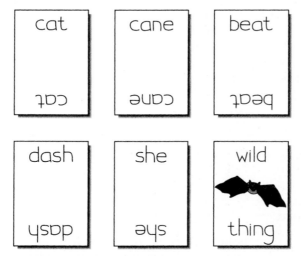

FIGURE D.2 Wild Things game cards.

Object of Game:

The first one to get rid of her cards wins.

Procedures

1. Deal five cards face down to each player.
2. Place the rest of the deck face down in the center of the table.
3. Turn the top card face up beside the deck to form a discard pile.
4. The person to the left of the dealer begins play.
5. Each player plays (discards) or draws *only one card;* then it's the next person's turn.
6. To play a card, the player must be able to match the pattern of the top card on the discard pile (VC, VCC, VVC, VCE, or CV). The player must read the pattern and word on her card out loud to the approval of the other players or lose her turn. *Example:* If *hunt* is the top card on the discard pile, a player must discard a VCC word like *mask* and say, "VCC, mask."
7. If a player does not have a word that follows suit she may play a card having a word beginning with the same first letter as the top card on the discard pile. This now changes the suit. *Example:* If *hunt* was down and the player discarded *ham,* the next player must play a VC word or another *h* word. She must also call out the pattern and the word.

8. A player may change the suit anytime by playing a wild card and calling out the suit she wishes to change to. *Example:* After playing a wild card, the player says, "I want to change it to VCE words."
9. If a player does not have a playable card, she must draw one card from the deck and lose a turn. She may not play again until her next turn.

Value of Game

Discriminating among five vowel patterns.

Adaptations of Game

Use the five *r* patterns as suits: *ar, er, ir, ur,* and *or.* The player not only reads the word but calls out the pattern as well. Another adaptation is the use of phonograms as suits, such as *at, ack, am, an,* and *ap.* See Figure D.3.

FIGURE D.3 Phonograms as Wild Things game cards.

Appendix E

More Ideas for Language Experience

1. Have the children see how long they can make this sentence: "The bear chased the girl." They may change the sentence or the words in any way they wish. After they have made the sentence as long as they wish, they may also add more sentences.
2. Ask students to think of ideas for making the classroom more attractive.
3. Ask pupils to choose one picture (from a large set of pictures) to tell or write a story about. Give them a day or two to think about their ideas. Then have them come one at a time to a quiet corner to tell you the story (or to tell it into a tape recorder). Let the child hold the picture while telling the story.
4. Find pictures that tell a story, for example, a crying child who is obviously lost. Have children tell or write (or both) what is happening now, what happened just before the picture, and what is going to happen after the picture.
5. Make a "touch book" with a different texture on each page: sandpaper, wax paper, silky fabric, and so on. Number each page and pass around the book. When a child has a turn with the book, he is to write down the page number and also at least five words that describe how the material feels. The child then hands in the paper to the teacher and passes on the book. (This is an excellent activity for a learning center.) Some children may need help from a large chart of "touch words" to select words for their own lists.
6. Ask pupils to make up one or two sentences that describe you, the teacher. Have fun reading them aloud, while at the same time discussing the kinds of words and phrases that can be used to describe a person's appearance and personality. Have the children use suggestions from your discussion to develop a paragraph about themselves.
7. Have the children make up a story or just tell about their own drawings or paintings. Take dictation during the telling or use a tape recorder. Or have them write their story after telling it.

8. Develop a class story based on an event that occurs during the school day, such as an unusual fire drill or an animal that gets into the room. The teacher takes dictation from the class.

9. Read two or three Dr. Seuss books to the children and discuss the imaginary animals he created. Have them create their own imaginary animals on paper and tell or write about them.

10. Have the children close their eyes and imagine an imaginary character, such as a strange animal or funny person. Have them describe their characters one at a time and help weave them together into a story as they describe them. You may either stop here or write the characters' names on the board and have the children make up a story about them. They may use part of the story already created if they wish.

11. Have some of the children bring in toys to explain to the others. Have them pretend they are toy manufacturers and, together, think of ways to improve the toys. Accept even their wildest impossible ideas; in fact, encourage such ideas. If you wish, you can then have them write a story about a toymaker and how he tried to make the best toy in the world.

12. Have children read each other's palms. Encourage them to tell exactly what adventures their partners will have, exactly how they will make their fortunes, and so on.

13. Have each person write a detailed description of a character from a familiar story—one they've all read in class, favorite bedtime stories, and so on. Then have each person read his description and let the rest of the class guess who was described.

14. Make up "balloon adventures" about a helium-filled ballon and its travels around the world. An effective starter is to bring such a balloon to school and release it.

15. Have the children get in groups of four or five. Put several words on the chalkboard that might suggest a story, such as *sailboat, waves, rocks,* and *beach.* Each person in a group should start a story and then pass it on to another person in his group until the teacher says "time." When each person has added something to each of the stories, have the children read the stories to see how similar and different they are.

16. Give each child a newspaper comic with the words cut out. Have them write their own dialogue.

17. Have a class puppet who talks to the children every day. Have it tell about an adventure it had (the teacher had), about something it saw one of them doing that it didn't think was such a good idea, about how proud it is of them, and so on. Let the children make up adventures for it.

18. After practicing with some what-if questions (such as "What if all the trees in the world were cut down?"), have students write their own what-if stories.

19. After a period of spontaneous drama, have the children write the story they created.

20. Write a title on the board, such as "The Danger Zone" or "Flying Is for the Birds." Have each person write three sentences as a beginning of a story. Then have the children put their names on the papers, fold the papers in half twice, and put them in a large box. They will then blindly pick one from the box and finish the story. Finally they will hand the story to the person who began the story, so that all may see how their stories turned out.

21. Give each child five 3″ × 5″ index cards or other small pieces of paper. Have the students write WHO, WHEN, WHAT, WHERE, and WHY on the five cards. After WHO, they are to write the name and description of a character they have created. After WHAT, they should tell something the character did. After WHEN and WHERE, they should tell the time and place of the action. After WHY, they should explain why the character did what he or she did (the motive).

    For example, WHO, Bill Robertson, a jeweler, age 40, tired-looking, graying hair, nail biter; WHAT, stole some of his own jewelry; WHEN, during a summer day when no customers were in the store; WHERE, in his own jewelry store in Chicago in a run-down shopping area; WHY, he wanted to claim he was robbed and collect the insurance money so he could send his daughter to college.

    Have the children put the cards in separate boxes: a WHO box, a WHAT box, a WHEN box, a WHY box, and a WHERE box. Mix the contents in the boxes and let the children each select five new cards—one from each box. They are to use their new cards, but only the ones that help them think of a story.

22. Have students create a story from a single WHERE sentence. Give each child a sentence on a piece of paper, for example, "I went to the circus" or "I went to a farm" or "I went to a grocery store." It is all right if several children have the same sentence, but they should all begin with "I went to. . . . "

    Show them how to create a story from a sentence. Put this sentence on the board: "I went to the new shopping mall." Under the sentence write the words when, who, what, why. Then show them how to ask questions that will help them describe their trip. For instance; When did you go? Whom did you go with? What did you do there? Why did you do these things?

23. Have students create a story from a single WHO sentence. (This is similar to 22.) Work with WHO sentences such as, "I saw Mrs. Twilliger, the lady who sells strange things." Ask questions about where, when, what, and why. For example, Where did you see Mrs. Twilliger? When did you see her? What was she doing when you saw her? Why was she doing it?

24. Have students create a story from a single WHAT sentence, for example, "He was dropping cotton balls from an airplane." Ask who, when, where, and why questions.

25. Have students create a story from a single WHEN sentence, for example, "It was on a dark, foggy night at the beginning of a summer vacation." Ask where, who, what, and why questions.

26. Have students create a story from a single WHY sentence, for example, "She was tired of having those kids tramp across her lawn and pick her flowers." Ask who, where, what, and when questions.

27. Have students create new adventures for their favorite cartoon characters, such as Snoopy and Charlie Brown. This is especially good shortly after they have seen a Charlie Brown TV special.

28. Have the children create new adventures for their favorite TV character.

29. Have students create a newspaper story about a game they have played on the playground. Be sure to have them include the who, what, when, and where in their stories, and the why if it's appropriate.

30. Have the children make up crazy titles and put them in a grab box for other children to pick from blindly. An example of a crazy title would be "The Lion Who Ran the People Zoo" or "The Girl Who Walked Backwards."

Appendix F

Book Projects for Children, Teachers, and Cooperative Groups

These projects are to be modeled by the teacher and/or selected by students from file cards.

Oral Projects

1. Try to interest others in a book you have read by reading an interesting part to the class. Practice before you read to them.
2. Read an exciting part of a book to the class. Stop reading right in the middle of the action. Practice before you read to them.
3. Tell about one character in the book. Tell why he or she is such an interesting person. Make the others in the class want to know more about that character.
4. Show on a globe or map how you would get from your home to where the story took place. Tell how you would travel there. Then tell something about the place. Tell a little bit about why the place was important to the story. Make the others in the class wish they could go there.
5. Pretend you are one of the characters in the book. Describe yourself and tell one or two things you do in the story. If others have already read the book, ask them to guess who you are.
6. Find an important object in the book you just read. Show it to the class and have them guess what it is and why it might be important in the story. Give them a few hints, but don't tell them too much.
7. Play Twenty Questions with the class. Have them think of the object or person you have in mind that was important in the story. First tell them whether it is animal, vegetable, or mineral. Then allow them 20 yes/no questions. After the game, give them some hints as to why the object or person was important, but don't tell them too much.
8. Tell the class some interesting facts you learned about a country you read about. Then ask them three or four questions to see what facts they can remember.

471

9. Tell how you would have done something differently from the way a person in the story did it.

10. Prepare and present a TV commercial for your book. Try to interest others in "buying" your book.

11. Read to the class two or three poems from a book of poems you have read. Be sure to practice several times before you do this. You may wish to use the tape recorder for practicing.

12. Find someone else who has read the same book of poetry. Together, read two or three poems to the class. You might try different arrangements, as with a song; for example, one person could read the first verse, the other person could read the second verse, and both could read the third verse together.

13. See if you can recite from memory a favorite poem from a poetry book you have just read.

14. Dress up as a character in the book and tell about yourself or about one of the adventures you had.

15. After reading a book of folktales, see if you can learn one of the stories well enough to tell it to the class.

16. Look up an author in *The Junior Book of Authors* or *More Junior Authors* (in the reference section of the library). Tell the class a few interesting things about him or her.

17. Make up another adventure for one of the characters. Tell the adventure to the class.

18. Make up a new ending for the book. Tell your ending to the class after you first tell a little bit about the beginning and the middle. Don't tell them the real ending, though.

19. Have a panel discussion about a book that three or four of you have read. Tell how you agree and disagree about some of the characters or about part of the story.

20. Tell about an adventure you had that was similar to one a character in the book had.

21. Meet in small groups to chat about books you have read.

Drama Projects

1. Pantomime a scene from your book. Have the class guess what you were doing. Tell them only enough to get them interested in the book.

2. Plan so that you and a friend read the same book; then prepare and present a skit about part of the book. You may have to make up some of your own dialogue, or you can say what the characters said in the book.

3. Tape-record a skit based on the book. You may have to make up some of your own dialogue and make your voice sound like several different people. Play the tape recording to the class.

4. Put on a puppet play about one part of the book.

5. Play Meet the Author. Find someone who has read the same book. One person pretends to be the author and the other interviews her. The interviewer asks questions about the book, about the author's life (if you can find that information), and so on.

6. Pretend you are the author of the book and are trying to get someone to publish it. Tell the publishing staff (your class) why it would be a good book to publish. Let them ask you questions.

7. Play charades with the class. Act out each word of the book's title. See how long it takes the class to guess the title.

8. If several others have read this book, pantomime a scene from the book *by yourself*. Then ask the class to guess the title of the book. See if they can also guess the author.

9. Pretend you are a character in the book you have read. Find someone who will pretend to be a character in a different book. In front of the class, carry on a conversation between the two characters. You might tell each other about some of your adventures or about some of the people you know (those who were described in the books).

10. Put on a play by yourself in which you play two or three parts. Make name cards for each character. Each time you switch parts, hold up one of the cards.

11. Find some dolls you can use to represent characters in your book. Put on a doll play about one part of your book.

12. Put on a play with one or two others. Have the class guess the title and author of the book.

Written Projects

1. Write a magazine advertisement for the book you have read. Put the ad on the bulletin board. Be sure to tell where the book can be found and a few things about why it's a marvelous book.

2. Write a letter to a friend and try to persuade him to read the book.

3. Make up a new table of contents for your book. Use your imagination to invent chapter titles that would interest someone else in reading the book.

4. Read two or three chapters of the book. Write down what you think will happen in the next chapter. Then write briefly about how close your guess was.

5. Make a brief outline of your book. For example:

Tom Sawyer
   I. Tom plays, fights, and hides
       A. Tom tricks Aunt Polly
       B. Siddy gets Tom in trouble
       C. Tom fights with a new boy
       D. Tom returns home late at night
   II. The glorious whitewasher

6. Write about something that happened in the book in the same way a newspaper reporter would describe it. A reporter tries to answer these questions: who? what? when? where? why? Don't forget to make up a snappy headline for your newspaper article.
7. Write a pretend letter to a character in the book. Tell the character how his or her life is the same as or different from yours.
8. Send a letter or e-mail message to the author. Send it in care of the publisher.
9. Make a short diary for one of the characters in the book. Describe three or four days as if you were the person in the book.
10. Pretend you are one of the characters in the book. Write a letter to another character in the book.
11. Add another chapter to the book. Tell what happened next or what adventure was left out.
12. Write an ending to the book that is quite different from the one the author wrote.
13. Write about two books you have read on the same topic. Tell how the books are similar and different.
14. See how good your memory is. Describe the important details in one chapter. Draw a line under your description; then reread that chapter. Write down any important details you left out.
15. Write about an adventure you had that was like an adventure a character in the book had. Tell how the two adventures were alike and different.
16. Read in an encyclopedia or in another factual book about a person, place, or thing described in your book. Write down some of the things you learned in this way that you did *not* learn from the book itself.
17. Try to make a list from memory of all the characters in the book. List both their first and last names. Draw a line under your list. Now skim through the book to see if you remembered all of them. Write down any you didn't remember. How good was your memory for names?
18. Write about the character in the story that you would most like to have for a friend. Tell why he or she would be a good friend. Also write about the character that you would *not* like to have for a friend. Tell why.
19. Write about how you would have solved a problem differently from the way a character in the book solved it.
20. Pick two characters from the story. Write about how they were alike and how they were different.
21. Make a list of words or phrases in the story that helped you almost be able to see or hear or smell or feel or taste something described in the story.
22. Write a poem that tells about one adventure in the book.

Art and Craft Projects

1. Make clothes for a doll to match a character in the book. Display it for the rest of the class to see. Make sure you put a card by it with the name of the book, the author, and your name.

2. Make an object that is important in the book you just read. Have the class guess what it is and why it might be important in the story. Give them a few hints, but don't tell them for sure.
3. Make a flannel board or bulletin board display about your book.
4. Make a comic strip about one of the scenes in your book. Put it on the bulletin board.
5. Make a diorama (a small stage) that describes a scene in the book. Use a cardboard box for the stage. Make the objects and people in your scene out of clay, cardboard, pipe cleaners, papier-mâché, or any other material.
6. Make a mobile representing five or six characters in the book.
7. If the book doesn't have a book jacket, make one for it. Be sure to put a picture on it and all the necessary information. A manila folder might be good to use.
8. Make a "movie" of one scene in your book. Use a long piece of butcher paper. After you draw a sequence of several pictures, roll the butcher paper. Then ask two people to unroll it as you describe the scene to the class.
9. Make a picture of one scene in the book. Put it on the bulletin board. Below it put the title and author and two or three questions about the scene. Try using crayon, chalk, or charcoal.
10. Do 9, but use tempera, watercolor, or acrylic.
11. Do 9, but use collage materials (bits of paper, cloth, or other materials).
12. Study the illustrations in the book. What techniques did the artist use? See if you can illustrate a part of the book that was not illustrated. Try to use some of the same techniques the artist did. Put your illustration on the bulletin board. Be sure to name the illustrator you imitated.
13. Make a time line of the story showing main events rather than dates. Draw pictures to illustrate the main events.
14. Read half or more of the book. Then draw three pictures to show three different ways the book might end. Put them on the bulletin board, along with a card giving the title, author, your name, and Three Ideas on How This Book Might End.
15. Make a scrapbook of things related to the book. Be sure to label what you put in your scrapbook.
16. Make a map to show where the characters went in the story.

Demonstration Projects

1. Demonstrate a science principle you learned from your book by performing an experiment in front of the class.
2. Show the class how to make something you learned to make from reading your book.
3. Show the class how to do something you learned to do from reading your book.

Appendix G

Additional Comprehension Practice

These activities are designed to be used during interactive reading experiences or to be followed by interactive applications.

Practice in Developing Images or Associations

1. When reading a story aloud to children, occasionally have them close their eyes and picture what you're reading. Once in a while you may wish to pause to discuss their "pictures" or to write a descriptive word or phrase on the board.
2. Have students first read a passage silently and then draw a picture of what they see in their heads.
3. Ask the children first to read a passage silently and then tell what they "saw."
4. Have students first read a passage silently and then tell what personal experiences it made them remember.
5. Arrange for the children first to read a passage silently and then pantomime what they "saw."
6. Have one child read a passage aloud while other children pantomime the picture they "see."

Practice in Following a Sequence

1. Have the children work in pairs. Each member of the pair should read silently the same set of directions. Then one person should attempt to follow the directions while the other person judges whether she followed the directions correctly.

2. Provide children with directions for making things—paper airplanes, paper costumes for dolls, cookies, and so on. Have them work in pairs so they can check each other's comprehension of the directions.

3. Have students read a story and then decide in what order to place pictures depicting events in the story.

4. Ask the children to read a story and then tell it to or act it out for some other children.

5. Provide a child with a set of directions for a game; then have her explain the game in sequence to some other children.

6. Ask the children to read informative passages about sequential occurrences, such as the water cycle or the cycle of life for a butterfly, and then explain the cycle to some other children or depict the cycle in a sequential drawing.

Practice in Finding Important Details

1. Help the children change a story into a brief newspaper report. Help them write it as a reporter does, telling who, why, what, where, and when. The same activity can be used for a historical event described in a social studies book.

2. Help the children change a story into a telegram of 25 words or less. Show them how to include only the most important details. You can use the same activity for a historical event described in a social studies book.

3. After students have decided on the main idea for a passage, have them find or remember details that support their decision.

4. Ask the children to scan a reading selection from a basal reader, social studies book, or science text to find highly factual information. This is best done orally in small groups, with the first child to find it reading the answer.

5. Develop students' appreciation for literary devices by having them read aloud some sentences, phrases, or words that help paint a picture for the reader.

Practice in Drawing Inferences

This thinking process can be practiced even on reading passages as simple as this:

One hot day Roy went on a boat ride.
He went with his teacher and his school friends.

To give children practice at *literal thinking,* the teacher might simply ask, "What kind of day was it when Roy went on a boat ride?" But to give children practice in *inferential thinking,* the teacher could ask, "What season of the year do you think it is—winter, summer, spring, or fall?" To answer this question, they would have to make inferences based on the words *hot, teacher,* and *school.* Robert may say "summer" because of the word *hot.* Jill may say, "No, it can't be summer because Roy is going with his teacher and school friends." Frank may then say, "I'll bet it's either spring or fall." All three children will be engaged in inferential thinking. The teacher has helped them communicate with the author rather than merely absorb the author's words.

Practice in Determining Main Ideas

Try reading the following selection aloud and then having the children choose the title that best describes what the author has told them.

In 1888 a terrible snowstorm hit New York City. Tall poles snapped, and electric wires fell into the street. People were killed by electric shock. Some were killed by the falling poles. And nearly a thousand died in the fires that broke out.

The mayor saw that he must do something to make his city a safe place to live. He asked electricians to put electric wires safely underground. Then the mayor sent men out to take down the wooden poles.

These electric wires were the beginning of America's amazing underground city in New York. Today the narrow streets and the sidewalks hide more than four million miles of wire. In some places there are so many wires and pipes that two fingers cannot be pushed between them.*

1. A terrible snowstorm
2. How some people were killed
3. Putting wires underground
4. How an amazing underground city began

Since the first three ideas all lead up to the fourth one, perhaps you would agree that Number 4 is the best title. This type of exercise gives children specific practice in determining main ideas. Other types of experiences include these:

1. After students have read a selection, ask them questions such as these:
   What do you think the author was trying to tell you?
   What was this story really about?
   Was there one big idea the author was talking about?
   If you were the author, what is the one thing you'd want the readers to remember from this article more than anything else?
2. After students have read a story or an article, have them capture the big idea with a two-line or four-line verse. You'll need to do this together and also

From "Air Pudding and Wind Sauce" in *Keys to Reading* (p. 250), 1972, Oklahoma City, OK: Economy Company. Adapted from "Amazing Underground City" by Edward Hymoff, August 1963, *Boys' Life.*

provide them with the first line. Here's an example for "Goldilocks and the Three Bears":

Goldilocks bothered the bears.
She even broke one of their chairs.
But she'll never do that again.
Not even now and then.

3. After older children have read a story, let them decide on the basic theme: (a) people against nature, (b) people against people, or (c) people against themselves.
4. After students have read a selection, have them decide whether the title tells what the story was really about. Or you might ask them if it tells what the author was really trying to say. Then have them create a better title—one that describes better what the author was talking about.

Practice in Recognizing Details That Support Main Ideas

Let's look again at the article in the previous section on New York City's amazing underground city. Mr. Hymoff, the author of this article, didn't simply tell the reader, "Now I'm going to tell how an amazing underground city began." Instead he chose to present as many details as he thought necessary to illustrate and lead up to this idea. To help children realize what the author has done, the teacher will often need to have children reconstruct the author's purpose and procedures. You can do this with questions like these:

1. Why do you think this article is called "Amazing Underground City"?
2. What can you find in this article that seems to be "amazing"?
3. Was the author, Mr. Hymoff, trying to just tell about the underground city, or was he trying to tell you how this underground city began? Or was he doing both? What can you find in the article to prove your point?
4. Mr. Hymoff tells us that in 1888 a terrible snowstorm hit New York City. Can you find anything in the first paragraph that would explain why he used the word *terrible?*
5. How did the amazing underground city begin?

Practice in Predicting

1. After students have read part of a story, have them guess what is going to happen next.
2. Let the children draw or pantomime what's coming next, after they have read a certain portion of a story.

3. Have students continue a story in writing; then read the rest of the story and discuss how their endings differed.
4. Have older children read a dittoed portion of a newspaper editorial or other passage presenting an argument; have them discuss what they think the author would have said next. Then read the rest of the editorial to them so that they can see how well they predicted. (You can do the same thing with an informative passage rather than an argumentative one.)

Practice in Understanding Cause and Effect

Cause-and-effect relationships are the nuclei of many stories and articles. Event B happens because of Event A; Event F occurs because of the personality of Character D; and so on. Unless children recognize such relationships, their understanding of an article or story will have little depth. In "The Amazing Underground City," for example, they would not really understand why the "mayor saw that he must do something to make his city a safe place to live" unless they connect this with the electric wires falling into the street. The teacher's role is again one of asking thoughtful questions—this time questions that encourage children to notice the cause-and-effect relationships:

1. Why did the mayor see that he must do something to make his city a safe place to live?
2. What caused the electric wires to fall into the street in the first place?
3. Why did so many people die in the snowstorm of 1888?
4. Why did the mayor have the electricians put the wires under the ground?
5. What kind of person do you think the mayor was? Do you think this had anything to do with what he decided to do after the storm of 1888?

Practice in Distinguishing Between the Factual and the Nonfactual

This form of critical thinking can be practiced through at least eight types of activities:

1. Distinguishing between literal and figurative expressions
2. Distinguishing between real-life stories and fantasies
3. Distinguishing between real-life stories and satire
4. Distinguishing between factual statements and opinions

5. Recognizing differences between observations an author is making and inferences he is making
6. Recognizing differences between observations an author is making and judgments he is making
7. Detecting an author's bias and how this influences his statements
8. Deciding on the author's competence and how this may influence the accuracy of his statements

Here are some corresponding sample learning activities for the critical-thinking activities:

1. Discuss the meaning of figurative phrases such as "shouting my head off" or "pulling my leg." Have the children think of others they have heard. Have them picture in their heads or on paper what the words seem to mean and what they really mean. The same type of thing can be done with metaphors you and the children discover in descriptive passages. For example, in the sentence "John flew down the hallway to his classroom," what does *flew* seem to mean and really mean? (Other examples, Bill didn't get the *point* of my poem. That book is hard to *swallow*. I *plowed* right through my homework.)
2. After students have read a fanciful story in their basal readers or library books, ask them whether it was a real-life story or a make-believe one. Have them explain their answers.
3. Read aloud to the children *The Enormous Egg* by Oliver Butterworth. This book includes satire that most children in third through sixth grades will enjoy and understand. Ask them to discover how the author satirizes ("makes fun of" or "pokes fun at") advertisers, politicians, and others. Another book useful for this type of experience is Jean Merrill's *The Pushcart War*. Discuss how Merrill creates imaginary characters and situations that are very like real people and real situations. Help the children understand that authors sometimes do this to avoid criticizing people directly.
4. Show students how to tell the difference between factual statements and opinions. Use these nonsense statements as illustrations:
   a. A snurtzle has two eyes and three fleb pads. (factual)
   b. Snurtzles are very good at swinking. (opinion)
   c. A snurtzle can swink 50 gallons a day. (factual)
   d. It is clear that snurtzles are always flumptuous. (opinion)
   Ask what makes them sure that statements (b) and (d) are opinions. Then present them with a list of actual statements and have them decide which statements seem factual and which seem to be opinions. Have them justify their answers. (*Note:* For this type of exercise, a factual statement is not necessarily a truthful statement.) Then have them look for factual statements and opinions in their basal readers, library books, or social studies textbooks.

5. Have the children learn to distinguish between observations and inferences by discussing two-part statements such as these:
   Noticing: Jimmy Smith took the milk out of Mrs. Jones's refrigerator. (observation)
   Guessing: Jimmy stole the milk. (inference)
   Noticing: Jimmy Smith took the milk out of Mrs. Jones's refrigerator. (observation)
   Guessing: Mrs. Jones asked Jimmy to keep her milk while she was on vacation. (inference)

6. Have students learn to distinguish between observations and judgments by discussing three-part statements such as these:
   Noticing: Jimmy Smith took the milk out of Mrs. Jones's refrigerator. (observation)
   Guessing: Jimmy *stole* the milk. (inference)
   Judging: Jimmy is a thief. (judgment)
   Guessing: Mrs. Jones asked Jimmy to keep her milk while she was on vacation.
   Judging: Jimmy is a nice kid.
   After they complete sentences such as these, have them look for other examples in their basal readers, library books, or social studies book.

7. Have the children study magazine ads with the intention of detecting these three propaganda tricks:
   Expert appeal: "Four out of five doctors recommend No-Ache aspirin."
   Winner appeal: "More people buy Shuvvy than any other car."
   Star appeal: "Hefty Breakneck, star tackle for the Podunk Tigers, uses Left Tackle deodorant. Shouldn't you?"
   Ask them why the advertisers use these tricks. Have them talk about the times they have used these tricks in their own lives. For instance,
   Expert appeal: "If you don't believe me, just ask my mother."
   Winner appeal: "But Mom, all the kids are wearing Squishtight jeans."
   Star appeal: "Frankie Hackshaw is in sixth grade and he wears 'em."
   Ask them whether authors may sometimes use tricks like these to get them to believe something or do something. If possible, demonstrate this technique in a basal anthology, library books, or social studies text.

8. Have the children compare information in two science books or encyclopedias, one published recently and one published several decades ago; have them see how many disagreements they can find about topics such as Mars or atoms. Show them where to find the copyright date in books. Discuss the importance of currency for some information.

Practice in Creative Thinking

1. Ask the children, before or during the reading of a story, to imagine how they might solve the main character's problem. Then, when they have finished the story, have them discuss or write about how they might have solved the problem in a different way.

2. Have students discuss how the main character's problem was similar to one they have right now. Encourage them to tell how they might solve those personal problems. At a later date, encourage them to tell how they actually did solve them.

3. Encourage the children to share their feelings about stories or books through drama, poetry, painting, and other media. For instance, a child can pretend she's one of the characters in the story; she can describe herself and tell about one or two things she did in the story. Two children who have read the same book may enjoy dramatizing a scene from the book. Another child may decide to make a diorama (a small stage) describing a scene in her book.

4. Give students time to construct things (castles, dragons, rockets, and so on) they have read about.

5. Let students share their favorite passages from stories by reading aloud to each other. Give them practice time and assistance so that the experience will be a positive one for both the audience and the readers. Encourage them to give their own original interpretation to the reading.

Appendix H
Six Common Sentence Patterns for Syntax Development

Pattern 1

Here are some examples of Pattern 1 (read them aloud, if possible):

Noun + *Be* verb + Prepositional phrase

> The girl was inside the house.
> My friend was outside the car.
> The bear was in the zoo.
> Bob was behind the door.
> The doctor was in the hospital.
> His doctor was under the table.
> A nurse was near the bed.
> The flebonk was in the malps.

> Now you make up two or three.

Pattern 2

Here are examples of Pattern 2 (read them aloud, if possible):

Noun + Intransitive verb + Adverb or Prepositional phrase (optional)

> The boy walked slowly.
> The boy walked.

Susan walked.
That girl played under the house.
This girl played in the park.
My mother worked in the morning.
The giant spoke grumpily.
That flebonk lived in the malps.

Now it's your turn. Make one of them nonsensical if you can.

Pattern 3

These are examples of Pattern 3:

Noun + Linking verb + Adjective

The candy seemed sweet.
That candy was sweet.
His shirt looked dirty.
Your dress was pretty.
The monkey seemed clever.
That child was cruel.
Alice appeared snobbish.
That flebonk smelled yucky.
My flebonk tasted delicious.

Pattern 4

Here are examples of Pattern 4:

Noun + Linking verb + Noun

The dog was his friend.
The dog became his friend.
The dog remained his friend.
Bob was a snob.
That girl became my sweetheart.
Her brother remained a fink.
Your costume was a scream.
My flebonk became a skiddle.
His skiddle remained a nurgle.

Pattern 5

These are examples of Pattern 5:

Noun + Transitive verb + Noun

The monkey climbed the ladder.
My father drove a car.
This motor ran the pulley.
Jim owned this place.
The train jumped the track.
Your sister liked my brother.
Her flebonk zagged his delbur.
His delbur zagged a flurtop.

Pattern 6

Here are examples of Pattern 6:

Noun + Transitive verb + Noun + Noun

The woman gave her dog a bone.
The woman fed her son a steak.
My father spared the beggar a dime.
The king granted Columbus an audience.
The club awarded Felix a prize.
Mr. Jones offered Mother a hand.
My uncle left my sister a fortune.

Appendix I

Sample Lesson on Dictionary Guide Words

Say something like this to your students:

> "Now that you've learned how to alphabetize so well, you're ready to learn how to use guide words. Let's look at some guide words in your dictionary. At the top of page 216 are the words *fast* and *fatten*. Can you find them? These are the guide words for page 216. These two words tell you that all the words on this page begin with the letters *f—a*. Can you tell me why I know that's true? Can you prove it to me?"

> "These two guide words tell you that some of the words on this page start with *f—a—s* and some of them start with *f—a—t*. Can you prove this to me?"

> "These two guide words tell you that none of the words on this page start with *f—a—s—s*. How do I know that? Can you prove this to me?"

> "These two guide words tell you that none of the words on this page start with *f—a—t—u*. How do I know that? Can you prove this to me?"

Write *father, fatal, fashion,* and *favor* on the board. Then ask:

> "Would you expect to find the word *father* on this page? Why? Prove it. Would you expect to find the word *fatal?* Why? Prove it. Would you expect to find the word *fashion?* Why not? Can you prove it? Would you expect to find the word *favor?* Why not? Can you prove it?"

> "What guide words do you find on page 285? What things do these two guide words tell you? Do you see the word I've just written on the chalkboard? Would you expect to find this word on this page? Prove it. What guide words do you find on page 95? What things do these two guide words tell you? Without looking at the page, tell me one word that you think will be there. Tell me one word you're sure will not be there."

> "On this worksheet is a list of words. After each word I'd like you to write the two guide words you find in the dictionary on the page where the word appears. Let's do the first one together."

Appendix J

Observation Checklist for Reading and Language Disabilities

A student should display several of the behaviors in each category to be considered disabled. See also the RAD Test in Appendix K.

General Behavior

_____ (1) Shows average or above-average intelligence in some way; for example, does well in science reasoning or mathematical reasoning, shows sense of humor, or has ingenious ways of getting into trouble

_____ (2) Often has trouble expressing himself/herself

_____ (3) Often shows poor eye-hand coordination

_____ (4) Appears nervous or anxious in many situations

_____ (5) Tends to get frustrated easily

_____ (6) Withdraws when things get too difficult

_____ (7) Has far too much energy (or sometimes far too little)

_____ (8) Has trouble concentrating

_____ (9) Has trouble remembering directions, names, or other details

_____(10) Has trouble making lasting friendships

Reading Behavior

_____ (1) Standardized reading-achievement score: at least 1 year below grade level in Grades 2 and 3, and 2 years below in later grades

_____ (2) Standardized individual diagnostic score: at least 1 year below grade level in Grades 2 and 3, and 2 years below in later grades

_____ (3) Informal reading inventory: at least 1 year below grade level in Grades 2 and 3, and 2 years below in later grades

_____ (4) BAF Test: 40% error in Grades 3 and above (see Appendix L)

_____ (5) Essential sight words: 40% error in Grades 3 and above

_____ (6) Has considerable trouble concentrating on reading task even when working directly with teacher

_____ (7) Frequently guesses wildly at words

_____ (8) Forgets words shortly after learning to read them

_____ (9) Asks teacher to decode words rather than using clues

_____(10) Transposes letters or words or syllables while reading

_____(11) Loses place in reading passage easily

Appendix K

The RAD Test—Rapid Assessment of Disablement

Directions for Group Administration

Note: This test is not a diagnostic test. Its purpose is to provide a means of quickly determining which children in a group *may* have a specific language disability. The test is designed for second grade and above.

Part A: Visual-Kinesthetic Memory

Directions: Print the following words or letters at least 1½″ high, using heavy black felt-tip pen on white cardboard about 3″ × 8″:

1.	bad	6.	hobby
2.	your	7.	eighty
3.	top	8.	minnow
4.	nuts	9.	whenever
5.	JKBF	10.	stumbles

Show each card one at a time in the order given. (Do not print the number on the card. Just say the number as you show it.) Expose the card for about 10 seconds while students hold their pencils high over their heads.

After you have turned the card facedown, count 5 more seconds and say, "Write word number 1." The children are then to write the word next to the number 1 on their test (see Figure K.1). Give them about 15 seconds to write the word; then ask them to raise their pencils above their heads again.

Repeat this procedure for each of the 10 words. Do not show a word again after you have turned over the card.

RAD Test

Student's Name _____   Grade _____

Teacher's Name _____   Date _____

Part A:

1. _____   6. _____

2. _____   7. _____

3. _____   8. _____

4. _____   9. _____

5. _____   10. _____

Part B:

1. puick	qnick	quick	pnick	kciuq
2. fypt	tqyf	ftyq	fyqt	tyqf
3. was	saw	sam	mas	zaw
4. dceb	dbce	bedc	peqc	bdec
5. buddles	dubbles	selbbub	bubbles	bnbbles
6. mommy	wowwy	ymmom	mymmo	mowwy
7. thoutgh	tghuoht	thought	thuoght	thuohgt
8. snrronud	surround	dnuorrus	sunnourd	surruond
9. nurring	runners	running	gninnur	rurring
10. evyerone	oneevery	evenyoue	everyone	evenyone

FIGURE K.1   RAD Test

Part B: Auditory Memory and Visual Discrimination

Directions: Tell students to turn their test page face down. Say each of these words or series of letters twice.

1. quick
2. fyqt
3. saw
4. bdec
5. bubbles
6. mommy
7. thought
8. surround
9. running
10. everyone

After you have said a word or series of letters twice, count 5 seconds and say, "Turn over your paper and find Part B, Number (x). Draw a circle around the word or letters I just said."

Allow about 10 seconds for them to circle a word or series of letters. Then say, "Put your pencil down and turn over your paper. Listen for the next word or letters."

Repeat this procedure for each of the 10 words or series of letters. Do not say a word or series of letters more than twice.

Directions for Scoring RAD Test

To derive a score from this test, simply add the number of correct items in the 20-item test. Then compare the papers in the bottom third of the group with those in the top third. Disabled learners will usually stand out. This is not a precise assessment, but it gives you a way to determine quickly which children need closer observation. Do the test results coincide with your observations on the Observation Checklist in Appendix J? If so, you have candidates for special instruction as described in Chapter 13.

Appendix L
Phonics Tests

Phonics Test One: The BAF Test

The BAF Test uses nonsense words and is not suitable for children who have not yet succeeded at the primer level or above. It consists of two parts and must be administered individually. Normally this test would be given to children above Grade 2 who are considered remedial readers. You have permission to enlarge and reproduce it (see Figures L.1 and L.2).

Part I: Consonant Letters, Digraphs, and Clusters

The children should be encouraged to try decoding each nonsense word without your help. If they miss one, simply circle it and have them continue. Be sure to pronounce the first one for them /baf/ and have them pronounce it correctly before they continue. It is also a good idea to correct the second one if they miss it (*caf* is pronounced /kaf/). *Note:* Consider a word wrong *only* if the target letter, digraph, or blend is wrong. For example, for 1c /daf/ is correct. So is /dap/ but not /paf/, since the target letter is *d*.

Part II: Vowel Letters, Vowel Digraphs, and Vowel Clusters (for those whose instructional level is at least primer)

This part of the inventory should also be administered individually. You will need to enlarge and reproduce a copy of this test for each child. The children should be encouraged to try decoding each nonsense word without your help. If they miss one, simply circle it and have them continue. Be sure to pronounce the first one for them /baf/ and have them pronounce it correctly before they continue.

Name of Student _____

Directions (to be read or told to the student):

These words are nonsense words. They are not real words. I'd like you to think about what sounds the letters stand for; then read each word out loud without my help. Don't try to go fast; read the list slowly. If you have any trouble with a word, I'll just circle it and you can go on to the next one. The first word is /baf/. Now you say it . . . All right, now go on to the rest of the words in row 1.

A	B	C	D	E	F	G
Consonant Letters						
1. baf	caf	daf	faf	gaf	haf	jaf
2. kaf	laf	maf	naf	paf	raf	saf
3. taf	vaf	waf	yaf	zaf	baf	bax

A	B	C	D	E	F	G	H
Consonant Digraphs							
4. chaf	phaf	shaf	thaf	whaf	fack	fant	fank
Consonant Clusters							
5. blaf	braf	claf	craf	draf	dwaf	flaf	fraf
6. glaf	graf	fand	plaf	praf	quaf	scaf	scraf
7. skaf	slaf	smaf	snaf	spaf	splaf	spraf	squaf
8. staf	straf	swaf	thraf	traf	twaf		

FIGURE L.1 BAF Test, Part I.

Directions (to be read or told to the student):

These words are silly words. They are not real words. I'd like you to think about what sounds the letters stand for; then read each word out loud without any help. Don't try to go fast; read the list slowly. If you have any trouble with a word, I'll circle it and you can go on to the next one. The first word is /baf/. Now you say it. . . . All right, now go on to the rest of the words in row 1.

A	B	C	D	E	F	G
1. baf	bafe	barp	baif	bawf		
2. bef	befe	berf	beaf			
3. bof	bofe	borf	boaf	bouf	boif	boof
4. bif	bife	birf				
5. buf	bufe	burf				

FIGURE L.2 BAF Test, Part II.

Phonics Test Two: The Phonogram Phonics Test

This test will give you an idea of how well a student can recognize patterns of letters at the end of one-syllable words or at the end of syllables in multisyllable words (see Figure L.3).

Directions:

1. Read the first two words to your student and explain that most of these words are not real words. Tell the student you want to find out how well he or she knows the sounds that the letters stand for.
2. Have the student read the entire first row across the top of the page without help. Tell the student to say "I don't know" whenever necessary.
3. Circle each one that the student misses, using another copy for recording.
4. This test is recommended for Grade 2 or higher.

High-Frequency Phonogram Test

Name of Student _____   Grade _____

zab	zack	zace	zail	zay	zall	zed	zell	zeak
zear	zid	zick	zice	zight	zob	zock	zoke	zold
zout	zorn	zore	zub	zuck	zy	zad	zamp	zade
zain	zar	zen	zeal	zew	zend	zig	zill	zide
zag	zand	zake	zark	zaw	zam	zame	zang	zash
zan	zank	zet	zim	zent	zeam	zing	zime	zod
zong	zone	zud	zump	zunt	zap	zate	zest	zat
zane	zug	zeat	zin	zish	zint	zeep	zatch	zeed
zog	zum	zip	zink	zone	zope	zun	zut	zive
zot	zuff	zunk	zeet	zung	zow	zown	zab	zack

FIGURE L.3   Phonogram phonics test.

Appendix M

Informal Assessment Procedure for Essential Sight Words

Have the child use a ruler or an index card under each row and read each row from left to right. The child should recognize these words through visual memory within 1 second.*

the	of	and	a	to	in	1–6
is	you	that	it	he	was	7–12
for	on	are	as	with	his	13–18
they	I	at	be	this	have	19–24
from	or	one	had	by	words	25–30
but	not	what	all	were	we	31–36
when	your	can	said	there	use	37–42
an	each	which	she	do	how	43–48
their	if	will	up	other	about	49–54
out	many	then	them	these	so	55–60
some	her	would	make	like	him	61–66
into	time	has	look	two	more	67–72
write	go	see	number	no	way	73–78
could	people	my	than	first	water	79–84
been	called	who	oil	its	now	85–90
find	long	down	day	did	get	91–96
come	made	may	part	over	new	97–102
sound	take	only	little	work	know	103–108
place	years	live	me	back	give	109–114
most	very	after	things	our	just	115–120
name	good	sentence	man	think	say	121–126
great	where	help	through	much	before	127–132
line	right	too	means	old	any	133–138
same	tell	boy	following	came	want	139–144
show	also	around	form	three	small	145–150
set	put	end	does	another	well	151–156
large	must	big	even	such	because	157–162
turned	here	why	asked	went	men	163–168
read	need	land	different	home	us	169–174
move	try	kind	hand	picture	again	175–180
change	off	play	spell	air	away	181–186
animals	house	point	page	letters	mother	187–192
answer	found	study	still	learn	should	193–198
American	world	high	every	near	add	199–204
food	between	own	below	country	plants	205–210
last	school	father	keep	trees	never	211–216
started	city	earth	eyes	light	thought	217–222
head	under	story	saw	left	don't	223–228
few	while	along	might	close	something	229–234
seemed	next	hard	open	example	beginning	235–240

*Note: From *The Reading Teachers' Book of Lists* (3rd ed.) by Edward B. Fry, J. E. Kress, and D. L. Fountou Kidis, 1993, Englewood Cliffs, NJ: Prentice Hall. Copyright 1993 by Prentice Hall. Reprinted with permission.

Appendix N

More Than 200 Patterned Books

Aardema, Verna *Bringing the Rain to Kapiti Plain*
Adams, Pam *This Old Man*
Ahlberg, Janet and Allen *Each Peach, Pear, Plum*
Alain *One, Two, Three, Going to Sea*
Aliki *Go Tell Aunt Rhody*
    Hush Little Baby
    My Five Senses
Asbjornsen, Peter *The Three Billy Goats Gruff*
Asch, Frank *Monkey Face*
Atwood, Margaret, and Maryanne Kovatsky *Princess Prunella and the Purple Peanut*
Balian, Lorna *The Animal*
Barohas, Sarah E *I Was Walking Down the Road*
Barrett, Judi *Animals Should Definitely Not Wear Clothing*
Barton, Byron *Building a House*
    Buzz, Buzz, Buzz
Baskin, Leonard *Hosie's Alphabet*
Battaglia, Aurelius *Old Mother Hubbard*
Baum, Arline and Joseph *One Bright Monday Morning*
Bayer, J. A. *My Name Is Alice*
Baylor, Byrd *Everybody Needs a Rock*
Becker, John *Seven Little Rabbits*
Beckman, Kaj *Lisa Cannot Sleep*
Bellah, Melanie *A First Book of Sounds*
Bennett, David *One Cow Moo Moo*
Berenstain, Stanley and Janice *The B Book*
Bonne, Rose, and Alan Mills *I Know an Old Lady*
Brand, Oscar *When I First Came to This Land*
Brandenberg, Franz *I Once Knew a Man*

Briggs, Raymond *Jim and the Beanstock*
Brooke, Leslie *Johnny Crow's Garden*
Brown, Marcia *The Three Billy Goats Gruff*
Brown, Margaret Wise *A Child's Good Night Book*
    Four Fur Feet
    The Friendly Book
    Goodnight Moon
    The Important Book
    Runaway Bunny
    Where Have You Been?
Burningham, John *Mr. Gumpy's Outing*
Cameron, Polly *I Can't, Said the Ant*
Campbell, Rod *Dear Zoo*
Carle, Eric *The Grouchy Ladybug*
    The Mixed Up Chameleon
    Polar Bear, Polar Bear, What Do You Hear?
    The Very Busy Spider
    The Very Hungry Caterpillar
    The Very Quiet Cricket
Carter, D *How Many Bugs in a Box*
Charlip, Remy *Fortunately*
    What Good Luck!
Cook, Bernadine *The Little Fish That Got Away*
Dalton, Anne *This Is the Way*
Degan, Bruce *Jamberry*
de Regniers, Beatrice *Catch a Little Fox*
    The Day Everybody Cried
    How Joe the Bear and Sam the Mouse Got Together
    The Little Book
    May I Bring a Friend?
    Willy O'Dwyer Jumped in the Fire
Domanska, Janina *If All the Seas Were One Sea*
Duff, Maggie *Jonny and His Drum*
    Rum Pum Pum
Dunrea, Oliver *The Broody Hen*
Edens, Cooper *Caretakers of Wonder*
Einsel, Walter *Did You Ever See?*
Emberley, Barbara *Drummer Hoff*
    Simon's Song
Emberley, Barbara and Ed *One Wide River to Cross*
Emberley, Ed *Klippity Klop*
Enderle, Judith Ross *Six Creepy Sheep*
Ets, Marie Hall *Elephant in a Well*
    Play with Me

Flack, Marjorie *Ask Mr. Bear*

Fox, Mem *Hattie and the Fox*

Gag, Wanda *Millions of Cats*

Galdone, Paul *The Gingerbread Boy*

    Henny Penny

    The Little Red Hen

    The Three Bears

    The Three Billy Goats Gruff

    The Three Little Pigs

Gerstein, Mordicai *Roll Over*

Ginsburg, Mirra *Across the Stream*

    The Chick and the Duckling

Goss, Janet, and Jerome Harste *It Didn't Frighten Me*

Greenburg, Polly *Oh Lord, I Wish I Was A Buzzard*

Grossman, Bill *My Little Sister Ate One Hare*

Gwynne, Fred *The King Who Rained*

Hale, S. J. *Mary Had a Little Lamb*

Higgins, Don *Papa's Going to Buy Me a Mockingbird*

Hill, Eric *Spot Goes to the Beach*

    Where's Spot?

Hoffman, Hilde *The Green Grass Grows All Around*

Hutchins, Pat *The Doorbell Rang*

    Good-Night Owl

    Rosie's Walk

    Titch

Ipcar, Dahlov *I Love My Anteater with an A*

Joose, Barbara *Mama, Do You Love Me?*

Joslin, Sesyle *What Do You Do, Dear?*

    What Do You Say, Dear?

Joyce, Irma *Never Talk to Strangers*

Kamen, Gloria *"Paddle," said the Swan*

Katz, Bobbie *Nothing but a Dog*

Keats, Ezra Jack *Over in the Meadow*

Kellogg, Steven *Can I Keep Him?*

    The Mysterious Tadpole

Kent, Jack *The Fat Cat*

Kessler, Eleanor and Leonard *Is There a Horse in Your House?*

Kimmel, Eric *The Greatest of All*

    The Old Woman and Her Pig

Klein, Lenore *Brave Daniel*

Kovalski, Maryann *The Wheels on the Bus*

Kraus, Robert *Good Night Little ABC*

    Whose Mouse Are You?

Krauss, Ruth *Bears*
>*The Carrot Seed*
>*A Hole Is to Dig*

Langstaff, John *Frog Went A-Courtin'*
>*Gather My Gold Together: Four Songs for Four Seasons*
>*Oh, A-Hunting We Will Go*
>*Over in the Meadow*

Laurence, Ester *We're Off to Catch a Dragon*

Lexau, Joan *Crocodile and Hen*

Lobel, Anita *King Rooster, Queen Hen*

Lobel, Arnold *A Tree Full of Pigs*

MacDonald, Amy Rachel *Fister's Blister*

Mack, Stan *10 Bears in My Bed*

Mars, W. T. *The Old Woman and Her Pig*

Martin, Bill *Brown Bear, Brown Bear, What Do You See?*
>*Fire! Fire! Said Mrs. McGuire*
>*Freedom Books*
>*A Ghost Story*
>*The Haunted House*
>*Instant Readers*
>*Little Owl Series*
>*Monday, Monday, I Like Monday*
>*Polar Bear, Polar Bear, What Do You Hear?*
>*Sounds of Language*
>*Wise Owl Series*
>*Young Owl Series*

Martin, Bill, and John Archambault *Chicka Chicka Boom Boom*

Mayer, Mercer *If I Had . . .*
>*Just for You*
>*What Do You Do with a Kangaroo?*

McGovern, Ann *Too Much Noise*

McMillan, Bruce *One Sun: A Book of Terse Verse*

McNalley, Darcie *In a Cabin in a Wood*

McNaughton, Colin *Who's That Banging on the Ceiling?*

Memling, Carl *Riddles, Riddles from A to Z*
>*Ten Little Animals*

Misumura, Kazue *If I Were a Cricket*

Moffett, Martha *A Flower Pot Is Not a Hat*

Mosel, Arlene *Tikki, Tikki, Tembo*

Murphy, Jill *Peace at Last*

Neitzel, Shirley *The Dress I'll Wear to the Party*
>*The Jacket I Wear in the Snow*

Nodset, Joan *Who Took the Farmer's Hat?*

Numeroff, Laura Joffe *If You Give a Moose a Muffin*
    If You Give a Mouse a Cookie
O'Neill, Mary *Hailstones and Halibut Bones*
Patrick, Gloria *A Bug in a Jug*
Peek, Merle *Mary Wore Her Red Dress*
Peppe, Rodney *The House That Jack Built*
Petersham, Maud and Miska *The Rooster Crows . . . Rhymes and Jingles*
Pinkwater, Daniel *The Big Orange Splot*
Polushkin, Maria *Mother, Mother, I Want Another*
Preston, Edna Mitchell *Where Did My Mother Go?*
Quackenbush, Robert *Poems for Counting*
    She'll Be Comin' Round the Mountain
    Skip to My Lou
Raskin, Ellen *Spectacles*
Rockwell, Anne *Boats*
Rokoff, Sandra *Here Is a Cat*
Rosen, Michael *We're Going on a Bear Hunt*
Rosetti, Christina *What Is Pink?*
Rounds, Glen *Old MacDonald Had a Farm*
Scheer, Julian, and Marvin Bileck *Rain Makes Applesauce*
    Upside Down Day
Schulz, Charles *You're My Best Friend Because*
Sendak, Maurice *Chicken Soup with Rice*
    Where the Wild Things Are
Seuss, Dr. *Dr. Seuss's ABC*
Sharmat, Marjorie *The Terrible Eater*
Shaw, Charles B. *It Looked Like Spilt Milk*
Shaw, Nancy *Sheep in a Jeep*
Shulevitz, Uri *One Monday Morning*
Skaar, Grace *What Do the Animals Say?*
Sonneborn, Ruth A. *Someone Is Eating the Sun*
Spier, Peter *The Fox Went Out on a Chilly Night*
Stover, JoAnn *If Everybody Did*
Titherington, Jean *Pumpkin, Pumpkin*
Tolstoy, Alexei *The Great Big Enormous Turnip*
Vaughan, Marcia *The Sandwich That Max Made*
    Wombat Stew
Viorst, Judith *Alexander and the Terrible, Horrible . . . Day*
    I Used to Be Rich Last Sunday
    If I Were in Charge of the World
    I'll Fix Anthony
Waber, Bernard *Dear Hildegarde*
Waddell, Martin *Can't you Sleep, Little Bear?*
    Let's Go Home, Little Bear

Walsh, Ellen Stoll *Mouse Paint*
Watson, Clyde *Father Fox's Pennyrhymes*
Welber, Robert *Goodbye, Hello*
West, Colin *"Pardon?" Said the Giraffe*
Westcott, Nadine *I Know an Old Lady Who Swallowed a Fly*
    The Lady with the Alligator Purse
Wildsmith, Brian *Brian Wildsmith's ABC*
    The Twelve Days of Christmas
    What the Moon Saw
Williams, Barbara *If He's My Brother*
Williams, Sue *I Went Walking*
Winthrop, Elizabeth *Shoes*
Withers, Carl *A Rocket in My Pocket*
Wolkstein, Diane *The Visit*
Wondriska, William *All the Animals Were Angry*
Wood, Audrey *King Bidgood's in the Bathtub*
    The Napping House
Wood, Don and Audrey *The Little Mouse, the Red Ripe Strawberry, and the . . .*
    Bear
    Quick as a Cricket
Wright H. R. *A Maker of Boxes*
Zaid, Berry *Chicken Little*
Zemach, Harve *The Judge*
Zemach, Margot *Hush, Little Baby*
    The Teeny Tiny Woman
Zolotow, Charlotte *Do You Know What I'll Do?*

Appendix O

Favorite Books from the Fulton-May Library

Read-Aloud Books for Children Ages 3–6

Anamalia Graeme Base
Big Keith Haring
Big Red Barn Margaret Wise Brown
Blueberries for Sal Robert McCloskey
Brown Bear, Brown Bear, What Do You See? Eric Carle
Buzz Said the Bee W. C. Lewison
Caps for Sale Esphyr Slobodkina
Cars and Trucks and Things That Go Richard Scarry
The Cat in the Hat Dr. Seuss
The Cat on the Mat Brian Wildsmith
Clap Your Hands Lorenda Cauley
Cloudy with a Chance of Meatballs Judi and Ron Barrett
Five Little Ducks Pamela Paparone
Flying Donald Crews
Going on a Plane Anne Civardi
Goodnight Moon Margaret Wise Brown
Harold and the Purple Crayon Crockett Johnson
Home for a Bunny Margaret Wise Brown
How Do Dinosaurs Say Goodnight? Jane Yolen and Mary Teague
If You Give a Mouse a Cookie Laura Numeroff
Polar Bear, Polar Bear, What Do You Hear? Bill Martin
Runaway Bunny Margaret Wise Brown
Ten Apples Up on Top! Theo. LeSieg

Read-Along Books for Children Ages 3–6

A Cat and a Dog Claire Masurel
Dirty Little Boy Margaret Wise Brown
Go, Dog, Go! P. D. Eastman
Good Night, Monkey Boy Jarrett Krosoczka
Good Thing You're Not an Octopus Julie Markes
Hop on Pop Dr. Seuss
Snow Day Mercer Mayer
The Very Busy Spider Eric Carle
The Very Hungry Caterpillar Eric Carle

2001–2004 Children's Choices for Beginning Readers Ages 5–8

Albert's Impossible Toothache Barbara Williams
Babar's Little Circus Star Laurent de Brunhoff
Big Pumpkin Erica Silverman
The Buggiest Bug Carol Diggory Shields
Busy Little Mouse Eugenie Fernandez
Can You Make a Piggy Giggle? Linda Ashman
Captain Bob Sets Sail Roni Schotter
Cave Boy Cathy East Dubowski
Chicken Chuck Bill Marten, Jr.
Crazy Hair Day Barney Salzberg
The Dirty Little Boy Margaret Wise Brown
Do Your Ears Hang Low? Carolyn Jayne Church
Doggie Dreams Nancy Kapp Chapman
Doggie Night Meredith Hooper
Down by the Cool of the Pool Tony Mitton
Dr. Pompo's Nose Saxton Freymann and Joost Elffers
Drip, Drop (An I Can Read Book) Sarah Weeks
Duck on a Bike David Shannon
Excuse Me—Are You a Witch? Emily Horn
Farm Flu Teresa Bateman
The Forgetful Bears Larry Weineberg
Franklin Says "I Love You" Paulette Bourgeois
Froggy Goes to Bed Jonathan London

The Giant Zucchini Catherine Siracusa
Giraffes Can't Dance Giles Andreae
Good Night, Monkey Boy Jarrett J. Krosoczka
Good Thing You're Not an Octopus! Julie Markes
The Great Gracie Chase: Stop That Dog Cynthia Rylant
Happy Thanksgiving Rebus David Adler
Hello, House Lynn Munsinger
How Do Dinosaurs Say Good Night? Jane Yolen
I Know an Old Lady Who Swallowed a Fly Steven Gulbis
I Stink! Kate McMullan
If Dinosaurs Came to Town Dom Mansell
If You Take a Mouse to School Laura Numeroff
I'm Not Going to Chase the Cat Today! Jessica Harper
Leon the Chameleon Melanie Watt
Little Buggy Kevin O'Malley
The Magic Hat Mem Fox
Makeup Mess Robert Munsch
Megatooth Patrick O'Brien
Mmm, Cookies! Robert Munsch
Mouse in Love Robert Kraus
The Mouse That Snored Bernard Waber
My Somebody Special Sara Weeks
Never Spit on Your Shoes Denys Cazet
One Dark Night Hazel Hutchins
A Plump and Perky Turkey Teresa Bateman
The Practically Perfect Pajamas Eric Brooks
The Princesses Had a Ball Teresa Bateman
Professor Wormbug in Search for the Zipperump-a-Zoo Mercer Mayer
A Pup Just for Me/ A Boy Just for Me Dorthea P. Seeber
Sheep in a Shop Nancy Shaw
Shoe Fly! Iza Trapani
Sidney Won't Swim Hilde Schuurmans
Sleep Tight, Ginger Kitten Adele Geras
Snow Day Mercer Mayer
Snug as a Bug Amy Imbody
Some Things Are Scary Florence Parry Heide
Spiders Carolyn Otto
Spike in the Kennel Paulette Bogan
Splish! Splash! Animal Baths April Pulley Sayre
Tatty Ratty Helen Cooper
10-Step Guide to Living with Your Monster Laura Numeroff
Trick-or-Treat on Milton Street Lisa Bullard
The Tub People Pam Conrad
Tyrannosaurus Rex Don Lessem
Very Boring Alligator Jean Graelley

What Gramas Do Best/ What Grampas Do Best Laura Numeroff
Where Do Balloons Go? An Uplifting Mystery Jamie Lee Curtis
Widget Lyn Rossiter McFarland
Wimberly Worried Kevin Henkes
The Witch Who Wanted to Be a Princess Lois Gambling

2001–2004 Children's Choices for Intermediate Readers Ages 8–10

Crickwing Jannel Cannon
The Dinosaurs of Waterhouse Hawkins Barbara Kerley
Experiments in Science: How Does It Work? David Glover
Goldilocks Returns Lisa Campbell Ernst
Halloween Motel Sean Diviny
Horses Dorothy Hinshaw Patent
How the Animals Saved the People: Animal Tales from the South Retold by J. J.
    Reneaux
How to Talk to Your Cat Jean Craighead George
It's Raining Pigs and Noodles Jack Prelutsky
Jazz Cats David Davis
Joining the Boston Tea Party Diane Stanley
Just One More Wendi Silvano
Little Yau Jannell Cannon
Lunch Box Mail and Other Poems Jenny Whitehead
Mountain Dance Thomas Looker
The Music Teacher from the Black Lagoon Mike Thaler
Tales from the Dragon's Cave: Peacemaking Stories for Everyone Arlene Williams
The Terror of the Pink Dodo Balloons Lawrence David and Barry Gott
*Twisters and Other Terrible Storms: A Nonfiction Companion to Twisters on Tues-
    day* Will Osborne

2001–2004 Children's Choices for Advanced Readers Ages 10–13

Act I, Act II, Act Normal Martha Weston
Alice Alone Phyllis Reynolds Naylor
Bad Girls Jacqueline Wilson
Becoming Joe DiMaggio Maria Testa
Coraline Neil Gaiman
Fossil Fish Found Alive: Discovering the Coelacanth Sally Walker
Hello, Goodbye, I Love You: The Story of Aloha, A Guide Dog for the Blind Pamela
    Bauer Mueller

Locomotion Jacqueline Woodson
Magic Can Be Murder Vivian Vande Veide
Money Hungry Sharon Flake
Rat Jan Cheripko
The Secret School Avi
The Sisters Club Megan McDonald
Star in the Storm Joan Hyatt Harlow
Teen Angst? Naaah . . . A Quasi-Autobiography Ned Vizzini
Under the Ice Kathy Conlan
The Waterstone Rebecca Rupp

Classic Children's Choices for Advanced Readers Ages 10–13 and Young Adults

Aliens for Breakfast Jonathan Etra and Stephanie Spinner
Anansi Goes Fishing Eric Kimmel
Babar's Little Circus Star Laurent de Brunhoff
The Carrot Seed Ruth Krauss
Even That Moose Won't Listen to Me Martha Alexander
Falling Up Shel Silverstein
Flat Stanley Jeff Brown
The Giver Lois Lowry
Harry Potter and the Chamber of Secrets J. K. Rowling
Harry Potter and the Goblet of Fire J. K. Rowling
Harry Potter and the Prisoner of Azkaban J. K. Rowling
Harry Potter and the Sorcerer's Stone J. K. Rowling
The Jungle Book Rudyard Kipling
Lon Po Po: A Red Riding Hood Story from China Retold by Ed Young
Ramona the Brave Beverly Cleary
Sarah, Plain and Tall Patricia MacLachlan
Superfudge Judy Blume
The Tale of Peter Rabbit Beatrix Potter
Where's Waldo Martin Handford

Categories of Books

Adventure and Danger

The Big Buck Adventure Shelly Gill and Deborah Tobola
Bubble Bath Pirates Jarrett Krosoczka
The City of Ember Jeanne duPrau

Dare to Be Scared: Thirteen Stories to Chill and Thrill Robert San Souci
Fire Storm Jean Craighead
Frosty: The Adventures of Morgan Horse Ellen Feld
The Man Who Walked Between the Towers Mordicai Gerstein

Biography

The Fantastic Journey of Pieter Bruegel Pieter Bruegel
Girl in a Cage Jane Yolen and Robert Harris
How Ben Franklin Stole the Lightning Rosalyn Schanzer
Mahalia: A life in Gospel Music Roxanne Orgill
Martin's Big Words: The Life of Dr. Martin Luther King Doreen Rappaport
Peaceful Protest: The Life of Nelson Mandella Zona McDonough
Sacagawea Louise Landau
The Sky's the Limit: Stories of Discovery by Women and Girls Catherine Thimmesh
Ten Kings and the World They Ruled Milton Meltzer

Comic Novels and Cartoons

Betty and Veronica Digest Archie Comics
Captain Underpants and the Big, Bad Battle of the Bionic Booger Boy Dav Pilkey
The Horrible Trouble with Hally Tosis Dav Pilkey
Into the Air: The Story of the Wright Brothers' First Flight Robert Burleigh
Little Vampire Goes to School Joann Star
Millions to Measure David Schwartz

Folktales

Adelita: A Mexican Cinderella Story Tomie DePaola
Anansi and the Moss-Covered Rock Eric Kimmel
Can You Guess My Name? Traditional Folk Tales from Around the World Retold
    by Judy Sierra
Hayyim's Ghost Eric Kimmel
Jack Outwits the Giants Paul Johnson
Keepers of Life: Discovering Plants Through Native American Stories Michael
    Kaduto
Keepers of the Animals: Discovering Plants Through Native American Stories
    Michael Kaduto
The Legend of the Loon Kathy-jo Wargin
Lessons from the Wolverine Barry Lopez
Mrs. Frisby and the Rats of Nimh (Aladdin Fantasy) Robert O'Brien
Mystic Horse Paul Goble
Quiver Stephanie Spinner
Robin Hook, Pirate Hunter! Eric Kimmel

Sense Pass King: A Story from Cameroon Katrin Tchana

The Tale of Despereaux: Being the Story of Mouse, a Princess, Some Soup and a Spool of Thread Kate diCamillo

Thirteen Moons on Turtle's Back: A Native American Year of Moons Joseph Bruchac

Thunder Rose Jerdine Nolan

A Trip to Dinosaur Time Michael Foreman

Under the Quilt of Night Deborah Hopkinson

Valadeores (Legends of the Americas) Patricia Petersen

What About Me? Ed Young

Will Rogers: An American Legend Frank Keating

Yonder Mountain: A Cherokee Legend Robert Bushyhead and Kay Thorp Bannon

Geography

Chang and the Bamboo Flute Elizabeth Hill

A Full Hand Thomas Yezerski

I Am Rosa Parks (Puffen Easy to Read) Rosa Parks

The Kite Rider Geraldine McCaughrean

Magnificent Voyage: An American Adventure on Captain James Cook's Final Expedition Laurie Lawlor

Monkey for Sale Sanna Stanley

One Leaf Rides the Wind: Counting in a Japanese Garden Celeste Mannis

Zulu Dog Antone Perreira

History and Historical Fiction

Ashes of Roses Mary Auch

Charlotte Janet Lunn

Crossing the Panther's Path Elizabeth Alder

Doomed Queen Anne Meyer

Galen: My Life in Imperial Rome Marissa Moss

Heading for Better Times: The Arts of the Great Depression Duane Damon

The House in the Mail Rosemary and Tom Wells

Man with the Silver Oar Robin Moore

The Midwife's Apprentice Karen Cushman

Red Midnight Ben Mikaelsen

When Marian Sang: The True Recital of Marian Anderson Munoz Ryan

The Winter People Joseph Bruchac

Mystery and Detective Stories (for oral or silent reading)

The Box Car Children Mysteries: Books 5–8 Gertrude Warner

Cam Jansen and the Mystery of the Television Dog David Adler

The Dead Man in Indian Creek Mary Hahn

Gumshoe Goose, Private Eye (Puffen Easy To Read) Mary Kwitz
The Hamster of Baskervilles: A Chet Gecko Mystery Bruce Hale
Look for Me by Moonlight Mary Hahn
The Mysterious Cases of Mr. Pin Mary Monsell
The Mysterious Matter of I. M. Fine Dianne Stanley
Mystery of the Lobster Thieves Elaine Willoughby
Piet Potter on the Run: Story and Pictures Robert Quackenbush
Robert Quackenbush's Treasury of Humor Robert Quackenbush
Sherlock Chick's First Case Robert Quackenbush
Spy Cat Peg Kehret
Utterly Me, Clarice Bean Lauren Child
Vampire State Building Elizabeth Levy
Wait Till Helen Comes: A Ghost Story Mary Hahn
Young Cam Jansen and the Missing Cookie David Adler

Pure Humor

Alice in Blunderland Phyllis Reynolds
Don't Let the Pigeon Drive the Bus Mo Willems
Henry's Awful Mistake (*Parents Magazine* Read-Aloud Original) Robert Quack-
enbush
It's Not My Fault Nancy Carlson
My Lucky Day Keiko Kasza
Olivia . . . and the Missing Toy Ian Falconer
Sideways Stories from Wayside School Louis Sachar
Six Hogs on a Scooter Eileen Spinelly
What Got You Started, Mr. Fulton? Robert Quackenbush

Realism

A Corner of the Universe Ann Martin
Double Dutch Sharon Draper
Home at Last Susan Middleton Elya
Left for Dead: A Young Man's Search for the USS Indianapolis Pete Nelson
The Recess Queen Alexis O'Neill
Refugee Boy Benjamin Zephaniah
This Place I Know: Poems of Comfort Georgia Heard (Editor)
The White Swan Express: A Story About Adoption Jean Okimoto

Rhymes and Poetry

ABC Math Riddles Jannelle Martin
Bow Wow Meow Meow Douglas Florian
Busy, Busy Mouse Virginia Kroll
Ferocious Girls, Steamroller Boys and Other Poems in Between Timothy Bush

Hey Pancakes Tamson Weston
The Kingfisher Book of Family Poems Belinda Holly
Paul Revere's Ride: The Landlord's Tale Henry Wadsworth Longfellow
Read-Aloud Rhymes for the Very Young J. Preluski

Science

Brilliant Bees Linda Glaser
The Case of the Monkeys That Fell from the Trees: And Other Mysteries in Tropical Nature Susan Quinlan
Fabulous, Fluttering, Tropical Butterflies Dorothy Hinshaw
The Incredible Record-Setting Deep Sea Dive of the Bathysphere Brad Matsen
Killer Rocks from Outer Space: Asteroids, Comets, and Meteorites Steven Koppes
Probing Volcanoes Laura Lindop
Saving Birds: Heroes Around the World Pete Salmansohn and Stephen Kress
Sea Horses Sally Walker
What Do You Do with a Tail Like This? Robin Page and Steve Jenkins
The Woods Scientists Susan Morse

Special Picture Books

Cassie's Word Quilt Faith Ringgold
The King's Equal Catherine Paterson
Let's Rock! Rock Painting for Kids Linda Kranz
Lon Po Po: A Red Riding Hood Story from China Ed Young
Lottie's New Beach Towel Petra Mathers
Nothing at All Denys Cazet
Peep! Kevin Luthardt
A Picture Book of George Washington (Biography) David Adler
A Picture Book of Martin Luther King, Jr. David Adler
Pigs Rock Melanie Davis Jones
Plane Song Diane Siebert
Truck Board Book Donald Crews
Voices of the Heart Ed Young

Sports

Arthur and the Goalie Ghost Marc Brown
Choosing Up Sides John Ritter
The Lucky Baseball Bat Matt Christopher
Pitchers' Duel Clair Bee
A Strong Right Arm: The Story of Mamie "Peanut" Johnson Y. Green
The Team That Couldn't Lose Matt Christopher
Wilma Unlimited: How Wilma Rudolph Became the World's Fastest Woman Cathleen Krull

Internet Sites for Other Excellent Books

http://www.cbcbooks.org
Children's Book Council, a joint project of the IRA and the American Library Association, provides a comprehensive list of recommended books.

http://www.reading.org
International Reading Association gives a current list of Teachers' Choices and Children's Choices for each year and each age group.

http://www.nsta.org.ostbc
These outstanding science books are recommended by the National Science Teachers Association. Look under "SciLinks" for ways to extend and expand specific science books.

http://www.ala.org/productsandpublications
American Library Association provides a list of the Newberry Medal and Honor books, whose authors are recognized for making the most distinguished contribution to American literature for children. You can also find the Caldecott Medal and Honors winners for the artists of the most distinguished American picture books.

http://superkids.com

http://www.CreativeThink.com
These are two sources for books and vocabulary builders in Spanish, French, and English, to encourage critical and creative thinking and imagination building.

http://www.afb/info

http://www.nbp.org/bookclub.html
These are two of the best sources for books in Braille and large print.

http://www.cde.state.co.us
The Colorado State Library provides a list of 50 multicultural books every child should know, preschool through age 12.

http://www.ncss.org
The National Council for the Social Studies provides an exciting list of recommended books in every social studies genre.

http://www.ncte.org
The National Council of Teachers of English identifies many exciting nonfiction books that have been selected for the Orbis Pictus Award.

http://www.udel.edu
The University of Delaware maintains a well-organized list of books with social studies themes for history, geography, economics, and civics at all grade levels.

http://www.guysread.com
Here is an Internet site that maintains an age-appropriate list of books boys have rated as their most favorite.

http://www.multcolib.org/Kids/booksforgirls.html
Here are books recommended by the Multnomah County Library in Portland, Oregon, including a list of books especially for girls.

Glossary

action research Classroom experiments implemented by teachers to test new ways of learning and teaching.

alphabetic principle The principle that oral speech sounds, or phonemes, can be represented by one or more letters to produce written words. Translating the written words back into the correct letters and into the correct series of phonemes allows the written words to become oral.

artifacts For purposes of assessment, something that can be observed or collected by a teacher or a student to demonstrate the student's comprehension of specific skills and concepts.

assessment The gathering of information about one or more students' reading and other concepts and skills through visual observations, oral observations, work samples, and tests.

basal readers The former name for today's level books. They are fiction and nonfiction anthologies at various levels of reading difficulty.

basic sight words A list of common, frequent words.

bilingual Capable of speaking two languages.

changing-direction method The search for a new direction in which teachers can work together to improve a situation and drop old solutions.

children at risk Students who might have considerable difficulty in school because of a lack of educational stimulation in the home or because of a host of other societal inabilities to meet their needs.

collaboration Whenever teachers or students "labor" together to reach a common goal.

collaborative learning A highly flexible learning process that engages students in groups that cooperate in solving real or imaginary problems; brainstorming is often used.

comprehension strategies Problem-solving procedures for students to use to understand an author's message or meaning.

concept An idea formed from experiences with a variety of samples, details, examples, and characteristics. For example, terms such as *canine, puppy, Lassie, golden retriever, fur,* and *wagging tail* might be grouped together in a child's mind to gradually produce the *concept of dog.*

consonant blend The sound of two consonants in sequence that are recognized as two phonemes rather than one, as /sk/ in *skill* or /tr/ in *trade.* This is contrasted with a *digraph,* such as /th/ in *thin,* which produces only one phoneme.

constructivists Students and teachers who construct their own meanings based on their own learning experiences.

515

context clues Clues in the author's message that students need to search for in order to comprehend a set of circumstances or facts that surround a particular event or situation.

critical reading Mentally processing an author's text by making inferences, judgments, criteria for judgments, or other evaluation processes.

decoding Translating written letter patterns into oral subvocal language sounds.

default A type of oral reading miscue in which the reader creatively begs the teacher to pronounce a hard word (e.g., pronounces only the first letter, says "uhmm" several times, looks for pity, or tries other humorous approaches).

digraph See *consonant blend.*

diphthong A glided vowel sound typically represented by the letter combinations *oy, oi, ow,* and *ou,* as found in the words *boy, oil, cow,* and *out.*

direct instruction A teaching philosophy characterized by explicit teacher-directed instruction, in contrast to indirect instruction and discovery learning. Those who rely on direct instruction have research support, but few have bothered to research the advantages of indirect teaching.

discovery instruction Indirect teaching strategies whereby teachers create learning opportunities for students to discover new skills and information in reading, writing, speaking, and listening. Inductive and deductive reasoning are used as problem-solving tools.

diverse classroom One in which some students do not share the cultural background and language of the teacher and their peers.

Ell students English-language learners whose home language is not English and who need extra linguistic assistance.

engaged learners Students who have become individually involved in reading, writing, speaking, listening, and other learning processes.

essential sight words The top 100 words, which make up about 50% of the words used by average American students and adults. Understanding and spelling these words is particularly important.

evolution method A process of creatively improving what has already been introduced, making it better and better, as when a teacher improves a lesson plan in ways that cause students to understand and develop a clearer and clearer image.

explicit learning The process of understanding an idea at least to the extent of being able to express it clearly; often linked to *direct instruction.*

expository structures Patterns used by nonfiction authors to explain concepts, events, procedures, and so forth. Explanation patterns include cause and effect, time sequence, description, definitions, problem and solution.

flexible reading Reading at different speeds and intensities depending on the difficulty of the text.

fluency Reading with ease, at an appropriate rate and speed for the type of text being read, and a high level of comprehending the author's message.

grapheme One or more letters that stand for one speech sound, or phoneme.

graphic organizers For teaching purposes, drawings that help explain relationships through lines, boxes, circles, and other shapes.

graphophonic cues Letter patterns or letter-sequence cues as to how a written word is pronounced.

high-frequency words Words that occur in the language far more often than most other words. For the United States the 1,000 most frequently used English words represent about 75% of the words normally used.

implicit learning The process of understanding an idea without necessarily being able to express it clearly.

indirect instruction Teacher-developed instruction that uses discovery learning, inductive and deductive learning, and problem solving to lead students to new skills and knowledge.

ineffective substitution A miscue that does not match the syntax and/or meaning of the author's true text.

inferential thinking Using one's understanding of text to grasp the author's implied message by reading between the lines.

instant words Normally refers to high-frequency written words, based on students' reading materials in school. The top 100 words are the most important to learn.

intuitive learning The process of understanding an idea through experience and insight rather than through direct instruction.

level books A new name for the former basic readers; anthologies designed for various levels of difficulty.

literacy The ability to read and write to sufficiently perform well in school and survive well in society.

literature Fiction, nonfiction, and poetry that has been written well for the appropriate audience.

metacognition A state of awareness that allows people to observe their own emotions and intellectual processes, especially their comprehension; put simply, understanding what you know and don't know.

miscue analysis Analyzing a student's reading ability, especially decoding, by studying the student's oral reading errors called miscues.

miscues Oral reading mistakes that show how students are understanding what they are reading. Miscues include word substitutions, omissions, insertions, defaults, and self-corrections. Only three of these have proven to be valid indicators of comprehension: ineffective substitutions, defaults, and self-corrections.

modifications To revise instruction, both format and content, to better meet the needs of students having learning difficulties.

objectives Very specific goals that usually lead to individual improvement. Teachers often have specific objectives for their teaching.

observations Information gathered by a teacher from watching children's behavior or listening to them; gathered informally or through anecdotal notes or observation checklists.

onset The letter(s) coming in front of a *rime*; a *rime* is the vowel and the letters that go with it. For example, the letters *st* in the word *stem* are an onset, and *em* is the rime. See *rime*.

oral blending Combining two or more phonemes into a single word or word part, for example, /sl/ + /ip/ = /slip/. This ability is essential for phonics.

phonemes The smallest units of language sound. The spoken word *seat* has three phonemes: /s/, /e/, /t/.

phonemic awareness The understanding that spoken words are composed of individual language sounds; a necessary precursor to learning phonics and the alphabetic principle.

phonogram The same thing as a rime. *It* is the unit that provides the actual rhyming sound, for example, r*at*, c*at*, sc*at*, th*at*, f*at*, s*at*, sp*at*.

phonological awareness Awareness of sentences, compound words, syllables, alliteration, and, of course, phonemes.

portfolio A collection of your students' work that they wish to share with you, the teacher, and with their peers.

predictable text A selection written with recurring patterns, with pictures that match the text, and with familiar phrases and other devices that help the reader easily decode the text.

print concepts Ideas related to written language, such as letter names, letter sounds, letter shapes, words, compound words, sentences, onsets, and rimes.

reapplication method Creatively looking at something specific in a different way, like using a penetrating pen not for writing but for bringing more air into the soil for roses.

revolution method A creative, overall change that yields a brand new way of thinking, such as seeing Johnny in a completely new way after receiving information from his mother.

rime A synonym for *phonogram*, made up of the rhyming unit such as *eat* in *seat, cheat, feat, beat, cleat, heat, meat.*

role players Young children who have learned enough to pretend they are reading or writing.

scaffolding A gradual process of helping learners by first modeling for them; then solving a problem with them; then letting them solve it with nothing but prompts; then merely suggesting the name of the strategy; and finally just asking them what they should do.

schemas The notions, minitheories, or cognitive frameworks that we generate in our minds to explain or categorize our personal experiences. We grow in wisdom as we expand and modify our schemas.

schematic cues A unit of understanding generated by the reader on the basis of prior knowledge and schemas—triggered by the author's graphophonic, semantic, and syntactic cues.

semantic cues Meaning-laden words and messages provided by the author or speaker.

sentence structures Patterns used in a language to arrange words in sentences. The English language is based primarily on a noun-verb relationship.

shared reading Reading that is shared interactively among students and teacher.

sight words Any words that can be decoded instantly through the use of visual memory. Instant sight words are the top 100 or 200 high-frequency words in the English language.

specific learning disability A disorder in the ability to understand written or spoken language that results in difficulty when listening, speaking, reading, writing, and performing some forms of mathematics; also called learning disabled.

structural analysis Analyzing words by detecting root words, prefixes, and suffixes, as in *pre-determin-ed*.

struggling reader Usually a student who does not understand that reading is communicating with an author and thus has not gained the motivation to understand an author. There are also other reasons for a child to become a struggling reader.

syntactic cues Sentence-pattern order, arrangement of parts of speech, and the general arrangement of a sentence to make sense of the author's message.

synthesis method With respect to creative teaching, combining two ways to teach an idea by using two types of media. For example, students might take turns talking about Pygmies while showing a movie about Pygmies without the sound.

text Written material—passages, a book, informative document, a story, a poem.

think-aloud assessment Listening to students (or a modeling teacher) problem solve as they read or write out loud.

trade books Books sold by publishers to the general public, as contrasted to textbooks sold to students; can also include library books and books purchased from a book club.

vowel diagraphs Two vowels appearing together but representing one vowel sound or phoneme, as /ea/ in *heal*.

vowel patterns A consistent arrangement of vowels and consonants, as in *ape, cape, tape,* and *grape*—all indicators of a VCE vowel pattern (vowel, consonant, silent *e*). The other *major* patterns are these:

VC—*it, bit, slit*
VCC—*math, bath, path*
VVC—*eat, heat, beat*
CV—*go, he, try*

vowel phoneme The language sound represented by the letters *a, e, i, o, u,* or *y* (as in *gym*).

webbing Using lines, circles, and other shapes to demonstrate relationships or associations among words, concepts, events, or relationships.

Index

About the Authors

Frank May has been an educator since his 21st birthday, at which time he taught at an elementary school in Dayton, Ohio. While teaching eighth-grade gymnastics in the morning and sixth-grade everything else in the afternoon, he learned both the joy and the challenge of being a teacher. When he moved to New York City and taught fourth and fifth graders at a downtown private school, he learned how to teach children of the very wealthy, which he said was "eeeen-ter-esting." Following that and while completing his Master's degree program at the original University of Chicago, he taught fifth grade at the Laboratory School founded by John Dewey and there he truly learned how to teach—from several experienced and devoted teachers and professors.

By this time his goal was to teach all of the grades from K to 8 so he could someday become competent enough to prepare teachers to teach *creatively* and *successfully*. In Greensboro, North Carolina, he taught the combined grades of one through three. Fulfilling his desire to "Go West," he found *model* teachers at Jefferson School in Pullman, Washington, home of Washington State University, and taught all the grades there from fifth through eighth. And finally, he felt ready to become a professor of education and worked on a rigorous doctoral program at the original University of Wisconsin, with what he considered to be some of the finest educators ever.

While working on his courses and dissertation, he was able to teach several education courses and discover how much he enjoyed his role of teaching teachers. This discovery led to a position of professor at Washington State University—in the same city in which he had taught children. But two years later, somewhat against his wishes, he was "commanded" by his Wisconsin mentor to "come back and teach, and carry on our research." In the *long* run this led to his happily teaching and researching at five universities, but the one he has enjoyed *the most* has been Portland State University, where his students have generally been exceptionally eager to learn.

Has he been successful as a professor? Semester after semester, quarter after quarter, he has been seen as a favorite of the students—for both his teaching and his writing. He is the author of numerous professional articles and books and has directed a large number of federal research projects. Frank is a happy man—and often a happy-go-lucky man. He loves his family—his amazing wife, Louise, two daughters, Ivey and Gretchen, and five sons, Dell, Richmond, Ben, Lee, and Steve. And how he loves to write.

Dr. Louise Fulton's career in the field of education reads like a who-dunnit mystery in which she finds a new clue every step of the way—then uses all those clues to solve yet another case. The first major case occurred in the famous race track city of Talladega, Alabama, where she taught third-graders to read, write, listen, and speak, while developing their problem-solving skills like a good detective should.

The second major case also occurred in Talladega, this time as a high school teacher of English, reading, and physical education. The third case was the most difficult, for she became a teacher of deaf and blind children at The Alabama School for the Deaf and Blind. That was followed by a ten-year period as a professor at Talladega College, after which she taught at California State University at San Bernardino. There she continues to offer her popular courses on teaching K-12 regular and special education students.

But teaching is only one facet of her career. Her other contributions include such things as these: Author of six books and numerous articles; Coordinator of Special Education Programs; Founder and Director of the California Transition Center for Children with Autism; Fulbright Senior Award Winner to conduct research at several universities in Japan; World Ballot winner for President of the Division of International Special Education and Services; volunteer of her services in more than ten Asian and European countries. You can see why Dr. Fulton is a most loved and admired educator inside and outside of the United States. As you will also see, Dr. Fulton has poured her energy and inventive talents into the development of *Teach Reading Creatively*.